Accessibility and Diversity in Education:

Breakthroughs in Research and Practice

Information Resources Management Association
USA

Volume I

Published in the United States of America by
IGI Global
Information Science Reference (an imprint of IGI Global)
701 E. Chocolate Avenue
Hershey PA, USA 17033
Tel: 717-533-8845
Fax: 717-533-8661
E-mail: cust@igi-global.com
Web site: http://www.igi-global.com

Copyright © 2020 by IGI Global. All rights reserved. No part of this publication may be reproduced, stored or distributed in any form or by any means, electronic or mechanical, including photocopying, without written permission from the publisher. Product or company names used in this set are for identification purposes only. Inclusion of the names of the products or companies does not indicate a claim of ownership by IGI Global of the trademark or registered trademark.

Library of Congress Cataloging-in-Publication Data

Names: Information Resources Management Association, editor.
Title: Accessibility and diversity in education : breakthroughs in research
 and practice / Information Resources Management Association.
Description: Hershey, PA : Information Science Reference (an imprint of IGI
 Global), [2020] | Includes bibliographical references and index. |
 Summary: ""This book examines emerging methods and trends for creating
 accessible and inclusive educational environments and examines the
 latest teaching strategies and methods for promoting learning for all
 students. It also addresses equal opportunity and diversity requirements
 in schools"--Provided by publisher"-- Provided by publisher.
Identifiers: LCCN 2019026518 (print) | LCCN 2019026519 (ebook) | ISBN
 9781799812135 (hardcover) | ISBN 9781799812142 (ebook)
Subjects: LCSH: Educational equalization. | Inclusive education. |
 Multicultural education.
Classification: LCC LC213 .A336 2020 (print) | LCC LC213 (ebook) | DDC
 379.2/6--dc23
LC record available at https://lccn.loc.gov/2019026518
LC ebook record available at https://lccn.loc.gov/2019026519

British Cataloguing in Publication Data
A Cataloguing in Publication record for this book is available from the British Library.

The views expressed in this book are those of the authors, but not necessarily of the publisher.

For electronic access to this publication, please contact: eresources@igi-global.com.

Editor-in-Chief

Mehdi Khosrow-Pour, DBA
Information Resources Management Association, USA

Associate Editors

Steve Clarke, *University of Hull, UK*
Murray E. Jennex, *San Diego State University, USA*
Ari-Veikko Anttiroiko, *University of Tampere, Finland*

Editorial Advisory Board

Sherif Kamel, *American University in Cairo, Egypt*
In Lee, *Western Illinois University, USA*
Jerzy Kisielnicki, *Warsaw University, Poland*
Amar Gupta, *Arizona University, USA*
Craig van Slyke, *University of Central Florida, USA*
John Wang, *Montclair State University, USA*
Vishanth Weerakkody, *Brunel University, UK*

List of Contributors

Addison, Mark Antony / *Western Michigan University, USA* 390
Alegre de la Rosa, Olga M. / *University of La Laguna, Spain* 599
Aleshina, Ekaterina / *Penza State University, Russia* 291, 296
Alisat, Laurie / *University of Calgary, Canada* 995
Amaral, Maryan / *Aero, Inc., USA* 509
Angulo, Luis M. Villar / *University of Seville, Spain* 599
Ash, Anthony / *University of North Carolina Charlotte, USA* 782
Bagnato, Karin / *University of Messina, Italy* 356
Bateman, David F. / *Shippensburg University, USA* 550
Benedict, Amber Elizabeth / *University of Florida, USA* 143
Bowman, Nicky / *University of Missouri, USA* 102
Brookfield, Stephen / *St. Thomas University, USA* 738
Brownell, Mary T. / *University of Florida, USA* 143
Bruyere, Susanne / *Cornell University, USA* 215
Chamblin, Michelle / *Molloy College, USA* 972
Clarke, Veronika Bohac / *University of Calgary, Canada* 995
Cline, Jenifer / *Great Falls Public Schools, USA* 550
Coffey, Heather / *University of North Carolina at Charlotte, USA* 782
Cooley, Derek / *Godwin Heights Public Schools, USA* 121
Crosby-Cooper, Tricia / *National University, USA* 163
Curran, Christina M. / *University of Northern Iowa, USA* 906
Ehlinger, Emily / *University of Minnesota, USA* 34
Epler, Pam / *Grand Canyon University, USA* 940
Ford, Theron N. / *John Carroll University, USA* 1022
Foster, Monika / *Edinburgh Napier University, UK* 822
Gaona, Alma Rosa García / *Universidad Veracruzana, México* 535
Gibbon, Thomas C. / *Shippensburg University, USA* 550
Gilic, Lina / *St. John's University, USA* 972
Glimps, Blanche Jackson / *Tennessee State University, USA* 1022
Golden, Thomas / *Cornell University, USA* 215
González, Alfredo Mendoza / *Universidad Juárez Autónoma de Tabasco, México* 535
Gower, Wendy Strobel / *Cornell University, USA* 215
Griffin, Cynthia C. / *University of Florida, USA* 143
Gulley, Ann / *Auburn University at Montgomery, USA* 495
Gupta, Sanjeev Kumar / *All India Institute of Speech and Hearing, India* 431
Hadley, Wanda / *Western Michigan University, USA* 390

Name	Affiliation	Page
Hagelkruys, Dominik	*University of Vienna, Austria*	272
Hawbaker, Becky Wilson	*University of Northern Iowa, USA*	906
Heineke, Amy J.	*Loyola University, USA*	757
Hosfelt, Patricia D.	*Frederick County Maryland Public Schools, USA*	550
Hsu, Jennifer	*Grand Valley State University, USA*	390
Hu, Luanjiao	*University of Maryland at College Park, USA*	197
Huang, Liujuan	*Guangming Experimental School, China*	865
Huang, Ying	*Changzhen Elementary School of Guangming District, China*	865
Ikuta, Shigeru	*Otsuma Women's University, Japan*	464
Ishitobi, Ryoichi	*University of Tsukuba, Japan*	464
Jackson, Keonta N.	*Texas A&M University – Commerce, USA*	446
Jackson, Nykela H.	*University of Central Arkansas, USA*	666
Johnson, Ronn	*Creighton University Medical School, USA & VA Nebraska-Western Iowa Health Care System, USA*	680
Kennedy, Adam S.	*Loyola University, USA*	757
Keough, Penelope Debs	*National University, USA*	179
Kim, Ji Youn Cindy	*University of Iowa, USA*	680
Lee, JoJo Yanki	*University of San Diego, USA*	680
Li, Jiacheng	*East China Normal University, China*	865
Li, Yan	*East China Normal University, China*	865
Lin, Jing	*University of Maryland at College Park, USA*	197
Lopez, Ann E.	*University of Toronto, Canada*	613
Luján-Mora, Sergio	*University of Alicante, Spain*	52
Mary, Latisha	*Université de Lorraine, France*	630
Mkrttchian, Vardan	*HHH University, Australia*	291, 296
Motschnig, Renate	*University of Vienna, Austria*	272
Myers, Jonte A	*University of Florida, USA*	143
Nakui, Haruka	*Abiko Special Needs Education School for the Mentally Challenged, Japan*	464
Nemoto, Fumio	*University of Tsukuba, Japan*	464
Nkabinde, Zandile P.	*New Jersey City University, USA*	806
O'Connor Jr., Johnny R.	*Lamar University, USA*	446
Odia, Agnes Anuoluwapo	*University of Benin, Nigeria*	80
Odia, James Osabuohien	*University of Benin, Nigeria*	80
Olan, Elsie L.	*University of Central Florida, USA*	613
Pacis, Dina	*National University, USA*	163, 179
Pendergast, Mark O.	*Florida Gulf Coast University, USA*	19
Perez, Luis	*Eye on Access, USA*	495
Pfannenstiel, Kathleen Hughes	*American Institutes for Research, USA*	240
Pluta, Rebecca Magee	*Special Education Advocate, USA*	578
Preast, June L.	*University of Missouri, USA*	102
Prickett, Logan	*Auburn University at Montgomery, USA*	495
Raasch, Jennifer	*Clemson University, USA*	1
Raghunandan-Jack, Nadira	*Charter School Sector, USA*	649
Rankin, Jenny Grant	*University of Cambridge, UK*	843
Ritter, Zachary S.	*University of Redlands, USA*	712
Robles, Teresita de Jesús Álvarez	*Universidad Veracruzana, México*	535

Rodríguez, Francisco Alvarez / *Universidad Autónoma de Aguascalientes, México* 535
Rose, Chad A. / *University of Missouri, USA* 102
Roth, Kenneth Robert / *California State University, USA* 712
Rudstam, Hannah / *Cornell University, USA* 215
Ruffin, Tiece / *University of North Carolina – Asheville, USA* 891
Russell, Carol / *Emporia State University, USA* 404
Sanchez-Gordon, Sandra / *National Polytechnic School of Ecuador, Ecuador* 52
Sanders, Jennifer "JC" / *Independent Researcher, USA* 240
Schwilk, Christopher L. / *Shippensburg University, USA* 550
Talbot, Donna / *Western Michigan University, USA* 390
Tseng, Margaret / *Marymount University, USA* 578
Uduigwome, George / *Los Angeles Unified School District, USA* 320
Urushihata, Chiho / *University of Tsukuba, Japan* 464
Van Looy, Sara / *Cornell University, USA* 215
Wang, Jun / *University of Florida, USA* 143
Webster, Nicole / *Pennsylvania State University, USA* 782
Whitten, Elizabeth / *Western Michigan University, USA* 121
Wright, Michelle F. / *Masaryk University, Czech Republic* 368
Yamaguchi, Kyoko / *Abiko Special Needs Education School for the Mentally Challenged,
    Japan* 464
Young, Andrea / *Université de Strasbourg, France* 630
Zheng, Binyao / *Kennesaw State University, USA* 865

Table of Contents

Preface xv

Volume I

Section 1
Accessibility Laws and Frameworks

Chapter 1
Laws, Finance, and Policies of Higher Education Accessibility 1
Jennifer Raasch, Clemson University, USA

Chapter 2
Evaluating the Accessibility of Online University Education 19
Mark O. Pendergast, Florida Gulf Coast University, USA

Chapter 3
Expanding Notions of Access: Opportunities and Future Directions for Universal Design 34
Emily Ehlinger, University of Minnesota, USA

Chapter 4
Design, Implementation and Evaluation of MOOCs to Improve Inclusion of Diverse Learners 52
Sandra Sanchez-Gordon, National Polytechnic School of Ecuador, Ecuador
Sergio Luján-Mora, University of Alicante, Spain

Chapter 5
Accessibility to Higher Education in Nigeria: The Pains, Problems, and Prospects 80
James Osabuohien Odia, University of Benin, Nigeria
Agnes Anuoluwapo Odia, University of Benin, Nigeria

Section 2
Disabilities: General

Chapter 6
Creating Inclusive Classroom Communities Through Social and Emotional Learning to Reduce Social Marginalization Among Students 102
    June L. Preast, University of Missouri, USA
    Nicky Bowman, University of Missouri, USA
    Chad A. Rose, University of Missouri, USA

Chapter 7
Special Education Leadership and the Implementation of Response to Intervention 121
    Derek Cooley, Godwin Heights Public Schools, USA
    Elizabeth Whitten, Western Michigan University, USA

Chapter 8
Leveraging Professional Development to Prepare General and Special Education Teachers to Teach within Response to Intervention Frameworks 143
    Amber Elizabeth Benedict, University of Florida, USA
    Mary T. Brownell, University of Florida, USA
    Cynthia C. Griffin, University of Florida, USA
    Jun Wang, University of Florida, USA
    Jonte A Myers, University of Florida, USA

Chapter 9
Implementing Effective Student Support Teams 163
    Tricia Crosby-Cooper, National University, USA
    Dina Pacis, National University, USA

Chapter 10
Best Practices Implementing Special Education Curriculum and Common Core State Standards using UDL 179
    Penelope Debs Keough, National University, USA
    Dina Pacis, National University, USA

Chapter 11
Access to Higher Education for People with Disabilities: A Chinese Perspective 197
    Luanjiao Hu, University of Maryland at College Park, USA
    Jing Lin, University of Maryland at College Park, USA

Chapter 12
Beyond Handicap, Pity, and Inspiration: Disability and Diversity in Workforce Development
Education and Practice 215
Hannah Rudstam, Cornell University, USA
Thomas Golden, Cornell University, USA
Susanne Bruyere, Cornell University, USA
Sara Van Looy, Cornell University, USA
Wendy Strobel Gower, Cornell University, USA

Chapter 13
Characteristics and Instructional Strategies for Students With Mathematical Difficulties: In the
Inclusive Classroom 240
Kathleen Hughes Pfannenstiel, American Institutes for Research, USA
Jennifer "JC" Sanders, Independent Researcher, USA

Chapter 14
Inclusion of Users with Special Needs in the Human-Centered Design of a Web-Portal 272
Renate Motschnig, University of Vienna, Austria
Dominik Hagelkruys, University of Vienna, Austria

Chapter 15
Providing Quality Education for Persons With Disabilities Through the Implementation of
Individual Educational Programs Managed by the Intelligent Agents in the Sliding Mode 291
Vardan Mkrttchian, HHH University, Australia
Ekaterina Aleshina, Penza State University, Russia

Chapter 16
Digital Control Models of Continuous Education of Persons with Disabilities Act (IDEA) and
Agents in Sliding Mode 296
Vardan Mkrttchian, HHH University, Australia
Ekaterina Aleshina, Penza State University, Russia

Section 3
Disabilities: Learning and Developmental

Chapter 17
Specific Learning Disabilities: Reading, Spelling, and Writing Strategies 320
George Uduigwome, Los Angeles Unified School District, USA

Chapter 18
Coping Strategies of Primary School Students With Specific Learning Disabilities 356
Karin Bagnato, University of Messina, Italy

Chapter 19
School Bullying and Students with Intellectual Disabilities... 368
Michelle F. Wright, Masaryk University, Czech Republic

Chapter 20
Marginality and Mattering: The Experiences of Students With Learning Disabilities on the College Campus 390
    Wanda Hadley, Western Michigan University, USA
    Jennifer Hsu, Grand Valley State University, USA
    Mark Antony Addison, Western Michigan University, USA
    Donna Talbot, Western Michigan University, USA

Chapter 21
Understanding Nonverbal Learning Disabilities in Postsecondary Students with Spina Bifida 404
    Carol Russell, Emporia State University, USA

Chapter 22
Use of Assistive Technology to Empower Persons with Intellectual Disabilities 431
    Sanjeev Kumar Gupta, All India Institute of Speech and Hearing, India

Chapter 23
The Use of iPad® Devices and "Apps" for ASD Students in Special Education and Speech Therapy 446
    Johnny R. O'Connor Jr., Lamar University, USA
    Keonta N. Jackson, Texas A&M University – Commerce, USA

Chapter 24
Handmade Content and School Activities for Autistic Children with Expressive Language Disabilities 464
    Shigeru Ikuta, Otsuma Women's University, Japan
    Ryoichi Ishitobi, University of Tsukuba, Japan
    Fumio Nemoto, University of Tsukuba, Japan
    Chiho Urushihata, University of Tsukuba, Japan
    Kyoko Yamaguchi, Abiko Special Needs Education School for the Mentally Challenged,
        Japan
    Haruka Nakui, Abiko Special Needs Education School for the Mentally Challenged, Japan

Section 4
Disabilities: Physical

Chapter 25
Improving Access to Higher Education With UDL and Switch Access Technology: A Case Study 495
    Luis Perez, Eye on Access, USA
    Ann Gulley, Auburn University at Montgomery, USA
    Logan Prickett, Auburn University at Montgomery, USA

Volume II

Chapter 26
Wheelchair Access and Inclusion Barriers on Campus: Exploring Universal Design Models in Higher Education 509
    Maryan Amaral, Aero, Inc., USA

Chapter 27
Addressing Accessibility of MOOCs for Blind Users Hearing Aid for Screen Orientation 535
    Teresita de Jesús Álvarez Robles, Universidad Veracruzana, México
    Alfredo Mendoza González, Universidad Juárez Autónoma de Tabasco, México
    Alma Rosa García Gaona, Universidad Veracruzana, México
    Francisco Alvarez Rodríguez, Universidad Autónoma de Aguascalientes, México

Chapter 28
The Educational Rights of Students with Chronic Disease 550
    Thomas C. Gibbon, Shippensburg University, USA
    Jenifer Cline, Great Falls Public Schools, USA
    Christopher L. Schwilk, Shippensburg University, USA
    Patricia D. Hosfelt, Frederick County Maryland Public Schools, USA
    David F. Bateman, Shippensburg University, USA

Chapter 29
Educating Students with Chronic Illness: How the Old Service Model Fails 578
    Margaret Tseng, Marymount University, USA
    Rebecca Magee Pluta, Special Education Advocate, USA

Section 5
Diversity and Culturally Responsive Teaching

Chapter 30
Social Inclusion and Intercultural Values in a School of Education 599
    Olga M. Alegre de la Rosa, University of La Laguna, Spain
    Luis M. Villar Angulo, University of Seville, Spain

Chapter 31
Critical Practices for Teaching and Learning in Global Contexts: Building Bridges for Action 613
    Ann E. Lopez, University of Toronto, Canada
    Elsie L. Olan, University of Central Florida, USA

Chapter 32
The Role of Multi-Media in Expanding Pre-Service Teachers' Understanding of Culturally and Linguistically Diverse Classrooms and Furthering Their Professional Identities 630
    Latisha Mary, Université de Lorraine, France
    Andrea Young, Université de Strasbourg, France

Chapter 33
Teacher Preparatory Programs and Culturally Responsive Teaching 649
    Nadira Raghunandan-Jack, Charter School Sector, USA

Chapter 34
Fusing Culturally Responsive Teaching, Place Conscious Education, and Problem-Based
Learning With Mobile Technologies: Sparking Change 666
    Nykela H. Jackson, University of Central Arkansas, USA

Chapter 35
A Forensic Psychological Perspective on Racism in Schools of Educational Leadership: Impact
on Organizational Culture 680
    Ronn Johnson, Creighton University Medical School, USA & VA Nebraska-Western Iowa
        Health Care System, USA
    JoJo Yanki Lee, University of San Diego, USA
    Ji Youn Cindy Kim, University of Iowa, USA

Chapter 36
Channeling Race: Media Representations and International Student Perceptions 712
    Kenneth Robert Roth, California State University, USA
    Zachary S. Ritter, University of Redlands, USA

Chapter 37
Using Narrative and Team-Teaching to Address Teaching About Racial Dynamics 738
    Stephen Brookfield, St. Thomas University, USA

Chapter 38
Preparing Urban Educators to Address Diversity and Equity through Field-Based Teacher
Education: Implications for Program Design and Implementation 757
    Adam S. Kennedy, Loyola University, USA
    Amy J. Heineke, Loyola University, USA

Chapter 39
#UrbanLivesMatter: Empowering Learners through Transformative Teaching 782
    Nicole Webster, Pennsylvania State University, USA
    Heather Coffey, University of North Carolina at Charlotte, USA
    Anthony Ash, University of North Carolina Charlotte, USA

Chapter 40
Multiculturalism in Special Education: Perspectives of Minority Children in Urban Schools 806
    Zandile P. Nkabinde, New Jersey City University, USA

Chapter 41
Exploring Intercultural Awareness: International Student Mobility in China and the UK through a
Non-Essentialist Lens 822
    Monika Foster, Edinburgh Napier University, UK

Chapter 42
Data System-Embedded Analysis Support's Implications for Latino Students and Diverse Classrooms 843

Jenny Grant Rankin, University of Cambridge, UK

Section 6
Inclusive Classrooms and Campuses

Chapter 43
Creating Inclusive Classroom: Innovative Practices by Chinese Banzhurens 865

Jiacheng Li, East China Normal University, China
Yan Li, East China Normal University, China
Ying Huang, Changzhen Elementary School of Guangming District, China
Liujuan Huang, Guangming Experimental School, China
Binyao Zheng, Kennesaw State University, USA

Chapter 44
Equity and Inclusion in Today's Diverse and Inclusive 21st Century Classroom: Fostering Culturally Responsive Pre-Service Teachers with the Tools to Provide Culturally Responsive Instruction 891

Tiece Ruffin, University of North Carolina – Asheville, USA

Chapter 45
Cultivating Communities of Inclusive Practice: Professional Development for Educators – Research and Practice 906

Christina M. Curran, University of Northern Iowa, USA
Becky Wilson Hawbaker, University of Northern Iowa, USA

Chapter 46
Supporting Secondary Students with Disabilities in an Inclusive Environment 940

Pam Epler, Grand Canyon University, USA

Chapter 47
Assessing the Functions of Behavior for Students with Autism in the Inclusive Classroom Environment 972

Lina Gilic, St. John's University, USA
Michelle Chamblin, Molloy College, USA

Chapter 48
An Integral Analysis of Labeling, Inclusion, and the Impact of the K-12 School Experience on Gifted Boys 995

Laurie Alisat, University of Calgary, Canada
Veronika Bohac Clarke, University of Calgary, Canada

Chapter 49
A Comparison of "Inclusiveness" in Two Liberal Arts Catholic Universities: What Nurtures an Inclusive Campus Climate? 1022
    Theron N. Ford, John Carroll University, USA
    Blanche Jackson Glimps, Tennessee State University, USA

Index xx

Preface

Providing an inclusive educational environment is rapidly becoming critical for pre-service teachers as many students now come from diverse economic and racial backgrounds, and/or present different learning abilities and behavioral challenges. Educators, including teachers, administrators, and academicians, now require a set of dispositions, skills, and practices that honor students' differences, are representative of deep content knowledge, and result in the delivery of high quality, rigorous instruction. An inclusive education centers on creating a classroom community that is comprised of diverse students, including those with varying abilities, from differing races and ethnicities, and bringing with them a variety of cultural and familial backgrounds.

The cultural composition of American public schools has changed over recent years, and as such, it is vital that educators become equipped with the appropriate cross-cultural competencies required to effectively teach and meet the needs of diverse students. Today's inclusive classrooms require educators to understand differences in culture, language, and ability and how these differences can affect a child's aptitude for learning.

However, the vast majority of educators are unprepared for the diversity that they will ultimately face in schools. Therefore, it is critical for teachers to acknowledge that diversity is an important element in education and can have a massive impact on the classroom atmosphere as well as student achievement. Teacher education programs must endeavor to prepare educators to interact more effectively with diverse populations and enhance students' achievement at the same time.

Additionally, it is critical for teachers to model the knowledge, skills, and attitudes of culturally competent professionals as without that it will be difficult for students to apply the knowledge, skills, and attitudes that foster cross-cultural competence. The challenge that educators face today is clear as they strive to differentiate learning environments and academic achievement for all students.

The everchanging scene surrounding the varied applications of different educational areas can make it very challenging to stay on the frontline of ground-breaking research trends. That is why IGI Global is pleased to offer this two-volume comprehensive reference that will empower teachers, administrators, principals, higher education faculty, curriculum developers, instructional designers, policymakers, students, researchers, and academicians with a vigorous understanding of education policies and inclusion barriers.

This compilation is designed to act as a single reference source on conceptual, methodological, and technical aspects, and will offer insight into emerging topics including but not limited to educational technology, differentiated learning, inclusive pedagogy, special education, and online learning. The chapters included in this publication will provide readers with the tools that are necessary for future research and discovery within education.

Accessibility and Diversity in Education: Breakthroughs in Research and Practice is organized into six sections that provide comprehensive coverage of important topics. The sections are:

1. Accessibility Laws and Frameworks;
2. Disabilities: General;
3. Disabilities: Learning and Developmental;
4. Disabilities: Physical;
5. Diversity and Culturally Responsive Teaching; and
6. Inclusive Classrooms and Campuses.

The following paragraphs contain a summary of what to expect from this invaluable reference source:

Section 1, "Accessibility Laws and Frameworks," opens this wide-ranging reference source by highlighting the latest trends in educational policy and special educational laws. The first chapter in the section, "Laws, Finance, and Policies of Higher Education Accessibility," by Prof. Jennifer Raasch of Clemson University, USA, explores and explains the complex interconnections of laws, finances, and policies in supporting accessibility on campuses and offers potential guidelines for further institutional policies and procedures related to students with disabilities. The next chapter is titled "Evaluating the Accessibility of Online University Education," by Prof. Mark O. Pendergast of Florida Gulf Coast University, USA, and examines the requirements of accessibility laws, the formation of the accessibility initiative, and the resulting WCAG 2.0 standard. Chapter 3 in this section is titled "Expanding Notions of Access: Opportunities and Future Directions for Universal Design," by Prof. Emily Ehlinger from University of Minnesota, USA, and studies several different frameworks of universal design that are specific to the context of instruction and learning, as well as the scholarship and theory related to implementation of these frameworks in postsecondary classroom environments. The next chapter, "Design, Implementation, and Evaluation of MOOCs to Improve Inclusion of Diverse Learners," by Prof. Sandra Sanchez-Gordon from National Polytechnic School of Ecuador, Ecuador and Prof. Sergio Luján-Mora from the University of Alicante, Spain, presents accessibility requirements that need to be considered in the design, implementation, and evaluation of massive open online courses (MOOCs) to ensure they are inclusive of all students. The last chapter in this section, "Accessibility to Higher Education in Nigeria: The Pains, Problems, and Prospects," by Profs. James Osabuohien Odia and Agnes Anuoluwapo Odia of the University of Benin, Nigeria, considers the issues and challenges that are associated with low accessibility to university education in Nigeria and also suggests ways to address these issues and challenges for the future.

Section 2, "Disabilities: General," discusses emerging research on disabilities and how they create diversity within educators' classrooms. The first chapter in this section, "Creating Inclusive Classroom Communities Through Social and Emotional Learning to Reduce Social Marginalization Among Students," by Profs. June L. Preast, Nicky Bowman, and Chad A. Rose from University of Missouri, USA, looks at how we can identity the key components of social and emotional learning (SEL), provide guidance in implementation, and describe how SEL can help reduce the social marginalization among youth with disabilities and those at-risk for disability identification. Another chapter in this section titled "Implementing Effective Student Support Teams," by Profs. Tricia Crosby-Cooper and Dina Pacis from the National University, USA, discusses the historical aspects, purpose and processes, and challenges of student support teams (SST) and also presents strategies for teachers and educators to effectively implement and work within the SST process. Another significant chapter within this section is titled "Best

Preface

Practices Implementing Special Education Curriculum and Common Core State Standards using UDL," by Profs. Penelope D. Keough and Dina Pacis of the National University, USA, which provides a model for collaboration between general education and special education teachers using universal design for learning (UDL) and shows how the curriculum can be accessed by students with special needs. Also included in this section is "Beyond Handicap, Pity, and Inspiration: Disability and Diversity in Workforce Development Education and Practice," by Profs. Hannah Rudstam, Thomas Golden, Susanne Bruyere, Sara Van Looy, and Wendy Strobel Gower from Cornell University, USA, focuses on 10 misconceptions that have fueled the marginalization of disability in diversity and inclusion efforts. The final chapter in this section, "Digital Control Models of Continuous Education of Persons With Disabilities Act (IDEA) and Agents in Sliding Mode," by Prof. Vardan Mkrttchian from HHH University, Australia and Prof. Ekaterina Aleshina from Penza State University, Russia, covers models of continuous education and how they will affect persons with disabilities and what this will mean for the future of education.

Section 3, "Disabilities: Learning and Developmental," presents chapters that examine challenges for students with intellectual and developmental disabilities including nonverbal learning disabilities and students with autism. The first chapter included in this section, "Specific Learning Disabilities: Reading, Spelling, and Writing Strategies," by Prof. George Uduigwome from the Los Angeles Unified School District, USA, discusses best practices in providing support for students diagnosed with reading (dyslexia), writing (dysgraphia), and spelling (dysorthographia) deficits and explains that early intervention is key to providing students with learning disabilities a meaningful learning experience. Another important chapter contained in this section, "School Bullying and Students with Intellectual Disabilities," by Prof. Michelle F. Wright from Masaryk University, Czech Republic, aims to explore multidisciplinary research concerning school bullying among students with intellectual disabilities and to make recommendations for public policy and prevention programs as well as future research. Also included within this section is a chapter titled "Marginality and Mattering: The Experiences of Students With Learning Disabilities on the College Campus," by Prof. Wanda Hadley from Western Michigan University, USA; Prof. Jennifer Hsu of Grand Valley State University, USA; and Profs. Mark Antony Addison and Donna Talbot from Western Michigan University, USA, which discusses students' access and adjustment to the campus culture and how this experience influences their identity development. One of the closing chapters included in this section, "The Use of iPad® Devices and 'Apps' for ASD Students in Special Education and Speech Therapy," by Prof. Johnny R. O'Connor Jr. of Lamar University, USA and Prof. Keonta N. Jackson from Texas A&M University – Commerce, USA, examines the various uses of iPads and other applications ("apps") for students with autism spectrum disorders (ASD) in special education and speech therapy settings. The final chapter in this section, "Handmade Content and School Activities for Autistic Children With Expressive Language Disabilities," by Prof. Shigeru Ikuta from Otsuma Women's University, Japan; Profs. Ryoichi Ishitobi, Fumio Nemoto, and Chiho Urushihata of University of Tsukuba, Japan; and Profs. Kyoko Yamaguchi and Aruka Nakui of Abiko Special Needs Education School for the Mentally Challenged, Japan, considers how different multimedia such as audio, movies, web pages, HTML files, and PowerPoint files can be used to help children with expressive language disabilities and autism spectrum disorders (ASD) learn more effectively.

Section 4, "Disabilities: Physical," includes chapters on improving access to education for students with physical handicaps, including blind students and those restricted to wheelchairs, and how to help educate students with chronic illnesses. The first chapter in this section, "Improving Access to Higher Education With UDL and Switch Access Technology: A Case Study," by Prof. Luis Perez from Eye on Access, USA and Profs. Ann Gulley and Logan Prickett of Auburn University at Montgomery, USA, presents an in-depth case study of the creative use of a mobile technology system by a diverse learner who is blind and has significant fine and gross motor impairments. The next chapter, "Wheelchair Access and Inclusion Barriers on Campus: Exploring Universal Design Models in Higher Education," by Prof. Maryan Amaral from Aero, Inc., USA, explores the barriers to inclusive education that students with disabilities face and propose solutions to create more inclusive and welcoming campuses that facilitate the success of all students. Also included in this section is "Addressing Accessibility of MOOCs for Blind Users: Hearing Aid for Screen Orientation," by Prof. Teresita de Jesús Álvarez Robles from Universidad Veracruzana, Mexico; Prof. Alfredo Mendoza González of Universidad Juárez Autónoma de Tabasco, México; Prof. Alma Rosa García Gaona from Universidad Veracruzana, México; and Prof. Francisco Alvarez Rodríguez of Universidad Autónoma de Aguascalientes, México, which examines a set of guidelines for designing hearing messages that help blind students to maneuver a massive online open course's (MOOC's) interface. This chapter is followed by "The Educational Rights of Students With Chronic Disease," by Prof. Thomas C. Gibbon from Shippensburg University, USA; Prof. Jenifer Cline of Great Falls Public Schools, USA; Prof. Christopher L. Schwilk from Shippensburg University, USA; Prof. Patricia D. Hosfelt of Frederick County Maryland Public Schools, USA; and Prof. David F. Bateman from Shippensburg University, USA, which discusses the consideration for education in the least restrictive environment, and key components in the development of both IEP's and Section 504 plans, issues related to providing a free appropriate public education, and the Family and Educational Rights Privacy Act. The final chapter in this section, "Educating Students With Chronic Illness: How the Old Service Model Fails," by Prof. Margaret Tseng from Marymount University, USA and Prof. Rebecca Magee Pluta of Special Education Advocate, USA, illuminates the need for schools to break away from the traditional administrative special education mold when responding to the challenges of educating frequently absent students with chronic illness.

Section 5, "Diversity and Culturally Responsive Teaching," discusses current perspectives on multiculturalism in education and tackles the challenge of addressing race and racism in the classroom. The first chapter in this section, "Social Inclusion and Intercultural Values in a School of Education," by Prof. Olga M. Alegre de la Rosa of University of La Laguna, Spain and Prof. Luis M. Villar Angulo from University of Seville, Spain, aims to analyze the contextual and personal factors associated with student teachers' inclusive and intercultural values to minimize barriers to learning and participation for students. Another chapter included in this section, "Teacher Preparatory Programs and Culturally Responsive Teaching," by Prof. Nadira Raghunandan-Jack from Charter School Sector, USA, focuses on culturally responsive educational programs within higher education institutions and also includes a framework for recommendation and improvements for higher education institutions to implement in order to further refine and strengthen teacher preparatory programs. Also included in this section is "Channeling Race: Media Representations and International Student Perceptions," by Prof. Kenneth Robert Roth of California State University, USA and Prof. Zachary S. Ritter from University of Redlands, USA, which examines how media representations can flavor cross-cultural interactions, and the implications these interactions may have for campus climate, diversity initiatives, and the increasingly multicultural and globalized work place. Another important chapter in this section, "#UrbanLivesMatter: Empowering Learners Through Transformative Teaching," by Prof. Nicole Webster of Pennsylvania State University, USA and Profs. Heather Coffey and Anthony Ash from University of North Carolina at Charlotte, USA, discusses the need for professional development embedded in culturally responsive teaching, multicultural education, and critical literacy, all of which have the power to incite social action. The final chapter within this section, "Data System-Embedded Analysis Support's Implications for

Preface

Latino Students and Diverse Classrooms," by Prof. Jenny Grant Rankin from University of Cambridge, UK, highlights study findings that can significantly improve teachers' ability to use data to help Latino students thrive in diverse classrooms.

Section 6, "Inclusive Classrooms and Campuses," explores strategies for educators of all levels of education who are looking to make their classrooms more diverse and inclusive. The first chapter in this section, "Creating Inclusive Classroom: Innovative Practices by Chinese Banzhurens," by Prof. Jiacheng Li from East China Normal University, China; Prof. Yan Li of East China Normal University, China; Prof. Ying Huang from Changzhen Elementary School of Guangming District, China; Prof. Liujuan Huang of Guangming Experimental School, China; and Prof. Binyao Zheng from Kennesaw State University, USA, discusses inclusive education throughout China and offers practical applications, limitations on research, and future research directions. Another chapter included in this section is "Equity and Inclusion in Today's Diverse and Inclusive 21st Century Classroom: Fostering Culturally Responsive Pre-Service Teachers With the Tools to Provide Culturally Responsive Instruction," by Prof. Tiece Rufin from the University of North Carolina – Asheville, USA. It shares the odyssey of one African American teacher educator at a predominately white institution in a diverse learner's course fostering culturally responsive pre-service teachers with the tools to provide culturally responsive instruction for today's diverse and inclusive 21st century classroom. A noteworthy chapter included in this section, "Supporting Secondary Students With Disabilities in an Inclusive Environment," by Prof. Pam L. Epler from Grand Canyon University, USA, informs and educates secondary (Grades 6-12) pre-service teachers on how to provide content and design assignments for students within the special education curriculum. Finally, the last chapter included in this section, "A Comparison of 'Inclusiveness' in Two Liberal Arts Catholic Universities: What Nurtures an Inclusive Campus Climate?" by Prof. Theron N. Ford, Independent Researcher, USA and Prof. Blanche Jackson Glimps from Tennessee State University, USA, looks retrospectively at Madonna University and compares it to John Carroll University to highlight differences in how each has dealt with the issue of inclusiveness.

Although the primary organization of the contents in this work is based on its six sections, offering a progression of coverage of the significant concepts, practices, technologies, applications, social issues, and emerging trends, the reader can also find specific contents by utilizing the extensive indexing system listed at the end of the publication.

Section 1
Accessibility Laws and Frameworks

Chapter 1
Laws, Finance, and Policies of Higher Education Accessibility

Jennifer Raasch
Clemson University, USA

ABSTRACT

Historically, educational accessibility in higher education appeared to be a dynamic and fluid scale with individual rights and accessibility on one side while institutional policies and procedures balanced the other side. Additional weights were applied to both sides of the scale. United States (U.S.) federal laws applied weight to the individual rights and accessibility side. Meanwhile, financial considerations applied weight to the institutional policies side. U.S. universities may have found this balancing act difficult through ongoing legal cases and law revisions. Critical Disability Theory (CDT) provides an alternative viewpoint to review education accessibility. CDT also encourages participation by more campus stakeholders to resolve accessibility issues and promote full accessibility on university campuses. This chapter will explore and explain the complex interconnections of laws, finances and policies in supporting accessibility on campuses and discuss potential guidelines for future institutional policies and procedures related to students with disabilities.

INTRODUCTION

Historically, educational accessibility in higher education appeared to be a dynamic and fluid scale with individual rights and accessibility on one side while institutional policies and procedures balanced the other side. Additional weights were applied to both sides of the scale. United States (U.S.) federal laws applied weight to the individual rights and accessibility side. Meanwhile, financial considerations applied weight to the institutional policies side. U.S. universities may have found this balancing act difficult through ongoing legal cases and law revisions.

Critical Disability Theory (CDT) provides an alternative viewpoint to review education accessibility. CDT also encourages participation by more campus stakeholders to resolve accessibility issues and promote full accessibility on university campuses. U.S. universities could become the role model for accessible spaces and curriculum.

DOI: 10.4018/978-1-7998-1213-5.ch001

This chapter will explore and explain the complex interconnections of laws, finances and policies in supporting accessibility on campuses and discuss potential guidelines for future institutional policies and procedures related to students with disabilities. The goals for this chapter are:

- Provide an overview of landmark federal disability laws.
- Review of recent legal cases impacting accessibility issues in U.S. universities.
- Examine accessibility finances in higher education.
- Discuss alternative CDT inspired institutional policies for the future of campus accessibility.

SOCIAL ACTIVISM BACKGROUND

Disability rights and laws were born out of civil activism and advocacy groups. Historically, people with disabilities were supported by family and friends without much public awareness and resources. Students with disabilities were educated at home. Ward and Meyer (1999) noted that public advocacy groups such as the American Foundation of the Blind began in the 1920s and post World War I veterans required rehabilitation services. Disability advocate groups continued to expand as American industrialism increased. From the 1930s to the 1950s, disability advocacy enlarged as people with disabilities lived longer lives due to the advances in treating disabilities along with better rehabilitation services. They desired more independent living environments as well. McDonald and Oxford (2005) noted that Ed Roberts became disabled from polio and was a key leader for independent living rights. Ed Roberts fought for accessibility rights to attend college in California in the late 1960s and early 1970s. Also during the 1960s and 1970s, Scotch (1989) explained how the smaller advocacy groups became more connected and organized to protest for equal rights which gained national media attention. During the

Figure 1. Historical factors impacting accessibility in higher education

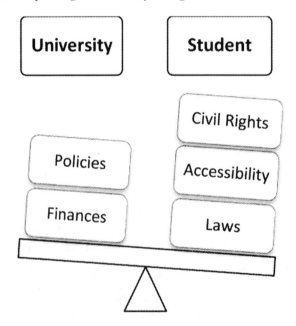

Figure 2. CDT inspired accessibility framework

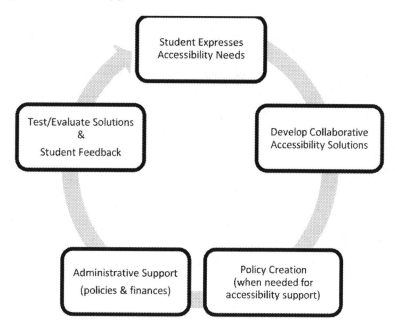

same time period, federal laws were developed and passed to support disability rights. A new era of individual and educational rights were achieved and continued to mature through the remainder of the twentieth century. Individuals with disabilities had transitioned from medical abnormalities outside normal society to empowered community members with a focus on removing environmental barriers.

Overview of Landmark U.S. Federal Laws Supporting Accessibility

An overview is presented of the historic landmark U.S. federal laws as they pertain to higher education accessibility issues. Basic descriptions of the laws significance and impact on higher education are noted. It is important to acknowledge that educational accessibility rights were achieved in the U.S. primary and secondary grades (K-12) first. These important laws paved the way for K-12 students to graduate from secondary schools and have the opportunity to proceed into higher education institutions. A few of the crucial K-12 laws will be noted but not discussed in great detail. An in-depth discussion of the nuances of the presented laws is beyond the scope of this chapter. However, the entire content of the presented laws are readily accessible through U.S. government websites. A good starting point for additional information is: www.ada.gov.

1968: Architectural Barriers Act (ABA)

From the post World War I 1920s to the Civil Rights Movement in the 1960s and 1970s, various activist groups fought for public rights for individuals with disabilities. Due to their persistence, a key U.S. federal law was passed to provide accessibility to public places. In 1968, postsecondary institutions were impacted by the U.S. federal law passed for the Architectural Barriers Act (ABA), 42 U.S.C. §§ 4151 *et seq.* (1968). Ward and Meyer (1999) emphasized the importance of the passage of the ABA law which required publicly accessible buildings and included individuals with disabilities in the general community of activities and events. This crucial law mandated structural changes to public spaces so individuals with disabilities could access them easily. Architectural designs shifted focus to accessibility in all public spaces through universal design principles. The Architectural Barriers Act of 1968 was a major achievement in disability rights and an important first step toward accessing educational facilities.

1973: Section 504 of the Rehabilitation Act

Additional U.S. federal laws were added in the 1970s to support disability rights and further impacted postsecondary education. In 1973, Section 504 of the Rehabilitation Act (§ 504), 29 U.S.C. § 794 (1973), connected federal aid and assistance programs to non-discrimination and reasonable accommodations for equitable treatment of students with disabilities. Section 504 introduced the need for reasonable accommodations in higher education courses and programs without modifying the key components of the programs. Many U.S. postsecondary institutions accepted U.S. federal financial funding and participated in federal programs which gave Section 504 traction in higher education. The concept of reasonable accommodations opened new educational opportunities to individuals with disabilities. Classroom accommodations forced more accessibility to course curriculum and learning materials for students.

Important Note: Dayton (2015) also noted the Education of the Handicapped Act (EHA), Pub. L. No. 94-142 § 2, 89 Stat. 773 (1975), established a federal Bureau of Education for the Handicapped. A new federal level organization assigned to disability education requirements gained national public interest in students with disabilities and their educational options. Although this law applied to students in K-12 grades, EHA paved new educational paths that lead more students with disabilities to seek entry into postsecondary institutions.

1990: Americans With Disabilities Act (ADA)

In 1990, the Americans with Disabilities Act (ADA), 42 U.S.C. § 12101 (1990), increased legal requirements in the private sector and clarified public institutions' responsibilities. The ADA law also made public transportation accessible and created the TDD/telephone relay services. Dayton (2015) explained that federal funding could no longer be used as a reason for discrimination against individuals with disabilities in public and private facilities. The ADA law forced all higher education institutions (public and private) to be accessible to individuals with disabilities for education activities and public events. The ADA law broadened the scope and reach of mandated accessibility for individuals with disabilities.

Important Note: Prior U.S. federal K-12 education laws culminated in the Individuals with Disabilities Education Act (IDEA), 20 U.S.C. § 1401 (1990), and included an addition of transitional services and training for entering the workforce or a university after graduation. IDEA promoted further educational services to K-12 students with disabilities and encouraged further advocacy for enrollment in higher education degree programs.

1998: Section 508 of the Rehabilitation Act (and Other Assistive Technology Laws)

Jaeger (2006) stated Section 508 of the Rehabilitation Act was added in 1998 and required federal websites to be accessible for individuals with disabilities by 2001. Many universities received federal aid for students through financial aid assistance and other federal programs. In order to maintain the federal aid

Laws, Finance, and Policies of Higher Education Accessibility

funding sources, many university website pages were modified and made accessible through assistive technologies such as screen reader software.

Other disability laws related to assistive technologies impacted postsecondary education as well. Day and Edwards (1996) explained the Technology-Related Assistance Act for Individuals with Disabilities Act (Tech Act), 29 U.S.C. § 2201 *et seq.* (1988), defined assistive technology as technology devices which assisted or improved the daily activities or functional tasks of individuals with disabilities. The Tech Act of 1988, amended in 1994, encouraged development of assistive technologies and technology training for individuals with disabilities. In 1998, the Assistive Technology Act (AT Act), 29 U.S.C § 3001 (1998), was passed and amended in 2004. Alper and Raharinirina (2006) mentioned the AT Act refined the previous terms and increased programs created by the Teach Act.

2016: Americans With Disabilities Act Amendments Act (ADAAA)

In 2016, the amended ADA law was published. The Americans with Disabilities Act Amendments Act (ADAAA) incorporated the ADA Amendments Act of 2008 (P.L. 110-325) and the updated 2010 ADA Standards for Accessible Design (U.S. Department of Justice, 2016). The amended law broadened the definition of disability again after prior court cases had narrowed the definition and law interpretation. The expansion of the definition of disability and interpretation of the law was written to incorporate more of the spirit of the law to stop discrimination against individuals with disabilities and increase accessibility. Again, the ADAAA supported higher education accessibility to course curriculum, public events and campus buildings for students with disabilities.

These key laws related to disability rights and postsecondary education accessibility provided a federal and state framework to implement reasonable accommodations and accessible public spaces on U.S. campuses. Individuals with disabilities have filed complaints about a lack of compliance with these laws. When complaints occurred, the U.S. Office for Civil Rights investigated the circumstances of the complaints.

KEY ACCESSIBILITY THEMES FROM RECENT LEGAL CASES

Office for Civil Rights

The Office for Civil Rights (OCR) working with the U.S. Department of Education ensured accessible education for all students and equity of rights in U.S. schools (both K-12 and postsecondary). An official complaint was filed in cases where students (or parents) felt discrimination occurred or education institutions were not in legal compliance with federal and state disability laws (available on the OCR Web site: http://www.hhs.gov/ocr/). Legal action was taken by OCR to resolve the filed complaints. OCR employees presented aspects of recent OCR cases from higher education institutions at an OCR Legal Year in Review session at the fall South Carolina AHEAD conference (Office for Civil Rights, 2015, October). Three key themes emerged from the discussed cases and investigations.

Equity in Campus Procedures

The first key theme revealed no tolerance for discrimination and required equity in campus procedures. From admissions applications (OCR 11-15-2032) to housing and dining accommodations for campus residents (OCR 05-12-2192 and OCR 11-14-2256), the OCR lawyers expressed the importance of fair treatment for all students regardless of ableness.

Physical and Electronic Accessibility

The second key theme discussed was accessibility for both physical locations and electronic course materials. Facilities (OCR 05-14-2467), campus Websites (OCR 15-13-6002) and online learning systems (OCR 08-15-2040) received continued monitoring for accessibility. OCR resolutions supported disability rights and equity in educational environments accessibility.

Reasonable Academic Accommodations

The third key theme revolved around reasonable academic accommodations. The OCR lawyers reiterated that documentation guidelines for accommodations (OCR 11-14-2247) and essential program or course requirements (OCR 05-11-2011) must be reasonable. For example, third party medical evaluation requirements should fit with the disability type and include minimum requirements to provide evidence of the disability. In summary, students' access to needed accommodations, facilities, assistive technologies and academic materials was essential to the educational learning process and campus life.

U.S. federal laws and OCR investigations with resolutions provided guidelines and standards of accessibility for postsecondary institutions. The U.S. Department of Justice (DOJ) heard law cases as well. In recent years, the DOJ has reviewed several cases on electronic learning environments which provided accessibility standards for higher education institutions.

Additional Education Technology Legal Cases

Newer education technologies caused accessibility problems for individuals with disabilities. The U.S. Department of Justice dealt with two complaints filed by the National Federation of the Blind (NFB) and the American Council of the Blind (ACB) related to electronic book readers (specifically the Kindle DX). On December 22, 2009, a Letter of Resolution (DJ. No. 202-57-146) was issued to Case Western Reserve University which stated that the university would not purchase or require any electronic book readers without full accessibility to students with visual impairments (U.S. Department of Justice, 2009). On January 08, 2010, a settlement agreement was reached with the Arizona Board of Regents and Arizona State University to also utilize electronic readers that were fully accessible by students with visual disabilities (United States of America, 2010). These national concerns prompted the U.S. Department of Justice and the U.S. Department of Education to send out a letter on June 29, 2010 which reminded university presidents across the U.S. to provide accessible technologies such as electronic book readers to all students.

Students filed complaints against non-accessible course materials posted on the Internet by higher education institutions as well. Miami University in Oxford, Ohio operated edX™ which offered massive open online courses (MOOCs) to students. In April 2015, a settlement agreement (DJ No. 202-36-255) was reached between the United States and edX™ Incorporated to modify the edX™ products so they conformed to accessibility guidelines (United States of America, 2015). EdX™ was also tasked with developing guidelines and training related to accessibility for course content providers and employee technical support services (United States of America, 2015). MOOCs course content was challenged again when the National Association of the Deaf (2015) filed complaints against Massachusetts Institute of Technology (Civil Action No. 3:15-cv-300024-MGM) and Harvard University (Civil Action No. 3:15-cv-30023-MGM) for a lack of closed captioning on video content. Without the closed captioning option, the public video content was not accessible to individuals who were deaf or hard of hearing. At the time this chapter was written, a settlement had not been reached in these cases.

Another recent legal case involved high stakes national testing for law school entry. The U.S. DOJ chose to intervene in a lawsuit filed in California. In May 2014, a Consent Decree was reached with the Law School Admission Council (CV 12-1830-EMC) which incorporated more reasonable guidelines to request testing accommodations and improved accessibility options to exam materials (California Department of Fair Employment and Housing, 2015).

The variety of education related court cases demonstrated the U.S. Department of Justice, U.S. Department of Education and the Office for Civil Rights expected and enforced education equality and accessibility for individuals with disabilities. United States governmental authorities and federal laws have repeatedly worked to improve equity and accessibility for students with disabilities in education. Postsecondary institutions received several legal examples that emphasized all students deserved equal learning environments with accessible learning resources. Additionally, university administrators, faculty and staff were responsible for understanding and implementing federal and state disability laws into university and departmental policies. Since accessibility for all students is federally and state mandated, university administrators must obtain and budget monetary funding to support accommodations and accessible facilities.

ACCESSIBILITY FINANCE RESEARCH

University accessibility funding covered a broad range of campus projects from facilities management to technology acquisitions to faculty training on universal design principles to accessible online content. The broad range of accessibility issues on a university campus usually required crossover into multiple university departments and generally more than one budget to cover all accessibility costs. Research in financial budgeting for accessibility in U.S. higher education institutions was minimal at a local, state and federal level. Previous financial budgeting for accessibility issues and student accommodations established no transparent processes from the federal expenditures to the state and then into the university levels. Limited information on accessibility costs for all three levels appeared to be available from past research studies and U.S. government database collections.

Federal Issues

The U.S. Department of Education (U.S. Department of Education, 2016) provided federal funding for the K-12 environment to support the IDEA law with grants to states of approximately $11.5 billion in 2014. The funding was increased to $11.7 billion in 2016. Conversely, federal funding for adults (including university students) was funneled through Rehabilitation Services with Vocational Rehabilitation (VR)

State Grants of about $3.1 billion in 2014 and $3.4 billion in 2016. Within universities, not all students with disabilities were registered with VR. Therefore, some students never received federal benefits and monetary funding. Some college students with disabilities probably benefited from VR funds through (U.S. Department of Education, 2016):

- Protection and Advocacy of Individual Rights (PAIR) which received about $17.7 million in 2016.
- American Printing House for the Blind which received approximately $24.9 million in 2016.
- National Technical Institute for the Deaf which received about $67 million in 2016.

Adults (including university students) also benefited from the Office for Civil Rights (OCR). The U.S. Department of Education (2016) provided federal funding for OCR employee salaries and department expenses with approximately $98.4 million in 2014 with 544 employees. This budget was increased to $130.7 million in 2016 with 754 employees. For a contrasting budget beneficial to university students (regardless of ableness), Student Aid Administration (SAA) which managed student loans to attend universities received a departmental budget of approximately $1.2 billion in 2014 with 1,320 employees; $1.6 billion in 2016 with 1,350 employees (U.S. Department of Education, 2016). The SAA served a larger population of students than OCR which could have accounted for the employee staffing and budgeting differences. None the less, OCR required about half the number of employees of SAA but the federal budget is less than half for OCR. After a review of federal budgets, some inequalities in federal funding for accessibility initiatives with adult students appeared. Therefore, university student accessibility expenses and budgets depended more heavily on state and university budgets.

Important Note: More research data on K-12 school budgets and funding for students with disabilities is available at the national and state levels. The budgetary spending is more clearly designated and categorized as well.

State and Local Issues

Some U.S. states provided education budgets which were obtained through an Internet search. However, those budgets provided only general information about operating expenses. The budgets were not specifically listing funds for higher education student accommodations and accessibility initiatives. Likewise, departmental data from universities for the disability services operating budget and support funding for accessibility was not easily obtainable through Internet searches. Therefore, another measurement to compare universities' expenditures was utilized. The U.S. Department of Education (2014) maintained the Integrated Postsecondary Education Data System (IPEDS) which contained financial information for many U.S. universities. A comparison of some universities from the Southern U.S. provided statistics for core expenses per FTE (full-time equivalent or headcount) enrollment by function and the percent of distribution to core expenses for fiscal year 2014. Disability support and services were typically structured under Academic Affairs or Student Affairs departments in the U.S. so statistics related to academic support and student services became informative for evaluation of university funding on a common measurement. The U.S. Department of Education (2014) IPEDS data listed the following percentage expenses per FTE enrollment range for academic support (4% - 14%) and student services (2% - 8%). IPEDS data also displayed the following core expenses per FTE enrollment for academic support ($2,060 - $6,561) and student services ($833 - $2,201). States such as California and Texas had slightly higher statistics which demonstrated that U.S. universities funded academic support and student services differently. Higher education students are likely to receive different levels of support in various U.S. postsecondary institutions based on national and state statistics of funding.

Assistive Technologies

Assistive technologies (AT) appeared in many varieties from motorized wheelchairs for mobility disabilities to captioning for hearing impairments to screen readers and educational learning strategies for learning differences. A comprehensive overview of the various types of AT and all the vendors who provided AT products were not provided in this chapter. For more information about assistive technologies and the vendors who sold them, a few informative resources were available through:

- **AbleData:** Tools & Technologies to Enhance Life (http://www.abledata.com/).
- **Assistivetech.net:** National Public Website on Assistive Technology (http://assistivetech.net/).
- **Disability.gov:** Guide to Assistive and Accessible Technologies (https://www.disability.gov/resource/disability-govs-guide-assistive-technology/).

Financial data for assistive technologies tended to be compiled at individual institutions and not available for public review and research. State and national data was more difficult to locate and appeared to be general information without a clear application for higher education. For example, the U.S. Department of Health and Human Services Administration for Community Living (2016) listed a 2016 Budget Table with a heading for Consumer Information, Access and Outreach which contained Assistive Technology funding for $34,000. Domin and Smith (2012) offered another example from an AT ACT Data Brief which noted 10% of assistive technology reutilization was for education and 6,809 individuals received transition training on assistive technology to improve the transition into employment or postsecondary education.

Research literature recommended further studies related to AT costs. Lenker, Harris, Taugher and Smith (2013) noted AT users wanted cost compared on long-term life performance and quality for the best AT solution implementation instead of the least expensive AT available. Also, AT users wanted the opportunity to work with AT vendors to improve AT products and support services. Schraner, De Jonge, Layton, Bringolf and Molenda (2008) encouraged a more holistic approach to evaluation and calculation of AT costs based on a comparison between no AT assistance, the current AT usage status and the optimal AT solution with environmental factors added to the formula. For example, a student who has reading disabilities or learning differences required another person to read educational materials (such as English and history homework) or was provided with a screen reader software. The short-term cost of the screen reader was more expensive than providing a reader for a couple of hours after classes. However, the long-term cost of the acquired screen reader software with environmental factors added was less expensive than the student dropping out of school due to poor grades (no AT intervention) or additional tutor expenses with advanced course work in a university program (current AT solution). Therefore, the screen reader software (optimal AT solution) was less expensive and more effective long-term to support this individual with a disability. This type of calculation formula focused on long-term and more aspects of an AT solution and implementation. With limited statistical data and research studies on AT costs in higher education, more research conducted to understand the complex nature of AT short-term and long-term costs would be valuable to university planning.

SOLUTIONS AND RECOMMENDATIONS

U.S. federal laws clearly supported disability rights and higher education accessibility to buildings, academic curriculum, public events and mass transportation. Social equality demands Kantian ethics of universal human rights for all people (Sandel, 2009). However, some U.S. higher education institutions may still struggle with inclusive policies, financial budgeting for accommodations and collaborative problem solving for accessibility challenges on campus.

Future Institutional Policy Considerations

Critical disability theory (CDT) can offer a new conceptual framework to critically review and implement long term solutions to accessibility issues. As disability laws and rights developed, higher education institutions trying to balance all the institutional policies, financial budgeting, new federal laws and students rights to create an accessible campus may have been a difficult task (See Figure 1). However, critical disability theory provides empowerment to the student with disabilities to state accommodation needs (See Figure 2). Then, other campus stakeholders can provide support and problem solving to find a reasonable solution to the accessibility challenges. Further support to the student is provided by campus administrators. Campus leaders can create policies and allocate funding to support new accessibility initiatives on campus. Lastly, a review of the solution and feedback from the student with disabilities allows for testing the solution in an appropriate environment and fine tuning it to properly assist the student. Hopefully, the feedback process and fine tuning will also allow the accessibility solution to be utilized with other students who have the same accessibility needs and challenges on campus. All students can have equitable access to campus resources with critical campus planning to remove all environmental barriers and a revised problem solving framework such as CDT.

Critical Disability Theory Background

Critical disability theory evolved over time from three other theoretical frameworks and years of social activism for individuals with disabilities. The three guiding pedagogies are medical impairment to social justice perspective, disability studies and empowerment issues. From a social justice lens, Rocco and Delagado (2011) recommended movement away from traditional medical and economic issues toward the recognition of identity markers and social constructs for individuals with disabilities. Goodley (2011) explained disability studies included discussions about inclusive learning environments and equity in education. From empowerment issues, Morris (1997) explained the difference between care for individuals with disabilities and independence while Kelly (2013) suggested accessible care was a complex mixture of emotions, actions, empowerment and coercion. Meekosha and Shuttleworth (2009) broadly defined critical disability theory as an examination of past social, political and intellectual paradigms which described life experiences of people with disabilities and clarified prospective improvements for social, political and economic equity in the future.

From a critical disability theory perspective, three areas of accessibility support continue to change due to societal influences from within and outside the university: accommodations acquisition, assistive technologies and financial budgeting for support services. Educational leaders and accessibility support staff need to critically review university policies and implement revisions to achieve an accessible learning environment for all students. Students with disabilities and accessibility support staff must continue to be advocates for resolving accessibility challenges with campus collaboration from a broad spectrum of campus community members.

Efficient Accessibility Facilitation Procedures

Bolt, Decker, Lloyd and Morlock (2011) noted that students found accommodations helpful in both high school and college but more students used them in college. In April 2012, the Association on Higher Education And Disability (AHEAD) posted new Documentation Guidance on their website due to ADA amendments and revisions (AHEAD, 2015). The Documentation Guidance provided a paradigm shift for registering students with accessibility services in higher education. Before 2012, documentation guidelines suggested that students needed to acquire documentation of a disability from a qualified 3rd party (such as a medical doctor or licensed psychologist). Then, students (and possibly parents, siblings, friends or K-12 teachers) were interviewed for additional information on the nature of the disability and potential accommodation needs. Some students found providing the documentation difficult for a variety of reasons such as young age diagnosis with no current affiliation with the doctor, lack of health insurance to visit a doctor or high cost of additional medical testing. As noted earlier in this chapter, more recent OCR cases supported an individual's rights to disability services and support resources with a minimum requirement for documentation of a disability. Therefore, the new AHEAD Documentation Guidance was posted in 2012 which shifted the primary source of documentation to a student's interview with university staff. Then, family, friends or even former teachers and education professionals' testimonies could be supplied. Lastly, documentation from a qualified 3rd party was requested. From a CDT perspective of empowerment, this shift reflected precedence for vocalizing the student's personal narrative for needed accommodations as an important first step in registering for disabilities support services on campus.

The major paradigm shift in the Documentation Guidance impacts registration of students for accessibility services on university campuses across the U.S. More students can register for services if documentation from a 3rd party is no longer the primary gatekeeper. Policy changes are inevitable as the disability laws continue to develop and court cases are resolved. University administrators should anticipate potential concerns and requests for increased staff and funding along with providing communication channels to explain policy changes to campus faculty, staff and students. University administrators should strategically plan department growth and additional support resources for students with disabilities.

An increase in students utilizing accessibility services may require some streamlining of the accommodation registration processes. More technology processes, or a new disabilities registration system, may be required to make the registration process more timely and efficient. Policy and practice revisions require planned collaboration and visionary leadership. Campus leaders for accessibility need to plan and implement effective internal changes to campus processes to comply with new legal standards and accommodation documentation guidelines. Critical review of current policies and procedures, incorporated with purposeful process improvements, are essential to adequately support students with disabilities in higher education programs. Accessibility support staff also should to be open to new campus department partnerships to review and streamline student registration processes.

Assistive Technology Consortium Contracts

Assistive technologies (AT) continually develop and advance at a rapid rate. Heiman and Shemesh (2012) recommended AT as a mandatory resource in postsecondary education with a critical need to offer alternative learning formats for academic studies. The disability studies aspect of CDT encourages inclusive learning environments with accessible curriculum for all students. Some students with disabilities depend on assistive technologies to complete college course work and required exams. Assistive technology purchases and maintenance licenses necessitates some collaboration between accessibility services and the campus technology department. An essential support services partnership indicates accessibility department staff must schedule meetings and coordinate AT projects with the technology department administrators. Many times, technology department administrators also have experience with technology contract negotiations and establishing larger consortiums for better pricing. A larger state or multi-institutional consortium for expensive accommodations such as captioning or transcription services could benefit higher education institutions but also K-12 schools, state agencies and community services. A strong coordination between the technology staff and student disability support staff is critical to supply high quality technology support services to students with disabilities along with the necessary training to faculty, staff and students. Additionally, students with various disabilities can assist the support staff with testing revised websites and new vendor products for accessibility issues. A collaborative evaluation process would empower students with disabilities to build adequate solutions to accessibility challenges and provide valuable feedback to support staff.

Training workshops and developmental resources for universal design should be offered to faculty and staff. Universal design applied to curriculum and course materials establishes guidelines which facilitate learning for a variety of learning styles and disability types (CAST, Inc., 2015). Technology staff and student disability support professionals must engage in regular strategic planning sessions and coordinate training workshops to campus community members. Accessibility services staff should utilize the technology support department expertise to organize equipment replacement strategies, streamline regular processes and test pilot new technologies across campus. A strong partnership between the technology department and accessibility support professionals on campus will benefit the faculty, staff and students as well as streamline required technology processes with long-term economical solutions.

Accommodations Financing Strategy Changes

Lasher and Greene (2001) wrote a chapter on university budgeting factors and explained several types of budgeting models including incremental, formula, program, zero-based, performance, incentive and cost-center. Incremental budgeting was a traditional model utilized in many universities to create a line-item or departmental budgeting system. According to Lasher and Greene (2001), an incremental budget was rolled over annually with minimal changes.

Incremental budgeting may work well to finance accessibility services for the core costs such as staff salaries and benefits, office operations, standard computer replacements and annual software licenses. However, it will not account for changes in funding due to fluctuating accommodations costs. Students can register each semester for accommodations and utilize accommodations by course so financial budgets change based on what types of accommodations students need each semester for each course. The selection of an appropriate finance model and budgeting strategies is more difficult with continually fluctuating accommodation costs. However, CDT encourages social justice and supporting individuals with disabilities to have equal educational resources (such as needed accommodations) as other students at U.S. universities.

Therefore, a different financial model is needed to estimate costs for accommodations by semester. Formula budgeting could predict some of the more expensive accommodation costs. Lasher and Greene (2001) explain formula budgeting is effective at predicting costs based on current and future needs with a specific mathematical formula. With services such as captioning, sign language interrupting, assistive technologies and testing centers, a formula based on the number of students who receive the accommodation each semester and the number of courses being taken by the student could be utilized to develop a cost accommodation formula and estimate semester short-term funding requirements. For example, a student who has requested a sign language interpreter and is taking 4 courses (or 12 credit hours) would spend approximately 12 hours in class each week. The formula of 12 hours x 15 weeks (in a semester) x $40 interpreter hourly rate = $7,200.00 for one student per semester. Similar formulas could be applied to captioning and other required specialized assistive technologies.

While formula budgeting could develop short-term cost analysis by accommodation type, university administrators also need a strategy for long-term predictive models to estimate accessibility funding. A review of state and local primary school (K-12) funding for disabilities offers strategies to figure upcoming average costs for higher education institutions. Parrish and Wolman (2004) and Dhuey and Lipscomb (2013) explain various types of U.S. state funding structures including census-based funding and resource-based funding for special education and K-12 students with disabilities. According to Dhuey and Lipscomb (2013), resource-based funding is state financial aid provided based on educational resources used in a school or district while census-based funding is state financial aid provided based on a school district total student enrollment. In higher education institutions, a review of the state allotted funding from a resource-based or census-based district funding structure could provide some average yearly trends for education expenditures on students heading into postsecondary education programs. A long-term predictive education cost model could be developed with current state funding data from K-12 grades (or just secondary grade schools) expenses across the local state. In summary, one financial model and funding strategy is not likely to establish the needed resources for supporting accessibility services in postsecondary institutions. A combination of financial models will be more effective to create short-term and long-term funding strategies for higher education accessibility static and fluctuating costs.

In the current reduced U.S. federal and state funding education environment, university administrators must attempt to plan financially and secure reliable resources. Disability services is shifting more quickly toward accessibility services which focuses on universal design that is appropriate for all students regardless of ableness. To follow this critical service shift, financial planning should also transition to a more proactive model. Access service administrators should review past data to see growth trends in factors such as testing center usage. This data could provide valuable information for strategic growth planning and future funding requirements. Also, training offerings should be frequent and open to all campus stakeholders. With more knowledge about accessibility best practices and assistive technology options, campus stakeholders can utilize the purchased specialized technologies to enhance course work and improve learning opportunities. Accessibility through assistive technologies at campus events should be increased as well. Accessibility services staff must actively pursue and obtain community partnerships. Community collaboration builds good will for a university and increases opportunities for campus growth, community leadership and shared research interests. Community members and college access services departments could potentially benefit in cost sharing for captioning services, assistive technologies, accessible meeting spaces and other critical accessibility resources. University administrators and accessibility service professionals must communicate with fellow colleagues at other institutions and professional organizations to establish purchasing partnerships as much as possible. A multiple institutional rate or state contracts for assistive technologies, captioning and other disability support resources could potentially lower annual costs or allow the current established funding to purchase more resources.

FUTURE RESEARCH DIRECTIONS

Limited information appears to be publically available on higher education finances related to accessibility and accommodation issues. K-12 education funding is more transparent from the federal budget to the state budgets to the local districts and schools. Higher education funding is more complex to investigate through the levels of interconnections and myriad of governmental funded programs. Additional research on accessibility and accommodations funding in postsecondary institutions and the interconnections with federal and state budgets would be useful information. With more informed knowledge of monetary flow and interconnection levels of funding, higher education institutions could develop better long-term strategies for financing accessibility and more expensive accommodations along with identifying strategic partnerships. More transparency in costs for accommodations and accessibility initiatives might also provide clear reasoning to petition federal and state legislators for additional funding support. Clear instances of vital technology consortiums or shared specialized programs and services might be easily identifiable with more specific funding and costs information available. University administrators are continually assessing current funding and institutional resources without simplified methods to compare accessibility costs. Perhaps worse, university administrators have limited means to plan better financial funding in the future with minimal compiled data on current costs of accommodations and accessibility initiatives. Research studies to improve the overall financial knowledge base on higher education accessibility and develop more efficient funding best practices are essential to stable long-term financial planning in higher education institutions.

CONCLUSION

In conclusion, federal and state laws grant people with disabilities civil rights of equity and access in educational environments. Recent legal cases continue to support disability laws, individual civil rights and education accessibility. However, financial and strategic planning becomes more challenging for academic administrators due to the annual changes in student enrollments and the diverse types of disability accommodation needs on campus. Despite the obstacles, university administrators and student support professionals must develop proactive strategies to fund and support accessibility across the institution. Critical disability theory (CDT) provides an alternative lens to critically review campus support services. CDT focuses on social justice, disability studies and empowerment. From a CDT perspective, students with disabilities face environmental accessibility challenges with a broad range of campus support services and collaborative problem solving teams. With a CDT framework approach in mind, some suggestions to contemplate for future policy and financial planning include:

- Review past data to aid in predicting future growth trends.
- Implement new financial planning strategies and cost analysis models.

- Increase access to and training for assistive technologies.
- Develop community and multiple institution consortiums to decrease costs for resources.
- Supply additional research studies on higher education accessibility financial issues.

Additionally, accessibility department staff and campus technology services should collaborate with colleagues and professional organizations to simplify the processes for providing accommodations (especially during the institutional transfer process) and cultivate rich training resources for assistive technologies.

Disability rights, services and support have improved over the past fifty years but more improvements are required in higher education. Some campuses continue to experience facilities that lack proper accessibility requirements. In addition, online information does not always utilize universal design principles to provide easy accessibility through assistive technologies. Furthermore, some faculty and campus support staff still do not understand how to assist students with disabilities to improve their learning opportunities and facilitate required accommodations. These obstacles can be removed with adequate funding, strategic academic goals and campus stakeholder collaboration so all students experience an equal and accessible postsecondary education environment. Education professionals can create a higher quality learning environment for current and future students by implementing equitable policies, strategic financial planning and accessibility best practices.

REFERENCES

AHEAD. Association on Higher Education and Disability. (2015). *Supporting accommodation requests: Guidance on documentation practices-April 2012*. Retrieved from http://www.ahead.org/learn/resources/documentation-guidance

Aleeha Dudley v. Miami University, et al., No. 1:14-cv-038 (S.D. Ohio 2015).

Alper, S., & Raharinirina, S. (2006). Assistive technology for individuals with disabilities: A review and synthesis of the literature. *Journal of Special Education Technology*, *21*(2), 47–64. doi:10.1177/016264340602100204

Americans with Disabilities Act, 42 U.S.C. § 12101 (1990).

Architechtural Barriers Act, 42 U.S.C. §§ 4151 *et seq.* (1968).

Assistive Technology Act, 29 U.S.C. § 3001 *et seq.* (1998).

Bolt, S. E., Decker, D. M., Lloyd, M., & Morlock, L. (2011). Students perceptions of accommodations in high school and college. *Career Development for Exceptional Individuals*, *34*(3), 165–175. doi:10.1177/0885728811415098

California Department of Fair Employment and Housing. (2015). *Consent Decree in DFEH v. LSAC in the United States District Court for the Northern District of California San Francisco Division*. Retrieved from http://www.dfeh.ca.gov/consentdecreeindfehvlsac.htm

CAST, Inc. (2015). *National Center on Universal Design for Learning: About UDL learn the basics* [Website page]. Retrieved from http://www.udlcenter.org/aboutudl

Day, S. L., & Edwards, B. J. (1996). Assistive technology for postsecondary students with learning disabilities. *Journal of Learning Disabilities*, *29*(5), 486–492, 503. doi:10.1177/002221949602900503 PMID:8870518

Dayton, J. (2015). *Higher education law: Principles, policies, and practice*. Lexington, KY: Wisdom Builders Press.

Department of Fair Employment and Housing v. Law School Admission Council, No. CV 12-1830-EMC (N. D. California San Francisco Div. 2014).

Dhuey, E., & Lipscomb, S. (2013). Funding special education by total district enrollment: Advantages, disadvantages, and policy considerations. *Education Finance and Policy*, *8*(3), 316–331. doi:10.1162/EDFP_a_00098

Domin, D., & Smith, F. A. (2012). *Using AT Act data to understand, plan, and improve programs* (AT Act Data Brief, 3). Retrieved from http://www.catada.info/at-act-data-brief

Education of the Handicapped Act, Pub. L. No. 94-142 § 2, 89 Stat. 773 (1975).

Goodley, D. (2011). *Disability studies: An interdisciplinary introduction*. Thousand Oaks, CA: Sage.

Heiman, T., & Shemesh, D. O. (2012). Students with learning disabilities in higher education: Use and contribution of assistive technology and website courses and their correlation to students hope and well-being. *Journal of Learning Disabilities*, *45*(4), 308–318. doi:10.1177/0022219410392047 PMID:21252373

Individuals with Disabilities Education Act, 20 U.S.C. § 1401 (1990).

Jaeger, P. T. (2006). Assessing Section 508 compliance on federal e-government Web sites: A multi-method, user-centered evaluation of accessibility for persons with disabilities. *Government Information Quarterly*, *23*(2), 169–190. doi:10.1016/j.giq.2006.03.002

Kelly, C. (2013). Building bridges with accessible care: Disability studies, feminist care scholarship, and beyond. *Hypatia*, *28*(4), 784–800. doi:10.1111/j.1527-2001.2012.01310.x

Lasher, W. F., & Greene, D. L. (2001). College and university budgeting: What do we know? What do we need to know? In J. Yeager, G. Nelson, E. Potter, J. Weidman, & T. Zullo (Eds.), ASHE reader on finance in higher education (2nd ed.; pp. 475-502). Boston: Pearson.

Lenker, J. A., Harris, F., Taugher, M., & Smith, R. O. (2013). Consumer perspectives on assistive technology outcomes. *Disability and Rehabilitation. Assistive Technology*, *8*(5), 373–380. doi:10.3109/17483107.2012.749429 PMID:23350880

McDonald, G., & Oxford, M. (2005). History of independent living. *Independent Living Research Utilization (ILRU)*. Retrieved from http://www.ilru.org/sites/default/files/History_of_Independent_Living.pdf

Meekosha, H., & Shuttleworth, R. (2009). What's so "critical" about critical disability studies? *Australian Journal of Human Rights*, *15*(1), 47–75.

Morris, J. (1997). Care or empowerment? A disability rights perspective. *Social Policy and Administration*, *31*(1), 54–60. doi:10.1111/1467-9515.00037

National Association of the Deaf v. Harvard University and the President and Fellows of Harvard College, Civil Action No. 3:15-cv-30023-MGM (U.S.D. MA June 25, 2015). (n.d.). Retrieved from http://creeclaw.org/wp-content/uploads/2015/06/2015-06-25-33-DOJ-Amicus-Brief.pdf

National Association of the Deaf v. Massachusetts Institute of Technology, Civil Action No. 3:15-cv-300024-MGM (U.S.D. MA June 25, 2015). (n.d.). Retrieved from http://creeclaw.org/wp-content/uploads/2015/06/2015-06-25-34-DOJ-Amicus-Brief.pdf

Office for Civil Rights. (2015, October). *Legal Year in Review*. Conference session presented at the meeting of South Carolina University & College Council of Educators Empowering Disabled Students (SUCCEEDS), Columbia, SC. Retrieved from http://www.scahead.org/

Parrish, T. B., & Wolman, J. (2004). How is special education funded? Issues and implications for school administrators. *NASSP Bulletin*, *88*(640), 57–68. doi:10.1177/019263650408864005

Rehabilitation Act (§ 504), 29 U.S.C. § 794 (1973).

Rocco, T. S., & Delgado, A. (2011). Shifting lenses: A critical examination of disability in adult education. *New Directions for Adult and Continuing Education*, *132*(132), 3–12. doi:10.1002/ace.426

Sandel, M. J. (2009). *Justice: What's the right thing to do?* (1st ed.). New York, NY: Farrar, Straus and Giroux.

Schraner, I., De Jonge, D., Layton, N., Bringolf, J., & Molenda, A. (2008). Using the ICF in economic analyses of assistive technology systems: Methodological implications of a user standpoint. *Disability and Rehabilitation*, *30*(12-13), 916–926. doi:10.1080/09638280701800293 PMID:18484387

Scotch, R. K. (1989). Politics and policy in the history of the disability rights movement. *The Milbank Quarterly*, *67*(2), 380–400. doi:10.2307/3350150 PMID:2534157

Technology-Related Assistance Act for Individuals with Disabilities Act, 29 U.S.C. § 2201 *et seq.* (1988).

United States of America. (2010). *Settlement agreement*. Retrieved from http://www.ada.gov/arizona_state_university.htm

United States of America. (2015). *Settlement agreement between the United States of America and edX Inc. under the Americans with Disabilites Act DJ No. 202-36-255*. Retrieved from http://www.justice.gov/sites/default/files/opa/press-releases/attachments/2015/04/02/edx_settlement_agreement.pdf

U.S. Department of Education. (2016). *Fiscal year 2016 budget summary and background information*. Retrieved from http://www2.ed.gov/about/overview/budget/budget16/summary/16summary.pdf

U.S. Department of Education, Institute of Education Sciences, National Center for Education Statistics. (2014). *IPEDS: Look up by institution*. Retrieved from http://nces.ed.gov/ipeds/datacenter/InstitutionByName.aspx

U.S. Department of Health and Human Services, Administration for Community Living. (2016). *FY 2017 ACL Budget Table: Administration for Community Living FY 2017 President's Budget*. Retrieved from http://www.acl.gov/About_ACL/Budget/ACL-FY2017-budget-table.aspx

U.S. Department of Justice. (2009). *Letter of Resolution: DJ No. 202-57-146 Case Western Reserve University*. Retrieved from http://www.ada.gov/case_western_univ.htm

U.S. Department of Justice. (2010). *Dear college or university president*. Retrieved from http://www.ada.gov/kindle_ltr_eddoj.htm

U.S. Department of Justice, Civil Rights Division. (2016). *Information and technical assistance on the Americans with Disabilities Act*. Retrieved from https://www.ada.gov/2010_regs.htm

Ward, M. J., & Meyer, R. N. (1999). Self-determination for people with developmental disabilities and autism: Two self-advocates perspectives. *Focus on Autism and Other Developmental Disabilities, 14*(3), 133–139. doi:10.1177/108835769901400302

KEY TERMS AND DEFINITIONS

Ableness: The amount or status that an individual is able or disabled (traditionally-physically able or disabled).

Assistive Technology: A device (machine or electronic) utilized to assist individuals with disabilities in daily activities or tasks.

Critical Disability Theory: A theory developed from social justice activism, empowerment issues and disability studies with a critical review of concerns from individuals with disabilities.

Disability: A physical impairment or learning difference that limits an individual's daily activities or tasks.

Disability Law: United States federal and state laws developed to protect the rights of individuals with disabilities.

Education Accessibility: The level of availability and access to all educational resources by a student.

Education Finance: Funding, budgeting and monetary issues in education systems.

Higher Education/Postsecondary: Institutions (universities or colleges) that provide education and degree programs after an individual completes (graduates) from primary and secondary school (K-12 grades in the U.S.).

Institutional/Educational Policies: Official practices and procedures developed by postsecondary schools to facilitate daily operations.

This research was previously published in Disability and Equity in Higher Education Accessibility edited by Jennie Lavine, Roy Y. Chan, and Henry C. Alphin, Jr.; pages 135-152, copyright year 2017 by Information Science Reference (an imprint of IGI Global).

Chapter 2
Evaluating the Accessibility of Online University Education

Mark O. Pendergast
Florida Gulf Coast University, USA

ABSTRACT

The rights of disabled students are protected law in nearly every country. However, the lack of awareness of the laws and the need to make web pages accessible has created barriers to fully implementing the intent of these laws. These laws typically go beyond web pages to include all instructional devices including e-readers, social networking sites, and smart phone apps. This paper takes a look at the requirements of accessibility laws, the formation of the accessibility initiative, and the resulting WCAG 2.0 standard. Accessibility testing tools for websites and web content are discussed and then used to measure the level of compliance for a number of universities. It was found that almost all university sites checked had multiple accessibility errors. Finally, a number of recommendations are made based on the compliance issues found and on the terms of several U.S. Department of Justice consent decrees.

INTRODUCTION

For years advocates for the disabled have been fighting to apply the Americans with Disabilities Act to ecommerce, mobile apps, and by extension to universities (Loten 2014). In the past such claims were often dismissed because of a lack of guidance for websites provided by the Department of Justice (DOJ). This changed on March 6, 2014 when the DOJ announced a consent decree against H&R Block that their website, mobile apps, and tax preparation products were not accessible to the disabled. The DOJ alleged that H&R Block failed to make these services accessible and therefore violated Title III of the ADA. The consent decree requires that H&R Block adopt accessibility measures conforming to WCAG 2.0 (Paulding 2014). In addition to adopting WCAG 2.0, H&R Block must meet a number of administrative requirements including appointing an accessibility coordinator; maintaining a disabled-accessible mechanism for website visitors to make comments and complaints; testing all web content for accessibility; training at least 5% of their customer service personnel to respond to disabled website users; and retaining a third party consultant to conduct annual evaluations. Paulding (2014) went on

DOI: 10.4018/978-1-7998-1213-5.ch002

to note that these "aggressive requirements" may have reflected the fact that the National Foundation for the Blind (NFB) initiated the lawsuit and had significant input into writing the terms of the decree. Paulding (2014) also added that "owners and operators of websites should note that similar commitments may be necessary to resolve web accessibility litigation in the future."

Time will tell if this consent decree has a direct effect on universities, but judging by the number and type of lawsuits listed by (Carlson 2015), administrators ought to pay attention. Carlson (2015) lists over two dozen universities and community colleges that have recently settled lawsuits. Many of the suits were filed by the NFB on behalf of students and deal directly with nonconforming technology. The growing use of inaccessible technologies such as certain e-readers, social media sites, and smart phone apps place universities at greater risk of a lawsuit. Parry (2010a) detailed the problems faced by a blind journalism student at Arizona State University. These included a Facebook App, use of a Kindle E-reader, and an online workbook used in a Spanish class. These problems ultimately resulted in a lawsuit against Arizona State that was settled by the Department of Justice. Babu (2015) tested several of Facebook's interaction features and found that functions like reading, writing, friending, and posting messages to be significantly challenging. Participants in his study needed additional time, effort, and occasionally sighted help.

In the United States, the rights of disabled students are protected primarily by the Americans with Disabilities Act (ADA) and sections 504 and 508 of the Rehabilitation Act of 1973. Yu (2003) asserts that the concept of accessible design is becoming an important aspect of web design, however, the lack of awareness of the laws and the need to make web pages accessible have created barriers to fully implementing the intent of these laws. In general, American universities have an office dedicated to creating policies and ensuring that students receive proper accommodations for their disabilities, but it is up to the student to ask for accommodations and to complain when they do not receive them. A study (Roberts, et al, 2011) performed in 2011 found that disabled students perceived that their disability had a negative impact on the ability to succeed in online courses, but most stated that their requests for accommodation were met. Whether or not the accommodation requests can be met equally well for massive open online courses (MOOCS) remains to be seen. IT Staff and faculty members may or may not be aware of the myriad of rules that can come into play when they post class notes on the web, use a learning management system to support their course, or how the blind actually perceive their work. Asakawa (2005) provides some insights into what the web looks like as viewed through screen readers and how designers can improve their experience. He concluded that web designers should experience how disabled users access the web in order to fully understand accessible and usable sites.

This paper takes a look at the requirements of accessibility laws in several countries, the formation of the World Wide Web Consortium's accessibility initiative, and the resulting WCAG 2.0 standard. Accessibility testing tools for websites and web content are discussed and then used to measure the level of compliance for a number of universities in both a vertical and horizontal manner. Finally, a number of recommendations are made based on the compliance issues found and on the terms of several DOJ consent decrees.

BACKGROUND

A University's and therefore a faculty member's responsibility to accommodate students with disabilities are dictated by several laws, each of which apply to different situations and are often open to interpretation. Most Universities will have a set policy created by their legal department to help guide faculty members. Different countries have different laws pertaining to accessibility. A university may have to satisfy the requirements of multiple countries if it conducts online learning or exchange programs with that country. (WebAIM 2015) provides a synopsis of accessibility guidelines in various countries.

Australia

In 1992 Australia passed the Disability Discrimination Act (DDA). This act provides rules that directly apply to web accessibility. Section 24 provides that it is unlawful to discriminate on the grounds of disability by refusing to make goods or services available. This act was tested by a lawsuit directed at the Sydney Organizing Committee of the Olympic Games for not having a website that was accessible as required by the DDA. In their defense, SOCOG stated that the "Alt" label problems were being resolved, the website was too big causing an unjustifiable hardship, and it would take a person year of effort to fix the problem. These reasons were repudiated by expert witnesses (Worthington 2000). The SOCOG lost the case and was ordered to make changes. They refused and were fined $20000 Australian Dollars (Byrne, 2005) (Australian Human Rights Commission 2000). Although the fine was relatively small compared to the cost of compliance, the case did set a world wide precedent.

Canada

In 1977 Canada passed the Canadian Human Rights Act (CHRA), to be administered by the Canadian Human Rights Commission (Canada 2014).

All individuals should have an equal opportunity with other individuals to make for themselves the lives that they are able and wish to have and to have their needs accommodated, consistent with their duties and obligations as members of society, without being hindered in or prevented from doing so by discriminatory practices based on race, national or ethnic origin, colour, religion, age, sex, sexual orientation, marital status, family status, disability or conviction for an offence for which a pardon has been granted.

In addition to the CHRA, Canada has created a number of initiatives to help with implementation of the law. Government Online Initiative (GOL) is a project begun in 2005 to provide Canadians with enhanced access to citizen centered service in the official language of their choice. The Government of Canada Internet Guide supports the GOL by providing guidance as to the implementation and maintenance of sites. Finally, Canada's Common Look and Feel provides guidelines for sites that must adhere to government wide statues and provides information on accessibility (Canada 2013).

European Union

The EU Charter of Fundamental Rights (European Union 2009) has two articles relating to accessibility, one, Article 21 prohibits discrimination based on the ground of disability, the other, and Article 26 provides recognition of the rights of disabled persons for independence and integration into society. Further, in 1999 the EU began *eEurope – An information Society for All* initiative. This initiative has three key objectives: bring every citizen, home, school, and business into the online information age; create a digitally literate Europe; ensure the process in socially inclusive.

A component of eEurope is e-participation for the disabled. The initiative stipulated that by the end of 2001 the Commission of Member States should commit themselves to making all public websites accessible to persons with disabilities (European Union 1999). In addition to the EU initiatives, each country in the union has their own laws and regulations for accessibility.

United Kingdom

The UK passed the Disability Discrimination Act (DDA) in 1995(United Kingdom 1995). In 2004 the entire act became enforceable. The parts of the act that dealt with websites have been in force since 1999. The Special Needs Act of 2001 filled a gap in the 1995 law dealing with education. Until 2001, universities did not have to ensure accessibility for the disabled. In 2001, the Special Education Needs and Disability Act (SENDA) was passed and added as part 4 of the DDA (Sloan 2002). Also in 2002, the Disability Rights Commission created a Code of Practice. This document provides guidance for service providers and disabled persons and became law in 2011 (United Kingdom 2011).

United States

The Individuals with Disabilities Education Act (IDEA) is a federal law that governs early intervention, special education and related services for disabled schoolchildren ages 3-21 (or until high school graduation) (University of Chicago, 2015). The ADA is a federal civil rights law designed to provide equal opportunity for qualified individuals with disabilities, including students. Section 504 of the Rehabilitation Act of 1973 is a law that protects individuals from discrimination based on their disability in connection with any public or private program or activity receiving federal financial assistance. Section 508 of the Rehabilitation Act of 1973 is a law that requires that electronic and information technology that is developed by or purchased by the Federal Agencies be accessible by people with disabilities (Thatcher, 2011). In K through 12, the school is responsible for identifying students with disabilities, testing those students, and providing services. At the post-secondary level, the student must locate the office that provides services for students with disabilities, register with that office, request accommodations, and provide documentation to support the need for accommodations. Also at the post-secondary level, the student must, once approved, request an accommodation in each instance that it is needed. Colleges are not responsible for knowing a student's schedule and arranging accommodations without some form of initiation from the student. Ingeno (2013) it was noted that by the time a student "self identifies" in an online course, there is not enough time to redesign all the materials.

The 1998 version of section 508 created binding, enforceable standards that are incorporated into the federal procurement process. Section 508 does not directly apply to private sector websites or to public sites which are not U.S. Federal agency sites (Thatcher, 2011). Therefore, universities generally do not have to comply with the standards. However, the standards can be used by a university to assess whether the technology they employ is accessible. A list of standards can be found at (U.S. Access Board 2014).

HIPPA protects the privacy of individually identifiable health information (U.S. HHS 2014). This law limits what medical information a faculty member or mentor can be given about a student with disabilities. In order to protect student's privacy most universities will not disclose the exact nature of the disability, instead, a list of appropriate learning accommodations will be given to the faculty member. A student is free to share disability information, but a faculty member should not ask for it. This can make providing accommodations more difficult.

WEB ACCESSIBILITY INITIATIVE (WAI)

Fortunately, there exists an organization that is working to make a global set of standards for accessibility, the World Wide Web Consortium (W3C). W3C's Web Accessibility Initiative (WAI) group has developed an international standard for accessibility, the Web Content Accessibility Guideline (WCAG) which is currently in version 2 (WCAG 2.0). WCAG 2.0 has been recognized by the International Standards Organization and was approved as ISO/IEC 40500:2012 standard. In order for a website to conform to the WCAG 2.0 the site must a set of requirements (W3C.org 2014): Conformance level, one of the three conformance levels must be met, A, AA, or AAA; Conformance levels are for full web pages; if visiting series of web pages is required to complete a process, then all web pages must be compliant; only accessibility-supported mechanisms for accessing content are used to meet the criteria; Non-interference, technologies (scripts, videos, animations, etc.) that are not accessibility supported can be used so long as the information they provide is available in an accessible format and they do not block access to the rest of the page.

One outcome of the creation of these standards has been the development of web accessibility validation tools. AChecker and Wave, are programmed to check web pages (HTML, CSS, JavaScript) against WCAG and other standards developed by governments and international organizations. While universal standards and compliance checking tools are a good start, Lewthwaite (2014) cautions that this approach may lead to counterproductive results for persons whose disabilities do not meet Western disability and accessibility norms. These persons may benefit more from a holistic approach that blends digital and physical solutions.

COMPLIANCE CHECKING TOOLS

AChecker

With AChecker (Inclusive Design Research Centre, 2009) the user can check webpage content by either providing a URL, uploading a file, or with a cut and paste of the HTML code itself into the tool. AChecker allows the user to specify which WCAG standard (1 or 2) and which conformance level (A, AA, AAA) to test against. AChecker also allows for testing against the USA ADA Section 508 and the Italian Stanca Act criteria. For the purposes of this paper, the WCAG 2.0 AA and ADA Section 508 guidelines were selected. AChecker classifies errors as one of three types:

1. **Known Problems:** Problems that have been identified with certainty as accessibility barriers;
2. **Likely Problems:** Problems that have been identified as probable barriers, but require a human to make a decision;
3. **Potential Problems:** Problems that AChecker cannot identify, that require a human decision.

Wave Checker

The Wave Checker is a tool created by WebAim.org (Web Accessibility in Mind). WebAim has been in existence since 1999 and is dedicated to expanding the potential of the web for individuals with disabilities. They do this by providing software tools, training, performing research, and consulting directly with industry and government. The Wave Checker tool (WebAIM, 2014) combines the WCAG 2.0 and Section 508 tests into one comprehensive test. WAVE is different from many evaluation tools in that it checks the page *after* CSS styles have been applied to it. WAVE reports problems using six categories:

1. **Errors:** Obvious problems that must be repaired;
2. **Alerts:** Likely problems that should be checked;
3. **Features:** HTML constructs that aid accessibility;
4. **Structural Elements:** Not necessarily a problem, but should be checked;
5. **HTML5 and ARIA:** Accessibility of rich internet applications;
6. **Contrast Errors:** Indicate low contrast between text and background.

Features, Structural elements, and HTML5/ARIA are not necessarily errors, but should be checked to be sure they convey the right meaning. Errors, Alerts, and Contrast errors must be addressed. WAVE displays the website being tested and tags the errors with red/green/yellow icons. Wave also generates a textural report of errors. For each error an explanation is available to clarify why it matters, how to fix it, and how WAVE located the error on the page, and links to the relevant section 508 guidelines.

Microsoft Office Accessibility Checker

Since Office version 2010, PowerPoint and Word have included an accessibility checker (Microsoft 2015a). This checker looks for many of the same errors that might be present on web pages, e.g. missing ALT text, contrast, meaningful hyperlink text, slide titles, and more. Problems are categorized as Errors, Warnings, or Tips. Errors that are checked include (Microsoft 2015b): all objects have alternative text; tables specify column header information; all slides have titles; long documents use styles to provide structure. Warnings include: hyperlink text is meaningful, use of floating objects, blank cells in tables, and table structure

Adobe PDF Accessibility Checker

According to (Adobe 2015), the accessibility features in Acrobat Reader (PDF) are in part dependent on the quality of the PDF file being read. To this end, Adobe has created an Accessibility checker as part of the Acrobat Pro DC product. The Adobe Accessibility checker has a feature that will aid in fixing the document, either by an automatic change or by prompting the user for missing information. The accessibility checker follows the WCAG 2.0 rules, e.g. Alt information must be present, PDF forms must have label tags, and table structures cannot be complex.

UNIVERSITY IMPLEMENTATION

Nearly all universities have a statement regarding the rights of individuals to access an education. New York University states:

New York University is committed to providing equal educational opportunity and participation for students with disabilities. It is the University's policy that no qualified student with a disability be excluded from participating in any University program or activity, denied the benefits of any University program or activity, or otherwise subjected to discrimination with regard to any University program or activity.

Lofty goals aside, it is up to each university to form and implement their own policies and procedures to help students with disabilities. In the United States it is up to the student to request assistance under the ADA. At most universities this requires them to register with an adaptive services office and present documentation about their disability. Once this is done the office determines what assistance they are entitled to. This assistance usually takes the form of accommodation requests being sent to the faculty member so that they can provide extra services that the student may need.

A learning management system can provide facilities to help with many of these accommodations, (Pendergast 2015). The faculty is still responsible for ensuring their course content is compatible with the various adaptive technologies in use. For the visually impaired this includes screen magnifiers, screen readers like ChromeVox (Google 2014), and braille readers. For the hearing impaired common technologies include speech to text, closed captioning software, and video relay interpreters (VRI). Many of these technologies are available free of charge, some (such as screen magnifiers) are included in operating systems; others would need to be purchased by the student or the university. It is the faculty member's responsibility to ensure course content is compatible to the technology being used and provide accessibility standards dictated by law (Lazar, Hochheiser 2013). Special care needs to be taken by faculty members when creating online course content. Even with the use of adaptive technologies, improperly created pages can be difficult or impossible to read for those with sight limitations. Audio and video content without transcripts are not useable by hearing impaired students. E-readers with text to speech features can be of help so long as the menu/functions of the device are also accessible.

A good practice is to check html using one of the many accessibility tools. In addition to accessibility, all html pages should be checked for validity. Validity checkers will find missing tags, broken links, obsolete tags, and other errors that might make it hard for screen readers to work correctly. An example of such a checker can be found at http://validator.w3.org/.

Faculty will also need to ensure that linked pages in formats other than HTML are compatible with adaptive technologies. In particular, faculty should make sure that their PowerPoint, Word, and PDF files are accessible. A first step is to run the accessibility checker contained in Microsoft and Adobe tools

Unless a university has a proactive policy for ensuring accessibility, chances are that compliance will be spotty. The next section tests this assumption by running WCAG and Section 508 tests on a sample set of university homepages.

TESTING THE CURRENT STATE OF UNIVERSITY SITES

WCAG 2.0 guidelines were first published in 2008 and various web page testing tools have been around for nearly as long. Given that, it would seem likely that most official university created web pages would be WCAG 2.0 AA compliant. To verify this supposition two sets of tests were performed, a horizontal test of university home pages; and a vertical test of pages needed to access the content within the Canvas LMS.

Horizontal Website Test

For this test 24 universities were selected; some public, some private, some large, and some small. All are accredited and based upon their reputations should have the resources to maintain compliant websites. Each homepage was tested using AChecker for both WCAG 2.0AA and Section 508. All universities homepages tested showed multiple known, likely, or potential problems for the WCAG 2.0 AA standard with the exception of New York University. The NYU homepage did not have any know, likely, or potential problems. Carnegie Mellon University and the University of Montana did not have any known or likely, but did have some potential problems. On average, the 24 universities tested had 19 known, 1 likely, and 448 potential problems. Table 1 details the results.

AChecker has 165 different error codes for WCAG2.0 AA, 61 Known, 16 Likely, and 88 Potential. A closer examination of the results shows that 16 of the 61 of the "known" errors accounted for the

Table 1. Homepage AChecker.ca for WCAG2.0 AA results from May 7, 2015

University	Home Page	Known Problems	Likely Problems	Potential Problems
Arizona	http://www.arizona.edu/	5	12	418
Bradley	http://www.bradley.edu/	33	2	275
Brigham Young	http://home.byu.edu/	9	0	842
UCLA	http://www.ucla.edu/	5	0	428
Carnegie Mellon	http://www.cmu.edu/	0	0	187
Colorado State	http://www.colostate.edu/	15	0	554
Delaware	http://www.udel.edu/	10	0	819
Florida Gulf Coast	http://www.fgcu.edu/	27	0	295
Galluadet University	http://www.gallaudet.edu/	5	0	546
Georgia	http://www.uga.edu/	14	0	919
Harvard	http://www.harvard.edu/	10	0	526
Indiana	http://www.iu.edu/	45	1	325
Louisville	http://louisville.edu/	4	0	492
Montana	http://www.umt.edu/	0	0	327
New York University	http://www.nyu.edu/	0	0	0
North Carolina State	https://www.ncsu.edu/	1	8	376
Oklahoma	http://www.ou.edu/	68	2	271
Pittsburg	http://www.pitt.edu/	39	1	520
Syracuse	http://www.syr.edu/	14	0	554
Tennessee Knoxville	http://www.utk.edu/	7	0	323
Texas	http://www.utexas.edu/	93	0	511
Tufts	http://www.tufts.edu/	11	0	182
Wake Forrest	http://www.wfu.edu/	30	0	448
Wisconsin	http://www.wisc.edu/	20	0	626
Average		**19**	**1**	**449**

majority of the problems. Errors 301, 303, and 304 all deal with insufficient contrast between text and background colors. This has an adverse effect on students with color blindness or limited vision. Errors 48 and 49 indicate an incorrect or missing "lang" attribute on the HTML tag. This tag assists screen readers, search engines, and browsers. Errors 188, 57, 213 all deal with the need for a label tag to be associated with each input tag. The label tag is used by screen readers to tell users what is expected of them when they enter input into a form control. Errors 116, 117 indicate that the physical tags bold and italic formatting tags have been used as opposed to logical tags. Screen readers do better with logical tags such as "em" tag (for emphasis) and strong (important text). Errors 37, 38 both deal with header tags being out of order, a good document will have a heading 1 followed by a heading 2, followed by a heading 3. Not a heading 1 followed directly by a heading 3. Errors 1, 7, and 174 all deal with missing text or missing alt text on images and links.

For the section 508 test all universities showed multiple errors with the exception of New York University. NYU did not have any know, likely, or potential problems. Indiana University and the Tufts only had 1 known problem, but many likely and potential problems. On average, the 24 universities tested had 10 known, 14 likely, and 47 potential problems. Table 2 details the results.

AChecker has 51 different error codes for Section 508, 17 Known, 12 Likely, and 22 Potential. A closer examination of the results shows that 4 of the 17 of the "known" errors occur on 25% or more of the homepages. 21 of the 24 schools broke error number 90; this check requires that a noscript section must exist for every script section within the body of the document. Errors 1 and 7 indicate the Alt text for an image is missing. Error 57 indicates an input field does not have an associated label field.

Given that NYU homepage had no errors or warnings for either the WCAG2.0 or section 508 tests a few more of NYU's webpages were tested for errors. What was discovered was that all webpages tested on their university webserver were error free (according to AChecker), however, webpages on servers sponsored by individual colleges had errors. This indicates that NYU had different policies or procedures in place based on what entity controlled the web content.

Based on the results obtained from AChecker it appears that most universities have not made a conscientious effort to insure that all their webpages meet WCAG2.0 or Section 508 standards. The sheer number of pages on university web servers and the dynamic nature of much of their content make bringing them into compliance a large task.

Vertical Website Test

The horizontal tests just examined the homepages of select universities. Almost all were discovered to have multiple errors. To further explore the nature of accessibility errors and the effort needed to correct them, a second set of tests were performed on the series of pages a student must navigate in order to access a page within a course. This test began with a Florida Gulf Coast University's homepage, LMS login page, and then several pages within a demo course. The demo course pages were chosen because they were did not require passwords to access them and therefore were reachable by the accessibility checker software. In addition to the LMS pages a few pages commonly linked to online courses were tested. This included a publisher's student website, the Wall Street Journal, CNN, and New York Times. The Wave Checker was used for this test. The results are shown in Table 3. As you can see, none of the pages looked at in the vertical test were totally error free. What was particularly disconcerting is that a visually impaired person would have trouble getting past the login page, let alone the course content.

Table 2. Homepage AChecker.ca for Section 508 results from May 11, 2015

University	Home Page	Known Problems	Likely Problems	Potential Problems
Arizona	http://www.arizona.edu/	3	17	42
Bradley	http://www.bradley.edu/	30	18	50
Brigham Young	http://home.byu.edu/	11	13	67
UCLA	http://www.ucla.edu/	7	11	50
Carnegie Mellon	http://www.cmu.edu/	3	3	19
Colorado State	http://www.colostate.edu/	19	14	52
Delaware	http://www.udel.edu/	7	15	81
Florida Gulf Coast	http://www.fgcu.edu/	22	16	70
Galluadet University	http://www.gallaudet.edu/	8	13	54
Georgia	http://www.uga.edu/	6	15	67
Harvard	http://www.harvard.edu/	19	22	47
Indiana	http://www.iu.edu/	1	11	48
Louisville	http://louisville.edu/	10	15	32
Montana	http://www.umt.edu/	7	11	53
New York University	http://www.nyu.edu/	0	0	0
North Carolina State	https://www.ncsu.edu/	11	22	32
Oklahoma	http://www.ou.edu/	8	9	37
Pittsburg	http://www.pitt.edu/	5	40	73
Syracuse	http://www.syr.edu/	4	24	69
Tennessee Knoxville	http://www.utk.edu/	6	9	45
Texas	http://www.utexas.edu/	9	12	55
Tufts	http://www.tufts.edu/	1	4	19
Wake Forrest	http://www.wfu.edu/	25	7	50
Wisconsin	http://www.wisc.edu/	10	5	24
Average		**10**	**14**	**47**

CONCLUSION AND RECOMMENDATIONS

In 2010 the Chronicle of Higher Education published a table ranking 183 college websites according to their accessibility for blind students (Gunderson 2010). Dr. Gunderson reviewed home pages, admissions office pages, as well as other pages linked directly to the home page. Most colleges had less than 60% of their pages meet his criteria for accessibility. A similar study by Erickson (2013) found that less than 1% of the pages tested met Section 508 standards. The findings of this paper show that colleges have not made very much progress in the last 5 years.

There are two basic strategies that a college or university can take when addressing accessibility of their institution, reactive (personalized) or proactive (institution wide). The results of this and previous studies seem to indicate that most universities have adopted a reactive personalized strategy. IDEA and ADA laws in the United States require K-12 educators to take a proactive strategy; one where individuals

Table 3. Vertical accessibility for the Wave Checker

Page	Errors	Alerts	Features	Structure	HTML5	Contrast
FGCU Homepage (www.fgcu.edu)	13	20	16	35	0	6
LMS login page (canvas.fgcu.edu)	10	16	5	15	0	1
Student demo course home	0	4	3	16	9	0
Modules	21	142	8	16	461	0
Canvas Help	7	13	9	49	37	2
Submitting assignments	0	2	2	5	15	0
Sample survey	0	2	2	10	16	0
Text book student website	18	10	5	9	0	0
Wall Street Journal (wsj.com)	13	46	2	221	7	39
Cable News Network (cnn.com)	10	14	10	38	3	27
New York Times (nytimes.com	14	20	43	251	24	30

Collected May 26, 2015.

with needs are identified and individualized educations plans are adopted for them. In higher education, it is up to the student to seek help that is needed.

Under the reactive personalized strategy, the university has an office whose primary function it is to help students with special needs be successful with their studies. They acquire for students specialized hardware and software, determine what accommodations they are entitled to, and work with faculty and staff to make sure their needs are met. Lawsuits can occur when student's needs cannot be met using reasonable accommodations. A typical scenario of such lawsuits is detailed in (University of Minnesota, Duluth 2013). In their scenario a university that relies on web based content or collaboration technology fails to ensure all such materials are accessible. A disability rights organization or a student discovers the inaccessible content and files a lawsuit. Commonly this progresses into a campus wide audit of accessibility. In the end, the university agrees to terms much broader than the original complaint and agrees to a campus wide review and repair of all technologies, making them WCAG 2.0AA compliant.

The National Federation of the Blind versus Penn State is an example of such a case (Cummings 2011). Under this suit Penn State was required to: conduct a full accessibility audit of its "complete technology environment"; establish a policy statement to guide development and implementation of accessible technologies across all disciplines; conduct institution wide training on the policy and its procedures; develop procedures that require the university to only purchase technology that is accessible; designate a person on each campus to monitor the university's accessibility compliance; and maintain a rich set of web resources that will provide ADA tools and training for webmasters. This settlement is similar to the one imposed on H&R Block (Paulding 2014).

A proactive institution wide strategy entails that the institution to actively look for and correct deficiencies in their operations, create policies to help ensure only accessible content is created or purchased, and train faculty and staff in the rules related to compliance and tools that can be used to create ADA compliant materials. As lawsuits such as NFB vs Penn State become more common, universities (perhaps motived by state legislatures) will need to adopt proactive strategies. Establishing an organization wide policy to ensure all technology in use meets WCAG 2.0AA standards would seem to be a fairly straightforward, though costly, thing to do. However, the organizational structure of many universities conspires against this. Parry (2010b) identifies the decentralized manner in which ADA compliance is handled is a vulnerability for universities. He went on to report that of 183 colleges and universities surveyed, one third said compliance rested with individual professors, one quarter to programs or departments, and only 1 in 6 had a central office to review compliance for every course. As an example Florida Gulf Coast University has two separate organizations responsible for computing technology; one for the administrative side of the house; the other for the academic side. Each organization has their staff, budget, web servers, and responsibility to support departments. Faculty work with administrative computing for their desktop and research needs, and academic computing for classroom needs. In addition, each college and organizational unit has their own webmaster. On top of all that, the academic freedom granted to faculty allows them to create and post their own pages and select their own learning supplements. Student organizations are also allowed to create and post materials on the university website.

Webmasters ultimately have control and responsibility for what goes on their servers. They rarely have authority over every staff and faculty member who uploads to the server but they can control what is on the server. Some proactive steps that a university ore college webmaster can take include: Provide a script or mechanism that will check each html page for WCAG 2.0AA compliance before uploading to the web server; employ a web crawler (spider) that will periodically check all pages on the webserver for compliance. The crawler needs to also check offsite linked materials for compliance and flag those that are not; maintain a pool of part-time web developers (IT, IS, CS students) who have the capability to make the minor repairs files in order to make them compliant.

University and college administrators need to do their part as well. Some of the policies they could institute should include: training faculty and staff on disability requirements; make sure authoring tools (web and otherwise) contain WCAG 2.0AA compliance checking functions; provide procedures for purchasing equipment and a list of compliant technology; use only compliant learning management systems, collaboration, and social network tools and apps; actively solicit feedback from disabled faculty and staff about their preferences and experiences; provide a mechanism for them to anonymously report ADA violations; and create and enforce university and college policies for technology use and acquisition.

In the end, it is up to faculty and staff to make a conscientious effort to only use accessible materials. Faculty should work with textbook publishers to ensure that all content made available to students on their websites is ADA compliant. In particular, make sure presentation and multimedia learning supplements are compliant. If they are not, then get permission to create compliant versions for use in their course. They should also be wary of new devices and apps. Make sure they are completely accessible from power on to accessing your content. Moore (2014) provides a number of strategies to help create compliant materials. These include the use of tagged PDF materials and using a flat navigational structure. Alpine (2013) recommended making eLearning accessibility part of the culture of an institution. Adopting a proactive strategy for ADA compliance should reduce the risk of legal problems, eliminate many problems and frustrations for students, and help the university establish the reputation as an accessible institution.

DISCLAIMER

You must not rely on the information in the report as an alternative to legal advice from an appropriately qualified professional. If you have any specific questions about any legal matter you should consult an appropriately qualified professional.

REFERENCES

W3C.org. (2014). Website Accessibility Initiative. Retrieved from http://www.w3.org/standards/web-design/accessibility

Adobe. (2015). Adobe Accessibility. Retrieved from http://www.adobe.com/accessibility.html

Alphin, H. C. (2013). E-Learning Accessibility Model: A Culture of Collaboration and Outcomes Assessment. *International Journal of Online Pedagogy and Course Design*, *3*(3), 18–42. doi:10.4018/ijopcd.2013070102

Asakawa, C. (2005). What's the Web Like If You Can't See It. *W4A '05 Proceedings of the 2005 International Cross-Disciplinary Workshop on Web Accessibility*. Retrieved from http://www.ra.ethz.ch/cdstore/www2005-ws/workshop/wf01/1-asakawa.pdf

Australian Human Rights Commission. (2000). Bruce Lindsay Maguire vs Sydney Organizing Committee for the Olympic Games. Retrieved from http://www.humanrights.gov.au/bruce-lindsay-maguire-v-sydney-organising-committee-olympic-games

Babu, R. (2015). Blind Students' Challenges in Social Media Communication: An Early Investigation of Facebook Usability for Informal Learning. *International Journal of Online Pedagogy and Course Design*, *5*(1), 58–73. doi:10.4018/ijopcd.2015010105

Byrne, J. (2005). Bruce Maguire versus Sydney Organizing Committee for the Olympic Games (SOCOG). Retrieved from http://ezinearticles.com/?Bruce-Maguire-Versus-Sydney-Organising-Committee-for-the-Olympic-Games-%28SOCOG%29&id=92115

Canada Justice Laws. (2014). Canadian Human Rights Act. Retrieved from http://laws-lois.justice.gc.ca/eng/acts/H-6/

Canada Treasury Board Secretariat. (2013). Web Standard for the Government of Canada. Retrieved June 5, 2015, from http://www.tbs-sct.gc.ca/ws-nw/index-eng.asp

Carlson, L. (2015). Higher Ed Accessibility Lawsuits Complaints and Settlements. Retrieved from http://www.d.umn.edu/~lcarlson/atteam/lawsuits.html

Cummings, J. (2012). NFB and Penn State resolve U.S. Dept. of Justice civil rights complaint. Retrieved from http://www.educause.edu/blogs/jcummings/nfb-and-penn-state-resolve-us-dept-justice-civil-rights-complaint

Erickson, W., Trerise, S., Lee, C., Vanlooy, S., Knowlton, S., & Bruyere, S. (2013). The Accessibility and Usability of College Websites: Is your Website Presenting Barriers to Potential Students? *Community College Journal of Research and Practice*, *37*(11), 864–876. doi:10.1080/10668926.2010.484772

European Union (1999). eEurope – an Information Society for all. Retrieved from http://europa.eu/legislation_summaries/information_society/strategies/l24221_en.htm

European Union (2009). EU Charter of Fundamental Rights. Retrieved from http://ec.europa.eu/justice/fundamental-rights/charter/index_en.htm

Formstack. (2014). See if your website is 508 Compliant. Retrieved from http://www.508checker.com/

Google. (2014). ChromeVox User Guide. Retrieved from http://www.chromevox.com/

Guides, C. (2014). Improving accessibility to your course. Retrieved from http://guides.instructure.com/m/5834/l/92747-improving-the-accessibility-of-your-course

Gunderson, J. (2010). Best and Worst College Websites for Blind Students. *The Chronicle of Higher Education, 12*(December). Retrieved from http://chronicle.com/article/BestWorst-College-Web/125642/

Inclusive Design Research Centre. (2009). *AChecker API*. Retrieved from http://achecker.ca/

Ingeno, L. (2013). Online Accessibility a Faculty Duty. *Inside Higher Ed*. Retrieved from https://www.insidehighered.com/news/2013/06/24/faculty-responsible-making-online-materials-accessible-disabled-students

Lazar, J., & Hochheiser, H. (2013, December). Legal aspects of interface accessibility in the U.S. *Communications of the ACM, 56*(12), 74–80. doi:10.1145/2500498

Lewthwaite, S. (2014). Web accessibility standards and disability: Developing critical perspectives on accessibility. *Disability and Rehabilitation, 36*(16), 1375–1383. doi:10.3109/09638288.2014.938178 PMID:25009950

Loten, A. (2014). Accessibility Claims Expected over Websites, Wall Street Journal, October 15. Retrieved from http://www.wsj.com/articles/accessibility-claims-expected-over-websites-1413411990

Microsoft. (2015a). Creating accessible PowerPoint Presentations. Retrieved from https://support.office.com/en-nz/article/Creating-accessible-PowerPoint-presentations-6f7772b2-2f33-4bd2-8ca7-dae3b2b3ef25

Microsoft. (2015b). Rules use by the Accessibility Checker. Retrieved from https://support.office.com/en-nz/article/Rules-used-by-the-Accessibility-Checker-651e08f2-0fc3-4e10-aaca-74b4a67101c

Moore, E. (2014, June 30). Improve Accessibility in Tomorrow's Online Courses by Leveraging Yesterday's Techniques. *Faculty Focus*. Retrieved from http://www.facultyfocus.com/articles/online-education/improve-accessibility-tomorrows-online-courses-leveraging-yesterdays-techniques/

Parry, M. (2010a). College Lock out Blind Students Online. *The Chronicle of Higher Education*. Retrieved from http://chronicle.com/article/Blind-Students-Demand-Access/125695/

Parry, M. (2010b). ADA Compliance Is a 'Major Vulnerability' for Online Programs. *The Chronicle of Higher Education*. Retrieved from http://chronicle.com/blogs/wiredcampus/ada-compliance-a-major-vulnerability-for-online-programs/28136

Paulding, M. (2014). DOG Consent Decree Provides Guidance on Web Accessibility Compliance Under ADA, Info Law Group. Retrieved from http://www.infolawgroup.com/2014/03/articles/lawsuit/doj-consent-decree-provides-guidance-to-web-accessibility-compliance-under-ada/

Pendergast, M. (2015). Leveraging Learning Management System to Accommodate Students with Disabilities: Issues and Experiences with the Canvas LMS. *Proceedings 18th Southern Association for Information Systems Conference*, Hilton Head Island, SC, USA.

Roberts, J. B., Crittenden, L. A., & Crittenden, J. C. (2011). Students with disabilities and online learning: A cross-institutional study of perceived satisfaction with accessibility compliance and services. *The Internet and Higher Education, 14*(4), 242–250. doi:10.1016/j.iheduc.2011.05.004

Sloan, M. (2002). TechDis Briefing Paper: Intuitional Websites and Legislation. Retrieved from http://www.ukoln.ac.uk/web-focus/events/workshops/webmaster-2002/talks/phipps/word2000-html/

Thatcher, J. (2011). Web Accessibility for Section 508. Retrieved from http://jimthatcher.com/webcourse1.htm

United Kingdom. (1995). Disability Discrimination Act. Retrieved from http://www.legislation.gov.uk/ukpga/1995/50/contents

United Kingdom Equality and Human Rights Commission. (2011). Equality Act Codes of Practice. Retrieved from www.equalityhumanrights.com/equality-act-codes-practice

University of Chicago. (2015). IDEA, ADA, and Section 504. Retrieved from https://disabilities.uchicago.edu/idea-ada-and-section-504

University of Minnesota Duluth. (2013). Higher Ed Accessibility Lawsuits. Retrieved from http://blog.lib.umn.edu/itsshelp/news/2013/10/higher-ed-accessibility-lawsuits.html

U.S. Access Board. (2014). Web-based Intranet and Internet Information and Applications (1194.22). Retrieved from http://www.access-board.gov/guidelines-and-standards/communications-and-it/about-the-section-508-standards/guide-to-the-section-508-standards/web-based-intranet-and-internet-information-and-applications-1194-22

U.S. Department of Health and Human Services. (2014). Health Information Privacy. Retrieved from http://www.hhs.gov/ocr/privacy/

WebAIM. (2014). Web Accessibility Evaluation Tool, WAVE. Retrieved from http://webaim.org

WebAIM. (2015). World Laws. Retrieved from http://webaim.org/articles/laws/world/

Worthington, T. (2000). Olympic Failure: A Case for Making the Web Accessible. Oxford University Computing Laboratory. Retrieved from http://www.tomw.net.au/2000/bat.html

Yu, H. (2003). Web accessibility and the law: issues in implementation. In M. Hricko (Ed.), *Design and implementation of web-enabled teaching tools* (pp. 1–24). Hershey, PA, USA: IGI Publishing. doi:10.4018/978-1-59140-107-0.ch001

This research was previously published in the International Journal of Online Pedagogy and Course Design (IJOPCD), 7(1); edited by Chia-Wen Tsai and Pei-Di Shen; pages 1-14, copyright year 2017 by IGI Publishing (an imprint of IGI Global).

Chapter 3
Expanding Notions of Access:
Opportunities and Future Directions for Universal Design

Emily Ehlinger
University of Minnesota, USA

ABSTRACT

This chapter focuses on disability access in higher education and the role that Universal Design has played in improving meaningful participation and inclusion of students with disabilities. The purpose of this chapter is to provide an overview of several frameworks of Universal Design that are specific to the context of instruction and learning, as well as the scholarship and theory related to implementation of these frameworks in postsecondary classroom environments. Scholarship on how current Universal Design frameworks might be expanded to address a broader set of access and equity issues, as well as the limitation of the current research about its application and effectiveness are also discussed. The chapter closes with a synthesis of opportunities and future directions for research, scholarship, and practice related to the development and implementation of Universal Design frameworks in higher education.

INTRODUCTION

The landscape and number of students with disabilities participating in higher education in the United States has changed dramatically over the past several decades. Students with disabilities comprised about 11% of the national undergraduate population as of the 2011-2012 academic year (Snyder, de Brey, & Dillow, 2016), compared to just 6% in 1995-1996 (Horn & Berktold, 1999). Despite gains in access to postsecondary education, students with disabilities are still less likely to go to college, and those who do are less likely to persist to their degree than their peers without disabilities (Erickson, Lee, & von Schrader, 2014; Newman, Wagner, Knokey, Marder, Nagle, Shaver, & Wei, 2011). Additionally, many students who are identified as having a disability in primary and secondary education choose not to disclose their disability when they go on to college. Nationally representative data from the National Longitudinal Transitional Study-2 (NLTS2) has revealed that nearly two-thirds of students who were

DOI: 10.4018/978-1-7998-1213-5.ch003

identified as having a disability in high school did not disclose their disability once they transitioned to college (Newman et al., 2011).

Students previously diagnosed with a disability may choose not to disclose to their postsecondary institutions for a variety of reasons, including misunderstanding their responsibility to disclose in college, lack of knowledge about how to access services (Getzel, 2008), fear of stigma, or desire to shed or disassociate with their disability identity (Marshak, Van Wieren, Ferrell, Swiss, & Dugan, 2010). While some students may no longer need services related to their disability, data regarding persistence of students who do disclose still indicate that this population is experiencing disparate postsecondary outcomes in comparison to their peers. Legal mandates to prevent discrimination and provide accommodations have improved postsecondary access for students with disabilities. Still, the data on educational outcomes and disclosure continue to raise important questions about what institutions can do to more broadly support students with disabilities.

Frameworks of Universal Design (UD) have been proposed as mechanisms to enhance access and inclusion by designing educational environments, courses, and programs to meet the needs of diverse student populations, including those with disabilities (Burgstahler, 2008b). While originally focused on designing environments to reduce physical barriers for individuals with disabilities (e.g. through curb cuts and manual doors), UD eventually gave rise to several other frameworks that are specific to teaching and learning (Schelly, Davies, & Spooner, 2011). These UD frameworks focus on improving flexibility and variation in curriculum, pedagogy, and support resources to enhance cognitive, as well as physical, access for students with disabilities and other diverse learners (Rao, Ok, & Bryant, 2014). The intention of UD is to consider access needs from the design process through implementation. Thus, the use of UD in postsecondary environments may be particularly vital for those students who choose not to disclose or seek out individual accommodations (Silver, Bourke, & Strehorn, 1998).

This chapter will explore the role that Universal Design has played in enhancing meaningful access in postsecondary environments for a wide range of student populations, including students who do not identify, have not disclosed, or have not been diagnosed with a disability. While issues related to disability access and the use of UD in higher education are not unique to the United States, this chapter will focus primarily on the U.S. to provide a more focused context for this topic. This chapter will begin with an overview of the legal landscape of disability access and representation in higher education. The rise and development of UD frameworks will then be discussed with an overview of several models and corresponding principles as well as the limitations of UD documented in scholarly literature. The chapter will close with a discussion of opportunities and new directions for UD in continuing to meet the promise of broader accessibility and inclusion for students with disabilities and other historically underserved populations.

CONTEXT OF DISABILITY ACCESS IN POSTSECONDARY EDUCATION

The Americans with Disabilities Act (ADA), as amended in 2008 (ADAAA), defines a person with a disability as having "a physical or mental impairment that substantially limits one or more major life activities, a person who has a history or record of such an impairment, or a person who is perceived by others as having such an impairment" (ADAAA: Definition of Disability, 2008, p. 7). Major life activities include "caring for oneself, performing manual tasks, seeing, hearing, eating, sleeping, walking, standing, lifting, bending, speaking, breathing, learning, reading, concentrating, thinking, communicating, and working" as well as a number of "major bodily functions" (ADAAA: Definition of Disability, 2008, p. 7).

Postsecondary institutions are guided by the ADA, as well as Section 504 of the Rehabilitation Act of 1973, which prohibit discrimination on the basis of disability and require that institutions provide students with reasonable accommodations (U.S. Government Accountability Office, 2009; Newman, Wagner, Knokey, Marder, Nagle, Shaver, & Wei, 2011). Students with disabilities who meet the academic qualifications of their institution and give sufficient notice of their disability can be provided reasonable accommodations which do not substantially alter the requirements or nature of the academic program (Simon, 2011). Examples of reasonable accommodations can include extended time on tests or recording class lectures (Simon, 2011). Institutions are not required to provide individual aides and services (such as tutors) or personal devices (such as wheelchairs) to students with disabilities (U.S. Government Accountability Office, 2009). Accommodations may vary by institution but must be tailored to each student's needs (U.S. Government Accountability Office, 2009).

In order to receive reasonable accommodations, students with disabilities are required to identify themselves to their institution and seek out accommodations. This process stands in contrast to that of primary and secondary schools, which are guided by the Individuals with Disabilities in Education Act (IDEA) of 1990. Under IDEA and the 2004 Individuals with Disabilities in Education Improvement Act (IDEIA), primary and secondary institutions are required to identify and evaluate students with disabilities and provide them with free and appropriate public education (Wolanin & Steele, 2004). Once students go on to attend postsecondary education, the responsibility is instead shifted to the student to disclose and provide documentation of their disability (Hadley, 2011). If a student has not previously been diagnosed with a disability, it is their responsibility to seek out and pay for testing (U.S. Department of Education Office of Civil Rights, 2011).

Shifting Demographics of Disability

Both the legal landscape and demographics of students with disabilities participating in higher education have shifted over the last several decades. The United States Government Accountability Office (2009) has noted the shift in students reporting orthopedic and mobility impairments from over 25% of the population of students with disabilities in 2000 to 15% in 2008 according to data from the National Postsecondary Student Aid Study (p. 11). The largest proportions of primary disabilities reported in 2008 were mental health and psychiatric disabilities, at 24%, as well as Attention Deficit Disorder (ADD), at 19% (U.S. Government Accountability Office, 2009).

Data from the National Center for Education Statistics (NCES) has indicated that the most prominent disability types reported at postsecondary institutions during the 2008-2009 academic year were specific learning disabilities (31%), ADD/Attention Deficit and Hyperactivity Disorder (ADHD) (18%), and mental health or psychiatric disabilities (15%) (Raue & Lewis, 2011). Differentiation in these two data sets likely exists because of how disability type was reported (i.e., self-reports versus data reported from documentation at the institution; U.S. Government Accountability Office, 2009). Both data sets illustrate the high number of students with less-apparent (often referred to as "hidden" or "invisible") disabilities being served at postsecondary institutions.

The high representation of students with learning disabilities in education is documented in scholarly literature (Madaus, 2011), and is also reflected in data analyzed under IDEA, which identified learning disabilities as the most prevalent disability reported for students ages 6-21 in 2011 (U.S. Depart-

Expanding Notions of Access

ment of Education, 2014). Yet, scholars also note the important growth in other populations pursuing postsecondary education, including students with mental health conditions (Madaus, 2011), veterans with disabilities, and students with Autism Spectrum Disorders (ASD; Simon, 2011; U.S. Government Accountability Office, 2011). Postsecondary institutions are already serving students with an array of disability types, including a large percentage of students with less-apparent disabilities. The potential increase in students with mental health conditions, veterans with disabilities, ASD, and other disability types will challenge institutions to address a new array of student needs, as well as training for the faculty and staff who serve them.

Whether or not students go on to disclose their disability and receive accommodations in college, instructors have been and will continue to be challenged to identify new ways to provide meaningful access and engagement in their classrooms. Universal Design has been thought to be one promising practice, in conjunction with accommodations, to proactively address the needs of emerging populations, whether or not they identify as having a disability. The following section discusses the context and development of UD frameworks in postsecondary education and the ways in which corresponding principles have been conceptualized to reduce barriers for students with disabilities and students more broadly.

UNIVERSAL DESIGN IN INSTRUCTION AND LEARNING

Universal design frameworks have been explored and implemented to respond to the overall growing number of students with disabilities, including those that are less-apparent, as well as the growing number of students from historically underserved racial and ethnic backgrounds, international students, and students of non-traditional age pursuing higher education (Zeff, 2007). UD focuses on reducing barriers beginning at the design process, for example in the development of a course, through consideration of diverse populations as opposed to focusing only on reducing individual barriers through accommodations (Rose, Harbour, Johnston, Daley, & Abarbanell, 2006). Since the focus on reducing barriers for students begins at the design phase, UD has been widely viewed as a proactive way of serving students with disabilities as opposed to having to rely on individual accommodations once a barrier has been identified (Burgstahler, 2008b).

Originally conceptualized by Ronald Mace (1988), the creation of UD was influenced by the Architectural Barriers Act of 1968 and Americans with Disabilities Act (Pliner & Johnson, 2004). UD focused primarily on designing physical environments to be accessible to all people, regardless of a disability (Rao, Ok, & Bryant, 2014). UD eventually gave rise to concepts of Universal Instructional Design (UID; Pliner & Johnson, 2004), Universal Design for Learning (UDL; Rose, Harbour, Johnston, Daley, & Arbarbanell, 2006), and Universal Design for Instruction (UDI; McGuire & Scott, 2006), among other adaptations and models. These UD models focus on enhancing aspects of teaching and learning to improve access for students with disabilities and other populations in classroom environments (Rao et al., 2014).

With regard to serving students with disabilities, the intent of UD models has been to reduce the need for and number of steps that students must take to obtain support or individual accommodations, the extent to which students must rely on external supports to succeed, the need to segregate students from their peers, and the requirement for students to disclose their disability (Higbee & Goff, 2008; Pliner & Johnson, 2004). As noted earlier, another important aspect of UD principles and application is the specific focus on diverse learners. Scholars note that the intent of UD is not to lump all students into one category of universal learners, but to instead be flexible and responsive to the needs of diverse students

(Higbee & Goff, 2008). Though UID, UDI, and UDL have sometimes been used interchangeably in the literature, each framework has also been described separately with overlapping principles and practices (Rao, Ok, & Bryant, 2014).

Silver, Bourke, and Strehorn (1998) originally coined the term Universal Design for Instruction (UDI) as a way to translate UD into the context of postsecondary education. Silver et al. conducted focus groups with instructors from the University of Massachusetts to define UDI from a faculty perspective and to explore practices and barriers to implementation in the classroom. The researchers recruited participants through the Office of Learning Disabilities Support Services (LDSS) Faculty and Friends Network, which was comprised of faculty who had been recognized by students with disabilities as providing extraordinary accommodations (Silver et al., 1998, p. 48). A total of 13 faculty members participated in this study. Demographic characteristics of faculty participants were not included. LDSS staff conducted three 1.5-hour focus groups with two research assistants. Silver et al. identified the following practices of UID from the focus groups:

- Hold high expectations for all learners;
- Demonstrate interest in seeing all students succeed;
- Be intentionally responsive to diverse learning needs and styles;
- Use diverse teaching methods to benefit all learners;
- Expect that high standards will be maintained;
- Acknowledge need for learners to receive instruction and be assessed in different ways as a matter of good teaching;
- Identify ways to teach and deliver instruction creatively; and
- Recognize diverse learners and styles in the way that students show up in their classrooms.

Strategies that faculty identified for enhancing UID and success of students with disabilities included team-based and cooperative learning; peer-editing; contextual, constructive, and criterion-based learning; prompting and cueing; distributing materials prior to class; putting materials on reserve for student access outside of class; providing extended time on projects and tests; consistency between teaching and testing; computer assisted learning; and online instruction and assessment (Silver et al., 1998, p. 49). Barriers to implementing UID included difficulty in changing teaching strategies due to pressure to conform to the status quo of the university, encountering faculty attitudes of elitism and gate keeping, the time-consuming nature of implementing UID, and lack of awareness about needs of diverse learners and alternative pedagogical methods (Silver et al., 1998).

Universal Design for Learning (UDL) was developed by the Center for Applied Technology (CAST) and is rooted in findings from cognitive neuroscience (Rose, Harbour, Johnston, Daley, & Arbarbanell, 2006). CAST was originally interested in the way that UD was being applied to architecture and saw application to the k-12 learning environment (Zeff, 2007). Rose et al. (2006) have asserted that broadening access must go beyond information by also extending to pedagogy. While their work in developing UDL initially focused on k-12 teaching and learning, their focus gradually began to expand to postsecondary education (Zeff, 2007). UDL identifies three primary brain networks involved in learning (recognition, strategic, and affective) to provide three principles for designing learning (Center for Applied Special Technology, 2014); Rao, Ok, & Bryant, 2014). UDL is differentiated from the general concept of UD because it focuses on the process of teaching and learning, not on access to information or physical structures (Rose et al., 2006).

UDL centers on three primary teaching and learning principles that include multiple means of action and expression, representation, and engagement in the learning process (Meyer, Rose, & Gordon, 2014). The principle of multiple means of representation focuses on presenting and representing information for learners (Meyer et al., 2014). Multiple means of representation may include the way that course content is presented, the way that course material is organized, and the way that content connects to other aspects of students' learning (Rose et al., 2006). For example, instructors may implement multiple means of representation by varying how content is delivered, including through lecture, small group discussions, and individual or group assignments (Zeff, 2007). Guidelines for the principle of multiple means of representation include providing "options for comprehension," "options for language, mathematical expression, and symbols," and "options for perception" (Meyer et al., 2014, p. 54).

A core aspect of the principle of multiple means of action and expression is allowing students to respond to content and express what they know in various ways (Meyer et al., 2014; Rose et al., 2006). This principle is intended to support students who may need to express their learning in different ways due to a disability or other factor related to their identity or learning style. Multiple means of expression may include providing several ways for students to demonstrate their learning or access in-class supports, like tutoring (Rose et al., 2006). Guidelines for the principle of multiple means of action and expression include providing "options for executive functions, expression and communication, and options for physical action" (Meyer et al., 2014, p. 55). Multiple means of engagement acknowledges that not all students engage in learning in the same way, develop similar internal motivation, or are engaged by the same reward structure (Rose et al., 2006). For example, an instructor may implement multiple means of expression by offering different kinds of assignments and activities, including presentations, blogging, social media exercises, or writing papers (Zeff, 2007). Guidelines for the principle of multiple means of engagement include providing "options for self-regulation," "options for sustaining effort and persistence," and "options for recruiting interest" (Meyer et al., 2014, p. 52).

Conceptually similar to UID, Scott, McGuire, and Shaw (2001, 2003) developed Universal Design for Instruction (UDI). Utilizing the first seven principles of UD established by The Center for Universal Design (CUD; 2007) at North Carolina State University, Scott et al. (2003) also integrated the work of Chickering and Gamson (1987), the Center for Applied Special Technology (CAST), and other scholars to create the following nine principles that became known as UDI:

1. Equitable use.
2. Flexibility in use.
3. Simple and intuitive.
4. Perceptible information.
5. Tolerance for error.
6. Low physical effort.
7. Size and space for approach and use.
8. Community of learners.
9. Instructional climate (pp 375 & 376).

As noted earlier, each principle within UD frameworks are intended to reduce particular barriers for students and enhance access to a certain element of the course. In the case of UDI, the first principle of equitable use focuses on providing equal or equivalent, accessible instruction for all students (Scott, McGuire, & Shaw, 2003). Examples of equitable use may include posting electronic copies of class notes to benefit students with a variety of disabilities, as well as students who are English language learners (Scott et al., 2003). The second principle, flexibility in use, focuses on providing variation in use of instructional methods; for example, using lectures, group work, online discussion boards, and other ways of engaging students in the content (Scott et al., 2003). Principle three, simple and intuitive means providing predictable and straightforward instruction; for example, by providing detailed assignment rubrics and comprehensive course syllabi (Scott et al., 2003). Principle four, perceptible information, focuses on clear and effective communication in instruction; such as selecting books that can be used in hard copy and electronic format with accessible technology (Scott et al., 2003).

The fifth principle, tolerance for error, focuses on accounting for individual learning paces and skills; for example, by breaking large assignments down into smaller sections that allow for constructive feedback for students to integrate into the final product (Scott et al., 2003). Principle six, low physical effort, focuses on reducing non-essential physical energy; for example, by allowing use of computers and word processors to write essays and assignments (Scott et al., 2003). Principle seven, size and space approach, focuses on designing accessible instruction regardless of physical characteristics; for example, arranging classroom seating in a circle instead of in rows so that all students can see the person who is speaking (Scott et al., 2003). Principle eight, A community of teachers and learners, focuses on fostering interactions between students and instructors; for example, by structuring discussions, study groups, and other interactions in and outside of class. The ninth principle, instructional climate, focuses on designing welcoming and inclusive instruction; for example, by highlighting respect for and value of diversity in the syllabi and course content (Scott et al., 2003).

In an initiative to further understand the validity of UDI, McGuire and Scott (2006) explored the perceptions of effective teaching and instructional strategies by conducting four focus groups with students with learning disabilities at three Northeastern colleges. Participants were from a community college in New York, a community college in Massachusetts, and a research university in Connecticut. Each institution was participating in the University of Connecticut's Universal Design for Instruction project. The campus' disability service offices identified potential participants and a total of 23 students joined the study. Fifteen participants chose to provide demographic information; nine identified as men and four identified as women. Participants ranged in ages from 19 to 42. Racial and ethnic background was not specified. The four focus groups were conducted at the students' home institution.

In response to being asked about instructional strategies that supported their learning, participants identified practices that were categorized into the following themes: clear expectations, advanced organizers and supports, information in multiple formats, a welcoming classroom climate, connecting teaching with real life experiences, frequent and formative feedback, supporting individual learning needs within the group, and effective assessment strategies (McGuire & Scott, 2006). Themes regarding instructor attributes that positively impacted learning also surfaced. These qualities included being approachable and available, being focused on the subject, making personal connections, and holding challenging standards for learning (McGuire & Scott, 2006). McGuire and Scott asserted that the research findings from this study align closely with the nine principles of UDI and that the themes were pervasive across the four focus groups. Although the authors noted that participants articulated challenges and barriers regarding their experiences with instruction, related themes were not reported in the findings.

Bowe (2000) elaborated on the original seven principles of UD to provide further guidance for how UD could translate into designing materials and curricula for courses. Bowe laid out the following tips for instructors to implement UD in the classroom:

- Become aware of your own culture's teachings and how those affect you as an educator.
- Provide students with options for demonstrating knowledge and skills.
- Offer instruction, and accept student work, at a distance.
- Alert students to availability of digitized texts (e-books).
- Offer students information in redundant media.
- Provide the support students need to improve accuracy and speed.
- Translate important materials to other languages as needed by your students
- Choose physically accessible locations for your classes (pp. 5-6).

One notable aspect of Bowe's tips is the call for instructors to reflect on their own cultural background. This aspect of self-reflection has been less obviously integrated into principles of UD in teaching and learning. Bowe noted that reflecting on one's own cultural background can help instructors to become aware of their own biases and identify the areas in which students' values or ways of learning may differ from their own. Bowe's tip about cultural self-reflection points to the importance of instructors considering their own identity as well as that of their students when implementing UD.

Expanding further on the work of previous scholars and researchers who developed principles related to UDI, UDL, and UID and the work of Chickering and Gamson (1987), researchers involved in a partnership called Curriculum Transformation and Disability (CTAD) at the University of Minnesota proposed eight principles of UID (Higbee & Goff, 2008). These principles include:

1. Creating a welcoming classroom.
2. Determining essential course components.
3. Communicating clear expectations.
4. Providing constructive feedback.
5. Exploring the use of natural supports in learning (such as technology) to support all learners.
6. Designing teaching methods that consider diverse learning styles, abilities, ways of knowing, previous experience, and background knowledge.
7. Creating multiple ways for students to demonstrate knowledge.
8. Promoting interactions between students and faculty (Fox, Hatfield, & Collins, 2003; Higbee & Goff, 2008, p. 2).

Higbee and Goff (2008) have contended that UID is not simply good teaching. UID requires that instructors broaden their thinking around effective teaching by taking into consideration the ways in which student identity shapes their learning experiences and by ensuring that no student is marginalized or excluded in the learning environment (Higbee & Goff, 2008). Additionally, scholars have noted that UID and other UD frameworks shift away from viewing disability as an individual problem that needs to be fixed to focusing on elements in the environment that need to be changed to provide greater access to people with disabilities (Evans, 2008). While UD models do shift the frame on traditional views of disability, some scholars have asserted that social justice, the ways in which environments are disabling, as well as the ways in which disability oppression and ableism intersect with other forms of oppression, must be a central focus to properly implementing UD (Evans, 2008; Hackman, 2008). The following section discusses the ways in which social justice and diversity have become a part of the conversation about UD, the need for more research on the impact of UD on other historically underserved populations, and scholarship focusing on the integration of other teaching and learning frameworks to enhance UD.

Universal Design and the Intersections of Diversity and Social Justice

Universal Design frameworks have been highlighted for their capacity to serve a wider array of student populations than those protected by disability rights laws in postsecondary education. UD has also been utilized to extend beyond the access provided by civil rights legislation to create inclusion in learning environments through a focus on teaching and learning. (Pliner & Johnson, 2004). Despite the intention of UD to meet the needs of a wide population of students, less is known about the extent to which this intention is in fact a real outcome of UD. In attempts to enhance UD frameworks and their full capacity to address inequities for underserved students, several scholars have written about the ways in which theories related to intersectionality, power, and privilege could be more firmly integrated into UD.

For example, Knoll (2009) has utilized a feminist analysis to explore issues of intersectionality, power, and privilege in the context of UD. While universally designed environments are something to strive for, Knoll has asserted that the experiences of people with disabilities are not universal and that the intersection of other identities and individual experiences must be taken into account. Knoll has cited the work of Wendell (1997) to discuss "double-oppression," in which marginalization based on a second aspect of identity, such as gender or race, occurs in addition to a disability (p. 124). Knoll has integrated concepts from disability studies and feminist disability scholarship as well as physical-object privileges (how spaces and items are physically created and made accessible to people without disabilities) and social-privilege (how society grants access to resources or capital to people without disabilities) to discuss opportunities to expand on UD's use in the classroom environment (p. 124).

Knoll (2009) has noted the importance of utilizing universal design as well as accommodations to maximize access for all students. Knoll has suggested that instructors' willingness to use UD and make modifications to a course without an accommodation letter may reduce barriers for students who cannot afford to pay for disability assessments. Knoll has also discussed the role that students, as well as the instructor, can play in implementing UD through practices such as interdependency. Interdependency raises students' awareness of physical-object and social privileges by asking them to take mutual responsibility for creating an accessible learning environment (Knoll, 2009). Examples of interdependency include involving students in writing notes that are visible to the class as the instructor speaks, reading out loud, and determining adjustments to make the classroom space more accessible (Knoll, 2009).

Although scholars have recognized that students who have other underrepresented identities in addition to a disability may experience the academic environment differently, the scholarship exploring these experiences remains very small. Some existing literature has illuminated the experience of double oppression, as noted by Knoll (2009), of students who are marginalized in other ways in addition to their disability. For example, in a study of African American males with disabilities at a historically Black college, Banks and Hughes (2013) found that negative stereotypes and messages that students experienced related to their disability, such as perception of diminished intellectual ability, were further exacerbated by the perception of incompetency and other negative cultural messages they received about their race. Their findings revealed that African American males with disabilities were often trading one stereotyped identity for another. Stereotypes about participants' race, gender, and disability were not only held by their peers, but were also sometimes exhibited by faculty who conveyed messages of low expectations for students' performance, pity, or at times hostility (Banks & Hughes, 2013).

Although there has been some discussion in the literature about the differing experiences of students of color with disabilities, less is known about whether or not UD itself addresses barriers related to these experiences. Further research is needed in this area to understand how the experience of the classroom and UD frameworks changes for students with disabilities who have other underrepresented identities. Several scholars have already posited that UD frameworks must pay greater attention to addressing other forms of oppression in order to truly reduce barriers for a diverse student population. Scholars have also called for greater attention to and integration of frameworks related to multicultural education and social justice to enhance implementation of UD.

For example, Hackman (2008) has suggested that the integration of Social Justice Education (SJE) and Critical Multicultural Education (CME) frameworks has the potential to enhance UD practices, particularly in serving students from historically marginalized groups, whether they have a disability or not. Hackman contends:

Unless educators have an awareness of students' social identities and the connection of power and privilege to those identities, as well as cultural competency in relating to those identities, there is a strong likelihood that even in a classroom where UID is deeply integrated, students from non-dominant groups will be alienated (p. 26).

Scholars such as Hackman have suggested that UID could be enhanced with greater attention to the dynamics of power and privilege in the context of classroom accessibility.

While reducing barriers related to physical and informational access have been a critical aspect of accommodations and UD, greater attention must be given to reducing systemic barriers related to ableism, racism, heterosexism, and other forms of oppression (Hackman, 2008). Additionally, scholars such as Liasidou (2014) have posited that UD frameworks may benefit from further integration into a social justice framework in design of both pedagogy and the curricula. Social justice and social responsibility have been somewhat absent from discussion on UD in a few different ways. For example, Hackman has argued that highlighting the history of exclusion of students with disabilities and other populations in education could make a stronger argument for the importance of UD (Hackman, 2008). This argument has not always been a part of the dialogue on why UD frameworks should be integrated into postsecondary education.

Despite the focus on self-advocacy in the disability rights movement, UD has also lacked a focus on activism and social responsibility that are more present in other education frameworks like Social Justice Education (Hackman, 2008). More discussion, research, and scholarship is needed to understand how UD frameworks may fit within or be enhanced by social justice and multicultural teaching frameworks. The rich history of the disability rights movement, which helped to spur disability civil rights legislation, provided a foundation for viewing disability in the context of systemic oppression. Still, as several scholars have noted, UD is often not embedded or discussed in the context of historical inequity or social justice. Additionally, while there have been more calls to be attentive to the intersection of other forms of oppression and the ways in which race and other aspect of identities affect students' experiences in the postsecondary environment, research on this topic is significantly lacking.

Limitations in the Research of Universal Design

Although UD and its application to postsecondary education have been widely discussed in the literature and applied at universities across the United States, research about the topic in general remains limited in providing in-depth information about appropriate implementation and evidence of effective outcomes. Roberts, Park, Brown, and Cook (2011) have argued that research on UID in particular has yielded limited evidence that these instructional practices actually improve educational outcomes for students with disabilities and other underrepresented populations. Roberts et al. pointed to a lack of studies utilizing mixed methods and experimental design to validate the effectiveness of UID. Other scholars have also noted the need for more studies to include the voices of students themselves to better understand how UD practices are perceived and experienced in postsecondary classrooms (Gibson, 2012; Liasidou, 2014).

Rao, Ok, and Bryant (2014) have argued that another limitation of the literature on UD models is the lack of consistency in addressing what practices can be considered universally designed and what principles actually result in effective practice. Current literature on UD models includes limited detail about the actual implementation and operationalization of the principles, making it difficult to replicate or evaluate effectiveness (Rao et al., 2014). Without these details, scholars and practitioners will be greatly challenged in enhancing both implementation and evaluation, as well as improving on existing frameworks of UD. Additionally, Rao et al. have called for researchers to include more detailed demographic information about study participants; including disability type, race, gender, and English language learner status, and also to disaggregate data to better assess what interventions are effective for which learners. Further consideration and exploration must also be made into whether or not UD frameworks address deeper classroom inequities that span across identities and other forms of oppression.

OPPORTUNITIES AND FUTURE DIRECTIONS FOR UNIVERSAL DESIGN

Although there are limitations in the research and opportunities for further developing UD, the concepts and theories that surround them have gained national and international traction over the past few decades. Universal Design for Learning in particular, with its grounding in cognitive neuroscience, has been a part of broader education policy considerations and dialogues. For example, UDL was highlighted in the Higher Education Opportunity Act (HEOA) in 2004 (Asselin, 2012) and became a significant theme in the reauthorization of the HEOA, signed into law in 2008. Within the bill, congress defines Universal Design for Learning as:

a scientifically valid framework for guiding educational practices that - (A) provides flexibility in the way information is being presented, in the ways students respond or demonstrate knowledge, and skills, and in the ways students are engaged; and (B) reduces barriers to instruction, provides appropriate accommodations, supports, challenges, and maintains high achievement expectations for all students, including students with disabilities and students who are limited English Proficient (HEOA: Universal Design for Learning, 2008, p.12).

The bill includes provisions for integration of instructional strategies, teaching techniques, as well as technology that reflect UDL principles in teacher preparation programs, grants for institutions to assess the effectiveness of this integration, and grant funding for professional development of teacher candidates to build skills necessary to utilize UD (Council for Exceptional Children, 2008).

Additionally, Universal Design was integrated into the United Nations (UN) Convention on the Rights of Persons with Disabilities, adopted in 2006 and entered into force in 2008 (United Nations, n.d.). The convention had 82 signatories and is considered the first comprehensive treaty for human rights in the 21st century (United Nations, 2006). Universal design is included in Article 4 of the General Obligations:

Expanding Notions of Access

> *To undertake or promote research and development of universally designed goods, services, equipment and facilities, as defined in article 2 of the present Convention, which should require the minimum possible adaptation and the least cost to meet the specific needs of a person with disabilities, to promote their availability and use, and to promote universal design in the development of standards and guidelines (UN, n.d., p. 6).*

In addition, the convention has also highlighted the need for access to education and the need for reasonable accommodations for individuals with disabilities. Increasing access to education to students with disabilities continues to be a global issue. Concepts related to Universal Design have been a focus in education outside of the United States as well, for example with Inclusive Design and Inclusive Education in the United Kingdom and Barrier Free Design, Accessible Design, and Design-For-All in other parts of the world (Ostroff, 2011).

In the United States, national data indicate that the populations of students accessing higher education are growing and changing. Representation of students with disabilities has increased and now includes a large percentage of students with mental health disabilities, Autism Spectrum Disorders (ASD), and other less apparent disabilities. Proper implementation of UD in teaching and learning could be a vital tool for ensuring equitable educational outcomes for these growing populations. Enhancing design in postsecondary courses has the capacity to create broader educational equity for students with disabilities and others who have previously been underserve in postsecondary education. The design process must be conducted through a broad reaching and collaborative effort involving multiple experts in the collegiate environment. For example, practitioners such as instructional designers may play an important role in the design process, particularly as institutions expand options for online and hybrid courses and instructors explore options for transforming their courses into flipped and active learning environments. These online and hybrid environments pose unique access challenges through ensuring that technologies and course delivery formats, as well as materials are accessible while also ensuring that instruction and teaching techniques are inclusive.

Ideas and efforts focused on a collaborative approach to UD implementation involving multiple constituencies are not new and have been documented widely in colleges and universities across the United States. In a collaborative approach to UD implementation, disability offices will likely play a vital role in identifying potential needs of changing populations and illuminating unknown access barriers that may arise in the academic environment. Similarly, offices and departments that focus on specific underserved populations will also play a critical role in identifying the potential issues and considerations for truly inclusive changes to and implementation of UD. Offices of teaching and learning as well as instructors themselves will play a significant role in implementation and knowledge sharing to create greater capacity within the institution itself. Ultimately, administrators also will play a vital role in creating greater buy in and making resources available that support wider efforts for implementation of UD.

Prior research focused on the faculty perspective on implementing universal design indicates that there may be some barriers in both developing knowledge of proper implementation of UD and gaining institutional buy-in for broader change and opportunities for training on how to modify courses for universal design (Lombardi & Murray, 2013; Silver, Bourke, & Strehorn, 2006). Attitudinal barriers about students with disabilities may pose additional barriers to the adoption of UD on a wider scale. For example, attitudes of seeing students with disabilities as burdensome in the classroom or unfit for success at postsecondary institutions more broadly may hamper the broader implementation of UD (Burgstahler, 2008a). While effective and broad implementation of UD is both challenging and not well understood, a holistic approach to implementing universal design with multiple stakeholders, including administrators, may be vital to ensuring that barriers are also reduced for instructors who are on the front lines of implementation.

Postsecondary institutions may benefit from exploring what is already being done in their courses with regard to accessibility and design. Without opportunities to research and share what is being done within and across departments, instructors may have limited opportunities to learn from one another and benefit from wider institutional knowledge. For example, institutions may consider implementing faculty mentoring programs focused on teaching and learning or regular faculty research symposia to reduce siloing and isolation of knowledge, especially at larger institutions where faculty interaction across disciplines may be more limited. Institutions may also consider the role that graduate students and staff instructors have in teaching and implementing innovative course design. These groups should not be left out of opportunities to partake in professional development or showcase their work with regard to teaching and learning and should also be seen as playing a vital role in implementing UD.

Additionally, though innovative course design and implementation may be occurring in the vein of UD, the specific terminology may be absent from the conversation. Some postsecondary publications targeted to audiences of instructors and practitioners regularly feature the voices of faculty who are making innovative changes in their classroom to enhance equity and inclusion, though often are not articulating these changes by using the words Universal Design. With the discussion from scholars of the limitations of the word "universal" and the need to broaden the focus of UD to further encompass ideas of social justice and equity, the language of UD may also need to grow and change within institutions and more widely. Still, many scholars have argued that good teaching alone does not necessarily equate to access for students with disabilities and other student populations (Higbee, 2008). Regardless of the language used, instructors must purposefully and intentionally integrate UD, as well as other facets of multicultural teaching and social justice education to ensure that instructors are producing outcomes of greater access and inclusion.

Finally, the need for greater and more in-depth research on the efficacy of Universal Design cannot be understated. Research focusing on UD is critical to creating a broader understanding of how practitioners can put theory into practice to effectively implement UD principles. This need has been documented in the literature by a number of scholars but the body of research has yet to expand substantially. Postsecondary institutions and higher education as a whole continue to grapple with questions of how to create more faculty buy-in and knowledge for implementing UD, as well as what these practices can and should look like in different disciplines, from science, technology, engineering, and math (STEM) courses, to second language learning. If a major barrier to implementation of UD is related to buy-in and lack of information on research-based practices across an array of disciplines, then further scholarly research on the efficacy and practical implementation of UD will continue to be an imperative. Individual institutions must consider what incentives exists for instructors to conduct research focused on teaching and what mechanisms or systems are in place that already support instructors in these endeavors.

The body of literature on UD and its broader adoption within institutions and in higher education more widely will not happen without research beginning within and across individual institutions. Where there currently are not incentives or mechanisms in place for promoting research on teaching and learning, institutions may consider how such mechanisms may add greatly to institutional understanding and capacity, as well as scholarly knowledge about effective approaches to implementing UD. In acknowledging that this research will not appear on its own, a critical question to be asked in discussions on UD is who will contribute to expanding this body of knowledge and how will that knowledge be utilized to enhance buy-in among postsecondary institutions and higher education more broadly?

CONCLUSION

Universal design techniques in teaching and instruction show great promise in making learning environments accessible for students regardless of whether they disclose a disability. However, further research is needed to better understand how instructors implement universal design principles and practices into their courses, how they evaluate whether or not these practices are effective, and the extent to which principles related to social justice and multiculturalism are actually integrated into UD practices. A more complete understanding of the implementation and evaluation of UD is critically important to expand upon and enhance access provided by legal mandates and provisions for individual accommodations.

Individual accommodations are and will likely continue to be a vital aspect of ensuring access, particularly for students with disabilities. The inclusion of universal design in national legislation and international dialogues, such as in the Higher Education Opportunity Act and the United Nations Convention on Human Rights, reinforce the idea that access cannot and should not just be an individual pursuit of a student with a disability. We as a society and as postsecondary institutions have a responsibility to ensure that we are playing an active role in reducing barriers that continue to exist for students with disabilities and other historically underserved populations. As with Universal Design, focusing on access and inclusion from the beginning of the design phase, whether in courses, the creation of physical spaces, or the development and facilitation of support programs, is one significant way for institutions to play an active role in enhancing educational equity more broadly.

REFERENCES

Americans with Disabilities Act Amendments Act of. 2008, Pub. L. No. 110-325, 42 U.S.C. § 12102. (n.d.). Retrieved from https://www.ada.gov/pubs/adastatute08.pdf

Americans with Disabilities Act Amendments Act of 2008: Definition of Disability, 42 C.F.R. § 12102 (2008).

Americans with Disabilities Act of 1990, 42 U.S.C. § 12101 *et seq.* (1991). Retrieved from http://www.ada.gov/archive/adastat91.htm

Asselin, S. (2012). Universal design for access and equity. In National Council of Professors of Educational Administration (Ed.), *NCPEA handbook of online instruction and programs in education leadership* (pp. 148-159). Retrieved from: https://cnx.org/exports/d302309d-1341-4020-90fd-ec4492502fe7@24.1.pdf/ncpea-handbook-of-online-instruction-and-programs-in-education-leadership-24.1.pdf

Banks, J., & Hughes, M. S. (2013). Double consciousness: Postsecondary experiences of African American males with disabilities. *The Journal of Negro Education*, 82(4), 368–381. doi:10.7709/jnegroeducation.82.4.0368

Bowe, F. (2000). *Universal design in education: Teaching nontraditional students.* Westport, CT: Bergin & Garvey.

Burgstahler, S. E. (2008a). Promoters and inhibitors of universal design in higher education. In S. E. Burgstahler & R. C. Cory (Eds.), *Universal design in higher education: from principles to practice* (pp. 3–20). Cambridge, MA: Harvard Education Press.

Burgstahler, S. E. (2008b). Universal design in higher education. In S. E. Burgstahler & R. C. Cory (Eds.), *Universal design in higher education: from principles to practice* (pp. 3–20). Cambridge, MA: Harvard Education Press.

Center for Applied Special Technology. (2014, July 31). *About universal design for learning.* Retrieved from: http://www.udlcenter.org/aboutudl/whatisudl

Chickering, A. W., & Gamson, Z. F. (1987). Seven principles for good practice in undergraduate education. *AAHE Bulletin, 39*(7), 3–7.

Council for Exceptional Children. (2008, August). *Higher education opportunity act reauthorization: Summary of selected provisions for individuals with exceptionalities and the professionals who work on their behalf.* Retrieved from: https://www.aucd.org/docs/CEC%20Higher%20Education%20short.pdf

Erickson, W., Lee, C., & von Schrader, S. (2014). *Disability statistics from the 2012 American Community Survey (ACS).* Ithaca, NY: Cornell University Employment and Disability Institute. Retrieved from http://www.disabilitystatistics.org

Evans, N. J. (2008). Theoretical foundations of universal instructional design. In J. L. Higbee & E. Goff (Eds.), Pedagogy and student services for institutional transformation: Implementing universal design in higher education (pp. 11-23). Minneapolis, MN: Regents of the University of Minnesota.

Getzel, E. E. (2008). Addressing the persistence and retention of students with disabilities in higher education: Incorporating key strategies and supports on campus. *Exceptionality, 16*(4), 207–219. doi:10.1080/09362830802412216

Gibson, S. (2012). Narrative accounts of university education: Sociocultural perspectives of students with disabilities. *Disability & Society, 27*(3), 353–369. doi:10.1080/09687599.2012.654987

Hackman, H. W. (2008). Broadening the pathway to academic success: The critical intersection of social justice education, critical multicultural education, and universal instructional design. In J. L. Higbee & E. Goff (Eds.), Pedagogy and student services for institutional transformation: Implementing universal design in higher education (pp. 25-48). Minneapolis, MN: Regents of the University of Minnesota.

Hadley, W. M. (2011). College students with disabilities: A student development perspective. *New Directions for Higher Education, 2011*(154), 77–81. doi:10.1002/he.436

Higbee, J. L. (2008). A faculty perspective: Implementing universal design in a first-year classroom. In S. E. Burgstahler & R. C. Cory (Eds.), *Universal design in higher education: From principles to practice* (pp. 3–20). Cambridge, MA: Harvard Education Press.

Higbee, J. L., & Goff, E. (2008). Pedagogy and student services for institutional transformation: Implementing universal design in higher education. Minneapolis, MN: Regents of the University of Minnesota.

Higher Education Opportunity Act of 2008, Public. L. No. 110-315, §§103-710, 122 Stat. 3078 (2008). Retrieved from: https://www.gpo.gov/fdsys/pkg/PLAW-110publ315/pdf/PLAW-110publ315.pdf

Higher Education Opportunity Act of 2008: Universal Design for Learning, Pub. L. No. 110-315, §103, 122 Stat. 3078 (2008). Retrieved from: https://www.gpo.gov/fdsys/pkg/PLAW-110publ315/pdf/PLAW-110publ315.pdf

Horn, L., & Berktold, J. (1999). *Students with disabilities in postsecondary education: a profile of preparation, participation, and outcomes (NCES 1999–187)*. Washington, DC: U.S. Department of Education, National Center for Education Statistics. Retrieved from https://nces.ed.gov/pubs99/1999187.pdf

Individuals with Disabilities Education Act, 20 U.S.C. § 1400, *et seq.* (2004). Retrieved from http://idea.ed.gov/download/statute.html

Knoll, K. R. (2009). Feminist disability studies pedagogy. *Feminist Teacher, 19*(2), 122–133. doi:10.1353/ftr.0.0031

Liasidou, A. (2014). Critical disability studies and socially just change in higher education. *British Journal of Special Education, 41*(2), 120–135. doi:10.1111/1467-8578.12063

Lombardi, A., Murray, C., & Dallas, B. (2013). University faculty attitudes toward disability and inclusive instruction: Comparing two institutions. *Journal of Postsecondary Education and Disability, 26*(3), 221–232.

Mace, R. (1988). *An introduction to the Americans with disabilities act. A teleconference tape*. Architectural Association.

Madaus, J. W. (2011). The history of disability services in higher education. *New Directions for Higher Education, 2011*(154), 5–15. doi:10.1002/he.429

Marshak, L., Van Wieren, T., Ferrell, D. R., Swiss, L., & Dugan, C. (2010). Exploring barriers to college student use of disability services and accommodations. *Journal of Postsecondary Education and Disability, 22*(3), 151–165.

McGuire, J. M., & Scott, S. S. (2006). An approach for inclusive college teaching: Universal design for instruction. *Learning Disabilities-Multidisciplinary Journal, 14*(1), 21.

Meyer, A., Rose, D. H. R., & Gordon, D. (2014). *Universal design for learning: Theory and practice*. Wakefield, MA: CAST Professional Publishing.

Newman, L., Wagner, M., Knokey, A.-M., Marder, C., Nagle, K., Shaver, D., … Schwarting, M. (2011). *The post-high school outcomes of young adults with disabilities up to 8 years after high school. A report from the national longitudinal transition study-2 (NLTS2)* (NCSER 2011-3005). Menlo Park, CA: SRI International. Retrieved from: https://ies.ed.gov/ncser/pubs/20113005/pdf/20113005.pdf

Ostroff, E. (2011). Universal design: an evolving paradigm. In K. H. Smith & W. Preiser (Eds.), *Universal design handbook* (2nd ed.; pp. 1.3–1.11). McGraw-Hill, Inc.

Pliner, S. M., & Johnson, J. R. (2004). Historical, theoretical, and foundational principles of universal instructional design in higher education. *Equity & Excellence in Education, 37*(2), 105–113. doi:10.1080/10665680490453913

Rao, K., Ok, M. W., & Bryant, B. R. (2014). A review of research on universal design educational models. *Remedial and Special Education, 35*(3), 153–166. doi:10.1177/0741932513518980

Raue, K., & Lewis, L. (2011). *Students with disabilities at degree-granting postsecondary institutions (NCES 2011–018). U.S. Department of Education, National Center for Education Statistics.* Washington, DC: U.S. Government Printing Office. Retrieved from http://nces.ed.gov/pubs2011/2011018.pdf

Roberts, K. D., Park, H. J., Brown, S., & Cook, B. (2011). Universal design for instruction in postsecondary education: A systematic review of empirically based articles. *Journal of Postsecondary Education and Disability, 24*(1), 5–15.

Rose, D. H., Harbour, W. S., Johnston, C. S., Daley, S. G., & Abarbanell, L. (2006). Universal design for learning in postsecondary education: Reflections on principles and their application. *Journal of Postsecondary Education and Disability, 19*(2), 135–151.

Schelly, C. L., Davies, P. L., & Spooner, C. L. (2011). Student perceptions of faculty implementation of universal design for learning. *Journal of Postsecondary Education and Disability, 24*(1), 17–30.

Scott, S. S., McGuire, J. M., & Shaw, S. F. (2001). *Principles of universal design for instruction.* Storrs: University of Connecticut, Center on Postsecondary Education and Disability. Retrieved from http://udi.uconn.edu/index.php?q=node/12

Scott, S. S., McGuire, J. M., & Shaw, S. F. (2003). Universal design for instruction: A new paradigm for adult instruction in postsecondary education. *Remedial and Special Education, 24*(6), 369–379. doi:10.1177/07419325030240060801

Section 504 of the Rehabilitation Act of 1973, 29 U.S.C. § 701 (1973). Retrieved from: http://www.dol.gov/oasam/regs/statutes/sec504.htm

Silver, P., Bourke, A., & Strehorn, K. C. (1998). Universal instructional design in higher education: An approach for inclusion. *Equity & Excellence, 31*(2), 47–51. doi:10.1080/1066568980310206

Simon, J. A. (2011). Legal issues in serving students with disabilities in postsecondary education. *New Directions for Student Services, 2011*(134), 95–107. doi:10.1002s.397

Snyder, T. D., de Brey, C., & Dillow, S. A. (2016). *Digest of Education Statistics 2014 (NCES 2016-006).* Washington, DC: National Center for Education Statistics, Institute of Education Sciences, U.S. Department of Education. Retrieved from http://nces.ed.gov/pubsearch/pubsinfo.asp?pubid=2016006

The Center for Universal Design. (1997, April 4). *The principles of universal design, version 2.0.* Raleigh, NC: North Carolina State University. Retrieved from: https://www.ncsu.edu/ncsu/design/cud/about_ud/udprinciplestext.htm

United Nations. (2006). *Convention on the rights of persons with disabilities.* Retrieved from: http://www.un.org/disabilities/convention/conventionfull.shtml

United Nations. (n.d.). *Convention on the rights of persons with disabilities and optional protocol.* Retrieved from: http://www.un.org/disabilities/documents/convention/convoptprot-e.pdf

United States Department of Education, Office for Civil Rights. (2011). *Students with disabilities preparing for postsecondary education: Know your rights and responsibilities.* Washington, DC: U.S. Department of Education Office for Civil Rights. Retrieved from http://www2.ed.gov/about/offices/list/ocr/transition.htmlhttp://www.gao.gov/products/GAO-10-33

United States Government Accountability Office. (2009). *Higher education and disability: Education needs a coordinated approach to improve its assistance to schools in supporting student need*. Washington, DC: U.S. Government Accountability Office. Retrieved from: http://www.gao.gov/new.items/d1033.pdf

Wendell, S. (1997). Toward a Feminist Theory of Disability. In L. J. Davis (Ed.), *The disability studies reader* (pp. 261–278). New York, NY: Routledge.

Wolanin, T. R., & Steele, P. E. (2004). *Higher education opportunities for students with disabilities: A primer for policymakers*. Washington, DC: The Institute for Higher Education Policy; Retrieved from http://www.ihep.org/sites/default/files/uploads/docs/pubs/opportunitiesstudentsdisabilities.pdf

Zeff, R. (2007). Universal design across the curriculum. *New Directions for Higher Education, 2007*(137), 27–44. doi:10.1002/he.244

This research was previously published in Disability and Equity in Higher Education Accessibility edited by Jennie Lavine, Roy Y. Chan, and Henry C. Alphin, Jr.; pages 204-221, copyright year 2017 by Information Science Reference (an imprint of IGI Global).

Chapter 4
Design, Implementation and Evaluation of MOOCs to Improve Inclusion of Diverse Learners

Sandra Sanchez-Gordon
National Polytechnic School of Ecuador, Ecuador

Sergio Luján-Mora
University of Alicante, Spain

ABSTRACT

This chapter presents accessibility requirements that need to be considered in the design, implementation and evaluation of Massive Open Online Courses (MOOCs) to ensure they are inclusive. Accessibility requirements take in account particular needs, preferences, skills and situations of diverse learners, e.g. people with disabilities, elderly people and foreign students. The accessibility needs have to be considered in the design and implementation of MOOCs' interfaces, contents and learning/assessment activities. Due to its open and massive nature, with an adequate implementation, MOOCs can overcome inclusion barriers for the benefit of potential learners worldwide, both able and disabled. For evaluation, there are accessibility evaluation tools that identify accessibility problems in the content, semantic and structural elements of a website that can be used to evaluate the level of accessibility of MOOCs. Additional expert-based and user-based evaluations are always recommended in order to achieve valid results.

INTRODUCTION

Humankind is diverse. Hence, there is also great diversity among learners, especially in the context of Massive Open Online Courses (MOOCs). This diversity imposes accessibility needs associated to students with different types of disabilities, elderly students with combined disabilities, and foreign students with cognitive issues due to lack of proficiency in the second language.

DOI: 10.4018/978-1-7998-1213-5.ch004

Persons with Disabilities

According to the World Report on Disability made by the World Health Organization (2011), more than one billion people live with some form of disability. This is around 15 per cent of the world's population. This fact makes this community the world's largest minority.

The World Report on Disability is a guide to implement the United Nations' Convention on the Rights of Persons with Disabilities (CRPD). The CRPD entered into force in 2008 after decades of work by the United Nations to change attitudes towards viewing persons with disabilities as capable of claiming their rights as well as being active members of society. The CRPD simply guarantees that the same rights recognized in the Universal Declaration of Human Rights of 1948 are respected for persons with disabilities.

The CRPD stresses that persons with disabilities should be able to live independently and participate fully in all aspects of life. To this end, signatories should take appropriate measures to ensure that persons with disabilities have access to the physical environment, to transportation, to information and communications technology, and to other facilities and services open or provided to the public.

Of particular importance in the context of this chapter is Article 24 of the CRPD. This article recognizes the right to education for persons with disabilities. Signatories must make sure that persons with disabilities are able to get access not only to general education but also to tertiary education, vocational training, adult education and lifelong learning without discrimination and on an equal basis with others (United Nations, 2008).

As of April 2015, 154 countries or regional integration organizations have signed and ratified the CRPD, Kazakhstan being the latest one so far (United Nations, 2015). When a country signs and ratifies a convention, it becomes a legal promise and it often leads the government to adapt and change its own laws to support the goals of the ratified convention.

Nevertheless, Morales (2007) reports that in Spain only 3.6% of the population with disabilities completes higher education while the correspondent percentage for general population is 20%. Besides, 84% of Spain college students with disabilities state that they face several barriers through their studies.

In the same line, Molina (2007) presents the following data from Colombia: only 2.3% of the population with disabilities has some level of higher education (technical, technological or professional), 1% completes their higher education and 0.1% obtains graduate degrees.

That is, higher education penetration among population with disabilities has a long way to go before reaching similar levels than general population. Part of the problem is that higher education institutions might not have had accessibility in mind when getting facilities and equipment.

The adaptations of facilities and equipment to make a college campus accessible might be costly. A study made in the European Higher Education Area (EHEA) about standards and indicators for disability (Diez et al., 2011), describes 31 indicators such as: ensure students with disabilities have priority accessible rooms in residential accommodations or rooms near buildings where classes are taught; ensure computer labs are accessible to students with disabilities (e.g. appropriate sits or space for wheelchairs, height adjustable desks, alternative keyboards); ensure that classrooms and labs consider the needs of students with disabilities (e.g. physical access, adequate sound and light conditions); ensure that the aisles are wide enough to allow a person with a physical disability or a wheelchair user to get around them; ensure that alarms and security devices are available in both sight and hearing formats; ensure that campus maps and signs are available in Braille and long print.

There are also attitudinal and communication barriers with teachers, fellow students and administrative personal in educational institutions. People often do not known how to interact and communicate with persons with disabilities, thus prefer to avoid contact. Finally, adaptations in policies, procedures, curricula, learning and assessment activities must be put in place in order to accommodate students with disabilities.

In this context, online learning -and more specifically MOOCs- are a great opportunity for persons with disabilities than would not be able to engage in learning otherwise. Moreover, in a MOOC environment the situation of a person with disabilities may go unnoticed; hence the person can be treated truly equally by their teachers and peers. Best of all, currently the design and implementation of inclusive MOOCs is pedagogically, technically and financially feasible.

Elder People

Another human group that deserves special attention is the elderly population. Velasco (2010) explains that humanity is assisting in the past four decades to an unprecedented fact in its history: the aging of the population; consisting in the presence of an increasing number of elderly, especially in Europe, where birth rates and life expectancy have operated in reverse order in the last years. This fact raises cultural changes, economic burdens and social demands.

Worldwide life expectancy has increased from 50 years in 1900 to 66 years today. By 2050, general life expectancy might increase to 76 years. In Japan and Spain, life expectancy is already 82 years old. The general increase of life expectancy due to better health care and environment conditions is provoking an increase in the fraction of the elderly population. Currently, one in ten people is 60+ years old (600 million people). Moreover, the world's older population is expected to exceed one billion by 2020. By 2030, 13% of the population (i.e. one in eight people) will be 65+ years old, of an estimated total of 8.321 billion people. That is, 1.165 billion of people will be 65+ years old. In United States, older adults (65+ years old) already are the largest population group according to the latest census report (Werner, 2011).

Waldmeir (2014) reports that by 2050, China could have nearly 500 million people aged over 60, more than the total population of USA. Local governments across China are investing in elderly education as one way to achieve healthy old people. At Shanghai University of the Elderly the average students' age is 65 years old. There are five universities for elder people in Shanghai that serve more than five million students.

Various authors have stated that e-learning is an opportunity to help older people to become integrated with the rest of society (Tsai et al., 2014; Githens, 2007; Notess & Lorenzen-Huber, 2007). In this context, MOOCs bring great opportunities to enhance the quality of life of older people by enabling lifelong learning and inclusion in learning communities, which in turn favors cognitive stimulation, a sense of belonging, and social engagement.

However, MOOCs can present some barriers that could hamper full participation by elderly students due to diminish capacities related to natural aging such as vision decline, hearing loss, decremented motor skills and cognition issues (Sanchez-Gordon & Luján-Mora, 2013).

Foreign Students

Regarding the languages in which MOOCs are offered, Shah (2014) presents the following data from the MOOC aggregator Class Central: 80% of MOOCs are offered in English, followed by 8.5% of courses offered in Spanish, of a total offer of 13 different languages.

Similarly, a quick review made in April 2015 of the leading MOOC platform Coursera shows that from a total of 1,117 courses, 794 are offered in English (71%), Chinese is the second language with 126 courses (11.3%) and Spanish is the third language with 49 courses (4.4%). These data may seem discouraging in terms of language diversity, but actually it shows a positive trend, since a year before, from a total of 585 courses hosted on Coursera, 515 of them were offered in English, corresponding to 90% of the offered courses back then.

Students taken a course offered in a language different from their own might face difficulties due to their level of proficiency in the course language, e.g., non-native speakers read at slower speed, which leads to information overload and cognitive problems. This causes them to take longer to perform certain learning/assessment activities as well. Non-native speakers also experience stress related to workload and visibility of their written responses in essays, forums and textual chats. For these reasons, the language barrier discourages many potential users to participate in MOOCs (Sanchez-Gordon & Luján-Mora, 2014a).

Chapter Objectives

The accessibility needs of diverse learners must be taken in account in the design, implementation and evaluation of MOOC interfaces, contents and learning/assessment activities. This chapter focuses on learners with disabilities, elderly learners and foreign learners in the context of MOOCs.

The main objectives of this chapter are:

- Identify MOOCs' potential users accessibility needs.
- Specify accessibility requirements for non-disabled learners, learners with disabilities, elderly learners and foreign learners.
- Explain how to design and implement accessible MOOCs.
- Explain how to evaluate the level of accessibility of MOOCs.

BACKGROUND

Massive Open Online Courses

MOOCs can be simply defined as:

Online courses with no formal entry requirement, no participation limits, and free of charge. (Gaebel, 2013)

Oxford dictionary defines MOOC as:

A course of study made available over the Internet without charge to a very large number of people. (Parr, 2013)

With a brief history of seven years, MOOC is relatively a new phenomenon and its definition is still evolving. The term was coined in 2008 by Dave Cormier and Bryan Alexander to refer to the course "Connectivism and Connective Knowledge" organized by George Siemens and Stephen Downes of University of Manitoba, with 2,300 online students. The first MOOC to get really massive was "Introduction to Artificial Intelligence", offered in 2011 and organized by Sebastian Thrun of Stanford University and Peter Norving of Google. It got a registration of 160,000 students. In 2012, "Circuits and Electronics", organized by Anant Agarwal of the Massachusetts Institute of Technology, registered 120,000 students (Daniel, 2012; Adams, Yin, Vargas, & Mullen, 2014).

Since then, the concept has evolved in such a way that to date every letter of the acronym has several interpretations (Sanchez-Gordon & Lujan-Mora, 2014b):

- The term MASSIVE implies that a MOOC should support access to a very large number of users and have the capacity to scale in the number of users in several orders of magnitude, for example, going from 1,000 to 100,000 students, without significantly affecting its functioning and quality.
- The term OPEN has several meanings. First, it means open enrollment, i.e. the course should be open to all users with no prerequisites nor previous studies. Second, open also comes from the concept of Open Educational Resources. In this sense, open means that the course is based on "open content" and the content generated by the course should also be published with an open license, so it could be reused by others. In addition, open also means that access to the content and learning/assessment activities of the course should be free. Also, open is often interpreted as not using just a closed platform but the entire cloud, i.e. social networks, multimedia repositories, web portals, blogs, wikis. Finally, open can also mean that the platform hosting the MOOCs is under open source licenses, so code adaptation and improvement of the platform is possible and all changes should be also shared.
- The term ONLINE implies that the course is delivered via Internet. That is, instructors and students interact and communicate, as well as access to content and learning/assessment activities on the Internet. But the character of online goes beyond the fact that communication is mediated by a computer network: when a user enrolls in a MOOC, they are not only a student of the course, but also a user of a software system designed to provide a service to their satisfaction.
- Finally, the term COURSE implies that there is learning objectives, learning outcomes, content and educational activities. In general, a course is a space in which an instructor leads a group of students in learning about a specific topic. A traditional course takes place in spaces such as classrooms or laboratories, in a specific period and uses educational resources. A course is not necessarily part of an official curriculum towards a professional degree or certification. A course can also be taken by personal interest and growth in the context of lifelong learning, as might be the case of elderly students.

The first MOOCs did not use specific platforms. For instance, the MOOC "Connectivism and Connective Knowledge" was based on various blog aggregators. However, currently MOOCs are hosted in specific platforms. In principle, any educational institution can become a MOOC provider if they develop their own platform or use a local instance of an open platform, such as edX.

To date, the main MOOC platform providers are: Coursera, edX and Udacity (USA); MiriadaX and Unimooc (Spain); FutureLearn (United Kingdom); Open2Study (Australia); Iversity (Germany). These providers and others offer hundreds of MOOCs in several knowledge areas to potential learners, with almost 17 million of users registered worldwide, distributed as following (Shah, 2014):

- Coursera: 10.5 million
- edX: 3.0 million
- Udacity: 1.5 million
- MiriadaX: 1.0 million
- FutureLearn: 800,000
- Others: 200,000
- **Total:** 17.0 million

Human-Computer Interaction

Preece et al. (1994), in their classic book, states that the term human-computer interaction (HCI) was adopted in mid-1980s as a mean to acknowledge the need of a field of study dedicated to the communication between human and computers. They propose important challenges: keep abreast of changes in technology and ensure designs offer good HCI, and explain that that goal of HCI is produce usable, safe and functional systems. Usability is a key concept in HCI that is concerned with designing and implementing digital products in such a way that are easy to use and easy to learn.

Horton & Sloan (2014) explains that when usability is envisioned in terms of a large and diverse population, including persons with disabilities, it becomes accessibility.

Accessibility

The International Organization for Standardization (ISO) defines accessibility as:

The usability of a product, service, environment or facility by people with the widest range of capabilities. (ISO, 2012)

The inventor of the World Wide Web and director of the World Wide Web Consortium (W3C), Tim Berners-Lee, states:

Accessibility is the art of ensuring that, to as large an extent as possible, facilities (such as, for example, web access) are available to people whether or not they have disabilities of one sort or another. (W3C, 1999)

The W3C created the Web Accessibility Initiative (WAI) with the aim of studying the problems of accessibility in the web, develop guidelines and provide resources. The WAI is recognized as an international authority on web accessibility. W3C recognizes that accessibility depends on several components working together. WAI has developed three sets of guidelines (WAI, 2014):

- **Content:** WCAG - Web Content Accessibility Guidelines.
- **Authorship:** ATAG - Authoring Tool Accessibility Guidelines.
- **User tools:** UAAG - User Agent Accessibility Guidelines.

The WCAG defines how to make web content accessible to disabled persons. These guidelines include website conformance requirements and define three levels of conformance: A, AA and AAA. WCAG establishes four principles that give the foundation for web content accessibility:

- **Perceivable**: the information and components of the user interface should be presented to users so they can perceive them.
- **Operable**: the components of the user interface and navigation must be operable.
- **Understandable**: the information and manipulation of the user interface must be understandable by the users.
- **Robust**: content must be robust enough to be reliably interpreted by a wide variety of user agents, including assistive technology software or devices.

These principles are known by the acronym **POUR**. This chapter uses the POUR principles to categorize accessibility needs of potential MOOC users.

The W3C created the ATAG to address the software people use to create websites. The ATAG defines how web development tools should help website developers produce content that is accessible and conforms to the WCAG. The ATAG compliant tools provide web developers with a means to produce accessible websites, prompt the developer for accessibility related information and provide ways to verify the content is accessible. The tools themselves should also be accessible to disabled persons.

The UAAG explains what is required for the accessible design of user agents. User agents are web browsers, media players and assistive technology software that disabled persons use to interact with computers.

WCAG, ATAG and UAAG work together to make the web accessible. Smith (2012) gives the following example to illustrate the combination of the three sets of guidelines: for alternative text on images, the WCAG would require images be accompanied by descriptive text, the ATAG would require that the web design software verify that images on the website contain alternate text, and the UAAG would require the browser to display the alternate text in a manner that works with screen reading software.

Current versions of the three set of guidelines are: WCAG 2.0 released in 2008, ATAG 2.0 released in 2015 and UAAG 1.0 released in 2002. In addition, WCAG 2.0 was approved as the standard ISO/IEC 40500 in 2012. UAAG 2.0 is currently in draft stage.

DESIGN, IMPLEMENTATION, AND EVALUATION OF ACCESSIBLE MOOCS

Issues, Controversies, Problems

In 2013, the president of edX Anant Agarwal stated:

MOOCs are transforming education in both quality and scale. MOOCs make education borderless, gender-blind, race-blind, class-blind and bank account-blind (...) MOOCs are democratizing education. (Agarwal, 2013)

In 2012, the co-founder of Coursera Daphne Koller said in a TED Talk:

If we could offer a top quality education to everyone around the world for free, what would that do? Three things. First it would establish education as a fundamental human right, where anyone around the world with the ability and the motivation could get the skills that they need to make a better life for themselves, their families and their communities. Second, it would enable lifelong learning. It's a shame that for so many people, learning stops when we finish high school or when we finish college. By having this amazing content be available, we would be able to learn something new every time we wanted, whether it's just to expand our minds or it's to change our lives. And finally, this would enable a wave of innovation, because amazing talent can be found anywhere. (Koller, 2013)

Nevertheless, Palin (2014) presents data that shows that most current MOOCs beneficiaries live in developed countries and have university studies. For instance, on Coursera, 28% of users are from United States.

Perna et al. (2013) made a study on sixteen courses of University of Pennsylvania in Coursera that concluded that most students come from United States, with a few students from Central and South America; and very few students from Africa.

Liyanagunawardena, Williams & Adams (2013) compiled data confirming that the majority of MOOC students come from United States and Europe with limited participation from the rest of America, Asia and even less from Africa. The difference is overwhelming, especially because most of the world's population is concentrated in those continents.

Guo & Reinecke (2014) presents learning analytics of four MOOCs on the platform edX, where the top-five list of countries with the most certificate-earning students were: United States (22%), India (17%), Spain (11%), Russian Federation (8%) and United Kingdom (6%).

On the other hand, Martinez-Cruz (2014) reports an interesting success case where students from El Salvador, motivated by a teacher, enrolled on 2012 to the second version of "Circuits and Electronics" and got a 27.6% of certificate attainment for this country, compared to the global percentage of 5.8% from 97 different countries.

Despite of this last experience, for now, MOOCs are elitist.

Bohnsack & Puhl (2014) conducted a study that determined that none of the current MOOC platforms is fully accessible: most lack of correct HTML syntax (e.g., language definition, heading structure and labels in input fields) and accessible design (e.g., clean interface, keyboard navigation, links to skip to main content). These authors concluded that accessibility was not in focus when these platforms were built.

Al-Mouh et al. (2014) conducted an experiment that included a heuristic evaluation of ten Coursera MOOCs with respect to WCAG 2.0. All the evaluated MOOCs failed to comply with A, AA and AAA accessibility levels.

Calle-Jimenez et al. (2014) described some of the challenges that exist to make accessible MOOCs on Geographical Information Systems (GIS). These kinds of MOOCs, by nature, have inherent problems of accessibility.

Aboshady et al. (2015) presents the following results regarding the awareness and use of MOOCs among medical undergraduates in Egypt as a developing country: one-fifth of Egyptian medical undergraduates have heard about MOOCs but only 6.5% actively enrolled in courses. Students who actively participated showed a positive attitude towards the experience, but better time-management skills and faster Internet connection speeds are required.

Finally, in February 2015, the National Association of Deaf filed federal lawsuits against Harvard and M.I.T. (Lewin, 2015), saying both universities violated antidiscrimination laws by failing to provide closed captioning in their online lectures, courses, podcasts and other educational materials, including MOOCs provided through edX.

So for now, MOOCs are not accessible enough.

Hence, the promise of democratizing education and giving access to education to everyone is yet to be fulfilled. Therefore, it is necessary to analyze the problem and propose solutions to improve inclusion of diverse learners, both able and disabled, in MOOCs.

SOLUTIONS AND RECOMMENDATIONS

There are several strategies to improve the level of accessibility of MOOCs.

One option is to avoid certain types of features, content and learning/assessment activities that are not readily accessible to diverse learners, e.g., people with disabilities, elderly students and foreign students. However, this is not a good solution because it leads to a general reduction of features offered to MOOC learners in general. Besides, it generates the idea that in order to make a MOOC accessible, it is necessary to reduce its functionality. That may induce some users to perceive accessibility as a negative thing.

A second option is to develop a generic version of the MOOC and several alternative versions for different categories of disabilities. This path is not suitable, because the development, maintenance and support of multiple versions are expensive and in most cases not possible. Also, this does not solve the problem of segregation.

A better strategy is to apply universal design to define MOOC features, content, and learning/assessment activities. Universal design "is the design of products and environments to be usable by all people, to the greatest extent possible, without the need for adaptation or specialized design" (Mace et al., 1996). Next sections identify MOOCs users' accessibility needs, specify MOOCs' accessibility requirements, and explain how to design, implement and evaluate accessible MOOCs

Diverse Learners Accessibility Needs

For identifying MOOCs potential users' accessibility needs, this section considers people with the widest range of capabilities, including people with permanent, temporary or progressive disabilities:

- A permanent disability might be congenital (i.e. person born blind) or acquired (i.e. person that become blind due to an accident).
- A temporary disability starts and ends in some point of a person's life. Examples of temporary disabilities are: people recovering after surgery (i.e. eye, ear, throat), with trauma injuries (i.e. broken bones in upper limbs), and circumstantial situations such as parents with their baby in arms, foreign students, or students in a silent library.
- A progressive disability appears and develops over time. Examples of progressive disabilities are: vision, hearing, motor, cognitive, and psychosocial progressive loss due to natural aging, as is the case of elderly students. Progressive disabilities might develop combined.

Accessibility needs of potential MOOC users can be organized according to the four POUR principles proposed by the WCAG: perceivable, operable, understandable and robust.

Accessibility Needs to Perceive

The main senses considered in the perceivable category are vision and hearing.

People with full use of their vision are able to read text, view images, understand the visual meaning of colors, and in general they can use their eyes to make sense of information that is presented to them (WebAIM, 2015).

On the other hand, MOOC users with visual disabilities cannot properly access visual information or use the mouse, and they need to mainly rely on audio information. There are three main types of users with visual disabilities:

- Blind people that uses text-to-speech software, also known as screen readers, and optionally audio descriptions (Christensen, 2001).
- Users with low vision that use magnifiers and screen readers (Prougestaporn, 2010).
- Users with color-blindness that need alternatives to color conveyed-information.

The web enables several kinds of audio interactions among people that can hear, such as engage in voice chats, watch videos, hear music, listen web radio broadcasts and podcast (WebAIM, 2015).

MOOC users with hearing disabilities cannot properly access to audio information, such as speech, music or sounds. For them, it is important to make auditory content available in alternative format. There are three main types of users with hearing disabilities:

- People with mild, moderate or severe hearing loss that uses captions and transcripts. Hearing loss generally affects to elderly people.
- People with post-lingual deafness (after the acquisition of language) that lip-read and also use captions and transcripts.
- People with pre-lingual deafness (deafness impaired the ability to acquire a spoken language) that uses captions and transcripts and optionally videos in sign language.
- People with deaf-blindness. In this case, touch is the main form of communication. These users use text-to-Braille devices.

Although touch, smell and taste are not significant on the web, they might be necessary to perform learning or assessment activities outside the MOOC platform. For instance, a video lecture can instruct the student to perform an experiment at home where they have to taste different kind of foods to classify them by type of flavor, and then perform statistics calculations with the data obtained. If a student has some kind of taste disability, they won't be able to perform this activity. Hence, alternative activities must be designed.

Accessibility Needs to Operate

Users generally rely on the use of mouse and standard keyboard to input information and navigate through and interact with web content.

Nevertheless, MOOCs users with motor disabilities in upper limbs have inability or difficulty using mouse and keyboard. Moreover, users with visual disabilities have also difficulties using mouse.

Hence, the user interface components and navigation must be operable not only with mouse and standard keyboard, but also with assistive technology devices and software, e.g., voice recognition software, mouth stick, head wand, single-switch access, sip and puff switch, track-ball mouse, adaptive keyboard, on-screen keyboards (Burgstahler, 2002; WebAIM, 2015).

Additionally, it is important to consider that these users require extra time to input information and also to navigate and interact with the MOOC.

Accessibility Needs to Understand

Any user might potentially experience problems understanding web content or how to operate a web interface. The frequency and level of difficulty of such problems increase if the user has some cognitive, psychosocial or speech disability.

In general terms, a user with a cognitive disability has more difficulties with one or more types of mental tasks than the average user. Cognitive disabilities include difficulties with memory, problem-solving, attention, reading, linguistic/verbal comprehension, math comprehension, and visual comprehension (Pouncey, 2010; WebAIM, 2015).

A common cognitive disability is dyslexia (10% of the global population has it). Dyslexia is a neurological condition that impairs a person's ability to read, recognize words, spell correctly and decode written information (Kalyvioti & Mikropoulos, 2013).

The disabilities arising from mental health conditions are called psychosocial disabilities. Conditions leading to psychosocial disabilities include depression, psychosis, epilepsy, post-traumatic stress disorder and dementia. Depression can cause the affected person to suffer greatly and function poorly at work, at school and in their family. Dementia is a syndrome in which there is deterioration in memory, thinking, behavior and the ability to perform everyday activities. Dementia generally affects to elderly people.

Speech disabilities includes: lack of speech, slurred, slowed, hoarse, stuttered or rapid speech. In these cases, the person's articulation, voice quality, or fluency patterns impair listeners' ability to understand the intent of the speaker. At present, users input information mostly using mouse and keyboard. However, it is very likely that different forms of voice activated user computer interfaces become more popular in the near future, especially in circumstances in which the use of mouse and keyboard is not the best option (for example, when there is also a motor impairment). Users with speech disabilities uses communication devices that produce either synthetic or digital speech output based on their textual input (Hasselbring & Williams, 2000). Additionally, users with speech disabilities might have difficulties performing learning/assessment activities involving oral communication.

There is also needs associated to users level of proficiency of the course language. This circumstance might affect the understanding of platform functionality, course content and learning/assessment activities. Language proficiency issues affects users taking MOOCs in a language different to their native one; including users born deaf whose native language is sign language (Holcomb & Kreeft, 1992). In addition, MOOC contents and activities might be culturally bound, hence they need to be reviewed to make sure they don't conflict with cultural and religion backgrounds of foreign users. This applies also for people born deaf who belong to a culture proper of their community.

In addition, users with low levels of digital literacy, or literacy in general, may find difficult to perform MOOC tasks such as navigate course contents, post in forums, or perform assessment activities. Digital literacy levels of users from developing countries tend to be low. For instance, Sri Lanka has a computer literacy rate of 20.3%, even though literacy rate is 91% (Satharasinghe, 2004). Users with low levels of digital literacy may find difficult to perform MOOC platform general tasks, e.g., sign up, sign in, sign out, update their profile; as well as course tasks such as enroll, navigate course contents, post in forums, or perform assessment activities. Social network skills are part of digital literacy and are necessary to understand and successfully participate in MOOCs (McAuly et al., 2010).

Besides blind users, screen readers also help users with low levels of literacy or cognitive disabilities. Screen readers are an example of how the same assistive technology can help users with different accessibility needs (Perez-Gonzales et al., 2014).

Accessibility Needs to Robust Access

Users should be allowed to choose their own technologies to access web content. If a web content requires a particular software or hardware technology, e.g., certain browser, media player, plug-in or assistive technology, it may exclude some types of users who either don't want to use that technology or can't use it.

Robust access is also related to having adequate access to technological resources, e.g., electricity supply, affordable and quality internet, updated computer devices.

In countries of sub-Saharan Africa, 36% of the population does not have regular access to electricity. In Burundi, 97% of the population lives without electricity, and those who have access to electricity only get it on certain days of the week (Legros et al., 2009).

Only around one-third of the total world population has regular access to Internet. Whereas in most European countries (Norway, Sweden, Denmark, Finland, United Kingdom, Germany, Belgium, France), Japan, Canada and United States, the number of Internet users is 80% or above; in countries such as Burundi, Ethiopia, Guinea, Myanmar, Niger, Sierra Leona, Somalia, and Timor-Leste is less than 2% (World Bank, 2014). Internet connection speed in many developing countries is not sufficient to download large files or watching videos in an acceptable way.

Also, users in developing countries might have difficulties to have adequate access to affordable and updated computers, laptops, tablets or smart phones (Post, 2006).

MOOC's Accessibility Requirements

In the previous section, accessibility needs of potential MOOC users have been identified. This section presents the corresponding MOOC accessibility requirements and their related disabilities. It is important to note that in general the compliance of these accessibility requirements favors not only users having the related disabilities but non-disabled users as well.

Accessibility Requirements to Perceive

These are requirements mainly oriented to solve the needs of users with difficulties to perceive, such as blind users (B), users with low vision (V), users with hearing loss or post-lingual deafness (H), users with pre-lingual deafness (D), and users with deaf-blindness (DB). Users with cognitive disabilities (CG) including dyslexia (DX) and users with low levels of foreign language proficiency (L) might also beneficiate from the compliance of these requirements. Table 1 lists the specification of accessibility requirements to perceive.

Accessibility Requirements to Operate

These are requirements oriented to solve the needs of users with motor disabilities (M), visual disabilities: blind (B) and low vision (V), and hearing disabilities: pre-lingual deafness (D) and deaf-blindness

Table 1. Accessibility requirements to perceive

Code	Accessibility Requirement	Related Disabilities
P1	Provide explanatory alternative text for non-textual elements such us, images, sensitive areas of image maps, audio content and speech content.	B, DB, V, DX
P2	Provide informative titles for links.	B, DB, CG, DX
P3	Use labels for form fields.	B, DB
P4	Make sure tables are comprehensible when read sequentially.	B, DB, CG
P5	Do not use nested tables.	B, DB, CG
P6	Provide mechanisms to stop and resume animations and other moving content.	CG
P7	Provide textual narratives for images and audio descriptions for videos.	B, DB, CG
P8	Include explanatory hidden text content for screen readers.	B, DB
P9	Support text and images resizing up to 200% at least.	V, CG, DX
P10	Provide adequate ratio contrast between foreground and background colors of at least 4:5:1.	V
P11	Do not use color as the only mechanism to convey information.	B, DB, V, CG
P12	Provide captioning to video content.	L, H, D, CG
P13	Make sure content in documents, presentations and files in pdf format comply with accessible rules.	B, V, H, D, DB, CG, DX
P14	Provide alternative video content in sign language.	D
P15	Provide textual transcripts of audio content.	H, D, CG
P16	Simplify textual content.	D, DB, CG, DX

Table 2. Accessibility requirements to operate

Code	Accessibility Requirement	Related Disabilities
O1	Make sure all the functionality is fully operable by keyboard.	M, B, V, DB
O2	Provide proper spatial distribution of the elements of the web pages.	M, CG, DX
O3	Design and implement web pages to be error-tolerant.	M, B, V, DB, CG, DL
O4	Provide mechanisms for skipping over long lists of links.	M, B, DB, CG, DX
O5	Provide mechanisms for skipping over long content.	M, B, DB, CG, DX
O6	Make sure learning/assessment activities do not have time limits or provide extra time.	M, B, V, D, DB, CG, DX, P, L, DL

(DB). These requirements also benefits users with cognitive disabilities (CG) including dyslexia (DX), users with low levels of digital literacy or literacy in general (DL) and users with low levels of foreign language proficiency (L). Table 2 lists the specification of accessibility requirements to operate.

Accessibility Requirements to Understand

These are requirements oriented to solve the needs of users with cognitive disabilities (CG) including dyslexia (DX), psychosocial disabilities (P), speech disabilities (S), low levels of foreign language proficiency (L), cultural/religion background (CU), and low levels of digital literacy (DL). In addition, blind users (B), low vision users (V), hear loss and post-lingual deaf users (H), pre-lingual deaf users (D), and blind-deaf users (BD) might also beneficiate of the compliance of these requirements. Table 3 lists the specification of accessibility requirements to understand.

Accessibility Requirements for Robust Access

These are requirements oriented to solve the needs of users with limited access to: base software (SW), electricity (E), affordable and quality internet (I), and updated computer devices (HW); which are usual limitations in developing countries. Table 4 lists the specification of accessibility requirements for robust access.

Accessibility Requirements Model

The integration of the POUR accessibility requirements sets up the accessibility requirements specification model for MOOCs. Figure 1 presents a partial view of the associated UML Use Case Model. The actor Learner can specialize in Blind, Low Vision, Dyslexia, and so on. The actor Learner performs the use case MOOC Platform Tasks including the use case Manage Profile, which has a use case extension Manage Accessibility Preferences. When the actor Learner performs the use case Navigate MOOC content, the appropriate use case extensions are executed. The alternative accessible interfaces are created by the actor Platform Developer. The alternative accessible content formats are created by the actor Content Author.

Table 3. Accessibility requirements to understand

Code	Accessibility Requirement	Related Disabilities
U1	Make sure relevant data is included in graphs.	CG, P, V
U2	Use consistent structure for web pages.	CG, P, DL, B, D, DB,
U3	Make sure content have only short, simple, clear paragraphs focused on a single idea at a time.	CG, P, DX, L, DL, B, D, DB
U4	Make sure content is logically and consistently organized.	CG, P, DX, L, DL, B, D, DB
U5	Provide a glossary for complicated, unusual, technical vocabulary.	CG, P, DX, L, CU, DL, D, BD
U6	Avoid content with non-literal text, such as sarcasm, satire, parody, allegory, metaphor, slang, and colloquialisms.	CG, P, L, CU, D, BD
U7	Provide conceptual explanations of mathematical expressions.	CG
U8	Use correct spelling and grammar.	CG, DX, L, D, BD
U9	Use consistent navigation mechanisms, including links to home page and previous page, a navigation bar and a website map.	CG, P, B, DB, D, DL
U10	Provide options to disable multimedia elements and automatic refreshing of content.	CG, P, B, DB
U11	Use adequate text font and text size.	DX, V
U12	Use adequate line spacing and line length.	DX, V
U13	Make sure text is left-aligned.	DX, V
U14	Use white space adequately.	DX, V
U15	Include a search option.	CG, P, L, DL, D
U16	Provide appropriate error messages and feedback.	CG, P, L, DL, D, DB
U17	Use appropriate examples and study cases.	CG, P, L, CU, D, BD
U18	Provide positive feedback to learning/assessment activities.	CG, P, CU
U19	Use appropriate vocabulary in video lectures.	CG, P, L, CU, D, BD
U20	Provide option to start, stop and resume relaxing music.	P
U21	Provide option to switch to relaxing colors.	P
U22	Provide alternative mechanism using written communication to voice chats or video conferences that require user's synchronic participation using vocal communication.	CG, P, S, L, H, D, BD
U23	Provide alternative mechanism using written communication to assignments that imply creation of audio content using vocal communication.	S, L, D, BD
U24	Provide alternative mechanisms to learning/assessment activities, such as texting chats and forums that require user's participation via written statements.	L, DL
U25	Provide alternative mechanism to assignments, such as essays and academic papers that involves users' creation of text content.	L, DL
U26	Select content, examples and learning/assessment activities that are not strange or offensive to users with diverse cultural backgrounds.	P, CU, D, DB
U27	Provide mechanisms to curate post in forums.	CG, L

Table 4. Accessibility requirements for robust access

Code	Accessibility Requirement	Related Disabilities
R1	Ensure content or learning/assessment activities do not requires a particular software technology.	SW
R2	Ensure there is no data loss in case of power failure.	E
R3	Make sure content can be downloaded, so users can work offline.	I
R4	Provide a mechanism to synch back offline work.	I
R5	Avoid heavy content in the web pages.	I, HW
R6	Provide mechanisms to allow views of videos with different levels of quality.	I, HW
R7	Provide an option to enable loading only text content in the web pages.	I, HW
R8	Make sure learning/assessment activities do not require downloading or uploading big volumes of data.	I, HW
R9	Ensure maximum compatibility with outdated hardware or software.	SW, HW
R10	Ensure maximum compatibility with future hardware or software.	SW, HW

Figure 1. UML use case model – partial view
Source: Authors, 2015

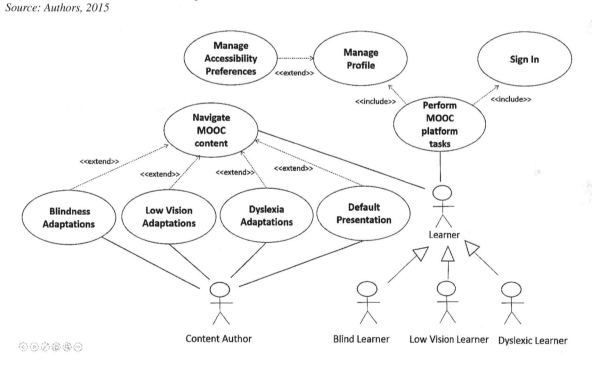

Design and Implementation of Accessible MOOCs

Although currently there are accessibility options in most operating systems, special-purpose applications and assistive technologies for several disabilities, many of them require the user to explicitly invoke them. Also, the potential negative psychological effects caused by the introduction of an assistive technology that change how a user interacts with a computer may lead to the user rejection of that assistive technology or computer use altogether (Stephanidis et al., 2001; Sloan et al., 2010).

As an alternative, this chapter proposes satisfying the MOOC users accessibility needs with an approach based in user profiling and the use of questionnaires that combines explicit user-invoked adaptations with automatic adaptive content presentation.

Adaptive content presentation involves personalizing the contents delivered to the user to enhance their accessibility (Stephanidis, 1998). To successfully achieve this, it is necessary an accurate detection of the particular user accessibility needs through user profiling and a mechanism that allows transparent selection and presentation of the appropriate adaptations according to the registered needs (Sloan et al., 2010).

On one hand, the design allows authors to configure parameters and define features so the MOOC can adapt to diverse potential learners. On the other hand, the design allows MOOC users to manage their accessibility user profile by selecting a combination of accessibility issues that best suit their current life situation and optionally taking quick questionnaires to define specific accessibility preferences (e.g., text size, color contrast, line spacing). The use of an accessibility user profile represents an improvement compared with current approaches used in websites and web applications, where the user must manually select specific technical adaptations. Nevertheless, the Accessibility Preferences user interface has an "Advanced Options" feature that provides more savvy users with freedom to select specific adaptations if desired. Figure 2 shows a user interface prototype to select accessibility preferences.

Figure 2. User interface prototype to select accessibility preferences
Source: Authors, 2015

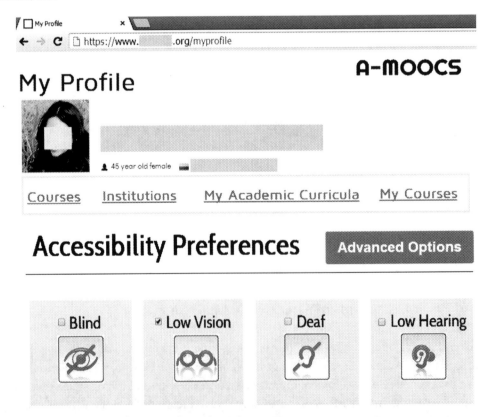

Design, Implementation and Evaluation of MOOCs

The user does not need to know what adaptations should be applied to the MOOC to make it more accessible for them. User needs to know only their reality and keep it updated in their profile. From that, the adaptive content presentation engine automatically applies all the necessary adaptations.

The architecture of the adaptive content presentation extension is composed of three layers, as illustrated in Figure 3. The Presentation Layer receives the course content in the appropriate format from the Logic Layer, where the adaptive engine resides. To select the appropriate content format, the adaptive engine scans the user profile and applies the necessary adaption rules to the course contents. The Persistence Layer contains three databases for storing user profiles, adaptation rules and course contents.

The course contents' database must contain several alternative formats for the same content, as illustrated in Figure 4. The user must be able to access any of the available alternative formats for any course content if desired.

To populate the course contents' database with several alternative formats for the same content, authors use ATAG compliant tools that offer functionality to produce accessible content. These tools provide wizards and forms to guide authors through actions such as:

Figure 3. Three-layer architecture
Source: Authors, 2015

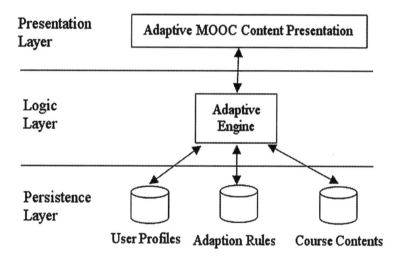

Figure 4. Example of alternative formats for same course content
Source: Authors, 2015

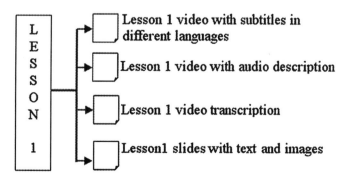

When a multimedia object is inserted, the title and the alternative text are requested.

When a video is inserted, different tracks of captions can be defined.

The structure of the web page can be organized with different levels of headings.

When a graph is inserted, it is possible to create an accompanying data table using the values used to create the graph.

Accessibility checking is an integrated function that helps make authors aware of web content accessibility problems during the authoring process, so they can be immediately addressed.

As an example of the adaption ruleset, Box 1 shows an extract of the adaption ruleset sequence to be executed if the user accessibility preferences profile indicates dyslexia. This adaption ruleset sequence is based on the research on dyslexia developed by De Santana et al. (2012).

Figure 5 shows the implementation of a default presentation of a typical lesson of a MOOC course that includes text content and a graph. In this default presentation, there are some accessibility issues, such as small text size, justified text, poor color contrast, meaning conveyed only by color, graph without data.

Figure 6 shows the implementation of the same lesson adapted to a low vision user profile. The requirements applied in this use case scenario are:

P10: text has a contrast ratio of at least 4.5:1.
P11: button and graph includes border pattern.
U1: graph includes data.
U9: better text font and bigger text size.

In the next scenario for user with both low vision and dyslexia, the additional requirements applied are:

U11: sans serif text font and bigger text size.
U12: bigger line spacing, smaller line length.
U13: text left-aligned.
U14: better use of white space.

Box 1.

```
FOR UserPreference[i] {
            #adaption ruleset sequence for dyslexia
            IF UserPreference[i] EQUALS dyslexia
            THEN
            {
                #U11 Text font without serif
                TextFont = p {font-family: Verdana, Arial, Calibri, Sans-serif} AND
                #U11 Text size minimum 12
                TextSize=12 AND
                #U12 Line spacing of minimum 1.5
                LineSpacing=1.5 AND
                #U12 Line length of maximum 80
                LineLength = 80 AND
                #U13 Text without justification
                TextJustification=Unjustified AND
                #More rules here
                ...
            }
} NEXT i
```

Figure 5. Accessibility implementation: Default presentation
Source: Authors, 2015

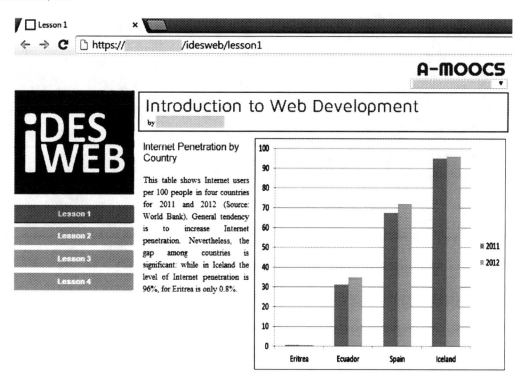

Figure 6. Accessibility implementation: Low vision adaptation
Source: Authors, 2015

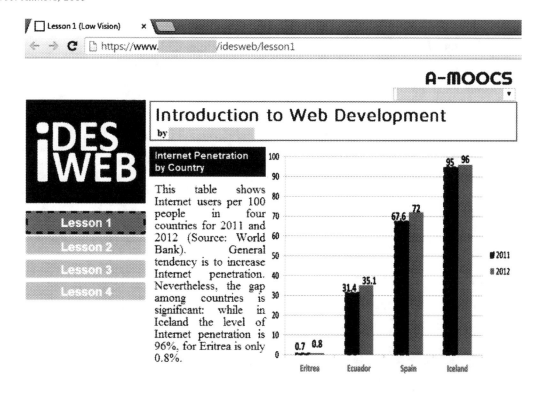

Figure 7. Accessibility implementation: Low vision and dyslexia adaptation
Source: Authors, 2015

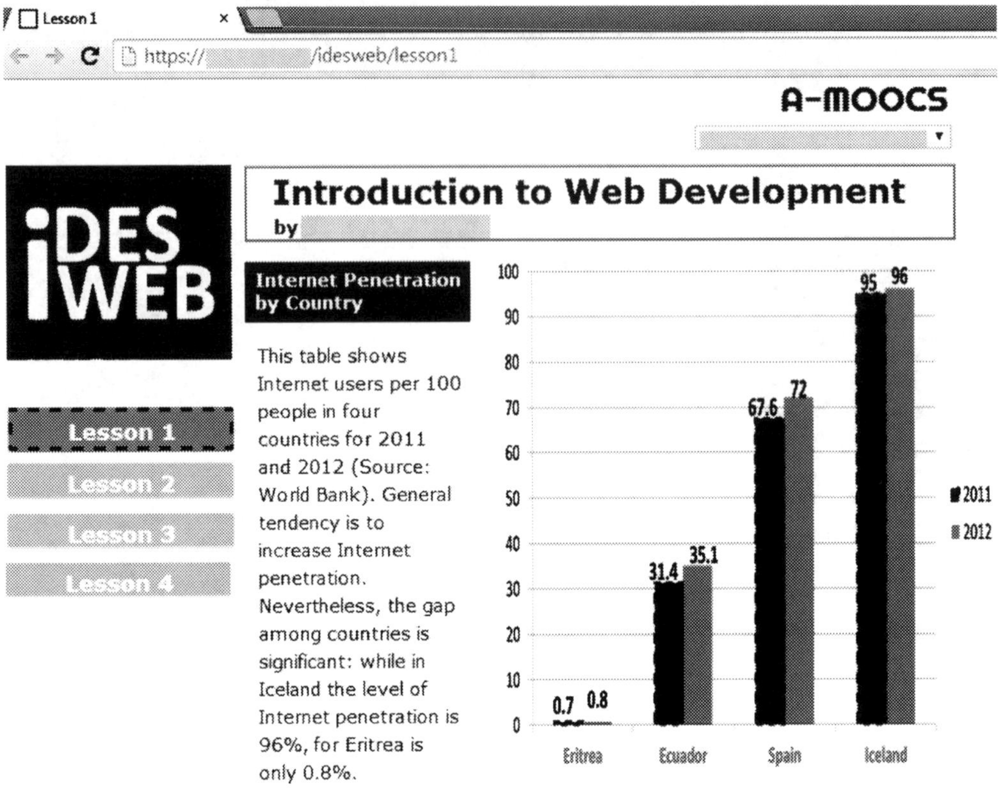

These adaptations improve legibility, readability, and reduce visual stress caused by dense paragraphs, as illustrated in Figure 7.

Finally, the adaption for a blind person is shown in Figure 8. A table with the data that generated the graphic has been added. The requirements applied in this use case scenario are:

P1: graph has alternative text.
P4: table is structured in a way that can be read by a screen reader.
O5: there is an option to skip to main content.

In order to make the table accessible to screen readers, the correct HTML tags must be used to define the table structure (Calle-Jimenez et al., 2014).

Accessibility Evaluation of MOOCs

In July 2014, WCAG released the Website Accessibility Conformance Evaluation Methodology WCAG-EM 1.0. The WCAG-EM describes a procedure to evaluate existing websites to determine their level of accessibility. The procedure is composed of five sequential steps: define the evaluation scope, explore the target website, select a representative sample, audit the selected sample, and report the findings.

Figure 8. Accessibility implementation: Blindness adaptation
Source: Authors, 2015

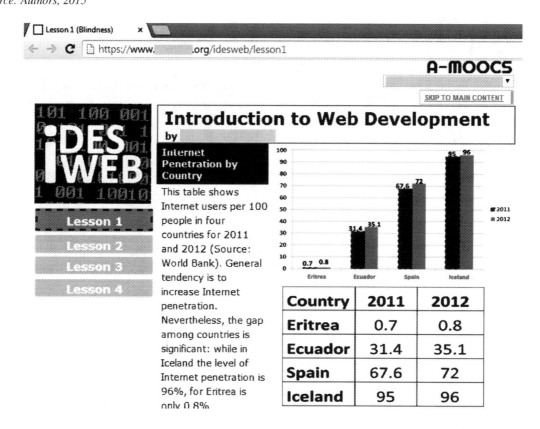

Besides, the WCAG-EM also includes considerations to guide evaluators through the evaluation process. This chapter proposes the adoption of WCAG-EM to use it during the design and implementation stages of MOOCs including automated, expert-based and user-based accessibility evaluations.

While most accessibility checks are not fully automatable, automated tools can significantly assist evaluators during the accessibility evaluation process and contribute to more effective evaluation. Accessibility evaluation tools are software applications or online services that help determine if a website meets accessibility requirements. There are several open web accessibility tools available, e.g., WAVE, AChecker, TAW, Total Validator, eXaminator and Accessibility Audit of Chrome Developer Tools.

The accessibility evaluation tools not necessarily produce reliable results since not all the accessibility problems can be automatically detected. Besides, a tool can produce fail positives that need to be discarded by expert-based and user-based evaluation. These tools are best exploited when used by experts on the subject of accessibility. When developers don't have expertise in accessibility, they tend to rely on the tool results only.

Accessibility evaluation tools are a useful resource to identify accessibility problems but they cannot solve them. Developers have to solve them by making changes on the web content to improve accessibility based on the automated evaluations results, but also on the evaluation results obtained with the help of accessibility experts and potential users with different types of disabilities. It is recommended to involve potential learners with aging-related disabilities and foreign language learners. These users may help to identify additional accessibility barriers that are not easily discovered by expert-based evaluation alone.

FUTURE RESEARCH DIRECTIONS

Continuing research is essential for improving inclusion of diverse learners in MOOCs. As Howard A. Rosenblum, CEO of the National Association of the Deaf stated, "Online content represents the next frontier for learning and lifelong education" (NAD, 2015).

For future work, next step is to formally validate the specified accessibility requirements. This validation will ensure that the accessibility requirements specification model is complete, correct, consistent, clear, unambiguous, and truly reflects MOOC potential users' needs.

Also, future work includes developing extensions for authoring tools that allow MOOCs creators to design and implement courses with improved accessibility.

CONCLUSION

Software solutions and educational content must adapt to users, not the other way around. This is the best cost-effective way to design a solution, especially in scenarios where large numbers of diverse users are expected to access and use a product, as is the case in MOOCs.

That is why this chapter proposed a specification of accessibility requirements for MOOCs based on the accessibility needs of potential users; and the design, implementation and evaluation of MOOCs using this specification.

More important, with this approach the particular situation of a person with disabilities may go unnoticed for both instructors and peer students, so the person with disabilities can be treated truly equally, hence assuring real inclusiveness.

REFERENCES

Aboshady, O., Radwan, A., Eltaweel, A., Azzam, A, & Aboelnaga, A. (2015). Perception and use of massive open online courses among medical students in a developing country: multicentre cross-sectional study. *BMJ open*. Retrieved from http://bmjopen.bmj.com/content/5/1/e006804.short

Adams, C., Yin, Y., Vargas, L., & Mullen, C. (2014). Snapshots from the Lived World of Massive Open Online Courses (MOOCs): A phenomenological study of learning large. *Proceedings of the 9th International Conference on Networked Learning*.

Agarwal, A. (2013). Online universities: It's time for teachers to join the revolution. *The Guardian*. Retrieved from http://www.theguardian.com/education/2013/jun/15/university-education-online-mooc

Al-Mouh, N., Al-Khalifa, A., & Al-Khalifa, H. (2014) A First Look into MOOCs Accessibility. *Proceedings of the 15th International Conference on Computers Helping People with Special Needs ICCHP* (pp. 145-152). Springer. 10.1007/978-3-319-08596-8_22

Bohnsack, M., & Puhl, S. (2014). Accessibility of MOOCs. *Proceedings of the 15th International Conference on Computers Helping People with Special Needs ICCHP. Springer International Publishing*, 141-144. 10.1007/978-3-319-08596-8_21

Burgstahler, S. (2002). Real connections: Making distance learning accessible to everyone. Retrieved from https://www3.cac.washington.edu/doit/Brochures/PDF/distance.learn.pdf

Calle-Jimenez, T., Sanchez-Gordon, S., & Luján-Mora, S. (2014) Web Accessibility Evaluation of Massive Open Online Courses on Geographical Information Systems. *IEEE Global Engineering Education Conference EDUCON* (pp. 680-686). 10.1109/EDUCON.2014.6826167

Christensen, S. (2001). How We Work to Make the Web SPEAK. *Computers in Libraries*, *21*(9), 30–34.

Daniel, J. (2012). Making sense of MOOCs: Musings in a maze of myth, paradox and possibility. *Journal of Interactive Media in Education*, *2013*(3).

De Santana, V. F., De Oliveira, R., Almeida, L. D. A., & Baranauskas, M. C. C. (2012). Web accessibility and people with dyslexia: a survey on techniques and guidelines. *Proceedings of the International Cross-Disciplinary Conference on Web Accessibility*. 10.1145/2207016.2207047

Diez, E., Alonso, A., Verdugo, M.A., Campo, M., Sancho, I., & Sánchez, S. (2011). European Higher Education Area: standards and indicators of good practices for the attention of college students with disabilities. Retrieved from http://sid.usal.es/libros/discapacidad/26032/8-1/espacio-europeo-de-educacion-superior.aspx

Gaebel, M. (2013). MOOCs: Massive Open Online Courses. European University Association Occasional Papers. Retrieved from http://www.eua.be/Libraries/Publication/EUA_Occasional_papers_MOOCs.sflb.ashx

Githens, R. (2007). Older Adults and E-learning: Opportunities and Barriers. *The Quarterly Review of Distance Education*, *8*(4), 329–338.

Guo, P., & Reinecke, K. (2014). Demographic differences in how students navigate through MOOCs. *Proceedings of the first ACM Conference on Learning @ Scale* (pp. 21-30). 10.1145/2556325.2566247

Hasselbring, T., & Williams, C. (2000). Use of computer technology to help students with special needs. *The Future of Children*, *10*(2), 102–122. doi:10.2307/1602691 PMID:11255702

Holcomb, T., & Kreeft, J. (1992). ESL Literacy for a Linguistic Minority: The Deaf Experience. Retrieved from http://www.cal.org/caela/esl_resources/digests/ESLlit.html

Horton, S., & Sloan, D. (2014). Accessibility in Practice: A Process-Driven Approach to Accessibility. In Inclusive Designing (pp. 105-115). Springer International Publishing. doi:10.1007/978-3-319-05095-9_10

ISO. (2012). ISO 9241-171 Ergonomics of human-system interaction – Guidance on software accessibility.

Kalyvioti, K., & Mikropoulos, T. (2013). A Virtual Reality Test for the Identification of Memory Strengths of Dyslexic Students in Higher Education. *J. UCS*, *19*(18), 2698–2721.

Koller, D. (2012). What we're learning from online education. *TED Talk*. Retrieved from http://www.ted.com/talks/daphne_koller_what_we_re_learning_from_online_education/

Legros, G., Havet, I., Bruce, N., & Bonjour, S. (2009). *The energy access situation in developing countries*. United Nations Development Programme and World Health Organization.

Lewin, T. (2015). Harvard and MIT are sued over lack of closed captions. *The New York Times*. Retrieved from http://www.nytimes.com/2015/02/13/education/harvard-and-mit-sued-over-failing-to-caption-online-courses.html

Liyanagunawardena, T., Williams, S., & Adams, A. (2013). The impact and reach of MOOCs: A developing countries' perspective. *eLearning Papers*, 33.

Mace, R. L., Hardie, G. J., & Place, J. P. (1996). *Accessible Environments: Toward Universal Design*. The Center for Universal Design, North Carolina State University.

Martinez-Cruz, C. (2014). An experience using a Massive Open Online Course at the University of El Salvador. *Proceedings of the 5th International Conference on Quality and Accessibility of Virtual Learning CAFVIR* (pp. 536-538).

McAuly, A., Bonnie, S., Siemens, G., & Cormier, D. (2010). The MOOC Model for Digital Practice, Knowledge Synthesis Grants on the Digital Economy, *University of Prince Edward Island*. Retrieved from http://www.elearnspace.org/Articles/MOOC_Final.pdf

Molina, R. (2010). Higher education for disabled students. *The R Journal*, *34*(70), 95–115.

Morales, A. (2007). White Paper on University and Disability. *Royal Board on Disability*.

Mordini, E., Wright, D., Wadhwa, K., De Hert, P., Mantovani, E., Thestrup, J., & Vater, I. (2009). Senior citizens and the ethics of e-inclusion. *Ethics and Information Technology*, *11*(3), 203–220. doi:10.100710676-009-9189-7

National Association of the Deaf. (2015). NAD Sues Harvard and MIT for Discrimination in Public Online Content. Retrieved from http://nad.org/news/2015/2/nad-sues-harvard-and-mit-discrimination-public-online-content

Notess, M., & Lorenzen-Huber, L. (2007). Online learning for seniors: barriers and opportunities. *eLearn*, 2007(5). Retrieved from http://doi.acm.org/10.1145/1266885.1266893

Palin, A. (2014). Moocs: Young students from developing countries are still in the minority. *Financial Times - Online learning*. Retrieved from http://www.ft.com/cms/s/2/8a81f66e-9979-11e3-b3a2-00144feab7de.html#axzz3T66iShyI

Parr, C. (2013). MOOC makes Oxford online dictionary. *Times Higher Education*. Retrieved from http://www.timeshighereducation.co.uk/news/mooc-makes-oxford-online-dictionary/2006838.article

Perez-Gonzalez, D., Soto-Acosta, P., & Popa, S. (2014). A Virtual Campus for E-learning Inclusion: The Case of SVC-G9. *J. UCS*, *20*(2), 240–253.

Perna, L., Ruby, A., Boruch, R., Wang, N., Scull, J., Evans, Ch., & Ahmad, S. (2013). The Life Cycle of a Million MOOC Users. Retrieved from http://www.gse.upenn.edu/pdf/ahead/perna_ruby_boruch_moocs_dec2013.pdf

POST. (2006). ICT in Developing Countries. Parliamentary Office of Science and Technology Postnote, 261.

Pouncey, I. (2010). Web accessibility for cognitive disabilities and learning difficulties. Retrieved from http://dev.opera.com/articles/view/cognitive-disability-learning-difficulty/

Preece, J., Rogers, Y., Sharp, H., Benyon, D., Holland, S., & Carey, T. (1994). *Human-computer interaction*. Addison-Wesley Longman Ltd.

Prougestaporn, P. (2010). Development of a web accessibility model for visually-impaired students on Elearning websites. *International Conference on Educational and Network Technology ICENT* (pp. 20-24). 10.1109/ICENT.2010.5532117

Sanchez-Gordon, S., & Luján-Mora, S. (2013b). Web accessibility of MOOCs for elderly students. *Proceedings of the 12th International Conference on Information Technology Based Higher Education and Training ITHET* (pp. 1-6). 10.1109/ITHET.2013.6671024

Sanchez-Gordon, S., & Luján-Mora, S. (2014a). Web Accessibility Requirements for Massive Open Online Courses. *Proceedings of the 5th International Conference on Quality and Accessibility of Virtual Learning CAFVIR* (pp. 530-5350.

Sanchez-Gordon, S., & Luján-Mora, S. (2014b). MOOCs Gone Wild. *Proceedings of the IEEE 8th International Technology, Education and Development Conference INTED* (pp. 1449-1458).

Satharasinghe, A. (2004). Computer Literacy of Sri Lanka. Retrieved from http://www.statistics.gov.lk/CLS/index.htm

Shah, W. (2014). MOOCs in 2014: Breaking Down the Numbers. *edSurge*. Retrieved from https://www.edsurge.com/n/2014-12-26-moocs-in-2014-breaking-down-the-numbers/

Sloan, D., Atkinson, M., Machin, C., & Li, K. (2010). The potential of adaptive interfaces as an accessibility aid for older web users. *Proceedings of the International Cross Disciplinary Conference on Web Accessibility*. 10.1145/1805986.1806033

Smith, M. (2012). Application of the ADA to Websites: Congress Should Rely on the Standards Created by the World Wide Consortium. Retrieved from http://works.bepress.com/marad_smith/1

Stephanidis, C. (2001). Adaptive techniques for universal access. *User Modeling and User-Adapted Interaction, 11*(1-2), 159–179. doi:10.1023/A:1011144232235

Stephanidis, C., ... (1998). Adaptable and adaptive user interfaces for disabled users in the AVANTI project. Intelligence in Services and Networks: Technology for Ubiquitous Telecom Services, 153-166.

Tsai, H., Shillair, R., & Cotten, S. (2014). Social Support and 'Playing Around': An Examination of How Older Adults Acquire Digital Literacy with Tablet Computers. *Proceeding of the 42nd Research Conference on Communication, Information and Internet Policy*.

United Nations. (2008). *Convention on the Rights of Persons with Disabilities and Optional Protocol*. Retrieved from http://www.un.org/disabilities/documents/convention/convoptprot-e.pdf

United Nations. (2015). *United Nations ENABLE Rights and Dignity of Persons with Disabilities*. Retrieved from http://www.un.org/disabilities/

W3C. (1999). Weaving the Web Berners Lee. Retrieved from http://www.w3.org/People/Berners-Lee/Weaving/glossary.html

W3C. (2014). Website Accessibility Conformance Evaluation Methodology (WCAG-EM) 1.0. Retrieved from http://www.w3.org/TR/WCAG-EM/

Velasco, R. (2011). *Health and Longevity I: Aging.* CODEU, 14-16.

WAI. (2014). WAI: Web Accessibility Initiative. Retrieved from http://www.w3.org/WAI/

Waldmeir, P. (2014). China's elderly flock back to university. *Financial Times.* Retrieved from http://www.ft.com/cms/s/0/aa918952-7ac8-11e4-8646-00144feabdc0.html#axzz3RrTJjcZW

WebAIM. (2015). Constructing a POUR website. Retrieved from http://webaim.org/articles/pour/perceivable

World Bank. (2014). World Development Indicators: Internet users. 2013. Retrieved from http://data.worldbank.org/indicator/IT.NET.USER.P2

World Health Organization. (2011). *Word Report on Disability*. Retrieved from http://www.who.int/disabilities/world_report/2011/en/

ADDITIONAL READING

Bates, A. W. (2015). *Teaching in a Digital Agechnology, e-learning and distance education.* Routledge. 999

Horton, S., & Quesenbery, W. (2014). *A web for everyone: designing accessible user experiences.* Rosenfeld Media.

Langdon, P., Clarkson, P. J., & Robinson, P. (2008). *Designing inclusive futures.* Springer Science & Business Media. doi:10.1007/978-1-84800-211-1

Pomerol, J. C., Epelboin, Y., & Thoury, C. (2015). *MOOCs: Design, Use and Business Models.* John Wiley & Sons. doi:10.1002/9781119081364

KEY TERMS AND DEFINITIONS

Accessibility: Extend to which a person can use an object, reach a place or obtain a service.

ATAG: A set of guidelines to maximize the accessibility of authoring tools used to produce web content.

Disability: A condition that limits a person's activities or participation in a permanent or temporal fashion.

Diversity: The awareness and acceptance that there are differences among human beings that ought to be embraced in a positive way.

HCI: A discipline related to the communication between humans and computers, its design, implementation and evaluation.

MOOC: A type of online course that can accept massive number of students without pre-requisites.

UAAG: A set of guidelines to maximize the accessibility of user agents, such as browsers and video players.

WAI: An initiative of the World Wide Web Consortium to promote the accessibility of the Web.

WCAG: A set of guidelines to maximize the accessibility of web content.

Web Accessibility: The grade in which web content is accessible to diverse users.

This research was previously published in User-Centered Design Strategies for Massive Open Online Courses (MOOCs) edited by Ricardo Mendoza-Gonzalez; pages 115-141, copyright year 2016 by Information Science Reference (an imprint of IGI Global).

Chapter 5
Accessibility to Higher Education in Nigeria:
The Pains, Problems, and Prospects

James Osabuohien Odia
University of Benin, Nigeria

Agnes Anuoluwapo Odia
University of Benin, Nigeria

ABSTRACT

Accessibility to university education represents a vital instrument for personal empowerment as well as the economic growth and technological advancement of a country. It is against the backdrop of the relevance and benefits of higher education that the quests for admission to Nigerian universities have assumed an alarming dimension due to the increasing annual applications to enroll for the entrance examinations conducted by the Joint Admission and Matriculation Boards and the subsequent screening by the respective universities. Unfortunately, most of the candidates are unable to gain admission to the university. The chapter considers some of the issues and challenges associated with low accessibility to university education for people seeking admission into Nigerian Universities and also suggest the ways to address the problems.

INTRODUCTION

Education is an important tool in any society or nation for moving the nation towards development and advancement in all fields of human endeavor. It is generally conceptualized as the process of acquiring skills, knowledge and attitude which helps in making an individual useful to himself/herself, his community and the nation at large. Although it is a universal feature of society, educational systems vary according to organizational structures, pedagogical practices, and philosophical and cultural organizations. A meaningful education is a functional education, that is, an education that will not make its product or possessor redundant but rather make him/her to become a useful member of the society to which they

DOI: 10.4018/978-1-7998-1213-5.ch005

belong. According to Jaja (2013), education is the fabric of any culture; with it culture is transmitted, advanced and consolidated; thoughts are conceptualized and information is transmitted. It is therefore unimaginable to conceive a learning process without education. The importance of education cannot be over-emphasized, little wonder it is generally referred to as the best legacy parents can bequeath to their children.

Education may be formal or informal with unintended consequences. The ultimate aim is the shaping of human behavior (Hungerfold & Volk, 1999), all-round development of the individual and preparation for life in society (Obayan, 1980). Education, particularly higher education, is fundamental to the construction of a knowledge economy and society in all nations (World Bank, 1999). In fact, the advancement and application of knowledge has increasingly driven economic and social developments (Saint, Harnett & Strassner, 2003). Higher Education refers to the western type of education which is organized after college education or all organized learning activities at the tertiary level. The National Policy on Education (2004) in Nigeria defines tertiary education to include: universities, colleges of education, polytechnics and monotechnics. The objectives of tertiary education include the following:

- To contribute to national development through high-level relevant manpower training.
- To develop and inculcate proper values for the survival of the individual and society.
- To develop the intellectual capability of individual to understand and appreciate their local and external environment.
- To acquire both physical and intellectual skills which would enable the individuals to be self-reliant and become useful members of the society.
- To promote and encourage scholarship and community services.
- To forge and cement national unity; and
- To promote national and international understanding and interaction.

Higher education in Nigeria has a long history dating back to 1934 when Yaba Higher College was established and in 1948 when the first university, University of Ibadan, was established. Today in 2016, besides the Federal Government and private universities, almost all the States in Nigeria have one or more universities. Nevertheless, the desire to provide equal educational opportunities to all has been mere expression of intentions without accompanied determination and commitment in the implementation and actualization of the desire. This is because the challenge of access to higher education has been further exacerbated by anticipated increase in demand for higher education owing to the higher education participation rate.

According to the National Policy on Education (2004), access implies making it possible for everyone who is entitled to education to receive it. It is the right to receive formal education as distinct from informal education (Dada, 2004). UNESCO (2003) sees access in tertiary education ensuring equitable access to tertiary education institutions based on merit, capacity, efforts and perseverance. Although accessibility to higher education refers to the opportunity to participate in the education sector whether formal or informal (Ehiametalor, 2005). Access to university education in Nigeria has been plagued with numerous problems and challenges such as poor funding by government, limited spaces for prospective applicants due to federal character quota system, carrying capacity and educationally least developed States (ELDS) admission criteria, high cost, incessant strike action by academic university workers, low marketability of the university products, falling standard and quality as well as infrastructural decay, gender inequality and disproportionate female enrolment in university education. Other factors like the government discriminatory policies, increasing population, globalization, information technology, cost and course content package, socio-economic status and student-support programme, the education disparities between the north and south as well as religious and cultural practices have also affected accessibility to higher education in Nigeria (Mustapha, 2005; Aluede, 2006, Udwigwomen, 2003; Ilusanya, 2008; Agboola & Ofoegbu, 2010; Dambazau, 2015).

The demands for university education have become very high and competitive because of the immense benefits and economic prospects (Ubogu,2011). However, there are also attendant pains and difficulties in gaining admission in recent times that it has been advocated the country would need to more than double the existing universities to accommodate the teeming number of youths who cannot matriculate due to population explosion and the after-effects of universal basic education. Akubuilo and Okorie (2013) argued that while increase in the number of educational institutions may addressed the issue of access but other factors such as shortage of teaching staff, research grants, infrastructure, corruption, quality and weak technology are even more serious challenges still facing the Nigerian education system. Therefore, the objective of the chapter is to examine accessibility to higher education in Nigeria by considering the influencing factors and challenges, pains and problems, as well as the prospects of accessible and affordable higher education.

The rest of the chapter is structured into four sections as follows: the immediate section considers the background to higher education in Nigeria. Section three dwells on some of the lingering issues in the accessibility to higher education in Nigeria. This subsection also discusses the pains, problems, challenging dilemmas and prospects associated with university education. Section four addresses and proffers solutions to the challenges and problems of accessibility to higher education in Nigeria. The last section is the conclusion and suggestions for further research

BACKGROUND OF HIGHER EDUCATION IN NIGERIA

According to Adeoti (2015), the desire for higher education in Nigeria dates back to the second half of the 19th century when the well-to-do Africans in Lagos sent their children overseas for professional training. The returnee children upon completion of their studies demanded for the establishment of higher institution in Nigeria. The agitation led to the Yaba Higher College in 1934. The first five universities in Nigeria were established between 1948 and 1969- University College, Ibadan (1948), University of Nigeria, Nsukka (1960), Ahmadu Bello University, Zaria (1962), University of Ife (1962) and the University of Lagos (1962).The 1970s saw the mass establishment of universities by the military government owing to the need for national integration. Starting with University of Benin in 1970 the Federal Military Government established 7 other universities in Jos, Ilorin, Sokoto, Maiduguri, Kano now (Bayero University), Port Harcourt and Calabar in 1975. Between 1981 and 1985 additional seven Federal Universities of Technology were established at Owerri, Yola, Makurdi, Bauchi, Akure, Abeokuta and Minna (with Abeokuta and Makurdi being converted to universities of Agriculture (Idowu, 2012).During the fourth civilian regime of Olusegun Obasanjo from 1999 to 2007 over thirty universities were established. In fact between 1970 and 2015, the Federal Government built additional 42 universities while State Governments established 37 universities between 1970 and 2015 (Nwachukwu & Okolie,2015).

By the Nigerian Constitution of 1979, the Federal Government lost its central control over the university system and this accounted for the proliferation of State and private universities. The Federal Government of Nigeria through Section 18 of the 1999 Constitution guaranteed that government shall direct its policy towards ensuring equal and adequate educational opportunity at all levels. Section 42(2) of the Constitution of the Federal Republic of Nigeria (FRN,1999) dwells on the right to freedom from discrimination. Section 1 and sub-sections 4c and 5c of the National Policy on Education of 2004 stipulated that there is need for equality of educational opportunities to all Nigerian children irrespective of any real or imagined disabilities, each according to his or her ability and there will be the provision of equal access to educational opportunities for all citizens of the country at the primary, secondary and tertiary levels both inside and outside the formal school system.

The Universal Declaration of Human Right (1948) in Article 26 stated that everyone has the right to education. Similarly, the International Covenant on Economic, Social and Cultural Rights (1966) and the African Charter on Human and Peoples' Rights (1981) are international human rights instruments that provide for education as a fundamental human right. Thus, access to education is the right to be educated as provided by the Nigerian Constitution, the Universal Declaration of Human Rights, the Conference on Education for All (EFA), the Dakar Framework for Action, the Ouagadougou 1992 Declaration on Education of Women and Girls, the Amman 1996 Affirmation of the Pursuit of the Goals of Jomtien, the Durban 1998 State of Commitment on Inter-African Collaboration for the Development of Education and the African Union (AU) 1997 – 2006 decade of education in Africa

ISSUES OF HIGHER EDUCATION IN NIGERIA

The need for meaningful access to university education has recently become indispensable in Nigeria as a result of population increase and the level of awareness of the roles of the university education in the development of the individual and the nation at large (Chukwurah, 2011). Okojie (2010) revealed that apart from the low value of funding for universities between the years 2000 and 2009, there were also upsurge in degree students' enrolment. In fact Saint et al. (2003) found that between 1990 and 1997, the real value of government allocations for higher education declined by 27% even as enrolment grew by 79%. Education is a means by which a nation equips her citizens for all round development. It is a fulcrum for achieving progress in all aspects of human life, national growth and development. This is in consonance with the 1998 World Conference on Education Commitment that higher education should be geared towards development and progress (Mukoro, 2013). The establishment and development of higher education in Nigeria has been from the pre-independence era till day based on findings and recommendations of committees and commissions. For instance, the Asquith and Elliot Commissions of 1943 led to the establishment of the University of Ibadan in Nigeria in 1948.The Ashby Commission of 1960 led to the establishment of more universities and the expansion of the institutes in Enugu, Ibadan, Kaduna and Yaba (Osokoya, 1989). The commission also recommended the establishment of new institutes of Agriculture in Benin City, Port Harcourt and Kano respectively. In addition, the commission recommended the establishment of two more universities which were later established and located in Zaria in Kaduna State and Nsukka in Enugu State.

Access to university education in Nigeria when compared with the number of qualified applicants is low (Agboola & Ofoegbu, 2010). Consequently the gap between successful or qualified candidates and those admitted has continued to widen yearly. The higher education enrolment rate in Sub-Saharan Africa is less than 5% (Juman, 2007). Moreover, the higher education participation rate (HEPR) of Nigeria is low compare to developed countries like USA, Australia, Korea with 64%, 41% and 51% HEPR respectively (Daniel, Kanwar & Uvalic-Trumbic, 2006). The level of access to higher education in Nigeria compares poorly with that of South Africa (17%), Indonesia (11%) and Brazil (12%).The issue of low access started from the colonial period. Anyanwu (2010) stated that access to university education was very limited during the colonial period because the British administrators were not willing to incur the costs of maintaining academic quality. Hence between 1948 and 1959 less than one thousand Nigerians enrolled in the University College Ibadan but only three were women. The 1970s witnessed some increase in the established universities but without corresponding improvement in academic quality and funding.

The Joint Admission and Matriculation Board (JAMB) was created by Decree No.2 of 1978 to address the problem of multiple admissions into Nigerian universities and the inability of universities to predict their future fresh student population. JAMB was set up to ensure uniform standards for university admissions and to ensure that merit serves as the basis of selection of candidates for admission. But this was not to be as JAMB eventually became a political tool to equalize educational opportunities between the advantaged states in the south and disadvantaged states in the North by deliberately thwarting the pace of higher education development in southern States of Nigeria (Abdulkareeem & Muraina,2014). Obilade (1992) found a contradiction between the stated objectives of JAMB and what was done in practice. The JAMB's University Matriculation Examinations (UMEs) were harmonized for all candidates seeking admission to tertiary institutions with the Unified Tertiary Matriculation Examination (UTME) in 2009 whereby a candidate has the option of two universities, two polytechnics and two colleges of education as his or her choice of institutions. However, from 2014 a new system was introduced which allows an applicant to a choice of one University, one Polytechnic, one College of Education and one Computer Institute (Oseni, 2015) when applying for UTME.

The controversial quota system introduced by the Shagari's administration in 1981 compromised national unity. The system was introduced owing to the dissatisfaction with JAMB's first admission in 1978 which favoured more candidates from the South than the North because it was based on merit. The challenge of unequal access to university education, multiple admissions particularly by candidates from Southern Nigeria and the fact that educational opportunity was tied to employment opportunities, agitations and pressures from northerners eventually led to the liberalization of the admission process through the quota system for sake of regional equality and mass access. Although quota system was intended to help increase access to the academically disadvantaged northern States, it has since alienated candidates from southern States which lost significant admission slots in the federal universities from year to year.

Again, Saint, Hartnet and Strassner (2003) found significant differences in the academic performances between students admitted on merit and those admitted on other criteria. Akpan and Undie (2007) argue that the quota system has an inequitable effect in guiding and regulating admissions into universities. The criticisms of JAMB on the lack of relationship between JAMB entry scores and performance in degree examinations as well as defective admission criteria led the Federal Government in 2005 to allow universities to conduct Post University Matriculation Examinations (PUME) screening for candidates that have achieved a certain level of performance (180 or 200 score) in JAMB examinations. The reform gave universities the opportunity to have input in the candidates admitted by them and the students admitted through PUME are also adjudged to have better performance. However, the screening has not only increased the student's hurdles to pass additional examination before gaining admission to the university but there are also claims that the universities are exploiting the candidates in the fee charge to conduct the screening.

The National Universities Commission (NUC), established by the Federal Government in 1962 to take over the colonial government's Inter-University Council, became a statutory body through Decree No.1 of 1974 with the objectives of coordination, development and financing of universities. It has also been responsible for granting licenses for the establishment of private universities in Nigeria. Despite NUC's achievements in expanding access through her transformational policies and programmes, promoting equity among geo-political zones and gender, and improving efficiency in the governance and management of the university, NUC has been criticized by Academic Staff Union of Universities (ASSU) and other stakeholders for the proliferation of universities through indiscriminate granting of licenses and the negative impacts on the Nigeria's economy, and undermining and becomes cog in the wheel of progress in the development of the entire university system.

The mid to late 1990s saw an upsurge in the establishment of many private universities owing to political pressures and increasing demands for access and equal opportunity to education and the obvious facts that both the Federal and State governments could not meet the high demand for higher education (Obasi, 2007; Nwagwu, 2001). However, even with the increasing number of private universities, which are mainly targeted at the children of political and economic elites, the less privileged are still denied access to higher education in Nigeria owing to high costs. While the proprietors of private universities have the liberty to use their discretion in admitting students other than on merit or quota system, the federal universities face heavy sanctions if they fail to comply fully.

With regard to the issue of funding and infrastructure, Fafunwa (1971) cited in Adeoti (2015) stated that the bulk of the money to run the first university in Nigeria was provided by the colonial government; thus serving as precedence for the financing of universities in Nigeria. Idowu (2012:5) argued that between 1960s and 1975 all the universities in the country had been funded 100% by the federal and regional governments. However, following the military takeover and proliferation of universities, the resources available for universities' development have continued to dwindle over time and unfortunately less than the United Nations minimum recommended benchmark of 26%.

There is also the issue of declining quality of Nigerian universities (Adeogun & Gboyega, 2010). The decline in quality has been linked to proliferation of private universities as well as the poor state of the economy, weak internal capacity; poor governance, poor research activities, brain drain, political interference and poor funding (Oseni, 2015). Oni (2000) found both internal and external factors to be responsible for declining quality. The internal factors include strikes, lack of employee motivation, and weak accountability for educational performance while the external factors include shortages of teachers, corruption, inconsistent funding efforts by government and admissions based on quotas rather than merit. The military government between 1980 and 1990s as well as the low level of investment in research capacity and education are also responsible for quality decline (Akubuilo & Okorie, 2013). Little wonder, Anya (2013) and Okemakinde (2014) argued that the standards and performance of the Nigeria's university system has plummeted, suffered multiple vicissitudes since the 1980s. Okebukola (2008) observed that the depressed quality of education in Nigeria can be explained in part by the inadequate funding of the system. In fact, no Nigerian university has made the list of the global ranking of universities in recent times. Moreover, higher education in Nigeria has not been able to graduate persons with the requisite generic skills that can be associated with the development of the Nigeria state. More worrisome is the fact that the country is backward not only based on global ranking but she has also low ranking in the African continent (Akubuilo & Okorie, 2013). Nevertheless, the aspiration is where Nigerian universities begin to pay a critical role in the nation's future innovation, economic competitiveness and prosperity by connecting "knowledge creators with knowledge commercializers through technology incubators, entrepreneurial development curricula and nurturing relationships with community-based venture funds" (Sampson, 2004). Unfortunately, university education has not liberated

Nigerians from the bondage of parochialism, ethnicity, tribalism, oppression and injustice; education has not transformed Nigerians development (Jaja, 2013; Aghenta, 1983)

The issues of institutional and academic autonomy of Nigeria's university have been a contentious matter between government and ASUU in recent years. The struggle for institutional autonomy has been a long-standing issue in the university system in Nigeria. Arikewuyo (2004) recounted how past and present governments have encroached and eroded universities' autonomy by banning and unbanning staff and student unions at various times, removing the Vice Chancellor for not complying with government directives, dismissal, retiring and unjustly jailing of academics, integration of the universities into the civil service, creation of JAMB which eroded the power of universities to determine student intakes and criteria for admission, expanding the scope of operations of NUC which usurp the powers of the university's senate to regulate curriculum and syllabus and by reducing the powers of the governing council and senate of university in relation to being statutory employers and highest decision making body over academic matters.

The Pains of Denied Accessibility to University Education

The pains include: (1) the difficulty of gaining access because of the discriminatory admission policy, the requirements to pass other screening tests as well as the high entry fees (2) the horrible physical screening exercise of thousands of candidates for admission like the ones of the 2016/2017 session owing to the cancellation of PUME (3) cancellation of all diploma programmes in universities by the NUC which hitherto provided opportunities for students to subsequently gain access into university (4) admission into courses and institutions not applied for. The unnecessary delays and disruptions of academic activities through incessant strike actions so that a student knows when he is admitted into the university but cannot tell when she will graduate hindering planning. The decay, dwindling standards and low current ratings of Nigerian universities compare to other African and foreign universities are also a source of concern. Defective curriculum (Ajayi & Adeniji 2009) and the tag of un-employability of Nigeria's graduates and the fears and frustrations of not being able to get a job or fix-up after graduation even with fantastic certificate or result are other horrifying experience.

Admission into public universities in Nigeria is like the proverbial camel going through the needle's eye. Only a handful of students are able to gain admission into their preferred course at first or second sitting for JAMB. For many others, after long period of waiting or writing the entrance examination repeatedly, they are eventually offered admission into courses in universities not originally applied for or the ones the university think the students are qualified for. The candidate is giving a choice to either accept or reject such offer. Adelakun (2013) lamented that the current admission trend into higher education has not improved as recent developments showed that over a million candidates sat UTME annually but only a small percentage get admitted. Abang (1988) remarked the Nigerian universities lack a friendly teaching and learning for people with disabilities.

The PUME screening has been not favourable to some candidates seeking access to university education in Nigeria because of the lack of correlation between the scores obtained in JAMB and PUME. Hence some high-scoring candidates who could not repeat the same feat in PUME either miss Nevertheless, it has helped the universities to control the quality of admitting the best students admitted and guarantee their outputs. In fact, the accusations and counter accusations that the universities were usurping JAMB's functions by subjecting the prospective candidates to other examinations and exploiting them through PUME made the Minister of Education to ban universities from conducting any post UTME for admission into the university in the 2016/2017 session. Consequently, PUTME was replaced with a physical screening exercise where the University was not permitted to conduct any post UTME examination but screen candidates to rather confirm the UTME results and grades obtained in the O' level examinations (WAEC, NECO and NABTEB). As the universities and other stakeholders' apprehension rises on the way forward, JAMB came up with two proposed models for the screening exercise:

Model 1

- Screening of ONLY candidates recommended to JAMB and offered provisional admissions.
- No written examination conducted.
- Verification of course requirements (O' levels or A' levels) with maximum lifespan of five (5) years.
- Verification of valid JAMB results.
- Fees charged for Screening.

Model 2

- Screening of candidates before recommendation and presentation to JAMB for provisional admissions.
- No examination conducted.
- Verification of course requirements (O' levels or A' levels). Grades and UTME scores are weighted.
- Verification of valid JAMB results by checking: (i). Online result slip (ii). Print out (iii). Photo album (iv). Checklist (v). Biometrics
- Fees charged for Screening.

It was suggested that the weighted course requirements, grades and UTME scores put some candidates at a disadvantage. However, the weighting of grades and UTME scores are as follows:

Criteria for Scoring UTME Candidates in the 2016/2017 Screening Exercise

For instance, a candidate who scores 250 in JAMB examination and also had ordinary (O) level credits (3As, 1B and 1C) in five relevant subjects in one sitting will have a cumulative score of 10 + 18+ 4+3 + 33 or 68% while another candidate with a score of 260 in JAMB examination but (3As, 1B and 1C) in five relevant subjects in two sittings will have 3+18+4+3+ 35 or 63%. Given the example and where two O' level sittings were allowed for admission into a course, candidates with two sittings were dis-

Table 1. Number of sitting (Total Marks = 10%)

S/NO	Number of Sittings	Marks
1	One	10
2	Two	3

Table 2. O level results in five relevant subjects (Total Marks = 30%)

S/NO	O Level Grades	Marks
1	A1	6
2	B2, B3	4
3	C4,C5,C6	3

Table 3. Grading of JAMB UTME score (Total Marks = 60%)

S/NO	Range of UTME Scores	Marks
1	180-185	20
2	186-190	21
3	191-195	22
4	196-200	23
5	....	
6	246-250	33
7	...	
8	296-300	43
9	...	
10	376-380	59
11	381-400	60

Source JAMB (2016)

advantaged despite their higher score in JAMB. Again, the current policy of the government limits the ability of the universities to verify and authenticate the current state and preparedness of candidates to be admitted into university education particularly for students who left secondary schools after a long time and others who engaged in examination malpractices to pass their O' levels and /or JAMB examinations with fantastic results. The fears and frustrations have made some students to seek for admission in the private universities if they afford the cost or go to other African countries, UK, USA or Asian countries.

Criteria for Scoring Direct Entry

The ban of PUME without consultation with the various stakeholders not only set back the university timetable, as admission of the new students into 100 level is yet to be concluded six months after writing entrance examination, the 2016/2017 is likely going to be affected as well. Parents and the wards are apprehensive of the fate of the wards and way forward owing to the delay in the admission process in 2016.

The Problems of Higher Education in Nigeria

According to Baikie (1999), the problem of accessibility was created by noticeable disparities in education between sections of the country for instance between the north and south. The disparities in access

Table 4. Number of sitting (Total Marks = 10%)

S/NO	Number of Sittings	Marks
1	One	10
2	Two	3

Table 5. O level results in five relevant subjects (Total Marks = 30%)

S/NO	O Level Grades	Marks
1	A1	6
2	B2, B3	4
3	C4,C5,C6	3

Table 6. Grading of A level for IJMB, NCE score etc (Total Marks = 60%)

S/NO	Range of A Level Aggregates	Marks
1	15 Points	60
2	14	55
3	13	51
4	12	47
5	11	43
6	10	39
7	9	35
8	8	31
9	7	27
10	6	23
11	5	19
12	4	15
13	3	11

Table 7. Grading of A level for national diploma score, etc. (Total Marks = 60%)

S/NO	Range of A Level Aggregates	Marks
1	Distinction/Excellent	60
2	Upper Credit/Credits	50
3	Lower Credit/Merit	30
4	Pass	15

Source: JAMB (2016)

to higher education have been along geo-ethnic, gender and socio-economic dimensions. The North-South educational divide and imbalance has been blamed on the misguided educational policy of the colonial administration in Northern Nigeria (Mustapha, 2005), entrenched Islamic values and culture practices which excluded women from both higher education system and socio-economic and political roles (Aluede, 2006; Udwigwomen, 2003) and time-lag (Agboola & Ofoegbu, 2010). Ilusanya (2008) sees the issue of access as politics. He observes that variations in educational development between the southern and northern parts in Nigeria had necessitated the introduction of certain policies to engender even national representation in institutions nationally owned. The problem of multiple admissions into Nigerian universities and the inability of universities to predict their future fresh student population gave rise to the centralization of university admission through the creation of JAMB. Again, the need to correct this discrepancy resulted in the introduction of the quota system (Okebukola, 2002). Akpotu (2005) posited that the major obstacles to increased access to higher education in Nigeria are not prices but the reform policies of quota system, catchment area admission policy, poor and inadequate facilities and the limited absorptive capacity of Nigerian universities. Okoli (2015) gave the many challenges facing Nigerian universities from inception to include the struggle to grapple with issues of admission, accommodation, education policies, student unionism and funding. Ukpai and Ereh (2016) identified six current challenges affecting university education in Nigeria to include: (i)The challenge of over-emphasis on science and technology related courses at the detriment of humanities. (ii) The challenge of on-line registration (internet services). (iii) The challenge of persistent increase in school fees versus quality learning experiences. (iv) The challenge of deregulation of education. (v) The challenge of certificate racketeering and marketability of university products and (vi) The challenge of demand and supply of university education. Agboola and Ofoegbu (2010) argued that the measures which have taken to address the issues such as expansion of access, provision of human and material resources and quality at the tertiary education seem to have failed due to the continuing widened gap of education imbalance as the fear of domination by one group over the others have given way to the various admission criteria.

Although many universities have been established since the 1960s, the expansion has not translated to a broad-based access. In fact, Ukpai et al (2016) showed that less than 30% of the university seekers through JAMB were able to secure admission between 2010 and 2014. Anyanwu (2010) argued that the consequence of expansion has not been positive. Among the problems of higher education, particularly university education in Nigeria include (1) poor funding, (2) infrastructure decay and deficiency, (3) frequent government intervention and lack of university's autonomy (4) unpredictable educational imposed policy by the Federal Ministry of Education and the NUC. There are also incessant shut-downs as a result of striking university staff and students' gangsterism, cultism and other social vices (Osagie, 2009:12; Adedeji & Bamidele, 2002: 516). Obanya (2007) identified the challenges of higher education in Nigeria to include: expanding access, thereby responding to increasing social demand; ensuring continuity in university work as there have been many disruptions due to staff and student strikes; going beyond mere academics by dwelling on students' personality development; eliminating cultism among students, thus ensuring peace on campuses. There is also lack of relevance of academic programmes and curricula due to the inability of some specialized universities to match graduate output to national manpower requirements (Federal Ministry of Education, 2009)

Funding

The problem of poor funding started with the advent of the military in the 1970s and reached its apogee between 1990 and 1997 when the real value of government allocation for higher education nose-dived by 27% while enrolment grew by 79%. Inadequate funding has been described as the bane of tertiary education in Nigeria which has led to various strikes with adverse effect on the standard of education in Nigeria (Famurewa, 2014). The study by World Bank (2010) revealed problem of financing qualitative university education in Africa. Similarly, Okojie (2010) submitted that most federal universities'

Table 8. Admission demand and supply of Nigerian universities

Year	Application Demand	Admission supply	% Admitted
2010	1,256,465	346,605	27.5%
2011	1,434,704	360,170	25.12%
2012	1,436,473	397,067	27.6%
2013	1,685,084	392,559	23.3%
2014	1,479,513	361,400	24.6%

Source: Ukpai et al (2016)

administrators complain of inadequate funding because they were not allowed to charge undergraduate tuition fees. According to Obanya (2002) the inadequate funding has led to the problems to deterioration of physical facilities, internal and external brain drain among the intellectuals and overstretching of teaching, research and managerial capacities in Nigerian University system. Shina (2012) found funding issues to be a critical challenge in the effective discharging of university's administrators' functions. There has been also no progressive increase in the funding injected to the universities despite the increase in maintenance costs, students intake, inflation trends and overhead costs (Omopupa & Abdulraheem, 2013). For instance the proportion of the Federal Government funding to the universities was less than 7% of the total government expenditure between 2002 to 2008. This level of funding by the Nigerian government falls far below the 26% of government expenditure as recommended by UNESCO.

Decay Infrastructure

There is also the problem of decay and deficient facilities conducive for educational pursuit, teaching and learning. Lecture theatres, classrooms, laboratories, workshops and libraries in government's universities are insufficient and inadequate with inappropriate furnishings, power and water supply. Most of the equipment and machineries are old and outdated. The decay and stress on infrastructural resources in the universities is linked to the tremendous growth in the demand for higher education which has taken a negative toll on the quality of services provided by the institutions and the comparative quality of their products (Utomi, 2008). For instance in 2013, over 1.7million candidates sat for the Unified Tertiary Matriculation Examination (UTME) organized by the JAMB to gain access to institutions of higher education in Nigeria with half a million carrying capacity of all the tertiary institutions. Moreover, the mismanagement, corruption, misappropriation and mismanagement by the universities' administrators of the available funds from Tertiary Education Trust Fund (TETFUND), internally generated revenue and other government allocation have also constrained the provision and expansion of critical infrastructures, upgrade of laboratories and workshops and ICT facilities to global standard, development of the teachers' teaching and research capacities and promotion of high quality teaching and learning environment

Table 9. Fund disbursements to Federal Universities in Nigeria (2000-2009)

Year	Recurrent Grants (N)	Capital Grant (N)	Budget Allocation to GDP (%)	Budget Allocation to Govt Expenditure (%)
2000	28206218865.91	936785632.00	8.36	7.1
2001	28419719502.84	4226691359.00	7.00	7.6
2002	30351483193.00	NIL	6.82	6.4
2003	34203050936.33	NIL	7.20	6.6
2004	41492948787.01	11973338699.00	6.68	6.4
2005	49453098168.72	8822869440.00	6.80	6.3
2006	75400267475.00	6976416815.00	7.28	6.66
2007	81757053487.00	8808205850.00	7.68	6.4
2008	92219484808.00	14414135937.00	7.82	6.8
2009	98028449198.00	10571861732.00		7.0

Source: Okojie (2010), Jaja (2013)

Besides, equipment and consumables are absent, inadequate or outdated, financial problem, inadequate ICT facilities, demographic factors and personnel re-engineering/re-orientation. This is corroborated by Okojie (2009) of the increased enrolments and/or reduced funding in the needs assessment of Nigerian university that physical facilities for teaching and learning in the public universities were inadequate, dilapidated, over-stretched and improvised (Anya, 2013).

Gender Enrollment Disparity

Moreover, the higher education female gender equitable access rate in Nigeria is quite unimpressive (Mukoro, 2013). Anho and Onojetah (2007) reported that the cumulative undergraduate enrolment overtime in Nigeria from 1980-1999 revealed that there was a great disparity between enrolment of male and female. The gender disparity started even in the first admission into the University of Ibadan in 1948 when out of the 104 students admitted there were only three women (Fapohunda, 2011). Also, Emunemu and Ayeni (2003), Oyebade (2008) and Nwajiuba (2011) have shown that there is a very poor level of equitable accessibility to university education in Nigeria, whether on the part of women or other educationally disadvantaged like nomads, migrant fishermen and street children. The problem has further been compounded by the discrimination between types of higher institutions and certificate awarded such that most candidates prefer to go to the university rather than polytechnics and colleges of education, and to public university compare to private university. The average male enrolment is also higher than the female. There is also disparity in the gender enrolment in the universities in Nigeria across the

Table 10. Students enrolment and admission per gender

Sessions	Gender	Universities Enrolment	Admitted Students per gender	% Admitted
2000/2001	Male	238,456	26,665	11.2
	Female	177,835	19,101	10.7
2001/2002	Male	743,725	54,972	7.4
	Female	312,892	35,797	11.4
2002/2003	Male	580,338	31,942	5.5
	Female	414,042	19,903	4.8
2003/2004	Male	603,176	62,023	10.3
	Female	443,764	43,984	9.9
2004/2005	Male	484,217	60,049	12.4
	Female	353,834	45,906	12.9
2005/2006	Male	527,180	39,743	7.5
	Female	390,780	25,775	6.5
2006/2007	Male	521,170	42,953	8.2
	Female	391,180	28,044	7.2
2007/2008	Male	578,715	NA	
	Female	455,368	NA	

Sources: Adapted from JAMB for various years

geo-political zones and disciplines. Oseni (2013) attributes the male - female disparity to socio-cultural, customs and local traditions, religion, socio-economic and poverty, lapses in policies and processes of eliminating gender inequality, and high tuition and cost of education,

Quota System

With respect to admission to the university, issue of catchment areas, educationally least developed States. The federal character policy is a means to ensure fair and equal representation in various components of the units and communal groups in the country's educational institutions, agencies, status and influence, and positions of power. According to FRN (1996), it involves lowering the entry and promotional qualifications of states considered disadvantaged in educational opportunity. Federal character policy which is associated with the quota system of admission has been detrimental to candidates' access to university education (Akpan & Undie, 2007). According to them the quota system was introduced in an attempt to provide equal opportunity for candidates to be admitted into the university, but regrettably, the system has been greatly abused. It has also make access to the university very difficult for some candidates while giving others undue advantages to others because of the State of origin. It has made admission political, not based on merit and lower access of the qualified (Okebukola, 2006). Chukwurah (2011) argues that quota system policy of university admission is not favourable to non-indigenes of the states where the university is situated such that any student who misses the merit list has little or no chance of being admitted because of this policy. Moreover, the access to university was also restricted by the policy of 60:40 ratio of admission to science and liberal arts discipline respectively in the conventional universities and 70:30 ratio in polytechnics and colleges of technologies but a ratio of 80:20 for specialized universities (Ojogwu, 2004; JAMB, 2016). Consequently, there are increase in the number of Nigerian students seeking admissions and studying in universities outside the country, even in smaller African nations despite the skyrocketing costs and foreign exchange outflows implications on the Nigeria's economy. Some of the top oversea countries of study destination for Nigerian students are: United Kingdom, United States of America, Malaysia, Ghana, South Africa and Canada.

The Prospects of University Education

Education is a strong weapon for social, political and economic development of every nation. The importance of university education in one's life as a means for social mobility, self-development and self-actualization (Ene, 2007). Obanya (2009) argues that education in any society plays two major roles of conservation and transformation. According to him, conservation is the society's mechanism for building up and preserving its culture while transformation involves getting society to the next level

Table 11. Admission criteria guidelines

Criteria	2003	2015	2016
Merit	40%	45%	45%
Catchment Area	30%	35%	35%
Educationally Less Developed States	20%	20%	20%
Discretion	10%	-	

by taking advantages and advances in ideas, knowledge and technology. Adekola and Kumbe (2012) noted that education is one of the potent tools for human capital and societal development. Although primary and secondary education is essential but they are not sufficient to empower people and nations to compete successfully in the global economy nor solve the chronic problem of poverty, ill-health and illiteracy (Jonathan,2010).it is only through a strong and an appropriate higher education that learning and training can create people with enough wisdom to be used in advancing the issue of poverty and development in developing countries like Nigeria (Wolfensohn,2000). University education is perceived to confer greater benefits on the recipients and greater access to national resources or the 'national cake' by Nigerian ethnic groups.

According to Jonathan (2010), higher education such as university education is central to development and democracy, increased earned income, better working conditions, better health and longer life span. It is also very important because of its role in producing leaders in all areas of national life: government, business, innovation and invention (Nwachukwu & Okoli, 2015). Higher education at college and university plays vital role in cultural transmission, social integration, selection and allocation, and personal development (Broom & Selznick, 2004). Education creates skills which facilitate higher levels of productivity (Becker, 1975) and high value output necessary for economic growth and poverty reduction (Vener, 2004). It has positive effects on health, poverty reduction and eliminates hunger and gender equality as well as a condition for progress in other social sectors (UNESCO, 2012). Ukwueze and Nwosu (2014) found that higher education has the capacity to reduce poverty among Nigerian youths. They found that youth with higher education qualifications have a better chance of securing a job in a tough market compared to those who do not have higher education. Fapohunda (2011) found that higher education can aid women's empowerment and national development and help to reduce the widening gap between male and female. Higher education is one of the most powerful means that countries can use to reduce poverty and achieve social and economic development goals (Okojie, 1990; Zoë Oxaal,1997). According to Jaja (2013), university education provides skills and techniques necessary to improve human competencies, productivity and innovation for society's development. It brings about political enlightenment and national unity. It also provides sound citizenship as a basis for effective participation, adaptability to changing circumstances, self- confidence and development of the total man in order to contribute meaningfully to life in the society.

SOLUTIONS TO IMPROVING ACCESSIBILITY TO HIGHER EDUCATION IN NIGERIA

The issue of quota system or federal character or catchment areas or locality should be reviewed to create room for the best and successful candidates in the UME and PUME to be admitted into the universities. The 20% allocated to the educationally less developed States for over 25 years should be reduced to 10% to give room for candidates outside the ELDS that qualified to be admitted.

Also, colleges of education, monotechnics and polytechnics should be upgraded to bachelor's degree awarding institutions in order to reduce the pressures on the universities. The private universities should be supported by governments and encourage to admit more students while also charging fees that are affordable by the indigent students.

There is the need for a strong university-industry-government synergistic partnership and relationship where the research outputs and value-added innovations from the universities are geared towards enhancing advancements of industries and government business while the duo help to finance and support the teaching and research activities of the universities. All stakeholders must become involved in the financing of universities: parents and guardians, the society in general, private sector and nongovernmental agencies. In the face of the declining financial resource allocation to the education sector, there is the need for alternative sources of funding which will ensure qualitative education and standard growth in Nigerian tertiary institutions (Ogungbenle & Edogiawerie, 2016).The universities can improve their financial base through financial aid, endowment fund and gifts, development appeal fund and alumni fund), and by engaging in profitable ventures like: sale of services (sales of admission forms and general services, rental services and consultancy services) and business enterprises (agriculture-poultry, cattle, fishery, piggery farming-,manufacturing (simple food processing industry),commercial ventures(bakery, hotel and catering services, bookshop, printing, transport services, pure-water business, event management, broadcasting) and portfolio management (investment in profitable government securities, bonds, debentures and stock).They must also account and properly manage the internal revenue generated to supplement government and other external funds to the university.

Adequate funding scheme should be introduced by government to cushion and ameliorate the economic hardships of students in accessing higher education. Government should implement and sustain the provision of scholarships, bursaries and loans to ensure that all Nigerians particularly the less privilege, physically challenged with capacities to seek education at the tertiary level can actualize them. The soft loan could be paid back over some specified periods after the student has started to work.

There should be adequate provision of funds to repair dilapidated buildings and build new ones to accommodate more students. Moreover, as is the practice in other parts of the world, the Open Universities and Distant Learning (ODL) should be encouraged and implemented by the conventional universities in order to increase access to higher education in Nigeria.

With regard to curtailing the declining quality of university in Nigeria, there should be complete overhaul of mode of instruction, massive investment in infrastructures in higher education, review of school curricula to promote critical and relevant learning and effective monitoring and quality control to enhance and sustain quality in Nigerian higher education (Okemakinde, 2014). There should also be continuous equipping, training and development of the human resources capacity to curtail the massive brain and foster the delivery of effective and quality university education in Nigeria.

To enhance gender equitable and increase access of women to university education in Nigeria, there should be increased awareness campaigns for women's education; peg legal age of first marriage at a minimum of 18 years for women and institute stiff penalties for withdrawal of girls from school for early marriage and street trading and expanding facilities for "second chance" functional and literacy education for adult women and those women with special needs. Government at various levels must show sustained political commitment and support for a culture of promoting the education of the girl child. There should be increased advocacy, mobilization, building partnership with Non-Governmental Organizations (NGOs)/Community Based Organizations (CBOs) and gender sensitivity programmes to draw the attention of all stakeholders to the need to educate the girl to the university level.

The frequent policy reversal and summersault of government through the Ministry of Education, NUC and the lawmakers and collaboration between the various stakeholders to avoid further crisis in the educational sector in Nigeria. Government while acting as regulator through her monitoring agencies should allow the universities to devise ways and means to admit the best authenticated students as this has a long way to affecting their output as well as the educational standards and quality. The recent mess and delay in the 2016/2017 admission process by JAMB goes to show that she is not only incapable but bring to the fore the urgent need for reform of the body. The bracket suspension of the post university's entrance examination by the Minister of Education should be reversed considering the unpleasant and horrible experience in the physical clearance of the shortlisted candidates and the delays in the admission process. Again, the recent Senate resolution that JAMB result will now have a validity period of three years for the purpose of admission into Nigeria's university is retrogressive and will further devalue the falling academic standard and increase the challenges of admission and access to Nigerian universities.

SUGGESTION FOR FURTHER STUDIES

The demands for higher education particularly admission to university education in Nigeria have been high, competitive and restrictive in access because of various contending issues. Moreover, the banning of the entrance examination or PUME by the Minister of Education for admission of new students into the Universities for the 2016/2017 session and replacing it with the physical screening and two models for scoring for prospective candidates has not only caused unwarranted delay in the admission process but also suspense, fears, tension, subjectivity and bias, high costs in conducting the physical screening and rendering the university irrelevant in the admission of their students. It is suggested that other studies should examine the effects of the Minister's pronouncement on the admission process and compare with present admission criteria or models to writing entrance examination.

REFERENCES

Abdulkareeem, A. Y., & Muraina, M. B. (2014). Issues and challenges of access and management of admission to universities in Nigeria. *International Journal of Education and Research, 2*(6), 449–460.

Adedeji, S. O., & Bamidele, R. O. (2002). Economic impact of tertiary education on human capital development in Nigeria in the Nigerian Economic Society. In *Selected papers for the 2002 Annual conference* (pp. 499-550).

Adekeye, F. Bilewomo, A. & Ogundele, F. (2012, October 12). War against fake universities. *Tell Magazine,* 41.

Adekola & Kumbe (2012) Women education in Ogoniland and its implications for rural development in Rivers State, Nigeria. *Journal of Society and Communication.* 22.

Adelakun, A. A. (2013). Globalization of higher education in Nigeria: A panacea for access deprivation. *Journal of Educational Review, 6*(1), 7–12.

Adeogun, A. A., & Gboyega, G. I. (2010). Declining quality of Nigerian university graduates: Revitalizing quality assurance through foreign agencies' support US-China. *Educational Review, 7*(6), 45–53.

Adeoti, E. O. (2015). The role of National Universities Commission (NUC) in the development of the university education in Nigeria. Reflections and prospects. *Advances in Social Sciences Research Journal, 2*(3), 116–139. doi:10.14738/assrj.23.938

Agboola, B. M., & Ofoegbu, F. I. (2010). *Access to university education in Nigeria: A review*. Working paper, Department of Educational Studies and Management, University of Benin.

Ajayi, K. &Adeniji, A. (2009). Access to university education in Nigeria in B.G. Nworgu & E.I.

Akpan, C. P., & Undie, J. A. (2007). Access to university education in Nigeria: Issues and problems. In J.B. Babalola, G.O. Akpa, A.O. Ayeni et al. (Ed.), Access, equity and quality in higher education. NAEAP, Lagos.

Akpotu, N. E. (2005). Deregulating the Nigerian university system: Implications for equity and access. In G. O. Akpa, S. U. Udoh, & E. O. Fagbamiye (Eds.), *Deregulating the provision and management of education in Nigeria. Nigerian Association of Educational Administration and Planning* (pp. 57–62). NAEAP.

Akubuilo, F., & Okorie, E. U. (2013). Sustainability of tertiary education through quality assurance and development in Nigeria. *Journal of Education and Practice*, 4(15), 140–144.

Anya, O. A. (2013). *The idea and uses of university in the 21st century. 2013 Convocation Lecture*. Port Harcourt: University of Port Harcourt.

Anyanwu, O. (2010). Experiment with mass university education in post-civil war Nigeria, 1970-1979. *Journal of Nigeria Studies*, 1(1), 1–36.

Arikewuyo, M. O. (2004). *Democracy and university education in Nigeria:* Some constitutional considerations, higher educational management and policy. *A Journal of the Organization for Economic Co-operation and Development*, 16, 121-134.

Becker, G.S. (1975). Human capital: A theoretical and empirical analysis, with special reference to education. 2nd Edn., New York: National Bureau of Economic Research.

Chukwurah, C. C. (2011). Access to higher education in Nigeria: The University of Calabar at a glance. *Canadian Social Science*, 7(3), 108–113.

Dada, J. A. (2004). Access to education in democratic Nigeria: Issues and problems. In E.O. Uya, D. Denga, J. Umeh et al. (Eds.), Education for sustainable democracy: The Nigerian experience. Calabar: University of Calabar Press.

Dambazau, A. (2015). Education, security and national development: The case of Nigeria. In A. A. Aderinto, O. Adediran, & A. I. Alarape (Eds.), *Higher education and national development*. Ibadan University Press.

Ehiametalor, E. T. (2005). Issues of access, equity and private sector participation in the development of education. In G. O. Akpa, S. U. Udah, & E. O. Fagbamiye (Eds.), *Deregulating the Provision and Management of Education in Nigeria. Jos: The Nigeria Association for Educational Administration and Planning*. NAEAP.

Ene, A. C. (2007). Access to and equity in university education. In J. B. Babalola, G. O. Akpa, A. O. Ayeni, & O. Adedeji (Eds.), *Access, Equity and Quality in Higher Education*. NAEAP Publication.

Fafunwa, A.B. (1971). A history of Nigerian higher education. Lagos: Macmillan & Co.

Famurewa, I. O. (2014). Inadequate funding as the bane of tertiary education in Nigeria. *Greener Journal of Economics and Accountancy, 3*(2), 20–25.

Fapohunda, T. M. (2011). Empowering women through higher education in Nigeria. *European Journal of Humanities and Social Sciences, 9*(1), 389–406.

Federal Ministry of Education. (2009). *Roadmap for the Nigeria education sector.* Abuja, Nigeria.

Federal Republic of Nigeria. (1991). *Higher education in the nineties and beyond. Report of the commission on the review of higher education in Nigeria. The Gray Longe Commission.* Lagos: Government Printing Office.

Federal Republic of Nigeria. (1996). *The federal character official gazette.* Abuja Government Press.

Federal Republic of Nigeria. (2001). *Report of the committee on university autonomy and other related matters. (the 'Ijalaye Committee').* Abuja, Nigeria: National Universities Commission.

Federal Republic of Nigeria. (2004). National policy on education. Lagos: National Education Research and Development Council (NERDC) Press.

Idowu, A. (2012). *Funding the 21st century Nigerian university.* A paper delivered at the Annual Conference of the Committee of Directors of Academic Planning of Nigerian Universities (CODAPNU) held on October 24, at the National Universities Conference Room.

Ilusanya, R. (2008). Politics and development of tertiary institutions in Nigeria. *International Journal of Educational Management,5* & 6, 166-178.

Jaja, J. M. (2013). Higher education in Nigeria: Its gain, Its burden. *Global Journal of Human Social Science. Linguistics and Education, 13*(14), 21–29.

JAMB. (2016). Meeting on the modalities for screening of candidates for the 2016 admission exercise at Ukeje Hall. JAMB headquarters, Abuja.

Jonathan, F. F. (2010). *University as strategic partners in national development. 2010 Convocation Lecture. Port Harcourt.* Nigeria: University of Port Harcourt.

Mukoro, A. S. (2013). The phenomenon of gender inequality in access to and equity in university education in Nigeria. *Mediterranean Journal of Social Sciences, 4*(7), 129–136.

Nwachukwu, J. N., & Okoli, F. C. (2015). Problems and prospects of private ivory towers in Nigeria. *Singaporean Journal of Business Economics and Management Studies, 4*(6), 36–50. doi:10.12816/0017731

Obanya, P. (2002). *Revitalizing education in Africa.* Ibadan: Stirling-Horden Press.

Obanya, P. A. I. (2007) Thinking, talking and education. Ibadan, Evans Brothers, Nigeria Publishers Limited.

Obanya, P. A. I. (2009). *Dreaming, living and doing education.* Ibadan: Education Research and Study Group.

Obasi, I. N. (2007). Analysis of the emergence and development of private universities in Nigeria (1999-2006). Council for the Development of Social Science Research in Africa 2007 (ISSN 08517762) JHEA/RESA, 5(2&3), 39–66.

Obilade, S.O. (1992). JAMB and university admission in Nigeria. In T. Ajayi, & R.A. Alani, (Eds.), Contemporary issues in Nigerian education. Ijebu-Ode: Triumph Books Publishers.

Oduwaiye, R. O. (2008). Access and equity in Nigerian university education in challenges and way forward. In I.A. Njodi, A.A Fajonyomi, & K. Bulama (Eds.), Equity, quality and access to education in Nigeria: Problems and the way forward. Ibadan: His Lineage Publishing House.

Ogungbenle, S. K., & Edogiawerie, M. N. (2016). Budgetary allocation and development in Nigeria tertiary institutions. *Igbinedion University Journal of Accounting*, 2, 377–407.

Okebukola, P. (2002). *The state of university education in Nigeria*. Abuja: National Universities Commission.

Okebukola, P. A. O. (2006). *State of university education in Nigeria*. Ibadan: Heinemann.

Okebukola, P. C. (2008). Education reform: Imperatives for achieving vision 20-2020. *Paper presented at the National Summit on Education Organized by Senate Committee on Education*, Abuja.

Okemakinde, T. (2014). Transformation of higher education towards enhanced quality education in Nigeria. *European Journal of Humanities and Social Sciences*, 29(1), 1555–1570.

Okojie, J. (2009). List of approved universities in Nigeria in National Universities Commission (NUC) Monday 20th July bulletin. A publication of the office of the executive secretary.

Okojie, J. A. (2010). System and strategies for funding Nigerian universities. Retrieved from http://www.naps.org.ng/index

Okojie, M. I. (1990). Women in management. In J. Akande, F. D. Oyekanmi, & ... (Eds.), *The contribution of women to national development in Nigeria*. Lagos: NAUW.

Okoli, N. J. (2015). Impact of fees increase on university students' education in Nigeria. *Merit Journal of Education and Review*, 3(2), 115–118.

Oni, B. (2000). *The demand for universities graduates and employers' assessment of graduate skills in Nigeria*. Ibadan: Nigerian Institute of Social and Economic Research.

Osagie, A. U. (2009). *Change and choice: The development of private universities in Nigeria*. Benin City: Rawel Fortune Resources.

Oseni, M. (2015). Effectiveness and desirability of private higher education in Nigeria. *Journal of Educational and Social Research*, 5(1), 151–157.

Saint, W., Hartnett, T.A., & Strasser, E. (2003). Higher education in Nigeria: A status report. The World Bank, N. W. Washington D.C.

Sampson, D.A. (2004). Our universities: Accelerators for economic growth. *Economic Development America*, Winter.

Shina, O. (2012). Alternative perspective to funding public universities in Nigeria. *Sustainable Development*.

Ubogu, R. E. (2011). Financing higher education in Nigeria. *Journal of Research in Education and Society*, 2(1), 36–45.

Ukpai, U. E., & Ereh, C. E. (2016). Current challenges and the needed competences in the management of university education in Nigeria. *British Journal of Education*, 4(2), 74–86.

Ukwueze, E. R., & Nwosu, E. O. (2014). Does higher education reduce poverty among youths in Nigeria? *Asian Economic and Financial Review*, 4(1), 1–19.

UNESCO. (2003). *Education webmaster. World Conference on higher education framework and action*. Retrieved from www.jyu.fi/ unesco2003/conference.html

UNESCO. (2012). *Education and skills for inclusive and sustainable development beyond 2015: Thematic think piece*. UNESCO, UN task team on the post 2015 UNN development agenda.

Utomi, T. O. (2008). *Education, entrepreneurship and youth empowerment in the Niger Delta. Convocation Lecture*. Nigeria: Niger Delta University.

Vener, D. (2004). Education and its poverty-reducing effects: The case of Paraíba, Brazil. World Bank policy research, Working Paper, 3321.

World Bank. (2010). *Financing higher education in Africa*. Washington, D.C: World Bank.

Zoë Oxaal. (1997). *Education and poverty: A gender analysis, report prepared for the gender equality unit, Swedish international development cooperation agency (SIDA), Institute of development studies*. UK: University of Sussex.

This research was previously published in The Future of Accessibility in International Higher Education edited by Henry C. Alphin Jr., Jennie Lavine, and Roy Y. Chan; pages 104-124, copyright year 2017 by Information Science Reference (an imprint of IGI Global).

Section 2
Disabilities: General

Chapter 6
Creating Inclusive Classroom Communities Through Social and Emotional Learning to Reduce Social Marginalization Among Students

June L. Preast
University of Missouri, USA

Nicky Bowman
University of Missouri, USA

Chad A. Rose
University of Missouri, USA

ABSTRACT

A student's social and emotional skills are related to how well equipped they are to address and adapt to the academic, behavioral, and functional demands of the classroom. With the increased attention on academic outcomes, the opportunities to teach social and emotional learning (SEL) are limited. However, SEL approaches have demonstrated increases in functional, behavioral, and academic outcomes for school aged youth. This chapter is designed to identify the key components of SEL, provide guidance in implementation, and describe how SEL can help reduce the social marginalization among youth with disabilities and those at-risk for disability identification.

INTRODUCTION

A student's social and emotional skills are related to how well equipped they are to address and adapt to the academic, behavioral, and functional demands of the classroom (CASEL, 2012; Espelage, Rose, & Polanin, 2015, 2016). Students with age-appropriate social and emotional skills tend to acquire and maintain friendships and appropriately manage social problems more efficiently than those that do not possess these skills (Merrell & Gimpel, 1998). Effective implementation of appropriate social and emotional learning can be directly affected by school factors (CASEL, 2012), yet social and emotional instruction that extends beyond the classroom supports improved skill development for school-aged youth (Tolan, Guerra, & Kendall, 1995). However, to facilitate more inclusive classroom practices, the adoption of prosocial goals and supports is important to social and emotional development of school-aged youth with and without disabilities (Erdley & Asher, 1999).

While social and emotional development is critical for all students, specific implementation of a social and emotional curriculum may be more germane for individuals with disabilities (Espelage et al., 2015, 2016). Specifically, due to the varying degrees of educational support based upon individual needs, students with disabilities may receive different educational experiences and social opportunities in comparison to their peers without disabilities (Individuals with Disabilities Education Improvement Act [IDEIA], 2004; Maag & Katsiyannis, 2012; Yell, Shriner, & Katsiyannis, 2006). While these educational experiences may vary, the prevalence of students with disabilities who receive special education services within an inclusive environment continues to increase (National Center for Educational Statistics, 2015; Rose, Simpson, & Moss, 2015). Unfortunately, students with disabilities are often viewed as outsiders, have fewer friends, and have lower quality of social interaction due, in part, to the restriction of educational and social opportunities (Rose & Monda-Amaya, 2012), which may increase social marginalization. This level of marginalization may also be associated with social and communication skill deficits (Christensen, Fraynt, Neece, & Baker, 2012; Rose, Monda-Amaya, & Espelage, 2011; Rose, Forber-Pratt, Espelage, & Aragon, 2013; Swearer, Wang, Maag, Siebecker, & Frerichs, 2012), where social and emotional learning programs have proved promising in reducing this overrepresentation (Espelage et al., 2015, 2016). The purpose of this chapter is to describe the central tenants of social and emotional learning, explain how social and emotional learning can be embedded within positive behavior interventions and supports (PBIS) framework, highlight the outcomes associated with social and emotional learning, underscore the importance of social and emotional learning as an approach to reducing social marginalization among youth with disabilities, and provide recommendations for social and emotional program implementation.

SOCIAL AND EMOTIONAL LEARNING

"Social and emotional learning is the capacity to recognize and manage emotions, solve problems effectively, and establish positive relationships with others" (Zins & Elias, 2007, p. 234). A social and emotional learning approach is grounded in the notion that behaviors, both intrinsic and extrinsic, are linked to social and academic outcomes (Espelage et al., 2016; Durlak, Weissberg, Dymnicki, Taylor, & Schellinger, 2011). Five cluster areas have been identified by the Collaborative for Academic, Social, and Emotional Learning (CASEL) that encompass cognitive, affective, and behavioral competencies; self awareness, self management, social awareness, relationship skills, and responsible decision making (CASEL, 2012). Addressing the five cluster areas, as well as, improving student beliefs about self, school and others is the foundation for students who are more prepared to meet academic and social demands (CASEL, 2012). CASEL (2012) provided direction and definitions for each of the domains that serve as the foundation for implementing school-based social and emotional learning approaches (*see* Table 1).

Table 1. Description of social and emotional learning domains

Domain	Domain Description
Self Awareness	Ability to understand and be aware of one's own emotions and the effects of those emotions on one's behavior
Self Management	Skills necessary for an individual to regulate their own emotions, behaviors, and thoughts in a variety of settings
Social Awareness	Ability to understand and recognize societal and ethical standards for behavior and participating within those standards to provide empathy and awareness for those from different backgrounds
Relationship Skills	Ability to form healthy relationships with individuals from different backgrounds and maintain those relationships
Responsible Decision-Making	Ability to make appropriate decisions about one's behaviors and interactions after considering the ethical and societal implications for those choices

Note. Domains and Domain Descriptions defined by CASEL (2012).

Social and Emotional Learning and the Hidden Curriculum

With the legislative push for increased academic outcomes for school-aged youth, it is imperative that programmatic changes are not perceived as add-ons to existing curricular structures. Therefore, teacher buy-in is critical to the success of a social and emotional learning approach, because outcomes are grounded in their pedagogical dexterity in implementing such programs (Merrell, Gueldner, Ross, & Isava, 2008). While teachers are inundated with responsibilities related to their vocation, including academic outcomes, meeting academic standards through district- or state-based curricula, and preparing highly engaging lessons (Lauermann, 2014; Lauermann & Karabenick, 2013), much less attention is placed on the 'hidden curriculum.' The 'hidden curriculum' refers to common skills or environmental rules that are treated as common knowledge, but are rarely taught within schools (Lee, 2011; Myles & Simpson, 2001).

Although a majority of students can navigate the social tenants of the 'hidden curriculum' through social interactions, peer modeling, and meeting age-appropriate developmental milestones, the 'hidden curriculum' places a unique risk for students who are socially marginalized, including students with disabilities (Rose, Simpson, et al., 2015). The relevance of the 'hidden curriculum' is especially relevant for youth with disabilities because the percentage of youth with disabilities who primarily receive special education services alongside their peers without disabilities has doubled over the past two decades (National Center for Educational Statistics, 2015). Unfortunately, two of the most notable predictors of social marginalization among youth with disabilities are communication and social skill deficits (Rose et al., 2011). Therefore, in addition to providing students with access to the general curriculum through special education services and individualized education programs (Ruppar & Gaffney, 2011), the implementation of a social and emotional learning curriculum will help aid the development of these critical skills for youth with or at-risk for disability identification (Espelage et al., 2015, 2016).

SOCIAL AND EMOTIONAL LEARNING WITHIN A MULTI-TIERED SYSTEM OF SUPPORT

With the national push for multi-tiered systems of support, including Response to Intervention (RTI) and Positive Behavioral Interventions and Supports (PBIS; IDEIA, 2004), schools are beginning to establish graduated tiered systems to support academic and behavioral outcomes. According to the Office of Special Education Programs' Technical Assistance Center for Positive Behavioral Interventions and Supports (2016), PBIS is currently implemented in more than 21,000 schools nationwide. While social and emotional learning is not a direct component of the PBIS framework, it is tangentially related, and can be implemented within a tiered system of support (*see* Figure 1).

Specifically, a student's social and emotional skills defines not only how they will interact with others, but how they will succeed within the school environment. Schools are tasked with preparing youth to be educated and skilled adults, which includes academic, functional, and behavioral outcomes (Rose, Simpson, et al., 2015). Unfortunately, the area of social and emotional learning is not typically entrenched within a school's curricular materials. However, students who receive instruction within a school-wide social and emotional learning intervention tend to display higher social and emotional skills and behaviors, as well as decreased emotional distress and conduct problems, when compared to students who do not receive social and emotional learning interventions (Durlak et al., 2011). Teachers play an important role in implementing social and emotional learning programs for their students, and evidence suggests that teachers, who are trained, have a higher self-efficacy in implementing social and

Figure 1. The connection between social and emotional learning and PBIS

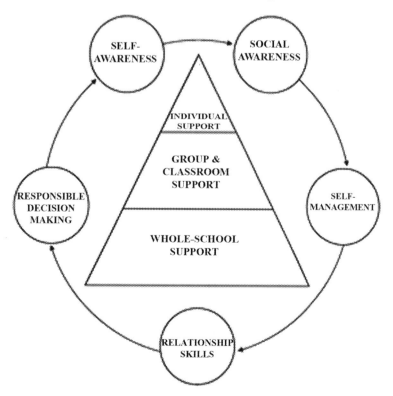

emotional learning programs within their classrooms (Durlak et al., 2011). Specifically, teachers set the tone for their classrooms by displaying socially and emotionally competent behavior and encouraging relationships with their students and exhibiting prosocial behavior (Jennings & Greenberg, 2009), which also increases the inclusiveness and acceptance within the classroom environment.

Social and emotional learning not only gives students the skills to interact appropriately with others, but it also influences learning behaviors of students. Prosocial behavior demonstrated in young students is predictive of academic achievement and social preference in older students (Caprara, Barbaranelli, Pastorelli, Bandura, & Zimbardo, 2000). Additionally, displays of antisocial behavior affects the teacher's acceptance of the student, the student's learning, and social opportunities (Masten & Coatsworth, 1998), all of which can be buffered or supported by social and emotional skill development.

School Belongingness

One of the primary goals at the school-wide level within a PBIS framework is to promote school belongingness. Consequently, social and emotional skills are are directly related to school belongingness, where positive attitudes towards schools is one of the fundamental areas to overall school success (Abbott et al., 1998) and the crux of inclusive education. Cooperative learning, in addition to proactive classroom management and interactive teaching, has been linked to positive attitudes toward learning and school (Hawkins, Doueck, & Lishner, 1988). A strong link has been shown between a student's sense of belonging in the school environment and their engagement in the classroom (Osterman, 2000). It is believed that student problem behavior can be prevented through social bonding to prosocial groups and activities (Abbott et al., 1998; Rose, Espelage, Monda-Amaya, Shogren, & Aragon, 2015). Schools play an integral role in developing a student's level of belongingness and can promote school belongingness by providing opportunities for active involvement and participation in school activities and school-level recognition for an individual's behavior (Catalano & Hawkins, 1996; Hawkins et al., 1992; Hawkins & Weiss, 1985; O'Donnell, Hawkins, Catalano, Abbott, & Day, 1995). Strong levels of school belongingness are believed to decrease a student's willingness to engage in inappropriate behaviors (e.g., violence, aggression, substance abuse, etc.; Abbott et al., 1998). A student's sense of connections to their school lessens as they grow older, impacting their academics, behavior, and health (Blum & Libbey, 2004), which demonstrates the necessity for implementing social and emotional learning curricula throughout a student's K-12 education.

Sense of belonging is directly related to how one situates him or herself within a peer group, school, or among friends. An increased sense of belonging has been documented as a buffer for increased victimization, perpetration, and aggression (Nipedal, Nesdale, & Killen, 2010; Poteat & Espelage, 2005). For example, schools that have a climate that is more positive and inclusionary, where equal emphasis is placed on academic outcomes and social and emotional needs often have students who maintain a higher sense of belonging (Johnson, 2009; Nipedal et al., 2010). Similarly, students who have stronger peer relationships and engage in fewer aggressive behaviors tend to have higher levels of belonging (Nipedal et al., 2010). Links have been shown between student at-risk behavior and their sense of belonging (Blum & Rinehart, 1996). Students with a higher sense of belonging display lower levels of depression, social rejection, and school problems (Anderman, 2002). Therefore, school climate and peer relations can increase a sense of belonging while decreasing aggressive behaviors; all of which can be supported through instruction within a social and emotional learning program.

Academic achievement, student belongingness, and positive behavior are promoted and enhanced when schools implement universal social and emotional learning programs (Durlak et al., 2011). Student social and emotional skills can be developed through direct instruction via social and emotional learning curricula and appropriate classroom management (Durlak et al., 2011; January, Casey, & Paulson, 2011; Kress & Elias, 2006; Weare & Nind, 2011; Zins, Bloodworth, Weissberg, & Walberg, 2004). Not only are student academic achievement and social adjustment improved by effective classroom instructional practices, but also by the positive interactions between the teacher and student (Hamre & Pianta, 2007; Mashburn & Pianta, 2006). Teachers often get overwhelmed when dealing with high levels of social-behavioral problems, which impacts achievement across the classroom (Stoiber, 2011). Self-control and cooperation, are central tenants of social and emotional learning, and are skills teachers consider important for student success (Lane, Givner, & Pierson, 2004). To demonstrate the importance of teachers' ability to implement social and emotional learning programs, a recent meta-analysis revealed that teacher-led social and emotional learning programs produced promising results for overall social and emotional learning skills, positive attitudes, increased social behavior, increased academic outcomes, decreased conduct problems, and less emotional distress (Durlak et al., 2011).

Benefits of Inclusion From a Social and Emotional Learning Perspective

Schools teach academics through curricula that address core subjects, but instruction and learning are also influenced by the structure of the school, relationships between teachers and students, and the social environment (Cartledge & Milburn, 1978; Saylor & Alexander, 1974). The school environment and the interactions of the individuals within it has direct effects on the academic and social progress of the students within that school (DeRosier & Mercer, 2009). As a result of the linkage between the academic and student progress of students, a curriculum beyond that of academics within schools has been explored by scholars (Myles & Simpson, 2001). As previously mentioned, this secondary curriculum has been termed the 'hidden curriculum' and encompasses the social skills and rules that are not directly taught in schools, but are expected from every individual (Lee, 2011). The social skills expected by all individuals should be taught and supported within the school and can be reinforced by social and emotional learning programs, which is especially germane for youth with disabilities within inclusive environments (Rose & Espelage, 2012; Son et al., 2014).

Participation in the general education classroom, and direct access to the general curriculum, not only provides higher levels of academic content, but it also provides students with more socialization opportunities than if they were receiving instruction in a more restrictive environment (Rose, Stormont, et al., 2015; Stainback, Stainback, & Ayres, 1996). In particular, students with disabilities have a greater chance of forming relationships with peers without disabilities if they receive special education services within an inclusive environment (Klingner, Vaughn, Schumm, Cohen, & Forgan, 1998; Vaughn & Klingner, 1998), thereby increasing the social and emotional outcomes within the 'hidden curriculum.'

To further support access to the 'hidden curriculum', students within inclusive environments are provided with more opportunities to participate in rich conversations that promote language development, as well as learn, practice, and validate social and communication skills among their same-aged peers without disabilities (Llewellyn, 2000). Peers view students with communication delays or social skills deficits less favorably than their peers with age-appropriate social and communication skills, as this subset of students display difficulties with initiating conversations, responding appropriately to the topic and maintaining a conversation (Hemphill & Siperstein, 1990; Rose et al., 2011). However, classrooms that promote social and emotional skills, such as inclusion, friendships, and relationships among students, regardless of disability, have students with lower risks of social marginalization (Frederickson & Furnham, 2004; Rose & Monda-Amaya, 2012; Savage, 2005). Inclusive classrooms alone might not provide the necessary skill instruction to aid students with disabilities in their social and emotional development, but the addition of social and emotional learning programs within inclusive settings promotes social and communication skills for all students (Rose, Stormont, et al. 2015; Espelage et al., 2015; 2016).

Outcomes Associated With Social and Emotional Learning

When the development of social and emotional skills is not addressed among school-aged youth who display social and communication skill deficits, they may experience challenges with age-appropriate social interactions later in life. Decreased competence in personal and/or social areas is predictive of increased externalizing and internalizing issues, such as aggression, bullying, delinquency, depression, and anxiety (Cole, 1990; Cook, Williams, Guerra, Kim, & Sadek, 2010; Espelage et al., 2015; Fox & Boulton, 2005; Holt & Espelage, 2007; Van Lier & Koot, 2010). Additionally, the presence of psychopathology interferes with the development of other future competencies and affects adjustment leading to adverse long-term outcomes (Van Lier & Koot, 2010; Zins & Elias, 2007). The long-term impacts of inadequate social and emotional skills are not limited to mental health, but also include physical health and academics (Cartledge, & Milburn, 1978; Renshaw et al., 2009; Zins et al., 2004). Similarly, problem behaviors and low social and emotional skills have been linked to lower grades (Casilias et al., 2012; Cobb, 1972; Wentzel, 1993), achievement (Brelau et al., 2009; Bursuck & Asher, 1986; DiPerna, 2006; DiPerna, Volpe, & Elliott, 2002, 2005; Duncan et al., 2007; Kwon, Kim, & Sheridan, 2012; Malecki & Elliott, 2002; Volpe et al., 2006), academic readiness (Denham, Bassett, Zinnser, & Wyatt, 2014), and increased risk of academic problems (King, Lembke, & Reinke, in press).

CASEL (2012) argues that social and emotional learning implementation through explicit classroom instruction, integration with existing academic curricula, and trained teachers results in improved social and emotional skill acquisition (i.e., self awareness, self management, social awareness, relationship skills, responsible decision making), increased intrapersonal and interpersonal attitudes, fewer challenging behaviors, less emotional distress, and improved academic outcomes. These outcomes are supported by extant literature, where in a recent meta-analysis, Durlak and colleagues (2011) noted that social and emotional learning programs resulted in improved attitudes, increased pro-social behaviors, and reduced emotional distress. In addition to these improved social outcomes, and in relation to the primary mission of schools, social and emotional learning programs promoted increased academic performance and outcomes (Algozzine & Algozzine, 2009; Durlak et al., 2011; Linares et al., 2005; Menzies & Lane, 2012; Putnam, Horner, & Algozzine, 2006). Therefore, social and emotional learning programs can directly impact outcomes related to the general curriculum (i.e., academic outcomes) and the 'hidden curriculum' (i.e., social norms and rules).

The Connection Between Social and Emotional Learning and Social Marginalization

While social and emotional learning programs have demonstrated improved outcomes related to the general and hidden curricula, schools are also faced with addressing issues related to social marginalization, including bullying (Espelage et al., 2015, 2016). Based on existing literature, it is clear that social and emotional learning and social marginalization are directly linked (Smith & Low, 2013). Unfortunately, proximal and distal psychosocial outcomes are associated with social marginalization, and schools are beginning to implement increased mental health supports for school-aged youth. For example, social marginalization has been linked to depressive symptoms, anger and hostility, delinquency, and lower self-esteem (Camodeca & Goossens, 2005; Cook et al., 2010; Rose & Espelage, 2012; Rose, Simpson, et al., 2015; Ttofi, Farrington, Lösel, & Loeber, 2011). These negative psychosocial outcomes point to the necessity of social and emotional learning, because students who are socially marginalized may have difficulties with emotional regulation (Kochenderfer-Ladd, 2004; Rose & Espelage, 2012; Shields & Cicchetti, 2001).

These negative psychosocial outcomes may be more detrimental for youth with disabilities, as they are often less resilient when faced with bullying or social marginalization (Hartley, Bauman, Nixon, & Davis, 2015). For example, in a large sample of middle and high school youth with disabilities, Rose, Simpson, and Preast (2016) reported that students who experience victimization, including social marginalization, have higher levels of depression and hostility, and lower levels of self-esteem. These psychosocial attributes, coupled with increased victimization, also predicted higher levels of proactive and reactive aggression. Rose and colleagues (2013) argued that comorbidity between disability identification and characteristics associated with specific disabilities (e.g., social and communication skill deficits) may lead to increased social marginalization, which is linked to detrimental psychosocial outcomes. By providing appropriate educational accommodations, social skills instruction, and peer models, with a focus on social and emotional learning within an inclusive environment, students with disabilities may experience less social marginalization and improved psychosocial outcomes (Martlew & Hodson, 1991; Rose, Espelage, & Monda-Amaya, 2009; Sabornie, 1994). Therefore, it is conceivable that the implementation of social and emotional learning can increase functional skill development, while improving the mental health and social relationships of school-aged youth.

IMPLEMENTING SOCIAL AND EMOTIONAL LEARNING PROGRAMS

Several variations of social and emotional learning programs are available for school-level implementation. Based on the PBIS framework, it is critical for schools to implement a universal-level social and emotional learning curriculum. One such program, *Second Step: Skills for Social and Academic Success* (Committee for Children, 2008, 2011) is a social and emotional learning curriculum designed to support youth in grades kindergarten through 8th grade. The elementary program (K-5) covers social and emotional skills related to academic learning, empathy, emotion management, and problem solving (Committee for Children, 2011); and the middle school program (6 – 8) builds upon the elementary program by addressing skills related to empathy and communication, bully prevention, emotion management, problem solving, substance abuse prevention, and goal setting (Committee for Children, 2008) through a series of lessons and instructional activities. This interactive and engaging program has demonstrated promising results in social and emotional skill development (Espelage, Low, Polanin, & Brown, 2013, 2015). Additionally, this program has resulted in promising results related to bullying involvement, willingness to intervene in bullying situations, and academic outcomes for youth with disabilities (Espelage, Rose et al., 2015, 2016). While this program is not the sole social and emotional learning curriculum, it maintains the basic tenets of implementation, which includes teacher training, teacher implementation, student practice and demonstration, and teacher reinforcement. Therefore, the success of this program, or any other social and emotional learning program, hinges on the pedagogical dexterity of the implementer, as well as school-level support for adequate and appropriate implementation.

Targeted Instruction

While a universal-level social and emotional learning program is essential to the development of social and emotional skills for all school-aged youth, some students may require additional, targeted instruction. Based on the evidence that suggests students with social and communication skill deficits have a higher likelihood for social marginalization (Rose et al., 2011), as well as increased likelihood for disability identification, it is recommended that schools take a two-step approach to identifying and supporting youth who have low social and emotional skills. First, schools should consider employing a brief screener to identify youth who could benefit from targeted instruction. For example, the Social Skills Improvement System – Performance Screening Guide (SSIS-PSG, Elliott & Gresham, 2007b) has documented success in identifying students with critical social and communication skill deficits (Gresham, Elliott, Cook, Vance, & Kettler, 2010). Similarly, the Social, Academic, and Emotional Behavior Risk Screener (SAEBRS; Kilgus, Chafouleas, Riley-Tillman, & von der Embse, 2013) is a 19 item screener to identify youth who are at risk for social, academic, and emotional behavior deficits. This screener has been used with youth in grades kindergarten through 12th, with high internal consistency (Kilgus, Riley-Tillman, Chafoules, Christ, & Welsh, 2014). By using a brief screener, schools can proactively identify students who could benefit from targeted social and emotional learning instruction.

Once students are identified, schools should provide small group, targeted instruction related to the skill deficits documented on the brief screener. For example, social skills deficits are often identified through the behavioral risk screener. Therefore, schools could elect to implement school-based social skills instruction as part of the students' daily curriculum by providing teacher-led lessons. While social skills represent a broad category of functional skills, Kauffman and Kinnealey (2015) identified seven critical domains. These domains are directly related to social and emotional learning, and include verbal presentation, nonverbal presentation, emotional response, play, awareness of self and others, interpersonal relationships, and feelings about self (*see* Table 2). Based on these domains, teachers could craft lessons that address each of the identified social skills, while meeting the individualized needs of the students identified to receive instruction.

In addition to homegrown approaches to social skills instruction, schools may elect to implement a commercially available program to support social skills acquisition. One such program is the Social Skills Improvement System: Classwide Intervention Program (SSIS-CIP; Elliott & Gresham, 2007a), which is a comprehensive social skills program that is designed as a targeted intervention to be implemented in classrooms or in small student groups from kindergarten through 8th grade. The SSIS-CIP (Elliott & Gresham, 2007a) addresses 10 critical social skills domains (*see* Table 3), and has recent evidence to suggest it has positive effects on teacher ratings of social skills and internalizing behaviors, including students who were rated with the lowest social skill proficiency (DiPerna et al., 2005). Unfortunately, even though students with disabilities are typically found to have lower social skills (Llewellyn, 2000; Miller, Rose et al., 2011; Son et al., 2014), this social skills programs has not been systematically and specifically evaluated for skills acquisition for students with disabilities. Therefore, adaptations and modifications may be necessary for any adopted program success for students with the most significant

Table 2. Kauffman and Kinnealey's (2015) social skills taxonomy

Category	Goal Description
Verbal Presentation	Modify use of words (content) that interfere with acceptance by others
Nonverbal Presentation	Modify use of behaviors (psychomotor) that interfere with acceptance by others
Emotional Response	Modify emotional reactions to frustrating, new, accidental, or unexpected occurrences or when transitioning from one situation to another
Play	Modify behaviors related to playing and working with others
Awareness of Self and Others	Improve conscious consideration and valuing of oneself and other people
Interpersonal Relationships	Initiate and maintain effective relationships with other people
Feelings About Self	Modify level of self-esteem

Note. This table retrieved from Kauffman and Kinnealey (2015, p. 5).

need. However, it is conceivable that this level of social skills instruction will reduce social marginalization of youth with disabilities because two of the most notable predictors are social and communication skill deficits (Rose et al., 2011).

CONCLUSION

The primary mission of schools is to support the academic, behavioral, and functional development of all school-aged youth. Unfortunately, current legislative mandates place a strong emphasis on academic outcomes, with far less attention paid to social and emotional learning. However, recent evidence suggests that social and emotional learning and academic outcomes are directly and tangentially linked. These links may be more germane for youth with disabilities because increasing numbers are being educated within an inclusive environment; yet they are often identified with social and communication

Table 3. SSIS-CIP social skills domains and domain descriptions

Domain	Domain Description
Listen to Others	Demonstrate an understanding of active listening
Follow the Steps	Demonstrate an understanding of following directions
Follow the Rules	Demonstrate an understanding of rules and the function of classroom, school, and social rules
Pay Attention to Your Work	Demonstrate the ability to stay on an assigned task
Ask for Help	Demonstrate the ability to show initiative and ask for assistance when necessary
Take Turns When Talking	Demonstrate the ability to communicate and cooperate with others
Getting Along with Others	Demonstrate the ability to cooperate and work with others
Stay Calm with Others	Demonstrate the ability to self-manage emotions
Do the Right Things	Demonstrate an understanding of responsible decision making
Do Nice Things for Others	Demonstrate the ability to show empathy to others

Note. Table adapted from Elliott and Gresham (2007a).

skills deficits. Unfortunately, these deficits often predict increased social marginalization. To support the social and emotional development of all youth, including students with disabilities, schools should consider implementing a tiered approach to social and emotional learning by establishing school-wide and targeted approaches to social and emotional skill development. When systematic implementation occurs, and teachers are adequately trained, students engage in more socially appropriate behaviors, have decreased detrimental psychosocial outcomes, report increased social and communication skills, and have improved academic outcomes. Most importantly, social and emotional learning teaches functional skills that are beneficial for lifelong success.

REFERENCES

Abbott, R. D., ODonnell, J., Hawkins, J. D., Hill, K. G., Kosterman, R., & Catalano, R. F. (1998). Changing teaching practices to promote achievement and bonding to school. *The American Journal of Orthopsychiatry*, *68*(4), 542–552. doi:10.1037/h0080363 PMID:9809114

Algozzine, B., & Algozzine, K. (2009). Facilitating academic achievement through schoolwide positive behavior support. In W. Sailor, G. Dunlap, R. Horner, & G. Sugai (Eds.), *Handbook of positive behavior support* (pp. 521–550). New York, NY: Springer. doi:10.1007/978-0-387-09632-2_22

Anderman, E. M. (2002). School effects on psychological outcomes during adolescence. *Journal of Educational Psychology*, *94*(4), 795–809. doi:10.1037/0022-0663.94.4.795

Blum, R. W., & Libbey, H. P. (2004). School connectedness – Strengthening health and education outcomes for teenagers. *The Journal of School Health*, *74*, 229–299.

Blum, R. W., & Rinehart, P. M. (1997). *Reducing the risk: Connections that make a difference in the lives of youth*. Bethesda, MD: Add Health.

Breslau, J., Miller, E., Breslau, N., Bohnert, K., Lucia, V., & Schweitzer, J. (2009). The impact of early behavior disturbances on academic achievement in high school. *Pediatrics*, *123*(6), 1472–1476. doi:10.1542/peds.2008-1406 PMID:19482756

Bursuck, W. D., & Asher, S. R. (1986). The relationship between social competence and achievement in elementary school children. *Journal of Clinical Child Psychology*, *15*(1), 41–49. doi:10.120715374424jccp1501_5

Camodeca, M., & Goossens, F. A. (2005). Childrens opinions on effective strategies to cope with bullying: The importance of bullying role and perspective. *Educational Research*, *47*(1), 93–105. doi:10.1080/0013188042000337587

Caprara, G. V., Barbaranelli, C., Pastorelli, C., Bandura, A., & Zimbardo, P. G. (2000). Prosocial foundations of childrens academic achievement. *Psychological Science*, *11*(4), 302–306. doi:10.1111/1467-9280.00260 PMID:11273389

Cartledge, G., & Milburn, J. F. (1978). The case for teaching social skills in the classroom: A review. *Review of Educational Research*, *48*(1), 133–156. doi:10.3102/00346543048001133

CASEL – Collaborative for Academic, Social, and Emotional Learning. (2012). *Effective social and emotional learning programs: Preschool and elementary school edition*. Chicago, IL: Author.

Casillas, A., Robbins, S., Allen, J., Kuo, Y. L., Hanson, M. A., & Schmeiser, C. (2012). Predicting early academic failure in high school from prior academic achievement, psychosocial characteristics, and behavior. *Journal of Educational Psychology, 104*(2), 407–420. doi:10.1037/a0027180

Catalano, R. F., & Hawkins, J. D. (1996). The social development model: A theory of antisocial behavior. In J. D. Hawkins (Ed.), *Delinquency and crime: Current theories*. Cambridge, UK: Cambridge University Press.

Christensen, L.L., Fraynt, R.J., Neece, C.L., & Baker, B.L. (2012). Bullying and adolescents with intellectual disability. *Journal of Mental Health Research in Intellectual Disabilities, 5*, 49-65. doi:10.1080/19315864.2011.637660

Cobb, J. A. (1972). Relationship of discrete classroom behaviors to fourth-grade academic achievement. *Journal of Educational Psychology, 63*(1), 74–80. doi:10.1037/h0032247

Cole, D. A. (1990). Relation of social and academic competence to depressive symptoms in childhood. *Journal of Abnormal Psychology, 99*(4), 422–429. doi:10.1037/0021-843X.99.4.422 PMID:2266218

Committee for Children. (2008). *Second step: Student success through prevention program*. Seattle, WA: Author.

Committee for Children. (2011). *Second Step*. Seattle, WA: Author.

Cook, C. R., Williams, K. R., Guerra, N. G., Kim, T. E., & Sadek, S. (2010). Predictors of bullying and victimization in childhood and adolescence: A meta-analytic investigation. *School Psychology Quarterly, 25*(2), 65–83. doi:10.1037/a0020149

Denham, S. A., Bassett, H. H., Zinnser, K. M., & Wyatt, T. M. (2014). How pre-schoolers social-emotional learning predicts their early school success: Developing theory-promoting, competency-based assessments. *Infant and Child Development, 23*(4), 426–454. doi:10.1002/icd.1840

DeRosier, M. E., & Mercer, S. H. (2009). Perceived behavioral atypicality as a predictor of social rejection and peer victimization: Implications for emotional adjustment and academic achievement. *Psychology in the Schools, 46*(4), 375–387. doi:10.1002/pits.20382

DiPerna, J. C. (2006). Academic enablers and student achievement: Implications for assessment and intervention services in the schools. *Psychology in the Schools, 43*(1), 7–17. doi:10.1002/pits.20125

DiPerna, J. C., Volpe, R. J., & Elliott, S. N. (2002). A model of academic enablers and elementary reading/language arts achievement. *School Psychology Review, 31*(3), 298–312.

DiPerna, J. C., Volpe, R. J., & Elliott, S. N. (2005). A model of academic enablers and mathematics achievement in the elementary grades. *Journal of School Psychology, 43*(5), 379–392. doi:10.1016/j.jsp.2005.09.002

Duncan, G. J., Dowsett, C. J., Claessens, A., Magnuson, K., Huston, A. C., Klebanov, P., ... Japel, C. (2007). School readiness and later achievement. *Developmental Psychology, 43*(6), 1428–1446. doi:10.1037/0012-1649.43.6.1428 PMID:18020822

Durlak, J. A., Weissberg, R. P., Dymnicki, A. B., Taylor, R. D., & Schellinger, K. B. (2011). The impact of enhancing students social and emotional learning: A meta-analysis of school-based universal interventions. *Child Development, 82*(1), 405–432. doi:10.1111/j.1467-8624.2010.01564.x PMID:21291449

Elliott, S. N., & Gresham, F. M. (2007a). *Social skills improvement system: Classwide intervention program*. Minneapolis, MN: Pearson.

Elliott, S. N., & Gresham, F. M. (2007b). *Social skills improvement system: Performance Screening Guide*. Minneapolis, MN: Pearson.

Erdley, C. A., & Asher, S. R. (1999). A social goals perspective on childrens social competence. *Journal of Emotional and Behavioral Disorders, 7*(3), 156–167. doi:10.1177/106342669900700304

Espelage, D. L., Low, S., Polanin, J., & Brown, E. (2013). The Impact of a Middle-School Program to Reduce Aggression, Victimization, and Sexual Violence. *The Journal of Adolescent Health, 53*(2), 180–186. doi:10.1016/j.jadohealth.2013.02.021 PMID:23643338

Espelage, D. L., Low, S., Polanin, J., & Brown, E. (2015). Clinical trial of Second Step© middle-school program: Impact on aggression & victimization. *Journal of Applied Developmental Psychology, 37*, 133–151. doi:10.1016/j.appdev.2014.11.007

Espelage, D. L., Rose, C. A., & Polanin, J. (2016). Social-emotional learning program to promote prosocial and academic skills among middle school students with disabilities. *Remedial and Special Education, 37*(6), 323–332. doi:10.1177/0741932515627475

Espelage, D. L., Rose, C. A., & Polanin, J. R. (2015). Social-emotional learning program to reduce bullying, fighting, and victimization among middle school students with disabilities. *Remedial and Special Education, 36*(5), 299–311. doi:10.1177/0741932514564564

Fox, C. L., & Boulton, M. J. (2005). The social skills problems of victims of bullying: Self, peer and teacher perceptions. *The British Journal of Educational Psychology, 75*(2), 313–328. doi:10.1348/000709905X25517 PMID:16033669

Frederickson, N. L., & Furnham, A. F. (2004). Peer-assessed behavioural characteristics and sociometric rejection: Differ- ences between pupils who have moderate learning difficulties and their mainstream peers. *The British Journal of Educational Psychology, 74*(3), 391–410. doi:10.1348/0007099041552305 PMID:15296547

Gresham, F. M., Elliott, S. N., Cook, C. R., Vance, M. J., & Kettler, R. (2010). Cross-informant agreement for rating for social skill and problem behavior ratings: An investigation of the Social Skills Improvement System – Rating Scales. *Psychological Assessment, 22*(1), 157–166. doi:10.1037/a0018124 PMID:20230162

Hamre, B. K., & Pianta, R. C. (2007). Learning opportunities in preschool and early elementary classrooms. In R. C. Pianta, M. J. Cox, & K. L. Snow (Eds.), *School readiness and the transition to kindergarten in the era of accountability* (pp. 49–83). Baltimore, MD: Paul H. Brookes Publishing.

Hartley, M. T., Bauman, S., Nixon, C. L., & Davis, S. (2015). Comparative study of bullying victimization among students in general and special education. *Exceptional Children, 81*(2), 176–193. doi:10.1177/0014402914551741

Hawkins, J. D., Catalano, R. F., Morrison, D. M., O'Donnell, J., Abbott, R. D., & Day, L. E. (1992). Seattle Social Development Project: Effects of the first four years on protective factors and problem behaviors. In J. McCord & R. Tremblay (Eds.), *The prevention of antisocial behavior in children* (pp. 139–161). New York: Guilford Press.

Hawkins, J. D., Doueck, H. J., & Lishner, D. M. (1988). Changing teaching practices in mainstream classrooms to reduce discipline problems among low achievers. *American Educational Research Journal, 25*, 31–50. doi:10.3102/00028312025001031

Hawkins, J. D., & Weiss, J. G. (1985). The social development model: An integrated approach to delinquency prevention. *The Journal of Primary Prevention, 6*(2), 73–79. doi:10.1007/BF01325432 PMID:24271382

Hemphill, L., & Siperstein, G. N. (1990). Conversational competence and peer response to mildly retarded children. *Journal of Educational Psychology, 82*(1), 128–134. doi:10.1037/0022-0663.82.1.128

Holt, M. K., & Espelage, D. L. (2007). Perceived social support among bullies, victims, and bully-victims. *Journal of Youth and Adolescence, 36*(8), 984–994. doi:10.100710964-006-9153-3

Individuals with Disabilities Education Improvement Act, H.R. 1350, 108th Congress (2004).

January, A. M., Casey, R. J., & Paulson, D. (2011). A meta-analysis of classroom-wide interventions to build social skills: Do they work? *School Psychology Review, 40*(2), 242–256.

Jennings, P. A., & Greenberg, M. T. (2009). The prosocial classroom: Teacher social and emotional competence in relation to student and classroom outcomes. *Review of Educational Research, 79*(1), 491–525. doi:10.3102/0034654308325693

Johnson, L. S. (2009). School contexts and student belonging: A mixed methods study of an innovative high school. *School Community Journal, 19*, 99–118.

Kauffman, N. A., & Kinnealey, M. A. (2015). Comprehensive social skills taxonomy: Development and application. *The American Journal of Occupational Therapy, 69*(2), 1–10. doi:10.5014/ajot.2015.013151 PMID:26122679

Kilgus, S. P., Chafouleas, S. M., & Riley-Tillman, T. C. (2013). Development and initial validation of the Social and Academic Behavior Risk Screener for elementary grades. *School Psychology Quarterly, 28*(3), 210–226. doi:10.1037pq0000024 PMID:23773134

Kilgus, S. P., Riley-Tillman, T. C., Chafouleas, S. M., Christ, T. J., & Welsh, M. E. (2014). Direct behavior rating as a school-based behavior universal screener: Replication across sites. *Journal of School Psychology, 52*(1), 63–82. doi:10.1016/j.jsp.2013.11.002 PMID:24495495

King, K. R., Lembke, E. S., & Reinke, W. M. (in press). Using latent class analysis to identify academic and behavioral risk status in elementary students. *School Psychology Quarterly*. PMID:25751497

Klingner, J. K., Vaughn, S., Schumm, J. S., Cohen, P., & Forgan, J. W. (1998). Inclusion or pull-out which do students prefer? *Journal of Learning Disabilities, 31*(2), 148–158. doi:10.1177/002221949803100205 PMID:9529785

Kochenderfer-Ladd, B. (2004). Peer victimization: The role of emotions in adaptive and maladaptive coping. *Social Development, 13*(3), 329–349. doi:10.1111/j.1467-9507.2004.00271.x

Kress, J. S., & Elias, M. J. (2006). School-based social and emotional learning problems. Handbook of Child Psychology. IV:2:15. doi:10.1002/9780470147658.chpsy0415

Kwon, K., Kim, E., & Sheridan, S. (2012). Behavioral competence and academic functioning among early elementary children with externalizing problems. *School Psychology Review, 41*, 123–140.

Lane, K. L., Givner, C. C., & Pierson, M. R. (2004). Teacher expectations of student behavior: Social skills necessary for success in elementary school classrooms. *The Journal of Special Education, 38*(2), 104–110. doi:10.1177/00224669040380020401

Lauermann, F. (2014). Teacher responsibility from the teachers perspective. *International Journal of Educational Research, 65*, 75–89. doi:10.1016/j.ijer.2013.09.005

Lauermann, F., & Karabenick, S. A. (2013). The meaning and measure of teachers sense of responsibility for educational outcomes. *Teaching and Teacher Education, 30*, 13–26. doi:10.1016/j.tate.2012.10.001

Lee, H. J. (2011). Cultural factors related to the hidden curriculum for students with autism and related disabilities. *Intervention in School and Clinic, 46*(3), 141–149. doi:10.1177/1053451210378162

Linares, L. O., Rosbruch, N., Stern, M. B., Edwards, M. E., Walker, G., Abikoff, H. B., & Alvir, J. M. J. (2005). Developing cognitive-social-emotional competencies to enhance academic learning. *Psychology in the Schools, 42*(4), 405–417. doi:10.1002/pits.20066

Llewellyn, A. (2000). Perceptions of mainstreaming: A systems approach. *Developmental Medicine and Child Neurology, 42*(2), 106–115. doi:10.1017/S0012162200000219 PMID:10698328

Maag, J. W., & Katisyannis, A. (2012). Bullying and students with disabilities: Legal and practice considerations. *Behavioral Disorders, 37*, 78–86.

Malecki, C. K., & Elliott, S. N. (2002). Childrens social behaviors as predictors of academic achievement: A longitudinal analysis. *School Psychology Quarterly, 17*(1), 1–23. doi:10.1521cpq.17.1.1.19902

Martlew, M., & Hodson, J. (1991). Children with mild learning difficulties in an integrated and in a special school: Comparisons of behaviour, teasing, and teachers attitudes. *The British Journal of Educational Psychology, 61*(3), 355–372. doi:10.1111/j.2044-8279.1991.tb00992.x PMID:1786214

Mashburn, A. J., & Pianta, R. C. (2006). Social relationships and school readiness. *Early Education and Development*, *17*(1), 151–176. doi:10.120715566935eed1701_7

Masten, A. S., & Coatsworth, J. D. (1998). The development of competence in favorable and unfavorable environments: Lessons from research on successful children. *The American Psychologist*, *53*(2), 205–220. doi:10.1037/0003-066X.53.2.205 PMID:9491748

Menzies, H. M., & Lane, K. L. (2012). Using self-regulation strategies and functional assessment-based interventions to provide academic and behavioral support to students at risk within three-tiered models of prevention. *Preventing School Failure*, *55*(4), 181–191. doi:10.1080/1045988X.2010.520358

Merrell, K. W., & Gimpel, G. A. (1998). *Social Skills of Children and Adolescents: Conceptualization, Assessment and Treatment*. Mahwah, NJ: Lawrence Erlbaum.

Merrell, K. W., Gueldner, B. A., Ross, S. W., & Isava, D. M. (2008). How effective are school bullying intervention programs? A meta-analysis of intervention research. *School Psychology Quarterly*, *23*(1), 26–42. doi:10.1037/1045-3830.23.1.26

Myles, B. S., & Simpson, R. L. (2001). Understanding the hidden curriculum: An essential social and youth with Asperger syndrome. *Intervention in School and Clinic*, *36*(5), 279–286. doi:10.1177/105345120103600504

National Center for Education Statistics. (2015). *The condition of education 2015*. Washington, DC: Author.

Nipedal, C., Nesdale, D., & Killen, M. (2010). Social group norms, school norms, and children's aggressive intentions. *Aggressive Behavior*, *36*, 195–204. PMID:20301137

ODonnell, J., Hawkins, J. D., Catalano, R. F., Abbott, R. D., & Day, L. E. (1995). Preventing school failure, drug use and delinquency among low-income children: Long-term intervention in elementary schools. *The American Journal of Orthopsychiatry*, *65*(1), 87–100. doi:10.1037/h0079598 PMID:7733220

Office of Special Education Programs' Technical Assistance Center for Positive Behavioral Interventions and Supports. (2016). *Positive Behavioral Interventions & Supports - OSEP*. Retrieved January 01, 2016, from https://www.pbis.org/

Osterman, K. F. (2000). Students need for belonging in the school community. *Review of Educational Research*, *70*(3), 323–367. doi:10.3102/00346543070003323

Poteat, V. P., & Espelage, D. L. (2005). Exploring the relation between bullying and homophobic verbal content: The Homophobic Content Agent Target (HCAT) Scale. *Violence and Victims*, *20*(5), 513–528. doi:10.1891/vivi.2005.20.5.513 PMID:16248488

Putnam, R., Horner, R. H., & Algozzine, R. (2006). Academic achievement and the implementation of school-wide behavior support. *Positive Behavioral Interventions and Supports Newsletter*, *3*, 1–6.

Renshaw, T. L., Eklund, K., Dowdy, E., Jimerson, S. R., Hart, S. R., Earhart, J., & Jones, C. N. (2009). Examining the relationship between scores on the Behavioral and Emotional Screening System and student academic, behavioral, and engagement outcomes: An investigation of concurrent validity in elementary school. *California School Psychologist*, *14*(1), 81–88. doi:10.1007/BF03340953

Rose, C. A., & Espelage, D. L. (2012). Risk and protective factors associated with the bullying involvement of students with emotional and behavioral disorders. *Behavioral Disorders*, *37*, 133–148.

Rose, C. A., Espelage, D. L., & Monda-Amaya, L. E. (2009). Bullying and victimisation rates among students in general and special education: A comparative analysis. *Educational Psychology*, *29*(7), 761–776. doi:10.1080/01443410903254864

Rose, C. A., Espelage, D. L., Monda-Amaya, L. E., Shogren, K. A., & Aragon, S. R. (2015). Bullying and middle school students with and without specific learning disabilities: An examination of social-ecological predictors. *Journal of Learning Disabilities*, *48*(3), 239–254. doi:10.1177/0022219413496279 PMID:23886583

Rose, C. A., Forber-Pratt, A., Espelage, D. L., & Aragon, S. R. (2013). The influence of psychosocial factors on bullying involvement of students with disabilities. *Theory into Practice*, *52*(4), 272–279. doi:10.1080/00405841.2013.829730

Rose, C. A., & Monda-Amaya, L. E. (2012). Bullying and victimization among students with disabilities: Effective strategies for classroom teachers. *Intervention in School and Clinic*, *48*(2), 99–107. doi:10.1177/1053451211430119

Rose, C. A., Monda-Amaya, L. E., & Espelage, D. L. (2011). Bullying perpetration and victimization in special education: A review of the literature. *Remedial and Special Education*, *32*(2), 114–130. doi:10.1177/0741932510361247

Rose, C. A., Simpson, C. G., & Moss, A. (2015). The bullying dynamic: Prevalence of involvement among a large-scale sample of middle and high school youth with and without disabilities. *Psychology in the Schools*, *52*(5), 515–531. doi:10.1002/pits.21840

Rose, C. A., Stormont, M., Wang, Z., Simpson, C. G., Preast, J. L., & Green, A. L. (2015). Bullying and students with disabilities: Examination of disability status and educational placement. *School Psychology Review*, *44*(4), 425–444. doi:10.17105pr-15-0080.1

Ruppar, A. L., & Gaffney, J. S. (2011). Individualized education program team decisions: A preliminary study of conversations, negotiations, and power. *Research and Practice for Persons with Severe Disabilities*, *36*(1), 11–22. doi:10.2511/rpsd.36.1-2.11

Sabornie, E. J. (1994). Social-affective characteristics in early adolescents identified as learning disabled and nondisabled. *Learning Disability Quarterly*, *17*(4), 268–279. doi:10.2307/1511124

Savage, R. (2005). Friendship and bullying patterns in children attending a language base in a mainstream school. *Educational Psychology in Practice*, *21*(1), 23–36. doi:10.1080/02667360500035140

Saylor, J. G., & Alexander, W. M. (1974). *Planning curriculum for schools*. New York: Holt, Reinhart, & Wintson, Inc.

Shields, A., & Cicchetti, D. (2001). Parental maltreatment and emotion dysregulation as risk factors for bullying and victimization in middle childhood. *Journal of Clinical Child Psychology*, *30*(3), 349–363. doi:10.1207/S15374424JCCP3003_7 PMID:11501252

Smith, B. H., & Low, S. (2013). The role of social-emotional learning in bullying prevention efforts. *Theory into Practice*, *52*(4), 280–287. doi:10.1080/00405841.2013.829731

Son, E., Peterson, N. A., Pottick, K. J., Zippay, A., Parish, S. L., & Lohrmann, S. (2014). Peer victimization among young children with disabilities: Early risk and protective factors. *Exceptional Children*, *80*(3), 368–384. doi:10.1177/0014402914522422

Stainback, W., Stainback, S., & Ayres, B. (1996). Schools as inclusive communities. In W. Stainback & S. Stainback (Eds.), *Controversial issues confronting special education: Divergent perspectives* (2nd ed.; pp. 31–43). Boston: Allyn & Bacon.

Stoiber, K. C. (2011). Translating knowledge of social-emotional learning and evidence-based practice into responsive school innovations. *Journal of Educational & Psychological Consultation*, *21*(1), 46–55. doi:10.1080/10474412.2011.549039

Swearer, S. M., Wang, C., Maag, J. W., Siebecker, A. B., & Frerichs, L. J. (2012). Understanding the bullying dynamic among students in special and general education. *Journal of School Psychology*, *50*(4), 503–520. doi:10.1016/j.jsp.2012.04.001 PMID:22710018

Tolan, P. H., Guerra, N. G., & Kendall, P. C. (1995). A developmental-ecological perspective on antisocial behavior in children and adolescents: Toward a unified risk and intervention framework. *Journal of Consulting and Clinical Psychology*, *63*(4), 579–584. doi:10.1037/0022-006X.63.4.579 PMID:7673535

Ttofi, M. M., Farrington, D. P., Lösel, F., & Loeber, R. (2011). Do the victims of school bullies tend to become depressed later in life? A systematic review and meta-analysis of longitudinal studies. *Journal of Aggression, Conflict and Peace Research*, *3*(2), 63–73. doi:10.1108/17596591111132873

Van Lier, P. A. C., & Koot, H. M. (2010). Developmental cascades of peer relations and symptoms of externalizing and internalizing problems from kindergarten to fourth-grade elementary school. *Development and Psychopathology*, *22*(3), 569–582. doi:10.1017/S0954579410000283 PMID:20576179

Vaughn, S., & Klingner, J. K. (1998). Students perceptions of inclusion and resource room settings. *The Journal of Special Education*, *32*(2), 79–88. doi:10.1177/002246699803200202

Volpe, R. J., DuPaul, G. J., DiPerna, J. C., Jitendra, A. K., Lutz, J. G., Tresco, K., & Junod, R. V. (2006). Attention deficit hyperactivity disorder and scholastic achievement: A model of mediation via academic enablers. *School Psychology Review*, *35*, 47–61.

Weare, K., & Nind, M. (2011). Mental health promotion and problem prevention in schools: What does the evidence say? *Health Promotion International*, *26*(suppl 1), i29–i69. doi:10.1093/heapro/dar075 PMID:22079935

Wentzel, K. R. (1993). Does being good make the grade? Social behavior and academic competence in middle school. *Journal of Educational Psychology, 85*(2), 357–364. doi:10.1037/0022-0663.85.2.357

Yell, M. L., Shriner, J. G., & Katsiyannis, A. (2006). Individuals with disabilities education improvement act of 2004 and IDEA regulations of 2006: Implications for educators, administrators, and teacher trainers. *Focus on Exceptional Children, 39*, 1–13.

Zins, J. E., Bloodworth, M. R., Weissberg, R. P., & Walberg, H. J. (2004). The scientific base linking social and emotional learning to school success. *Journal of Educational & Psychological Consultation, 17*(2-3), 191–210. doi:10.1080/10474410701413145

Zins, J. E., & Elias, M. J. (2007). Social and emotional learning: Promoting the development of all students. *Journal of Educational & Psychological Consultation, 17*(2/3), 233–255. doi:10.1080/10474410701413152

This research was previously published in the Handbook of Research on Classroom Diversity and Inclusive Education Practice edited by Christina M. Curran and Amy J. Petersen; pages 183-200, copyright year 2017 by Information Science Reference (an imprint of IGI Global).

Chapter 7
Special Education Leadership and the Implementation of Response to Intervention

Derek Cooley
Godwin Heights Public Schools, USA

Elizabeth Whitten
Western Michigan University, USA

ABSTRACT

Special education administrators provide leadership to guide the identification of learners with exceptionalities and ensure that staff working with special education students delivers instructional best practice. In order to execute these responsibilities, special education administrators must be effective leaders who collaborate with a variety of stakeholder including. Contrary to their general education counterparts, special education administrators must possess a specific body of procedural knowledge to identify low-performing groups of students. These procedures are often referred to Response to Intervention (RTI) or Multi-Tier Systems of Support (MTSS). Under IDEA (2004), students with and without disabilities can benefit from the same system of interventions and supports. This intersection has necessitated co-ordination of RTI models by both general and special education administrators. Special education and general education leaders will be challenged to blend models of leadership to address the high-stakes environment in our K-12 schools.

INTRODUCTION

Many decades ago, Berry (1941) stated that the differences in philosophy and administration between general and special education were only in that the emphasis was placed on students with disabilities. Today, there are more than 20,000 special education administrators practicing in the U.S. who continue to emphasize the importance of programs and services for students with disabilities. Although the difference some 70 years ago was merely between those students with and those student without disabilities,

DOI: 10.4018/978-1-7998-1213-5.ch007

special education administrators are now charged with providing equal educational opportunities for *all* students (Boscardin, 2007; Crockett, 2011; Crockett, Becker, & Quinn, 2009).

The practice of special education leadership is primarily responsible for the leadership and administration of programs and services for students with disabilities. Special education administrators provide leadership to guide the identification of learners with exceptionalities and ensure that staff working with special education students delivers instructional best practice. In order to execute these responsibilities, special education administrators must be effective problem-solvers who collaborate with a variety of stakeholders including parents, teachers, administrators, and the community.

Central to the practice of special education leadership is the "finely tuned recognition of and response to individual learning needs" (Crockett, 2011, p. 351). Effective special education administrators juxtapose the needs of all students with the needs of each individual learner. These administrators must navigate policy, ensure the delivery of instructional best practice, and understand the context in which they administer programs and services. Special education administrators ensure that students with disabilities benefit from educational programs in both the general and special education settings. As a result, special education administrators are being held responsible for educational access and accountability not only for students with disabilities but also for students without disabilities.

Crockett (2011) states that although once driven primarily by district-wide compliance, the administration of special education is now focused on delivering effective and responsive instructional models at all district levels. Crockett (2011) continues that the practice of special education administration includes:

(a) setting expectations for recognizing the individual capabilities of students with disabilities, (b) developing personnel who work collaboratively and effectively in responding to students' unique educational needs and (c) making the organization of schools work more flexibly on their behalf. (p. 359)

Of these three tasks, the process of identifying students with disabilities and the provision of coordinating special and general education programs is likely to be the most difficult challenge for special education administrators in public schools today (Boscardin, 2007; Crockett, 2011; Crockett et al., 2009; McHatton, Gordon, Glenn, & Sue, 2012; Passman, 2008).

Contrary to their general education counterparts, special education administrators must possess a *specific* body of procedural knowledge to identify low-performing groups of students (Crockett et al., 2009; Passman, 2008). Much of this specific knowledge is needed to provide early intervention services for at-risk students and to develop procedures for identifying students who are at-risk of being identified with a disability (Werts, Lambert, & Carpenter, 2009). These procedures are often referred to as Response to Intervention (RTI) or Multi-tier Systems of Support (MTSS).

BACKGROUND

Response to Intervention is a multi-tiered model of instruction designed to foster academic achievement for *all* students. It is based upon the use of evidence-based interventions and research-based curriculum, which are intended to address unique learning needs. If implemented successfully, RTI can serve as a model to prevent severe academic problems and provide a means to identify students with disabilities (Whitten, Esteves, & Woodrow, 2009).

Response to Intervention is often organized into a three-tiered model. Tier I is high-quality instruction in which approximately 85% of all students participate. Tier I instruction is often referred to as the general education curriculum. Tier II includes supplemental instruction for small groups of students, representing approximately 10% of the student population. Tier III includes specially designed instruction and interventions for approximately 5% of the student population. If students fail to make progress in one tier, they move on to the next tier of more intensive interventions. If students fail to respond to instruction in all three tiers, a referral for special education can be made. As a result, RTI is both a diagnostic tool and instructional model in which the needs of struggling learners can be met.

Among all administrators in education, special education administrators have primarily taken the lead to make certain that RTI is successfully implemented in schools at both the building and district levels. Given that there is no "right way" to implement RTI (Esteves & Whitten, 2014), special education administrators are faced with the complexity of designing the procedures, policies, and protocols to effectively implement RTI (Werts et al., 2009)

RTI AND LEADERSHIP

A number of recent federal, state, and local policies have included programs for decreasing or eliminating the number of students who qualify for special education services. The No Child Left Behind Act (NCLB), which was passed in 2001, mandates that schools provide high-quality instruction using evidence-based practices for all students. The reauthorization of Individuals and Disabilities Education Act (IDEA) in 2004 allowed for the creation of Multi-tier Systems of Support (MTSS) to address the needs of struggling learners and to identify students with disabilities. Coupled together, these two laws have created systematic reforms by merging general and special education to meet the needs of both general and special education students in one unified system (Sansosti & Noltemeyer, 2008).

Given that special education administrators have historically been responsible for the provision of programs and services for students with disabilities, they are uniquely positioned to take responsibility for implementing RTI for groups of students who similarly lack adequate academic achievement. Students who are non-disabled and underachieving are also likely to benefit from the mandates of IDEA (2004), which calls for the use of research-based interventions delivered in an RTI model. Under IDEA (2004), students with and without disabilities can benefit from the same system of interventions and supports. This intersection has necessitated coordination of RTI models by both general and special education administrators. Boscardin, McCarthy, and Delgado (2009) state that "as inclusive practices and accountability continue to shape American education, special education and general education leaders will be challenged to join together in solving the problems of practice inherent in a diverse, complex, high-stakes environment" (p. 68).

Special education administrators must determine which factors for implementing RTI are most effective. Although there is an abundance of literature that defines RTI and how its practiced in schools, there is less research on how to successfully implement it (Harlacher & Siler, 2011; O'Connor & Freeman, 2012; Sansosti, Goss, & Noltemeyer, 2011; Sansosti & Noltemeyer, 2008; Werts et al., 2009). Thus, special education administrators are more likely to be challenged with determining the "how" of RTI as opposed to the "what." Special education administrators encounter a number of challenges related to the implementation of RTI that includes the fidelity in which research-based instruction and evidence-based intervention is delivered, effective professional development supporting RTI practices, staff collaboration and buy-in, and the availability of resources and/or materials.

The ability for special education administrators to effectively implement RTI is dependent upon the leadership skills they possess. Thus, special education administrators are further confronted with selecting administrative interventions that lead to the successful implementation of RTI. Such interventions for managing school reform often rely upon theoretical models for change (Sansosti & Noltemeyer, 2008).

One such model of change is Fullan's (2001) Framework for Leadership. Frequently cited in the educational reform literature, Fullan (2001) describes his work as a set of dimensions that can improve leadership in education. Within his framework, Fullan (2001) stresses that effective leaders must understand the process of change, rely on relationships with and among staff, collaborate with stakeholders to create and share knowledge, and depend on a sense of moral purpose. Although there are a number of theoretical models for educational reform, Fullan's (2001) model is well suited to support special education administrators in that it directly applies to the implementation of RTI (Datnow, 2006; Sansosti & Noltemeyer, 2008).

Special Education Leadership

The practice of special education administration has been described as the "intersection" of special education, general education, and educational leadership (Lashley & Boscardin, 2003). Collaborating with many school personnel to achieve the shared intentions and goals of schools, special education administrators work on behalf of students with disabilities to provide equal access and high quality programming to ensure sufficient outcomes (Crockett, Billingsley, & Boscardin, 2012).

The skills special education administrators must possess in order to be successful are complex and multi-faceted. Special education administrators must possess a specific body of procedural knowledge, an in-depth knowledge of learner characteristics, disability criteria, and accommodations, modifications, and intervention plans. Special education administrators must also have the skills to successfully facilitate the problem-solving process, including mediation and negotiation skills. Working with a variety of school staff, parents, and the community, special education administrators must possess dispositions including compassion, flexibility, sensitivity to differences, and an ability to build relationships with others (Passman, 2008).

In a review of special education administration literature, Crockett, Becker, and Quinn (2009) found that a significant body of the literature is primarily focused on leadership roles and responsibilities. They define these roles and responsibilities as the "dimensions of the work of special education administrators and the programmatic issues they address in their positions" (p. 58). Central to this theme is a focus on providing support for improving instruction for both general and special education students. In order to provide this support, special education administrators must promote a collaborative partnership with teachers and administrators within general education. Effective special education administrators recognize that such partnerships are critical in meeting the needs of all students through high quality programming and equal educational access (Lashley & Boscardin, 2003).

Similar to other educational administrators, the roles and responsibilities of special education administrators are changing. The onset of higher standards and increased accountability necessitates the need for special education administrators to provide reliable and valid assessment data for students with disabilities (Baaken et al., 2007; Lashley & Boscardin, 2003; Voltz & Collins, 2010). Broadening this responsibility to all students, "special education and general education leaders will be challenged to join together to solve the problems inherent in a diverse, complex, high-stakes education environment" (Lashley & Boscardin, 2003, p. 73).

Boscardin (2007) provides a framework for the practice of special education administration based upon the premise that evidence-based leadership practices are needed to improve educational opportunities for students with disabilities. Within this framework, special education administrators employ leadership approaches and responsive leadership interventions that mimic the concepts applied to RTI. These concepts include:

1. The concept of multiple stages of administrative interventions to improve teaching in ways that lead to improved student achievement.
2. The implementation of differentiated administrative approaches.
3. Leadership provided by staff other than designated personnel.
4. Varied duration, frequency, and time of administrative interventions.
5. Traditional and non-traditional administrative decisions.
6. Situational conditions for decisions.
7. Urgency for administrative decisions.
8. The use of standard protocols for determining the use of specific administrative approaches or interventions. (p. 191)

This framework is not based upon a set of prescriptive actions, per se, but a set of conceptual processes that are guided by progress monitoring and problem solving at the building and district level. Within Boscardin's framework for leadership, *student*-progress monitoring is replaced with *system*-progress monitoring by using leadership interventions to respond rapidly to system needs.

Standards for Preparation and Practice

Several studies highlight the importance of articulated standards for the practice and preparation of special education administrations. Although there are a number of standards for educational administration in general, the standards authored by the Council for Exceptional Children are most frequently cited among special education administration and leadership.

Boscardin, McCarthy, and Delgado (2009) used an integrative approach to engage special education administrators to validate major knowledge and skill statements in special education leadership. Triangulating data from a literature review, Q-sort analysis, and surveys, the authors were able to prioritize and rate domains that are associated with special education leadership. Their work resulted in the 2009 edition of the Council for Exceptional Children's (CEC) Advanced Knowledge and Skills for Administrators of Special Education (2009). The standards are:

1. Leadership and Policy
2. Program Development and Organization
3. Research and Inquiry
4. Evaluation
5. Professional Development and Ethical Practice
6. Collaboration

These standards are intended to guide universities in developing standards for preservice programs as well as professional development opportunities for practitioners in the field.

In a similar study, Wigle and Wilcox (2002) investigated the competencies of special education directors by developing a survey based upon an earlier set of CEC standards. The results of this survey suggest that special education directors perceived themselves as having high levels of competence in the following areas: program development, collaboration, communication and advocacy, technology, and behavior management. The CEC standards provide a strong foundation to guide preparation and practice within this field.

Based upon historical themes in special education such as free appropriate public education (FAPE) and least restrictive environment (LRE), Crockett (2002) developed a framework for special education leadership. Crockett's (2002) five core principles are intended to guide institutions of higher education in the development and preparation of special education administrators. The core principles are:

1. Ethical practice: Ensuring universal educational access and accountability.
2. Individual consideration: Addressing individuality and exceptionality in learning.
3. Equity under law: Providing an appropriate education through equitable public policies.
4. Effective programming: Providing individualized programming designed to enhance student performance.
5. Establishing productive partnerships. (p. 163)

In sum, the literature on special education administration is quite limited. It is primarily based upon explanations, observations, and experiences of both practitioners and researchers in the field. Further explained, "the special education administrative knowledge base is informed primarily by theoretical or interpretive professional commentary rather than by data-based research studies that could guide effective leadership practice" (Crockett et al., 2009, p. 65). Some recommend a stronger empirical foundation to support this body of literature.

Response to Intervention

Since the first passage of the Individuals with Disabilities Education Act (IDEA) more than 30 years ago, the number of students identified as having a Learning Disability (LD) has increased more than 200% (Bradley, Danielson, & Doolittle, 2005). This dramatic increase has caused concern for the method in which students are identified as having learning disabilities (D. Fuchs, Fuchs, & Compton, 2004; Kavale, Kauffman, Bachmeier, & LeFever, 2008).

Traditional methods for identifying students as having LD rely upon "wait-to-fail" models in which the discrepancy between academic achievement and intelligence determines eligibility (D. Fuchs et al., 2004; Kavale et al., 2008). This discrepancy model has been criticized for an over-reliance on a single testing point and a wide variability in LD assessment procedures (Fletcher, Denton, & Francis, 2005; Mellard, Deshler, & Barth, 2004).

Resulting from mandates passed in IDEA (2004), one of the most commonly used methods for identifying students with LD is Response to Intervention (RTI). As a tiered model, RTI is designed to move poorly performing students through a series of increasingly intensive academic interventions. If students fail to respond to all tiers of intervention, schools must consider a referral for eligibility for special education services (Hollenbeck, 2007).

Special Education Leadership and the Implementation of Response to Intervention

Background

The process for identifying students with LD dates to the original passage of the Education for All Handicapped Children Act of 1975. This law was renewed in 1991 as the Individuals with Disabilities Education Act (IDEA). Under IDEA (1991), the process for identifying students with LD was largely unchanged. This process relied heavily upon the use of a discrepancy formula, which is calculated on the difference between a student's actual performance and expected academic achievement (Mellard et al., 2004). Before the reauthorization of IDEA in 2004, school districts were allowed to individually define the formulas they used within their districts. As a result, inconsistencies in formula definitions allowed for a variation in LD identification procedures and prevalence rates not only from state to state but from school district to school district (Kratochwill, Clements, & Kalymon, 2007). Because of these inconsistencies and lack of student progress, the reauthorization of IDEA in 2004 included major reform efforts that provided states and districts the option to replace the "wait-to-fail method" with a response to intervention model of support. Such models identify students who are not working at grade level, whereby the use of evidence-based instruction is immediately implemented (D. Fuchs, Fuchs, & Compton, 2012).

In 2002, the President's Commission on Excellence in Special Education concluded that the entitlement of special education services was based upon waiting for a student to experience academic failure. Subsequently, it was recommended that special education services should be provided only after a student had the opportunity to participate in instructional programs that were designed to prevent failure (Gresham, 2007). Along with the President's Commission, the National Summit on Learning Disabilities (2002) concluded that little evidence supported a continued reliance on the IQ-discrepancy model as a means for LD identification. Both groups determined that a preventative model such as RTI could provide an alternative for LD identification (Kavale et al., 2008). Based upon the recommendations from these national groups and others, congress included provisions for RTI as a method for the identification of students with LD in the reauthorization of IDEA (2004). Specifically, IDEA outlines that states, "may permit the use of a process based on the child's response to scientific, research-based intervention" (IDEA, § 300.307(a)(2)). These words gave way to the term "Response to Intervention".

Definitions and Components of RTI

The literature outlines a number of components that define RTI. Among these definitions, the most common component is the use of outcome data for decision-making regarding the effectiveness of an academic intervention (L. S. Fuchs & Vaughn, 2012; Gresham, 2007; Knotek, 2007; Kratochwill et al., 2007). Such decisions can be made about the academic achievement of individual students and groups of students within schools and districts. These decisions can also include eligibility determination of special education for students who fail to respond to interventions. The National Association of State Directors of Special Education (NASDSE) defines RTI as "the practice of (1) providing high-quality instruction/intervention matched to student needs and (2) using learning rate over time and level of performance to (3) make important education decisions" (Batsche et al., 2005, p. 5). Outlining similar components to the NASDSE definition, the Council for Exceptional Children (CEC; 2008) states that RTI shall include universal screening, high quality research based instruction, and progress monitoring. CEC organizes these core components within a tiered system of instructional delivery.

Using a practical application of RTI components, Fletcher and Vaughn (2009) recommend that school personnel implement universal screening and assessment of academic progress at regular intervals, progress monitoring using curriculum-based measurement and, the provision of increasingly intense interventions for students who do not respond to instruction. Those students who do not adequately respond to instruction may be referred for evaluations for special education, which most often includes eligibility determinations of LD.

A Multi-Tiered System

RTI is most frequently structured around a three-tier system of interventions. Tier I is the core academic curriculum. Effective for 80% to 85% of all students, these core instructional interventions are preventative and proactive. Tier II consists of targeted group interventions for approximately 10% to 15% of students who are at-risk for academic failure. Comprising the most intensive interventions, tier III is tailored for 5% to 10% of students on an individual basis or small group basis. Longer in duration than tier I and II, tier III interventions utilize assessment measures most frequently to monitor student achievement (Batsche et al., 2005; Whitten et al., 2009).

When using RTI as a framework to establish LD identification, poor instruction is ruled out and student failure is more likely to be attributed to the result of a disability. Inadequate growth "suggests that disability is responsible and that specialized instruction is necessary to boost academic achievement" (D. Fuchs et al., 2004, p. 217). Although originally intended as a framework for early reading intervention, RTI is widely used to ensure that high-quality instruction and interventions are matched to students needs (Mellard, Stern, & Woods, 2011).

RTI has been found to increase student achievement and decrease the number of students identified as having a disability (Burns, Appleton, & Stehouwer, 2005; Hughes & Dexter, 2011). In a review of 13 published field studies, Hughes and Dexter (2011) report that schools implementing RTI report academic improvement. In a separate review of 21 studies, Burns, Appleton, and Stehouwer (2005) conclude that within existing RTI models, less than 2% of the student population was identified as LD, whereas national LD prevalence rates are higher than 5%

Response to Intervention Models

RTI is often constructed into two different, yet related, models – the problem-solving model and the standard treatment protocol (D. Fuchs et al., 2004; Hollenbeck, 2007; Marston, 2005; Mellard et al., 2011). Implementing an RTI framework requires choosing one of these models or establishing a hybrid between the two. Problem-solving models are associated with a shared decision-making team that identifies a problem. These teams are responsible for choosing interventions to address the problem, evaluating the outcome of the intervention, and monitoring progress to ensure the effectiveness of the intervention that was chosen (Fletcher & Vaughn, 2009).

Problems are defined as the difference between the actual and desired level of academic performance (Gresham, 2007). As the difference between the actual and desired levels of performance gets larger, so does the problem.

The second type of model uses a standardized protocol to deliver instruction. Implemented with validated interventions, standard protocols are delivered in a fixed- duration trial (e.g. 10-15 weeks) to allow for more control. Typically scripted, these interventions guarantee the integrity of delivery (Gresham, 2007). The standard protocol "approaches feature the use of tightly structured teaching using commercially available instructional packages" (Kovaleski, 2007, p. 83) These protocols have a high probability of producing outcomes for larger numbers of students (Batsche et al., 2005).

Some consider the use of both models, combined into one hybrid approach, preferable to the exclusive use of one model. Batsche et al. (2005) state, "in considering problem-solving teams and standard protocol interventions, it appears that a merger of the two approaches at tier 2 is most desirable" (p. 24). Within a hybrid model, problem solving teams utilizing standard protocols can increase treatment fidelity with specific interventions (e.g. reading fluency) to counteract less precise methods such as brainstorming (Batsche et al., 2005).

Universal Screening and Progress Monitoring.

Fuchs and Vaughn (2012) state, "RTI's greatest accomplishment to date may be the dramatic increase in schools' routine reliance on screening to identify students at risk for reading and increasing math difficulties" (p. 196). As the principle means for identifying struggling students, screening consists of brief assessments targeted at skills, such as reading and math, that are predictive of future academic achievement (Jenkins, Hudson, & Johnson, 2007). Universal screening tools, typically conducted three times per year, are administered to all students and intend to provide information to staff that allows for efficiently identifying academic problems (Fletcher & Vaughn, 2009; Hughes & Dexter, 2011; Whitten et al., 2009).

After universal screening is completed and student are receiving tier I instruction, progress monitoring is needed to frequently assess student performance to gauge the effectiveness of the interventions (Hughes & Dexter, 2011; Whitten et al., 2009). Stecker, Fuchs, and Fuchs (2008) define progress monitoring as "a system of brief assessments that are given frequently, at least monthly, to determine whether students are progressing through the curriculum in desired fashion and are likely to meet long-term goals" (p. 11).

Currently, the recommended time period for progress monitoring is 8-10 weeks (McMaster & Wagner, 2007). One of the most well-known and widely used techniques for progress monitoring is curriculum-based measurement (CBM). Similar to techniques used for universal screening, CBM can determine whether a student is learning and it can determine at what rate the learning is occurring. CBM is highly standardized, requires a small amount of time to be administered, and can be repeated multiple times during a school year (McMaster & Wagner, 2007; Whitten et al., 2009).

Implementation of RTI

Since the reauthorization of IDEA in 2004, School districts across the country have begun to implement RTI. Castillo and Batsche (2012) report that "district implementation of the response to intervention (RTI) model has occurred at a surprising rate" (p. 14). Findings from a survey by Spectrum K12 Solutions (2011) show that RTI implementation continues to rise nationally with 94% of districts reporting some level of RTI implementation (up from 72% in 2009). Eighty-eight percent of districts use RTI to identify students for early intervention and 66% of districts use RTI to identify students for special education services.

The National Association of State Directors of Special Education (NASDSE) published one of the most widely cited models for district-wide implementation of RTI (Elliott & Morrison, 2008). Designed to provide concrete guidance to school districts, these "Blueprints" define three steps for implementing RTI. Districts engage in district level consensus and infrastructure building, followed by specific implementation, evaluation, and professional development plans.

Although a number of states have implemented RTI in various ways, despite recommmendations from national organziations, no single model has been widely accepted.

Professional Development

Professional development has been cited as the most frequent factor leading to the successful implementation of RTI. School personnel should have many opportunities to practice new skills with ongoing feedback (Harlacher & Siler, 2011). School personnel participating in district-level professional development should understand the relationship between RTI and achievement, empirically validated instructional practices, use of the problem solving model, and evaluation strategies for student performance difference, which include continuous progress monitoring methods (Batsche et al., 2005; Harlacher & Siler, 2011).

Special Education Leadership and RTI Implementation

Administrative support has been cited as one of the most critical components for the successful implementation of RTI (O'Connor & Freeman, 2012; Sansosti et al., 2011; Werts et al., 2009; Wiener & Soodak, 2008). Specifically, Sansosti, Goss, and Noltemeyer (2011) state that the "role of the special education director as a leader and change agent is critical to successful implementation of RTI" (p. 16). When implementing RTI, special education administrators must assign staff roles and responsibilities, develop and implement district policies, and carefully consider the use of time and resources when overseeing programs (O'Connor & Freeman, 2012; Werts et al., 2009).

Having influence on decisions that impact student learning, special education administrators play key roles in data-based decision making processes that impact RTI. Special education administrators must be knowledgeable about concepts, principles, and communicate a rationale for a school-wide process for making data-based decisions. Working at the district level, special education administrators must establish and maintain structures for sustaining data-based decision making processes that align with school improvement goals and objectives.

Special education administrators consider a number of factors when implementing RTI. Wiener and Soodak (2008) found that special education administrators attributed RTI success to "access to professional development, resources and materials for training and implementation, and guidelines for implementation" (p. 43). Further, special education administrators are generally optimistic about the results of RTI in terms of impact on instruction and collaboration. Viewing the primary benefit of RTI as the improvement of instruction, rather than decreasing the number of student classified as LD, special education administrators concede that additional benefits will be realized through ongoing implementation and change (Wiener & Soodak, 2008). Creating a shared knowledge and understanding of RTI, special education administrators must provide clear and specific support to staff during RTI implementation (O'Connor & Freeman, 2012).

Implementing Educational Change

Duke (2004) defines educational change as "any intentional change designed to improve teaching and learning" (p. 30). As an ambiguous term, change may refer to the process in which change is initiated or the change as an artifact itself. Thus, not only is the study of educational change concerned with the process of change, but also the product of change (Duke, 2004).

The volume of educational change research is immense. A recent search of the literature revealed an astounding 461,000 journal articles referring to the topic. In order to conceptualize, organize, and make meaning of this amount of information, a number of researchers associate change within a particular perspective, or schema. From these perspectives, models and/or frameworks for educational change are created. The terms educational reform, educational change, and school reform are used interchangeably.

House and McQuillan (2005) conceptualize the literature on school reform into three perspectives: technological, political, and cultural. Researchers who subscribe to the technological perspective of school reform focus on specific goals and tasks, efficiency, outcomes, and systemic rational processes. This perspective is based on how to complete a specific set of steps to efficiently complete a job. Emphasis is largely placed upon the economics of the market as a means to frame the need for change. The political perspective of education reform relies heavily on negotiation. Concepts such as power, authority, group conflict and compromise, and competing interests make up this perspective. Lastly, theorists who rely on a cultural perspective focus on a school system as a community. Concepts include shared meaning, values, and the importance of relationships. Each of these perspectives points to a different set of factors that are responsible for change. Schools do not operate within one of these perspectives exclusively. The interaction among all three perspectives explains the complexity in which change occurs in schools. These models are typically prescriptive, in which a set of specific steps or actions are followed in order to implement, manage, and lead change.

Ellsworth (2000) makes three assumptions about the nature of educational change. First, educational change can be understood and managed. When approached as such, it is often referred to as *planned* change. Second, educational change can be understood and managed when practitioners apply a set of tools from a number of different models of change. Such models can be referred to as a "toolbox" that allows leaders to effectively match certain tools with certain innovations of change. Lastly, effective and lasting change must address the concerns and priorities of multiple stakeholder groups. The success of an initiative is a direct result of the willingness of staff, parents, and the community to change themselves as individuals (Edgehouse et al., 2007).

Educational change models are used by leaders to gain a better understanding of the process of change. These models describe *why* change occurs, *how* change occurs, and *what* will occur as a result of the change (Duke, 2004; Edgehouse et al., 2007). Certain models concentrate on a specific part of the process of change such as problem solving, innovation, the change agent, or the intended users of change. Ellsworth (2000) presents an overview of each of the major models of educational change. Instead of defining each model by the steps or components within them, questions that each model is most likely to answer are presented:

- What attributes can I build into the innovation or its implementation strategy to facilitate its acceptance by the intended adopter? – Roger's (1995) Diffusion of Innovations
- What are the conditions that should exist or be created in the environment where the innovation is being introduced to facilitate its adoption? – Ely's (1990) Conditions of Change

- What are the implications of change for people or organizations promoting or opposing it at particular levels? – Fullan and Stiegelbauer's (1991) Meaning of Educational Change
- What are the essential stages of the facilitation process and what activities should the change agent be engaged during the each stage? - Havelock's (1995) Change Agent's Guide
- What stages will stakeholders go through during implementation and what will be the major concerns at each stage? – Hall, Hord, and Newlove's (1973) Concerns-Based Adoption Model
- What are the cultural, social, organizational, and psychological *barriers* to change that can promote resistance to the innovation and what can I do to lower these barriers and encourage adoption? – Zaltman and Duncan's (1997) Strategies for Planned Change
- What are the factors *outside* the immediate environment in which the innovation is being introduced that can affect its adoption? Reigeluth and Garfinkle's (1994) Systemic Change in Education (p. 37)

Although each question is intended to guide a user to a specific model, many have suggested that school leaders draw on relevant components from all of the models to build one holistic strategy to approach change (Edgehouse et al., 2007; Ellsworth, 2000; Fullan, 2001). When special education administrators choose a selected model, for example, they must begin by determining which of the answers they are seeking. Each innovation or initiative comes with a different set of challenges, and as a result, may present with a new set of questions. Educational change cannot be achieved in a linear systematic process. Schools work on many different goals and initiatives at the same time, which require levels of concurrent management and coordination, which must all be integrated simultaneously (Hargreaves, 2005).

Even with an immense knowledge base for guidance in the field, efforts to lead change are often ineffective. Hargreaves (2005) mentions several factors that make leading change difficult. Some of these factors include:

- The reasons for the change is poorly conceptualized or not clearly demonstrated.
- The change is too broad and ambitious.
- The change is too fast or too slow for people to cope with.
- The change is poorly resourced.
- There is no long-term commitment to the change.
- Key staff are not committed to the change.
- Leaders are too controlling or ineffectual.
- The change is pursued in isolation and gets undermined by other unchanged structures (p. 2).

These factors highlight that educational change is not simply a technical process, nor is it based only upon an understanding of the culture and people of an organization. "People fear change not just because it presents them with something new, uncertain, or unclear – because it has no obvious or common meaning for them" (Hargreaves, 2005; p. 2). In sum, special education administrators must master the technical process of change, understand the culture in which they attempt to lead change, and ensure that stakeholders involved in change find meaning and purpose.

School Improvement and RTI

After the need for change has been identified and a design has been selected, the next phase involves developing an implementation plan. An implementation plan is a set of guidelines that ensures that the design itself is put into place. Such plans are often called school improvement plans or continuous school improvement. School improvement plans "are not the designs themselves, but the provisions for moving the designs from the drawing board to the school" (Duke, 2004, p. 123).

School improvement is based upon strategies that focus on curriculum and instruction, organization development, and the decentralization of decision making (Hopkins, 2005). Such efforts have led to a focus on the process of how to effect change, which is based upon school-selected priorities for improvement. This process often emphasizes the roles and perspectives of teachers and other stakeholders. School improvement also stresses the importance of a school culture, teacher collegiality, and staff relationships (Fink & Stoll, 2005). Such relationships are productive when the interactions between leaders and the people they work with produce desirable results for all stakeholders within a school (Cardno, 2012).

School improvement is an effective model when used to implement RTI because both processes focus on student outcomes. Further, both school improvement and RTI use planning and frequent review of system-level effectiveness to determine progress toward goals. Both models utilize system-wide decision making and progress monitoring to improve schools (Bernhardt & Hebert, 2011; O'Connor & Freeman, 2012).

Not only does school improvement focus on enhancing educational outcomes for students, it also strengthens the capacity for schools to understand and manage change (Bernhardt & Hebert, 2011). School improvement allows schools to take control of change. Thus, schools that use school improvement are "no longer the 'victims' of change, but can take more control of the process." (Hopkins, 2005, p. 3). Similarly, the implementation of RTI also allows for special education administrators to take control of change.

The literature often highlights that leading change is a complex and difficult task. Special education administrators must consider that change takes place in a world of chaos, and that the process of change is a complex chaotic process in and of itself. In addition to an understanding of the process of change, and the application of selected models that assist in leading it, special education administrators should consider societal change forces, the political factors that influence or mandate change, and the emotional aspects of teaching, learning and leading change (Hargreaves, 2005).

RTI and the Process of Change

Response to Intervention is often viewed as an educational reform initiative. Sansosti and Noltemeyer (2008) state that, "RTI cannot be characterized by one educational program or curriculum, but rather a transformation in the way that systems, schools, and professionals operate" (p. 56). Key to the success of reform initiatives such as RTI is a need for school leaders to understand the process of change and how to manage it. The literature fails to adequately identify factors that contribute to the successful implementation of RTI. As a result, it is important to review models and theories of educational change in order to improve future practice (Hargreaves, 2005; (Ellsworth, 2000; Sansosti & Noltemeyer, 2008).

Fullan's Model for Educational Change

Examining the process of change, Fullan (2001) provides a framework for leaders to define and implement change. Fullan suggests that "*leading* in a culture of change means *creating* a culture of change" (emphasis added, p. 44). Leaders who create a culture of change produce "the capacity to seek, critically assess, and selectively incorporate new ideas and practices" (Fullan, 2001, p. 44). Change is not addressed with step-by-step manuals or protocols. Rather, Fullan (2001) places emphasis on an understanding and an insight of change, rather than steps for taking action. His model, called A Framework for Leadership, is organized into five domains.

The first domain of Fullan's framework is *moral purpose*. Moral purpose is simply defined as the drive to make a difference in the lives of students. Leaders exhibiting moral purpose possess characteristics such as integrity, conviction, responsibility, moral excellence, and trust. Fullan states, "leaders in all organizations, whether they know it or not, contribute for better or for worse to moral purpose in their own organizations and in society as a whole" (p. 15). If leaders use moral purpose to lead change effectively, Fullan (2001) states they must:

(1) have an explicit 'making-a-difference' sense of purpose, (2) use strategies that mobilize many people to tackle tough problems, (3) be held accountable by measured and debatable indicators of success, and (4) be ultimately assessed by the extent to which it awakens people's intrinsic commitment, which is none other than the mobilizing of everyone's sense of moral purpose. (pg. 20)

Fullan's second domain of his framework for leadership is *understanding change*. Fullan summarizes the concept of understanding change into six parts:

1. The goal is not to innovate the most.
2. It is not enough to have the best ideas.
3. Appreciate the implementation dip.
4. Redefine resistance.
5. Reculturing is the name of the game.
6. Never a checklist, always complexity.

Leaders who implement initiatives do not always make progress. Without buy-in from staff, good ideas are nothing more than ideas. Effective leaders must not only possess good ideas, but be able to implement them as well. After implementing a new initiative, leaders find themselves and their staff lacking skills to sustain innovation because they don't have the new skills to accompany it. Fullan (2001) describes this as the implementation dip. Building in differences and offsetting equilibrium creates capacity for change. Leaders should foster organizations that have creativity to get through this implementation dip. As leaders understand the process of change, they realize that if everyone thinks exactly alike, no one will be able to make suggestions as how to move forward.

The third domain to Fullan's (2001) model is *relationships*. Fullan states that to implement change effectively, "it is actually the relationships that make the difference" (p. 51). Fullan (2001) articulates that although the development of people is important, it is not enough to successfully lead change. The creation of relationships is crucial, but only if the result is greater coherence among staff, programs, and schools. Relationships should lead to the creation of additional resources, which can be accessed by staff, parents, and the community. The role of leadership is to "cause" a greater capacity among the individuals in the organization. Professional relationships are bolstered with the use of professional development to improve teaching and learning. Fullan (2001) proposes professional development that focuses on system-wide change to improve instruction.

The fourth domain of Fullan's model is *knowledge creation and sharing*. The process of knowledge creation and sharing is built upon the development of relationships among staff. Ultimately, the purpose of relationships is to then create and share knowledge for the betterment of the organization. Fullan describes schools as being in the business of learning, yet he states that districts are inept at learning from one other. Using what Fullan calls intervisitation and peer advising, administrators and teachers can learn best practice from colleagues within their own schools and in neighboring schools.

Through inter-visitation, groups of teachers and administrators visit to observe instructional best practice in other schools. Districts participate in instructional consulting services in which both in-house consultants and out-of-house consultants work with staff to improve instruction. When staff shares information about best practices, they express a need for more knowledge, including the practical implications when implementing a new project or initiative. Administrators and teachers should also request time to reflect on newly implemented practices, policies, and protocols. During peer advising, administrators and teachers participate in a mentor-mentee program in which experienced administrators collaborate with new administrators.

The last domain of Fullan's framework for leadership is *coherence making*. Based upon the premise that complex systems such as schools are continually generating overload and fragmentation, the act of maintaining coherence is necessary to lead change. Fullan describes this coherence making by using the work Pascale, Millemann, and Gioja (2000, p. 6, emphasis in original):

1. *Equilibrium* is a precursor to *death*. When a living system is in a state of equilibrium, it is less responsive to changes occurring around it. This places it at maximum risk.
2. In the face of threat, or when galvanized by a compelling opportunity, living things move toward the *edge of chaos*. This condition evokes higher levels of mutation and experimentation, and fresh new solutions are more likely to be found.
3. When this excitation takes place, the components of living systems *self-organize* and new forms of *repertoires* emerge from the turmoil.
4. Living systems cannot be *directed* along a linear path. Unforeseen consequences are inevitable. The challenge is to *disturb* them in a manner that approximates the desired outcome.

In schools, "the main problem is not the absence of innovations but the presence of too many disconnected, episodic, piecemeal, superficially adorned projects (Fullan, 2001, p. 109). The result is that staff becomes frustrated, disenchanted, and complacent to change. Leaders must ensure organizational coherence to successfully implement new initiatives.

When applying each of Fullan's (2001) five domains to lead change, leaders should be patient and deliberate by absorbing challenges and redefining new patterns along the path of change. Learning in context, leaders are able to attain specific knowledge because the learning takes place with the group of an organization. Thus, commitment from staff cannot be activated from top-level leadership. Leadership at many levels within the organization is needed for sustainable success. Fullan (2001) concludes that "ultimately, leadership in a culture of change will be judged as effective or ineffective not by who you are as a leaders, but by *what leadership you produce in others*" (emphasis in original, p. 137).

SOLUTIONS AND RECOMMENDATIONS

In the non-stop pursuit to improve school systems and school personnel, understanding the process of change is important for special education administrators to successfully implement RTI. Fullan (2007) describes this structure as a hierarchy of successive levels. That is, students cannot be successful without successful teachers; teachers cannot be successful without successful leaders; and leaders must sustain the betterment of all stakeholders through sustaining meaningful educational change. When organizations change, leaders are required to link of all the parts of the system together (Fullan, 2006). Given the lack of research on what makes the implementation of RTI successful, theoretical models of change can serve to guide future educational practice. Specifically, Fullan's (2001) model for change has been pivotal in guiding practitioners and researchers through the process of educational change (Datnow, 2006; Sansosti & Noltemeyer, 2008; Stoll, 2006). Within the study of RTI, Sansosti and Noltemeyer (2008) purport that "Fullan's model appears to have direct applicability to the current practice of RTI" (p. 57).

FUTURE RESEARCH DIRECTIONS

A number of topics can be further explored using this chapter as a basis. Research including a large population could provide insight and comparisons among states and possibly larger geographic regions as well as a means to determine differences among subgroups of the sample population. Analysis could also include a review of policies and laws that are specific to each state within the region.

Understanding the perceptions of staff working under the authority of special education administrators during the implementation of RTI could be explored. Future research could address the interactions among special education administrators and their staff to determine the effectiveness of NASDE's steps to implement RTI in greater detail.

Furthermore, a study that includes an analysis of actual practices during implementation, qualitative methods such as direct observation, interviews, and focus groups could allow for a comparison between self-reported perceptions and actual practice in the field. These methods could also provide analysis to determine where challenges arise during each step of implementation.

CONCLUSION

This chapter provides information for special education administrators and others who are responsible for leading the implementation of RTI in schools and districts. Special education administrators will need a set of skills to successfully implement RTI, to understand the process of change, and to identify challenges during implementation. Special education administrators should have an in depth knowledge of the process of change, implement a strategic and prescriptive process for RTI based upon a systematic plan to address all district structures, and recognize the challenges that may impede the process along the way.

REFERENCES

Baaken, J. P., O'Brian, M. O., & Shelden, D. L. (2007). Changeing roles and responsibilities of special education administrators. *Advances in Special Education, 17*, 1–15. doi:10.1016/S0270-4013(06)17001-4

Batsche, G. M., Elliot, J., Graden, J. L., Grimes, J., Kovaleski, J. F., Prasse, D., & Tilly, W. D. (2005). *Response to intervention: Policy considerations and implementation.* Alexandria, VA: National Association of State Directors of Special Education.

Bergstrom, M. K. (2008). Professional development in response to intervention: Implementation of a model in a rural region. *Rural Special Education Quarterly, 27*(4), 27–36.

Berkeley, S., Bender, W. N., Peaster, L. G., & Saunders, L. (2009). Implementation of response to intervention. *Journal of Learning Disabilities, 42*(1), 85–95. doi:10.1177/0022219408326214 PMID:19103800

Bernhardt, V. L., & Hebert, C. L. (2011). *Response to intervention (RtI) and continuous school improvement (SCI) using data, vision, and leadership to design, implement, and evaluate a schoolwide prevention system.* Larchmont, NY: Eye on Education.

Berry, C. S. (1941). General problems of philosophy and administration in the education of exceptional children. *Review of Educational Research, 11*(3), 252–260.

Betts, F. (1992). How systems thinking applies to education. *Educational Leadership, 50*(3), 38–41.

Boscardin, M. L. (2007). What is special about special education administration? Considerations for school leadership. *Exceptionality, 15*(3), 189–200. doi:10.1080/09362830701503537

Boscardin, M. L., McCarthy, E., & Delgado, R. (2009). An integrated research-based approach to creating standards for special education leadership. *Journal of Special Education Leadership, 22*(2), 68–84.

Bradley, R., Danielson, L., & Doolittle, J. (2005). Response to intervention. *Journal of Learning Disabilities, 38*(6), 485–486. doi:10.1177/00222194050380060201 PMID:16392688

Burns, M. K., Appleton, J. J., & Stehouwer, J. D. (2005). Meta-analytic review of responsiveness-to-intervention research: Examining field-based and research-implemented models. *Journal of Psychoeducational Assessment, 23*(4), 381–394. doi:10.1177/073428290502300406

Cardno, C. (2012). *Managing effetive relationships in education.* London, GRB. Sage (Atlanta, Ga.).

Castillo, J. M., & Batsche, G. M. (2012). Scaling up response to intervention: The influence of policy and research and the role of program evaluation. *Communique, 40*, 14–16.

Creswell, J. W. (2007). *Qualitative inquiry and research design: Choosing among five approaches.* Thousand Oaks, CA: Sage.

Crockett, J. B. (2002). Special education's role in preparing responsive leaders for inclusive schools. *Remedial and Special Education, 23*(3), 157–168. doi:10.1177/07419325020230030401

Crockett, J. B. (2007). The changing landscape of special education administration. *Exceptionality, 15*(3), 139–142. doi:10.1080/09362830701503487

Crockett, J. B. (2011). Conceptual models for leading and administrating special education. In J. M. Kauffman & D. P. Hallahan (Eds.), *Handbook of special education*. New York, NY: Routledge.

Crockett, J. B., Becker, M. K., & Quinn, D. (2009). Reviewing the knowledge base of special education leadership and administration from 1970-2009. *Journal of Special Education Leadership, 22*(2), 55–67.

Crockett, J. B., Billingsley, B. S., & Boscardin, M. L. (Eds.). (2012). *Handbook of leadership and administration for special education*. New York, NY: Routledge.

Datnow, A. (2006). Comments on Michael Fullan's "The future of educational change: System thinkers in action". *Journal of Educational Change, 7*(3), 133–135. doi:10.100710833-006-0005-4

Detgen, A., Yamashita, M., Davis, B., & Wraight, S. (2011). State policies and procedures on response to intervention in the Midwest Region. U.S. Department of Education, Institute of Education Sciences, National Center for Education Evaluation and Regional Assistance, Regional Education Laboratory Midwest.

Dillman, D. A., Smyth, J. D., & Christian, L. M. (2009). *Internet, mail, and mixed-mode surveys: The tailored design method* (3rd ed.). Hoboken, NJ: Wiley.

Duke, D. (2004). *The challenges of educational change*. Boston, MA: Pearson Education, Inc.

Edgehouse, M. A., Edwards, A., Gore, S., Harrison, S., & Zimmerman, J. (2007). Initiating and leading change: A consideration of four new models. *The Catalyst, 36*(2), 3–12.

Elliott, J., & Morrison, D. (2008). *Reponse to intervention blueprints: District level edition*. Alexandria, VA: National Association of State Directors of Special Education.

Ellsworth, J. B. (2000). *Surviving change: A survey of educational change models*. Syracuse, NY: ERIC Clearinghouse on Information and Technology.

Ervin, R. A., Schaughency, E., Goodman, S. D., McGlinchey, M. T., & Matthews, A. (2007). Moving from a model demonstration project to a statewide initiative in Michigan: Lessons learned from merging research-based agendas to address reading and behavior. In S. R. Jimerson, M. K. Burns, & A. M. VanDerHeyden (Eds.), *Handbook of response to intervention*. New York, NY: Springer. doi:10.1007/978-0-387-49053-3_27

Fanning, E. (2005). Formatting a paper-based survey questionnaire: Best practices. *Practical Assessment, Research & Evaluation, 10*(12).

Fink, D., & Stoll, L. (2005). Educational change: Easier said than done. In A. Hargreaves (Ed.), *Extending educational change* (pp. 17–41). New York, NY: Springer. doi:10.1007/1-4020-4453-4_2

Fletcher, J. M., Denton, C., & Francis, D. J. (2005). Validity of alternative approaches for the identification of learning disabilities: Operationalizing unexpected underachievement. *Journal of Learning Disabilities, 38*(6), 545–552. doi:10.1177/00222194050380061101 PMID:16392697

Fletcher, J. M., & Vaughn, S. (2009). Response to intervention: Preventing and remediating academic difficulties. *Child Development Perspectives, 3*(1), 30–37. doi:10.1111/j.1750-8606.2008.00072.x PMID:21765862

Fraenkel, J. R., & Wallen, N. E. (2006). *How to design and evaluate research in education* (6th ed.). New York, NY: McGraw-Hill.

Fuchs, D., & Fuchs, L. S. (2008). Implementing RTI: Response-to-intervention is an ambitious and complex process that requires administrators choose the right model. *District Administration, 44,* 73–76.

Fuchs, D., Fuchs, L. S., & Compton, D. L. (2004). Identifying reading disabilities by responsiveness-to-instruction: Specifying measures and criteria. *Learning Disability Quarterly, 27*(4), 216–227. doi:10.2307/1593674

Fuchs, D., Fuchs, L. S., & Compton, D. L. (2012). Smart RTI: A next-generation approach to multilevel prevention. *Exceptional Children, 78*(3), 263–279. doi:10.1177/001440291207800301 PMID:22736805

Fuchs, L. S., & Fuchs, D. (2007). A model for implementing responsiveness to intervention. *Teaching Exceptional Children, 39*(5), 14–20. doi:10.1177/004005990703900503

Fuchs, L. S., & Vaughn, S. (2012). Responsiveness-to-intervention: A decade later. *Journal of Learning Disabilities, 45*(3), 195–203. doi:10.1177/0022219412442150 PMID:22539056

Fullan, M. (2001). *Leading in a culture of change* (1st ed.). San Francisco, CA: Jossey-Bass.

Fullan, M. (2006). The future of educational change: System thinkers in action. *Journal of Educational Change, 7*(3), 113–122. doi:10.100710833-006-9003-9

Gresham, F. M. (2007). Evolution of the response-to-intervention concept: Empirical foundations. In S. R. Jimerson, M. K. Burns, & A. M. VanDerHeyden (Eds.), *Handbook of response to intervention*. New York, NY: Springer. doi:10.1007/978-0-387-49053-3_2

Hackett, J. (2010). Developing state regulations to implement the response-to-intervention requirements of IDEA: The Illinois plan. *Perspectives on Language and Literacy, 36*(2), 36–39.

Hamel, G. (2000). *Leading the revolution*. Boston, MA: Harvard Business School Press.

Hargreaves, A. (2005). Pushing the boundaries of educational change. In A. Hargreaves (Ed.), *Extending educational change* (pp. 1–16). New York, NY: Springer. doi:10.1007/1-4020-4453-4_1

Harlacher, J. E., & Siler, C. E. (2011). Factors related to successful RTI implementation. *Communique, 39,* 20–22.

Hollenbeck, A. F. (2007). From IDEA to implementation: A discussion of foundational and future responsiveness-to-intervention research. *Learning Disabilities Research & Practice, 22*(2), 137–146. doi:10.1111/j.1540-5826.2007.00238.x

Hopkins, D. (2005). Tensions in and prospects for school improvement. In D. Hopkins (Ed.), *Practice and theory of school improvement* (pp. 1–21). New York, NY: Springer. doi:10.1007/1-4020-4452-6_1

House, E. R., & McQuillan, P. J. (2005). Three perspective on school reform. In A. Lieberman (Ed.), *The roots of educational change* (pp. 186–201). New York, NY: Springer. doi:10.1007/1-4020-4451-8_11

Hughes, C. A., & Dexter, D. D. (2011). Response to intervention: A research-based summary. *Theory into Practice, 50*(1), 4–11. doi:10.1080/00405841.2011.534909

Individuals With Disabilities Education Act, 20 U.S.C. § 1400 (2004).

Jenkins, J. R., Hudson, R. F., & Johnson, E. S. (2007). Screening for at-risk readers in a response to intervention framework. *School Psychology Review, 36*(4), 582–600.

Kavale, K. A., Kauffman, J. M., Bachmeier, R. J., & LeFever, G. B. (2008). Response-to-intervention: Seperating the rhetoric of self-congratulation from the reality of specific learning disability identification. *Learning Disability Quarterly, 31*(3), 135–150.

Knotek, S. E. (2007). Consultation within response to intervention models. In S. R. Jimerson, M. K. Burns, & A. M. VanDerHeyden (Eds.), *Handbook of respoonse to intervention*. New York, NY: Springer. doi:10.1007/978-0-387-49053-3_4

Kotter, J. (1996). *Leading change*. Boston, MA: Harvard Business School Press.

Kovaleski, J. F. (2007). Potential pitfalls of response to intervention. In S. R. Jimerson, M. K. Burns, & A. M. VanDerHeyden (Eds.), *Handbook of response to intervention*. New York: Springer. doi:10.1007/978-0-387-49053-3_6

Kratochwill, T. R., Clements, M. A., & Kalymon, K. M. (2007). Response to intervention: Conceptual and methodological issues in implementation. In S. R. Jimerson, M. K. Burns, & A. M. VanDerHeyden (Eds.), *Handbook of response to intervention*. New York, NY: Springer. doi:10.1007/978-0-387-49053-3_3

Lashley, C., & Boscardin, M. L. (2003). Special education administration at a crossroads. *Journal of Special Education Leadership, 16*(2), 63–75.

Marston, D. (2005). Tiers of intervention in responsiveness to intervention: Prevention outcomes and learning disabilities identification patterns. *Journal of Learning Disabilities, 38*(6), 539–544. doi:10.1177/00222194050380061001 PMID:16392696

McHatton, P.A., Gordon, K.D., & Glenn, T.L., & Sue. (2012). Troubling special education leadership: Finding purpose, potential, and possibility in challenging contexts. *Journal of Special Education Leadership, 25*(1), 38–47.

McMaster, K. L., & Wagner, D. (2007). Monitoring response to general education instruction. In S. R. Jimerson, M. K. Burns, & A. M. VanDerHeyden (Eds.), *Handbook of response to intervention*. New York, NY: Springer. doi:10.1007/978-0-387-49053-3_16

Mellard, D. F., Deshler, D. D., & Barth, A. (2004). LD identification: It's not simply a matter of building a better mousetrap. *Learning Disability Quarterly, 27*(4), 229–242. doi:10.2307/1593675

Mellard, D. F., Stern, A., & Woods, K. (2011). RTI school-based practices and evidence-based models. *Focus on Exceptional Children, 43*(6), 1–15.

O'Connor, E. P., & Freeman, E. W. (2012). District-level considerations in supporting and sustaining RtI implementation. *Psychology in the Schools, 49*(3), 297–310. doi:10.1002/pits.21598

Passman, B. (2008). Case in point: Knowledge, skills, and dispositions. *Journal of Special Education Leadership, 21*(1), 46–47.

Pazey, B. L., & Yates, J. R. (2012). Conceptual and historical foundations of special education administration. In J. B. Crockett, B. S. Billingsley, & M. L. Boscardin (Eds.), *Handbook of leadership and administration of special education* (pp. 17–36). New York, NY: Routledge.

Sansosti, F. J., Goss, S., & Noltemeyer, A. (2011). Perspectives of special education directors on response to intervention in secondary schools. *Contemporary School Psychology*, 9-20.

Sansosti, F. J., & Noltemeyer, A. (2008). Viewing response-to-intervention through an educational change paradigm: What can we learn? *California School Psychologist*, *13*(1), 55–66. doi:10.1007/BF03340942

Skyttner, L. (2005). *General systems theory: Problems, persepctives, and practice* (2nd ed.). Hackensack, NJ: World Scientific Publishing Co.

Stoll, L. (2006). The future of educational change: System thinkers in action: Response to Michael Fullan. *Journal of Educational Change*, *7*(3), 123–127. doi:10.100710833-006-0004-5

Tilly, W. D. (2002). Best practices in school psychology as a problem as a problem-solving enterprise. In A. Thomas & J. Grimes (Eds.), *Best practices in school psychology* (Vol. 4, pp. 21–36). Bethesda, MD: National Association of School Psychologists.

Voltz, D. L., & Collins, L. (2010). Preparing special education administrators for inclusion in diverse, standards-based contexts: Beyond the council for exceptional children and the Interstate School Leaders Licensure Consortium. *Teacher Education and Special Education*, *33*(1), 70–82. doi:10.1177/0888406409356676

Werts, M. G., Lambert, M., & Carpenter, E. (2009). What special education directors say about RTI. *Learning Disability Quarterly*, *32*(4), 245–254. doi:10.2307/27740376

Whitten, E., Esteves, K. J., & Woodrow, A. (2009). *RTI success: Proven tools and strategies for schools and classrooms*. Minneapolis, MN: Free Spirit.

Wiener, R. M., & Soodak, L. C. (2008). Special education administrators' perspectives on response to intervention. *Journal of Special Education Leadership*, *21*(1), 39–45.

Wigle, S. E., & Wilcox, D. J. (2002). Special education directors and their competencies on CEC-identified skills. *Education*, *123*(2), 276–288.

Yell, M. L., & Walker, D. W. (2010). The legal basis of response to intervention: Analysis and implications. *Exceptionality*, *18*(3), 124–137. doi:10.1080/09362835.2010.491741

Zirkel, P. A., & Thomas, L. B. (2010). State laws and guidelines implementing RTI. *Teaching Exceptional Children*, *43*(1), 60–73. doi:10.1177/004005991004300107

KEY TERMS AND DEFINITIONS

Fullan's Framework for Leadership: This framework defines the process in which leaders can address change themes that will result in effective leadership (Fullan, 2001).

Implementation: "The process of achieving intended change" (Duke, 2004, p. 158).

Implementation of Response to Intervention: The process of putting systematic supports and structures, often organized into successive components or steps, into place to establish a comprehensive model of Response to Intervention. This primarily takes place at the school district level, but may also include a focus on individual school buildings (Elliott & Morrison, 2008; O'Connor & Freeman, 2012).

Individuals with Disabilities Education Act (IDEA) of 2004: Federal law that influences education regarding the determination of individuals with disabilities using response to intervention (Yell & Walker, 2010).

Response to Intervention: The practice of (1) providing high-quality instruction/intervention matched to student needs and (2) using learning rate over time and level of performance to (3) make important education decisions (Batsche et al., 2005).

Special Education: Instruction that is specifically designed, at no cost to parents, to address the unique needs of a child with a disability to ensure access to and progress toward the general education curriculum ("Individuals With Disabilities Education Act," 2004).

Special Education Administrator: A school administrator whose primary responsibility is leading, supervising, and managing the delivery of special education and related services (Crockett, 2007).

Student with a Disability: A child having mental retardation, a hearing impairment, a speech or language impairment, a visual impairment, an emotional disturbance, an orthopedic impairment, autism, a traumatic brain injury, an other health impairment, a specific learning disability, deaf-blindness, or multiple disabilities needing special education and related services ("Individuals With Disabilities Education Act," 2004).

This research was previously published in the Handbook of Research on Individualism and Identity in the Globalized Digital Age edited by F. Sigmund Topor; pages 265-286, copyright year 2017 by Information Science Reference (an imprint of IGI Global).

Chapter 8
Leveraging Professional Development to Prepare General and Special Education Teachers to Teach within Response to Intervention Frameworks

Amber Elizabeth Benedict
University of Florida, USA

Mary T. Brownell
University of Florida, USA

Cynthia C. Griffin
University of Florida, USA

Jun Wang
University of Florida, USA

Jonte A Myers
University of Florida, USA

ABSTRACT

This chapter examines the role professional development (PD) plays in preparing teachers to teach within Response to Intervention (RTI) frameworks, and how future PD efforts might be leveraged to strengthen the preparation of general and special education teachers to coordinate instruction and teach more effectively within multi-tiered instructional systems. This chapter highlights two PD approaches that directly address these issues. Prime Online and Project InSync are two PD innovations that have specifically addressed how PD can be designed to support general and special education teachers in deepening their shared knowledge and improving their ability to enact coordinated instruction across instructional tiers within RTI frameworks.

DOI: 10.4018/978-1-7998-1213-5.ch008

INTRODUCTION

Response to Intervention (RTI), a framework for improving instruction for all students, particularly those with academic and behavioral needs (Berkeley, Bender, Peaster, & Saunders, 2011; Detgen, Yamashita, Davis, & Wraight, 2011; Zirkel, 2011). RTI, also referred to as Multi-tiered Systems of Support (MTSS), involves a tiered instructional approach to prevention and intervention, and has evolved, in large part, as a result of concerns about the over-identification of students with disabilities due to poor instruction and inappropriate curriculum (e.g., Burns, Appleton, & Stehouwer, 2006; Lennon & Slesinski, 1999). According to the National Center on Response to Intervention [NCRI], effective prevention depends on high quality general education core instruction (i.e., tier 1) that is designed based on ongoing collection and analysis of student data and empirical research on instruction (see http://www.rti4sucess.org/). When tier 1 instruction is insufficient for supporting student learning, as determined through progress monitoring and data analysis, then students receive increasingly intensive academic and behavioral supplemental support according to their documented need in tier 2 instruction. General education teachers typically provide tier 2 instruction; however, if despite that support students continues to struggle, according to ongoing data collection and outcomes, then students receive tier 3 instruction, which is usually provided by the special education teachers. As students progress through the tiers, the instruction becomes more intensive and tailored to students' individual learning needs.

For each tier to promote student learning, instruction must focus on critical content, and evidence-based practices (e.g., Johnson, Mellard, Fuchs, & McKnight, 2006; RTI Action Network, 2009). For example, in a recent large scale efficacy trial, Gersten and colleagues (2015) found that students receiving instruction in tier 1, performing at the 35th percentile or lower, made significant gains on a standardized assessment after receiving teacher directed, systematic, small group instruction with extensive teacher feedback on whole number concepts and operations delivered in small groups, they made significant gains on a standardized assessment, and the effect size was moderate (effect size, $g = .34$). Other studies reveal that for teachers to use evidence-based supplemental instruction alone is insufficient without instructional coordination across tiers, as students remain in tier 1 while also receiving supplemental tier 2 or tier 3 instruction (Fuchs et al., 2008; Wonder-McDowell, Reutzel, & Smith, 2011). Moreover, when teachers provided evidence-based tier 1 instruction and supplemental instruction that was coordinated across the content taught, evidence based practices (EBPs) used, and assessment administered, students at risk for reading and mathematics failure made greater academic gains than when such instruction was absent. The studies described here and numerous others have shown that when RTI is implemented effectively, the approach can improve outcomes for students at risk for academic failure, reduce inappropriate identification for special education services, and improve the academic achievement of both struggling learners and those with learning disabilities (for a review see Klingner et al., in press).

Due to RTI's success as a research-based approach to identifying students with learning disabilities (LD), and supporting students who struggle to achieve, RTI was legitimized in the 2004 reauthorization of the Individuals with Disabilities Education Act (IDEA) as one approach that may be used by states to identify and serve students with disabilities. State education agencies across the country interested in improving the education of their students with disabilities and preventing the inappropriate identification of students are undertaking efforts to implement RTI. In 2011, Zirkel found that 46 states had language about RTI in their laws or guidelines. Further, in an implementation study conducted nationwide, 49 states were found to have some type of RTI commission, task force, or internal working group (Bradley, Daley, Levin, O'Reilly, Parsard, Robertson, & Werner, 2011). Clearly, states see the importance of RTI

Leveraging Professional Development to Prepare General and Special Education Teachers

for improving learning for students who struggle academically and behaviorally, and teacher educators and researchers want to ensure that professional development (PD) is designed to address teachers' current instructional contexts.

In this chapter, we examine what RTI demands of teachers, and discuss the role PD plays in preparing teachers to teach within an RTI framework. Specifically, we ponder the knowledge and skills teachers need for providing effective instruction within a RTI framework, and summarize what we have learned about the features of effective PD that could support the development of such knowledge and skills. We conclude the chapter with two PD innovations that are configured specifically to capture what we know about effective PD but also deliberately attend to the ways in which PD might be delivered to improve general and special education teachers' abilities to teach within an RTI framework.

WHAT DOES RTI DEMAND OF TEACHERS?

For general and special education teachers to work within a RTI framework, they need considerable knowledge and skills, particularly in the areas of reading, content area literacy, and mathematics, as these subjects pose some of the greatest barriers to the academic of learning of students with LD (Geary, 2004; Swanson & Jerman, 2006; Swanson & Saez, 2003). Research, however, has not yet revealed how to best support the development of those necessary knowledge and skill. Most studies conducted on effective RTI implementation have relied on research assistants and teachers trained to implement curriculum designed by researchers (e.g., (e.g., Burns & Symington, 2002; Fuchs et al., 2008). Although these studies have yielded positive results and clear ideas about instructional methods that help students with LD achieve, they do not help us understand how general and special education teachers working with district-provided curricula can learn to implement RTI instruction effectively. In research studies, RTI curricular materials are designed with effective implementation of evidence-based practices and instructional coordination across the different tiers in mind (e.g., Fuchs et al., 2008; Wonder-McDowell, Reutzel, & Smith, 2010), but in reality, many teachers do not work with well designed, cohesive curricula (Hawkins & Riley, 2008).

"America's love affair with local control and teacher autonomy has made curricular coherence a low priority" (Hawkins & Riley, 2008, p. 407). Many districts select commercially available curricula without considering to which degree these materials integrate an evidence-based approach to instruction or without considering how tier 2 and 3 curricula are coordinated with core curricula (Hill, King, Lemons, & Partanen, 2012). Under these conditions, general and special education teachers working together in a RTI framework are left largely to their own devices to determine a) when to integrate evidence-based strategies into the core curriculum, and b) how to design supplemental instruction for tiers 2 and 3 that builds on tier 1 instruction, is responsive to students' needs, and includes opportunities for pre-teaching and re-teaching.

To craft such coordinated, evidence-based instruction requires considerable knowledge and skills on the part of the teachers. Not only do general and special education teachers require knowledge of EBPs and the skill to implement them, they also must have extensive knowledge of the curriculum, as well as students' learning needs in literacy and mathematics (Benedict, Park, Brownell, Lauterbach, & Kiely, 2013; Brownell et al., 2012). As an illustration, consider Kate, a general education teacher, and Paige, a special education teacher working together within a fourth grade RTI framework. After analyzing data on the students' performance to tier 1 instruction, Kate and Paige realize that some of their struggling learners need to learn more powerful comprehension strategies, so Kate recommends using an EBP she learned about in her preservice teacher education reading course, Collaborative Strategic Reading (CSR). One of the steps of this strategy involves "Getting the Gist" or describing what the passage is mainly about. Kate knows that narrative text is more difficult to summarize than expository text since expository text often includes headers and has more clear topic sentences than narrative text. Consequently, Kate decides initially to model "Getting the Gist" by using expository text during whole group instruction administered in core. However, some of these students require further support. Fortunately, these students also work with Paige in tier 3 small group instruction. Paige understands that these students will need explicit instruction in summarizing if they are going to participate effectively in Kate's core instruction. Thus, in small group, Paige models steps for students that can be employed by those students to summarize the passages and helps them practice to mastery. Additionally, the oral reading fluency and word analysis skill assessments collected by Paige indicates that her students receiving tier 3 instruction need strategies for decoding and understanding multisyllabic words. Thus, Paige also provides explicit instruction in a decoding strategy designed to help students unpack multisyllabic words and decode them, and provides explicit instruction in helping students build words with prefixes and suffixes.

The example of Kate and Paige illustrates much of the knowledge and skill required for general and special education teachers to navigate and effectively deliver the typical 4th grade curriculum, while teaching within a RTI framework. Kate and Paige understand how reading proficiency develops and what types of skills and strategies students need to learn in fourth grade. They also understand the curriculum and the challenges it presents to their students, thereby allowing them to select materials most appropriate for teaching students the CSR strategy. Finally, Paige coordinates with Kate to develop more intensive instruction that would allow students to implement the CSR strategy effectively while reading connected text. Such knowledge and skill is not easily developed without carefully crafted, effective PD, a topic to which we now turn.

EFFECTIVE PROFESSIONAL DEVELOPMENT

What characterizes PD that impacts teacher knowledge and subsequently teachers' instructional practice as well as the outcomes of their students? Although much has been written about effective PD, the science supporting this literature is insufficient. Largely, the research on PD is qualitative, investigating how teachers' understandings or beliefs develop as a result of PD (e.g., Lewis, Perry, Hurd, & O'Connell, 2006; Shank, 2006; Stewart & Brendefur, 2005; Wood, 2007). Fewer studies have examined, using quasi-experimental or experimental methods, the impact of PD approaches has on quantitative measures of teacher knowledge, instructional practice, or student achievement or the linkages among these variables (Gersten, Taylor, Keys, Rolfhus, & Newman-Gonchar, 2014; Yoon, Duncan, Lee, Scarloss, & Shapley, 2007). In this section, we summarize key findings from quantitative research that investigates the impact of PD innovations on teacher and student outcomes. We focus our efforts on studies designed to improve teachers' knowledge and instructional skill in reading and mathematics, as these areas are typically the focus of RTI instruction. To the extent possible, we rely on findings of three key literature reviews, two of which were conducted for the Institute of Education Sciences (Gersten et al., 2014; Hill, 2012; Yoon et al., 2007). In addition, we integrated recent studies of content-focused PD that impact teacher and student outcomes (Bell, Wilson, Higgins, & McCoach, 2010; Bianscarosa & Dexter, 2010; Connor, Alberto, Compton, & O'Connor, 2014; Gersten et al., 2010; Hough et al., 2013; McCutchen et al.,

2002; McCutchen, Green et al., 2009; McMeeking, Orsi, & Cobb, 2012), and one of which that met the inclusion criteria that specifically examining the impact of research-based PD on the knowledge and instructional practices of teachers of students with disabilities (Brownell et al., 2013)..

Identifying themes from the research on effective PD that could be used to guide the development of future efforts in this area is challenging. The conceptual underpinnings of the various PD innovations vary widely from one study to the next; thus, it is difficult to draw conclusions about the characteristics of effective PD innovations. These variations reflect different assumptions about how one learns to become an effective teacher that may or may not be explicitly articulated. Some PD innovations focus the majority of their time on helping teachers learn how to implement specific strategies with far less attention to helping them understand the conceptual foundations of the intervention or the content knowledge needed for implementing the intervention successfully. Innovations focused on implementation seem more focused on changing teacher behavior or instructional practice than they are aimed at increasing the underlying knowledge teachers will need to support the appropriate use of the innovation. This view of learning to teach is a dominant one in special education, especially in PD approaches using expert-based coaching (e.g., Greenwood Tapia, Abbott, & Walton 2003; Kretlow, Wood, & Cooke, 2011). Other PD innovations place stronger emphasis on helping teachers acquire knowledge of the content, pedagogical skill in teaching the content, and an understanding of how students learn the content. These researchers assume that teachers learn to be more effective by acquiring a sort of specialized content knowledge – the type of knowledge teachers have about the content that allows them to enact it for their students (e.g., McCutchen, Abbott et al., 2002; McCutchen, Green, Abbott, & Sanders, 2009; Gersten, Dimino, Jayanthi, Kim, & Santoro, 2010). These two examples of how PD innovations vary in terms of their conceptual underpinnings make clear why it is difficult to compare effective PD innovations and draw conclusions about commonalities.

Despite such conceptual diversity, effective PD innovations that impact on teachers' knowledge, classroom practice, and student achievement, do share common features. They tend to be: a) multi-faceted, often combining two or more approaches to improving teachers' knowledge and instructional practice, b) intensive in terms of the quantity of time teachers are involved, and c) supportive in that they help teachers learn to implement new instructional practices and often analyze students' thinking and achievement growth. Additionally, those PD innovations that promoted gains in teachers' knowledge were content-focused; that is, they attend to deepening teachers' content knowledge and understandings of how they might enact that knowledge for students.

Multi-Faceted

Effective PD innovations included multiple components for improving teacher learning, such as some sort of course or institute where teachers focused on the content of the PD innovation combined with instructional coaching. As an example, Bianscarosa, and Dexter (2010) and Hough et al., (2013) investigated gains in teachers' instructional practice and their students' reading achievement after participation in the Literacy Collaborative, a PD innovation that involved a comprehensive approach to teaching reading and writing. The Literacy Collaborative involved a 40-hour upfront institute, 10 to 12 hours of follow-up training offered annually thereafter, and ongoing instructional coaching to support implementation of direct and embedded instruction in phonics, phonological awareness, vocabulary, word structure, fluent reading, and literal, inferential and critical thinking about text. Extensively trained literacy coaches worked individually with teachers, modeling for them, observing their instruction, and providing feedback.

In a three-year longitudinal study, Hough and colleagues (2013) showed that teachers participating in the Literacy Collaborative demonstrated more effective instructional practices when they had more exposure to coaching. Additionally, Biancarosa and colleagues (2010) used a hierarchical, crossed-level, value-added effects model to compare literacy learning over a 3-year period of Literacy Collaborative implementation. Using this analysis, they compared growth in student achievement from baseline to treatment. Results of the analysis reveal that the treatment effect for the intervention was .22 in the first year, .37 in the second, and .43 in the third, and the benefits of the treatment persisted during the fourth year, demonstrating the lasting effects of the Literacy Collaborative were maintained by the teachers over the summer from year-to-year.

Other multi-faceted PD innovations in special education, reading, science and mathematics have also indicated that such comprehensive, multi-faceted efforts accrue benefits in terms of gains in teacher knowledge and instructional practice as well as gains in student achievement (e.g., Brownell et al., 2013; Connor, Alberto, Compton, & O'Connor, 2014; Scher & O'Reilly, 2009). Brownell and colleagues (2013) randomly assigned groups of special education teachers to Literacy Learning Cohorts or a two-day PD institute that focused on word study and fluency. Teachers in the Literacy Learning Cohort received two days of content-focused PD. In addition, they participated in six monthly cohort meetings, were taught to reflect on videos of their instruction, and discussed their observations with a coach who worked with them to identify areas for improvement. Teachers participating in the Literacy Learning Cohort made significant gains in their word study and fluency instruction compared to teachers in the two-day PD institute alone, and hierarchical linear model analyses revealed that students of Literacy Learning Cohort teachers made significant gains in their word attack skills and decoding efficiency compared to students of teachers in the control group. This study and others suggest that if RTI is to be successful in improving teachers' knowledge and instructional skill, then teachers will need access to comprehensive and multi-faceted PD approaches.

What these studies do not make clear though is the type of multi-faceted support that is necessary. The PD innovations in the research literature vary considerably in terms of underlying assumptions about teacher learning. For instance, some studies assume that teachers can learn to use new knowledge through ongoing dialogue and analysis of their instructional practice and student learning (e.g., Gersten et al., 2010), and others assume that teachers will need opportunities to collaboratively discuss implementation and analyze student data with their peers and receive support from expert coaches to use evidence-based strategies in their classroom (Brownell et al., 2013). Clearly, further research comparing different types of PD approaches within a content area will be necessary if we are to better understand the most effective and efficient ways of helping general and special education teachers acquire the knowledge and instructional skill they need to support all learners throughout an RTI framework.

Extensive in Duration

Teachers need considerable time to fully integrate newly acquired knowledge and skills learned through professional learning experiences into practice. PD innovations found to be most effective at promoting the learning of teachers and their students are intensive in nature, providing teachers ample time to learn new content and integrate it into their instructional repertoire. Exactly how much time is necessary for teachers to engage in structured PD experiences in order to see evidence of changes in teachers' knowledge and instructional practice, or student achievement? The answer is more time than many teachers are provided by their districts within a typical school year. Yoon and colleagues (2007) reviewed the literature examining the impact of teachers' professional learning experiences on student achievement. They found that teachers who received substantial PD – an average of 49 hours in duration – boosted the academic performance of their students by nearly 21 percentile points. In addition, closer examination of effective PD innovations reveals that these innovations are also distributed over a 12 or more-month timeline. Ensuring that teachers not only have adequate time to familiarize themselves with new content upfront, but also spaced opportunities to practice to support teachers in integrating the newly acquired knowledge and skills into classroom practice.

Since the publication of Yoon and colleagues' report, additional research has confirmed these findings. All of the studies examined in this chapter engage teachers in PD experiences for extended periods of time. Some of the most extensive PD approaches involved helping teachers learn a rather substantial amount of technical content along with strategies for enacting that knowledge. For example, McCutchen, Green, et al. (2009) engaged 3rd, 4th, and 5th grade teachers in a 10-day summer institute to deepen their knowledge of phonology, orthography, and morphology as it relates to decoding and understanding words and reading them within connected text. The institute also provided teachers extensive training in strategies they could use for promoting students' word knowledge and support for helping teachers analyze students' knowledge of phonology and orthography by teaching them to analyze children's miscues and spelling errors. Following the institute were three full day follow-up sessions where content from the summer institute was reviewed and strategy implementation problems were addressed. In addition, McCutchen and colleagues regularly visited teachers' classrooms to observe teachers' use of strategies, consult with them about implementation issues, and assist with student assessment.

After participation in the PD, teachers significantly increased their linguistic knowledge compared to the control group teachers. Teachers' linguistic knowledge was correlated with student achievement gains. Multilevel analysis demonstrated a significant relationship between teacher knowledge and student achievement in vocabulary, narrative composition, and word attack, and the relationship was stronger for the lowest achieving students in the treatment group. Additionally, the amount of time that teachers dedicated to explicit vocabulary instruction correlated with improvements in lower performing students' spelling outcomes. This randomized control study demonstrates that intensive PD focused on deepening teachers' content knowledge is critical for improving teachers' literacy instruction, especially for teachers providing instruction for struggling learners.

McCutchen and colleagues (2009) findings have been replicated in almost all PD studies that demonstrate an effect on teacher and/or student outcomes (e.g., Bell, Wilson, Higgins, & McCoach, 2010; McMeeking, Orsi, & Cobb, 2012). Unfortunately, few teachers receive access to the intensive and sustained professional learning experiences required to promote changes and knowledge and practices necessary to move the needle on student learning (Hill, 2009; Sindelar, Brownell, & Billingsley, 2010). Wei, Darling-Hammond, and Adamson (2010) reported that according to responses on the 2003-2004 Schools and Staffing Survey only 23 percent of teachers received 33 or more days of PD in the content they taught. These scholars went on to criticize the current status of PD support for teachers in American schools stating that:

The intensity and duration of professional development offered to U.S. teachers is not at the level that research suggests is necessary to have noticeable impacts on instruction and student learning. While many teachers get a day or two of professional development on various topics each year, very few have the chance to study any aspect of teaching for more than two days. Most of their professional learning does not meet the threshold needed to produce strong effects on practice or student learning. (p. 20)

Clearly, the current status of PD in America is insufficient for improving instruction in general, and in particular, inadequate for the encouraging the coordinated use of knowledge general and special education teachers will need to implement RTI instruction effectively.

Implementation Support

In addition to a sufficient amount of time, effective PD innovations support teachers in enacting PD content in their classroom contexts. Our examination of the research revealed that the most successful PD efforts provided implementation supports at minimum on a monthly basis, if not more frequently. Usually these supports involved assistance to teachers in reviewing content and practices introduced initially in some type of PD institute or coursework where teachers experienced intensive knowledge development activities (Blank & de las Alas, 2009; Hill, 2012). Examples of implementation support include coaching, mentoring, professional learning communities, and study groups (e.g., Gersten et al., 2010; Brownell et al., 2013; Vescio, Ross, & Adams, 2008).

To illustrate, Gersten and colleagues (2010) formed a teacher study group as a means of supporting and sustaining teacher learning. In a randomized control field trial, they determined the impact of 16 interactive teacher study group sessions, each 75 minutes in duration, on first grade teachers' implementation of evidence-based decoding, vocabulary, and comprehension instruction. The teacher study group process was informal in nature, and was designed to foster discussion and collaboration among teachers through a recursive process. Steps of the process included: (a) debriefing about previous implementation experiences; (b) discussions of new PD content introduced in a text on effective vocabulary instruction; (c) collective review a lesson plan developed in core curriculum; and (d) collaborative revision of the curriculum plan to integrate newly learned EBPs. The teacher study group sessions assisted teachers in tailoring newly acquired content knowledge and practices to their unique instructional context. Results from the multilevel analyses indicated that the teachers participating in the teacher study group scored 0.86 standard deviations higher on the comprehension measure and 0.58 standard deviations higher on the vocabulary measure than teachers in the control group schools. Correlational analyses were used to explore the relationship between observation scores teachers' assessing quality for teaching vocabulary and comprehension instruction and students' academic growth. The researchers found several significant, moderately sized partial correlations between teacher knowledge, teacher practices, and student achievement. Confirmatory analysis of student performance demonstrated marginally significant effects in oral vocabulary for students whose teachers participated in the teacher study group sessions compared to students whose teachers were assigned to the control condition.

Content Focused

Numerous studies have established that effective PD focuses on how students learn content and strategies for promoting student learning of the content (e.g., Cohen & Hill, 2001; Gersten et al., 2010; McCutchen, Abbott et al., 2002; McCutchen, Green et al., 2009). McMeeking, Orsi and Cobb's (2012) demonstrated how content-focused PD could improve teachers' instructional practice and student achievement. Employing a quasi-experimental cohort control group design, they investigated the impact of a three-year, intensive mathematics PD innovation on changes in teacher knowledge and instructional practice, and gains in student achievement. Teachers participated in nine content-focused mathematics courses offered through two to three-week institutes. In addition, teachers received supplementary support through four

Saturday follow-up units over the course of a semester designed to review content previously addressed over the summer. Content included pedagogical practices for teaching math, techniques for differentiating instruction, and specific strategies for supporting English language learners.

McMeeking and colleagues (2012) found that providing mathematics teachers extensive and content-focused opportunities to learn resulted in statistically significant improvements in students' mathematical achievement. The more mathematics PD courses the teachers participated in, the greater the impact on student learning. Using an odds ratio estimate to calculate the effect of the treatment, the researchers found that when a teacher participated in one PD mathematics course, the odds improvement difference between their students and those students of teachers who did not participate in this coursework was 1.29, though this comparison was not significant. However, when teachers engaged in more than two PD courses, the difference between participating in two or more PD courses versus none was 1.95 and significant. That is to say, teachers who participated in two more PD courses were almost twice as likely to have students who made gains in mathematics achievement when compared to those students whose teachers did not participate in these PD courses.

PD Approaches That Improve Teachers' Abilities to Operate Within RTI Frameworks

The effective PD innovations discussed thus far can be characterized as multi-faceted, extensive in terms of time, supportive in terms of implementation, and content-focused. Studies of PD innovations that meet these criteria have been associated with positive gains in teachers' knowledge and instructional practice. Further, in some of the studies, student outcomes improve. Despite the promise of these approaches, not one of these studies deliberately addresses the issue of how to support general and special education teachers in designing, coordinating, and implementing evidence-based instruction within a RTI framework. In this section, we describe two PD innovations specifically designed to enable general and special education teachers to develop essential knowledge and skills for delivering effective instruction within RTI frameworks. The first innovation, *Prime Online*, illustrates how including general and special education teachers in shared professional learning opportunities improved their ability to meet the needs of all learners, including those with LD and mathematics difficulties. The second innovation, *Project InSync*, also includes both general and special education teachers. Like *Prime Online*, *Project InSync* provides opportunities for general and special education teachers to develop shared knowledge, however, the innovation's use of lesson study, a collaborative planning and analysis process, also offers a structure for helping teachers learn to coordinate their instruction across the various instructional tiers of RTI.

Prime Online: Promoting a Shared Knowledge Base

Prime Online PD program (Griffin et al., 2014) is a multi-faceted innovation designed to support the learning of general and special education teachers providing instruction to students who struggled to learn mathematics through online teacher PD. *Prime Online* aimed to deepen teachers' pedagogical content knowledge in mathematics and their ability to meet the learning needs of students with LD and other struggling learners receiving instruction within tiers 1 and 2 of the RTI framework. *Prime Online's* innovative use of online teacher learning allowed for teachers engaged in tier 1 and tier 2 mathematics instruction to collaborate with peers at other sites to collectively analyze student data and discuss problems of practice through online discussion forums. A study of *Prime Online* was conducted involving 23 Florida teachers and their students in 3rd through 5th grade mathematics across one state.

In addition to the content-focus, *Prime Online* provided teachers with considerable implementation support over time. *Prime Online* was developed using an online learning software program (i.e., Moodle; Dougiamas, 1999) and delivered over one calendar year (May through April) with breaks in the program aligned with a teacher's school schedule. The PD program consisted of 35 learning modules, each taking approximately one week for the teachers to complete. Learning modules included a consistent format with four components: (1) Introduction, (2) Anticipatory Activity, (3) Content and Discussion, and (4) Classroom Connections. The *Introduction* offered an overview of the week's activities, goals, objectives, and references to materials needed to complete learning tasks. The *Anticipatory Activity* helped teachers reflect on and connect their prior experiences and knowledge to the new content they were about to learn. The *Content and Discussion* section of the modules consisted of readings, video-recordings, web-quests, and other activities accompanied by prompts used to foster online forum discussions and support among teachers throughout the week. Finally, the *Classroom Connections* portion of each module contained an application assignment in which teachers applied what they learned during the week to their classroom practices. Within this component, teachers tried out their new learning by designing and implementing tier 1 and tier 2 lessons tailored to the needs of their students experiencing mathematics learning difficulties.

The 35 modules were arranged into three integrated content-focused segments. Segment One addressed the foundations for inclusive elementary mathematics classrooms concentrating on effective instruction for tiers 1 and 2. Specifically, this segment addressed mathematics content standards (Common Core State Standards, 2012; National Council of Teachers of Mathematics [NCTM], 2000; 2006); the nature of mathematics LD and difficulties; and tools for understanding struggling mathematics learners, including RTI, assessment, progress monitoring, and instructional decision-making. Segment One also emphasized instructional differentiation, student self-regulation, and evidence-based mathematics practices.

Segment Two (see Pape et al., 2015 for further details) focused on 3rd through 5th grade mathematics content and pedagogy, including the topics of (a) number sense and building conceptual understanding of multiplication and division; (b) differentiated mathematics instruction for multiplication and division; (c) fraction and decimal number representation; and, (d) addition, subtraction, multiplication and division of fractions and decimal numbers. Teachers were provided opportunities to connect their enhanced mathematics content knowledge to their current mathematics instruction by reflecting and acting on implementation problems they were encountering in the classroom. At the same time, teachers learned a process for uncovering and addressing the instructional needs of students with LD and other struggling learners in their classrooms. This process was introduced in Segment Two, and emphasized in Segment Three.

In Segment Three, teachers participated in an inquiry process designed to help them study the impact of their classroom mathematics instruction on students with LD and other struggling learners receiving tier 1 and tier 2 instruction. This teacher inquiry process involved five steps: 1) developing a "wondering", or question, 2) collecting data, 3) analyzing data, 4) taking action, and, 5) sharing results with others (Dana & Yendol-Hoppey, 2014). In this segment, teachers read about the process, designed plans to study their mathematics instruction, and implemented their plans with students. Later, they shared their students' progress in small online discussion forums of three to four teachers. Teachers used student data to inform these conversations. During the final weeks of Segment Three, teachers presented their findings within synchronous online meetings. Teachers gave their own presentations and fielded questions from other teachers, and also participated in other online sessions as an audience member.

As a result of teachers' involvement in *Prime Online,* teachers' content knowledge for teaching mathematics and their reported use of practices associated with the PD improved significantly over time as measured by a validated knowledge measure and a researcher created survey. In addition, changes in teachers' self-reported beliefs about mathematics teaching, teaching students with LD and other struggling learners, and using teacher inquiry were more closely aligned with beliefs they might need to work effectively within RTI frameworks. In addition, *Prime Online* teachers found the PD experience to be rigorous and time intensive but also enjoyable, reporting consistently high levels of satisfaction with the PD program throughout the year. The highest ratings on the satisfaction survey were for items pertaining to teacher learning with their peers in discussion forums, and the applicability of their learning to the classroom. The teachers reported that they enjoyed learning from each other as they discussed the program content and activities in relation to their particular schools, classrooms, and students. In addition, *Prime Online* teachers reported that the opportunities to adapt and apply what they were learning to their own classrooms were most useful. Despite gains in teachers' learning and practice, quantitative analysis of the students' performance on the mathematics portion of the Florida Comprehensive Assessment Test (FCAT) revealed no difference between students taught by teachers who received *Prime Online* and those whose teachers did not receive the PD. However, this finding is not surprising given the complexities associated with using state standardized achievement measures as an index of growth for students with LD (Jones, Buzick, & Turkan, 2010).

Prime Online is a fine example of PD designed to assist both general and special educators teaching mathematics to struggling learners within tiers 1 and 2. The collaborative online community provided frequent opportunities for teachers to participate in online discussions with their *Prime Online* teacher colleagues working in similar classroom settings. The online forums enabled them to merge the knowledge special education teachers typically have about teaching students with LD, and the knowledge typically held by general education teachers about mathematics content and pedagogy, promoting a shared knowledge base for all teachers providing instruction to diverse learners within the RTI framework.

Project InSync: Promoting Coordinated Instruction Throughout the Tiers

In addition to developing shared knowledge of instruction, teachers providing RTI instruction must also be able to coordinate instruction across the instructional tiers in terms of goals, content, use of evidence-based practices, and use of student assessments if their instruction is going to maximize student learning in the supplemental tiers (Fuchs et al., 2008; Wonder-McDowell et al., 2011). *Project InSync* is a multi-faceted, extensive PD innovation that addresses the development of shared knowledge for teaching through the use of content-focused institutes. This innovation deliberately focuses on developing general and special education teachers' ability to plan for and implement coordinated instruction across the tiers by using a lesson study (LS) framework. LS is a collaborative approach to planning and evaluating instruction that was developed in Japan and credited for reforming their elementary mathematics instruction (e.g., Lewis, Perry, & Murata, 2006; Saito & Atencio, 2013). In LS, teams of teachers collaboratively plan, teach, observe, and analyze the effectiveness of lessons designed to meet students' learning needs (Hiebert, Morris, Berk, & Jansen, 2007; Lewis, Perry, Hurd, & O'Connell, 2006; Takahasi & Yoshida, 2004).

In a qualitative study examinig *Project InSync's impact on teacher learning,* teams of nine 4th and 5th grade general and special education teachers participated in over 50 hours of PD focused on the knowledge and skill needed for teaching advanced word study (WS; Benedict, 2014). Five PD institutes were designed to deepen the teachers' knowledge of effective word study subject matter, EBPs (e.g., Moats,

2009; Henry, 2010), and how to plan for coordinated instruction (Bean, 2009; Wonder-McDowell, et al., 2010). The first workshop introduced the teachers to the importance of coordinating instruction within an RTI framework, and helped teachers understand their individual roles in such instruction. The next four institutes addressed the subject matter associated with effective advanced WS (i.e., alphabetic knowledge, multisyllabic decoding, and morphological awareness). Additionally, teachers learned strategies for deliberately designing tier 1 instruction with the needs of their most struggling learners in mind as well as strategies for aligning and intensifying instruction in tiers 2 and 3. Teachers learned strategies for collecting and analyzing student data for use to make instructional decisions.

After each PD institute, *Project InSync* teachers participated in an LS session that incorporated a planning framework that assisted teachers in planning coordinated, tiered instruction. First, the LS team came together to analyze curriculum and student data to develop instructional goals. Once teachers determined what students needed to learn, they collaborated to determine what should be taught and how. When the plan was complete, one teacher taught the lesson while the remaining members of the LS team observed and collected information about the lesson's quality, paying careful attention to the students' responsiveness to instruction. Finally, the LS team reconvened to analyze the impact of instruction on promoting student learning. During this reconvening, they discussed the ways in which instruction could be improved. The LS collaborative planning process was utilized to actively support teachers in integrating newly acquired knowledge and skills from the PD institutes within the context of their classroom practices (e.g., Lewis, 2002, Fernandez & Yoshida, 2004). Furthermore, LS served as a mechanism to promote coordinated tiered instruction. During the planning phase of LS, teachers used an Aligned Planning Framework as a tool to assist them in coordinating instructional goals, lesson content, strategies, and practice activities across each tier. In addition, the framework assisted teachers in thinking about ways they could intensify and individualize instruction for learners receiving supplemental instruction in tiers 2 and 3.

Qualitative analysis of teachers' discourse while engaging in the collaborative planning and debriefing aligned LS sessions revealed that teachers' learning occurred in three phases. In Phase 1, teachers focused most of their planning discussions on making sense of the new content. Specifically, teachers' talk focused on using content they had acquired in the PD and trying to select activities that they thought reflected that content. Instead of discussing strategies they learned in the PD institute, they tended to focus on instructional strategies that were familiar to them but not necessarily effective. Additionally, both general and special education teachers failed to show how the strategies they selected addressed students' learning needs. In fact, their discussions of students' learning needs seemed simplistic. They talked mostly about students not having knowledge, but could not talk specifically about students' strengths and needs as they related to advanced WS. During the collaborative debriefing session, teachers' discourse revealed attempts at making some tentative connections between WS content and the instructional actions they took to teach the content to their students. Moreover, one teacher was beginning to identify connections between the WS instruction and students' improved spelling performance, and this teacher became a leader in the group.

During Phase 2, the teachers began to discuss how they could integrate both content and strategies they had learned in the PD institute to meet students' needs in tier 1 instruction. The teachers were beginning to use the Aligned Planning Framework to support them in thoroughly designing their lesson. They engaged in detailed planning – carefully thinking through each instructional scenario. In doing so, their understandings for WS content and pedagogy became more integrated. Teachers began to think about the content and strategies they were planning from the perspective of their students. They did not, however, differentiate their instruction, or contemplate how they could coordinate instruction across the tiers. During the collaborative debriefing session, teachers began to engage in more substantive critique of the content of their instruction as well as the instructional practices and materials they selected to use. Teachers seemed to integrate their understandings of WS content and pedagogy with their understandings of their students and how they were learning.

During Phase 3, teachers collaboratively developed three aligned tiered WS lessons. This time teachers considered how well their instructions were coordinated across the instructional tiers. Moreover, for the first time, they considered how struggling learners' needs could be addressed early on in the planning process as they deliberately designed tier 2 and tier 3 instructions to review and reteach skills first introduced during tier 1 instruction. Thus, their discussions of WS content, pedagogical practices for teaching the content, struggling learners, and alignment were more interwoven than they had been previously – demonstrating stronger knowledge integration. Further during the debriefing period, teachers' engaged in a more fine-grained critique of their instruction. They began to consider carefully how their instruction could be improved to meet their students' learning needs within each instruction tier.

This study of *Project InSync* brings to light some important insights for developing teachers' knowledge and skill for teaching within an RTI framework. For one, this innovation illuminates that teachers would need some avenue for acquiring the knowledge of reading and EBPs they would need to support students who struggled, but simply acquiring the knowledge would be insufficient. Secondly, teachers would need extended learning opportunities and explicit planning and lesson evaluation frameworks if they were to use the knowledge they were acquiring to plan and evaluate the success of coordinated instruction across the instructional tiers. Students' morphological knowledge as measured by a researcher created morphological assessment was demonstrated to improve as well. However, these findings are only preliminary and there was no comparison group. Currently, schools do not provide this type of extended PD development support to teachers, and may struggle to find the resources to do so. How PD approaches can be organized to deliver such multi-faceted, extended, collaborative PD remains a question, but clearly it is a question we must answer if we want students who are not achieving well to make better academic gains in schools.

CONCLUSION AND THE FUTURE OF PD FOR RTI FRAMEWORKS

The diverse literature base of PD research draws attention to the fact that effective professional learning experiences for teachers involve a lot of moving components, that for the most part, are useful at cultivating teacher growth. Effective PD efforts are multi-faceted, combining two or more approaches to deepen teachers' knowledge and improve instructional practice. These professional learning experiences are extensive in terms of time and intensive in terms of implementation supports, providing teachers ample time to learn and practice new content and instructional practices. The most substantive PD innovations, PD efforts that engaged teachers in 49 hours of professional learning or more, were most effective at bolstering teacher learning, and as a result, improving their students' academic outcomes. In addition, the most effective PD efforts support teachers in integration and implementation, utilizing some form of teacher study group, induction, or coaching as a strategy. Finally, the most effective PD efforts demonstrate that ensuring these professional learning opportunities are content-focused is critical. PD efforts that deepen teachers' knowledge for subject-matter content, and how students learn that content, seem imperative for deepening teachers' knowledge and improving implementation of effective instructional practice.

What we know less about is just how PD efforts should be constructed to: (a) most effectively and efficiently develop teachers' knowledge and skill for providing tiered instruction, and (b) help teachers learn to coordinate their instructional efforts across tiers. Across the literature in reading and mathematics, PD efforts varied considerably in terms of how they were constructed. For example, how Gersten et al (2010) approached teacher learning was different from the more expert driven approaches that Brownell and colleagues (2013) and McCutchen and colleagues (2009) used to promote teacher knowledge. Gersten and colleagues (2010) assumed that teachers would be able to learn to implement EBPs in vocabulary if they could discuss those practices collaboratively and plan for their implementation collaboratively. Brownell and colleagues and McCutchen and colleagues assumed that teacher learning depended on having access to expert knowledge and intensive support for implementing that knowledge. Additionally, the time teachers spent in PD varied considerably across studies cited in this literature review. This variability in how PD research is conceptualized and enacted does not result in an evidence base capable of providing teacher educators and district instructional leaders explicit guidance on how to structure teachers' professional learning opportunities to maximize teacher and student growth.

Furthermore, it is evident that there is little research to inform how PD innovations can be constructed to meet the needs of general and special education teachers collaborating to teach within RTI frameworks. The PD innovations showcased within this chapter, *Prime Online* and *Project InSync*, the only two we could identify that addressed the shared knowledge teachers would need to implement RTI successfully, and *Project InSync*, was the only PD innovation that provided explicit guidance and support for how general and special education teachers could plan and implement coordinated instruction across the tiers and examine its impact on student learning. Although these two PD approaches illustrate that general and special education teachers will need substantial opportunities to jointly learn content and apply strategies for enacting that content, and explicit support for planning coordinated instruction, two studies hardly comprise a knowledge base.

It is clear that future research efforts are needed that can identify the most effective and efficient approaches for supporting the development of the type of knowledge and skill general and special education teachers will need to operate within RTI frameworks for instruction. Since RTI is implemented in so many states and districts across the country (Berkeley et al., 2011; Zirkel, 2011), it seems imperative that the research community in general and special education take up this important problem and generate the research needed to improve how teachers plan for and implement RTI instruction. These research approaches must help teachers learn how to identify the critical content and EBPs that must be taught to students with disabilities and other struggling learners, as well as how to best provide learning supports for implementing this knowledge and instructional practice. It is essential researchers also be committed to determining how such PD can be organized to address the current conditions of teachers work and school environments. As indicated earlier, teachers currently have little access to content focused PD (Hill, 2009) despite the fact that such PD has been shown repeatedly to be effective. More research is needed devoted to determining ways that technology, including online teacher learning, can be harnessed to provide teachers with the opportunities they need to acquire the necessary content knowledge and EBPs for improving the diverse learning needs of students. *Prime Online* provides one example of how this might be done, but many more examples will be needed to form a knowledge base for PD. Additionally, we urge researchers to identify how implementation supports can be structured to assist general and special education teachers in using their newly acquired knowledge in coordinated ways to plan and deliver tiered instruction. As *Project InSync* demonstrated, LS approaches that are modified to provide explicit support for instructional coordination can be helpful, but more research is needed to determine the quantitative impact of such an approach on teachers' delivery of coordinated and evidence-based instruction, and on student outcomes. Moreover, how can these collaborative approaches, such as the LS approach described in this chapter, be implemented efficiently in schools? Can technology be harnessed to improve teachers' ability to plan and analyze instruction collaboratively?

These questions and many others must be addressed in research if education is to amass the knowledge base need to inform PD innovations designed to improve RTI instruction. Without such a research base on PD, it is unlikely that schools will be able to create the sorts of PD supports that can provide general and special education teachers with the knowledge and skill needed to teach successfully within an RTI framework. Thus, the promise of RTI instruction for many students who continue to struggle in school depends on furthering the research base.

REFERENCES

Bean, R. M. (2009). *The reading specialist: Leadership for the classroom school and community*. New York: Guilford.

Bell, C. A., Wilson, S. M., Higgins, T., & McCoach, D. B. (2010). Measuring the effects of professional development on teacher knowledge: The case of developing mathematical ideas. *Journal for Research in Mathematics Education, 41*(5), 479–512.

Benedict, A. (2014). *Learning together: Teachers' evolving understandings during ongoing collaborative professional development* [Doctoral dissertation]. Gainesville, FL: University of Florida.

Benedict, A., Park, Y., Brownell, T. M., Lauterbach, A. A., & Kiely, M. T. (2013). Using lesson study to align elementary literacy instruction within the RTI framework. *Teaching Exceptional Children, 45*(5), 22–31.

Berkeley, S., Bender, W. N., Peaster, L. G., & Saunders, L. (2011). Implementation of response to intervention: A snapshot of progress. *Journal of Learning Disabilities, 42*(1), 85–95. doi:10.1177/0022219408326214 PMID:19103800

Biancarosa, G., Bryk, A. B., & Dexter, E. (2010). Assessing the value-added effects of Literacy Collaborative professional development on student learning. *The Elementary School Journal, 111*(1), 7–34. doi:10.1086/653468

Blank, R. K., & de las Alas, N. (2009). *Effects of teacher professional development on gains in student achievement: How meta-analysis provides scientific evidence useful to education leaders*. Washington, DC: Council of Chief State School Officers.

Bradley, M. C., Daley, T., Levin, M., O'Reilly, F., Parsad, A., Robertson, A., & Werner, A. (2011). *IDEA National Assessment Implementation Study (Final Report NCEE 2011-4027)*. National Center for Education Evaluation and Regional Assistance.

Brownell, M. T., Kiely, M. T., Corbett, N., Boardman, A. G., Haager, D. S., & Dingle, M. P. (2013). Literacy learning cohorts: Effective professional development for special education teachers. *Paper presented at the Annual Meeting for American Education Research Association*, San Francisco, CA.

Brownell, M. T., Lauterbach, A., Benedict, A., Kimberling, J., Bettini, E., & Murphy, K. (2012). Preparing teachers to effectively deliver reading instruction and behavioral supports in response to intervention frameworks. In B. G. Cook, M. Tankersley, & T. J. Landrum (Eds.), *Advances in learning and behavior disorders* (pp. 247–278). Bingley, UK: Emerald Group Publishing Limited.

Burns, M. K., Appleton, J. J., & Stehouwer, J. D. (2005). Meta-analytic review of responsiveness to intervention research: Field-based and research-implemented models. *Journal of Psychoeducational Assessment*, 23(4), 381–394. doi:10.1177/073428290502300406

Burns, M. K., & Symington, T. (2002). A meta-analysis of pre-referral intervention teams: Student and systematic outcomes. *Journal of School Psychology*, 40(5), 437–447. doi:10.1016/S0022-4405(02)00106-1

Cohen, D. K., & Hill, H. (2001). *Learning policy: When state education reform works*. New Haven, CT: Yale University Press. doi:10.12987/yale/9780300089479.001.0001

Common Core State Standards Initiative. (2012). Retrieved from http://www.corestandards.org

Connor, C. M., Alberto, P. A., Compton, D. L., & O'Connor, R. E. (2014). *Improving reading outcomes for students with or at risk for reading disabilities: A synthesis of the contributions from the Institute of Education Sciences Research Centers (NCSER 2014-3000)*. Washington, DC: DOE, National Center for Special Education Research. Retrieved from http://ies.ed.gov/ncser/pubs/20143000/pdf/20143000.pdf

Dana, N. F., & Yendol-Hoppey, D. (2014). *The reflective educator's guide to classroom research: Learning to teach and teaching to learn through practitioner inquiry*. Corwin Press.

Detgen, A., Yamashita, M., Davis, B., & Wraight, S. (2011). *State policies and procedures on response to intervention in the midwest region. (Issues & Answers Report, REL 2011-No. 116)*. Washington, DC: DOE, National Center for Education Evaluation and Regional Assistance. Retrieved from http://ies.ed.gov/ncee/edlabs/regions/midwest/pdf/REL_2011116.pdf

Dougiamas, M. (1999). Developing tools to foster online educational dialogue. *Teaching in the disciplines/learning in context*, 119, 123.

Fuchs, L. S., Fuchs, D., Craddock, C., Hollenbeck, K. N., Hamlett, C. L., & Schatschneider, C. (2008). Effects of small-group tutoring with and without validated classroom instruction on at-risk students' math problem-solving: Are two prevention better than one? *Journal of Educational Psychology*, 100(3), 491–509. doi:10.1037/0022-0663.100.3.491 PMID:19122881

Geary, D. C. (2004). Mathematics and learning disabilities. *Journal of Learning Disabilities*, 37(1), 4–15. doi:10.1177/00222194040370010201 PMID:15493463

Gersten, R., Dimino, J., Jayanthi, M., Kim, J. S., & Santoro, L. E. (2010). Teacher study group: Impact of the professional development model on reading instruction and student outcomes in first grade classrooms. *American Educational Research Journal*, 47(3), 694–739. doi:10.3102/0002831209361208

Gersten, R., Rolfhus, E., Clarke, B., Decker, L. E., Wilkins, C., & Dimino, J. (2015). Intervention for First Graders With Limited Number Knowledge Large-Scale Replication of a Randomized Controlled Trial. *American Educational Research Journal, 52*(3), 516–546. doi:10.3102/0002831214565787

Gersten, R., Taylor, M. J., Keys, T. D., Rolfhus, E., & Newman-Gonchar, R. (2014). *Summary of research on the effectiveness of math professional development approaches.* Washington, DC: U.S. Department of Education, Institute of Education Sciences, National Center for Educational Evaluation and Regional Assistance, Regional Educational Laboratory Southeast. Doi:10.3102/0002831214565787

Greenwood, C. R., Tapia, Y., Abbott, M., & Walton, C. (2003). A building-based case study of evidence-based literacy practices: Implementation, reading behavior, and growth in reading fluency, K-4. *The Journal of Special Education, 37*(2), 95–110. doi:10.1177/00224669030370020401

Griffin, C. C., Dana, N. F., Pape, S. J., Bae, J., Prosser, S., & Algina, J. (2014, April). Prime Online: Teacher professional development for inclusive elementary mathematics classrooms. *Paper presented at the annual meeting of the American Education Research Association*, Philadelphia, PA.

Hawkins, L. J., & Riley, M. N. (2008). Local educational authorities and IDEIA. In E. L. Grigorenko (Ed.), *Educating individuals with disabilities: IDEIA 2004 and beyond* (pp. 403–420). New York: Springer Publishing Company.

Henry, M. K. (2010). Unlocking literacy: effective decoding and spelling instruction. Baltimore, MD: Paul H. Brookes.

Hiebert, J., Morris, A. K., Berk, D., & Jansen, A. (2007). Preparing teachers to learn from teaching. *Journal of Teacher Education, 58*(1), 47–61. doi:10.1177/0022487106295726

Hill, D. R., King, S. A., Lemons, C. J., & Partanen, J. N. (2012). Fidelity of implementation and instructional alignment in response to intervention research. *Learning Disabilities Research & Practice, 27*(3), 116–124. doi:10.1111/j.1540-5826.2012.00357.x

Hill, H. C. (2009). Fixing teacher professional development. *Phi Delta Kappan, 90*(7), 470–476. doi:10.1177/003172170909000705

Hill, S. (2012). *Leap of faith a literature review on the effects of professional development on program quality and youth outcomes.* National Institute on Out-of-School Time.

Hindin, A., Morocco, C. C., Mott, E. A., & Aguilar, C. M. (2007). More than just a group: teacher collaboration and learning in the workplace. *Teachers and Teaching: theory and practice*, 13(4), 349-376.

Hough, H. J., Kerbow, D., Bryk, A., Pinnell, G. S., Rodgers, E., Dexter, E., ... Fountas, I. (2013). Assessing teacher practice and development: The case of comprehensive literacy instruction. *School Effectiveness and School Improvement: An International Journal of Research. Policy & Practice, 24*(4), 452–485.

Individuals with Disabilities Education Act (IDEA) of 2004, 20 U.S.C. §1400 *et seq.* (2004). International Reading Association/ National Institute of Child Health & Human Development. The Reading Writing Connection. Retrieved from www.reading.org/Libraries/.../reading-writingconnection_final.pdf

Johnson, E., Mellard, D. F., Fuchs, D., & McKnight, M. A. (2006). *Responsiveness to Intervention (RTI): How to Do It* [RTI Manual]. National Research Center on Learning Disabilities.

Jones, N. D., Buzick, H. M., & Turkan, S. (2013). Including students with disabilities and English learners in measures of educator effectiveness. *Educational Researcher*, *42*(4), 234–241. doi:10.3102/0013189X12468211

Klingner, J. K., Brownell, M. T., Mason, L., Sindelar, P., & Benedict, A. with Griffin, C., Lane, K., Israel, M., Oakes, W., Menzies, H., Germer, K., Park, Y. (in press). Teaching Students with Special Needs in the New Millennium. In D. Gittomer & C. Bell (Eds)., Handbook of Research on Teaching. American Educational Research Association. Washington, D.C.

Kretlow, A. G., Wood, C. L., & Cooke, N. L. (2011). Using in-service and coaching to increase kindergarten teachers' accurate delivery of group instructional units. *The Journal of Special Education*, *44*(4), 234–246. doi:10.1177/0022466909341333

Lennon, J. E., & Slesinski, C. (1999). Early intervention in reading: Results of a screening and intervention program for kindergarten students. *School Psychology Review*, *28*(3), 353.

Lewis, C., Perry, R., Hurd, J., & O'Connell, M. (2006). Teacher collaboration: Lesson study comes of age in North America. *Phi Delta Kappan*, *88*(4), 273–281. doi:10.1177/003172170608800406

Lewis, C., Perry, R., & Murata, A. (2006). How should research contribute to instructional improvement: A case of lesson study. *Educational Researcher*, *35*(3), 3–14.

McCutchen, D., Abbott, R. D., Green, L. B., Beretvas, N., Cox, S., Potter, N. S., & Gray, A. L. (2002). Beginning literacy: Links among teacher knowledge, teacher practice, and student learning. *Journal of Learning Disabilities*, *35*(1), 69–86. doi:10.1177/002221940203500106 PMID:15490901

McCutchen, D., Green, L., Abbott, R. D., & Sanders, E. A. (2009). Further evidence for teacher knowledge: Supporting struggling readers in grades three through five. *Reading and Writing*, *22*(4), 401–423. doi:10.100711145-009-9163-0

McMeeking, L. B., Orsi, R., & Cobb, R. B. (2012). Effects of a teacher professional development program on the mathematics achievement of middle school students. *Journal for Research in Mathematics Education*, *43*(2), 159–181. doi:10.5951/jresematheduc.43.2.0159

Moats, L. (2009). Knowledge foundations for teaching reading and spelling. *Reading and Writing*, *22*(4), 379–399. doi:10.100711145-009-9162-1

National Center on Response to Intervention. (2010, March). *Essential Components of RTI – A Closer Look at Response to Intervention*. Washington, DC: U.S. Department of Education, Office of Special Education Programs.

National Center on Response to Intervention National Council of Teachers of Mathematics. (2000). *Principles and standards for school mathematics*. Reston, VA: Author.

National Council of Teachers of Mathematics. (2006). *Curriculum focal points for prekindergarten through grade 8 mathematics: A quest for coherence*. National.

Pape, S. J., Prosser, S. K., Griffin, C. C., Dana, N. F., Algina, J., & Bae, J. (2015). *Prime online*: Developing grades 3-5 teachers' content knowledge for teaching mathematics in an online professional development program. *Contemporary Issues in Technology & Teacher Education, 15*(1). Retrieved from http://www.citejournal.org/vol15/iss1/mathematics/article1.cfm

RTI Action Network. (2009). *Learn about RTI.* Retrieved from http://www.rtinetwork.org/learn/what/whatisrti

Saito, E., & Atencio, M. (2013). A conceptual discussion of lesson study from a micro- political perspective: Implications for teacher development and pupil learning. *Teaching and Teacher Education, 31*, 87–95. doi:10.1016/j.tate.2013.01.001

Scher, L., & O'Reilly, F. (2009). Professional development for K-12 math and science teachers: What do we really know? *Journal of Research on Educational Effectiveness, 2*(3), 209–249. doi:10.1080/19345740802641527

Shank, M. J. (2006). Teacher storytelling: A means for creating and learning within a collaborative space. *Teaching and Teacher Education, 22*(6), 711–721. doi:10.1016/j.tate.2006.03.002

Sindelar, P., Brownell, M., & Billingsley, B. (2010). Special education teacher education research: Current status and future directions. *Teacher Education and Special Education, 33*(1), 8–24. doi:10.1177/0888406409358593

Stewart, R. A., & Brendefur, J. L. (2005). Fusing lesson study and authentic achievement: A model for teacher collaboration. *Phi Delta Kappan, 86*(9), 681–687. doi:10.1177/003172170508600912

Swanson, H. L., & Jerman, O. (2006). Math disabilities: A selective meta-analysis of the literature. *Review of Educational Research, 76*(2), 249–274. doi:10.3102/00346543076002249

Swanson, H. L., & Saez, L. (2003). Memory difficulties in children and adults with learning disabilities. In H. L. Swanson, K. R. Harris, & S. Graham (Eds.), *Handbook of learning disabilities* (pp. 182–198). New York: Guilford.

Vescio, V., Ross, D., & Adams, A. (2008). A review of research on the impact of professional learning communities on teaching practice and student learning. *Teaching and Teacher Education, 24*(1), 80–91. doi:10.1016/j.tate.2007.01.004

Wei, R. C., Darling-Hammond, L., & Adamson, F. (2010). *Professional development in the United States: Trends and challenges.* Dallas, TX: National Staff Development Council.

Wonder-McDowell, C., Reutzel, D. R., & Smith, J. A. (2011). Does instruction alignment matter? Effects on struggling second-grade students' reading achievement. *The Elementary School Journal, 112*, 259–279. doi:10.1086/661524

Wood, D. (2007). Teachers' learning communities: Catalyst for change or a new infrastructure for the status quo? *Teachers College Record, 109*(3), 699–739.

Yoon, K. S., Duncan, T., Lee, S. W.-Y., Scarloss, B., & Shapley, K. (2007). *Reviewing the evidence on how teacher professional development affects student achievement (Issues & Answers Report, REL 2007–No. 033)*. Washington, DC: DOE, National Center for Education Evaluation and Regional Assistance. Retrieved from http://ies.ed.gov/ncee/edlabs

Zirkel, P. A. (2011). State laws and guidelines for RTI: Additional implementation features. *National Association of School Psychologists, 39*(7), 30–32.

This research was previously published in the Handbook of Research on Professional Development for Quality Teaching and Learning edited by Teresa Petty, Amy Good, and S. Michael Putman; pages 42-61, copyright year 2016 by Information Science Reference (an imprint of IGI Global).

Chapter 9
Implementing Effective Student Support Teams

Tricia Crosby-Cooper
National University, USA

Dina Pacis
National University, USA

ABSTRACT

Pre-service teachers in a K-12 setting, encounter students in need of academic and behavioral supports. One method of providing supports to struggling students in the general education and special education setting is through the problem-solving process of pre-referral intervention, hence forth referred to as Student Support Teams (SST) within Response-to-Intervention. During the SST process, student's academic and/or behavioral difficulties are considered through a multidisciplinary approach. Research demonstrates the use of a multi-tiered problem solving approach as a means to provide supports for students prior to special education eligibility and placement. Additionally, there are concerns regarding implementation and teacher perceptions (Powers, 2001) on the effectiveness of the intervention and collaboration between general education and special education teachers (Graden, 1989). This chapter discusses historical aspects, purpose and process, best practices, and challenges of SSTs, while presenting strategies for teachers and educators to effectively implement the SST process.

INTRODUCTION

Ms. Lincoln, a first year teacher, referred a student in her 3rd grade class to the SST for reading difficulties. During the meeting Ms. Lincoln was asked to present her concerns. At which time, she replied, 'this student has been referred in first grade to the SST, but nothing to date has happened. This student needs to be tested and placed in special education. Why is this process taking so long?' The school psychologist responded to this question by asking Ms. Lincoln what interventions she has implemented?

DOI: 10.4018/978-1-7998-1213-5.ch009

Too often across the country teachers refer students to the Student Study Team (SST) as the first step towards special education placement. A study conducted by Powers (2001) noted that 63% of teachers believed that the SST process was a hoop they needed to jump through in order to get the student special education services. At the same time, there is a notion that teacher's must complete a certain number of SST's prior to the student being assessed for, and if needed, placed in special education. Though the data from the SST process can help struggling students, the function of the SST is not to qualify a student for special education services. Student study teams are a multidisciplinary team of individuals working collaboratively to address academic and behavioral concerns of students within a Response-to-Intervention framework (RTI). Response to intervention uses a multi-tiered approach to identify and support students with academic and behavioral needs (RTI Action Network) within the general education setting.

Response to intervention consists of three tiers – Tier 1 includes high quality research based classroom instruction in the general education setting (RTI Action Network). Tier 2 consists of targeted interventions for students who demonstrated difficulty at Tier 1. Students in Tier 2 are presented with additional academic supports in a small-group setting of 3-5 students with increased frequency and duration. Progress monitoring data is obtained from the implemented interventions. Student study teams take place at this Tier. Tier 3 includes intensive interventions with progress monitoring for students who did not respond to interventions at Tier 2. These interventions consist of increased frequency and duration of interventions in a small-group setting of 2-3 students. Special education referrals can take place in Tier 3 if the student does not show progress from the implemented interventions. "RTI is designed for use when making decisions in both general education and special education, creating a well-integrated system of instruction and intervention guided by child outcome data" (RTI Action network).

Student Study Teams were originally known as pre-referral teams. These teams, examined student difficulties for both academic and behavioral concerns through instructional support in the classroom environment. Pre-referral teams, grew out of a mandate from the Education for all Handicapped Children's Act of 1975 (PL. 94-142) requiring the use of these teams in the special education referral and placement process. Pre-referral Intervention Teams were mandated as a form of protection during the special education evaluation procedure suggesting that professionals using multiple criteria would make less biased referral decisions (Ysseldyke & Algozzine, 1983). Over the years, MDT's have had many names such as, Pre-referral Intervention Teams (PIT; Graden, Casey, & Bronstrom, 1985); Intervention Assistance Teams (IAT; Graden, 1989), Instructional Consultation Teams (ICT; Rosenfield & Gravois, 1996), Child Study Teams (CST; Moore, Fifield, Spira, & Scarlato, 1989), Mainstream Assistance Teams (MAT; Fuchs, Fuchs, & Bahr, 1990), Teacher Assistant Team (TAT; Chalfant, 1979), and Student Study Team (SST; Chalfant, Pysh, & Moltrie, 1979). Despite the variations in name and some procedural characteristics, the function remains the same - develop interventions for students struggling in the general education setting (Burns, et al., 2005). Student Study Teams are consistent in both general education and special education with the main focus to assist students struggling academically and behaviorally in the general education setting with general education curriculum (District of Columbia State Improvement Grant).

Background

The student body in the United States has grown more diverse and multifaceted over time. As such, meeting the needs of various students' academic and behavioral difficulties has become a major aspect of education, both in the general education and special education settings. Concerned with student achievement, there was a push by researchers and policymakers to help school districts improve "reading achievement through scientifically-proven methods of instruction" (US Department of Education, 2008). This push was due to the inability of the President's Commission (2002) to identify data that supported classification procedures, noting that assessments used for the identification of specific learning disability (SLD) were not informative, did not evaluate progress, or assist in the determination of educational need (Crosby-Cooper, 2009). As a result of the Commission's findings, the federal response by the House (H.R. 1350) and Senate (S. 1248) committee reports encouraged Local Education Agencies (LEA) to adopt a Response to Intervention (RTI) model (Federal Register, 2006; Crosby-Cooper, 2009). Through the inception of No Child Left Behind (NCLB, 2001), there was an increased accountability, on the part of districts, to ensure a high quality education for all students. The need for effective collaboration between educational specialists and teachers increased, as they worked together to provide high quality classroom instruction for struggling students. The No Child Left Behind Act (NCLB) is the reauthorization of the Elementary and Secondary Education Act (ESEA, 1965) which requires evidence-based practices for student achievement with state systems for accountability. Under NCLB, educational agencies must demonstrate program effectiveness through scientifically-based research in conjunction with progress monitoring. Additionally, the Individuals with Disabilities Education Improvement Act (IDEIA, 2004), required an increased role in data-based decisions, the use of scientifically-based reading programs, and an evaluation component to determine the student's intervention response (Crosby-Cooper, 2009). In 2011, the Every Student Succeeds Act (ESSA) was approved. This act sought to improve the perceived gaps of NCLB. Under ESSA, the need for data based decision making is reinforced, while the overuse of standardized tests and a one-size-fits-all mandate in the schools is rejected. This change comes in the form of an increased focus on teaching and learning. The Every Student Succeeds Act (2011) includes a program called *Race to the Top*. This program is comprised of 4 specific areas. One of these areas is the building of data systems that measures student growth and success. The data from *Race to the Top* informs teachers, educators, and principals how they can improve instruction and supports for the student. Student Study Teams fit into the building of data systems, as it is a multi-disciplinary data-based collaboration that measures student growth and success through the implementation of evidence based interventions and progress monitoring.

SST PURPOSE ROLES AND FUNCTIONS

Ms. Lincoln is of the understanding that the student study team is a direct pathway for student identification into special education. This was expressed at the SST meeting when Ms. Lincoln shared her frustration that she had done her job by presenting the student to the SST and informing the team that this student requires special education services. Ms. Lincoln is not alone in her perception regarding the purpose of the SST.

The purpose of an SST is to assist school staff in the problem-solving process of developing and implementing interventions. Determining special education eligibility is an aspect of SST based on progress monitoring data, but it is not the primary function of an SST (Graden, 1989). The SST process begins when the teacher, staff members, or parents recognize that the student is struggling in their learning environment. The SST meeting provides everyone with an opportunity to share concerns and develop a plan. The agreed upon interventions vary depending on the child's needs. Each element in the SST process provides essential information that assists the team in developing a successful intervention plan based upon student strengths. The SST process should create a learning environment that contributes to the achievement, well-being, and success of the student. Follow-up meetings are scheduled to ensure accountability of the plan and make adjustments to promote student success. If the data show that the student is not benefitting from the evidence-based interventions and may benefit from special education supports, the team then recommends a formal special education assessment. The SST intervention plan requires the participants to look at the students in a holistic manner. This team is an efficient and effective way to bring together all resources in the best interest of helping each student reach their potential. The SST is different than a parent-teacher conference which focuses on improving communication and addressing specific class problems (Understanding Special Education, 2016).

In order to adhere to the true intent of the SST, the following people should be in attendance during the meeting. The *scheduler* manages the case file throughout the SST process. They ensure that relevant dates are logged into the file, schedule meetings and support the teacher throughout the process. Follow up is critical so that all referrals are addressed and all members of the SST are invited and have responded. The *facilitator* is responsible for calling the meeting to order. They introduce the team members and review the purpose of the meeting. A summary of the students learning challenges is reported by the teacher the facilitator guides a problem solving effort. The facilitator should keep the conversation going, an allotted time amount for each agenda item helps to keep the meeting on track. The *recorder* is to keep a record of the problem solving process and note any contribution made by the members of the team. The *referring person* is most frequently the Teacher, but can also be the parent, school administrator, or educational specialists. Parents must be contacted prior to requesting an SST. Every school site should have a referral packet. The referral packet contains information on the specific learning concerns in observable and measurable terms. It should also contain information on the expected behavior (academic, attendance and/or social). The referring team member should attend all team meetings, collaborate with the team to problem solve solutions and agree to share the responsibility for implementing the action plan developed for the student. The *Parent and student* (when appropriate) should be prepared to share any developmental history as well as any other contributing factors which may impact the student's learning. Student strengths, any interventions implemented in the home as well as any concerns and perceptions should be shared. The parent and student are considered an integral part of the collaborative process as well as a team member. *Invited Specialists* –Selected for their expertise in specific areas of concern, can comprise of the school counselor, classified staff, district foster youth staff, county social workers, or private therapists. Parents may also invite to the meeting any specialists, or support personnel who may have worked with the student to the meeting. These team members are also considered in the collaborative process and a team member. The *administrator* is typically a school principal, assistant principal, site instructional coordinator, or administrative designee. They would be required to review any readiness assessments and determine whether an SST is appropriate based on the assessments and referral information. This person facilitates the collaboration, focusing on the student involvement in the general education process. S/he also provide support to students, their families and the teacher.

BEST PRACTICES OF STUDENT STUDY TEAM (SST)

During the SST meeting, Ms. Lincoln noted interventions that she had previously implemented to assist the student. These interventions consisted of extra tutoring during recess and lunch, sending the student to a different classroom, consulting with the resource (special education) teacher and other grade-level colleagues, peer assisted learning strategies (PALS), and peer tutoring. When asked about the effectiveness of the interventions, Ms. Lincoln stated that she has not seen any change in the student's performance and that is why we were meeting today.

Intervention effectiveness cannot be determined without assessment of the student's response. At the same time, the effectiveness of the intervention increases when the general education teacher and special education teacher work collaboratively (Graden, 1989). The perception of the intervention effectiveness, is based on the degree to which the implementer (typically the teacher) believes that the intervention will solve the problem (Telzrow & Beebe, 2002). Interventions are considered more acceptable when they match the intervention context. When examining the integrity of the implemented intervention, it is crucial to consider the amount of time, resources, and skill held by the intervention implementer (Telzrow & Beebe, 2002). Taking into account time, resources, and skill is important in a problem-solving model as teachers will be responsible for implementing the intervention as planned. If teachers do not find the intervention acceptable in relation to time, resources, and skills, the teacher may not implement the interventions as described (Telzrow & Beebe, 2002).

For an intervention to be implemented as described, the teacher must consider the intervention acceptable. Elements of intervention acceptability include the perception of intervention effectiveness, the complexity of the intervention, the effectiveness of the intervention based on progress monitoring data, and whether or not the intervention matches the behavior of concern (Telzrow and Beebe, 2002). Interventions that are easier to implement are considered more acceptable. Complex interventions that require a lot of time, materials, and staff are less likely to be implemented, or implemented with integrity (Gresham, 1989).

An important element in the implementation of SSTs is treatment integrity. Once the team agrees to the intervention, the next step is to ensure that the intervention implemented is done with integrity (Telzrow & Beebe, 2002). Treatment integrity is the degree to which an intervention is implemented as originally developed (Gresham, 1989). The intervention must also be instrumental in determining that the changes in the behavior of concerns are a direct result of the intervention (Crosby-Cooper, 2009).

Treatment integrity in relation to SST implementation is extremely important. The relationship between treatment integrity and SSTs is based on operational definitions and reliability measures (Gresham 1996). Moreover, treatment integrity is the extent to which behavioral concerns are specifically defined, and interventions are implemented as planned. In other words, what does the behavior look like, what does the behavior not look like, how often (frequency) does the behavior take place, how long (duration) does the behavior last, what days of the week or times of the day (patterns) is the behavior present.

A common methodology used to address student concerns within the SST process is the problem-solving model (PSM). Problem-solving is defined as an, "…approach to intervention rather than a focus on failure of deviance" (Deno, 2002 p. 38). Behavioral consultation is the best known approach in the problem-solving model. The four main characteristics of this model are, problem identification, problem analysis, plan implementation, and plan evaluation (Crosby-Cooper, 2009; Ruby, Crosby-Cooper, Vanderwood, 2011).

In the PSM, the team examines the concerns and needs of each student, brought to the SST, and designs an individualized intervention plan to address those concerns. According to Fuchs, Mock, Morgan, and Young (2003), intervention effectiveness is not determined based on certain characteristics, nor does any intervention work for all students within a specific subgroup. With the PSM, there is a trial and error approach regarding the effectiveness of the intervention which is measured by progress monitoring data, as not every student will respond to every intervention attempted. Additionally, environmental variables that may be contributing to the student's difficulties are explored instead of within child variables (Fuchs et al., 2003).

A distinct characteristic of problem-solving SSTs is the use of evidence based data decision making. Evidence based decisions focus on formative evaluation of the intervention which allows educators to document how well a student is responding to a specific intervention. During the problem-solving SST, goals are specified and formative evaluations of the student's progress are monitored. One formative evaluation process is progress monitoring. Progress monitoring provides a visual depiction of the student's response to the intervention. Data points representing the student's response to the intervention are collected over a specified period of time. These evidence based data points are graphed and analyzed to inform and modify interventions as a means to review student performance (Deno, 2002). Progress monitoring is essential to the SST process. Evidence based data is used to determine if the student is moving toward established goal(s), or if changes to the intervention(s) are necessary (e.g., increase, decrease, and change completely).

When conducting an SST, it is important that the team focus on a specific skill. Through the interventions, the team can assist the student in acquiring a new skill, or strengthening a current skill. The SST designs, implements, and evaluates the effectiveness of the evidence based intervention – thus yielding successful outcomes by way of best practice standards. Identifying a skill in concrete, observable, and measurable terms allows practitioners a clearer path to understand the target skill (Crosby-Cooper, 2009; Ruby, Crosby-Cooper, & Vanderwood, 2011). The Problem Solving Rubric by Upah and Tilly (2002) is one method of determining the effectiveness of the intervention. This rubric consists of 12 components that are scored based on an ordinal scale of 1 to 5 with 5 considered best practice. Scores of 3, 2, or 1 are considered ineffective and unacceptable. These components are, behavioral definition, baseline data, problem validation, problem analysis, goal setting, intervention development, measurement strategy, decision-making plan, progress monitoring, formative evaluation, treatment integrity, and summative evaluation. The Problem Solving Team Rubric is presented in conjunction with the four stages in the problem-solving process (Kratochwill & Bergan 1990). These stages are; problem identification, problem analysis, plan implementation, and plan evaluation:

- *Problem identification* is the first stage of the problem-solving model and consists of defining the behavior of concern by determining "...the discrepancy between the current performance and desired performance..." (Kratochwill & Bergan 1990, p. 48).
- *Problem analysis* is the second stage in the problem-solving model which focuses on "...conditions that may influence the behavior rather than on specific skill acquisition" (Kratochwill & Bergan 1990, p. 112).
- *Treatment Implementation* is the third stage in the problem-solving model. This stage consists of making preparations to implement the plan, ensuring the resources needed are available, and ensuring that the individual implementing the plan has the required skills prior to implementation. This stage also monitors the student's behavior and the treatment integrity of the plan. Monitoring the implementation of the plan can be done through interviews and/or observations ((Kratochwill & Bergan 1990).
- *Treatment evaluation* is the fourth and final stage in the problem-solving model. After a predetermined time has passed, the treatment is evaluated to determine its effectiveness, and consider if the treatment should be continued or terminate (Kratochwill & Bergan 1990).

It is important that suggested interventions are evidence based. As part of the implementation plan, a method to monitor student progress must be utilized. One of the tools widely used to monitor student progress is Curriculum-Based Measurement (CBM). According to Shinn and Bamonto (1998), CBM is a set of simple standardized short fluency measures used to determine the effectiveness of an intervention. CBM has been used with teachers in both special education and general education and is designed as an outcome measure of student achievement. CBM is a formative evaluation of a student's academic performance allowing for the continued monitoring of student's progress. In 2002, the President's Commission stated that the use of 1-or 2-minute assessments "…enhances instructional outcomes and results for children with learning and behavioral difficulties" (p.24). In addition to the use of progress monitoring, assuring that the intervention is implemented as designed is critical. Too often, summative evaluations are used to evaluate a student's educational program, making it too late to make any changes. A summative evaluation provides information regarding the efficacy of the intervention assessing whether or not the intervention did what it was supposed to do. Relying on summative evaluations does not take into consideration the modification of the intervention. Modifying the intervention is important to ensuring the student's success (Crosby-Cooper, 2009).

When adhering to best practices, ongoing training must be implemented to ensure appropriate referrals, development of support plans, and evidence based progress monitoring data to ensure student success. Research by Burns and Symington (2002) investigated the effectiveness of SSTs under controlled conditions with highly trained staff in a problem-solving model. When the SST process is structured, includes standardized procedures, problems are systematically identified and analyzed, evidence-based interventions are implemented with integrity, and progress was monitored systematically, there is a decrease in referrals to special education (Crosby-Cooper, 2009). There have also been suggestions that teachers and staff should be provided with SST training on a yearly basis (Powers, 2001).

CHALLENGES OF STUDENT STUDY TEAM (SST)

During the SST meeting, when the parent and student excused themselves from the room, Ms. Lincoln expressed frustration regarding the SST process. She indicated that though she has implemented interventions and mentioned her concerns with administration and colleagues, she has not received any support or assistance in meeting the needs of the student. She also expressed her frustration regarding the lack of immediate improvement in the student's performance based on modifications implemented in the classroom.

There are several challenges that may contribute to the lack of SST effectiveness. Research conducted by Flugum and Reschly (1994) concluded that in general SSTs typically fail to develop a behavioral definition of the academic or behavioral problem. The lack of a behavioral definition affects the team's ability to measure the behavior(s) of concern, develop an intervention, graph the results of the intervention, or compare progress monitoring data to baseline. In addition, Telzrow and colleagues (2000) noted the lack of standardized training regarding intervention implementation and documentation contributed to inconsistent and ineffective SSTs. Another challenge under the problem-solving model, is that students typically wait long periods of time for their concerns to be addressed (Fuchs et al., 2003). These long waits are the result of SSTs meeting irregularly and in a reactive fashion, with more time spent admiring the problem instead of focusing on a solution (Powers, 2001). Powers noted that in Southern California more than 60% of schools have SSTs, but less than 40% are implemented regularly. Powers further stated that while 62% of SSTs were regularly scheduled, only 30% had a consultant to follow-up and support the classroom teacher in implementing an intervention. At the same time, while one-third of the teams followed-up to examine student's progress, less than 12% collected evidence based progress monitoring data (Powers, 2001). In another study conducted by Telzrow et al. (2000), the authors noted that, "… reliable implementation of problem-solving approaches in schools remains elusive" (p. 458). Additional challenges regarding the effectiveness of SSTs in applied settings stem from limited time set aside for teams to meet and plan supports for the student (Tilly, 2002).

CONCLUSION

The school psychologist and administer/designee explain to Ms. Lincoln the purpose of the SST and the importance of gathering evidence-based information to document student progress towards the desired outcome. Current implanted interventions are discussed regarding effectiveness based on progress monitoring data. The team discusses an additional intervention taking into consideration Ms. Lincoln's skill level, time, and resources. Ms. Lincoln agrees with the new intervention, with the support of the team. The team agrees to meet again in 6-weeks to discuss the student's progress and data from the new intervention.

Though there are challenges with the SST, as has been previously noted the most prevalent challenge is that the SST is perceived as a gateway for immediate special education placement. While a student may eventually qualify for special education services after going through the SST process, the primary purpose of the SST is to increase the students skill set using evidence-based interventions and progress monitoring data. Despite these roadblocks, adhering to the best process and plan with the use of evidence based data to determine effectiveness should be the goal of the team. Regardless of the effectiveness of the problem-solving process and evidence based data decisions, it is the teacher who is an essential component of the process. Participating as a referring teacher, a case manager, or supporting a fellow teacher, are all behaviors of best-practice in the SST process.

One solution to the challenges schools face in implementing SSTs is ensuring school-based teams are trained and provided on-going consultative support (Burns, Peters, Noell, 2008). Providing teachers the support, resources, and skills needed with the use of evidence based interventions, and progress monitoring, will prove beneficial for both the student and the teacher. Best practices allows for the teacher to focus on the intervention, rather than the students deficit. Adhering to the four stages of the problem-solving model in conjunction with data-based decision making will yield more accurate information regarding the effectiveness of the intervention or treatment.

Pre-service and first year teachers face a multitude of challenges. The increase in accountability has placed a sense of urgency on the field of education which further adds to the complexity of teaching and learning. Ensuring that all students are achieving can be challenging given the diversity of today's U.S. population. Providing the supports needed for any student who is demonstrating academic and/or behavioral difficulty adds to the pressure pre-service and first year teachers face. In an effort to provide the resources and knowledge these new educators need to support students who are experiencing challenges, educational specialists and administrators must implement effective SSTs. Through the problem-solving process of the SST, well developed plans are implemented by the teacher, with support from the SST, in an effort to provide the student with the tools to achieve the desired skill. Ongoing progress monitoring of the student's response to the intervention should be addressed in follow-up meetings to determine the effectiveness of the intervention.

FUTURE RECOMMENDATIONS AND RESEARCH

Pre-service teachers are exposed to evidence-based assessment and interventions in their methods courses. However, connecting evidence-based assessments and interventions to the SST is not consistent. Typical student teaching experiences are based on the needs of the classroom under the guidance of the Master teacher. As such, we are recommending that pre-service teachers, as part of their student teaching, engage in the SST process to connect theory to practice. We further recommend that throughout the teacher education program, pre-service teachers are presented with video scenarios depicting academic and behavioral difficulties to identify the student's academic/behavioral concerns in preparation to present a summary of the student's evidence-based assessment to the SST. Further, the use of role playing in the teacher education program would also allow opportunity for the pre-service teacher to learn how to engage in the SST process and contribute to the team.

It is important for the success of the student, the team, and the teacher, that information regarding the purpose and process of the SST is widely disseminated. Results from various studies on the implementation of SSTs show that the purpose and function of SSTs has fallen below standard in applied settings. Because of this, additional studies on the implementation is critical (Telzrow et al., 2000). Future research should investigate the training and support schools need to increase the effectiveness of SSTs in typical school and district settings (Burns et al., 2005; Buck et. al., 2003; Burns & Symington, 2002; Crosby-Cooper, 2009). Finally, the roles and perceptions of the function and purpose of the SST should continue to be examined with a focus on ESSA.

RESOURCES

The following are a list of resources and their descriptions which will support teachers, educational specialists, and administrators towards ensuring that SST's team meetings have access to effective data, data analysis as well as classroom strategies and behavior management tools. These resources will help the problem solving dialogue that occurs during SST's as well as support the development and implementation of the SST plan.

Table 1. Evidence based supports

Screening and Progress Monitoring Resources
Dynamic Indicators of Basic Early Literacy Skills (DIBELS) – are a set of procedures and measures for assessing the acquisition of early literacy skills from kindergarten through sixth grade. They are designed to be short (one minute) fluency measures used to regularly monitor the development of early literacy and early reading skills.
The DIBELS measures were specifically designed to assess the Big Ideas in Reading. These research-based measures are linked to one another and predictive of later reading proficiency. The measures are also consistent with many of the Common Core State Standards in Reading, especially the Foundational Skills. Combined, the measures form an assessment system of early literacy development that allows educators to readily and reliably determine student progress.
www.dibels.uoregon.edu
AIMSWEB- **aims**web is the leading assessment and RTI solution in school today—a complete web-based solution for universal screening, progress monitoring, and data management for Grades K-12. **Aims**web provides guidance to administrators and teachers based on accurate, continuous, and direct student assessment. It supports identification of at-risk students early, as well as monitoring and reporting student progress.
www.aimsweb.com
Progress Monitoring Research- The Office of Special Education Programs (OSEP) funded the Research Institute on Progress Monitoring (RIPM) to develop a system of progress monitoring to evaluate effects of individualized instruction on access to and progress within the general education curriculum. RIPM's funded activities have ended and the center is now disseminating the findings from its five years of research and development.
www.progressmonitoring.org
Intervention Resources
Intervention Central – Response to Intervention (RTI) resources. Intervention Central provides teachers, schools and districts with free resources to help struggling learners and implement Response to Intervention and attain the Common Core State Standards.
www.interventioncentral.org
The Florida Center for Reading Research – The Florida Center for Reading Research (FCRR) is a multidisciplinary research center at Florida State University. FCRR explores all aspects of reading research—basic research into literacy-related skills for typically developing readers and those who struggle, studies of effective prevention and intervention, and psychometric work on formative assessment.
www.fcrr.org
Interventions: Evidence-Based Behavioral Strategies for Individual Students – This book was originally published in 1993. Since that time, research has continued to confirm that the proactive, positive and instructional approaches suggested in the original edition are far more effective in managing and motivating students than traditional authoritarian and punitive approaches.
Randy Sprick Ph.D.
Academic Skills Problems Fourth Edition- This practitioner guide and text presents an effective, problem-solving-based approach to evaluating and remediating academic skills problems. The text provides practical strategies for working with students across all grade levels (K–12) who are struggling with reading, spelling, written language, or math. Step-by-step guidelines are detailed for assessing students' learning and their instructional environment, using the data to design instructional modifications, and monitoring student progress.
Edward S. Shapiro Ph.D.
Academic Skills Problems Fourth Edition Workbook- A companion to Academic Skills Problems, Fourth Edition, this workbook provides practice exercises and reproducible forms for use in direct assessment and intervention. The workbook includes teacher and student interview forms, a complete guide to using the Behavioral Observation of Students in Schools (BOSS), tools to support RTI, and exercises in administering assessments and scoring, interpreting, and graphing the results.
Edward S. Shapiro Ph.D.
Strategies for Teaching Students with Learning and Behavior Problems – This text focuses on presenting content for preparing teachers to meet the needs of elementary and secondary students with learning and behavior problems in a variety of settings. It provides hands on applications and classroom strategies and information using current research on best practices through the use of embedded video clips, web links, and step-by-step instructional strategies. Text integrates the Common Core State Standards (CCSS), RTI, emphasis on higher level thinking, including reading comprehension and complex texts as well as problem solving, fractions, and algebra, and classroom management and positive behavior support.
Sharon Vaughn Ph.D.

continued on following page

Table 1. Continued

Other Resources
Eunice Kennedy Shriver National Institute of Child Health and Human Development - The NICHD, the National Institute for Literacy, and the ED also united to form the Partnership for Reading, an effort to distribute evidence-based reading research—such as the findings of the National Reading Panel—to those who could benefit the most from it. The Partnership aimed to ensure that the methods of reading instruction used in the classroom reflect evidence-based methods, such as those put forth by the National Reading Panel. Publications developed under this partnership are still relevant and available despite termination of the National Institute for Literacy.
https://www.nichd.nih.gov/research/supported/Pages/nrp.aspx
What Works Clearing House – The goal of the WWC is to be a resource for informed education decision making. To reach this goal, the WWC identifies studies that provide credible and reliable evidence of the effectiveness of a given practice, program, or policy (referred to as "interventions"), and disseminates summary information and free reports on the WWC website.
http://ies.ed.gov/ncee/wwc/
Schools for Success – Schools for success is a web-based SST guide that can be used to assist school districts, educators, and parents regarding the purpose of SST and the delivery of Response-to-Intervention (RTI)
Stephanie Holleran, Psy.D.
www.schools4success.com
Behavior Management
Tools for Teaching- Tools for Teaching integrates the management of discipline, instruction and motivation. The text provides strategies to helps reduce student disruptions, while helping teachers to increase responsible behavior, motivation and independent learning.
Fred Jones Ph.D.
Teacher's encyclopedia 500 solutions for 100 problems - This book gives specific guidelines and ideas about classroom and behavior management. Useful for School Psychologists, to write behavior plans, and to make recommendations in psychological reports, this is also an excellent resource for regular and special educators
Randy Sprick Ph.D. and Lisa Howard Ph.D
CHAMPs A Proactive and Positive Approach to Classroom Management: Volume 1 - The CHAMPs book Volume 1 outlines general classroom management strategies and tasks for success along with specific intervention correction procedures within module 7.
Randy Sprick, Ph.D.
Mickey Garrison, Ph.D.
Lisa M. Howard, M.S.
CHAMPs A Proactive and Positive Approach to Classroom Management: Volume 2 - This CHAMPs Volume 2 book is inclusive of a CD of reproducible forms & visuals for classroom use. The book also outlines developing a function-based intervention (beginning on page 371).
Randy Sprick, Ph. D.
RIDE: Responding to Individual Differences in Education- A multi-media web based program with 104 research based interventions across six critical areas of behavior.
Ray Beck Ed.D
Skillstreaming- This resource includes a four-part training approach: modeling, role-playing, performance feedback, and generalization—to teach essential pro-social skills to children and adolescents.
Arnold P. Goldstein, Ph.D. Ellen McGinnis, Ph.D.
Stop & Think- This nationally recognized social skills program addresses four developmental levels and helps students learn interpersonal, survival, problem-solving, and conflict resolution skills.
Howard M. Knoff, Ph.D
Tough Kid Tool Box- Ready-to-use, classroom-tested materials to help motivate and manage even the toughest to teach students.
Randy Sprick, Ph.D.
Lisa M. Howard, M.S.
William R. Jenson, Ph.D.
Ginger Rhode, Ph. D. H. Kenton Reavis, Ph.D.

REFERENCES

Baer, D. M., Wolf, M. M., & Risley, T. R. (1968). Some current dimensions of applied behavior analysis. *Journal of Applied Behavior Analysis*, *1*(1), 91–97. doi:10.1901/jaba.1968.1-91 PMID:16795165

Beck, R. (1997). *Project RIDE: Responding to individual differences in education.* Longmont, CO: Sopris.

Buck, G. H., Polloway, E. A., & Cook, K. W. (2003). Pre-referral Intervention processes: A survey of state practice. *Council for Exceptional Children*, *69*(3), 349–360. doi:10.1177/001440290306900306

Burns, M. K., Peters, R., & Noell, G. H. (2008). Using performance feedback to enhance implementation fidelity of the problem-solving team process. *Journal of School Psychology*, *46*(5), 537–550. doi:10.1016/j.jsp.2008.04.001 PMID:19083371

Burns, M. K., & Symington, T. (2002). A meta-analysis of pre-referral intervention teams: Student and systematic outcomes. *Journal of School Psychology*, *40*(5), 437–447. doi:10.1016/S0022-4405(02)00106-1

Burns, M. K., Vanderwood, M. L., & Ruby, S. (2005). Evaluating the readiness of pre- referral intervention teams for use in a problem solving model. *School Psychology Quarterly*, *20*(1), 89–105. doi:10.1521cpq.20.1.89.64192

Chalfant, J. C., Pysh, M. V., & Moultrie, R. (1979). Teacher assistance teams: A model for within-building problem solving. *Learning Disability Quarterly*, *2*(3), 85–95. doi:10.2307/1511031

Civic Impulse. (2016). *S. 1177 — 114th Congress: Every Student Succeeds Act.* Retrieved from https://www.govtrack.us/congress/bills/114/s1177

Crosby-Cooper, T. (2009). *Examining the effectiveness of student study teams in applied settings.* (Doctoral Dissertation) Retrieved from http://www.proquest.com/en-US/products/dissertations/individuals.shtml

Deno, S. (2002). Problem solving as "best practice.". In A. Thomas & J. Grimes (Eds.), *Best Practices in School Psychology IV* (4th ed.; pp. 37–55). Washington, DC: National Association of School Psychologists. District of Columbia State Improvement Grant. Student Support Teams-Research Synopsis. Retrieved from http://www.dcsig.org/files/100605/StudentSupportTeams_ResearchSynopsis.pdf

Education for all Handicapped Children's Act of 1975 (PL. 94-142). (n.d.). Retrieved from www.fcrr.org

Flugum, K. R., & Reschly, D. J. (1994). Pre-referral interventions: Quality indices and outcomes. *Journal of School Psychology*, *32*(1), 1–14. doi:10.1016/0022-4405(94)90025-6

Fuchs, D., & Fuchs, L. (2005). *Operationalizing response-to-intervention (RTI) as a method of LD identification.* Retrieved from http://www.state.tn.us/education/speced/seoperrifuchcase.pdf

Fuchs, D., & Fuchs, L. (2006). Introduction to Response to Intervention: What, why, and how valid is it? *Reading Research Quarterly*, *41*(1), 93–99. doi:10.1598/RRQ.41.1.4

Fuchs, D., Fuchs, L.S., & Bahr, M.W. (1990). Mainstream Assistance Teams: A scientific basis for the art of consultation. *Exceptional Children*, *57*(2), 128-139.

Fuchs, D., Mock, D., Morgan, P. L., & Young, C. L. (2003). Responsiveness-to- intervention: Definitions, evidence, and implications for the learning disabilities construct. *Learning Disabilities Research & Practice, 18*(3), 157–171. doi:10.1111/1540-5826.00072

Fuchs, L. S., Deno, S. L., & Mirkin, P. (1984). The effects of frequent curriculum-based measurement and evaluation on pedagogy, student achievement and student awareness of learning. *American Educational Research Journal, 21*(2), 449–460. doi:10.3102/00028312021002449

Graden, J. L. (1989). Redefining "pre-referral" intervention as intervention assistance: Collaboration between general and special education. *Exceptional Children, 56*(3), 227–231.

Graden, J. L., Casey, A., & Bonstrom, O. (1985). Implementing a prereferral intervention system: II. The data. *Exceptional Children, 51*, 487–496. PMID:3987765

Gresham, F. (2001). *Response to intervention: An alternative approach to the identification of learning disabilities.* Paper presented at the Learning Disabilities Summit, Washington, DC.

Gresham, F. (2004). Current status and future directions of school-based behavioral interventions. *School Psychology Review, 33*, 326–343.

Gresham, F. M. (1989). Assessment of treatment integrity in school consultation and pre-referral intervention. *School Psychology Review, 18*(1), 37–50.

Holleran, S. E. (2013). *Re-conceptualizing student study teams within a response to intervention framework: A web-based guide for educators* (Doctoral Dissertation). Retrieved from http://www.proquest.com/en-US/products/dissertations/individuals.shtml

Holleran, S. E. (2013). *Schools for Success*. Retrieved from http://www.schools4success.com/

House Committee on Education and the Workforce. (Report 108-077). To accompany H.R. 1350 (pp 107-108), Filed April 29, 2003.

Individuals with Disabilities Education Act. (2006). *34 C.F.R. 300 (Regulations) Civic Impulse. (2016). S. 844 — 112th Congress: Race to the Top Act of 2011.* Retrieved from https://www.govtrack.us/congress/bills/112/s844

Individuals with Disabilities Education Act (2006). 34 C.F.R. 300 (Regulations Implementing IDEA (1997) (Federal Register. (2006)).

Intervention Central. (n.d.)Retrieved from www.interventioncentral.org

Jankowski, E. A. (2003). Heartland area education agency's problem solving model: An outcomes-driven special education paradigm. *Rural Special Education Quarterly*, 2-9. Retrieved from http://www.questia.com/library/journal/1P3-597475431/heartland-area

Jenson, W., Rhode, G., & Reavis, K. (2010). *Tough Kid Tool Box*. Eugene, OR: Pacific Northwest Publishing.

Jones, F., Jones, P., & Jones, J. (2000). *Tools for Teaching: Discipline, Instruction, Motivation*. Santa Cruz, CA: F.H. Jones & Associates.

Knoff, H. (2010). *Stop and Think*. Little Rock, AK: Project Achieve Press.

Kratochwill, T. R., & Bergan, J. R. (1990). *Behavioral consultation in applied settings: An individual guide*. New York, NY: Plenum Press.

Marston, D., Muyskens, P., Lau, M., & Canter, A. (2003). Problem-solving model for decision making with high-incidence disabilities: The Minneapolis experience. *Learning Disabilities Research & Practice, 18*(3), 187–200. doi:10.1111/1540-5826.00074

Moore, K. J., Fifield, M. B., Spira, D. A., & Scarlato, M. (1989). Child study team decision making in special education: Improving the process. *Remedial and Special Education, 10*(4), 50–58. doi:10.1177/074193258901000409

National Reading Panel. (n.d.). *The Partnership aimed to ensure that the methods of reading instruction used in the classroom reflect evidence-based methods*. Retrieved from www.nationalreadingpanel.org

Office of Civil Rights and the U.S. Department of Education (2000). *Civil Rights Compliance Report*. Author.

Pennypacker, J. (1983). A review of Strategies and tactics of human behavioral research. *Applied Behavior Analysis, 16*(4), 461–464. doi:10.1901/jaba.1983.16-461

Peterson, L., Homer, A. L., & Wonderlich, S. A. (1982). The Integrity of Independent Variables in Behavior Analysis. *Journal of Applied Behavior Analysis, 15*(4), 477–492. doi:10.1901/jaba.1982.15-477 PMID:7153187

Powers, K. M. (2005). Problem solving student support teams. *California School Psychologist, 6*(1), 19–30. doi:10.1007/BF03340880

President's Commission on Excellence in Special Education. (2002). *A new era: Revitalizing special education for children and their families*. Washington, DC: Author.

Ruby, S., Crosby-Cooper, T., & Vanderwood, M. (2011). Fidelity of Problem Solving in Everyday Practice: Typical Training May Miss the Mark. *Journal of Educational & Psychological Consultation, 21*(3), 233-258.

Shappiro, E. (2010). Academic Skills Problems: Direct Interventions and Assessments (4th ed.). Florence, KY. Guilford Press.

Shinn, M. R., & Bamonto, S. (1998). Advanced applications of curriculum-based measurement: "Big ideas" and avoiding confusion. In M. R. Shinn (Ed.), Advanced applications of curriculum-based measurement (pp. 1-31). New York, NY: The Guilford school practitioner series.

Sprick, R. (2009). *CHAMPS A Proactive and Positive Approach to Classroom Management* (Vol. 2). Eugene, OR: Pacific Northwest Publishing.

Sprick, R., Garrison, M., & Howard, L. (1998). *CHAMPS A Proactive and Positive Approach to Classroom Management* (Vol. 1). Eugene, OR: Pacific Northwest Publishing.

Sprick, R., & Howard, L. (2002). *Teacher's Encyclopedia of Behavior Management: 100+ Problems/500+Plans*. Eugene, OR: Pacific Northwest Publishing.

Sprick, R., & Howard, L. (2012). *The Teacher's Encyclopedia of Behavior Management*. Eugene, OR: Pacific Northwest Publishing.

Sprick, R. S., & Garrison, M. (2008). *Interventions: Evidence-based behavioral Strategies for individual students* (2nd ed.). Eugene, OR: Pacific Northwest Publishing.

Telzrow, C., McNamara, K., & Hollinger, C. (2000). Fidelity of problem solving implementation and relationship to student performance. *School Psychology Review*, 29, 443–461.

Telzrow, C. F., & Beebe, J. J. (2002). Best practices in facilitating intervention adherence and integrity. In A. Thomas & J. Grimes (Eds.), *Best Practices in School Psychology IV* (4th ed.; pp. 503–516). Bethesda, MD: National Association of School Psychologists.

Tilly, W. D. III. (2002). Best practices in school psychology as a problem-solving enterprise. In A. Thomas & J. Grimes (Eds.), *Best Practices in School Psychology IV* (4th ed.; pp. 21–36). Washington, DC: National Association of School Psychologists.

Understanding Special Education. (n.d.). *Student Study Team*. Retrieved from http://www.understandingspecialeducation.com/student-study-team.html

Upah, K. R. F., & Tilly, D. W. III. (2002). Best practices in designing, implementing, and evaluating quality interventions. In A. Thomas & J. Grimes (Eds.), *Best Practices in School Psychology IV* (4th ed.; pp. 503–516). Bethesda, MD: National Association of School Psychologists.

U.S. Department of Education. No Child Left Behind. (2008). *Reading first: Student achievement, teacher empowerment, national success*. Retrieved from www.ed.gov/nclb/methods/reading/readingfirst.pdf

Vaughn, S., & Bos, C. (2015). *Strategies for Teaching Students with Learning and Behavior Problems*. Retrieved from https://www.pearsonhighered.com/program/Vaughn-Strategies-for-Teaching-Students-with-Learning-and-Behavior-Problems-Enhanced-Pearson-e-Text-with-Loose-Leaf-Version-Access-CardPackage-9th-Edition/PGM296487.html

West, Goldstein, A., & McGinnis, E. (2011). *Skillstreaming. Champaign, IL. Research Press What Works Clearing House*. Retrieved from http://ies.ed.gov/ncee/wwc/

Ysseldyke, J. E., & Algozzine, B. (1983). LD or not LD: That's not the question. *Journal of Learning Disabilities*, 16(1), 29–31. doi:10.1177/002221948301600112 PMID:6833864

KEY TERMS AND DEFINITIONS

Behavioral Consultation: Includes four stages – problem identification, problem analysis, treatment implementation, treatment evaluation.

Data-Based Decision Making: Data-based decision making focuses on formative evaluation of the intervention and allows educators to determine how well a student is responding to a specific intervention.

Individuals with Disabilities Education Improvement Act (IDEIA): Mandates in increased roles in data-based decision making. The use of scientifically based reading programs and an evaluation component regarding the student's response to the interventions.

Multi-Disciplinary Team (MDT): This process examines both academic and behavioral concerns.

No Child Left Behind (NCLB): The reauthorization of the Elementary and Secondary Education Act. Which requires evidence based practices for student achievement with state systems for accountability.

Response-to-Intervention (RTI): RTI is a multi-tiered approach to the early identification in support of students with learning and behavior needs.

Student Study Team (SST): The primary purpose of the SST is to assist the team in planning, developing, and implementing interventions in the general education setting.

This research was previously published in Preparing Pre-Service Teachers for the Inclusive Classroom edited by Jennifer Courduff, Patricia Dickenson, and Penelope Keough; pages 248-262, copyright year 2017 by Information Science Reference (an imprint of IGI Global).

Chapter 10
Best Practices Implementing Special Education Curriculum and Common Core State Standards using UDL

Penelope Debs Keough
National University, USA

Dina Pacis
National University, USA

ABSTRACT

The purpose of this chapter is to provide a model for collaboration between general education and special education teachers using Universal Design for Learning (UDL) to align common core state standards with instruction for students with special needs. A history of how UDL came to be and how it is now a strategic tool to support all learners is explored. Best practices are offered as supportive instructional strategies. An example of how UDL can be aligned with Common Core State Standards and the goal(s) found in an Individual Educational Plan (IEP) will also be provided. This model supports collaboration between general education and special education teachers in an effort to ensure that general education curriculum can be accessed by students with special needs.

INTRODUCTION

In the 2014-2015 academic year, 45 states began full implementation of Common Core State Standards. These standards were developed to transform American public education (National Governors Association Center for Best Practices [NGA Center] and Council of Chief State School Officers [CCSSO]. Specifically, the Common Core State Standards identify the key knowledge and skills that teachers must cover in the classroom. These key knowledge and skills are the foundation of state assessments which will provide evidence of student preparedness to be career and college ready (Conley, 2011).

DOI: 10.4018/978-1-7998-1213-5.ch010

Best Practices Implementing Special Education Curriculum and Common Core State Standards using UDL

One of the critical points of conversation during the development, adoption and implementation of CCSS for state LEA's was the need to ensure " students with disabilities are challenged to excel within the general education curriculum and be prepared for success in their post-school lives, including college and/or careers" (San Diego County Office of Education, 2013, np). This increased the urgency for special education teachers and school administrators to understand the CCSS and how they differ from prior standards (Shaefer, 2014; Staskowski, 2012). Additionally, the challenge to link individualized education programs (IEP) for students with disabilities directly to the grade level standards in CCSS has increased the challenge of special education teachers and school administrators. Student IEP's tied to standards is not new, it has been a requirement of federal law for well over a decade, but it continues to be a work in progress with the ongoing change and evolution of K-12 education. The CCSS initiative expects all students to meet grade level standards, but it does not address the specifics of writing IEP's. How to meld special educations mandate of individualized instruction with the goal of CCSS has been a struggle. Educators worry about unreasonable expectations as well as the concern that the focus on standards may crowd out some of the very important functional training students with disabilities may need (Samuels, 2010).

In an effort to increase access to general education curriculum for learners with disabilities, it is critical that teachers understand the barriers excluding these learners from access to the curriculum. This chapter will introduce the model Universal Design for Learning (UDL) as a means for collaboration between special education and general education teachers as they work towards aligning IEP goals with CCSS to design curriculum supporting student needs. Universal Design for Learning has become popular in recent years being defined quite simply as the planning of teaching and learning strategies to meet the needs of a broader population of students with diverse learning styles and abilities (Kurtts et al., 2009; Pisha & Coyne, 2001). The process of UDL provides teachers the means to remove preexisting barriers which may exist in curriculum, providing learners with a means to access and engage in the curriculum (Rose & Mayer, 2002; Orkwis & McLane, 1998). The principals of UDL foster student engagement, representation and evaluation in multiple ways, thereby lending itself to appropriately designing IEP goals complete with all three required components of time, task and measurement intact.

Much of the premise of UDL is based on brain research and how brain waves interact during higher order thinking processes. "What is most significant about our brains is not the band of neurons themselves, but the astonishing interconnectivity between them" (Meyer, Rose, & Gordon, 2014, p. 52). Going deeper into investigating cognitive mapping and the brain, we can explore Vygotsky's Zone of Proximal Development and Benjamin Bloom's Taxonomy or Depth of Knowledge. More will be uncovered to support UDL as a tool for aligning CCSS with IEP goals in regard to theorists just mentioned, but for now, a strong case has to be made for the "how to" incorporation of UDL in the Education Specialist's classroom to make certain CCSS and the student's with special needs IEP is being addressed.

Going deeper into the meaning of UDL and CCSS, one has to reach back several decades when the Center for Applied Special Technology determined that learning had to be learner centered and curriculum needed to be changed for the learner to grasp rather than the other way around. The learner did not need to change in order to penetrate the curriculum. Hence access to learning was a concept developed by CAST early on; developing a system that would remove barriers to learning! (Wakefield, 2011).

"Standards driven reform is a means of closing the achievement gap between enfranchised groups and disenfranchised (including special needs-groups) according to Fuchs et al, 2010 (as cited in Cash, 2006, p. 303). What Education Specialists are looking for is a formula, a template if you will, that allows them to align CCSS with each student's IEP goals. This becomes even more crucial when the site administrator steps into the special education classroom and either does not see the CCSS posted anywhere in the room, or sees a lesson conducted by the teacher that does not challenge higher order thinking skills, albeit a class comprised of students designated moderate severe disabilities.

This chapter will introduce UDL, as well as provide a model for how UDL can be used to support instruction that will deliver assessment based curriculum to students with special needs while remaining aligned to CCSS and the student's IEP.

GUIDELINES FOR UDL

Before we can examine the literature, the guidelines for UDL need to be presented. They are guided by three principles:

Principle I: Provide Multiple Means of Representation (the "what" of learning).
Principle II: Provide Multiple Means of Action and Expression (the "how" of learning).
Principle II: Provide Multiple Means of Engagement (the "why" of learning) (Wakefield, 2011, p. 5).

LITERATURE REVIEW

Providing an education for all students can be achieved through the implementation of the Universal Design for Learning (UDL). UDL removes roadblocks to learning through the use of built-in environments that benefit all learners (CAST, 2014). Originally developed by Robert L. Mace, architect, product designer, educator and advocate for individuals with disabilities, challenged traditional design in an effort to make the world a more useable place for everyone (The Center for Universal Design, College of Design, North Carolina State University, 2008).Examples of the work Mace helped pioneer are onscreen captioning for television to support those with hearing difficulties, and universal symbols which help facilitate meaning for those with difficulty reading, non-English speakers, and non-readers (Burgstahler, 2012). The original components of Universal Design became the principals from which UDL were eventually founded. These elements are comprised of the following:

1. Equitable use;
2. Flexibility in use;
3. Simple and intuitive use;
4. Perceptible information;
5. Tolerance for error;
6. Low physical effort;
7. Size and space for approach and use (Connell et al, 1997).

"The Universal Design for Learning Framework encourages creating flexible designs from the start that have customizable options, which allow all learners to progress from where they are and not where we would have imagined them to be" (Thompson, 2013, p. 10). Thompson (2013) studied at risk students, grades three through six, where the subject of implementation of Universal Design for Learning combined with RTI. Response to Intervention is a tiered system to support students who are struggling.

Only when all interventions have been implemented unsuccessfully is the student referred for special education assessment. Teachers initially participated in focus groups, then were interviewed using three key questions regarding the use of Universal Design for Learning in a mathematics classroom:

1. Since "learners differ in the ways that they perceive and comprehend information that is presented to them, "what non-traditional strategies/methods/techniques are provided for students to learn mathematics?
2. Given the fact that "learners differ in the ways that they can navigate a learning environment and express what they know", how is this done in mathematics to take in the uniqueness of each student?
3. It is an accepted fact within the Universal Design for Learning principles that "learners differ markedly in the ways in which they can be engaged or motivated to learn." How are learners motivated to learn mathematics using *Multiple Means of Engagement?* (p. 83-84). A wonderful resource for UDL is the National Center on Universal Design for Learning. The website highlights multiple means of engagement (See http://www.udlcenter.org/).

Additional methodology in the Thompson (2013) study included a review of the Louisiana school district's archival documents concerning the implementation of UDL combined with RTI when teaching elementary mathematics to students at risk. The results of the study showed students at risk, grades three through six, made significant gains in mathematics at the elementary level.

In another study (2006), not conclusive to the positive effects of aligning UDL to special education curriculum, but nonetheless important to this chapter studied directors' attitudes and factors implementing UDL in special education in Kentucky.

The methodology consisted of disseminating a survey to determine managerial behaviors. There was a 50% respondent rate based on N = 176. Of the 89 responders, results were used for descriptive purposes, and to ascertain general opinions of the Department of Special Education in Kentucky.

Thirty-six of the original 176 directors benefitted from having training in UDL principles. These directors guide the training of pre-service teachers in schools. The UDL training helps to inform their work as they develop, implement and facilitate UDL for preservice teachers. Specifically, directors are able to address UDL principles as a pathway to support preservice teachers in using UDL as a tool to align IEP goals with Common Core State Standards.

The fact that monies were spent in 36 districts in Kentucky to look at the attitudes of special education directors as well as other factors concerning leadership issues when implementing UDL in their schools, points to the importance of UDL as a tool to align special education curriculum with Common Core State Standards.

Segura (2016) set out to investigate teachers' perceptions of best practices when implementing CCSS in Special Education. Her method was to send a survey to K-8 special education teachers nationwide. The survey results evidenced there were:

1. Challenges implementing the CCSS in special education curriculum, and
2. Supports needed to address IEP goals when aligning them with CCSS.

The study used quantitative, i.e. descriptive statistics, and qualitative in the form of open ended questions which were analyzed using a constant comparative model.

Strategies favored by special education teachers in the Segura (2016) study to align CCSS to the special education curriculum were think alouds with modeling, graphic organizers which helped build vocabulary, building connections, and cooperative learning. The main challenges teachers faced in the above study were time, various needs in the classroom, aligning curriculum to CCSS, high caseloads and selecting most effective best practices.

A study conducted by (Nash, 2014) within an inclusive high school math class that implemented CCSS showed that instructional strategies used by special education resource teachers were based on Constructivism. The theory of Constructivism allows for multiple means of engagement which is the first principal of UDL. This is in keeping with the premise of this chapter that UDL is the tool to align CCSS with IEP goals.

When considering best practices for preservice teachers and how IEP goals are aligned with CCSS using the UDL process, constructivism emerges as a significant instructional strategy. The constructivist strategy compliments Universal Design for Learning through multiple means of engagement, representation, action & expression. This supports preservice teachers as they engage students, provide content (representation) and assess (action & expression) core curriculum for students with disabilities.

CONSTRUCTIVIST FOCUS

Woolfolk (2013) defines constructivism as a lens which emphasizes the active role a learner must take in order to build understanding and make sense of concepts which are taught. For example, to provide multiple means of engagement the preservice teacher may use constructivism to provide options for self-regulation. This allows students to work in cooperative groups assigning various roles that support self-efficacy and leadership. Engagement also allows for options to sustain effort and persistence. Constructivism lends itself to this practice. The preservice teacher providing multiple means to "vary demands and resourced to optimize challenge" (Meyer et al., 2014, p.114.) "Brainiac" games, math puzzles plus "word finds" (on a particular topic) at various levels can accommodate and meet the learning demands of the learner and thereby optimizing the challenge for further engagement. Constructivism allows for individual choice and autonomy, especially when the pre-service teacher has planned for various learning centers. The student has the option to choose their level of interest, capability to accomplish the task, and engage in full hands-on learning when actively involved in a learning center.

When the pre-service teacher is considering multiple means of representation, he/she provides options for comprehension. Constructivism supports this comprehension by activating or supplying needed background knowledge allowing the student to make meaning. This can be illustrated in group discussions by students actively completing a Venn diagram around a particular topic. This "highlights patterns, critical features, big ideas, and relationships (Meyer et al., 2014, p. 120). Additionally, representation can be accomplished through constructivism by presenting options for language, mathematical expressions and symbols through multiple media. Students can construct their own stories, poems, and mathematical illustrations to explain a procedure (even simplified equations) and even create videos to present constructs.

Multiple means of representation is further accomplished through constructivism by providing options for perception in that it "offers ways of customizing the display of information and offers alternatives for auditory and visual information" (Meyer et al., 2014, p. 122). The preservice teacher allows students to create (see Bloom's Taxonomy) dioramas, pictures of math problems to assist problem solving, compose songs to convey content, and last, but not least, compose videos to illustrate poignant information. When considering multiple means of action & expression, constructivism provides various ways for students to demonstrate knowledge. Action & expression provides options for executive functions, expression and communication, and physical action.

The pre-service teacher can design a lesson objective using constructivism by incorporating a visual means of students demonstrating knowledge gained by allowing assessment of the objective to consist of various hands-on activities to show mastery. For example, students can present a skit that shows concepts have been grasped. Or, compose a video, write a poem, construct a diagram, complete a learning center and/or even sing a song. There are so many more constructivist activities to show mastery other than trite pencil/paper exams, multiple choice questions and/or laborious essay responses.

The preservice teacher, when aligning CCSS with IEP goals using UDL must also be aware of creating depth of inquiry in the lesson. Inquiry refers to "systematic, intentional study of one's own professional practice" (Dana, Burns, & Wolkenhauer, 2013, p. 16.) Depth of Inquiry looks to how the preservice teacher designs the lesson using CCSS with the alignment of IEP goals and multiple means of engagement, representation and action & expression. In designing the lesson, the pre-service teacher must know the learners well. In other words, he/she must know the audience for whom the lesson is designed. Pre-assessment determines prior knowledge the instructor must base the lesson upon. Learner modalities must be considered. Differentiation for learners whose language is other than English must be considered as well as accommodations and modifications for students with disabilities.

Once the preservice teacher has a basis for who the learners are, actual teaching must occur. Teaching is an activity! This is where the pre-service teacher must decide how the lesson is to be presented; how it will unfold and how it will be offered to the learner for their full comprehension and understanding.

Designing the lesson is a *process*. As stated above, it begins with knowledge of the learner, must involve some pre-assessment, and revolve around a clear, concise objective that is measureable! It may look great on paper, but it is the ultimate "map", if you will, that the pre-service teacher takes into the classroom that is fully aligned to CCSS/IEP goals, but is able to be delivered according to the multiple means of engagement, representation, and action & expression.

IMPORTANCE OF UNIVERSAL DESIGN FOR LEARNING AND CCSS

The Segura (2016) study brings to the forefront the importance of this chapter and the need for special education teachers, and general education teachers to understand how to match CCSS with curriculum for students with special needs and align with IEP goals.

For example the following exemplifies one CCSS for writing in grade 5:

W.5.4: Produce clear and coherent writing (including multiple paragraph texts) in which the development and organization are appropriate to task, purpose, and audience. (p. 20).

When considering the CCSS for writing (w.5.4) one then reviews the students' individual IEP goals, attention must be given to any and all writing goals noted in the students' IEP. Several key elements to consider when aligning the CCSS to the IEP goals are: the level of students, i.e. are they capable of working within the framework of the CCSS with ease and or are accommodations/modifications needed?

Figure 1. Relationship of UDL to IEP individual education plan (IEP)

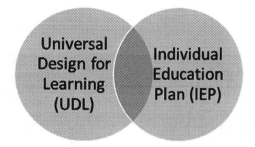

And application of Universal Design for Learning which allows students with special needs to achieve CCSS W.5.4 by:

1. Multiple means of Engagement
2. Multiple means of Representation
3. Multiple means of Action and Expression (p. 6).

In other words, the Universal Design for Learning can bring about the accomplishment of achieving the CCSS, W.5.4 by *multiple means*. The student who is non-verbal may produce "clear and coherent writing" through the use of technology. The student who is cognitively delayed may show "organization" is evidenced by a drawing, figure, or chart that is appropriate to the writing prompt. The special education instructor may use multiple means of action and expression by incorporating daily task sheets as evidence of students qualifying as moderate severe disabled when assessing the lesson objective aligned with writing W.5.4.

The illustration below represents the relationship of Universal Design for Learning with the Individual Education Plan (IEP).

BLOOMS TAXONOMY

A discussion of aligning Common Core State Standards with IEP goals would not be complete unless Bloom's Taxonomy was addressed since IEP goals are asking students to perform specific tasks, which are measurable, and based on their assessed need(s). Blooms Taxonomy assists preservice teachers by providing a framework for developing IEP goals.

The diagram is taken from Forehand, M. (2005). Bloom's taxonomy: Original and revised; In M. Orey (Ed.), Emerging perspectives on learning, teaching, and technology.

According to Woolfolk (2013): "The 2001 revision of Bloom's taxonomy added a new dimension-to recognize that cognitive processes must process *something*; you have to remember or understand or apply some form of knowledge…We now have the six processes of *remembering, understanding, applying, analyzing, evaluating,* and *creating* acting on four kinds of knowledge-*factual, conceptual, procedural, and metacognitive* (p. 516). Why is Bloom's Taxonomy so important to the alignment of special education curriculum, based on students with special needs IEP goals and the Common Core State Standards?

Figure 2. Comparison of older version of Bloom's Taxonomy to newer version
Retrieved May 29, 2016, from http://epltt.coe.uga.edu/

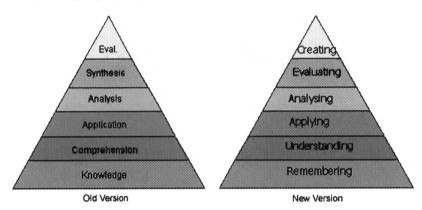

In a message from the State Board of California Education, Dr. M. Kirst, President, and the Superintendent of Schools, Tom Torlakson, emphasis is on the cognitive processes noted in Bloom's taxonomy:

The standards identify what it means to be a literate person in the 21st century. Students learn to closely and attentively read and analyze critical works of literature and an array of nonfiction text in an exploding print and digital world. They use research and technology to sift through the staggering amount of information available and engage in collaborative conversations, sharing and reforming viewpoints through a variety of written and speaking applications. Teachers and schools, districts and county offices of education, are encouraged to use these standards to design specific curricular and instructional strategies that best deliver the content to their students (Schaefer, 2016, p.8)

Not only does Bloom's Taxonomy set the stage for higher order thinking, which one may question if one puts limitations on students with special needs, but Bloom's Classification of verbs for the Cognitive Domain assist with writing IEP goals as stated previously (see illustration below taken from Chard-Yaron, 1997, p. 7). One example of an IEP goal utilizing Bloom's is as follows: *Jay a 5th grade will **organize** a multi-sentence paragraph by using topic sentence first in 4 out of 5 trials as measured by teacher records.* The CCSS mentioned on page 4 (W.5.4) refers to organization in writing. Therefore an appropriate Bloom's Taxonomy verb was selected to illustrate the student's task towards meeting the CCSS at the 5th grade level.

The following is an example of verbs that can be used when writing Individual Education Goals.

BEST PRACTICES FOR PRESERVICE TEACHERS

The following provides steps to consider when aligning Common Core State Standards with Individual Education Plan goals using Universal Design as the tool. As previously discussed in this chapter, Universal Design for Learning (UDL) provides Multiple Means in the following areas:

- Multiple Means of Action & Expression

Best Practices Implementing Special Education Curriculum and Common Core State Standards using UDL

Table 1. *An example of Bloom's classification of verbs*

comprehension-interpret information in one's own words classify, describe, restate, discuss, explain, translate express, report **analysis-break down knowledge into parts and show relationships among parts** analyze, appraise, categorize, compare, contrast, criticize, diagram, differentiate, discriminate, distinguish, examine, question, test	**Knowledge-recall of information** arrange, list define, name duplicate, reproduce label **application-use knowledge or generalization in a new situation** apply, choose, practice, demonstrate, dramatize, prepare employ, illustrate, schedule interpret, operate, sketch, solve, use
Evaluation-make judgments on basis of given criteria appraise, argue, assess, attack, choose, compare, defend, estimate, evaluate, judge, predict, rate, score, select, support, value	**Synthesis-bring together parts of knowledge to form a whole and build relationships for new situations** arrange, assemble, collect, compose, construct, create, design, formulate, manage, organize, plan, prepare, propose, set up, synthesize

- Multiple Means of Representation and
- Multiple Means of Engagement (Meyer, et al., 2014, p. 111)

In order to make the following steps useful to the reader, a conceptual understanding of what each category means is paramount.

Principle 1: Action and Expression in UDL refer to strategic, goal-directed learners in which the instructor provides: options for executive functions such as appropriate goal setting, supportive planning and strategy development and enhance capacity for monitoring progress, options for expression and communication, and options for physical action to vary the methods for response and navigation and optimize access to tools and assistive technologies (Meyer et al., 2014, p. 111)

Action and Expression require a great deal of strategy, practice, and organization which may differ among various learners (Wakefield, 2011, p. 22). The following are some options for action and expression the preservice teacher can utilize to see whether learning modalities are varied for differentiated learning:

1. A variety of different methods for physical action and a variety of methods for student expression and communication such as multi- media for communication.
2. Scaffold instruction in order to reach the "Zone of Proximal Development" so students at a lower level can ultimately achieve advanced knowledge (Wakefield, 2011).

   Principle 2: Representation in UDL refers to resourceful, knowledgeable learners in which the instructor provides: options for comprehension, options for language, mathematical expressions and symbols plus options for perception including ways of customizing the display of information. One offers alternatives for auditory information and alternatives for visual information.

   Principle 3: Engagement in UDL refers to purposeful, motivated learners in which the instructor provides: options for self-regulation, options for sustaining effort/persistence, options for recruiting interest composed of individual choice and autonomy, optimize relevance, values and authenticity, and minimize threats and distractions.

In regard to self-regulation, the preservice teacher is wise to develop the learner's intrinsic motivation and foster the learner's ability to control their own emotions and self-regulation. This can be done by modeling and prompting in a variety of methods (Wakefield, 2011, p. 32). Some examples to accomplish self-regulation are prompts that remind or guide are:

1. Self-regulatory goals that accomplish reduction of frequency of outbursts or aggression, and increase the length of time on task.
2. Use of "shaping" to foster self-reflection and self-reinforcement to gradually remove a reinforcer so that intrinsic motivation is the end result.

In psychological terms, "shaping is a process of building new responses by beginning with behavior the student already exhibits at some level and reinforcing successive approximations of that behavior" (Kauffman, 2005, p. 304).

In summary, the reader can equate "multiple means of engagement" to creating motivated learners through various constructivist strategies. Multiple means of representation refers to how the learner can express their knowledge. Multiple means of action and expression to be the various ways learners can be assessed based on the learner's goals.

The following model will work for pre-service teachers working to align Common Core State Standards with IEP goals using Universal Design for Learning as a tool for multiple means of Engagement, Representation and Action & Expression.

Additional strategies for the UDL principal of Engagement, options in self-regulation, sustaining effort and persistence, and recruiting interest, are noted below when preservice teachers are implementing IEP goals tied to CCSS and UDL practices.

1. **Token Economy**: This is a reward system which encourages self-regulation, motivation, sustained effort and interest. Students earn token rewards when they are observed engaged in these behaviors.

Table 4. Model to align CCSS with IEP goals using UDL

IEP Goal	CCSS	Multiple Means of Engagement	Multiple Means of Representation	Multiple Means of Representation	Multiple Means of Action & Expression
Within 1 yr. John will write two paragraphs that include a topic sentence with supporting detail as measured by teacher records/ observation with 80% accuracy.	w.5.4- Produce clear and coherent writing (including multiple paragraph texts) in which the development and organization are appropriate to task, purpose, and audience	Strategy supporting UDL: Interactive Writing 1.Providing active learning experiences. 2. Talking to establish a purpose. 3. Composing and constructing the text. 4. Rereading, revising, and proofreading. 6. Revisiting text to support word solving. 7. Summarizing and extending the learning.	Strategy supporting UDL: Assistive Technology where student exhibits assessed need. Dictate to "dragon speech" when assessed need of student requires such. Visual representation of main idea and supporting details for students in M/S category	Strategy supporting UDL: Allow final student product to be produced via Assistive Technology where assessed need is warranted. Illustrations of final project from students qualified as M/S. Media acceptable to present final project by student

2. **Positive Reinforcement**: This is another reward system which supports self-regulation and motivation, sustained effort and interest. In this reward system tokens are not necessarily utilized, but verbal praise is provided when the behaviors are exhibited.
3. **Modeling**: Pre-service teachers demonstrate the desired behavior that promote self-regulation and motivation, sustained effort and interest. Think-Alouds are another form of modeling. The think-aloud strategy asks students to say out loud what they are thinking about when reading, solving math problems, or simply responding to questions posed by teachers or other students. Effective teachers think out loud on a regular basis to model this process for students. In this way, they demonstrate practical ways of approaching difficult problems while bringing to the surface the complex thinking processes that underlie reading comprehension, mathematical problem solving, and other cognitively demanding tasks by:
4. **Constructivist Technique**: Hands on learning to promote engagement.
5. **Learning Centers**: Built on constructivist activities, learning centers provide sustained hands on learning which supports interest and student engagement.
6. **Technology**: Various forms of media can support self-regulation, motivation, sustained effort and interest.

The UDL principal of representation focuses on the resourceful and knowledgeable learner. The goal of this principal is to provide options in comprehension, language, mathematical expressions, symbols and options for perception. The following are some recommended strategies for the UDL principal of Representation which a preservice teacher can consider when implementing IEP goals tied to CCSS and UDL practices.

To promote comprehension preservice teachers may use the following strategies:

Graphic Organizers/nonverbal representation (e.g., pictures, graphs, charts [K-W-L], three dimensional objects, concept maps/Thinking Maps, diagrams [Venn]). Graphic organizers can be utilized across the content areas. Graphic Organizers can be used to promote higher order thinking skills..

Action and expression provides for executive functions, communication, and physical action. This goal is the assessment portion of UDL where students are asked to express or show (action) their learning. The following are some recommended strategies for this UDL principal which a preservice teacher can consider when implementing IEP goals tied to CCSS and UDL practices such as:

Reciprocal Teaching/Comprehension text processing (e.g., summarizing, questioning, clarifying, and predicting)

The Reciprocal Teaching strategy involves a role reversal: students become teachers of reading strategies. Palincsar and Brown (1984) argue that Reciprocal Teaching should always train students in . . .

Predicting upcoming information.
Asking questions.
Identifying and clarifying confusing information.
Summarizing as a means of self-review.
Steps to Reciprocal Teaching:
Select a well-structured text selection for the exercise. Distribute copies of the selection to the class.
Explain the four reading skills that you will demonstrate: summarizing, questioning, clarifying, and predicting.
Model each of these skills by analyzing the first paragraph of the document.

Divide the class into small groups. Assign each student in the groups one of the remaining paragraphs. Have the student "teach" the four reading skills to the group, using their assigned paragraph. Encourage discussion within the groups both during and after the student presentations. Ask students to identify the skills that were most and least effectively used.

Thoughtful Classroom Discourse

Talk is important. Children whose families talk to them often on a variety of topics come to school with more vocabulary than children who come from homes where talk is limited. Assist children who lack vocabulary by providing them with the same sort of highly interactive, language-rich environment that children with a large vocabulary have. Engage these students in conversations on a wide range of topics, calling attention to the different types of meaning of interesting words in their daily interactions with text (both written and oral), and promote curiosity about words and the different meanings that words can have in different contexts.

Cooperative Learning (e.g., numbered heads together, three step interview, Think-Pair-Share, number lines, Jigsaw)

SUGGESTED SOLUTIONS AND RECOMMENDATIONS

In order to support the preservice teacher who needs to align CCSS with IEP goals using UDL, better vertical articulation and alignment between preservice teacher programs in higher education and the Pk-12 system needs to occur. Additional professional development around the UDL principals as a tool for aligning CCSS and the writing of IEP goals needs to be ongoing. This additional professional development provides the backdrop for expert collaboration between administration and educators at the school site. By collaborative professional development, support from school administrators is garnered to build collaborative school communities between general education and special education teachers.

Preservice teachers will always be looking for answers: how to best serve students with special needs in the inclusive classroom, how to design lessons so that all students can learn and how to survive those first few years without undue stress and anxiety. The authors of this chapter propose that aligning Common Core State Standards with Universal Design for Learning will accomplish goals, not only for preservice teachers, but goals so that all students in the inclusive classroom can learn.

What is needed is a new mindset so that preservice teachers can expand their thinking to deliver lessons on a broader scope, using Universal Design for Learning to encompass all modalities of learning while using the Common Core State Standards as a base and matching them to the individual IEP goals. This chapter has presented an alignment chart to show how CCSS, IEP goals and Universal Design for Learning are connected. The preservice teacher will do well to make sure all three components are in continual alignment.

A discussion of alignment of CCSS, IEP goals and UDL to deliver meaningful lessons to all students is somewhat limited in written form. An important solution to the implementation of this alignment of all three components has to happen in the inclusive classroom. An ideal solution and recommendation is to offer a "lab" classroom where the preservice teacher has the opportunity to practice delivering a lesson conforming to CCSS, aligned with IEP goals using UDL. The guidance and supervision of a seasoned mentor teacher is a requirement that would further this implementation. The support of a veteran teacher while the preservice teacher carries out suggested strategies found in this chapter while practicing the use of UDL to implement CCSS aligned with IEP goals is invaluable in the inclusive classroom.

FUTURE RESEARCH DIRECTIONS

Preservice programs for teachers working with students with special needs will continue to search for methods that align Common Core State Standards with IEP goals. Professional development collaboratively developed between preservice teacher programs and school districts needs to be explored. Universal Design for Learning is an effective tool for this alignment and should continue to be explored as such for special education program curriculum and design.

Future research in the area of preservice teacher mentoring and supervision while implementing UDL's alignment with IEP goals and CCSS is needed. The effectiveness of the mentoring/supervision process is only as good as the professional development and training an institute of higher education (IHE) can provide. One institution is now using inter-rater reliability to make certain all supervisors of preservice teachers are evaluating candidates in the same manner. The IHE uses a formative and summative assessment along a 4-point rubric that identifies whether the preservice teacher is at the following four stages: beginning, emerging, applying or integrating. The passage from preservice teacher to fully credentialed teacher is dependent upon the summative assessment.

It is the authors' opinion that more IHEs will use inter-rater reliability of the evaluative tools for preservice teaching to determine whether they are able to implement effective lesson planning. Using UDL as a vehicle to align CCSS with IEP goals will ensure the preservice teacher is successful in the inclusive classroom instructing all students.

CONCLUSION

In conclusion, this chapter is a model of how Universal Design for Learning is a tool to align Common Core State Standards with IEP goals. This model supports collaboration between general education and special education teachers in an effort to ensure that general education curriculum can be accessed by students with special needs. A history of how UDL came to be and how it is now a strategic tool to support all learners were explored. Best practices are offered as supportive instructional strategies. An example of how UDL can be aligned with Common Core State Standards and the goal(s) found in an Individual Educational Plan (IEP) are provided.

REFERENCES

Burgstahler, S. (2012). *Universal Design of Instruction (UDI): Definition, principles, guidelines, and examples.* Retrieved from University of Washington, DO-IT (Disabilities, Opportunities, Internetworking, and Technology) website: http://www.washington.edu/doit/Brochures/Academics/instruction.html

Busy Teachers Café. (n.d.). *Comprehension Strategies.* Retrieved May 30, 2016 from http://www.busyteacherscafe.com/literacy/comprehension_strategies.htmlhttp://www.busyteacherscafe.com/literacy/comprehension_strategies.html

California Department of Education Special Education Symposium. (n.d.). Retrieved from http://aisep4ca.org

CAST. (2011). *Universal Design for Learning Guidelines version 2.0.* Wakefield, MA: Author.

CAST, Inc. (2014). *UDL Studio.* Retrieved May 30, 2016 from http://udlstudio.cast.org/http://udlstudio.cast.org/

Center for Universal Design, College of Design, North Carolina State University. (2008). *About the center: Ronald L. Mace.* Retrieved from http://www.ncsu.edu/ncsu/design/cud/about_us/usronmace.htm

Color in Colorado. (n.d.). *Cooperative Learning Strategies.* Retrieved May 30, 2016 from http://www.colorincolorado.org/article/cooperative-learning-strategies

Conley, D. T. (2011). Building on the Common Core. *Educational Leadership*, 68(6), 16–20.

Connell, B. R., Jones, M., Mace, R., Mueller, J., Mullick, A., Ostroff, E., & ... (2013). *Inquiring into the common core.* Thousand Oaks, CA: Corwin.

Dees, J. (n.d.). *How to Get Students to Participate in Class Discussions.* Retrieved May 30, 2016 from http://www.thereligionteacher.com/how-to-get-students-to-participate-in-class-discussions/http://www.thereligionteacher.com/how-to-get-students-to-participate-in-class-discussions/

Forehand, M. (2005). Bloom's taxonomy: Original and revised. In M. Orey (Ed.), *Emerging perspectives on learning, teaching, and technology.* Retrieved May 29, 2016, from http://epltt.coe.uga.edu/

GOS Organizers. (n.d.). Retrieved May 30, 2016 from http://members.whro.net/~pterry/vwc/week7/Gos.htm

Kauffman, J. M. (2005). *Characteristics of Emotional and Behavioral Disorders of Children and Youth* (8th ed.). Upper Saddle River, NJ: Pearson.

Kelly, M. (n.d.). *Top 10 Mnemonic Devices.* Retrieved May 30, 2016 from http://712educators.about.com/od/creativethinking/tp/mnemonics.htm

Kurtts, S., Matthews, C., & Smallwood, T. (2009). (Dis)Solving the difference: A physical science lesson using Universal Design. *Intervention in School and Clinic*, 44(3), 151–159. doi:10.1177/1053451208326051

McKeown, M., Beck, I., Omanson, R., & Pople, M. (1985). Some effects of the nature and frequency of vocabulary instruction on the knowledge and use of words. *Reading Research Quarterly, 20*(5), 522–535. doi:10.2307/747940

Meyer, A., Rose, D., & Gordon, D. (2014). *Universal Design for Learning theory and practice*. Wakefield, MA: CAST.

Nagy, W., & Herman, P. (1987). Breadth and depth of vocabulary knowledge: Implications for acquisition and instruction. In M. McKeown & M. Curtiss (Eds.), *The Nature of Vocabulary Acquisition* (pp. 19–35). Hillsdale, NJ: Erbaum.

Nagy, W. E., & Anderson, R. C. (1984). The number of words in printed school English. *Reading Research Quarterly, 19*(3), 304–330. doi:10.2307/747823

Nash, A. M. (2014). *Resource teachers' perceptions on common core standards and constructivist instructional strategies for students with learning disabilities* (3642377). Available from ProQuest Dissertations & Theses Global. (1626042051). Retrieved from http://ezproxy.nu.edu/login?url=http://search.proquest.com/docview/1626042051?acc ountid=25320http://ezproxy.nu.edu/login?url=http://search.proquest.com/docview/16 26042051?accountid=25320

National Center on Universal Design for Learning. (2012). *National Center on Universal Design for Learning*. Retrieved June 24, 2016. http://www.udlcenter.org/aboutudl/whatisudlhttp://www.udlcenter.org/aboutudl/whatisudl

National Governors Association Center for Best Practices (NGA Center), & Council of Chief State School Officers (CCSSO). (2013). *Common Core State Standards for English language arts and literacy in history/social studies, science, and technical subjects*. Washington, DC: Author.

National Governors Association Center for Best Practices (NGA Center), & Council of Chief State School Officers (CCSSO). (2010a). *Application to students with disabilities*. Washington, DC: Author. Retrieved from http://www.corestandards. org/assets/application-to-students-with-disabilities.pdf

National Governors Association Center for Best Practices (NGA Center), & Council of Chief State School Officers (CCSSO). (2010b). *Common Core State Standards for English Language Arts and literacy in history/social studies, science, and technical subjects*. Washington, DC: Author. Retrieved from http://www.corestandards.org/the-standards

National Governors Association Center for Best Practices (NGA Center), & Council of Chief State School Officers (CCSSO). (2010c). *Common Core State Standards for English language arts & literacy in history/social studies, science, and technical subjects. Appendix A: Research supporting key elements of the standards*. Washington, DC: Author. Retrieved from http://www.corestandards. org/assets/Appendix_A.pdf

No Child Left Behind Act (NCLB), 20 U.S.C. § 6301 et seq (2002).

Orkwis, R. (2003). *Universally designed instruction (ERIC /OSEP Digest, ERIC Document Reproduction Service No. ED475386)*. Arlington, VA: ERIC Clearinghouse on Disabilities and Gifted Education. Retrieved from http://files.eric.ed.gov/fulltext/ED475386.pdf

Orkwis, R., & McLane, K. (1998). *A curriculum every student can use: Design principles for student access (ERIC/OSEP Topical Brief, ERIC Document Reproduction Service No. ED423654)*. Reston, VA: ERIC/OSEP Special Project. Retrieved from http://eric.ed.gov/?id=ED423654http://eric.ed.gov/?id=ED423654

Palincsar, A. S., & Brown, A. L. (1984). Reciprocal teaching of comprehension-fostering and and comprehension-monitoring activities. *Cognition and Instruction, 1*(2), 117–175. doi:10.12071532690xci0102_1

Partnership for Assessment of Readiness for College and Careers. (n.d.). *PARCC frequently asked questions updated—September 2013*. Retrieved from https://www.parcconline.org/sites/parcc/files/PARCCFAQ_9-18-2013.pdf

Pisha, B., & Coyne, P. (2001). Smart from the start: The promise of universal design for learning. *Remedial and Special Education, 22*(4), 197–203. doi:10.1177/074193250102200402

Reading Educator. (n.d.). *Reciprocal Teaching*. Retrieved May 30, 2016 from http://www.readingeducator.com/strategies/reciprocal.htm

Rose, D. H., & Meyer, A. (2002). *Teaching every student in the digital age: Universal design for learning*. Alexandria, VA: Association for Supervision and Curriculum Development.

Rose, D. H., & Meyer, A. (2006). *A practical reader in universal design for learning*. Cambridge, MA: Harvard Education Press.

Samuels, C. (2010). Special Educators Look to Tie IEPs to Common Core. *Education Week, 30*(15), 8–9.

Schaefer, K. (2014, March 21). *Aligning IEP's and the CCSS: A deeper dive* [Webinar]. California Department of Education Special Education Symposium. Retrieved from http://cde.videossc.com/archives/032114/

Segura, L. (2016). *Special educators' beliefs about best instructional practices needed for common core implementation* (10044092). Available from ProQuest Dissertations & Theses Global. (1776183908). Retrieved from http://ezproxy.nu.edu/login?url=http://search.proquest.com/docview/1776183908?accountid=25320

Shared and Interactive Writing. (n.d.). Retrieved May 30, 2016 from http://www.sachem.edu/dept/curriculum/languagearts/sharedinteractivewriting.html

Stahl, S., & Fairbanks, M. (1986). The Effects of Vocabulary Instruction: A Model-Based Meta-Analysis. *Review of Educational Research, 86*(56), 72-110.

Staskowski, M. (2012). Overview of the Common Core State Standard initiative and educational reform movement from the vantage of speech-language pathologists. *Seminars in Speech and Language, 33*(02), 95–101. doi:10.1055-0032-1310310 PMID:22538706

Takemae, N. (2015). *Acquisition and application: Universal design for learning with teacher candidates in special education: General curriculum and the dual major in elementary education and special education: General curriculum* (3708190). Available from ProQuest Dissertations & Theses Global. (1696782161). Retrieved from http://ezproxy.nu.edu/login?url=http://search.proquest.com/docview/1696782161?accountid=25320

Teacher Vision. (n.d.a). *Think Aloud Strategy.* Retrieved May 30, 2016 from https://www.teachervision.com/skill-builder/problem-solving/48546.html

Teacher Vision. (n.d.b) *Building Vocabulary.* Retrieved May 30, 2016 https://www.teachervision.com/skill-builder/teaching-methods/48607.html?page=1https://www.teachervision.com/skill-builder/teaching-methods/48607.html?page=1

Vanderheiden, G. (1997). *The principles of universal design.* Retrieved from North Carolina State University, the Center for Universal Design website: http://www.ncsu.edu/ncsu/design/cud/about_ud/udprinciplestext.htm

Walker-Thompson, M. (2014). *Special education teachers' knowledge and use of brain-based teaching, common core state standards, formative feedback practices and instructional efficacy for the diverse learning needs of students in high and low proficiency groups* (3581567). Available from ProQuest Dissertations & Theses Global. (1590933593). Retrieved from http://ezproxy.nu.edu/login?url=http://search.proquest.com/docview/1590933593?accountid=25320

Wiggins, G., & McTighe, J. (2005). *Understanding by Design.* New York, NY: Pearson.

Woolfolk, A. (2013). *Educational Psychology.* Retrieved May 30, 2016 from http://r.search.yahoo.com/_ylt=A86.J76L1E1XWgYAwicnnIlQ;_ylu=X3oDMTByb2lvbXVuBGNvbG8DZ3ExBHBvcwMxBHZ0aWQDBHNlYwNzcg--/RV=2/RE=1464747276/RO=10/RU=http%3a%2f%2fcdlyjd.com%2fpdfdocument-readbook%2feducational-psychology-woolfolk-2013-12th-edition-pearson.pdf/RK=0/RS=1yVX4YhTArQVIlh4MexT3hpqkrM-

Woolfolk, A. (2013). *Educational Psychology.* Upper Saddle River, NJ: Pearson.

KEY TERMS AND DEFINITIONS

Bloom's Taxonomy: A classification system created by Bloom that addressed six domains: remembering, understanding, applying, analyzing, evaluating, creating on four kinds of knowledge – factual, conceptual, procedural, and metacognitive.

Collaboration: Collaboration is a working group with a common goal. The term is often used when general education teachers and special education teachers work together.

Common Core State Standards: The standards are designed to be robust and relevant to the real world, reflecting the knowledge and skills that our young people need for success in college and careers.

Constructivism: A hands-on instructional method which aligns with the kinesthetic learning modality. Constructivism encourages student motivation, engagement and creativity.

Individuals with Disabilities Education Act (IDEA): Transitioned from PL94-142 in 1990 to oversee the educational and support of students with disabilities. IDEA was revised in 1997 and the latest revision was in 2004.

IEP Goal: Written as part of the individual education plan based on student assessed need and must include time, task, and measurement.

Individual Education Plan (IEP): Mandated by the Individual Education ACT (2004) to be held annually for students with special needs includes such items as present levels of performance, individual educational goals, placement recommendation, accommodations and modifications, extended school year as well as transition plan when appropriate.

Special Education: Began with PL94-142, Education for All Handicapped Children Act (1975) to level the playing field for students with disabilities. It became IDEA in 1990 which mandates and oversees laws concerning children with disabilities.

This research was previously published in Preparing Pre-Service Teachers for the Inclusive Classroom edited by Jennifer Courduff, Patricia Dickenson, and Penelope Keough; pages 107-123, copyright year 2017 by Information Science Reference (an imprint of IGI Global).

Chapter 11
Access to Higher Education for People with Disabilities:
A Chinese Perspective

Luanjiao Hu
University of Maryland at College Park, USA

Jing Lin
University of Maryland at College Park, USA

ABSTRACT

This chapter focuses on a series of related questions centered on access issue for people with disabilities in Chinese higher education: what is the representation for people with disabilities in Chinese higher education? What factors contribute to the impediment of access for higher education for people with disabilities? What educational legislation exist that provide educational guidelines for people with disabilities? What cultural traditions underlie the lack of educational attainment for people with disabilities in China?

INTRODUCTION

In China, people with disabilities are visible and invisible at the same time. Visible in the sense that they are subjects of attention and discussion when spotted in "unexpected" public locations; invisible in the sense that the need for social participation of people with disabilities is generally neglected by the public (Tinklin, Riddell, & Wilson, 2004; Barnes, 2007). This invisibility extends to the education sector. In the discussion of factors causing educational inequality, disability/ability is seldom mentioned or studied in China.

Higher education is nowadays regarded as a prerequisite for success in the labor market in the era of knowledge society. China underwent a great expansion of higher education enrollment from 1999 to 2005, and it is increasingly crucial for young people to obtain higher education credentials. The long tradition of valuing education as a way for social mobility also greatly affects Chinese way of thinking

DOI: 10.4018/978-1-7998-1213-5.ch011

and investing in education. Higher education attainment significantly determines chances for better employment opportunities and higher income. While admitted students into Chinese higher education reached the total number of 7.2 million in 2014 (Ministry of Education, 2015), people with disabilities as a population is being left behind. Compared to the admitted millions to higher education in 2012, a number of 8,363 people with disabilities were admitted in 2012 (China's Disabled Persons Federation, 2015). In the National Education Development Annual Report released in 2015 by the Ministry of Education, special education is still categorized together with pre-school education. There was no data in regards to people with disabilities in higher education throughout the Report.

Various barriers persist, impeding the educational attainment for people with disabilities. Not much research has been done to look into the higher education access for this population in China. To fill the gap in literature, this article aims to examine the issue of higher education access for people with disabilities. The article focuses on a series of related questions centered on issues of access for people with disabilities in higher education: What is the representation of people with disabilities in Chinese higher education? What factors contribute to the impediment of access for this population? What educational legislations exist that provide educational guidelines for people with disabilities? What cultural traditions underlie the lack of educational attainment for them?

As guidance for answering these questions, the article uses three frameworks: inclusive education, education as a basic human right, and social model and medical model for defining disability. The article starts with the definition and theoretical frameworks. Then it moves to examine the access to elementary and secondary education for children with disabilities. This is followed by attempts to analyze the context of Chinese higher education, specifically the expansion of university enrollment starting in 1999. The ensuing section of the article looks at the College Entrance Examination (CEE), Physical Examination policies, and the role these policies play in affecting the fairness of the higher education access. Finally, the barriers that impede the access to higher education for people with disabilities are examined. The article concludes with reflections and policy recommendations.

DEFINITION AND BACKGROUND

To start with, let us look at the definitions for disability. In Oxford Dictionary, "disability" is defined as "a physical or mental condition that limits a person's movements, senses, or activities" or "a disadvantage or handicap, especially one imposed or recognized by the law". In the Chinese Law on the Protection of Disabled Persons (LPDP, 1990), people with disabilities are referred to as "*Can Ji Ren*", meaning "people who suffer from abnormalities of loss of a certain organ or function, psychologically or physiologically, or in anatomical structure and has lost wholly or in part the ability to perform an activity in the way considered normal." "*Can Ji Ren*" as the Chinese definition of people with disabilities refers to those with visual, hearing, speech or physical disabilities, intellectual disabilities, psychiatric disabilities, multiple disabilities and/or other disabilities.

In this article, the authors will use the Chinese phrase "*Can Ji Ren*" as an interchangeable term to refer to people with disabilities. Here, "*Can Ji*" means disability or disabled, and "*Ren*" means person or people. Together "*Can Ji Ren*" means disabled people or people with disabilities. The major organization for "*Can Ji Ren*" in China is the China's Disabled Persons' Federation (CDPF), established in 1988 by Deng Pufang, the son of a powerful political leader—Deng Xiaoping. The logo for the organization incorporates the acronym of *"Can Ji Ren"*—CJR in a flowery pattern as a representation of people with disabilities.

This article uses many data of various sources, mainly from China's Ministry of Education, the annual statistical bulletins from CDPF, and the Second National Survey of People with Disabilities conducted in 2006. The different data sources pose a challenge to this study, as some of the data show inconsistencies comparing with each other. The research conducted by Stratford and NG in 2000 also commented that the data on people with disabilities in China could never be as accurate as in some western countries due to the population size and uneven distribution of these people in rural and urban China. As a result, one needs to be critical about the accuracy of the data considering the possible underestimation or the scope of the data-collecting process.

The development of education system for people with disabilities in China has a late start and remains relatively stagnant in its improvement. The first special higher education institution for *Can Ji Ren* was not established until 1987. It was around the mid-1980s that higher education for *Can Ji Ren* began to develop and slowly *Can Ji Ren* began to enroll in regular higher education institutions (HEI), though with very limited numbers. Despite availability of different but often disparate sources of data, one difficulty of the study remains—there is a lack of data in the Ministry of Education for people with disabilities who are enrolled in Chinese higher education institutions. The few limited sources the authors found were from CDPF, the national umbrella organization for people with disabilities. The numbers suggest that *Can Ji Ren* are greatly underrepresented in higher education compared to their peers without disabilities. These numbers will be examined later in the article.

Overall, the lack of representation for people with disabilities in higher education can be attributed to an array of factors. To start with, there is a low enrollment rate in primary education for children with disabilities of school age. Comparing to their non-disabled peers who have achieved almost 100 percent enrollment ratio in primary education, only about 55.6% of the children with disabilities (age 6-17) are enrolling in school in 2007 (Chen, Lin, Zhang, Song, & Zheng, 2011). The illiteracy rate for people with disabilities is over 40 percent, much higher than their nondisabled peers. As the majority of the people with disabilities are found in the rural or remote areas of China, access to educational provision is limited for the disabled population in these areas (Chen et al, 2011). There is usually a lack of human rights education in China and the educational rights of individuals with disabilities are not deemed fundamental. Research show that some parents in rural or remote areas do not consider it necessary to send their children with disabilities to schools, as the children are often considered incapable of learning or taken as a burden for their family draining resources (Deng & Guo, 2007).

The second factor has to do with high dropout rate among children with disabilities. As children with disabilities progress in school, they drop out and few of them complete junior secondary level and even fewer proceed to senior secondary level (Deng & Guo, 2007). This is supported by statistics from the Ministry of Education, which shows significant dropouts for children with disabilities in the secondary education level. As shown in the Annual Education Report released in 2015 by the Ministry of Education, the number of students with disabilities enrolled in primary education, junior secondary education, and senior secondary education levels are respectively: 283000, 102000, and 9883, exhibiting a drastic declining trend as one advance further in the education levels. Again, no data for people with disabilities in higher education is provided in the Report. Data from previous years displayed a similar pattern, with students with disabilities drop out drastically in the secondary education levels.

The third factor is related to the country's deeply ingrained social stigma and discrimination associated with disability. Low educational aspiration and expectation are found for people with disabilities.

Can Ji Ren are viewed as deficit and incompetent in many tasks partly due to a heavy influence from the medical model of disability (Zhang, 2006). A research project conducted from 2003 to 2006 by Deng and Guo found that the ideological atmosphere was unfavorable towards students with disabilities in schools. It was even hard for teachers and administrators to convince parents of children with disabilities to send their children to schools in some rural areas. Even if they are enrolled in schools, children with disabilities are not challenged or supported with the adequate resources for them to succeed in schools (Deng & Guo, 2007). With a lack of social outcry for respect, equal treatment, and necessary accommodations for this population, people with disabilities often find themselves in the lower ladder of the social order.

Besides the cultural traditions and values, the low educational attainment for people with disabilities can be further explained by the legislative emphasis in the country's disability law. The educational guidelines laid out in the legislations demonstrate a clear emphasis on basic education and vocational education for *Can Ji Ren*. Access to higher education is neglected in both the legislative and institutional level. Limited access and inadequate accommodations are provided in higher education for *Can Ji Ren*. Regulatory guidelines for higher education admission demonstrate that students with specific disabling conditions would be denied access to certain academic programs in regular higher education institutions. These legislations, regulations, and institutional practices have seldom been challenged and reflected upon by policymakers and educators. As a result, the representation of people with disabilities in Chinese higher education remains staggering low. More detailed explanations of the above-mentioned barriers will be provided in the ensuing sections.

CONCEPTUAL FRAMEWORKS

As it is widely acknowledged in the international educational arena, education is a fundamental human right and it is the bedrock for the exercise of all other human rights. Education cultivates individual freedom, facilitates empowerment and produces significant development benefits (UNESCO). It is conducive to both public good and personal profit. Article 26 in the Universal Declaration of Human Rights (UDHR, 1948) stated:

Everyone has the right to education. Education shall be free, at least in the elementary and fundamental stages. Elementary education shall be compulsory. Technical and professional education shall be made generally available and higher education shall be equally accessible to all on the basis of merit.

The Jomtien Declaration (1990) included an article which called for countries to universalize access and promote equity as it stated: "Steps need to be taken to provide equal access to education to every category of disabled persons as an integral part of the education system." The Jomtien Declaration realized that educational disparities existed and many different groups of population are vulnerable to discrimination and exclusion. These groups include girls, the poor, street and working children, disabled people and many other groups. Other international instruments that clearly reiterate education as a human right and also promote Inclusive Education (IE) include the Standard Rules on the Equalization of Opportunities (1993), the Salamanca Statement and Framework for Action on Special Needs Education (1994), etc. One key point in the Standard Rules emphasized governments' responsibility in providing education for disabled persons by providing clear policy, flexible curriculum, quality materials, ongoing teacher training and other support. While the Salamanca Statement stated that "schools need to accommodate all children; disabled children should attend their neighborhood school; inclusion is essential to human dignity and the enjoyment of full human rights."

Inclusive Education (IE) is not another version of Special Education. As the context and our culture evolve, the definition for Inclusive Education has expanded and adapted accordingly. One widely accepted definition for IE was raised in the Agar Seminar in 1998. It listed IE as: broader than formal schooling; it includes the home, the community, non-formal and informal systems; it acknowledges that all children can learn; it enables education structures, systems and methodologies to meet the needs of all children; it acknowledges and respects differences in children: age, gender, ethnicity, language, disability, HIV/TB status etc.; it is a part of a wider strategy to promote an inclusive society. These general principles in IE are relevant throughout different stages from early childhood, basic, secondary, higher education, and vocational training. The purpose of IE is to achieve an inclusive society (Stubbs, 2002), which can be defined as a society "built upon ideals of social justice where participation and success are irrespective of race, gender, socioeconomic status, ethnicity, age and disability so that disadvantaged is not reproduced" (Nunan, George & McCausland, 2000, p.63-64).

In the context of China, the Constitution states that "the nation and society should arrange employment, living, and education for the blind, the deaf, and the other disabled citizens." The Compulsory Education Act (1987) writes that "all levels of governments are responsible in setting up special schools and special classes for disabled children and youth." Also, the Law on the Protection of Disabled Persons (LPDP) acknowledges education as a human right and emphasizes the compulsory education level (primary and junior secondary education) for children with disabilities:

(Article 18) The state shall guarantee the right of disabled persons to education. The state, society, schools and families shall provide compulsory education for disabled children and juveniles. The state shall exempt disabled students who accept compulsory education from tuition and reduce sundry fees or exempt them from such fees according to actual situations. The state shall set up grant-in-aid to assist students who are poor and disabled.

However, it can be seen that the laws in China lacks an IE element as it does not require regular school system to adapt to certain special needs of children with disabilities. According to the Law on the Protection of Disabled Persons (LPDP), regular mainstream schools would admit the disabled children, but on the condition that children with disabilities be able to adapt themselves to life and study in schools, where little or no accommodations in terms of special curricula or teaching strategies or other resources is provided (Human Rights Watch, 2013).

As defined in the LPDP (Law on the Protection of Disabled Persons, 1990), people with disabilities in China are "people who suffer from abnormalities of loss of a certain organ or function, psychologically or physiologically, or in anatomical structure and has lost wholly or in part the ability to perform an activity in the way considered normal." The official definition stated in the country's law for disability shows a heavy influence from the medical model. Within this model, it is assumed that people's disabilities are caused by mental or physical impairments. The focus is on the impairment aspect and doctors should be trained to cure such impairments or to alleviate their impacts. Disability defined under the influence of medical model is more considered as a medical problem, a disease and a tragedy. People with disabilities are viewed as victims of a disease, a problem, a permanent impairment. Thus, people with disabilities are in need of treatment in the medical model. They need to be changed or improved to be "normal" (Rieser & Mason, 1990). Such a model put more emphasis and responsibility on the people with disabilities instead of being concerned with the society's inclusive view. People with disabilities are implicitly isolated from the society due to their "abnormalities," which are perceived to be in need of correction and cure. Worse yet, this model has often led to another derogatory term, calling disabled people "Can Fei," meaning "useless" or "ruined" people.

An alternative model—the social model, favored by the United Nations since 1990, believes that disability is a socially constructed concept. The social model of disability focuses more on the rights and abilities of people with disabilities (Hernandez, 2008). In the social model, consideration about disabled people's own view of the situation is taken into consideration (Rieser & Mason, 1990). From disabled people's views, it is believed that the physical or mental impairments do not necessarily have to keep them from living good lives. The social model shifts some emphasis and responsibility to the society as a whole as it believes in the changing of social views on disability. Disability is less a physical impairment but more of a social construct. This model examines critically on the architectural barriers, inadequate pensions and other insufficiencies on the part of the society. One definition from the World Health Organization (2002) characterizes disability as "the umbrella term for impairments, activity limitations and participation restrictions." Such a definition is not just confined to medical-model's influence on the physical or mental impairments but also incorporates physical or mental disabilities' impact on the person's societal participation. So disability can be interpreted as part of a social construct, rather than merely an individual deficit (Podzimek, 2013). In China's case, the definition stated and persisted in the law for more than two decades shows a strong influence by the medical model and ignores the government and society's responsibility to provide more inclusive services to people with disabilities (Zhang, 2006).

ACCESS TO ELEMENTARY AND SECONDARY EDUCATION FOR CHILDREN WITH DISABILITIES

To understand the context of *Can Ji Ren*'s access to high education institutions, it is necessary to examine the access of these students to elementary and secondary education. Compulsory education in China includes six-year primary school education and three-year secondary school education. The Second National Survey of Persons with Disabilities in 2007 shows that as of 2006, about 2,460,000 children of school age (6-14) have one or more disabilities in China (Zhang, 2011). This figure from the National Survey conducted in 2007 is much lower than the number retrieved from 1987, which was 8.17 million (children with disabilities of school age), therefore we need to be careful with the data accuracy.

Putting aside the data issue, these children with disabilities get compulsory education in several forms: 特殊教育学校 (schools for special education), 小学附设特教班 (classes attached to primary schools), 小学随班就读 (followers in Primary schools) and 普通(职业)初中附设特教 (special classes attached to junior high or vocational schools). Within a decade (2003-2013), the number of schools of basic and secondary levels for *Can Ji Ren* of school age went from 1,551 to 1,933. This number, though showing an increase of 382 within 10 years, is truly unsatisfactory based on the time span and the number of *Can Ji Ren* of school age.

Can Ji Ren in China are not enjoying the same educational opportunities as those without disabilities and remain subject to education exclusion. China has been implementing compulsory education since 1986, but a good percentage of *Can Ji Ren* are still excluded out of basic education. By the end of 2005, about 53% of the school-aged *Can Ji Ren* are out of school (CDPF, 2012). In 2006, about 45.4 percent of disabled population aged 15 or above is illiterate (Zhang, 2011).

Access to Higher Education for People with Disabilities

The latest data from Ministry of Education shows in the year of 2013, about 368,103 school-aged *Can Ji Ren* enroll in different levels of education, with the enrollment number in primary education, junior secondary education, and senior secondary education being 259067, 99041, and 9995, respectively. One can see clearly that with the advancement in the academic track, the enrollment number decreases significantly.

At the primary education level, the general enrollment data for *Can Ji Ren* of school age in 2006 is only 62.01 percent (female) and 64.02 percent (male), falling way behind their counterparts without disabilities, as the enrollment rate for whom is about 99.7 percent (female) and 99.67 percent (male) (Chen et al, 2011).

An interregional gap is also shown in the enrollment data, meaning the educational opportunities for school-aged *Can Ji Ren* vary on a geographic base (Chen et al, 2011). *Can Ji Ren* of school age who are out of school are mostly centered in western and middle provinces of China, accounting about 82 percent (CDPF, 2012). While in contrast, the enrollment rate for those without disabilities from age 6 to 14 indicates an average of 99.7 percent enrollment rate with little gap among different geographic regions. This interregional gap is caused by a combination of the lack of education institutions for *Can Ji Ren* and the familial poverty issues in the western and middle provinces. The data also indicates an enrollment gap between *Can Ji Ren* of rural and urban areas (Chen et al, 2011). According to the Second National Survey of People with Disabilities in 2007, 20.7 million, accounting for 24.96 percent of the disabled population, reside in urban areas; and 62.2 million, accounting for 75.04 percent of the disabled population, reside in rural areas of China. Yet the enrolled number of *Can Ji Ren* from both areas at the primary level do not show much of a difference (Ministry of Education), which implies the urban disabled population, though not enjoying many educational opportunities themselves, are still having better chances of getting some education compared to their rural disabled counterparts, considering the rural/urban population gap.

Advancing to the Junior or Senior secondary school levels, *Can Ji Ren* in the urban areas exhibits a higher enrolled number compared with those of the rural areas. And the *Can Ji Ren* from the rural area exhibits a constant and continuous higher dropout number (Ministry of Education). By the senior secondary education level, the number of *Can Ji Ren* in rural area is incredibly low even to the point of being negligible (See Table 1). There is a chance that the *Can Ji Ren* from the rural areas might move to urban or town areas to further education, considering that more educational resources are centered in urban and town areas. However, it is clear that a huge gap of educational opportunities and attainments exists among disabled population in rural and urban areas of China.

As Chinese education is considered a model in reaching the Millennium Development Goal in terms of providing primary education to the children of school age, such enrollment or attainment achievement excludes *Can Ji Ren* of school age and therefore, should be considered inadequate. And as it is known, *Can Ji Ren* have to survive through primary and secondary education to proceed to the higher education level. Without an adequate enrollment and attainment rate at primary and secondary schools, a good amount of *Can Ji Ren* lose the opportunity to proceed to higher education.

MASSIFICATION OF HIGHER EDUCATION

To understand the access issue of higher education for people with disabilities we also need to examine China's higher education in general as a context. The higher education system in China has been going

Table 1. Enrollment number for Can Ji Ren in 2010

	Primary School				Junior Secondary School		Senior Secondary School		
Grade	1	2	5	6	1	3	1	2	3
Urban	15067	13531	13918	13581	12137	11844	3330	2625	2746
County & Towns	17340	16055	16355	15645	14928	15529	302	288	231
Rural	16163	18802	21458	19939	9567	10027	49	38	12

(Ministry of Education, 2015)

through a process of massification since 1999, as the system has witnessed unprecedented quantitative growth in its enrollment (World Bank Tertiary Enrollment Data, 2015). According to the data from the Ministry of Education in 2010, the number of higher education institutions (HEIs) doubled over the course of ten years: from 1,041 HEIs (2000) to 2,358 HEIs (2010), including HEIs providing Degree-level Programs and Non-university Tertiary institutions. And the number has stayed at about 7 million students admitted annually. The enrollment growth is achieved by the collective effort of both the public and the private sectors, as we saw the growing number of HEIs from 2000 to 2010. The increased provision of higher education could be attributed to both the marketization and internationalization of the Chinese higher education. While public HEIs increased enrollment dramatically, private sectors have also entered into the market, as well as overseas HEIs.

A close look into the context of higher education in China would not be complete without a touch on the national College Entrance Examination (CEE). CEE was established in 1955, not long after the founding of the People's Republic of China in 1949. It was halted during the ten-year Cultural Revolution (1966-1976) and did not resume until the year of 1977. The revival of the CEE is regarded as bringing the meritocratic admission criterion back into the higher education system after the Cultural Revolution (1966-1976) during which political status was used as the selection criterion. About 5.7 million students participated in CEE when it was again initiated in 1977, with less than 300,000 students being admitted into universities/colleges based on the CEE scores. CEE had been highly selective as the admission rate was very low before 1999, ranging from 2.5 to 5 percent of the age cohort (Lin, 1999). Due to the selectivity of the universities/colleges, people would usually consider those who are competent enough to make through the exam elites of the time and of the country. The massification started specifically from the late 1990s. In 2003, the gross enrollment rate of higher education reached 15 percent and Chinese higher education reached the stage of massification (Huang, 2005). This expansion process keeps on and continues to provide more chances for Chinese students in higher education. In 2012, the number of students taking the CEE reached the point of 9.15 million, with the admission rate increasing to 75 percent, about 23% of the cohort. The expansion of higher education also indicates the Chinese governmental emphasis on the higher education sector.

However, the emphasis shows little concern on providing higher education for people with disabilities. In the educational annual report from the Ministry of Education, we cannot locate any number of *Can Ji Ren* in HEIs. Before 2004, the data from the Ministry of Education for education for individuals with disabilities did not even constitute an independent category. Instead, education for people with disabilities was classified as a sub-category under the country's basic education sector, indicating that higher education for *Can Ji Ren* was negligible.

COLLEGE ENTRANCE EXAMINATION POLICIES

In the era of mass higher education, what are some of the effects of the College Entrance Examination policies on the access for people with disabilities (*Can Ji Ren*)? Are these policies promoting or exacerbating the fairness of education opportunities for *Can Ji Ren*?

To start, the College Entrance Examination policies refer to the criteria developed by the government, higher education institutions and community organizations for the authoritative distribution and regulation of higher education opportunities. These policies can include the provincial fixed-quota admission policies, province-specific CEE questions, independent enrollment policies of HEIs, admission recommendation policies of HEIs, and grade credit policies, etc. In all, many CEE policies have been considered conducive in maintaining of current familial socioeconomic status (Wang, 2010). The issue of access equity between rural and urban students in higher education draws nationwide attention, which has led to the changing of relevant policies. From 2013, decisions to increase higher education opportunities for students from rural areas were made in the executive meetings of the State Council. In 2014, the state government indicates that enrollment quota for poor rural areas should increase another 10 percent comparing with the previous year, meaning that an increase of 50,000 quota will be allocated to students from rural areas (Renmin, 2015). However, no attention is paid to (dis) ability as a factor causing inequitable access to higher education. No specific compensatory measures or special programs have been made to increase higher education opportunities for people with disabilities (*Can Ji Ren*).

In a global context, the majority of people with disabilities often suffer from poverty, in both developing and developed countries. Households with disabled family members are more likely to end up in poverty and lower socioeconomic status. A strong correlation between poverty and disability has been found in many researches (Podzimek, 2013). With no exception, Chinese households with a disabled member have demonstrated severe poverty issues. Based on a real-name system survey conducted by the Chinese Disabled Persons' Federation (CDPF), by the end of 2013, 12.3 million *Can Ji Ren* in rural China live under poverty line; 2.6 million urban-dwellers with disabilities live extremely poor and difficult lives. Extra medical expenses are usually required for *Can Ji Ren*, which exacerbate the poverty issue for these households. As the survey indicates, the disposable income for households with disabled member is only 56.7 percent of the nation's average level. With less disposable income, households with disabled children would have less monetary investment in education, therefore *Can Ji Ren* are less likely to proceed to higher level of education (Chen, 2015). Besides the poverty issue and the reproducing effects of CEE policies on the familial socioeconomic status, *Can Ji Ren* also suffers from a third barrier—examination of physical eligibility for entering higher education.

PHYSICAL EXAMINATION POLICY

Along with the CEE, students who aspire to further study in higher education in China are required to go through a mandatory physical examination. The purpose of the examination is to determine the physical eligibility for admission into higher education institutions. This annual nationwide physical examination takes place before the CEE, usually sometime in March or April, being strictly scheduled at the provincial level. Only hospitals and medical staff from specific certified levels could carry out the physical examination for all CEE takers.

In 2014, a disabled female student drew nationwide attention. Having met all other admission requirements except for the physical examination, the student was denied admission to a university in Fujian Province. The media coverage on the case attracted widespread public attention and caused heated discussion online. The major opinion online was opposing the university's decision on the student. When interviewed, the admission staff of the university responded that the student did not meet the state-established physical eligibility standards and therefore the denial decision was made correctly, based on the state regulation. Here the regulation that the admission staff refers to is "A Notice on the Dissemination of the Advisory Guideline on Physical Examination in College Admission into General Higher Education Institutions" (2003), stipulated by the Ministry of Education, and the Ministry of Health and China Disabled Persons' Federation (CDPF). In this Advisory Guideline, inadmissible physical conditions to HEIs or to specific majors within the HEIs were listed. The student was denied due to her wheelchair use.

Specifically, before the Advisory Guideline in 2003, what HEIs abided by was a regulation made and started implementation in 1985. It was through both the Ministry of Education and the Ministry of Health that the "Standards for the Physical Examination of Entrants into General Higher Education Institutions" were stipulated. The Standard (1985) includes three major areas of contents, one of which clearly stated that HEIs cannot grant admission to students with any of the fifteen categories of physical conditions along with one last category of "other provincial physical conditions or diseases that would affect the normal study (of the students)." According to this Standard, students whose hearing in each ear falls below two meters, or the sum of corrective visual acuity of two eyes is below 1.0 would be denied admission to HEIs. Also, students whose illness or disability falls out the listed fifteen categories will still be at the mercy of the HEIs in terms of admission decision. Other contents listed in the Standard are the majors or programs that HEIs could grant direct admission denial to students with certain disabilities or physical conditions, such as:

任何一下肢不能运用；两下肢不等长超过5公分；脊柱侧弯超过4公分；肌力二级以下；两下肢均跛行；显著胸廓畸形，不能录取野外、高空、高温、矿山、井下工作专业及刑侦、航船驾驶、运输类各专业，体育专业，艺术类的表演，舞蹈，电影等专业.

(Disabling conditions like) dysfunctional lower limb; the length of both lower limbs is lower than 5 centimeters; crippled walking of both limbs, etc., cannot be admitted into majors and programs in criminology, maritime, sports, performing arts, dancing, film, etc. (Article 6).

严重的口吃,口腔有生理缺陷及耳鼻喉科疾病之一而妨碍发言者,不能录取工科的运输、通信类各专业,民用航空专业,外交、外贸、外语各专业和医科各专业,体育各专业,艺术类的电影、戏剧、戏曲、音乐、管乐各专业及师范院校各专业和法律专业.

Those who have severe stutter, or physical defects on the mouth, or speech impediment due to other illnesses, could not be admitted into majors and programs related to transportation, telecommunication, aviation, foreign affairs, international trade, foreign languages, medical career, film, opera, music, wind instruments, teacher training, law, etc. (Article 15)

Such physical eligibility policies undoubtedly created a regulatory barrier for *Can Ji Ren* or students with certain diseases. It makes getting access to HEIs or getting into certain programs of study even more difficult for these students. In 2003, the Ministry of Education, Ministry of Health, collaborating with China Disabled Persons' Federation (CDPF), made an effort to expand the college access for students with certain illness or disability by changing some of the physical eligibility criteria and revise the Standard to the aforementioned Advisory Guideline, based on the guiding principle of being more human-rights-oriented. Several improvements were made in the Advisory Guideline in comparison with the previous Standard. For example, the inadmissible categories of physical conditions were reduced from fifteen to six. The Guideline also indicated explicitly that general HEIs could not deny access to students with physical disabilities who have met other admission requirements and can function well in their chosen programs of study. In addition, the Guideline transferred more liberty to individual HEIs to make their own admission decision. As the Advisory Guideline is no longer mandatory regulations, the HEIs do not necessarily have to rigidly abide by the Guideline. However, individual HEIs retain the power to decide their own admission standards on students' physical eligibility under the revised Guideline, on the condition that the institutions should be able to justify the admission decisions based on their own supplementary guideline while considering institution-specific teaching resources and educational goals. In the above case of the female disabled student in 2014, the university decided not to grant admission to the female student, referring to the Guideline for legal justification. In a way, equal access to HEIs for *Can Ji Ren* is not protected by the legislation. Granting admission to *Can Ji Ren* is more of a charity-based gesture rather than genuine recognition of the students' academic performance and their rights to education. In the above case, the female student was eventually admitted to another local university near her home, largely due to the widespread publicity of her case.

ACCESS TO HIGHER EDUCATION FOR *CAN JI REN*

The massification of higher education and the increasing opportunities in the twenty-first century creates a better environment for students across China. However, *Can Ji Ren* remain in a disadvantaged position. In the database from the Ministry of Education, there was simply no data for *Can Ji Ren* in senior secondary schools prior to 2007. With staggering low number of students who could proceed from secondary school to the next level, it is predictable that *Can Ji Ren* are hugely underrepresented in HEIs.

The laws in China do not put much emphasize on higher education level for people with disabilities, as the Law on the Protection of Persons with Disabilities (LPDP, 1990) states:

The principle of combining popularization with upgrading of quality shall be implemented in education of disabled persons, with emphasis on the former. Priority shall be given to compulsory education and vocational and technical education while efforts shall be made to carry out preschool education and gradually develop education at and above the senior middle school level (Article 20).

Over the years, the Chinese government showed some awareness for the higher education services for *Can Ji Ren*. Domestically, the Decree by the President of the People's Republic of China adopted in

1990, and the Regulations of Education of People with Disabilities (1994) both made clear that "institutions of higher learning must admit disabled students who meet the state admission requirements and shall not deny their admission because of their disabilities." The Law on the Protection of Persons with Disabilities (LPDP) outlines the educational rights among other basic human rights for this population. In a sense, the government shows its pledge on papers to better facilitate the participation of *Can Ji Ren* in education, employment and other aspects of life. Certain efforts were made and improvements in access for higher education were only seen in recent years. One example is that the government issued national regulations to guarantee that people with visual impairment could use Braille and electronic paper in the CEE in 2012. Though this regulation did not see its actual implementation until two years later in June of 2014 when the provision was actually provided. In its long history, China had its first batch of blind students sitting in the CEE with the assistance of Braille and Electronic exam paper (Human Rights Watch, 2014). Internationally, Chinese government ratifies the development and adoption of the Convention on the Rights of Persons with Disabilities (CRPD) in 2008, which is the latest international human rights treaty requiring state parties to "ensure an inclusive education system at all levels." However, the ratification of CRPD is more symbolic rather than real actions. Only when such a governmental commitment is also demonstrated in domestic laws and put into actual implementation by increasing educational provisions at all levels, do the ratification mean something substantial to the people with disabilities in China. As for higher education provision, the awareness and actual implementation is far from satisfactory.

For *Can Ji Ren* in China, there are two most common forms of higher education: regular HEIs and special HEIs. Of the limited number of *Can Ji Ren* who gained admission to HEIs from 2008 to 2012, approximately 89 percent of them were admitted to regular HEIs and 11 percent to special HEIs. This is easily understandable as there are more regular HEIs (over 2000) than special HEIs (14) in China. Again, we should note that the total numbers of admitted *Can Ji Ren* remain very minimal in these years. As CDPF (2015) indicated, the annual average admitted number of people with disabilities into HEIs is about 8,077 from 2008 to 2012, whereas the admitted number for those without disabilities is about 6.5 million every year (2008-2012). Other forms of HE for *Can Ji Ren* include Distance Learning through Online Universities, Self-taught Higher Education Examination, Television Universities, etc. Little data can be found for *Can Ji Ren* taking advantage of these types of higher education.

In terms of the financial aspect, HE in China since the 1990s has been more regarded as a personal benefit rather than a public good (Agelasto & Adamson, 1998). Most students finance their own higher education. While national financial aids in HEIs are available, limited aids are provided for people with disabilities. Yang's study (2010) shows that female students, students with college-educated fathers, and students from poorer household were to receive more aid. The amount of financial aid is also positively correlated with the selectivity of the higher education institutions. For *Can Ji Ren*, specific regional and provincial financial aids have been made available in recent years, funded by the Chinese Disabled Persons Federation (CDPF). The amount of the provincial financial aid provided by the local branches of CDPF is quite limited and differs geographically, with more resources centered in more developed municipalities or provinces (CDPF, 2015).

A major factor accounting for the low number of admitted people with disabilities (*Can Ji Ren*) every year is their low number in the graduating class of senior secondary schools in China, as shown in the database of the Ministry of Education. The number of *Can Ji Ren* enrolled in either regular high school or special education school does not exhibit a linear increasing pattern over the years (2008-2013). Instead, the numbers have been relatively stable after a sudden drop from 2008. A comparatively larger

Figure 1. Admission of disabled students by ordinary higher learning institute during Year 2001-2007. (China's Disabled Persons Federation, 2008)

number of *Can Ji Ren* tends to enroll in regular school system than the special education schools. From 2008 to 2012 (the Ministry of Education), an average of about 2,844 students successfully proceed to the senior year in special education high schools and the counterpart number for those in regular high schools is 6,038, which means every year, an average total number of 8,882 students with disabilities are eligible to proceed to HE level provided they all graduate. At the same time, the average number of admitted students with disabilities to different HEIs annually from 2008 to 2012 is about 8,077 (CDPF, 2015). This 8,077 number is an increase from previous years. The average number of admitted *Can Ji Ren* from 2001 to 2007 was about 3,658. The chart below shows the admitted number of disabled students in higher education (in both regular HEIs and special HEIs) from 2001 to 2007.

The data shows an increasing and high admission rate for students with disabilities. However, we have to be cautious since we are looking at a very small number of eligible students in graduating senior class. It has to be noted that the base of students with disabilities in China is huge, in the millions, hence the admission rate is very misleading. The fact is most students do not enroll in schools and they do not survive schools, especially to senior high school level.

As indicated above, the expansion of higher education in China did not boost significant enrollment increase for *Can Ji Ren*. From 2008 to 2012, the percentage of admitted *Can Ji Ren* among all admitted students of the year remains about 0.12 percent in average. Put it in another way, the ratio between admitted *Can Ji Ren* and their peers without disabilities has remained about 1:833 in HEIs for these years (2008-2012). This can be attributable to the low number of *Can Ji Ren* in graduating classes among senior secondary schools, as explained in the earlier section examining the primary and secondary education for children with disabilities.

As we look into higher education institutions, we see limited provision for *Can Ji Ren* as well. Overall, only a small number of special HEIs is available for *Can Ji Ren*. The first special HEI of the country—Changchun University Special Education School, was not established until 1987. Across the country, only 14 special HEIs were established, where a total of about 2,000 *Can Ji Ren* enrolled in them by the end of 2007 (CDPF, 2011). Approximately a total of 1,000 *Can Ji Ren* could be admitted into these special HEIs after the year of 2007 (CDPF, 2011). As for regular HEIs, there are 2,824 regular HEIs by the end of 2014 (Ministry of Education, 2015). Yet, little research has been done on the necessary accommodations provided in these higher learning institutions for people with disabilities. On the contrary, physical examination policies during admission process exclude a good number of students with disabilities from accessing regular HEIs. According to the disabled person's survey conducted in 1987, the number of children with disabilities reached 8.17 million. And the Second National Survey of Persons with Disabilities in 2007 shows a number of about 2.4 million children with disabilities are of school age (Zhang, 2011). Despite the inconsistency of data in the two national surveys, one can still see the fact that large numbers of children with disabilities are of school age, and the provision of higher education for people with disabilities in the country is far from satisfactory.

In addition, *Can Ji Ren* are not given high expectations in terms of educational attainment as attitudinal barriers have been visibly and invisibly enforced in the society as a whole. The attitudinal barriers are manifested in the admission practice of regular HEIs, as mentioned above. On the one hand, *Can Ji Ren* are subject to a stereotypic view that they are less competent or not as competitive as their non-disabled peers in the academic world or job market, due to their physical or other disability. Many HEIs have the inclinations to deny *Can Ji Ren* when it comes to admission decision (Du, 2005). Moreover, the physical examination policies further create access barriers. HEIs sometimes would deny admission to *Can Ji Ren* with the justification from the state-established physical eligibility standards. Disputes between people with disabilities and schools exist in different education levels (Guo, 2004). Some HEIs would tend to admit people with disabilities on consideration of equity or for the sake of their institutions' good reputation, but usually the admitted number remains very minimal (Du, 2005).

What's more, there is a lack of attention for higher education for *Can Ji Ren* either on governmental legislation or actual implementation. Most regulations and laws on the education provision for *Can Ji Ren* lay emphasis on compulsory education instead of HE level. As mentioned earlier, in the database from the Ministry of Education, education for people with disabilities was a sub-category of the Basic Education sector prior to 2003. It was not until 2004 that education for people with disabilities was separated into an independent sector in the database, but without any data for enrolled number of *Can Ji Ren* in senior secondary schools. It was until 2007 that there was data for *Can Ji Ren* in senior secondary education level. Though an emphasis is put on compulsory education level for *Can Ji Ren*, a huge lag between the legislative effort and actual implementation persists. Only a very small number of *Can Ji Ren* could survive the whole compulsory education process so as to reach the graduating class of senior high schools and proceed to the postsecondary education level.

CONCLUSION

Can Ji Ren in China are still subjects of educational exclusion as the Chinese educational environment for them remain discriminative and restrictive. While there are signs of progress in the development of provision for people with disabilities, areas of legislation, implementation, poverty reduction and social attitudes need much further attention. The massification of HE catalyzes an increase in the admission for many students, however, the increase for admitted *Can Ji Ren* remain quite minimal. Further research is needed in topics of special accommodations and accessibility in Chinese higher education. Governmental laws have been making some efforts to better guide the provision of education for people with disabilities. Yet, the efforts are far from enough as a significant gap between children with disabilities and those without disabilities remain in terms of education attainment and representation in higher education.

The underrepresentation of *Can Ji Ren* in HE is caused by multiple reasons: 1) poverty issues among households with disabled member resulting in less monetary investment in further education and less educational attainment, as a result, not enough *Can Ji Ren* have been able to survive the secondary education level to proceed to HE; 2) many of the CEE policies play a role in the reproduction of current familial socioeconomic status as they privilege students from developed areas or from higher socioeconomic status households, while about 75 percent *Can Ji Ren* in China reside in the rural areas and many of them suffer from poverty and education exclusion with no assistance from any compensatory policies; 3) the state-established physical eligibility standards along with the CEE policies create further regulatory and attitudinal barrier to *Can Ji Ren* who desire to further study in HE; 4) the negligence of relevant laws addressing the needs of people with disabilities' to proceed to HE level as most laws emphasize more on the compulsory education level; 5) an influence from a medical model where disability is more viewed as a problem of the individual, contributing to a stereotypic social view of people with disabilities being less competitive or competent, which produces an attitudinal obstacle for an inclusive environment for *Can Ji Ren* to participate.

Several policy recommendations can be drawn from this study: 1) Nationwide poverty reduction measures should be taken by the government at all levels. Nationwide financial aids should be better publicized and provided for *Can Ji Ren* who have demonstrated abilities to advance in their academic tracks. 2) At the legislative level, Chinese government needs to, first of all, revise the definition for disability, reducing the influence from the medical model of disability and incorporate the social model definition. Second, the government needs to make the laws less restrictive and more inclusive for *Can Ji Ren* to obtain education at different levels. Legislations should be more mandatory instead of being mere encouragement to enforce the educational provisions for people with disabilities at all levels, including the HE level. The provisions of higher education level for *Can Ji Ren* should be more visible in the national laws and regulations. 3) Further adjust the various CEE policies to reduce its negative effects on the fairness of granting access to HE for *Can Ji Ren*. 4) The Advisory Guideline made by the Ministry of Education, the Ministry of Health and CDPF should be eliminated, as it rigidly restricts the admission of *Can Ji Ren* into majors and programs of the various higher education institutions. 5) Top-down regulations and laws modification should be accompanied by the actual implementation at the down-to-earth levels. Public awareness to incorporate the social participation of *Can Ji Ren* requires more progressive promotion nationwide. Only through the combination of guiding theories in article and down-to-earth practices in reality can the people with disabilities in China be able to visibly participate in different life aspects as an organic and significant member in a healthy and inclusive society.

REFERENCES

Agelasto, M., & Adamson, B. (1998). *Higher Education in Post-Mao China*. Hong Kong: Hong Kong University Press.

Ministry of Education, Ministry of Health, and China Disabled Persons' Federation. (2013). A Notice on the Dissemination of the Advisory Guideline on Physical Examination in College Admission into General Higher Education Institutions. Retrieved from http://yz.chsi.com.cn/kyzx/zcdh/200809/20080903/8145649.html

Barnes, C. (2007). Disability, higher education and the inclusive society. *British Journal of Sociology of Education*, 28(1), 135–145. doi:10.1080/01425690600996832

Byrne, B., Dickinson, G. M., Diesfeld, K., Engelbrecht, P., Hancock, J., Harris, N., & Zhang, R. (2011). *The legal rights of students with disabilities: international perspectives* (C. J. Russo, Ed.). Rowman & Littlefield Publishers.

Chen, G., Lin, Y., Zhang, L., Song, X., & Zheng, X. (2011). *Livelihood situation of Disabled population in China*. Retrieved from http://www.ide.go.jp/English/Publish/Download/Jrp/pdf/152_03.pdf

Chen, X. G. (2015, February 27). The main path to realize the goal of "XIAOKANG" for the 85 million people with disabilities in China. *China Daily*. Retrieved from http://column.chinadaily.com.cn/article.php?pid=4783

China's Disabled Persons Service Net. (n. d.). Retrieved from http://www.cdpsn.org.cn/static/20130830CanJiRengdjy/index.html

China's Disabled Persons Federation. (2007). Chinese disabled persons development annual statistical bulletin. Retrieved from http://www.cdpf.org.cn/special/CDRS/content/2008-05/12/content_30262400_2.htm

China's Disabled Persons Federation. (2010). Chinese disabled persons development annual statistical bulletin. Retrieved from http://www.gov.cn/fwxx/CanJiRen/content_1839338.htm

Du, Y. H. (2005). Inequity in access to higher education in the process of massification. *Jianghuai Forum, 6*, 034.

Guo. Z. C. (2004). Case analyses of educational access for students with disabilities in China. *Chinese Teachers*, (2), 48-50.

Hernandez, V. T. (2008). Making good on the promise of international law: The Convention on the Rights of Persons with Disabilities and inclusive education in China and India. *Pac. Rim L. & Pol'y J., 17*, 497.

Huang, F. (2005). Qualitative enhancement and quantitative growth: Changes and trends of Chinas higher education. *Higher Education Policy, 18*(2), 117–130. doi:10.1057/palgrave.hep.8300076

Human Rights Watch. (2013). China: Revise Disability regulations for education: End Discrimination, Make Mainstream Schools Accessible. Retrieved from http://www.hrw.org/news/2013/05/18/china-revise-disability-regulations-education

Human Rights Watch. (2014). China: Exams accessible to the blink a breakthrough: education ministry announcement would reduce discrimination. Retrieved from http://www.hrw.org/news/2014/04/16/china-exams-accessible-blind-breakthrough

Lin, J. (1999). *Social transformation and private education in China*. Greenwood Publishing Group.

National Bureau of Statistics of China. (2006). 年第二次全国残疾人抽样调查主要数据公报 [Report of the 2006 Second National Survey of Disability, 2007].

Nunan, T., George, R., & McCausland, H. (2000). Inclusive education in universities: Why it is important and how it might be achieved. *International Journal of Inclusive Education*, *4*(1), 63–88. doi:10.1080/136031100284920

People's Republic of China Ministry of Education. (2015). Educational Statistics. Retrieved from http://www.moe.edu.cn/publicfiles/business/htmlfiles/moe/s8492/list.html

Podzimek, K. (2013). *Emerging from the shadows: quality of life research on students with disabilities in Monrovia*. Liberia.

Renmin Net. (2013, May 13). Numbers of College Entrance Examination takers and admitted students in Chinese history. *Ministry of Education*. Retrieved from http://edu.people.com.cn/n/2013/0503/c116076-21359059.html

Renmin Net. (2015, February 25). Li Keqiang: the urgency of promoting equity in educational access. *Ministry of Education*. Retrieved from http://edu.people.com.cn/n/2015/0225/c1053-26594015.html

Rieser, R., & Mason, M. (1990). *Disability equality in the classroom: a human rights issue*. London: Inner London Education Authority.

Ross, H., & Wang, Y. (2010). The college entrance examination in china: an overview of its social-cultural foundations, existing problems, and consequences: guest editors introduction. *Chinese Education & Society*, *43*(4), 3–10. doi:10.2753/CED1061-1932430400

Wikipedia. (n. d.). Sixth National Population Census of the People's Republic of China. Retrieved from http://zh.wikipedia.org/wiki/%E4%B8%AD%E5%8D%8E%E4%BA%BA%E6%B0%91%E5%85%B1%E5%92%8C%E5%9B%BD%E7%AC%AC%E5%85%AD%E6%AC%A1%E5%85%A8%E5%9B%BD%E4%BA%BA%E5%8F%A3%E6%99%AE%E6%9F%A5

Ministry of Education, Ministry of Health. (1985). Standards for the Physical Examination of Entrants into General Higher Education Institutions. Retrieved from http://210.28.182.158/edu/1/law/15/law_15_1139.htm

China's Disabled Persons Federation. (2012). Statistical Communique on the Development of the Work for Persons with Disabilities. Retrieved from http://www.cdpf.org.cn/sjzx/tjgb/200712/t20071202_357729.shtml

Stratford, B., & Ng, H. (2000). People with disabilities in China: Changing outlook—new solutions—growing problems. *International Journal of Disability Development and Education*, *47*(1), 7–14. doi:10.1080/103491200116093

Stubbs, S. (2002). *Inclusive Education: Where there are few resources*. Oslo: Atlas Alliance; URL www.atlas-alliansen.no

The World Bank. (2015). Gross tertiary school enrollment. Retrieve from http://data.worldbank.org/indicator/SE.TER.ENRR/countries?page=2

Tinklin, T., Riddell, S., & Wilson, A. (2004). Policy and provision for disabled students in higher education in Scotland and England: The current state of play. *Studies in Higher Education, 29*(5), 637–657.

UNESCO International Bureau of Education (2007). *Regional Preparatory Workshop on Inclusive Education East Asia: Hangzhou, China.* Retrieve from http://www.ibe.unesco.org/fileadmin/user_upload/Inclusive_Education/Reports/hangzhou_07/china_inclusion_07.pdf

UNESCO Education. (n. d.). Retrieve from http://www.unesco.org/new/en/right2education

United Nations. (n. d.). The Universal Declaration of Human Rights. Retrieved from http://www.un.org/en/documents/udhr/

Wang, H. (2010). Research on the influence of college entrance examination policies on the fairness of higher education admissions opportunities in China. *Chinese Education & Society, 43*(6), 15–35. doi:10.2753/CED1061-1932430601

World Education Forum: World Declaration on Education for All (Jomtien Declaration). Retrieved from http://www.unesco.org/education/wef/enconf/Jomtien%20Declaration%20eng.shtm

Xinhua Net. (2015). The replacement of national exam papers in the College Entrance Examination in 25 provinces next year, reducing provincial extra credits criterion. Retrieved from http://www.ln.xinhuanet.com/newscenter/2015-03/12/c_1114617825.htm

Yang, P. (2010). Who gets more financial aid in China? A multilevel analysis. *International Journal of Educational Development, 30*(6), 560–569. doi:10.1016/j.ijedudev.2009.12.006

Zhang, G. Z. (2006). Inclusion of person with disabilities in China. *Asia Pacific Disability Rehabilitation Journal, 17*(2). Retrieved from http://www.dinf.ne.jp/doc/english/asia/resource/apdrj/v172006/inclusionchina.html

This research was previously published in The Future of Accessibility in International Higher Education edited by Henry C. Alphin Jr., Jennie Lavine, and Roy Y. Chan; pages 70-87, copyright year 2017 by Information Science Reference (an imprint of IGI Global).

Chapter 12
Beyond Handicap, Pity, and Inspiration:
Disability and Diversity in Workforce Development Education and Practice

Hannah Rudstam
Cornell University, USA

Thomas Golden
Cornell University, USA

Susanne Bruyere
Cornell University, USA

Sara Van Looy
Cornell University, USA

Wendy Strobel Gower
Cornell University, USA

ABSTRACT

Individuals with disabilities represent a substantial portion of the U.S. population and workforce. Yet, disability is often not meaningfully included in diversity and inclusion efforts in the workplace or in higher education. This chapter focuses on ten misperceptions that have fueled the marginalization of disability in diversity and inclusion efforts. These ten misperceptions revolve around a range of issues: Legal, human and practical. We provide an overview of each misperception and discuss implications for diversity and workforce development practitioners, with a focus on higher education settings. In conclusion, we urge readers to consider their own organizations in light of each of these ten misperceptions.

DOI: 10.4018/978-1-7998-1213-5.ch012

INTRODUCTION

Over the past four decades, the concept of workforce diversity has evolved (Green & Kalev, 2010). Yet, one constant has remained throughout this evolution — disability continues to be seen as the "forgotten cousin" of workforce development and diversity programming. Despite the fact that close to one in five Americans report having a disability, and that more than half of those Americans with disabilities are in their working years, ages 18-64 (Erickson, Lee & von Schrader, 2014), disability is still perceived as somehow a "lesser" form of diversity. This has been demonstrated over the past two decades as various sectors of the contemporary workforce report being inadequately prepared and equipped to address disability issues in the workforce (AACB, 1992; Anderson, 2003; Folson-Meek, Nearing, Groteluschen, & Krampf, 1999; Muller & Haase, 1994). Others report that disability has simply been an "add-on" feature to broader diversity agendas and programs (Myers, 2009). Though disability often receives a passing reference in diversity efforts, it is rarely included with meaningful intent in implementation (AACSB, 1992; Muller & Parham, 1998).

What are the assumptions that have fueled this notion that disability is somehow a lesser form of diversity? How have these assumptions impacted workforce development efforts for people with disabilities? Most importantly, how have these assumptions impacted the field of workforce development generally? How might programming in the field itself be limited by not meaningfully including a major diversity population in our country today?

MISPERCEPTIONS FUELING THE MINIMIZATION OF DISABILITY IN DIVERSITY INITATIVES

The purpose of this chapter is twofold. First, we will identify and challenge some tacit assumptions that have historically fueled the positioning of disability as a set-aside piece of workforce diversity and workforce development efforts. Second, we will discuss how each identified misperception has impacted the field of workforce development practice and what workforce development educators and professionals must do to change this misperception.

Misperception #1: Disability Is Rare

The view of disability as a lesser diversity population is surprising, given the growing prevalence of disability among the U.S. population. Individuals people with disabilities represent one of the largest diversity populations in our country, in our schools, and in our workplaces today. There are currently about 56.7 million people with disabilities in the U.S., representing nearly 20% of the U.S. population (U.S. Census Bureau, 2014). Further, the number of people with disabilities in the U.S. is likely to increase, largely due to the aging of the U.S. population. It is estimated that by 2040 there will be about 82.3 million older persons in the U.S., twice as many as there were in the year 2000 (U.S. Administration for Community Living, 2015).

There is a clear connection between aging and disability. While the prevalence of disability is a little over one in ten among Americans in the working-age population of 21-64, it increases to one in four for Americans ages 65-74, and half of Americans over the age of 75 report having a disability (Erickson,

Lee, & von Schrader, 2014). The aging of the U.S. workforce and the concomitant rise in the number of people with disabilities in the workforce will intensify the need for workforce development professionals to develop competence in all areas of disability inclusiveness.

What Does This Mean for Educators and Workforce Development Practitioners?

The field of workforce development is limited by not including one of the largest diversity populations in our country today. The population of people with disabilities represents a large and untapped labor pool -- Americans with disabilities are employed at half the rate of their non-disabled peers, despite the fact that over one in ten are actively looking for employment (Erickson, Lee, & von Schrader, 2014). A large percentage of people who use workforce development systems will do so with a disability (Hoff, 2000). Further, given the increased prevalence of disability in the aging population and the likelihood that people will remain attached to the workplace longer, today's workplaces need to be inclusive and prepared to meet these human capital needs.

The intersection of labor supply and demand as it relates to disability requires two critical elements. On the demand side of the labor market equation, both pre-service and post-service discipline-focused curricula need to equip education practitioners to understand and manage disability as part of their respective practices for diverse populations. Myers (2009) articulated the need for disciplines and institutions to move beyond the limitation model of disability education, where disability education is provided as a "tag-on" and "one-up" experience, to an essential, integrated element of curricula, program and service design ensuring universal access for all people from the outset. Examples of these efforts can be seen in the well-established goals of undergraduate adapted physical education teacher preparation programs (Rizzo & Kirkendall, 1995; Rizzo, Broadhead, & Kowalski, 1997); the infusion of workforce diversity into a business school curriculum (Muller & Parham, 1998); and the incorporation of the human experience of disability within a graduate theological curriculum context (Anderson, 2003).

From the supply side of the labor market equation, workforce development professionals need to consider two important questions in developing and supporting inclusive workplace strategies and practices:

1. Are the workforce development strategies being employed fully accessible to people with disabilities?; and
2. Are all staff throughout the workforce development system prepared to include people with disabilities?

To address the first question, these strategies must move beyond simple physical access, to programmatic accessibility, and multi-cultural sensitivity—aligned with the call to more universal design (Myers, 2009). The second question is equally challenging to answer. Under the original Workforce Investment Act, and most recently the Workforce Innovations Opportunities Act, America's workforce development programs are all under the umbrella of America's Job Centers (formerly called One Stop Centers). Under this umbrella, a broad range of different services (job training, education, job-readiness and counseling programs) can be accessed by job seekers at a single point of entry—the American Job Center in their community. The challenge is that each program is unique. While these programs may have a similar intended purpose, the means by which they attain their ends, and the expertise required to support their end-users in achieving those ends, are very different. Some programs incorporated into America's Job Centers exclusively work with individuals with disabilities, like the state vocational rehabilitation program. However, the principle of universal design within the workforce development system is that any individual can avail themselves of resources they need to achieve their employment objectives, regardless of whether or not they have a disability—meaning that all facets of the Centers need to be equipped to manage the needs and supports of a diverse stakeholder audience. For more information on America's Job Centers and these workforce development programs, go to http://www.careeronestop.org or http://www.jobcenter.usa.gov.

Misperception #2: People with Disabilities Don't Need or Want to Work

People with disabilities continue to face significant barriers in their work lives and in their economic lives. The full-time/full-year employment rate for people with disabilities is 21.5%, as compared to 56.8% of people without disabilities, and the poverty rate among people with disabilities is 28.2%, as compared with 12.5% of people without disabilities (Erickson, Lee & von Schrader, 2014). The U.S. Social Security Disability Insurance (SSDI) Program provides monthly payments to eligible individuals with disabilities. In 2013, federal disability benefits were paid to about 10.2 million people. The average monthly payment for beneficiaries of SSDI was about $1,165 as of July, 2015 (U.S. Social Security Administration, 2015). Clearly, people with disabilities who cannot get and stay employed are at a far greater risk of living below the poverty level.

But do people with disabilities want to work? Are they actively trying to find work? In short: yes. Recent research shows that nearly 69% of people with disabilities surveyed reported that they are striving to work (Kessler Foundation and University of New Hampshire, 2015). This means that they are actively preparing for a job, looking for a job, seeking to work more hours, and trying to overcome barriers to employment (such as finding reliable transportation).

What Does This Mean for Educators and Workforce Development Practitioners?

A study conducted by Ali, Schur, and Blanck (2011) sought to better understand causes and specific elements of the low employment rates among people with disabilities. This study found that most research to date has focused on skill gaps, employment disincentives associated with disability entitlements and benefits, legislated accommodation requirements, and non-inclusive workplace cultures and employer attitudes—with little to no focus on the actual motivations and desire to work of currently non-employed people with disabilities. The findings of this study have considerable implications for educators and workforce development practitioners. Non-employed people with disabilities are as likely to want a job as their non-disabled peers, but are less likely to be actively searching. For educators preparing tomorrow's workforce, it reinforces that the population of people with disabilities are a viable, untapped labor pool that we need to include in the design of our workplace policies, practices, and cultures. Further, inclusion of disability as an element of diversity needs to be an essential element of training both for students preparing to enter the field via pre-service curricula and for professionals engaging in continuing education activities and post-service curricula.

For workforce development practitioners, the fact that people with disabilities are less likely to be actively searching for a job potentially speaks to a few possible considerations. A person's desire to work does not mean they have an incentive to work—to move them from knowing to doing. This requires workforce development professionals to consider motivational factors for each individual with a disability, and develop a keen knowledge of available resources that might provide incentives for individuals to move from just desiring work, to actively seeking and obtaining work.

Another consideration is that perhaps an individual with a disability simply lacks knowledge regarding job search strategies, or access to meaningful search supports. Individuals with disabilities often lack social capital and hence can be disadvantaged in finding job opportunities through connections in the community (Gilbride & Stensrud, 2008; Potts, 2005). While the purpose of the integration of America's workforce development system was to ensure universal access, workforce development practitioners should continue to assess and evaluate the degree to which all services and supports provided are accessible to individuals with disabilities, and customized to meet their unique support needs.

A final consideration is in understanding that the experience of disability is not homogenous. One size does not fit all when developing a plan and a package of services to support the job search of an individual with a disability. The successful workforce development practitioner will constantly be identifying emerging innovations in job search strategies to support the needs of individuals with disabilities. Systems change in the workforce development system will be necessary to ensure that programs and funding are available to meet the diverse needs of those with disabilities who will seek to use the system.

An important implication of this study was that non-employed people with disabilities are as likely to have job experience as their non-disabled counterparts, dispelling the myth that people with disabilities can't work. However, given the nature of the study, it did not explore prior arguments regarding skill gaps that may exist for the population of people with disabilities, which is an important consideration for educators and workforce development practitioners. The National Longitudinal Transition Study followed youth with disabilities for up to six years after high school; it clearly documents that youth with disabilities experience educational and skills gaps compared to their non-disabled counterparts. Youth with disabilities are less likely to enroll in postsecondary education, less likely to live independently, and more like to experience employment disparity compared to their non-disabled counterparts (Sanford, Newman, Wagner, Cameto, Knokey, Shaver, Buckley & Yen, 2011). While there are some noted improvements from earlier national longitudinal studies conducted by Blackorby and Wagner (1996), young people with disabilities continue to experience economic, employment and educational disparities. However, a study conducted by Karpur, Brewer and Golden (2013), comparing critical programmatic elements from the New York State Model Transition Program to the National Longitudinal Transition Study – 2 (NLTS-2), empirically demonstrated that several secondary school experiences were essential to post-school youth success and resulted in New York youth being twice as likely to have successful postsecondary outcomes compared with the national sample from the NLTS-2. These experiences included: career development activities; in-school work experiences; paid community work experiences; work- and postsecondary education-related goals in service planning documents; and connection and receipt of services from local community agencies. These secondary school experiences should be considered and planned for by both educators and workforce development practitioners to mitigate the skill gap for individuals with disabilities, to ensure their competitive advantage in the labor market.

Misperception #3: The American with Disabilities Act, as Amended (ADAAA) Has Eliminated Employment Discrimination for Individuals with Disabilities

Despite over 25 years of protections against employment discrimination, people with disabilities continue to face significant barriers in employment. Some of these barriers have to do with issues related to having a disability, such as finding reliable transportation or accessing higher education. A significant barrier, however, is that of negative employer expectations around hiring and accommodating people with disabilities (Kaye, Jans & Jones, 2011; Lengnick-Hall et al., 2008, Luecking, 2008; National Council on Disability, 2007). When considering employment barriers for people with disabilities, workforce professionals have tended to focus on "supply" issues—barriers having to do with characteristics of the job seeker with a disability. Instead, they may need to refocus their attention on the "demand" side—on barriers related to employers' reluctance to hire and retain workers with disabilities.

The U.S. Equal Employment Opportunity Commission (EEOC) charges of employment discrimination under the ADA provide some useful information about the characteristics of perceived disability discrimination in the years after the implementation of the ADA. The number of charges filed annually with the EEOC or state and local Fair Employment Practice Agencies has stayed relatively consistent at approximately 30,000 per year in the 25 years since the passage of the ADA (Bruyere et al., 2012). While lower in actual numbers than those filed for select other laws, like Title VII for gender, race or ethnicity, individuals with disabilities charge discrimination at a higher rate of charges filed per 10,000 individuals with in the relevant protected class in the workforce (Bruyere et al, 2012; Bjelland et al., 2010).

What Does This Mean for Educators and Workforce Development Practitioners?

The number of continuing level of disability discrimination charges confirms that workforce professionals need to work more closely with employers to assist them in proactively addressing workplace policies and practices where discrimination is occurring. The U.S. EEOC charge data discussed above also provides useful information on employer characteristics, where charges are most likely to occur. Not surprisingly, employers receiving charges under the ADA also have a higher likelihood of receiving charges under multiple statutes (Nazarov & von Schrader, 2014).

These findings point to the critical importance of workforce development professionals being able to speak to good workplace policies and practices that minimize discrimination of all forms across multiple protected classes, heightening the likelihood that not only people with disabilities, but other diverse individuals in the workforce are afforded equitable opportunities for hiring, retention, and advancement, and experience an overarching truly inclusive workplace climate.

The practice implications for educators' centers on the need to go beyond a legalistic notion of discrimination. Employment discrimination persists despite significant changes in regulatory framework both in the U.S. and globally. Curricula on disability issues need to expand beyond the law school. Understanding the human, organizational and business aspects of disability inclusiveness involves viewing these issues from a multi-disciplinary perspective.

Misperception #4: Unlike Other Diversity Populations, Employment Discrimination against Individuals with Disabilities Is Justified

People with disabilities tend to be one of the only diversity populations where it is still held that it is justified to blame the person for the discrimination they face in the labor market (Dipboye & Colella, 2005). Employers' unwillingness to hire people with disabilities is rooted in a number of misperceptions about the value and worth of workers with disabilities. These misperceptions include exaggerated beliefs about the costs of reasonable accommodations (Hernandez, et al, 2009), negative expectations of job performance potential (Florey & Harrison, 2000), and fear of litigation (Kaye, Jans & Jones, 2011). Research has shown, however, that many of these concerns are unsupported by evidence. Generally, people with disabilities do perform as well and are as productive on the job compared to those without disabilities (DePaul University, 2007; EARN, 2013). Similarly, the real cost of reasonable accommodations is far less than what most employers believe (Job Accommodation Network, 2014; Schur, et al, 2014). Half of all accommodations cost nothing and may be as simple as rearranging furniture or exchanging marginal (nonessential) job functions with a co-worker. When accommodations do bear a cost, the average amount is about $500. Considering the cost of losing a worker ranges between 20 – 100% of her annual salary, the cost of accommodation is always an excellent return on investment for employers (Center for American Progress, 2012; Job Accommodation Network, 2014). In addition, in a study comparing accommodation requests by people with and without disabilities using responses to the May 2012 U.S. Census Bureau Current Population Survey, results confirmed that most workplace accommodation requests come in fact from individuals without disabilities (von Schrader, Xu & Bruyèrec 2014). Workplace accommodations are therefore a critical part of the response of any employer in an effort to improve the productivity, and protect the well-being of its workforce.

What Does This Mean for Educators and Workforce Development Practitioners?

The findings above suggest that knowledge of how to create a workplace that affords individual employees accommodations to improve their productivity and well-being is imperative. This is only one, however, of a number of areas that workforce diversity professionals need to become aware of. Workplace practices must be examined across all aspects of the employment spectrum, including recruitment and hiring, retention and advancement, benefits/total compensation, technology and accessibility, disability inclusion practices, and metrics for an organization to self-assess its effectiveness across each of these dimensions (Bruyere, Switzer, VanLooy, von Schrader and Barrington, in press). In-depth research on recruitment and hiring practices of employers conducted by Cornell University in collaboration with the Society for Human Resource Management confirmed that select targeted practices can be effective in successfully increasing the hiring of individuals with disabilities. For example, practices such as internships for people with disabilities, strong management commitment, and explicit organizational hiring goals for individuals with disabilities, heightened the likelihood of successful hiring of a person with a disability in the past year by four to six times those employers who did report use such practices (Erickson, von Schrader, Bruyere, VanLooy, & Matteson, 2014).

Higher education practitioners need to reflect upon their talent acquisition and development practices. Are there any points in these processes where unquestioned assumptions about talent with disabilities creep into decision-making? Most higher education institutions would not tolerate HR-related decisions that were driven by unfounded negative assumptions about for example, gender or race. But are these automatic assumptions tolerated when it comes to disability? As a higher education practitioner, take a hard look at your practices. Ask yourself the following questions:

- Do we recruit faculty and staff from sources that include people with disabilities?
- Is our hiring process fully accessible?
- Do automatic negative assumptions about the capabilities of applicants with disabilities enter into our hiring decisions?
- Do we understand that needing an accommodation does not mean the person is unqualified to do the job?
- Do faculty and staff with disabilities trust us enough to come forward when they have an accommodation need?
- How often do faculty and staff have to leave their jobs because of a disability-related issue?

Misperception # 5: There Is a Well-Established Body of Research about Workforce Diversity Development and Disability

The lack of attention to disability in workforce development literature is surprising. As cited earlier, people with disabilities make up a significant portion of the population using workforce development systems. Yet there is almost no attention to disability issues in the research on workforce development or workforce diversity. Using two major research literature data bases (ProQuest and EBSCO), we conducted a search to determine how many research articles in workforce development or diversity included any mention of disability. To do this, we focused on articles published since 2005 and used the search term "workforce development" for one search and the term "workforce diversity" for another. For both these searchers, we set our search for the inclusion of these terms in the abstract and examined both all articles and peer reviewed-only articles for both these search terms. Our findings for this search, given in Table 1, illustrate the dearth of research attention given to disability in the workforce development and workforce diversity literature. These findings are even more alarming given the large number of people with disabilities who use major workforce services, such as American Job Centers and Manpower (Hoff, 2000).

Table 1. shows a serious omission in workforce diversity development research literature. The number of research articles from both peer-reviewed and nonpeer-reviewed sources that include disability in any way is minimal and far out of proportion to the number of people with disabilities who use these systems.

What Does This Mean for Educators and Workforce Development Practitioners?

Though a significant portion of those who use workforce development and diversity systems will be doing so with a disability, there is almost no presence of disability in these bodies of this research literature. This omission both precludes our understanding of a substantial number of users of workforce diversity development services and weakens the power of this research to improve practice.

Table 1. Number of Articles with and without Disability in Major Research Databases since 2005 (Search Date: August 23, 2015)

Key Search Terms	# of Articles: ABI/Inform ProQuest	# of Articles: EBSCO/Bus Source Complete
Workforce Development (All)	General: 13,294 Includes disability: 91	General: 1,184 Includes disability: 9
Workforce Development (Peer reviewed only)	General: 858 Includes disability: 13	General: 275 Includes disability: 1
Workforce Diversity (All)	General: 1,887 Includes disability: 235	General: 474 Includes disability: 6
Workforce Diversity (Peer reviewed only)	General: 337 Includes disability: 13	General: 186 Includes disability: 4

What Does This Mean to Practitioners in Higher Education?

This lack of research attention to disability in these fields means that higher education leaders may be compromised in their ability to create programs and services that meet the needs of all users. Whether higher education practitioners know it or not, twenty percent of those using their offerings will do so with a disability. With little disability-focused research in the diversity or workforce development literature, there is little evidence to use when planning efforts to enhance disability inclusiveness. What research questions might be needed to enable higher education practitioners to better plan disability programs and services? Here are a few suggestions:

- Faculty play a key role in the effectiveness of student accommodations. What are effective ways to communicate with faculty about disability inclusiveness?
- Distance learning has rapidly emerged as a major part of higher education learning experiences. Though distance learning has clear advantages for students with disabilities, the accessibility of online learning platforms has been uneven. How can higher education leaders ensure that their online learning experiences are fully accessible? What are the issues and barriers that can stand in the way of ensuring accessibility?

Misperception #6: Laws Preventing Employment Discrimination against Individuals with Disabilities Are Not Taken Seriously

There are currently four key laws that impact the employment and workforce development of people with disabilities: The Americans with Disabilities Act and its 2008 Amendments (ADAAA), Section 503 of the Rehabilitation Act (RA), the Workforce Innovation and Opportunities Act (WIOA) and Section 504 of the RA. Over the past several years, each of these laws have been strengthened to address employment and workforce development barriers for people with disabilities.

The ADA and ADAAA

The first of these three laws is Title I of the ADA, passed initially in 1990 and strengthened in 2008 with the ADA Amendments Act (ADAAA). The ADAAA defines disability being "a physical or mental impairment that substantially limits one or more major life activities" (EEOC, 2010). How disability is defined has been a key issue in the enforcement of the ADA and clarity as to how this definition should be interpreted was a critical factor in the drafting and passage of the ADAAA in 2008. With the broadening of how the definition of disability should be interpreted under the ADAAA, many more people became covered by its protection against disability employment discrimination. This broadened interpretation of the definition includes many people with disabilities that are not immediately obvious to others, such as mental illness, intellectual disabilities, multiple sclerosis or seizure disorders. The employment provisions of the ADAAA also include other elements. The ADAAA limits employers' disability inquiries. Job applicants and employees do not have to disclose a disability unless they are requesting a reasonable accommodation. Also, employers are required to provide qualified job applicants and employees with a reasonable accommodation unless this causes undue hardship. Reasonable accommodation is "any change in the work environment or in the way things are customarily done that enables an individual with a disability to enjoy equal employment opportunities" (U.S. Equal Employment Opportunity Commission, 2012). For more information on Title I (the employment provisions) of the ADAAA, go to http://www.eeoc.gov/eeoc/publications/fs-ada.cfm.

Section 503 of the RA as Amended

Applying to employers who have federal contracts of at least $10,000, Section 503 was also recently strengthened. The new Section 503 regulations, which took effect in March, 2014, require employers to work toward a goal of having a workforce that consists of at least seven percent of people with disabilities across all job categories in the organization. To show progress toward meeting this goal, employers must use a voluntary self-identification form to track the number of applicants and current employees who have disabilities. This form is confidential and cannot be used for human resource decisions, such as hiring or performance review. Section 503 also requires employers to create collaborations with disability agencies to recruit qualified individuals with disabilities into their workforce. For more information on Section 503, go to http://www.dol.gov/ofccp/regs/compliance/faqs/503_faq.htm.

Workforce Innovation and Opportunity Act (WIOA)

The Workforce Investment of Act of 1998 sought to consolidate all workforce development programs into a unified system, responsive to the needs of job seekers and employers (Bruyere, Golden & Cebula, 2010). This law was amended in 2014 with the passage of the Workforce Innovations and Opportunity Act (WIOA) which aimed, in part, to address further integration, streamlining, and seamlessness of workforce investment partners and programs, state and local coordination, common performance measures, and emphasis on preparing youth and job seekers to be competitive in the 21st century job-driven demand labor market. While final regulations are not expected until 2016, the proposed regulations definitely articulate very different expectations and architecture for how the workforce development system will operate, and ultimately how Americans seeking employment will be better prepared to meet the demand side challenges of the future labor market. WIOA was enacted in a policy environment proliferating Employment First initiatives—leveraging policies and practices that exclusively focus on integrated employment in the local economy at or above minimum wage as the first option for individuals with disabilities. This increased policy pressure at both the federal and state level will exert considerable force on the workforce development system to more effectively integrate the population of people with disabilities into the local labor market. For more information on WIOA, go to http://www.doleta.gov/wioa.

Section 504 of the RA

Applying to any program or activity that receives federal financial assistance, Section 504 covers most colleges and universities nation-wide. Federal financial assistance can include: grants, cooperative agreements or financial assistance to students. Section 504 closely mirrors the ADAAA and applies to such functions as faculty/staff employment, nondiscrimination in student admissions, program and physical accessibility, and modifications for individual students with disabilities. For more information about Section 504 of the RA, go to http://www.pacer.org/publications/adaqa/504.asp.

What Does This Mean for Educators and Workforce Diversity Practitioners?

First and foremost, educators and workforce diversity practitioners need to understand how these foundational pieces of legislation apply to policy and practice in their organizations. Regardless of the sector practitioners are being prepared for, at a minimum the ADA will intersect with their practice, on both a practical but also a compliance level. While WIOA may not have the broad sweeping impact that the ADA does on ensuring non-discrimination in the workplace, business and industry will likely work very closely with local workforce development systems and America's Job Centers to secure and tap into local labor supply. Understanding the constellation of workforce development programs, stakeholders they serve, and regulations governing how they operate, are critical. Similarly, while the new section 503 regulations pertain exclusively to federal contractors and subcontractors, it is an opportunity that workforce diversity practitioners should ready themselves to be able to leverage. In the new millennium, outsourcing by the federal government has been on the rise (Shane & Nixon, 2007), with over 200,000 organizations serving as federal contractors or subcontractors, employing approximately 25% of all U.S. workers (Shui, 2013). The contractors must meet the intended outcomes of the section 503 rules—including the seven percent aspirational employment goal for employees with disabilities. Workforce development professionals must be equipped to be at the strategizing table to support these contractors and subcontractors in identifying and promoting meaningful ways to include individuals with disabilities in their workforce (Rudstam, Golden, Strobel Gower, Switzer, Bruyere, & Van Looy, 2014).

Most higher education practitioners are already aware of laws covering the workplace and colleges/universities and have in place both employment, accessibility and accommodation processes for faculty/staff and for students. There are, however, some emerging considerations for leaders in higher education, such as the following:

- **Veterans with Disabilities on Campus:** The laws around employing and educating veterans with disabilities have recently been strengthened and are only recently fully enforceable. For example, the Vietnam Era Veterans Readjustment Assistance Act (VEVRAA) took effect in March, 2014 and covers (among other employers) any college/university receiving more than $100,000 in federal contracts/subcontracts (OFCCP, 2014). Also, the Post-9/11 GI Bill has recently offered additional education benefits to (among others) veterans with service-connected disabilities (U.S. DVA, 2015).
- **Online and Social Media Accessibility:** As more employment and education processes are being delivered online, the accessibility of online communications is imperative. Though the enforcement of online accessibility is still somewhat in flux, there are clear guidelines which higher education practitioners can follow to ensure that online offerings are fully accessibility. The accessibility of social media has been more difficult to address. There are several aspects of social media which are not fully accessible to users with disabilities. As yet, regulations and policies have yet to catch up in this area.

Misperception #6: If You Can't See a Disability, the Person Probably Does Not Have One

Try this short exercise: Go to google, perform a search for images, and enter the word "disability" as your search term. What do you see? It is likely that the vast majority of the images you see involve wheelchairs. When most people think of disability, they think of people with obvious disabilities, such as those who use wheelchairs or who have sensory disabilities. Yet, arguably, the majority of people with disabilities who have rights under the ADAAA are individuals with disabilities that are not immediately visible to others—who have nonobvious disabilities. Examples of prevalent nonobvious disabilities are multiple sclerosis, seizure disorders or mental illness.

Nonobvious disabilities have a unique dynamic in the workforce. Individuals with nonobvious disabilities are often taken less seriously than those with other disabilities, as if they do not have a "real" disability. They are also more likely to be blamed for their disability. Also, these disabilities might invoke more fear and misunderstanding on the part of the public.

Finally, there is the important issue of disclosure. For individuals with nonobvious disabilities, disclosure is a choice. Under the ADAAA, this is a legally protected choice. That is, employers cannot require applicants to disclose their disability during the hiring process. Similarly, employees cannot be required to disclose a disability unless they are requesting a reasonable accommodation. In this case, the employer has a right to collect some medical documentation pertaining to ensuring an appropriate accommodation in the workplace. For more information, go to EEOC document found at http://www.eeoc.gov/policy/docs/guidance-inquiries.html.

It is important to understand that there are different types of employer disability inquiry and disclosure. Under the ADAAA, employers cannot ask individual job applicants or employees about disabilities, except under certain very specific conditions. However, under RA Section 503, employers who are federal contractors are required to collect data about the number of people with disabilities in their applicant pool and among their employees. Called "invitation to voluntarily self-identify," this data collection is done by using a particular form and is confidential. Hence, it is not the same as a disability disclosure that can be tracked to the individual and can be used during HR processes, such as hiring, promotion or termination. For more information, go to http://www.dol.gov/ofccp/regs/compliance/faqs/503_faq.htm.

What Does This Mean for Educators and Workforce Development Practitioners?

Workforce development practitioners must be prepared to be as effective with individuals with nonobvious disabilities as they are with those who have obvious disabilities. Workforce development professionals must also thoroughly understand disability disclosure issues when dealing with employers. Workforce development practitioners cannot disclose a job-seeker's disability to an employer without the job-seekers' permission. Workforce development practitioners must also be prepared to support a job seeker with a disability in working through the decision to disclose or discuss a disability. Each person and each job application process can be unique. A job seeker can decide to disclose to one potential employer, but not to another. A key role of the workforce development professional is to ensure that the job seeker with a disability is making a choice that is right for her and right for the individual.

What Does This Mean to Higher Education Practitioners?

Many of those using higher education programs will do so with a disability that is not obvious to others, such as mental illness, learning disabilities or diabetes. For both employees and students, disability disclosure a legally protected choice (except when an employee or student requests an accommodation). This means that issues around organizational climate, such as trust and openness, come to the fore. Because of the many misperceptions and stigma linked to disabilities such as mental illness or learning disabilities, individuals with these invisible disabilities will not come forward if they believe there will be negative consequences or if there is emotional risk in doing so.

Higher education practitioners should consider some questions about the organizational climate on campus. What features of your organizational climate might inhibit or enable individuals to come forward if they need an accommodation? What is your messaging (both direct and indirect) around these types of disabilities? Do employees or students see others in the organization who are open and honest about their own nonobvious disabilities? Are there student or employee groups where individuals with nonobvious disabilities can share experiences and have a voice to organizational leaders? Or is there a culture of silence around these types of disabilities?

Misperception #7: Disability Is Deficit

The failure to fully include individuals with disabilities in workforce diversity development has been fueled in part by the tacit assumption that, unlike other diversity categories, disability is an inherent deficit. Challenging this subtle but powerful misperception involves a change in the conceptual lens we use to see disability. The first step in this change is recognizing that *disability is not simply a medical condition, it is a social construct.*

Historically, the exclusion of other diversity populations (such as African-Americans and women) has also been justified by an automatic assumption of deficit—by an unquestioned assumption that these individuals were simply not capable of making a full and equal contribution to the workforce (Green & Kalev, 2010). Today, few hold these beliefs regarding racial and gender diversity. Yet, many continue to hold them regarding disability, despite evidence that individuals with disabilities can and do perform as well as others in the workplace (DePaul University, 2007).

Seeing disability as a social construct, and not simply as a medical issue, involves recognizing that the most significant barrier individuals with disabilities face is often not the disability itself, but rather the attitudes of others toward the disability. With this recognition comes the questioning of other beliefs, such as:

- *The word "disabled" is an appropriate term.*
- Words matter. Over the past decade, person-first language has come to replace disability-first language. Individuals with disabilities need to be identified as people first and as having a disability second. Too often, a person's talents, abilities and interests were eclipsed by the label of "disability." Using person-first language (e.g. "a person/individual with a disability" instead of "a disabled man/woman") puts the person first and the disability second.
- *"Normal" is the opposite of "disabled."*
- The word "normal" when used in opposition to "disabled" conjures an image of people with disabilities as being "abnormal" – as being deserving of marginality.

- *Individuals with disabilities live with a constant wish they could escape their disability and become "whole."*
- A well-known image of disability involves a picture of a man in a wheelchair holding his head in anguish while his shadow stands with his hands raised in a posture that evokes the phrase, "Now I'm free!!!" This image is offensive to many individuals with disabilities who do not feel they are constrained or confined by their disability. More importantly, this image has justified a perception of limitation and deficit that has fueled the discrimination of individuals with disabilities in the workforce. Individuals with disabilities are not all clinging to the wish that they could be "whole." Many believe their disability has provided them with unique strengths: resilience, adaptability, problem-solving abilities and patience. The phrase, "My disability is part of who I am" expresses the disability pride that is now part of disability identity.
- *Individuals with disabilities are brave objects of inspiration to others.*
- Individuals with disabilities are often frustrated by comments that implicitly hold them to a higher moral standard. The key word in the phrase "object of inspiration" is, of course, the word object. These phrases evoke an idea about disability that does not acknowledge individuals with disabilities as being fully human. Though appearing appreciative, these phrases are based in the misperception that the worth is people with disabilities is to remind others of their good fortune. Acknowledge that individuals with disabilities span the range of all human capabilities. Just like anyone else, some people with disabilities are brave and inspirational, others are not.
- *Individuals with disabilities are all alike.*
- Finally, an undertone of the words and phrases used to describe disability is the idea that it's all about the disability--that having a disability is the only human characteristic that matters. Though a sense of disability community and disability pride has emerged over the past several decades, a key unifying theme of this community is that people with disabilities should be recognized for their individual talents, skills, interests and abilities.

What Does This Mean for Educators and Workforce Diversity Development Practitioners?

Workforce diversity development practitioners must be prepared to not only be "polite" when interacting with individuals with disabilities. They must also have a deeper empathy about the human experience of disability. The most important point here is to acknowledge the ongoing struggle individuals with disabilities face to simply be seen as not just people with disabilities, but individuals who have skills, talents, interests and career aspirations.

What does this mean for practitioners in higher education? Who you hire sends a powerful message about how your college/university views talent. Are individuals with disabilities seen at all levels of your workplace among your faculty and staff? Or if they are seen, are they only seen in unskilled positions? When your faculty/staff members do not look like your student population, there is a risk for a disconnect. For about twenty percent of your student population, going through life as a person with a disability has been a key part of their human experience and often a key part of their identity. If these students see no one on campus who looks like them or who shares this aspect of their life experience, they may hear a message that they have to choose between accepting who they are or being fully included in the culture.

Misperception # 7: Individuals with Disabilities Have a "Special" Place in the Workforce and Need a "Special" Form of Workforce Development

The word "special" has been used repeatedly to describe individuals with disabilities. Originally, the word was intended to evoke images of individuals with disabilities as simply being different, not necessarily as "less than." However, over the years, this notion of specialness has fueled the segregation of individuals with disabilities and funneled them into jobs that are more likely to be low-paying, dead-end, less secure, low-growth, and with few or no benefits (National Council on Disability, 2007; Kessler Foundation, 2010). Similarly, this notion of being "special" has fueled the idea that individuals with disabilities cannot compete in the open labor market and require a special labor market with lowered expectations of their performance and capabilities.

The notion of "sheltered workshops" or "work centers" emerged over 100 years ago to provide this special labor market (Hoffman, 2013). Sheltered workshops are defined as "facility-based day programs attended by adults with disabilities as an alternative to working in the open labor market" (Migliore, 2010). The Fair Labor Standards Act, Section 14c permits individuals working in sheltered workshops (or similar arrangements) to be paid subminimum wage in some situations (US Department of Labor, 2013). Sheltered employment workshops have been found to be not only costly, but also simply ineffective (Cimera, Wehman, West & Burgess, 2012). Many individuals with disabilities in these forms of segregated employment never find their way into real employment, even when they are in working in centers which are ostensibly designed to offer job preparation (National Disability Rights Organization, 2011). For these reasons, segregated employment or sheltered workshops are being phased out in many states (Hoffman, 2011). In 2014, the passage of WIOA also addressed this paradigm shift by limiting access to sheltered employment for youth under the age of 24, and requiring processes to ensure that individuals currently employed in those sheltered work environments are provided opportunities and choices regarding integrated employment (Chovaz, 2015). Despite the obvious problems with segregated workforce development, "special" employment continues to be associated with indivdiuals with disabilities.

What Does This Mean for Educators and Workforce Development Practitioners?

Educators and workforce development practitioners need to start from the assumption that individuals with disabilities can achieve competitive employment in the communities in which they live. Though workers with disabilities might use reasonable accommodations on the job, doing this does not make workers with disabilities less capable or less qualified than those who do not use accommodations (Job Accommodation Network, 2014).

There are several implications for practitioners in higher education. A confluence of trends has resulted in an increasing number of students with disabilities attending postsecondary institutions. Students now entering college as young adults are the first generation to have had the protections of the Individuals with Disabilities in Education Act throughout their primary and secondary school careers. The services offered them during their prior schooling are now bearing fruit in larger numbers of students with disabilities applying to college. Similarly, advances in assistive technology have enabled more students to participate in higher education. In addition to benefiting individuals with sensory disabilities, these advances have also been used by students with other disabilities, such as mobility, speech or learning disabilities. Higher education practitioners need to build in disability inclusiveness to the evaluation of their diversity efforts directed toward both students and employees.

Another implication for higher education practitioners centers on the need for better connections between the student disability services office and the career counseling office. With the strengthening of laws and the emerging awareness of the need for a disability inclusive workplace, many employers who recruit from colleges/universities are now actively recruiting graduating students with disabilities. Higher education practitioners need to consider the effectiveness of their career counseling services and/or disability services offices in building a bridge between students with disabilities seeking jobs and employers who are increasingly seeking to hire them. Also, disability services offices need to see their role as going beyond providing accommodations/modifications. Rather, they need expertise in supporting students with disabilities transitioning to work. They need to be able to provide coaching and support to these transitioning students around, for example, making disability disclosure decisions and requesting accommodations in the workplace.

Misperception # 8: Disability Awareness Training Will Be Enough

How can workforce development professionals build disability inclusiveness in their organizations? At first glance, the answer to this question is often: more training. However, several research studies suggest that traditional training alone is not a powerful way of bringing about sustainable organizational change (Robinson & Robinson, 2014, Roffe, 2007; Azmawani, Siew, Sambasivan & Wong, 2013).

The lessons learned from prior efforts to bring about organizational change to enhance workplace diversity reveal other interventions that are more effective than traditional training. Examining diversity efforts throughout the decades reveals a basic point about the effectives of these efforts (Green & Kalev, 2010; Rudstam, 2012). During the 1970s and 1980s, diversity efforts were focused on changing the individual through sensitivity training. In the 1990s, diversity efforts began to focus on the need to align with business imperatives rather than just on changing individual sensitivities. In the 2000s, a deeper awareness of how organization-level factors incentivized (or dis-incentivized) workplace diversity lead to the infusion of diversity into organizational practices, such as talent acquisition, mentoring, internships and hiring (Green & Kalev, 2010). Also, diversity efforts became more likely to take the form of greater accountabilities for leaders to hire and develop diverse talent. Finally, we have seen more attention to how diversity is interwoven with the subtle but powerful features of organizational climate—the everyday lived experience in the workplace. With this, diversity efforts have taken the form of employee resource groups who are not just "support groups" but who have a meaningful voice within business practices such as recruitment and customer outreach.

Efforts that focus only on changing individuals, such as awareness or sensitivity training, have little overall effect on bringing about sustainable diversity at the organization level. However, efforts which are based in a deeper understanding of the climate of the organization, and which take into account the obvious and subtle incentives that are at play in making decisions which lead to greater organizational diversity tend to be more effective. Finally, diversity efforts which are integral to organizational or business goals are more effective than those that are marginal to the aims of the workplace.

What Does This Mean for Educators and Workforce Development Practitioners?

Workforce diversity development professionals need to be prepared to suggest the full range of interventions to create workplaces that are disability inclusive. This will involve not only awareness training, but interventions such as mentoring, internships, and employee resource groups.

In higher education, investing in human intellectual capital is the cornerstone of organizational success. Employee turnover is very costly for all employers. However, it is particularly costly in the higher education workplace where specific expertise in teaching, research and grant-writing can often be extremely difficult to replace. Many of the employees with this expertise will, at some point in their careers, experience a disability that could mean that they will exit the workplace if they are not effectively accommodated. So for colleges and universities, the stakes are higher for finding innovative and engaging ways to create disability inclusiveness in the workplace.

Simply providing mandated staff training around diversity and inclusiveness will not be enough. Here are some suggestions for more innovative approaches to disability inclusiveness:

- Create more accountability. Set goals around disability inclusiveness in sourcing, recruiting and hiring.
- Give them a voice. Provide a confidential communication channel where faculty/staff with disabilities can provide feedback on their experiences. This communication can also be provided an Employee Resource Group.
- Look at suppliers and contractors. Though most colleges/universities have a supplier/contractor guidelines for diversity, these often do not meaningfully include disability.
- Why are employees leaving? Many employers *conduct exit interviews* where employees can provide confidential information about their decision to *leave the job*. Exit interviews can be a valuable source of data for determining whether disability issues came into play in a valued employee's decision to leave the job. What could have been done to prevent this separation?

Misperception # 9: Bringing about a Disability Inclusive Workforce Is Just about HR

Diversity and inclusion efforts are usually seen as being in the realm of HR practice. Yet, in most cases, HR professionals do not play the most important role in actually bringing about diversity and inclusion in the everyday lived experience of the workplace. A key theme that has emerged in the research about diversity and disability inclusion is the pivotal role played by face-to-face leaders—by managers/supervisors (M/Ss) (Osterman, 2008; Nishii & Bruyere, 2014; Leavitt, 2004; Huy, 2001; Buckingham & Coffman, 2004; Human Capital Institute, 2010).

M/Ss (not HR professionals) are often the key arbiters of those decisions that most powerfully impact diversity and inclusion: who gets hired; who gets developed or trained; who gets promoted; who gets coached; who is included in meetings or social events; who gets terminated. Also, M/Ss are frontline players for both accommodation processes and for performance management. Yet, they tend to be very difficult to reach for any organizational intervention, including those related to disability inclusiveness. So, too often, they are by passed by workforce diversity and inclusion efforts generally and disability inclusiveness efforts in particular.

These studies and others point to the importance of reaching and including M/Ss in any workforce development effort. This is even more critical for including people with disabilities in workforce development efforts. M/Ss are the key gatekeepers for fully including individuals with disabilities in the workplace. They tend to play the most powerful role in ensuring that employees with disabilities are mentored, coached, get formative feedback and have access to formal learning opportunities, such as classes or distance learning.

What Does This Mean to Workforce Development Practitioners?

Workforce diversity development practitioners need to develop proficiency in supporting employers as they develop strategies to bring about a more disability inclusive workforce. They need to be prepared to suggest ways that employers can meaningfully reach M/Ss about disability issues. Can disability be included during general M/S training efforts? Can the employers send out ongoing short communications—"blasts" to M/Ss about disability and employment? Can disability be included in other communications throughout the organization? Can disability inclusiveness be part of the M/Ss performance review criteria?

In the higher education workplace, the importance of face-to-face leaders in the full engagement of employees with disabilities is as important as in other sectors. Faculty/staff are often more likely to contact their own supervisor than their HR representative when a disability issue arises. Higher education diversity practitioners need to ask themselves some key questions:

- Do all leaders understand the importance of including disability in its diversity efforts?
- Is disability inclusiveness discussed in the on-boarding process for new faculty/staff?
- Do all leaders know what to do when notified of a disability?
- Are all leaders able to interact respectfully and effectively with employees and students with disabilities?

Misperception # 10: Disability Has Become a Major Part of the Higher Education Curriculum on Workforce Development or Human Resource Development

How can workforce development professionals learn about disability? To what extent is disability included in undergraduate and graduate education for workforce development professionals and other labor market sectors? Table 2 shows the number of colleges and universities from the U.S. News & World "Top Ten" list who provide learning experiences about disability in the undergraduate or graduate program. Generally, we see here that workforce development professionals who wish to include disability in their graduate or undergraduate curriculum must often seek informal learning experiences to do so. Less than half of these schools had courses specific to disability topics. However, these colleges were more likely to offer informal learning experiences, such as interest or research groups.

Table 2. The Number of Top 10 Business Colleges/Universities Offering Learning Experiences about Disability

	Undergraduate Program	Graduate Program
Has courses on disability issues	4 out of 10 schools	3 out of 10
Has extra-curricular learning experiences on disability issues	9 out of 10 schools	3 out of 10

What Does This Mean for Educators and Workforce Development Practitioners?

Often, workforce diversity development practitioners will have little formal preparation to address disability issues in their professional practice. For many, this could mean that when they enter their professional practice, they will have little understanding of the issues faced by about twenty percent of those who will be using their programs. This dearth of formal learning experiences about disability during higher education preparation will mean that workforce diversity development practitioners will need to get these learning experiences through continuing professional development. With the increase in the number of people with disabilities using workforce development services and programs, these continuing professional development experiences need to be readily available, updated, easy to find, and make sense for the broad range of workforce development professional practices.

CONCLUSION

The intent of this chapter is to bring home the notion that workforce development and diversity professional practice will be strengthened by including one of America's largest diversity populations: individuals with disabilities. To do this, workforce development and diversity practitioners may need to re-orient some basic assumptions about job-seekers with disabilities, understand regulatory issues, and commit to making changes in the concepts that underlie their practices.

Leaders in higher education generally have been at the forefront of diversity and inclusion efforts directed toward students as well as faculty and staff. The full inclusion of disability in these efforts will become more of an imperative for higher education in the future for several reasons. The number of students with disabilities on campus will increase as today's students with disabilities are better prepared for higher education than were prior generations. Also, with greater awareness and less shame, students with disabilities now expect accessibility, inclusion and equal opportunity during their higher education experience. Also, they will expect to see others like them among both the student body and among faculty and staff. Hence, in the higher education context (as in other employment settings), who you hire sends a message about what you stand for as an organization. Your employment practices are connected to your organizational capacity to connect with the increasing number of students who will be using your offerings with a disability.

Consider your own practices against each of the ten points discussed in this chapter. Where are you and where is your organization in "living" these ten points? How far have you come in bringing disability into the mainstream of your diversity and inclusion efforts? What are the areas where you are already strong? How can you further develop these strengths? In which areas might you need to further develop?

How you answer these questions will be key to whether you are prepared for a future where individuals with disabilities will increasingly expect that their employers, counselors and educators view them as not as broken, but as having the potential to fully contribute to the organization and to society.

REFERENCES

Ali, M., Schur, L., & Blanck, P. (2011). What types of jobs do people with disabilities want? *Journal of Occupational Rehabilitation*, *21*(2), 199–210. doi:10.100710926-010-9266-0 PMID:20924777

American Assembly of Collegiate Business Schools of Business (AACSB). (1992). Teaching diversity: Business schools search for model approaches. *Newsline*, *23*(1), 1–4.

Anderson, R. C. (2003). Infusing the graduate theological curriculum with education about disability: Addressing the human experience of disability in the theological context. *Theology Education*, *29*(1), 131–153.

Azmawani, R., Siew, I., Sambasivan, J., & Wong, F. (2013). Training and organizational effectiveness: Moderating role of knowledge management process. *European Journal of Training and Development.*, *37*(5), 472–488. doi:10.1108/03090591311327295

Barrington, L., Bruyère, S., & Waelder, M. (2014). Employer practices in improving employment outcomes for people with disabilities: A trans-disciplinary and employer-inclusive research approach. *Journal of Rehabilitation Research, Policy and Education*, *28*(4), 208-224. Retrieved from http://www.ingentaconnect.com/content/springer/rrpe/2014/00000028/00000004/art00002

Bjelland, M., Bruyère, S., von Schrader, S., Houtenville, A., Ruiz-Quintanilla, A., & Webber, D. (2010). Age and disability employment discrimination: Occupational rehabilitation implications. *Journal of Occupational Rehabilitation*, *20*(4), 456–471. doi:10.100710926-009-9194-z PMID:19680793

Blackorby, J., & Wagner, M. (1996). Longitudinal postschool outcomes of youth with disabilities: Finds from the National Longitudinal Transition Study. *Exceptional Children*, *62*(5), 399–413.

Bruyere, S. M., Golden, T. P., & Cebula, R. A., III. (2010). Legislation Affecting Employment for Persons with Disabilities. In R. Parker, E. Szymanski (Ed.), Work and Disability (ed., pp. 17-48). Austin, TX: Pro-Ed.

Bruyere, S., Switzer, E., VanLooy, S., von Schrader, S., & Barrington, L. (in press). Translating knowledge to practices and the way forward. In S. Bruyere (Ed.), *Disability and Employer Practice: Across the Disciplines*. Ithaca, NY: Cornell University ILR Press.

Center for American Progress. (2012). There are significant costs to replacing employees. *CAP Labor and Work Issues*. Retrieved from https://www.americanprogress.org/issues/labor/report/2012/11/16/44464/there-are-significant-business-costs-to-replacing-employees

Chovaz, M. (2015, July 10). APSE applauds WIOA Advisory Committee on increasing competitive integrated employment for people with disabilities. Association for Persons in Supported Employment Legislative News Brief. Retrieved from http://apse.org/apse-applauds-wioa-advisory-committee-on-increasing-competitive-integrated-employment-for-individuals-with-disabilities-acicieid

Dipboye, R. L., & Colella, A. (Eds.). (2005). *Discrimination at work: The psychological and organizational bases*. Mahwah, NJ: Lawrence Erlbaum Associates.

EARN. Employer Assistance Resource Network. (2013). Are employees with disabilities as productive as employees without disabilities? Retrieved from http://askearn.org/docs/brochures/pdf/FAQ_2-ACC.pdf

Erickson, W., Lee, C., & von Schrader, S. (2014). 2013 Disability Status Report: United States. Ithaca, NY: Cornell University Employment and Disability Institute (EDI).

Erickson, W., von Schrader, S., Bruyère, S., VanLooy, S., & Matteson, D. (2014). Disability-inclusive employer practices and hiring of individuals with disabilities. *Journal of Rehabilitation Research, Policy and Education, 28*(4), 309-328. Retrieved from http://www.ingentaconnect.com/content/springer/rrpe/2014/00000028/00000004/art00007

Florey, A. T., & Harrison, D. A. (2000). Responses to informal accommodation requests from employees with disabilities: Multi-study evidence on willingness to comply. *Academy of Management Journal, 43*(2), 224–233. doi:10.2307/1556379

Folson-Meek, S. L., Nearing, R. J., Groteluschen, W., & Krampf, H. (1999). Effects of academic major, gender, and hands-on experience on attitudes of preservice professionals. *Adapted Physical Activity Quarterly; APAQ, 16*, 389–402.

Gilbride, D., & Stensrud, R. (2008). Why won't they just do it. *Rehabilitation Education, 22*(2), 125–132. doi:10.1891/088970108805059462

Green, T., & Kalev, A. (2010). Discrimination reducing measures at the relational level. *Hastings Law Review, 59*, 1435–1462.

Hernandez, B., McDonald, K., Lepera, N., Shahna, M., Wang, A., & Levy, J. (2009). Moving beyond misperceptions: The provision of workplace accommodations. *Journal of Social Work in Disability & Rehabilitation, 8*(3-4), 189–204. doi:10.1080/15367100903202755 PMID:20183631

Hoffman, L. (2013). An employment opportunity or a discrimination dilemma?: Sheltered workshops and the employment of the disabled. *University of Pennsylvania Law Review*, Feb, 27.

Human Capital Institute. (2010). *Mid-level managers: The bane and salvation of organizations*. Retrieved from http://www.hci.org/Mid-level%2520Managers_DDI-Research#center

Huy, Q. N. (2001). In praise of middle managers. *Harvard Business Review, 79*(8), 72–79. PMID:11550632

Job Accommodation Network. (2013). Workplace accommodations: Low cost, high impact. Retrieved from http://askjan.org/media/lowcosthighimpact.html

Karpur, A., Brewer, D., & Golden, T. P. (2013). Critical program elements in transition to adulthood: Comparative analysis of New York State and the NLTS-2. *Career Development and Transition for Exceptional Individuals, 37*(2), 119–130. doi:10.1177/2165143413476880

Kaye, S., Jans, L., & Jones, E. (2011, December). Why don't employers hire and retain workers with disabilities? *Journal of Occupational Rehabilitation, 21*(4), 526–536. doi:10.100710926-011-9302-8 PMID:21400039

Kessler Foundation. (2015). *2015 National Disability and Employment Survey*. Retrieved from www.kesslerfoundation.org/sites/default/files/filepicker/5/KFSurvey2015_ExecutiveSummary.pdf

Leavitt, H. (2004). The plight of middle managers. *Harvard Business School Working Knowledge*. Retrieved from http://hbswk.hbs.edu/archive/4537.html

Lengnick-Hall, M. L., Gaunt, P. M., & Kulkarni, M. (2008). Overlooked and underutilized: People with disabilities are an untapped human resource. *Human Resource Management, 47*(2), 255–273. doi:10.1002/hrm.20211

Luecking, R. G. (2008). Emerging employer views of people with disabilities and the future of job development. *Journal of Vocational Rehabilitation, 29,* 3–13.

Migliore, A. (2010). Sheltered Workshops. In International Encyclopedia of Rehabilitation. Retrieved from http://cirrie.buffalo.edu/encyclopedia/en/pdf/sheltered_work shops

Muller, H. J., & Haase, B. (1994). Managing diversity in health services organizations. *Hospital & Health Services Administration, 14,* 415–434. PMID:10138715

Muller, H. J., & Parham, P. A. (1998). Integrating workforce diversity into the business school curriculum: An experiment. *Journal of Management Education, 22*(2), 122–148. doi:10.1177/105256299802200202

Myers, K.A. (2009). A new vision for disability education. *Interscience,* November-December, 15-21.

National Council on Disability. (2007). *Empowerment for Americans with Disabilities: Breaking Barriers to Careers and Full Employment.* Retrieved from http://www.ncd.gov/publications/2007/Oct2007

National Council on Disability. (2007). Empowerment for Americans with disabilities: Breaking barriers to careers and full employment. Washington, DC

Nazarov, Z., & von Schrader, S. (2014). Comparison of employer factors in disability and other employment discrimination charges. *Journal of Rehabilitation Research. Policy and Education, 28*(4), 291–308.

Nielson Group. (2014). Nielson Employee Resource Group Report. Retrieved from http://www.nielsen.com/content/dam/nielsenglobal/us/docs/about/2014-nielsen-employee-resource-group-report.pdf

Osterman, P. (2008). *The Truth about middle managers: Who they are, how they work, why they matter.* Boston, MA: Harvard Business School Press.

Potts, B. (2005). Disability and employment: Considering the importance of social capital. *Journal of Rehabilitation, 71*(3), 20–25.

Rizzo, T. L., & Kirkendall, D. R. (1995). Teaching students with mild disabilities: What affects attitudes of future physical educators? *Adapted Physical Activity Quarterly; APAQ, 12,* 205–216.

Rizzo, T. L., Broadhead, G. D., & Kowlaski, E. (1997). Changing kinesiology and physical education by infusing information about individuals with disabilities. *Quest, 49*(2), 229–237. doi:10.1080/00336297.1997.10484237

Robinson, D., & Robinson, M. (2014). *Performance Consulting: A Practical Guide for HR and Learning Professionals* (3rd ed.). Francisco, CA: BK Publishers.

Roffe, I. (2007). Competitive strategy and influences on e-learning in entrepreneur-led SMEs. *Journal of European Industrial Training, 31*(6), 416–434. doi:10.1108/03090590710772622

Rudstam, H., Golden, T. P., Strobel-Gower, W., Switzer, E., Bruyere, S. M., & Van Looy, S. (2014). Leveraging new rules to advance new opportunities: Implications of the Rehabilitation Act Section 503 new rules for employment service providers. *Journal of Vocational Rehabilitation, 41*, 193–208.

Sanford, C., Newman, L., Wagner, M., Cameto, R., Knokey, A. M., Shaver, D., ... Yen, S. J. (2011). *The post—high school outcomes of young adults with disabilities up to six years after high school: Key findings from the National Longitudinal Transition Study-2*. Washington, DC: Institute of Education Sciences, National Center for Special Education Research.

Schur, L., Nishii, L., Meera, A., Kruse, D., Bruyere, S., & Blanck, P. (2014). Accommodating employees with and without disabilities. *Human Resource Management*, July, 1.

Shane, S., & Nixon, R. (2007). U.S. contractors becoming a fourth branch of government. New York Times.

Shui, P. (2013). Innovative research on employer practices: Improving employment for people with disabilities. *Presentation at the Cornell University, ILR School, Employment and Disability Institute State-of-the-Science Conference*, Arlington, VA.

U.S. Census Bureau. (2014). *Report on the Recent U.S. Disability Statistics from the U.S. Census Bureau*. Retrieved from http://www.disabled-orld.com/disability/statistics/census-stats.php

U.S. Equal Employment Opportunity Commission. (2012). *Enforcement Guidance: Reasonable Accommodation and Undue Hardship under the ADA*. Retrieved from http://www.eeoc.gov/policy/docs/accommodation.html#general

U.S. Social Security Administration. (2015). Annual Statistical Report on the Social Security Disability Insurance Program. Retrieved from http://www.ssa.gov/policy/docs/statcomps/di_asr/2013/index.html

U.S. Department of Labor. (2013). *Fair Labor Standards Act, Section 14c Advisor*. Retrieved from http://webapps.dol.gov/elaws/whd/flsa/14c

von Schrader, S., & Nazarov, Z. E. (2014). Employer Characteristics Associated with Discrimination Charges Under the Americans with Disabilities Act. *Journal of Disability Policy Studies*. doi:10.1177/1044207314533385

von Schrader, S., Xu, X., & Bruyère, S. (2014). Accommodation requests: Who is asking for what? *Journal of Rehabilitation Research. Policy and Education, 28*(4), 329–344.

ADDITIONAL READING

Davis, L. (2011). Why is disability missing from the discourse on diversity? *The Chronicle of Higher Education*, (Sept): 25.

Erickson, W., von Schrader, S., Bruyère, S., VanLooy, S., & Matteson, D. (2014). Disability-inclusive employer practices and hiring of individuals with disabilities. *Journal of Rehabilitation Research, Policy and Education, 28*(4), 309-328. Retrieved from http://www.ingentaconnect.com/content/springer/rrpe/2014/00000028/00000004/art00007

Green, T., & Kalev, A. (2010). Discrimination reducing measures at the relational level. *Hastings Law Review, 59*, 1435–1462.

Kessler Foundation. (2015). *2015 National Disability and Employment Survey.* Retrieved from www.kesslerfoundation.org/sites/default/files/filepicker/5/KFSurvey2015_ExecutiveSummary.pdf

Lengnick-Hall, M. L., Gaunt, P. M., & Kulkarni, M. (2008). Overlooked and underutilized: People with disabilities are an untapped human resource. *Human Resource Management, 47*(2), 255–273. doi:10.1002/hrm.20211

von Schrader, S., & Nazarov, Z. E. (2014). Employer Characteristics Associated with Discrimination Charges Under the Americans with Disabilities Act. *Journal of Disability Policy Studies.* doi:10.1177/1044207314533385

KEY TERMS AND DEFINITIONS

Accommodation or Modification: Employers and colleges/universities are required to make changes so that a person with a disability can enjoy equal employment and education opportunities. The term for these changes is typically "accommodation" in a work setting, and "modification" in a higher education setting.

Disability: Historically, how we have defined "disability" has been at the heart of the struggle for disability rights and inclusion. A name has power in that it provides the automatic lens through which we formulate both a problem and a solution. When disability has been defined purely as a medical problem, we tend to respond by assuming we need to "fix" the person. Individual with disabilities have resisted the medical definition of a disability because they assert that the barriers they face lie not so much in their medical condition as in the barriers cast up by society: attitudes of others, inaccessible environments and exclusion from social life. Instead, a functional definition of a disability takes into account both the person's own condition as well as the attitudinal and physical barriers posed by the environment. The issue of defining "disability" was the key impetus behind the passing of the ADA Amendments Act of 2008 because many individuals were not being given the protections against discrimination intended by Congress when the original ADA was passed in 1990. The ADA uses a functional definition of disability as *a physical or mental impairment that substantially limits one or more major life activities*.

Deficit vs. Difference: Within the disability rights movement, there is controversy around the very term "disability." The "dis" prefix of this word automatically conjures an image of "less than." However, many individuals with disabilities do not view themselves as being limited (having a deficit), but as simply different--as having a unique way of operating in the world. In this view, disability is simply one more source of diversity of the human condition.

Disability Disclosure: Many disabilities are not obvious to others. For individuals with these disabilities, telling others about the disability is a choice. Under the ADA, this is a legally protected choice except in some limited circumstances, such as when a worker is requesting a reasonable accommodation.

Disability Prevalence: How many people in the U.S. and across the globe have a disability? Though this would seem to be a straightforward issue, it is not. Different data collection efforts use different definitions of disability. This means that there are widely varying statistics about the prevalence of disability across data collection efforts.

This research was previously published in Developing Workforce Diversity Programs, Curriculum, and Degrees in Higher Education edited by Chaunda L. Scott and Jeanetta D. Sims; pages 280-303, copyright year 2016 by Information Science Reference (an imprint of IGI Global).

Chapter 13
Characteristics and Instructional Strategies for Students With Mathematical Difficulties:
In the Inclusive Classroom

Kathleen Hughes Pfannenstiel
American Institutes for Research, USA

Jennifer "JC" Sanders
Independent Researcher, USA

ABSTRACT

This chapter explores mathematics education for students with mathematical difficulties (MD) and disabilities. Academic achievement measures have remained stagnant for this student population over the past 20 years (NAEP, 2013). The authors highlight Multi-Tiered System of Support and evidence-based strategies as a means to address the unique needs of students with disabilities within inclusion and general education contexts. Common characteristics of students with MD are challenges with working memory, number sense, symbols, basic fact computational fluency, word problem solving, and self-regulation. Educators can apply these specific recommendations to enhance mathematics instruction to address the critical factors for academic success for all students, but specifically students in special education or with MD. In order to implement these evidence-based strategies and ensure specially designed instruction is being provided, co-teaching models are reviewed as one way to provide instructional support in an inclusive setting.

INTRODUCTION

According to the National Center of Education Statistics (2011), 61% of students with disabilities are primarily served in the general education classroom 80% of the school day. Two pieces of educational legislation encourage students with disabilities to be served in the general education classroom;

DOI: 10.4018/978-1-7998-1213-5.ch013

Characteristics and Instructional Strategies for Students With Mathematical Difficulties

Individuals with Disabilities Education Act (IDEA) and Every Student Succeeds Act (ESSA, 2015) which reauthorized Elementary and Secondary Education Act (ESEA). IDEA states that students in special education need to be served in the least restrictive environment (LRE), which is often the general education classroom. In addition to LRE considerations, ESSA along with IDEA, states that all students, regardless of special education placement, are given state mandated assessments to measure progress on grade level standards/objectives. ESSA also stresses that students must demonstrate mastery and be exposed to grade level material and evidence-based instructional practices. Often, the best placement for exposure to grade level standards is within the general education classroom, rather than a separate resource or pullout classroom specifically for students in special education (e.g., resource room). While exposer to general core curriculum is necessary, students in special education often require specialized instruction in addition to core curriculum in order to gain mastery of grade level material. It is essential that special educators understand foundational mathematic skills and progressions to identify skill deficits and implement specialized instruction while accessing grade level material.

On a national level, mathematics continues to be an area that many students, not just those in special education, score lower in as compared to reading. In 2008, the U.S. Department of Education, National Mathematics Advisory Panel (NMAP), released a report describing the mathematical weaknesses of today's students. NMAP highlighted the high percentage of students lacking proficiency in such prerequisite skills as fractions or algebra by 12th grade, leading to an increased need for remedial mathematics classes in postsecondary settings. The National Assessment of Educational Progress (NAEP, 2015) reports that since 1990 mathematics scores have increased 28 points in Grade 4 and 22 points in Grade 8, but recent NAEP scores have remained virtually consistent from 2011-2013 and since 1990 have only seen a 15-point increase. In examining 2015 results, students in fourth and eighth grade scored lower or remained consistent with 2013 results. In fourth grade there was a score decrease for female, white students. In eighth grade score decreases were seen in male, black, Hispanic, students receiving free or reduced lunch and students with disabilities. In addition, the percentage of students scoring at or above proficient is also lower than 2013. As a nation, these results are alarming. Students, regardless of race, ethnicity, special education, or SES level are struggling with basic mathematical skills.

The disparity between students with disabilities and those without is discouraging and mathematics continues to be an area of struggle for students receiving special education support. Mathematics is not simply the computation of numbers; it involves reading, self-regulation skills, multi-step problem solving, vocabulary, and generalizations across topics. In addition, mastery of vital prerequisite skills is essential for higher level mathematics classes, which can be hindered by the complex demands of mathematics. As a result of the complexity, it is imperative that special educators have a conceptual understanding of mathematics and the trajectory of skills to best serve students within the inclusive mathematics classroom.

Having an understanding of characteristics of students with mathematical difficulties (MD) is important in identifying and breaking down specific skill deficits in order to remediate or pre-teach for success. Following an understanding of gaps in skills, the next step is to develop knowledge of evidence-based practices (EBPs) for specialized instruction of students receiving special education services, as well as those with mathematics difficulties as part of a Multi-Tiered System of Support (MTSS) in the general education inclusive setting.

The objectives and purpose of this chapter is to link EBPs in mathematics with evidence-based special education practice for special educators, interventionist, and small group differentiated instruction by a general educator. This chapter will present strategies linked to skills necessary for long-term success in mathematics: vocabulary instruction, word problem solving, arithmetic facts, and self-regulation strategies for students in special education, or those students at-risk for MD. Many of the characteristics and strategies presented will work with all students, the difference is that these are focused on students that continually progress at a much slower rate or are lacking foundational skills and continue to fall farther behind peers. The key for educators is to determine the area of weaknesses, as well as understand how mathematics skills connect and teach foundational skills to mastery. This includes the use of EBPs within a general education setting to teach both procedural fluency as well as conceptual understanding in order to decrease the academic achievement gap.

MATHEMATICAL INSTRUCTION IN GENERAL EDUCATION CLASSROOMS

Prior to reviewing characteristics of students with MD or at-risk, it is important to understand how mathematics are taught in general education settings. The methods of teaching mathematics vary between schools, classrooms, and teachers and are grounded in two instructional approaches, procedural and conceptual. Traditionally, general education core instruction tended to be more constructivist or investigational, allowing the students to develop conceptual understanding through discovery learning, with the mathematics educator acting as a facilitator. In special education settings, instruction tended to be more procedural, teaching algorithms and the use of tricks to solve. With the push for high stakes testing, both general education and special education focused on how to solve, with little teaching to the why, the building of conceptual understanding. Currently, there is a large push in the field to combine these two approaches to develop a conceptual understanding of the skills, as well as a procedural fluency for students that struggle, but educators often do not fully grasp the similarities within the instructional approaches.

Procedural

The procedural or algorithmic instructional approach is often rule based and explicit. The procedural approach was an integral component of mathematical curricula and classrooms until the late 1980s. In the traditional classroom, the educator is the leader and teaches the specific procedure or algorithm for solving problems. The role of the student is to be an active listener, to practice and to apply steps or strategy to solve specific types of problems (Blanton, Westbrook and Carter, 2005; Schmittau, 2004; Van Oers, 2001). For many educators, this is how mathematics was learned, for example the "rules" that you regroup when the answer is greater than 10 or that you simply count the digits to the right of the decimal point to determine where to insert the decimal point in the product. Procedural often means learning the rules of the mathematics without necessarily understanding the *why* this rule is true or *why* does it produce the correct answer (Lui & Bonner, 2016). The procedural approach is often favored in special education literature and classrooms because explicit instruction has been an effective approach for students with academic weaknesses and for students with specific learning disabilities (Gersten & Chard, 1999; Gersten et al., 2005; Scheurmann, Deschler, & Schumaker, 2009; Stein et al., 2006).

The procedural approach has often been viewed as prescriptive (Stein et al., 2006; Swanson & Jerman, 2006) and as one that builds declarative knowledge (Miller & Hudson, 2007), because students practice foundational skills such as facts and algorithms until they commit the answers to memory. The ability to retrieve information from memory, thus freeing the capacity of working memory, lends itself to support the procedural approach for remediating students with MD (Geary, 2005, 2004; Swanson & Jerman,

2006). Proponents of the procedural approach believe that students need explicit instruction and time to practice the steps in order to develop mastery of the foundational skills needed to solve problems (Stein et al., 2006). NMAP (2008) reported that when students do not have a firm understanding of the basic foundational skills, weaknesses become more apparent when they are presented with advanced, multi-step problems. When students are not taught foundational skills more time is spent in retrieval of basic skills (Miller & Hudson, 2007; Stein et al., 2006; Swanson & Jerman, 2006), thus procedural approach is often considered the best way to teach to mastery of these skills. Students need the foundational skill development and mastery in order to develop more sophisticated strategies and generalizations (rules), rather than just memorizing a traditional algorithm.

Conceptual

The conceptual approach or understanding of how skills connect and relationships across operations, as well as the comprehension of skills (National Council of Teachers of Mathematics; NCTM, 2014) centers on the framework that children develop their own way of learning and thinking. The conceptual approach was influenced by the work of Vygotsky and Davydov (Schmittau, 2004). These theorists completed extensive work in the area of applied learning. With a conceptual instructional approach, learning is student centered, with a focus on real-world problems in an interactive environment (NCTM, 2010). The role of the educator is to provide minimal support, allowing students to develop their own procedures and strategies for solving problems (Miller & Hudson, 2007; NCTM, 2002; Woodward, 2004). When students display deficits or an inability to solve problems, an educator may provide a scaffold, encourage peer tutoring, or provide additional mathematical tools and representations (Stein et al., 2006). Wood, Bruner, and Ross (1976) defined scaffolding as a type of assistance a child needs to make academic gains. Scaffolds can be provided by both teachers and peers. Scaffolds are flexible and are slowly faded when a student begins to master the skill. In a mathematics classroom in which the instructional approach is conceptual in nature, students are often at differing levels and are not all using the same method to arrive at the answer.

Instructional Approach Summary

For students receiving special education services or with MD it is essential that general core instruction, as well as intervention, determine the student's needs and utilize explicit, systematic procedural instruction to remediate skills, while still providing access to more conceptual understanding (Archer & Hughes, 2010; Bryant et al., 2014; Doabler et al., 2012; Gersten & Chard, 1999; Gersten et al., 2009; NCTM, 2002; NMAP, 2008). Using explicit instruction, cognitive strategies (Swanson & Sachs-Lee, 2000), and multiple representations (Gersten et al., 2009b; Miller & Hudson, 2007) to build both conceptual understanding and procedural knowledge of foundational skills results in students' ability to integrate these skills into problem solving and mathematical communications (Common Core State Standards for Mathematics, CCSSM, 2010). Explicit instruction of strategies, practice and application combined with a self-regulation strategy can help to remediate weaknesses in the area of strategy use, schematic models, numeracy skills and estimation (Gersten & Chard, 1999; Gersten et al., 2009). In addition, Griffin, League, Griffin, and Bae (2013) found that in elementary classrooms when educators provided multiple practice opportunities with feedback, strategy instruction (through conceptual models and procedural algorithms), use of manipulatives and pictorial representations all students scored much higher as compared to classrooms in which mathematics was strictly investigational. Mathematics instruction truly needs to blend procedural and conceptual instruction to best meet the diverse student ability levels and needs.

CHARACTERISTICS OF STUDENTS WITH MATHEMATICS DIFFICULTIES

Students struggling in mathematics often apply ineffective strategies and are weak in three areas: (1) retrieval or fluency, (2) procedures, (3) higher level, or conceptual understanding (Gray et al., 1999; Impecoven-Lind & Foegen, 2010; Jayanthi, Gersten, Baker, 2008). It is the role of a special educator to work with the general educator to improve these skill deficits, while still exposing students to grade level material. The collaboration between the special educator/ process expert and the general educator/ content expert can lead to an infusion of instructional strategies to differentiate and provide intensive intervention needed by students struggling in mathematics. One way to assist in the remediation and differentiation within general education is through a Multi-Tiered Support of System (MTSS). As part of the IDEA 2004 requirements, states are encouraged to utilize a MTSS or Response to Intervention (RtI) model to identify students needing additional support in academics, and provide evidence-based practices to diminish the gap in skills. RtI supports the notion that by providing "effective instruction early and intensively, [teachers can help students] make large gains in general academic achievement" (Lyon & Fletcher, 2001, p. 24), thus identifying and focusing instruction on foundational skill gaps to allow the student to fully access the general core mathematics curriculum.

Multi-Tiered System of Support

For schools that are implementing MTSS, universal screeners can assist in identification of students with MD, and additional progress monitoring and error analysis can aid a teacher in identification of specific skill weaknesses. Data-based decision making should guide instruction in the context of MTSS. For example, progress monitoring should be utilized to guide general core, as well as specialized instruction with a focus on whole numbers, fractions, algebraic readiness, problem solving, and arithmetic facts (NMAP, 2008). While components of these foundational areas can and should be embedded within general education core mathematics instruction, additional time outside of core is often needed for those students with more severe deficits (Fuchs & Deshler, 2007). Doabler et al. (2012) provided eight guidelines, see Table 1, to enhance core mathematics instruction, with the caveat that for students scoring much lower than peers, regardless of special education status, will need explicit, systematic instruction. The guidelines include: (1) streamline instruction to foundational content, (2) remediate and pre-teach prerequisite skills, (3) systematically select examples and increase difficulty, (4) scaffold instruction providing using the "I do, we do, you do" method (Archer & Hughes, 2010), (5) model and use think-alouds during all parts of instruction, (6) provide frequent and multiple opportunities for practice, (7) use multiple representations, especially visual, during all parts of instruction, and (8) provide feedback and fix errors quickly. By following these guidelines, both procedural fluency and conceptual understanding of skills can increase.

As schools implement MTSS, it is vital that educators understand the characteristics of mathematics difficulties to start intervention early and support prior to a formal special education evaluation. About three to six percent of school-aged children have an actual diagnosis or label of a mathematics disability (Geary, 2011; Shalev, Auerbach, Manor, & Gross-Tsur, 2000), but a growing number of students struggle and lack confidence in mathematics. When educators are able to correctly identify and address mathematics weaknesses early, a student may not require specialized instruction or special education services in the future.

The National Mathematics Advisory Panel (NMAP; 2008) identified key areas as a focus for mathematics instruction. These include streamlining mathematical trajectories and skills with a focus on building mastery of foundational skills early in a child's school career. Both NMAP (2008) and NCTM (2014, 2006, 2002) recommend that students build a deep understanding of whole numbers and algebra, specifically fractions, certain aspects of geometry and measurement. In addition, students should develop an "immediate recall of arithmetic facts" in order to solve multi-step, multiple operational computations (CCSSM, 2010). For students in special education or at-risk for a MD, overarching deficits often include: (a) working memory, (b) number sense, (c) symbols (d) basic fact computational fluency, (e) word problem solving, and (f) self-regulation. Addressing these six areas through the use of evidence-based practices and specially-designed instruction within mathematics interventions and general education core curriculum, can help remediate the skills hindering success in mathematics.

Working Memory

Working memory has advanced our understanding of cognition and how we store information. Working memory is defined as "a limited capacity system allowing the temporary storage and manipulation of information necessary for such complex tasks as comprehension, learning and reasoning." (Baddeley, 2000, p. 418). A growing body of research has linked MD and working memory deficits in students at various ages (Geary, 2004, 2005; Raghubar et al., 2010; Swanson, Kehler, & Jerman, 2010; Swanson & Jerman, 2006; Swanson, Jerman, & Zheng, 2008), and over time this deficit "could affect the procedural competencies" (Geary, 2005, p. 306) needed to solve mathematical problems. In mathematics, weaknesses in working memory can affect a child's ability to apply strategies to effectively solve whole-number computations and word problems (Geary, 1993, 2005; Raghubar, Barnes, & Hecht, 2009; Swanson & Jerman, 2006; Swanson et al., 2008).

Deficits in working memory are evident when students struggle to complete whole-number computations. All students begin with count all, but as students develop understanding of numbers they use the more efficient strategy of count on. For example, when a student is solving 7 + 2, the more efficient

Table 1. Guidelines to enhance core mathematics instruction

Streamline instruction to foundational content
Remediate and pre-teach prerequisite skills
Systematically select examples and increase difficulty
Scaffold instruction provides using the "I do, we do, you do" method (Archer & Hughes, 2010)
Model and use think-alouds during all parts of instruction
Provide frequent and multiple opportunities for practice
Use multiple representations especially visual, during all parts of instruction
Provide feedback and fix errors quickly

strategy is to "store" the number 7 and then count on 2 more to solve the problem (Geary, 2004; Siegler, 1988). This computation task requires a student to identify the greater number, start counting from 7, and then count on 2 more. Students with weaknesses in mathematics are not as efficient at solving whole number computations rather, students with MD continue to count all (i.e., start counting at 1, keep counting to 7, and then count 2 more) instead of using the more efficient count on strategy (Geary, 2004, 2005). These students struggle to apply strategies to solve whole number computations because they cannot fully "see" how the algorithm is applied and represented (Hecht et al., 2003; Swanson & Jerman, 2006; Swanson et al., 2008). Swanson and Jerman (2006) and Miller and Hudson (2007) identified computation deficits as a type of mathematical difficulty procedural in nature due to ineffective strategy application. The consequences of procedural mathematical difficulties are seen in accuracy and fluency weaknesses and impaired performance in basic arithmetic operations (Raghubar et al., 2010). In addition, working memory can also hinder and act as a "limited understanding of the meaning and application of arithmetic properties." (Bryant, Pfannenstiel, Bryant, Hunt, & Shin, 2014, p. 184). This is evident when students incorrectly understand or apply the commutative, associative, and distributive properties. See Figure 1 for instructional strategies related to working memory.

Number Sense

In addition to working memory weaknesses, another prevalent deficit for students with MD is number sense (Bryant, 2005; Bryant, Bryant, & Hammill, 2000). Gersten and Chard (1999) defined number sense as "the sense of what numbers mean and an ability to perform mental mathematics and to look at the world and make comparisons" (p. 19). A weakness in number sense is a significant predictor of MD (Bryant, 2005; Gersten, Jordan, & Flojo, 2005; Jordan, Kaplan, Locuniak, & Ramineni, 2007; Jordan, Glutting, & Ramineni, 2010). Number sense often involves counting and having a sense of flexibility with number discrimination, number transformation, number patterns, magnitude comparisons, and estimating (Bryant, 2005; Jordan et al., 2007). In the higher grades, a good foundation of number sense is needed for the application of more advanced "break-apart" strategies in multiplication and in conceptually understanding the concept of parts and wholes in fractions (Woodward, 2006). Number sense development should not be limited to mathematics curriculum in the early elementary grades; rather, number sense should be taught and reinforced every year.

Jordan et al. (2010) examined performance on number sense assessments in kindergarten students and the same students in third grade. The kindergarten students with a more developed number sense were far more successful in third grade than those with low scores on the kindergarten number sense assessment. A more developed number sense leads to flexibility of number decomposition (Siegler, 1988)

Figure 1. Working memory instructional strategies

Working Memory Instructional Strategies:
- Cue cards with steps and/or examples
- Highlighters, different colored pens/pencils to call attention to important words
- Minimizing steps
- Teacher modeling and think-alouds with all parts of process/steps illustrated
- Student verbalizing steps to complete problem

and an understanding of counting principles, such as cardinality, order, and abstraction (Geary, 2004). The mastery of number sense, flexibility in counting, and decomposing (i.e., 8 can be decomposed as 0 and 8, 1 and 7, 2 and 6, 4 and 4, 5 and 3, 2 and 1 and 5, etc.) of numbers directly relate to arithmetic facts because students need to comprehend the relationships between numbers (Bryant, 2005; Geary, 2004; Gersten et al., 2005; Siegler, 1988; Wagner & Davis, 2010; Woodward, 2004). Number sense also relates to fractions and the understanding that fractions are numbers (Siegler et al., 2010). Beyond fractions, flexibility with numbers can increase mastery of understanding of rational and irrational numbers needed in higher level mathematics (NMAP, 2008). See Figure 2 for instructional strategies related to the development of number sense. Thus, developing a strong number sense in students is vital for success in mathematics.

Symbols

Multiple representations are important to build conceptual understanding, but often educators move too quickly through manipulatives (concrete representations) to the symbolic (abstract) representation. As students' progress through school a "flexible understanding of symbolic equivalence relations is essential" (Jones, Inglis, Gilmore, & Evans, 2013, p. 34). Updated college readiness standards, as well as the National Council of Teachers of Mathematics (NCTM) content strands, stress the importance of writing numbers starting in kindergarten and moving into equations as early as Grade 1 (NCTM, 2006; National Governors Association Center for Best Practices & Council for Chief State School Officers, 2010). As students' progress through the grade levels, equations are written that include symbols such as the equal sign, and traditional operation signs for addition, subtraction, multiplication, and division. The higher the student progresses in grade level, the more sophisticated and elaborate the use of mathematic symbols become (e.g., negative and positive signs, fraction bar and division bar, a multiplication dot, inequality signs, radicals, exponents; Driver & Powell, 2015; Jones et al., 2013).

One of the earliest symbols used by students is the equal sign. For students with MD the equal sign typically means answer, rather than the same as or equal in amount (Blanton & Kaput, 2005; Powell, 2012). The other problem is that students rely on equations only written one way, often with the equal sign after the operation, $6 + 7 = 13$, rather than prior to the operation, $13 = 6 + 7$. By exposing students to "nonstandard equations, however may improve relational understanding of the equal sign." (Driver & Powell, 2015, p. 129). In addition to the equal sign, students need explicit instruction in mathematics symbols and how to accurately read equations. As recommended by Frye, Baroody, Burchinal, Carver,

Figure 2. Number sense instructional strategies

Number Sense Instructional Strategies:

- Use of manipulatives to decompose or break-apart numbers
- Developing flexibility in how to represent numbers (e.g. $7 = 1 + 6$; $3 + 1 + 3 = 5 + 2$)
- Counting with fluency forward and backward
- Skip counting
- Recognizing patterns in numbers
- Comparing numbers
- Ordering numbers

Jordan, & McDowell (2013), it is important to explicitly teach and link symbols with vocabulary and procedures and representations. Encouraging student verbalization of mathematics paired with explicit instruction of symbols can increase overall mastery of symbolic representation.

Basic Fact Computational Fluency

Working memory deficits and weaknesses in number sense and symbols affect basic fact computational fluency. Whole number computation is defined by NCTM (2000) as "having efficient and accurate methods for computing" (p. 152). A deficit in number sense can dramatically affect a student's ability to recall facts, resulting in weaknesses in whole number computational fluency, or the "ability to automatically retrieve...arithmetic facts" (Gersten et al., 2005, p. 294) and the automaticity is an integral component in mathematics curriculum (Schoenfeld, 2004). The inability to retrieve basic facts quickly has been labeled a processing delay, as well as a procedural delay (Bryant, 2005; Codding, Chan-Iannette, Palmer, & Lukito, 2009; Gersten et al., 2005; Hecht et al., 2003; Miller & Hudson, 2007; Pellegrino & Goldman, 1987; Woodward, 2006) and is often considered to be a hallmark of learning disabilities in mathematics (Geary, 2005; Gersten & Chard, 1999).

Hecht et al. (2003) explained that the underlying theory in procedural delays in mathematics is an immature development of (a) a conceptual knowledge of facts (i.e., an understanding "about the underlying principles that govern a domain"; p. 278). And (b) "memorized facts involving arithmetical relations among numbers" (p. 278). Conceptual knowledge is an understanding of similar characteristics in numbers and the ability to generalize number patterns to whole-number computations and conversions (Miller & Hudson, 2007). Whole-number computation involves a marriage between understanding a strategy and generalizability of when to apply the strategy (Pellegrino & Goldman, 1987). It is the ability to generalize computations to different processes and representations, and an ability to communicate how to solve whole-number computations (NCTM, 2002).

The NMAP (2008), NCTM (2014), and the CCSSM (2010) recommend that third-grade students demonstrate mastery, defined as 80% or better in accuracy, on all on addition and subtraction facts, as well as all products of two, one-digit numbers. Beyond basic fact mastery, students need to be able to extend fact knowledge to application of multi-step problems involving different operations. In a study examining whole number computations, a large decrease in fluency and ability often occurred between third and fourth grade. Furthermore, the findings suggested, "learning or retention of fourth grade level computation skill items" (p. 298) is pivotal to long-term mathematical success (Calhoon, Emerson, Flores, & Houchins, 2007). Automaticity in these areas is "important to estimation, mental calculation, and approximation skills" (Woodward, 2006, p. 287) and is a predictor of long-term mathematical success in more complex problem solving (NMAP, 2008). Thus, automaticity could lead to a deeper conceptual understanding and greater success in general education core mathematics.

Word Problems

Word problems are a mix of numbers and words in which students apply mathematics instruction in the context of problem solving (Wyndhamm & Saljo, 1997). Word problems have gained national attention because they are the tools used to measure mathematical concepts locally, nationally, and internationally (NAEP, 2009; NCTM, 2010; Trends in International Mathematics and Science Study, TIMSS, 2007). Word problems measure students' ability to generalize different mathematical structures conceptually in a format that may not be familiar or vastly different than a typical numerical representation alone (Cogan, Schmidt, & Wiley, 2001; Gersten, Chard, Jayanthis, Baker, Murphy, & Flojo, 2009; Pfannenstiel, Bryant, Bryant, & Porterfield, 2015; Schoenfeld, 2004; Wyndhamm & Saljo, 1997). Word problems connect the application of mathematics to the process of mathematics. This aligns to the mathematics practices completed by NCTM (2014) as well as the CCSSM (2010) that include the ability to make sense of problems, as well as the ability to "persevere in solving them, reason abstractly and quantitatively, model with mathematics," and to "look for and make use of structure." (p. 8). There are a total of eight mathematics practices (NCTM, 2014), but these four specifically focus on the ability of solving word problems, as well as attain a deeper understanding of and mathematical flexibility with numbers, concepts, and mathematics language (Gray, Pinto, Pitta, & Tall, 2005).

Difficulties in solving word problems can be a "major impediment for [students'] future success in any math-related discipline" (Gersten et al., 2009b, p. 26). Students with MD often struggle with word problems because they lack understanding of the language and vocabulary within the problems (Bryant, 2005; Fuchs, Fuchs, & Zumeta, 2008; Gersten et al., 2005), are unable to apply multiple steps within word problems (Parmer, Cawley & Frazita, 1996), and experience difficulty in selecting and using the correct algorithms to solve word problems (Hecht et al., 2003; Pfannenstiel et al., 2015). Students with MD have an inability to generalize strategies across different types of word problems (Gersten et al., 2009) and "infrequently abandon and replace ineffective strategies" (Montague & Dietz, 2009, p. 285), while increasing the time required to complete a problem and/or finding a solution more on luck than understanding the relationship of the numbers within the word problem. Students with MD require explicit instruction in the structure of word problems, identifying problem types, and applying a strategy to solve the problems (Gersten et al., 2009a; Jitendra, DiPipi, & Perron-Jones, 2002; Jitendra et al., 2009; Jitendra et al., 2013; Montague & Dietz, 2009). To foster an understanding of word problems, cognitive strategy instruction is essential (Gersten et al., 2009; Jitendra et al., 2002; Jitendra et al., 2009; Montague & Dietz, 2009; Van Garderen, 2007), as well as the mastery and accuracy of basic fact computational fluency to decrease the load on working memory, and allow for an abstract understanding of word problems (Jitendra et al, 2002; Van Garderen, 2007).

Self-Regulation

Teaching academic skills embedded with self-regulation strategies may contribute to academic achievement for students with mathematical difficulties (Burns et al., 2010; Codding et al., 2009; Montague, 2007; Rock, 2005). Self-regulation can be separated into three components, autonomy, relatedness and competence. Autonomy is one component of the self-determination, that "involves feeling that one is the owner or author of one's current behavior" (Filak & Sheldon, 2008, p. 714), and acting in a self-realizing way (Wehmeyer, Agran, & Hughes, 2000). Relatedness "involves feeling a meaningful connection between oneself and important others, rather than feeling like an object whose experiences are ignored and discounted" (Filak & Sheldon, 2008, p. 714). Competence is about ability and the perception that even challenging skills can be learned. In an academic setting "students demonstrate competence by achieving command of increasingly difficult material" (Filak & Sheldon, 2008, p. 714).

In inclusive mathematics classrooms, self-regulation can be infused easily within general education core mathematics instruction, as well as in small group and intervention. For example, Montague (2007) stated that self-regulation, or autonomy is often a weakness in students with learning difficulties, and teaching self-regulation may include, "self-instruction, self-questioning, and self-checking" (p. 75).

Educators can teach self-regulation by using tools, such as cue cards, to master word problem solving independently. Lee, Wehmeyer, Palmer, Soukup and Little (2008) also described the positive correlation between cue cards or simple visual prompts as self-regulation accommodations in the general education setting to increase success for students with learning difficulties. Self-regulation can also be brought into the mathematics instruction by offering choice in worksheets, writing goals related to mathematics achievement, or graphing progress alone or in conjunction with goals (Axtell, McCallum, Mee, Bell & Poncy, 2009; Burns, 2005; Flores, 2009; Flores, Houchins & Shippen, 2006; Jitendra, DiPi & Perron-Jones, 2002; Powell, Fuchs, Fuchs, Cirino, & Fletcher, 2009). Greater success for struggling students can be obtained when students become active participants by assisting in goal writing and progress monitoring (Konrad et al., 2007; Konrad & Test, 2007; Wehmeyer et al., 2004). For example, Rock (2005) used the self-regulation strategies of self-monitoring of behavior, time-on task and accuracy in the areas of mathematics and reading. By embedding self-regulation, it actively involved students in the process of data collection, and increased overall accuracy, productivity, and student engagement. In another study, Lee et al. (2008) conveyed that self-regulation strategy use was found to have a positive relationship in time on-task, work completion, and progress on educational goals.

Self-regulation in an academic setting involves using metacognitive strategies (Montague, 2007) for "planning, monitoring, and modifying" (Pintrick & DeGroot, 1990, p. 33), and effort in work completion (Konrad & Test, 2007; Pintrick & DeGroot, 1990; Rock, 2005). Mathematical challenges are becoming more evident in the upper grades because of the increased rigor of the mathematics curriculum (ESEA, 2001; NMAP, 2008). Many students often lack the self-regulation skills to manage both academics and life skills (Montague, 2007; Ryan, Reid, & Epstein, 2004). NMAP (2008) outlined the need to close the gap between struggling students and typically performing peers through interventions in number sense and computational fluency, while increasing motivation. Components of self-regulation can be used to increase student motivation in the demanding mathematics curriculum and is often the missing component in intervention (Auerbach, Gross-Tsur, Manor, & Shalev, 2008; Calhoon & Fuchs, 2003; Vostal, 2011).

In educational settings, self-regulation involves teaching students specific strategies for learning, thereby increasing management of one's actions. The self-regulation skills essential for mathematics success include the ability to identify a specific strategy to solve a problem and the ability to complete all steps while monitoring progress. In addition, building confidence by mixing previously mastered problems with new problems, as well as increasing difficulty, versus all new problem types, is another form of self-regulation that can lead to great gains (Vostal, 2011). Students with mathematical difficulties struggle to self-regulate the steps necessary to complete tasks (Miller & Hudson, 2007), and in paired peer interactions they tend to take a more passive role (Bottge, Heinrichs, Mehta, & Hung, 2002), thus often hindering their own learning and understanding of the material. Students with MD need to be taught how to be more active in their own learning and within peer groups. Gersten et al. (2009) found large effect sizes in explicit interventions with students taking an active role in data collection through graphing and goal setting. This echoes the need for students to be taught to self-regulate and understand how to become active in academic work. When students are active in regulating their own learning through strategy use, goal setting, and data collection, an increase of engagement and achievement is evident (Vostal, 2011).

EVIDENCE-BASED PRACTICES

For many years evidence-based practices were limited to the medical field. The most cited definition is from Sackett (1996) that defines EBPs as "the conscientious, explicit and judicious use of current best evidence in making decisions about the care of the individual." In the medical field, EBP was determined based upon randomized controlled trials. For the purpose of this chapter, EBPs are defined as "instructional techniques with meaningful research support that represent critical tools in bridging the research-to-practice gap and improving student outcomes." (Cook & Cook, 2011, p. 2). Many EBPs for mathematics are just good instruction, meaning they will assist all students in developing an understanding of the skills. For students struggling in mathematics, the key is to infuse EBPs in mathematics, with evidence-based special education professional practice. This is a strategy or intervention designed for use by special educators and intended to support the education of individuals with exceptional learning needs (Council for Exceptional Children, 2008). Educators need to be aware of both EBPs in mathematics, as well as special education instructional practices to meet the diverse needs of students in a general education setting.

Within the last decade, the field of education has stressed the important of using EBP for general core instruction, interventions and special education instruction. The What Works Clearinghouse (WWC, http://ies.ed.gov/ncee/wwc/mathhome.aspx) identifies reviews, and rates research in academics to determine levels of evidence to be used for students. In addition to the WWC, the National Center on Intensive Intervention (NCII, www.intensiveintevention.org) has also reviewed and rated evidence-based interventions specifically for use within MTSS. The gold-standard for high evidence, similar to the medical model, is a randomized controlled trial, meaning the participant sample is large enough to warrant a control and intervention group to determine effectiveness of a particular strategy or intervention (WWC). NCII still applies this gold standard, but the field of education has recently begun to examine other research designs, such as single-case studies with replication, to also rate effectiveness. NCII provides a chart that rates interventions based upon participants, study design, fidelity of implementation, measures, effect size, and meaningful outcomes. Educators face intense demands on their time, and by utilizing an intervention or strategy that has been proven to be an EBP, they are more likely to see student growth and success.

While EBPs can vary across skills in mathematics, researched-based high yield instructional strategies can be applied across general core instruction and standardized interventions (NCII, 2013). Numerous practice guides have been released from WWC to highlight the level of effectiveness to meet the needs of students at-risk for MD and receiving special education services (Gersten et al., 2009; Jayanthi, Gersten & Baker, 2008). The EBPs recommended for students with MD or receiving special education services includes using multiple representations, verbalized decision making, visual representations, heuristic strategies, ongoing formative assessment, motivational strategies, and explicit instruction. Pairing these general recommendations with specific skill strategies to provide specialized instruction can aid in knowledge gaps and long-term success in mathematics.

Multiple Representations

Interventions should include targeted strategy instruction that incorporates multiple representations (Gersten et al., 2009; Jayanthi et al., 2008; NMAP, 2008; Stein et al., 2006; Woodward, 2006). Multiple representations involve representing mathematical concepts in three ways: (a) concrete, (b) visual/pictorial, and (c) abstract. NMAP (2008), NCTM Core Standards (2010), and In Focus Grade 4-8 (2009) provide examples of multiple representations. Concrete representations involve the use of objects, such as manipulatives, to represent numbers and build models of concepts in operations, and fractions, decimals, and algebraic reasoning. Visual or pictorial representations can include pictures of the manipulatives, number lines, hundred charts, and drawings of models, such as area models of multiplication. Abstract representations refer to the numbers and symbols only, without the use of the concrete or pictorial scaffolds.

Representations should not be isolated, and students can utilize all representations within one lesson and across units or skill to understand a particular mathematical concept. Witzel, Mercer, and Miller (2003) found that students need to solve problems accurately at each stage prior to moving to fewer scaffolds or more abstract representations. This gradual transition leads to mastery of the content and conceptual understanding, not simply the process alone (Strickland & Maccini, 2010; Witzel, 2005). Gray et al. (1999) explained that students with a "flexible notion of process ... have a cognitive advantage; they derive considerable mathematical flexibility" (p. 120). To strengthen mathematical flexibility and the idea of choice in how to derive an answer, students need to master the process to understand the concept. The Center on Instruction's (2008) mathematical recommendations for teachers emphasizes the importance of both multiple representations and examples for scaffolding (Jayanthi et al., 2008). A combination of examples and non-examples presented through a carefully designed intervention using multiple representations can lead to accurate generalizations (Stein et al., 2006). Often general core classroom instruction transitions through multiple representations too quickly, or skips the pictorial/symbolic stage, thus not exposing students to the bridge between concrete and abstract and leading to confusion and surface level understanding of the skill (Jayanthi et al., 2008).

Mathematical Verbalization and Strategy Instruction

Merely teaching a student to solve a mathematical problem is not enough; understanding how an answer is obtained, as well as the ability to explain the process, are keys to success across a variety of mathematical curricula (Gray et al., 1999). Mathematics "goes beyond arithmetic" (Saracho & Spodek, 2009, p. 297) and encompasses processes at different levels (Pellegrino & Goldman, 1987). Mathematics instruction should allow for flexible thinking, different questioning strategies, various methods to arrive at the same answer (Dougherty, Bryant, Bryant, Darrough, & Pfannenstiel, 2014), and cognitive strategy instruction in word problem solving (Pfannenstiel et al., 2014). Strategy instruction combined with development of conceptual understanding shapes how students learn and the impact of ability levels on learning concepts and procedures in mathematics (Gray et al., 1999; Pellegrino & Goldman, 1987; Saracho & Spodek; 2009; Schmittau, 2004; Van Oers, 2001). The idea that mathematical activities happen simultaneously is defined as information processing.

Using procedural-only interventions or application interventions in isolation has been criticized as a limited approach for students receiving special education services or those with MD. Information processing is a bridge between the conceptual underpinning and the procedures for computation-type work. Aligning the procedural nature of special education research with more constructivist practices increases mathematical flexibility and generalization to other types of problems (Bottge et al., 2007; Grey et al., 1999; Jitendra et al., 2009), as well as greater success within the general education setting. Gray et al. (1999) explained the notion of schemas to switch between a "process, a concept output by that process, and a symbol that can evoke either process or concept" (p. 113). Students identified as low achievers tend to store nonessential information, resulting in poor and inefficient strategy use which takes up working memory space. The ability to move from counting to manipulating numbers is seen in average to high-average learners as a natural progression (Desoete, Stock, Schepens, Baeuens, & Roeyers, 2009; Gray et al., 1999; Morgan, Farkas, & Wu, 2009; Woodward, 2006). One way to remediate a weakness in this area is through strategy instruction, specifically in schema-based instruction. Linking schema-based and strategy instruction may be a missing component in procedural aspects of special education interventions, especially in word problem solving (Pfannenstiel et al., 2015). Specifically, it can assist students in understanding "the procedures or monitor their understanding to effectively solve novel problems." (Jitendra et al., 2013, p. 22). Connecting more efficient methods for solving problems, as well as teaching the underlying structure (Jitendra et al., 2013) may increase the visual ability and flexibility in understanding concepts and processes that are required in more advanced mathematical courses (Bottage, Rueda, Serlin, Hung, & Kown, 2007; Gray et al., 1999; Montague & Dietz, 2009).

Explicit, Systematic Instruction

Much of the effective instruction for students with MD or students receiving special education services is explicit and systematic. Explicit instruction is adopted from Direct Instruction, developed by Engelmann and Carnine in 1991. It includes teacher modeling, student practice with support, and then independent practice through clear, slightly scripted examples and non-examples of strategies in both reading and mathematics (Bryant, 2005; D. Bryant et al., 2000; Gersten et al., 2009; Impecoven-Lind & Foegen, 2010; Jayanthi et al., 2008; Scheurmann et al., 2009; Stein et al., 2006; Woodward, 2006). The use of explicit, systematic instruction results in positive effects and is more effective than traditional or mediated instruction (Gersten et al., 2009; Kroesbergen & Van Luit, 2003; Maccini, Mulcahy, & Wilson, 2007; Montague, Applegate, & Marquard, 1993). In a study completed by Kroesbergen, Van Luit, and Maas (2004) directly comparing constructivist-only mathematics instruction and explicit, systematic mathematics instruction, students receiving the explicit instruction proved to be more effective at solving multiplication problems. While all students made progress in automaticity and rate of improvement, explicit instruction resulted in greater gains and was proven to be more effective. It is important to include components of information processing within interventions. Students with MD need the structure of schema-based and explicit instruction in order to increase their ability in solving and understanding word problems and whole-number computation problems (Gersten et al., 2009; Jayanthi et al., 2008; Jitendra et al., 2013; Jitendra et al., 2002; Jitendra et al., 2009; Kroesbergen et al., 2004; Kroesbergen & Van Luit, 2003; NMAP, 2008; Stein et al., 2006).

Another vital component of explicit instruction is the use of carefully selected examples, allowing for an increase in difficulty and connection to real-world procedural computations (Jayanthi et al., 2008; NMAP, 2008). In addition, the selection of items to be included in modeling, guided practice, and independent practice is important to allow for mastery and confidence building for students that historically are easily frustrated and often do not complete work. The selection of items should include examples and non-examples, as well as items to increase generalization, and thus success across skills. Numerous studies (Axtell et al., 2009; Burns, 2005; Calderhead, Filter, & Albin, 2006) incorporated the traditional modeling, guided practice, independent practice found in Direct Instruction, as well as strategy instruction and immediate feedback. The addition of the strategy instruction, feedback and systematic selection of practice problems and examples increased fluency and accuracy in solving. Including components from information processing, while using multiple representations in a structured, balanced intervention can mean greater access to grade-level mathematics and long-term success in advanced mathematical courses

(Bottge et al., 2007; Gersten et al., 2009; Gray et al., 1999; Kroesbergen & Van Luit, 2003; Maccini et al., 2007; Montague et al., 1993; NMAP; 2008).

SPECIALLY DESIGNED INSTRUCTION

EBPs should be used as part of general core instruction, tiered intervention and in special education settings. For students with an IEP, general core instruction must be supplemented with additional specialized, individualized instruction. These services or supplements include specially designed instruction (SDI). SDI is what makes special education, special, meaning a child's disability requires instruction or instructional methodology that is individualized and different than typically developing peers (IDEA, 2004). In the area of mathematics, SDI should include EBPs, but should also be individualized to meet the students' unique needs resulting from the child's disability. Based upon research from Jayanthi, Gersten and Baker (2008) seven recommendations to guide SDI should be utilized with EBPs. These recommendations include: (1) using explicit instruction on a regular basis, (2) using multiple instructional examples, (3) have students verbalize decisions and solutions to a math problem, (4) have students visually represent the information in the math problem, (5) solve problems using multiple/heuristic strategies, (6) Provide ongoing formative assessment data and feedback and (7) provide peer-assisted instruction to students.

A challenge cited by many educators is the time to provide SDI within an inclusive mathematics class. NCII recommends that schools consider additional time outside of core general instruction to provide explicit, systematic instructional intervention within small groups. Another option to consider is the use of co-teaching to assist the general educator in differentiating and explicitly teaching strategies and evidence-based interventions during mathematics in the general education setting (Friend, Cook, Hurley-Chamberlain, & Shamberger, 2010). In co-teaching, the special educator should help guide SDI, while the general mathematics educator can connect and align with mathematics progressions and trajectories, thus allowing the special educator to not have the same understanding of the mathematics as the general educator and still be able to assist students. Both educators need to plan and work together closely in order to meet the diverse needs of all the students including students receiving special education support and those with a MD.

Co-Teaching

On method utilized by schools to assist in providing SDI inclusion support within the general education setting is co-teaching. In a co-taught classroom, a general and special educator, are responsible for differentiating and providing the legally mandated SDI for students with disabilities. With two professionals in the room, educators are able to utilize small group instruction, and can work directly to implement the intense and alternative instruction needed to address student mathematical gaps. As Friend et al. (2010) described, "The intent of co-teaching is to make it possible for students with disabilities to access the general curriculum while at the same time benefitting from specialized instructional strategies necessary to nurture their learning." (p. 11). There are three co-teaching approaches that can provide opportunities for small group instruction within the general education setting. The first is, *station teaching*. In station teaching, several stations or centers are set-up around the room for students to work in small groups and rotate through each station. See Table 2 for an example of station teaching in a grade 3 co-taught classroom. The teachers, both general and special education are at a station to provide instruction. Any additional stations are designed for independent/group work and should reinforce previously learned skills or provide additional practice.

Another co-teaching approach is *parallel teaching*. In parallel teaching, two teachers divide the class into two groups using data to determine grouping, and both teach the same lesson or skills. In this co-teaching approach, both teachers are being utilized and the class receives instruction in a smaller setting or group. Parallel teaching can be utilized for review or re-teach of content. For example, the objective is to graph a line using slope intercept form. The teachers provide instruction and demonstration of the skills. The very next day the teachers divide the class into two equal groups and provide guided practice of graphing linear equations given an equation in slope intercept form. The benefit of dividing the class is the opportunity to hear from each student. Teachers can provide immediate corrective feedback when working with a smaller group of students. Finding time to create small group situations also allows teachers time to become more familiar with their students.

A third approach to co-teaching with a goal of providing small group instruction is the *alternative approach*. In the alternative approach, a small group of students is pulled from the larger group based upon data, but rather than the same lesson, the two educators teach different lessons. This approach is often utilized when re-teaching is needed, but can also be very beneficial to provide pre-teach or enrichment for students. In all of these approaches, both the general and special educator are providing instruction to a smaller group of students (Friend et al., 2010). Data, not special education status, should guide groupings. In addition, groupings should be flexible to address the needs of the students, and allow the students to work with either teacher. The role of both educators, special and general, can vary and either can be the "lead" teacher (Friend et al., 2010; Scruggs, Mastropieri, & McDuffie, 2007).

Utilizing any of the three co-teaching small group approaches can be beneficial for all students, not just those that struggle, but can also be a challenge to implement. Teachers in a co-teaching partnership can implement SDI for students by planning with one another to collaborate on the mathematics concepts and skills. Teachers who co-plan have the advantage of putting both professionals' strengthens into action. General educators are the content experts and should be the one to map out the scope and sequence of the content, identify minimal levels of mastery for all students, and highlight concepts that may be challenging. The special educator in the partnership has the strengths of strategy and SDI, the process expert. This partner can support the students learning by providing ideas for alternative means of teaching the skills and adaptions to match the student's needs and abilities. Many co-teaching teams face the challenge of limited time when it comes to co-planning. It is recommended to use other resources and means in the quest to collaborate with one another (Friend et al., 2010). Co-planning does not have

Table 2. Example of station teaching in a grade 3 co-taught mathematics general education classroom

	Station 1 – General Education Teacher	**Station 2 – Special Education Teacher**	**Station 3 – Independent station**
First rotation	Today's lesson objective – comparing fractions with like numerators and unlike denominators.	Targeted re-teach based off of student work and campus benchmarks – subtraction of three-digit numbers with regrouping	Students work independently on computers or iPads on an individualized math program.
Second rotation	Today's lesson objective	Targeted re-teach – rounding to the tens and hundreds place in three-digit numbers	Computer math program
Third rotation	Today's lesson objective	Targeted re-teach – place value writing three-digit numbers in expanded form	Computer math program

to mean face-to-face meetings every day. Teachers can share information through file sharing. Teaching teams can also discuss ideas over messaging systems. In a review of co-teaching, Dieker and Murawski (2003), found that planning time and communication between educators is important to meet the diverse student needs. Co-teaching can be utilized elementary through secondary and both educators have to be open to being the lead, as well as the support (Weiss & Brigham, 2000). Co-teaching approaches have been found to be beneficial in meeting the diverse student needs in a mathematics inclusion classroom.

SPECIFIC EVIDENCE-BASED STRATEGIES

The following section highlights specific strategies to target skill areas that research has shown to be the most problematic for students in special education and for students with MD. These include: (a) fact instruction, (b) fractions, and (c) word problems.

Fact Instruction

Fact automaticity and fluency are skills that are essential across mathematics domains and are essential for students in special education and with MD to master. Mastery of basic mathematical operations (addition, subtraction, multiplication, division) to higher level, multi-step problems is how fluency is to reading comprehension (Calhoon, Emerson, Flores, & Houchins, 2007). NMAP (2008) linked fact mastery to success in multi-step problems, fractions, and algebra readiness. Mathematics interventions need to teach specific fact strategies to decrease cognitive load (Woodward, 2004), thus increasing the automaticity of solving facts. Increasing the automaticity is a "transition to memory-based processes [that] results in the quick solution of individual problems and reduction of the working memory demands" needed to solve facts (Geary, 2004, p. 7). Decreasing cognitive loads on working memory through efficient strategy instruction and using research-based instructional approaches is necessary for students with MD. However, instruction in basic facts within core instruction is limited, and students often require remediation of facts beyond the elementary level for success in the upper grades (Calhoon et al., 2007; NMAP, 2008). Thus, educators need evidence based, efficient, and effective interventions to assist students struggling with automaticity and accuracy in basic facts.

While educators often report that basic mathematical facts are an easier skill, full understanding of facts is a complex task (Boerst & Schielack, 2003). In order for students to master operational facts mastery of symbols and development of number sense are crucial. For students with MD or receiving special education support, research has shown this particular skill area to be one of the greatest deficits to overcome (Woodward, 2006). Using explicit, systematic instruction with specific strategies to learn facts is a highly effective evidence-based strategy (Bryant et al., 2013; Jayanthi et al., 2008; Woodward, 2006, Calhoon et al., 2007). As part of strategy instruction, multiple representations are of utmost importance in order to explain a strategy and to visually understand the steps. Part of the multiple representations should include manipulatives, number lines, hundred charts, part-part-whole mats and ten-frames (addition and subtraction), as well as equal groups and arrays (multiplication and division). Furthermore, when introducing the strategy, multiple representations should be used, as well as the number line so students develop a conceptual understanding of the strategy, rather than procedure alone (Jones et al., 2013; NCTM, 2006; Silbert et al., 2006; Woodward, 2006).

For many students with MD, either no strategy or ineffective strategies (e.g. finger counting, tally lines) are used to solve basic facts (Codding et al., 2009; Stein, Kinder, & Silbert, 2006). Strategy-based instruction allows an alternative path to mastery, rather than reliance on memorization or ineffective methods. The goal of strategy instruction is to provide a tool until a particular fact is memorized. As students become proficient with a particular strategy for a set of facts, the steps of the strategy will naturally become shorted as the student internalizes the steps (Codding et al., 2009). Prior to strategy instruction, it is imperative that the educator understand progressions in fact instruction. By reaching mastery in each skill area prior to the introduction of the next skill will increase generalization. To assist with development of number sense it is recommended that addition and subtraction be taught together, and multiplication and division paired. In teaching the inverse operations together mastery can be met quicker, while increasing student understanding of how numbers and operations are related (NCTM, 2006). Specific strategies and progressions for addition/subtraction are located in Table 3. Multiplication strategies and progression are in Table 4. It is important to note that these strategies build upon mathematical properties, such as associative, distributive, communicative, as well as the decomposition of numbers. In multiplication and division, the progression also builds upon ease of strategy. Easier facts or those that require more basic skills are introduced first, prior to more difficult or multi-step strategies (Stein et al., 2006). The importance of teaching multiplication and division together is evident, in that the strategy for solving division is to think multiplication. This is not the only progression possible. For example, in multiplication, if a student understands that part of six is five and one, rather than multiplying by six the student can decompose or distribute six through five and one and then add (e.g., $6 \times 9 = (5 \times 9) + (1 \times 9)$).

To increase symbol understanding it is significant that and when writing equations to write the equal sign on either side (e.g. $7 = 4 + 3$ and $4 + 3 = 7$) as well as provide practice in solving for the unknown by using fact knowledge (e.g., $3 + \_\_\_ = 7$; Driver & Powell, 2015). Instruction and mastery in decomposing of numbers and building upon previously mastered facts, builds generalization and flexible mathematical thinking to aid in multi-step problems seen in upper grades (Van De Wall, Lovin, Karp, Williams-Bay, 2013; Woodward, 2006).

Fact instruction and mastery of facts is imperative for long-term success. Correct mathematical vocabulary should be part of instruction. In addition and subtraction, explaining the numbers in relation to part-part-whole, lends itself to understanding the value of the digits and can increase understanding of multi-digit addition and subtraction. As students are learning facts, extending to power of ten facts can increase generalization. For example, if a student has mastered $5 + 8$ the power of ten fact, $50 + 80$ can be solved quickly. The same is true for 5×8 and 50×80 (Van De Wall et al., 2013). NMAP (2008) describes the need for students to master arithmetic facts as a key factor to success in higher mathematics. In order for all students to be successful in the mathematics classroom, educators must explicitly teach strategies using multiple representations until the fact is memorized. In addition, students should be explaining the steps and process and describe how to solve using correct mathematical vocabulary. This can lead to a deeper understanding of the mathematical process (NCTM, 2014) and mastery of number sense and basic arithmetic facts.

Fractions

Development of number sense, place value and magnitude comparison is vital in elementary grades so that students can then build flexibility to understand the concept and relationship of fractions and

Table 3. Addition and subtraction strategy progression

Fact Strand	Strategy	Instructional Example
Part-part-whole; introduction to equations and expressions	Break apart whole number, no mathematical symbols	Students are given concrete materials to represent the whole number. Students break apart into 2 groups to show the different parts.
+/-0	0 rule or generalization	Students use a ten-frame to build the greater number. Students are then directed to add or subtract 0 or nothing. Teach that any number added or subtracted from 0 equals the same number.
+/- 1, 2, 3, 4	Count on and count back	Students identify the greater number and then count-on 1, 2, 3 or 4 when adding. Students identify the whole number and then count back 1, 2, 3 or 4. Instructionally, students build the equations with concrete manipulatives, then move to a number line, prior to abstract representation.
Doubles and related facts	Count by 2s	Students first identify a doubles fact and understand that it is the same part added together. Students are taught to make groups of 2 to represent the double fact and then skip count to find the total or whole. Fact family activities are connected to write the inverse equations. Instructionally, students should make groups of 2 with concrete manipulatives and then link to the number line, showing "jumps" of 2 prior to abstract representation.
Doubles +1 Addition	Identify numbers that have a difference of 1, or are "neighbors on the number line"	Students first identify the number that is less, double it and then add on 1 more. Instruction is similar to the doubles strategy, but using a number line simultaneously with concrete manipulatives can assist students in understanding numbers that have a difference of 1.
Make 10 and related facts	Identify the pairs of numbers that result in a total of 10.	Students use a ten-frame to identify the different ways to make 10. As students identify the addition parts, fact family activities are connected to write the inverse equations. While multiple representation is recommended, many students may be able to begin strictly with a ten-frame using manipulatives to only represent the number added to 10 or number line only prior to abstract only representation.
Make 10 Plus More	Numbers 7, 8 or 9 added to 4, 5, or 6 that do not meet the criteria for doubles +1 facts or Make 10 facts.	Students first identify the greater number and make 10 from the lesser valued number. For example, in 9 + 7 the greater number, 9, becomes 10 by taking one away from 7. The student thinks, 10 + 6 is 16 so 9 + 7 is 16. This is a strategy that requires multiple steps and the use of previously mastered strategies so utilizing multiple representations is essential. Starting with a double ten-frame with manipulatives to show the movement from the lesser number to the greater number helps to illustrate this strategy. Scaffolding back to simply making the lesser number before moving to a number line is often needed prior to number line and abstract representation only.

decimals as numbers. As early as preschool, students begin to develop an understanding of magnitude comparison that is correlated with a later understanding of fractions. In a study testing the ability of students to place whole numbers and fractions on a number line, children that were accurate with whole numbers were also "superior at the corresponding tasks with fractions." (Frazio, Bailey, Thompson, & Siegler, 2014, p. 68). NMAP (2008) listed fractions as an essential concept for higher level mathematical understanding, much like whole number magnitude comparison is connected to fractions (Frazio et al., 2014). Yet, adults, high schoolers and middle schoolers often lack mastery and a deep understanding in fraction skills (Butler, Miller, Crehand, Babbitt, & Pierce, 2003; NCTM, 2007; NMAP, 2008). Fractions need to be well understood for mastery in the mathematical progression and link to ratios, rates, function, probability, and proportionality (Butler et al., 2003). The lack of a conceptual understanding can

Characteristics and Instructional Strategies for Students With Mathematical Difficulties

Table 4. Multiplication strategy progression

Fact Strand	Strategy	Instructional Example
× 0, 1	Generalization/rule	Students create models of equal groups. Based upon the models state the generalization that any number times 0 always equals 0. Any number times 1 always equals that number.
× 2, 5, 10	Skip count	Students create equal sized groups of 2, 5 or 10 and then skip count. Progress to skip counting on number line or hundreds chart.
×/÷ 9	Make 10 Minus the Factor	Students determine that 9 is also 10 minus 1 or 9 groups are equal to 10 equal-sized groups minus 1 equal-sized group. Using an array or area model, students multiply the factor by 10 and then subtract the one set of the other factor. $9 \times 7 = (10 - 1) \times 7$ $(10 \times 7) - (1 \times 7)$ $70 - 7 = 63$ Strategy for division is for students to think of it as a multiplication problem with a missing factor.
×/÷ 4/8	Double it Two Times/Double it Three Times	Students identify that 4 equals 2 times 2 and that 8 equals 2 times 2 times 2. For the 4s strategy, students double the other factor and double it again For the 8s strategy, student double the factor, double it again, and then double it a third time. $4 \times 7 = (2 \times 2) \times 7$ $2 \times 2 \times 7 = 2 \times 14$ $2 \times 14 = 28$ $8 \times 7 = (2 \times 2 \times 2) \times 7$ $2 \times 2 \times 2 \times 7 = 2 \times 2 \times 14$ 2×28 56 Division strategy for 4s is the half the dividend and half it again. For 8s, half it, half it again, and half it one more time.
×/÷ 6	Break-apart 6 and then put back together	Students decompose 6 into 1 and 5 or 2 and 4. The students show the decomposition by breaking apart an array or area model, finding the total and then putting it back together. Students then write the two new multiplication problems created and then add these products. $6 \times 8 = (1 + 5) \times 8$ $(1 \times 8) + (5 \times 8) = 8 + 40$ 48 Strategy for division is for students to think of it as a multiplication problem with a missing factor.
×/÷ 7	Break-apart 7 and then put back together	Students decompose 7 into 5 and 2. Using the array or area model and the distributive property to solve by multiplying the other factor times 5 and by 2. The final step is to add the products. $7 \times 6 = (5 + 2) \times 6$ $(5 \times 6) + (2 \times 6) = 30 + 12$ 42 Strategy for division is for students to think of it as a multiplication problem with a missing factor.
×/÷ 3	Break-apart 3 and then put back together	Students decompose 3 in 2 and 1 and then use the distributive property to solve. $3 \times 8 = (2 + 1) \times 8$ $(2 \times 8) + (1 \times 8) = 8 + 16$ 24 Strategy for division is for students to think of it as a multiplication problem with a missing factor.

lead to misconceptions that can hinder a student's ability to correctly compare fractions, place fractions on a number line, complete operations with fractions, write fractions as decimals, or "believe" that a fraction is a number (Siegler et al., 2010; Tzur & Hunt, 2015). Students with MD also try to apply or overgeneralize properties of whole numbers to fractions and decimals. For example, when comparing fractions students will often state that the greater the denominator, the greater the fraction (Siegler et al., 2010). With fractions, the whole idea of a value expressed as a single-digit can be a challenge for students with MD. As Siegler and Pyke (2013) describe, "Conceptual knowledge of fractions involves knowing what fractions are: that they are numbers that stretch from negative to positive infinity" (p. 1994). Also, students with MD struggle in understanding that a fraction is a number based upon the "numerator-denominator relation, rather than either number alone" (p. 1994). In fractions and decimals the only property that can be applied is in comparison or magnitude of numbers. With this in mind, it is imperative that fractions be taught both conceptually and procedurally to increase understanding and development of numerical properties (Fuchs et al., 2013; Osana & Pitsolantis, 2013; Siegler & Pyke, 2013). Students need to understand that fractions are a number and if "students do not see fractions as quantities, they have difficulty making sense of operations on quantities, such as adding or multiplying." (Kent, Empson, & Nielsen, 2015, p. 89). As recommended by Siegler et al. (2010), five recommendations are evident in the research for instruction in fractions for students in kindergarten through Grade 12. The five recommendations include: (1) build on equal sharing and proportionality to develop fractions, (2) use number lines to build understanding that fractions are numbers, (3) use models such as area, number lines, and visual representations to develop understanding of computations, (4) develop strategies through conceptual understanding for solving ratio, rate, and proportion problems, and (5) develop educators deep understanding of fractions and how to teach them.

Multiple representations have been cited as an instructional strategy for students with MD (Doabler et al., 2012; Jones et al., 2013; Gersten et al., 2009b), and are of great importance in teaching fractions (Siegler et al., 2010; Tzur & Hunt, 2015). In a study completed by Gabriel, Coche, Szucs, Carette, Rey and Content (2012), it was found that the use of concrete fractional pieces and numbers lines increased students in Grade 4 and 5 understanding and magnitude of fractions. An interesting caveat of this study was that students in the control group outscored on procedural only tasks, yet scored lower on conceptual understanding tasks. While educators will often teach the procedure in order for students to obtain an answer, this becomes a disservice to development of understanding. The lack of the conceptual understanding will often hinder ratio and proportional skills in middle and high school (Fuchs et al., 2013; Gabriel et al., 2012; Siegler et al., 2010), thus illustrating the important of number lines, fraction strips, and drawing models to justify answers.

In addition to the use of concrete representations, fraction instruction sequence as well as the vocabulary and models used can help students generalize to decimals, ratios and proportionality. Often fractions are taught as simply part of a whole, like 3 out of 4 written as $\frac{3}{4}$. The problem with teaching part of a whole is that it limits the understanding that a fraction and rational numbers "involves the coordination of many different but interconnected ideas and interpretations." (Lamon, 2006, p. 23). Fractions should be introduced to build upon prior knowledge, as in equal shares. An equal share is the idea that when you share an item, like a candy bar, everyone has to receive the same amount. Students quickly see that when you share with more people the piece of the item is smaller, thus proportional reasoning (Siegler et al., 2010).

Equal shares are a concept that links to division and begins with sharing one item or one set with two people, or one-half. Instructional trajectory of equal shares moves from unit fractions (i.e. fractions with a numerator of one, such as $\frac{1}{4}, \frac{1}{7}$) to non-unit fractions (i.e. $\frac{3}{4}, \frac{5}{10}$,). Concrete representations, pictures and number line should all be used to build understanding and to illustrate the shares. Through the use of equal shares and modeling, transitioning to fractional operations (i.e. addition, subtraction, multiplication, and division) is easier for students to grasp at a much younger age than the tradition algorithm. In addition, providing numerous practice opportunities to model fractions with concrete manipulatives, as well as drawing pictures, helps students to see fractions as a quantity, a number with a value (Kent et al., 2015). When students understand that a fraction is a number, transitioning to decimals becomes less of a challenge.

In addition to teaching fractions as part of a set and as part of a whole, students should also be taught fractions has part of a line. Teaching students to find where fractions fall on a number line will reinforce the understanding that fractions are numbers. Educators can then link fractions on the number line to decimals on the number line to help students make the connection between the different forms of the same rational number. See Figure 3 for an illustration of a number line that includes fractions, decimals, and whole numbers.

Word Problem Solving

Due to the high stakes nature of assessments in schools, students unable to solve and articulate a word problem often see many failures and challenges in upper mathematics classes. Word problem solving presents challenges for students with MD in syntax (i.e., language and vocabulary; Bryant, 2005; Fuchs et al., 2008; Gersten et al., 2005), schematic structure, particularly in multi-step problems (Parmer, Cawley & Frazita, 1996), selection and application of strategies and algorithms (Montague, Enders, & Dietz, 2011; NMAP, 2008). SDI in word problem solving should include schema-based strategy instruction in schematic organization (Gersten et al., 2009; Jitendra et al., 2002; Jitendra et al., 2009; Montague & Dietz, 2009; Pfannenstiel et al., 2015; Van Garderen, 2007).

Schema-based strategy instruction is the process of teaching the function or schema of the problem within a graphic organizer or diagram that can be applied across operations. Schematic diagrams are a visual representation of the relationship between elements and within the structure of the problem (Jitendra et al., 2002; Jitendra et al., 2009; Jitendra et al., 2013; Jitendra & Star, 2011) Schematic-based instruction (SBI) includes components of the four-step problem solving model: (1) understand the problem, (2) devise a plan, (3) solve, and (4) check and reflect (Lesh & Zawojewski, 2007), and explicitly teaches students that the plan or step 2 is a schematic diagram. By providing a diagram, students are better able to generalize across problem types and not be consumed with a type of plan. With a schematic diagram students are better able to recognize and verbalize the relationship in the number and determine

Figure 3. Illustration of a number line with fractions, decimals, and whole numbers

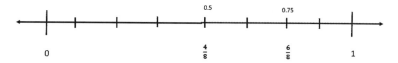

if/and/or how the numbers are changing. For example, a schematic diagram might include the number to start with and then have students identify if this number changed, meaning was something added or subtracted, and what is the result of the change. Teachers should use multiple representations to illustrate this relationship and change, thus drawing upon students understanding of how numbers are related and showing different ways to solve (e.g., adding to find the end or subtracting when the beginning or start and end is known, but the change is missing). While SBI stresses the importance of the structure and underlying relationship, it does not rely on key words (Jitendra et al., 2009). Key words tend to expire or are not true for every problem, "Karen went to an amusement park and took pictures. She deleted 14 pictures and downloaded the remaining 36. How many pictures did she take in all?" Using this word problem as an example, students will often focus on the word "delete" and subtract. Yet, in order to solve the students should add the numbers because the numbers presented are the change and the result, with the need to find the start. Key word instruction does not develop the deeper understanding of the structure of the word problem and can often lead to incorrect solutions as a result of a lack of understanding (Karp, Bush & Dougherty, 2014). An example of a schematic diagram can be found in Figure 4. This would be an example of a diagram to be paired with addition or subtraction problem types. This diagram assists students in identifying the unknown by examining the relationship and anchoring the student's understanding of the action that is taking place in the word problem. By completing a schematic diagram, like Figure 4, with known numbers the student can then determine if addition or subtraction should be used to solve based upon the relationship, not the words in the problem (Jayanthi et al., 2008).

CONCLUSION

The purpose of this chapter was to review evidence-based practices in mathematics for students in receiving special education support or students with MD served in an inclusive general education setting. Understanding characteristics of students with MD paired with mathematical trajectories can help to assist in planning and developing an appropriate Individualized Education Program or intervention within a system of tiered support. The goal of this chapter was not to review all skill areas or content to be covered within a general education core mathematics classroom, but rather key foundational areas in self-regulation, number sense, fact instruction, fractions, and word problem solving that can have the greatest impact in higher level mathematics. Utilizing EBPs and providing SDI within an inclusive general education setting exposes students to grade level standards while given the opportunity to fill gaps in learning and understanding for procedural fluency and conceptual understanding.

Students receiving special education services and with MD are increasingly being served in general education classes, which places demands on interventionists, whether they are general education or special education personnel. As more schools implement MTSS, the need for evidence-based instruction in mathematics is warranted in order to close the achievement gap. Core general mathematics instruction alone often does not provide enough opportunities for practice, is lacking in multiple representations, and is an environment where students with MD often take a more passive role (Bottge et al., 2002). For special educators or interventionists, becoming content experts in all core academic areas can be a challenge. Rather, each educator should work together to meet the needs of students and combine knowledge of content with process. Educators with an enhanced understanding of the characteristics of students with MD can provide specialized instruction with a focus on key areas linked to long-term success, while simultaneously providing all students access to general education curriculum.

Figure 4. Example of a schematic diagram

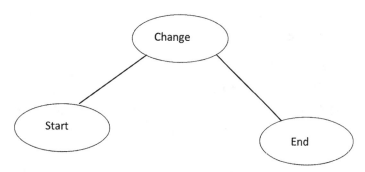

Phyllis earned $12 for washing the car. When adding the money she earned from washing the car to the money she already had in piggybank, Phyllis now has $35. How much money did Phyllis have in her piggybank before she washed the car?

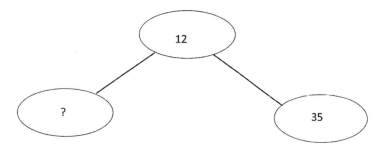

REFERENCES

Archer, A., & Hughes, C. (2010). *Explicit instruction: Effective and Efficient teaching*. New York: The Guilford Press.

Auerbach, J., Gross-Tsur, V., Manor, O., & Shalev, R. (2008). Emotional and behavioral characteristics over a six-year period in youths with persistent and nonpersistent dyscalculia. *Journal of Learning Disabilities, 41*(3), 263–273. doi:10.1177/0022219408315637 PMID:18434292

Axtell, P., McCallum, S., Mee Bell, S., & Poncy, B. (2009). Developing math automaticity using a class wide fluency building procedure for middle school students: A preliminary study. *Psychology in the Schools, 46*(6), 526-538. doi: 10.1002-pits.20395

Baddeley, A. (2000). The episodic buffer: A new component of working memory? *Trends in Cognitive Sciences, 4*(11), 417–423. doi:10.1016/S1364-6613(00)01538-2 PMID:11058819

Blanton, M., & Kaput, J. (2005). Characterizing a classroom practice that promotes algebraic reasoning. *Journal for Research in Mathematics Education, 36*(5), 412–446.

Blanton, M., Westbrook, S., & Carter, G. (2005). Using Valsiners zone theory to interpret teaching practices in mathematics and science classrooms. *Journal of Mathematics Teacher Education*, *8*(1), 5–33. doi:10.100710857-005-0456-1

Boerst, T. A., & Schielack, J. F. (2003). Toward understanding of "computational fluency.". *Teaching Children Mathematics*, *9*(6), 292–293.

Bottge, B., Heinrichs, M., Mehta, Z., & Hung, Y. (2002). Weighting the benefits of anchored math instruction for students with disabilities in general education classes. *The Journal of Special Education*, *35*(4), 186–200. doi:10.1177/002246690203500401

Bottge, B., Rueda, E., Serlin, R., Hung, Y., & Kwon, J. M. (2007). Shrinking achievement differences with anchored math problems: Challenges and possibilities. *The Journal of Special Education*, *41*(1), 31–49. doi:10.1177/00224669070410010301

Bryant, D. P. (2005). Commentary on early identification and intervention for students with mathematics difficulties. *Journal of Learning Disabilities*, *38*(4), 340–345. doi:10.1177/00222194050380041001 PMID:16122066

Bryant, D. P., Bryant, B., & Hammill, D. (2000). Characteristic behaviors of students with LD who have teacher-identified math weaknesses. *Journal of Learning Disabilities*, *33*(2), 168–177. doi:10.1177/002221940003300205 PMID:15505946

Bryant, D. P., Pfannenstiel, K. H., Bryant, B., Hunt, J., & Shin, M. (2014). Selecting and tailoring interventions for students with mathematics difficulties. In J. T. Mascolo, V. C. Alfonso, & D. P. Flanagan (Eds.), *Essentials of planning, selecting, and tailoring interventions for unique learners* (pp. 178–203). Hoboken, NJ: John Wiley & Sons, Inc.

Burns, M. (2005). Using incremental rehearsal to increase fluency of single-digit multiplication facts with children identified as learning disabled in mathematics computation. *Education & Treatment of Children*, *28*(3), 237–249.

Butler, F., Miller, S., Crehan, K., Babbitt, B., & Pierce, T. (2003). Fraction instruction for students with mathematics disabilities: Comparing two teaching sequences. *Learning Disabilities Research & Practice*, *18*(2), 99–111. doi:10.1111/1540-5826.00066

Calderhead, W., Filter, K., & Albin, R. (2006). An investigation of incremental effects of interspersing math items on task-related behavior. *Journal of Behavioral Education*, *15*(1), 53–67. doi:10.100710864-005-9000-8

Calhoon, M. B., Emerson, R. W., Flores, M., & Houchins, D. E. (2007). Computational fluency performance profile of high school students with mathematics disabilities. *Remedial and Special Education*, *28*(5), 292–303. doi:10.1177/07419325070280050401

Calhoon, M. B., & Fuchs, L. (2003). The effects of peer-assisted learning strategies and curriculum-based measurement on the mathematics performance of secondary students with disabilities. *Remedial and Special Education*, *24*(4), 235–245. doi:10.1177/07419325030240040601

Codding, R., Chan-Iannetta, L., Palmer, M., & Lukito, G. (2009). Examining a class wide application of cover-copy-compare with and without goal setting to enhance mathematics fluency. *School Psychology Quarterly, 24*(3), 173–185. doi:10.1037/a0017192

Cogan, L. S., Schmidt, W. H., & Wiley, D. E. (2001). Who takes what math and in which track? Using TIMSS to characterize U.S. students eighth-grade mathematics learning opportunities. *Educational Evaluation and Policy Analysis, 23*(4), 323–341. doi:10.3102/01623737023004323

Desoete, A., Stock, P., Schepens, A., Baeyens, D., & Roeyers, H. (2009). Classification, serration, and counting in grades 1, 2, and 3 and two-year longitudinal predictors for low achieving in numerical facility and arithmetical achievement? *Journal of Psychoeducational Assessment, 27*(3), 252–264. doi:10.1177/0734282908330588

Doabler, C., Fien, H., Nelson-Walker, N. J., & Baker, S. (2012). Evaluating three elementary mathematics programs for presence of eight research-based instructional design principles. *Learning Disability Quarterly, 35*(4), 200–211. doi:10.1177/0731948712438557

Dougherty, B., Bryant, D. P., Bryant, B., Darrough, R., & Pfannenstiel, K. H. (2014). Developing concepts and generalizations to build algebraic thinking. The reversibility, flexibility and generalization approach. *Intervention in School and Clinic, 50*(5), 273–281. doi:10.1177/1053451214560892

Driver, M., & Powell, S. (2015). Symbolic and nonsymbolic equivalence tasks: The influence of symbols on students with mathematics difficulty. *Learning Disabilities Research & Practice, 30*(3), 127–134. doi:10.1111/ldrp.12059

Engelmann, S., & Carnine, D. (1991). *Theory of instruction: Principles and applications*. Eugene, OR: ADI Press.

Flores, M., Houchins, D., & Shippen, M. (2006). The effects of constant time delay and strategic instruction on students with learning disabilities' maintenance and generalization. *International Journal of Special Education, 21*(3), 45–57.

Frazio, L., Bailey, D., Thompson, C., & Siegler, R. (2014). Relations of different types of numerical representations to each other and to mathematics achievement. *Journal of Experimental Child Psychology, 123*, 53–72. doi:10.1016/j.jecp.2014.01.013 PMID:24699178

Friend, M., Cook, L., Hurley-Chamberlain, D., & Shamberger, C. (2010). Co-teaching: An illustration of the complexity of collaboration in special education. *Journal of Educational & Psychological Consultation, 20*(1), 9–27. doi:10.1080/10474410903535380

Frye, D., Baroody, A. J., Burchinal, M., Carver, S. M., Jordan, N. C., & McDowell, J. (2013). *Teaching math to young children: A practice guide (NCEE 2014-4005)*. Washington, DC: National Center for Education Evaluation and Regional Assistance (NCEE), Institute of Education Sciences, U.S. Department of Education. Retrieved from the NCEE website: http://whatworks.ed.gov

Fuchs, D., & Deshler, D. (2007). Wat we need to know about responsiveness to intervention (and shouldnt be afraid to ask). *Learning Disabilities Research & Practice, 22*(2), 129–136. doi:10.1111/j.1540-5826.2007.00237.x

Fuchs, L., Fuchs, D., & Zumeta, R. (2008). A curricular-sampling approach to progress monitoring: Mathematics concepts and application. *Assessment for Effective Intervention, 33*(4), 225–233. doi:10.1177/1534508407313484

Fuchs, L., Schumacher, R. F., Long, J., Namkung, J., Hamlett, C. L., Cirino, P. T., ... Changas, P. (2013). Improving at-risk learners' understanding of fractions. *Journal of Educational Psychology*, 1–19. doi:10.1037/a0032446

Geary, D. (1993). Mathematical disabilities: Cognitive, neuropsychological, and genetic components. *Psychological Bulletin, 114*(2), 345–362. doi:10.1037/0033-2909.114.2.345 PMID:8416036

Geary, D. (2004). Mathematics and learning disabilities. *Journal of Learning Disabilities, 37*(1), 4–15. doi:10.1177/00222194040370010201 PMID:15493463

Geary, D. (2005). Role of cognitive theory in the study of learning disabilities in mathematics. *Journal of Learning Disabilities, 38*(4), 305–307. doi:10.1177/00222194050380040401 PMID:16122060

Geary, D. (2011). Cognitive predictors of achievement growth in mathematics: A five year longitudinal study. *Developmental Psychology, 47*(6), 1539–1552. doi:10.1037/a0025510 PMID:21942667

Gersten, R., Beckmann, S., Clarke, B., Foegen, A., Marsh, L., Star, J. R., & Witzel, B. (2009). *Assisting students struggling with mathematics: Response to Intervention (RtI) for elementary and middle schools (NCEE 2009-4060)*. Washington, DC: National Center for Education Evaluation and Regional Assistance, Institute of Education Sciences, U.S. Department of Education. Retrieved from http://ies.ed.gov/ncee/wwc/publications/practiceguides/

Gersten, R., & Chard, D. (1999). Number sense; rethinking arithmetic instruction for students with mathematical disabilities. *The Journal of Special Education, 33*(1), 18–28. doi:10.1177/002246699903300102

Gersten, R., Chard, D., Jayanthis, M., Baker, S., Murphy, P., & Flojo, J. (2009b). Mathematics instruction for students with learning disabilities: A meta-analysis of instructional components. *Review of Educational Research, 79*(3), 1202–1242. doi:10.3102/0034654309334431

Gersten, R., Jordan, N., & Flojo, J. (2005). Early identification and interventions for students with mathematics difficulties. *Journal of Learning Disabilities, 38*(4), 293–304. doi:10.1177/00222194050380040301 PMID:16122059

Gray, E., Pinto, M., Pitta, D., & Tall, D. (1999). Knowledge construction and diverging thinking in elementary & advanced mathematics. *Educational Studies in Mathematics, 38*(1/3), 111–133. doi:10.1023/A:1003640204118

Griffin, C., League, M., Griffin, V., & Bae, J. (2013). Discourse practices in inclusive elementary mathematics classrooms. *Learning Disability Quarterly, 36*(1), 9–20. doi:10.1177/0731948712465188

Hecht, S., Close, L., & Santisi, M. (2003). Sources of individual differences in fraction skills. *Journal of Experimental Child Psychology, 86*(4), 277–302. doi:10.1016/j.jecp.2003.08.003 PMID:14623213

Impecoven-Lind, L. S., & Foegen, A. (2010). Teaching algebra to students with learning disabilities. *Intervention in School and Clinic, 46*(1), 31–37. doi:10.1177/1053451210369520

Individuals with Disabilities Education Improvement Act of 2004, Pub. L. No. 108–446, [Amending 20 U.S.C. §§ 1400 et seq.]. (n.d.). Retrieved August 2, 2015, from http://www.ed.gov/policy/speced/leg/edpicks.jhtml?src=ln

Jayanthi, M., Gersten, R., & Baker, S. (2008). *Mathematics instruction for students with learning disabilities or difficulty learning mathematics: A guide for teachers.* Portsmouth, NH: RMC Research Corporation, Center on Instruction.

Jitendra, A., DiPipi, C., & Perron-Jones, N. (2002). An exploratory study of schema based word problem-solving instruction for middle school students with learning disabilities: An emphasis on conceptual and procedural understanding. *The Journal of Special Education, 36*(1), 23–38. doi:10.1177/00224669020360010301

Jitendra, A., & Star, J. (2011). Meeting the needs of students with learning disabilities in inclusive classrooms: The role of schema-based instruction on mathematical problem-solving. *Theory into Practice, 50*(1), 12–19. doi:10.1080/00405841.2011.534912

Jitendra, A., Star, J., Starosta, K., Leh, J., Sood, S., Caskie, G., ... Mack, T. (2009). Improving seventh grade students learning of ratio and proportion: The role of schema-based instruction. *Contemporary Educational Psychology, 24*(3), 250–264. doi:10.1016/j.cedpsych.2009.06.001

Jitendra, A. K., Rodriguez, M., Kanive, R., Huang, J., Church, C., Corroy, K. A., & Zaslofsky, A. (2013). Impact of small-group tutoring interventions on the mathematical problem solving and achievement of third-grade students with mathematics difficulties. *Learning Disability Quarterly, 36*(1), 21–35. doi:10.1177/0731948712457561

Jones, I., Inglis, M., Gilmore, C., & Evans, R. (2013). Teaching the substitutive conception of the equals sign. *Research in Mathematics Education, 15*(1), 34–39. doi:10.1080/14794802.2012.756635

Jordan, N., Glutting, J., & Ramineni, C. (2010). The importance of number sense to mathematics achievement in first and third grades. *Learning and Individual Differences, 20*(2), 82–88. doi:10.1016/j.lindif.2009.07.004 PMID:20401327

Jordan, N., Kaplan, D., Locuniak, M., & Ramineni, C. (2007). Predicting first-grade math achievement from developmental number sense trajectories. *Learning Disabilities Research & Practice, 22*(1), 36–46. doi:10.1111/j.1540-5826.2007.00229.x

Karp, K., Bush, S., & Dougherty, B. (2014). 13 Rules that expire. *Teaching Children Mathematics, 21*(1), 18–25. doi:10.5951/teacchilmath.21.1.0018

Kent, L., Empson, S., & Nielsen, L. (2015). Richness of childrens fractional strategies. *Teaching Children Mathematics, 22*(2), 84–90. doi:10.5951/teacchilmath.22.2.0084

Konrad, M., & Test, D. (2007). Effects of GO 4 IT...NOW! Strategy instruction on written IEP goal articulation and paragraph-writing skills of middle school students with disabilities. *Remedial and Special Education, 28*(5), 277–291. doi:10.1177/07419325070280050301

Kroesbergen, E. H., & Van Luit, J. E. H. (2003). Mathematics interventions for children with special educational needs; A meta-analysis. *Remedial and Special Education, 24*(2), 97–114. doi:10.1177/07419325030240020501

Kroesbergen, E. H., Van Luit, J. E. H., & Mass, C. (2004). Effectiveness of explicit and constructivist mathematics instruction for low-achieving students in the Netherlands. *The Elementary School Journal, 104*(3), 233–251. doi:10.1086/499751

Lamon, S. (2006). *Teaching fractions and ratios for understanding.* Mahwah, NJ: Lawrence Erlbaum Associates.

Lesh, R., & Zawojewski, J. (2007). Problem solving and modeling. In F. K. Lester (Ed.), *Second handbook of research on mathematics teaching and learning* (pp. 763–804). Charlotte, NC: Information Age.

Lui, A., & Bonner, S. (2016). Teacher's pedagogical content beliefs in mathematics. *Cognition and Instruction, 6*(1), 1–40. doi:10.1207/21532690cxi0601_1

Lyon, R., & Fletcher, J. (2001, Summer). Early warning system. *Education Matters,* 23-29.

Maccini, P., Mulcahy, C. A., & Wilson, M. G. (2007). A follow-up of mathematics interventions for secondary students with learning disabilities. *Learning Disabilities Research & Practice, 22*(1), 58–74. doi:10.1111/j.1540-5826.2007.00231.x

Miller, S., & Hudson, P. (2007). Using evidence-based practices to build mathematics competence related to conceptual, procedural, and declarative knowledge. *Learning Disabilities Practice, 22*(1), 47–57. doi:10.1111/j.1540-5826.2007.00230.x

Montague, M. (2007). Self-regulation and mathematics instruction. *Learning Disabilities Research & Practice, 22*(1), 75–83. doi:10.1111/j.1540-5826.2007.00232.x

Montague, M., Applegate, B., & Marquard, K. (1993). Cognitive strategy instruction and mathematical problem-solving performance of students with learning disabilities. *Learning Disabilities Research & Practice, 29,* 251–261.

Montague, M., & Dietz, S. (2009). Evaluating the evidence base for cognitive strategy instruction and mathematical problem solving. *Exceptional Children, 75*(3), 285–302. doi:10.1177/001440290907500302

Morgan, P., Farkas, G., & Wu, Q. (2009). Five-year trajectories of kindergarten children with learning difficulties in mathematics. *Journal of Learning Disabilities, 42*(4), 306–321. doi:10.1177/0022219408331037 PMID:19299551

National Center for Education Statistics. (2011). *The Nation's Report Card: A First Look: 2013 Mathematics and Reading (NCES 2014-451).* Institute of Education Sciences, U.S. Department of Education.

National Council of Teachers of Mathematics. (2002). *Standards and expectations.* Retrieved from http://www.nctm.org/standards/content.aspx?id=4294967312

National Council of Teachers of Mathematics. (2014). *Principles to actions. Ensuring mathematical success for all.* Reston, VA: The National Council of Teachers of Mathematics, Inc.

National Governors Association Center for Best Practices & Council for Chief State School Officers. (2010). *National Center on Intensive Intervention*. Retrieved from http://www.intensiveintervention.org/

National Mathematics Advisory Panel. (2008, March). *Foundations for success: The final report of the National Mathematics Advisory Panel*. Washington, DC: U.S. Department of Education. Retrieved from http://www.ed.gov/about/bdscomm/list/mathpanel/report/final-report.pdf

Osana, H., & Pitsolantis, N. (2013). Assessing the struggle to link form and understanding in fractions instruction. *The British Journal of Educational Psychology, 83*(1), 29–56. doi:10.1111/j.2044-8279.2011.02053.x PMID:23369174

Parmer, R. S., Cauley, J. F., & Frazita, R. R. (1996). Word problem solving by students with and without mild disabilities. *Exceptional Children, 62*(5), 415–429.

Pellegrino, J., & Goldman, S. (1987). Information processing and elementary mathematics. *Journal of Learning Disabilities, 20*(1), 23–57. doi:10.1177/002221948702000105 PMID:3805888

Pfannenstiel, K. H., Bryant, D. P., Bryant, B., & Porterfield, J. (2015). Cognitive strategy instruction for teaching word problems to primary-level struggling students. *Intervention in School and Clinic, 50*(5), 291–296. doi:10.1177/1053451214560890

Pintrich, P., & DeGroot, E. (1990). Motivational and self-regulated learning components of classroom academic performance. *Journal of Educational Psychology, 82*(1), 33–40. doi:10.1037/0022-0663.82.1.33

Powell, S. (2012). High-stakes testing for students with mathematics difficulty: Response format effects in mathematics problem solving. *Learning Disability Quarterly, 35*(1), 3–9. doi:10.1177/0731948711428773

Powell, S., Fuchs, L., Fuchs, D., Cirino, P., & Fletcher, P. (2009). Effects of fact retrieval tutoring on third-grade students with math difficulties with and without reading difficulties. *Learning Disabilities Research & Practice, 24*(1), 1–11. doi:10.1111/j.1540-5826.2008.01272.x PMID:19448840

Raghubar, K., Barnes, M., & Hecht, S. (2009). Working memory and mathematics: A review of developmental, individual difference, and cognitive approaches. *Learning and Individual Differences, 20*(2), 110–122. doi:10.1016/j.lindif.2009.10.005

Rock, M. (2005). Use of strategic self-monitoring to enhance academic engagement, productivity, and accuracy of students with and without exceptionalities. *Journal of Positive Behavior Interventions, 7*(1), 3–17. doi:10.1177/10983007050070010201

Ryan, J., Reid, R., & Epstein, M. (2004). Peer-mediated intervention studies on academic achievement for students with EBD. *Remedial and Special Education, 25*(6), 330–341. doi:10.1177/07419325040250060101

Saracho, O., & Spodek, B. (2008). Educating the young mathematician: A historical perspective through the nineteenth century. *Early Childhood Education, 36*(4), 297–303. doi:10.100710643-008-0292-x

Scheuermann, A., Deschler, D., & Schumaker, J. (2009). The effects of the explicit inquiry routine on the performance of students with learning disabilities on one-variable equations. *Learning Disability Quarterly, 32*(2), 103–120. doi:10.2307/27740360

Schmittau, J. (2004). Vygotskian theory and mathematics education: Resolving the conceptual-procedural dichotomy. *European Journal of Psychology of Education, 19*(1), 19–43. doi:10.1007/BF03173235

Schoenfeld, A. (2004). The math wars. *Educational Policy, 18*(1), 253–284. doi:10.1177/0895904803260042

Scruggs, T., Mastropieri, M., & McDuffi, K. (2007). Co-teaching in inclusive classrooms: A metasynthesis of qualitative research. *Exceptional Children, 73*(4), 392–416. doi:10.1177/001440290707300401

Shapiro, E. (2010). *Academic skills problems: Direct assessment and intervention* (4th ed.). New York: Guilford Publishing.

Siegler, R., Carpenter, T., Fennell, F., Geary, D., Lewis, J., Okamoto, Y., ... Wray, J. (2010). *Developing effective fractions instruction for kindergarten through 8th grade: A practice guide (NCEE #2010-4039)*. Washington, DC: National Center for Education Evaluation and Regional Assistance, Institute of Education Sciences, U.S. Department of Education. Retrieved from whatworks.ed.gov/publications/practiceguides

Siegler, R., & Pyke, A. (2013). Developmental and individual differences in understanding of fractions. *Developmental Psychology, 49*(10), 1994–2004. doi:10.1037/a0031200 PMID:23244401

Siegler, R. S. (1988). Strategy choice procedures and the development of multiplication skill. *Journal of Experimental Psychology. General, 117*(3), 258–275. doi:10.1037/0096-3445.117.3.258 PMID:2971762

Stein, M., Kinder, D., & Silbert, J. (2006). *Designing effective mathematics instruction: A direct instruction approach*. Columbus, OH: Pearson Merrill Prentice Hall.

Strickland, T., & Maccini, P. (2010). Strategies for teaching algebra to students with learning disabilities: Making research to practice connections. *Intervention in School and Clinic, 46*(1), 38–45. doi:10.1177/1053451210369519

Swanson, H. L., & Jerman, O. (2006). Math disabilities: A selective meta-analysis of the literature. *Review of Educational Research, 76*(2), 249–274. doi:10.3102/00346543076002249

Swanson, H. L., Jerman, O., & Zheng, X. (2008). Growth in working memory and mathematical problem solving in children at risk and not at risk for serious math difficulties. *Journal of Educational Psychology, 100*(2), 343–379. doi:10.1037/0022-0663.100.2.343

Swanson, H. L., Kehler, P., & Jerman, O. (2010). Working memory, strategy knowledge, and strategy instruction in children with reading disabilities. *Journal of Learning Disabilities, 43*(1), 24–47. doi:10.1177/0022219409338743 PMID:19749089

Swanson, H. L., & Sachs-Lee, C. (2000). A meta-analysis of single-subject design intervention research for students with LD. *Journal of Learning Disabilities, 33*(2), 114–136. doi:10.1177/002221940003300201 PMID:15505942

Trends in International Mathematics and Science Study. (2007). Retrieved from https://nces.ed.gov/surveys/international/ide/

Tzur, R., & Hunt, J. (2015). Iteration: Unit Fraction Knowledge and the French Fry Tasks. *Teaching Children Mathematics, 22*(3), 148–157. doi:10.5951/teacchilmath.22.3.0148

Van De Walle, J., Lovin, L. H., Karp, K., & Williams-Bay, J. (2013). *Teaching student-centered mathematics: Developmentally appropriate instruction for grades Pre-K-2* (2nd ed.; Vol. 1). Pearson.

Van Garderen, D. (2007). Teaching students with LD to use diagrams to solve mathematical word problems. *Journal of Learning Disabilities, 40*(6), 540–553. doi:10.1177/00222194070400060501 PMID:18064979

Van Oers, B. (2001). Educational forms of initiation in mathematical culture. *Educational Studies in Mathematics, 46*(1/3), 59–85. doi:10.1023/A:1014031507535

VanDerHeyden, A., & Burns, M. (2008). Examination of the utility of various measures of mathematics proficiency. *Assessment for Effective Intervention, 33*(4), 215–224. doi:10.1177/1534508407313482

Vostal, B. (2011). Engaging students with behavior disorders in mathematics practice using the high-p strategy. *Beyond Behavior*, 3–9.

Wagner, D., & Davis, B. (2010). Feeling number: Grounding number sense in a sense of quantity. *Educational Studies in Mathematics, 74*(1), 39–51. doi:10.100710649-009-9226-9

Witzel, B. (2005). Using CRA to teach algebra to students with math difficulties in inclusive settings. *Learning Disabilities (Weston, Mass.), 3*(2), 49–60.

Witzel, B., Mercer, C. D., & Miller, M. D. (2003). Teaching algebra to students with learning difficulties: An investigation of an explicit instruction model. *Learning Disabilities Research & Practice, 18*(2), 121–131. doi:10.1111/1540-5826.00068

Wood, D., Bruner, J., & Ross, G. (1976). The role of tutoring in problem solving. *Journal of Child Psychology and Psychiatry, and Allied Disciplines, 17*(2), 89–100. doi:10.1111/j.1469-7610.1976.tb00381.x PMID:932126

Woodward, J. (2004). Mathematics education in the United States: Past to present. *Journal of Learning Disabilities, 37*(1), 16–31. doi:10.1177/00222194040370010301 PMID:15493464

Woodward, J. (2006). Developing automaticity in multiplication facts: Integrating strategy instruction with timed practice drills. *Learning Disability Quarterly, 29*(4), 269–289. doi:10.2307/30035554

Wyndhamm, J., & Saljo, R. (1997). Word problems and mathematical reasoning- A study of childrens mastery of reference and meaning in textual realities. *Learning and Instruction, 7*(4), 361–382. doi:10.1016/S0959-4752(97)00009-1

This research was previously published in the Handbook of Research on Classroom Diversity and Inclusive Education Practice edited by Christina M. Curran and Amy J. Petersen; pages 250-281, copyright year 2017 by Information Science Reference (an imprint of IGI Global).

Chapter 14
Inclusion of Users with Special Needs in the Human-Centered Design of a Web-Portal

Renate Motschnig
University of Vienna, Austria

Dominik Hagelkruys
University of Vienna, Austria

ABSTRACT

Human-Centered Design focuses on the analysis, specification and involvement of a product's end users as driving elements in the design process. The primary research objective of the case-study presented in this paper is to illustrate that it is essential to include users with special needs into all major steps of designing a web-portal that provides services to these special users. But how can this be accomplished in the case of users with special cognitive and affective needs? Would the "classical" Human-Centered Design Process (HCD) be sufficient or would it need to be adapted and complemented with special procedures and tools? In this paper the design team shares the strategies they adopted and the experiences they gained by including users with dyslexia in the design of the LITERACY Web-Portal. Besides providing insight into the special effort and steps needed to adapt HCD for users with special needs, the paper encourages application designers to include end-users even though - or particularly because - they have needs that are special and critical for the adoption of the product.

INTRODUCTION

This paper discusses the process of designing a web-portal-interface that suits the needs of a special needs user group. It describes the strategies applied and experiences gathered while designing a specialized interface for users with dyslexia by applying and adapting the Human Centered Design (HCD) process. That process served as a guideline throughout the entire development phase of the "LITERACY-web-portal". In particular, the target group – dyslexic users – was included starting with the very early phases

DOI: 10.4018/978-1-7998-1213-5.ch014

and continuing until project completion. This approach was chosen because the project team wanted to confirm their hypothesis that end-user inclusion is a critical success factor for any software, especially for a special needs user-group. In fact, the acceptance of any software-tool hinges on the degree to which it manages to meet the (special) needs of the primary target groups (Nielsen, 1993). Since the Human Centered Design process (ISO 9241-210:2010) emphasizes end-user inclusion, it provides an optimal resource and starting point for the goals the LITERACY-portal-design project aimed to achieve.

Before it was possible to actively and directly include any users, it was necessary to apply the initial steps of the Human Centered Design process. The first step was to analyze the future user population by studying articles, looking at existing web-applications targeted at them, and personally talking to people with dyslexia. Based on the information gathered, potential tasks that would be performed on the Literacy Portal, were extracted and described. To achieve this, three core elements of the HCD process were employed: personas, context analysis, and task analysis.

Regarding the strategy, people with dyslexia were contacted and included as soon as possible in order to get a feeling not only for their special needs but also for their special strengths. Initial contact with persons with dyslexia followed extensive literature research and preparation of key questions, so as to have knowledgeable partners in the dialogue, to be as open as possible to learn from their life stories and experiences. Following this mindset, the design team considered it most helpful to engage in semi-structured interviews with dyslexic persons in various stages of life, and to gradually focus on some of their core issues that crystallized from the interviews such as finding work, using the internet, interacting in/with educational institutions, etc. Also, very early in the process dyslexic persons were asked about their preferences for screen designs and what terms they found relevant or interesting to look for on the LITERACY portal.

Regarding the experience gathered while designing the web-interface, the paper points to issues worth specific consideration in order to share the design team's experience with interested peers, and thus makes it reusable in the community of interface designers. In a nutshell, getting in contact with users with special needs may need special provisions, contacts with counseling centers, more time than talking to "ordinary" users, and an adaptation of methods and/or tools and procedures to accommodate for the particular special needs.

This paper is structured as follows: the next section discusses the background in which this research was conducted and provisions taken to maximize end-user inclusion in all aspects of the design process. Additionally, related work and studies that influenced different aspects of the research design are mentioned. The subsequent section describes applied design strategies and how people with dyslexia were included into the design-process through individual direct and indirect means of end-user inclusion during the early stages of the Human Centered Design process. The particular experiences gathered through inclusion of dyslexic users are highlighted throughout this section. The final sections summarize the work and experiences so far and give an outlook on further work. The contribution we make is a confirmation that the inclusion of end users in early stages of web-design is essential and that it should be done regardless of whether end-users have special needs or not. Furthermore, the paper illustrates some concrete techniques and steps to include end-users with dyslexia and thus can serve as an example or inspiration on how to accomplish and exploit end-user inclusion for increased usability of a web-portal.

Background and Related Work

As the British Dyslexia Association defined (BDA, 2013), "dyslexia is a specific learning difficulty that mainly affects the development of literacy and language related skills. It is likely to be present at birth and to be life-long in its effects. It is characterized by difficulties with phonological processing, rapid naming, working memory, processing speed, and the automatic development of skills that may not match up to an individual's other cognitive abilities." It often comes with other difficulties such as dyscalculia – numerical and math problems, dysgraphia and dysortographia – cognitive and motor writing difficulties, dyspraxia – coordination problems, and also attention deficit hyperactivity disorder (ADHD). These tend to be resistant to conventional teaching methods, but their effect can be mitigated by appropriately specific intervention, including the application of information technology and supportive counseling. Due to differences in languages and approaches of local bodies to defining and assessing dyslexia, it is hard to specify the prevalence of dyslexia in the population. Experts suggest 10% and more, which would make more than 70 million people - in Europe alone.

Human Centered Design (HCD) is a specific design approach, which sets the focus on the users of a product. The HCD-process is standardized (ISO 9241-210, 2010) and follows the philosophy that a product can only be good if it suits the needs of the people who use it. The HCD-process is inclusive and iterative and therefore heavily relies on the inputs, comments and suggestions of target groups. Unlike the often used and easier to plan top-down (waterfall) approach to design, in which the users do not see the product before it is in an advanced stage, Human Centered Design already includes target groups in the early stages of the development. This early and constant inclusion makes it possible to take the requirements and needs of the users into account, thus enabling suitable design choices.

The context in which HCD is applied is the LITERACY project, a European-wide research endeavor funded by the European Commission in the area of ICT under the FP7 program. Its aim is to create an advanced online portal, which will aid both dyslexic youths and adults. The portal is destined to provide personalized e-learning programs, useful tools and methods for helping people with dyslexia to improve their abilities in reading and writing. It will also provide entry to an accessible online community of peers. A specialized interface and Community Zone with programs and services will improve the skills of the users, drastically simplifying otherwise complicated tasks. This will be done by utilizing novel tools, which will be integrated with both existing and adapted ICT tools and hardware. Dyslexic users will be able to access this portal independently and receive real-time feedback on their progress.

The Human Centered Design process is a core element in creating this online portal, as it will allow the project team to fit the design of the portal to the specific needs of users with dyslexia.

There is a lot of quality work that influences different aspects of this article or discusses related topics. Certainly, a source of information that was used throughout various design steps was the book "Interaction Design: Beyond Human-Computer Interaction" (Rogers, 2011). It offers a broad variety of topics that not only focus on design aspects but also describes interaction processes or cognitive aspects. It served as a handy grounding while setting up testing sessions for the special target groups. Another work that provided great insights and helpful tips on how to assess users with special needs is the book "Assessing Learners with Special Needs: An Applied Approach" (Overton, 2012). The information provided by Overton helped with setting up tests and interpret their outcomes.

Another useful source is Harold Thimbleby's article "Understanding User-Centred Design (UCD) for People with Special Needs" (Thimbleby, 2008), which offers valuable insights into the complex topic of Human-Centered Design in a special needs context. It served as an initial stepping stone during the preparatory research phase.

Furthermore, there are various works that describe projects or relevant topics, like interface design for people with dyslexia or special needs in general. Notably there is the article "Web Accessibility: Designing for dyslexia" (Bell, 2009), which focuses on web-accessibility and interface design for people with dyslexia. Additionally, there is the article "Multimedia Software Interface Design for Special-Needs Users" (Lányi, 2009), focusing on interface design for people with special needs in a more general way. The paper "Designing with users, how?" investigates user involvement tactics for effective inclusive design processes (Lee, 2008) and describes the inclusive design processes on a general level. These papers and articles, among others, were a great source for designing the web-portal, as they provided insights and valuable tips.

Lastly there exists also a lot of material generated by other special needs projects. The information found while studying these other projects helped in estimating the work necessary and to identify potential problems. Notable examples are: "A mobile application concept to encourage independent mobility for blind and visually impaired students" (Liimatainen, 2012), "Under Watch and Ward at Night: Design and Evaluation of a Remote Monitoring System for Dementia Care" (Schikhof, 2008) and the AGID-Project (http://agid-project.eu/), which creates web-based training for professionals on the topics of ageing and intellectual disability by using a person-centered approach.

DESIGN STRATEGIES AND INCLUSION OF USERS

Strategies in the Design of the Literacy Portal

In order to create a successful online portal that suits the needs of its future users, specific methods and strategies that support the projects goals as well as the individual requirements of the target groups were chosen.

First of all the Human Centered Design approach, which heavily includes users already in the early design stages, was applied. Through this approach, it was possible to learn about the specific needs and preferences of dyslexic users and therefore eliminate potential problems in subsequent design-steps before they surfaced. This iterative process allowed the project team to step by step decrease the cognitive load and enhance the user experience.

Apart from the actual screen design of the portal it was also necessary to provide specific content for people with dyslexia. This not only includes theoretical input about dyslexia but also different ways to increase social inclusion of dyslexic youth and adults in the real world as well as in the virtual world. To achieve this goal the usage of a variety of means, like tips, life stories, e-learning, training and ways for community building, were proposed. These means will help people with dyslexia deal with problematic everyday situations, encourage them to work on their weaknesses, self-empower them and give them the possibility to get in contact with other people with dyslexia.

Additionally, to Human Centered Design the project-team also aimed at implementing a strength-based approach. This meant to not only tell users where they were weak and what they needed to improve, but also to seek to emphasize their strengths and encourage them to use them.

This strength-based approach is transported through Person-Centered Communication (Motschnig, 2014) and appreciative inquiry (Barret, 2005) in all contacts and dialogues. This means that all communication between the portal and the users is done in a way that fits the needs of the target groups, makes navigation as easy as possible, reduces the cognitive load and leaves them with a feeling of appreciation and motivation. The goal was to facilitate transparency and personalization as well as making the users feel respected through inclusion and participation. Including users into the design of the online portal according to the HCD process as achieved through different ways and techniques, can be roughly classified into indirect and direct methods.

Indirect Inclusion

Indirect methods include a series of different steps in the design process. Firstly, the topic of dyslexia and users with special cognitive and affective needs was researched online as well as in specialist literature and relevant studies, which provided initial ideas and guidelines for the design. The bandwidth of sources and literature collected through this process is quite broad and extensive. It ranges from specialist websites, like the website of the British Dyslexia Association, over national organizations, to papers and articles, like for example "What we know about dyslexia and Web Accessibility: A research review" (McCarth, 2009) to relevant expert literature like "Interacton Design: Beyond Human-Computer Interaction" (Rogers, 2011). Parts of it can be found as sources of this article and in the "additional reading" section. The life stories of dyslexics found in the process of research provided a lot of insight and proved to be valuable in later tasks of the HCD, i.e. task analysis. Based on this research specific accessibility and design criteria were created to guide further steps in the design of the online portal. Additionally, there were also the initial steps of the Human Centered Design process: Personas, Task analysis and Context analysis.

Personas are a commonly used technique in Human Centered Design. They are fictional characters that represent real users during the design process. Their description is based on important user-groups and their specific characteristics, motivation and expectations. Personas were already used in many IT-projects and various adaptations for special needs applications and revisions of the concept itself were proposed, such as in the paper "Revisiting Personas: The Making-of for Special User Groups" (Moser, 2012), which describes a decision diagram for the creation of Personas for elderly and children. For our purposes a similar approach that influenced our data collection process was used. In order to create Personas information was gathered through online resources and literature as well as interviews with dyslexics and experts. In the end ten different personas, which cover a wide range of users and include different types like students, parents or professionals, were identified. Based on these personas real life test users were contacted and selected, as we wanted to get people involved into the design process of the portal.

The Task analysis makes it possible to describe different use cases for users from their specific point of view. This is beneficial for the design process, because they describe what the users want to do and how the portal has to be designed to make it possible. By identifying major tasks that will potentially be done on the portal, a better understanding of how the interface should look and how it should respond, is generated. The collected tasks were stored in a database, in which they were organized in different categories and subcategories. Every task consisted of a short description, an example, parameters for frequency and priority, ideas for implementations and comments from different reviewers. Furthermore, every task is linked to one or several different personas. This provides a map of connections between different user groups and also helps identifying important design-goals.

The Context analysis represents a mixture of indirect and direct inclusion, as it is partly based on feedback from potential users and experts as well as research and the intended functionality of the portal. It showed that the Literacy Portal will be used in different environments and that the current state of mind of a user will have a huge impact on the reception of the information. Three important contexts were identified: assessment, everyday life and work. Each of these three contexts describes different usage conditions, which heavily affect the users in various ways and therefore result in shifting levels of cognitive load. The results of this analysis provided valuable information that was considered when designing the portal. These initial steps made it possible to outline target groups, set the main focus and identify potential problem areas.

Direct Inclusion

After acquiring knowledge about people with dyslexia and their challenges from indirect sources, further steps were taken to include them in more direct ways. The next steps of the human-centered design process chosen were interviews with dyslexics with the goal of selecting a screen design and conducting card-sorting. All of these activities were done with help of experts from the Psychological and Pedagogical Counseling Center in Brno. The Counseling Center shortlisted a number of their current and past clients, then contacted them via email, personally or even through television and 30 out of 40 invited responded positively. After a small workshop in Brno, that set a common vision for the direct inclusion, the Center also carried out interviews and participated in the analysis of the results. The help of psychologists and special pedagogues was essential for reaching people with dyslexia, mainly because dyslexia is a sensitive matter, often concealed and not admitted. The experts proved to be vital in selecting individuals who were open to sharing, which is described in the following sub-sections.

Interviews and Their Evolution

The first mode of the end user inclusion was dialogue in the form of an interview. The strategy was to apply appreciative inquiry: try to find the strengths of an interviewee, look for the conditions in which the strengths express themselves and try to replicate or create these conditions. Adoption of the Person-Centered Approach (Rogers, 1991; Motschnig, 2011) including active listening (Rogers, 1957), resulted in the creation of an atmosphere that was non-judgmental, empathic and open. Open also to the actual experience from the dialogue, so that the findings from the preparatory research were not held for rigid and directive constructs.

The interview process started with one prototypical unstructured interview with N., a manager of technical support, formerly a teacher of informatics for pupils with special needs. Through this initial interview a lot of information about strength, motivation, struggles, challenges and self-perception was derived, which helped to further structure and plan subsequent interviews. Based on this experience, a guide to conduct interviews with dyslexic users was generated and reviewed by an expert from the field of special pedagogy. This enabled scaling to a bigger number of interviews at the same time and supported data consistency. The guide summed up the strategy for interviewing, which consisted mainly of a non-judgmental approach, active listening and non-directive questioning. Furthermore, it gave an outline of topics (school life, work life, internet usage, hobbies) and examples of questions. Among the outcomes of the interviews was a collection of problems that adults with dyslexia encounter in their daily lives. They were related mainly to text in any form and medium. The top 12 problems as identified and reported by adults with dyslexia were that they:

- Read slowly;
- Have difficulties reading small letters;
- Get lost in text;
- Do not understand what they read or have to focus too hard to understand;
- Have problems moving to the next line;
- Do not see numbers or other data in text;
- Are unable to identify keywords in text thus evaluate it differently;
- Detest the amount of text they have to read in their job;
- Cannot focus deliberately;
- Miss important information in emails;
- Cannot write grammatically correct emails, yet these are requested by their employers;
- Form sentences differently – these make sense to them, not to others.

An example of an issue people with dyslexia could face at their workplace was explained by one of the interviewees, who used to work at a logistic firm. He described a problem concerning misidentifying numbers in emails: "I sent a lorry to load the goods at a wrong hour. It could be forgiven once, but it kept happening. My boss had to let me go. I never told anyone about my dyslexia because I was afraid I would lose my job."

Moreover, a majority of the respondents use the internet on a daily basis because they need it either for work or study. They prefer sites relevant to their professions. Two thirds of the respondents use Facebook and more than a half have Google Chrome set as their default browser, the rest choosing Internet Explorer, Mozilla Firefox or Opera. Sitemap were identified as helpful to users with dyslexia. Electronic diaries or schedulers and Skype came up in their lists of tools they only use sporadically. Half of the respondents use office suites such as MS Office or Open Office, often criticizing the abundance of functions as unclear. Two respondents use Google Translator, 3 respondents are working with a text-to-speech tool and 2 adjust texts to their needs. Some did not know that an adjustment of a text could help them read.

The troubles that adults with dyslexia have when interacting with the internet are:

- Advertisements
- Too much text
- Low contrast
- Too many homepage sections
- Moving text
- Flashing text

Some of the respondents described screen-readers and video tutorials as life-changers and shared various tricks they developed over time. The importance of a loving and willing parent or teacher was stressed, too, and they also explained how motivation from interests and hobbies can be transferred into reading.

The experiences gathered throughout these initial interviews motivated the design-team to collect the most useful questions into a simple yes-no questionnaire, which was shared online among the project-team and continuously expanded.

Moreover, through these interviews, a specific demand required by human-centered design was achieved – The project-team stepped into the shoes of users with dyslexia and got to know and understand their perspective and struggles first-hand (Norman, 2002).

As can be seen in the evolution of the interview, the iterative nature of the Human Centered Design was integrated into the process itself, as well. This might be helpful in cases such as the LITERACY project, when the end users have distinctly different, sometimes counter-intuitive mental models. This was also presented to us by experts in special pedagogy regarding the case of website background color choice (choosing bright strong yellow over much subtler tones of yellow).

Extending Interviews by Screen Design Choice

By the time interviewing started, five initial screen designs had been proposed. Each of them showed a different menu structure and three steps of going through it (the first screen, category choice and sub-category choice). Three of them, with the buttons in a grid, are based on suggestions of a dyslexia-expert and an IT specialist, both members of the LITERACY consortium. The fourth is a more modern book-flipping menu and the last one is a common vertical expanding menu, as briefly shown in the Figure 1.

As it was difficult to get in touch with future end users and arrange meetings, it was decided to join more activities of Human Centered Design together and on each interview meeting ask the interviewees to choose the screen design that is the most suitable for them. If they picked one, 2 points were assigned to it, and if they also picked a second choice it was assigned 1 point. Thus, the design-team was able to see how to proceed with the next prototypes. The results pointed to the vertical menu, which was chosen by the majority of the respondents. However, there is a difference between the genders. Whereas female participants strongly favored the vertical expanding menu (73%), the analysis of male participants showed a more even distribution of answers (see Figure 2).

Although the vertical expanding menu is still the winner, the three button menus combined (34%) and the book-flipping menu (31%) were very close. There was also difference between generations of users. Whereas respondents over the age 20 years preferred the vertical menu, the younger ones seemed to be used to different styles of menus such as the Apple's coverflow or smartphone and tablet button menus.

Figure 1. The five different screen designs, each showing the menu with main categories

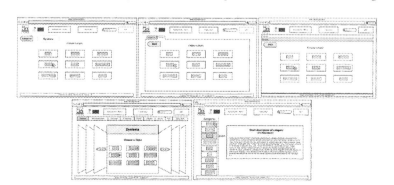

Figure 2. Overall screen design choice and gender preferences

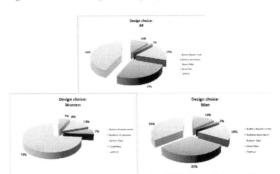

Extending Interviews by Card Sorting

The next step in the design process of the LITERACY portal, also executed at the interview meetings described in previous sub-sections, was card-sorting. It is a simple activity which yields complex results. A broad offer of content and functionality of the LITERACY-portal was assembled by the project-team and transcribed onto 60 paper cards. The interviewees were told to go through them, ask for clarifications, create their own cards if necessary and then sort any chosen cards into their own menu structure. These results were photographed, noted in an Excel spreadsheet and analyzed by an application called xSort.

A cluster tree generated by xSort identified 8 main categories, which represent content and functionality of the web portal. The design-team also received clues about naming of the (sub)categories and learned that 60 cards is not too much to handle for people with dyslexia as was feared prior to the testing. Quite the contrary, they accepted the task with engagement and enjoyed the creative work. Similarly, to the interviews, the card-sorting process was also iteratively improved, which is the fourth main learning taken from this activity.

Card-sorting also evaluated each function or piece of content planned for the portal. The respondents were free to omit any cards they would not want on the portal. The top 20 chosen to stay were Tests (27 votes), Dyslexia, Learning methods (26), Signs of Dyslexia, Reading (25), E-learning, Contact, Games (24), Second Language, Memory, ADHD, Complex aids, Tutorial (23), Training, Forum, Theories, Learning, Study aids (22) and Tips (21 votes). Based on these choices the professional partners were informed about which specific information and function they should focus on when creating content. More details about these improvements and results of the card-sorting are published in the article "A Case Study of Applying Card-sorting as an Initial Step in the Design of the LITERACY – Portal for People with Dyslexia" (Motschnig, 2013).

Excursion to a Class with Dyslexic Students

Another important opportunity for direct inclusion was a visit to a school in Budapest organized by dyslexia experts from the Hungarian Academy of Science. A sub-group of the project team (a team of 8 people) was taken to an English class at K-12 level of about 12 pupils between 17 and 19 years of age, each having a special need. After mutual introductions, when the pupils openly shared the challenges they face, some space for questions of the design-team was reserved.

Inclusion of Users with Special Needs in the Human-Centered Design of a Web-Portal

The questions mainly focused on their internet-usage habits and brought to light that they all use Facebook and can cope with it, but with variations. Some spent 5 minutes only to check agreements with friends, reading as little as possible, some browse for 5 hours. They hardly ever use discussion boards, reading in any form consumed too much of their energy.

Interestingly, one young lady was asked how it is for her to read transport schedules and responded that it would be better if they were pink. This shows the difference of the mental models that the design-team has to bridge. Furthermore, most of the students were creative and motivated in other than textual ways and claimed that they like photography, dance, music, fine arts and sports. Just as in the case of interviews, this encounter served as a way of further understanding the daily life of people with dyslexia with focus on their internet usage.

Final Choice of Menu-Design

In the second iteration of the previously described screen design choice, the users were asked to pick either the vertical menu or the button menu which were the top two menu styles chosen in the initial interviews. As this project was focusing on a special needs user group, the design-team opted to create simple clickable prototypes for both choices, so that the tester can judge the menu style not only by its aesthetic appeal and assumptions, but also by its clarity and usability. Furthermore, the users were able to work with a prototype in their native language, as all textual contents were translated into Czech as well as Hungarian. Conducting the testing in their native languages reduced the cognitive load for the participants and allowed them to focus on the actual design and functionality. Figure 3 displays the initial screens of the English language version of each prototype.

The testing sessions were administered by professionals from the Psychological and pedagogical centre in Brno and conducted in a face-to-face setting. The choice of menu-style of each participant was finalized in a two-step process. Initially the users were presented with screenshots of both designs and they had to pick the one that was more appealing to them, while also verbally describing their thought process. Following that the participants were able to use the clickable prototypes of each design and were asked to perform simple tasks. For this process the experts who administrated the testing sessions alternated which clickable prototype was shown first for every new participant. After both menu-designs were thoroughly tested, a second choice between the two was made. Figure 4 showcases the results of this testing process.

Figure 3. Menu-design prototypes

Figure 4. Results of the menu-design testing

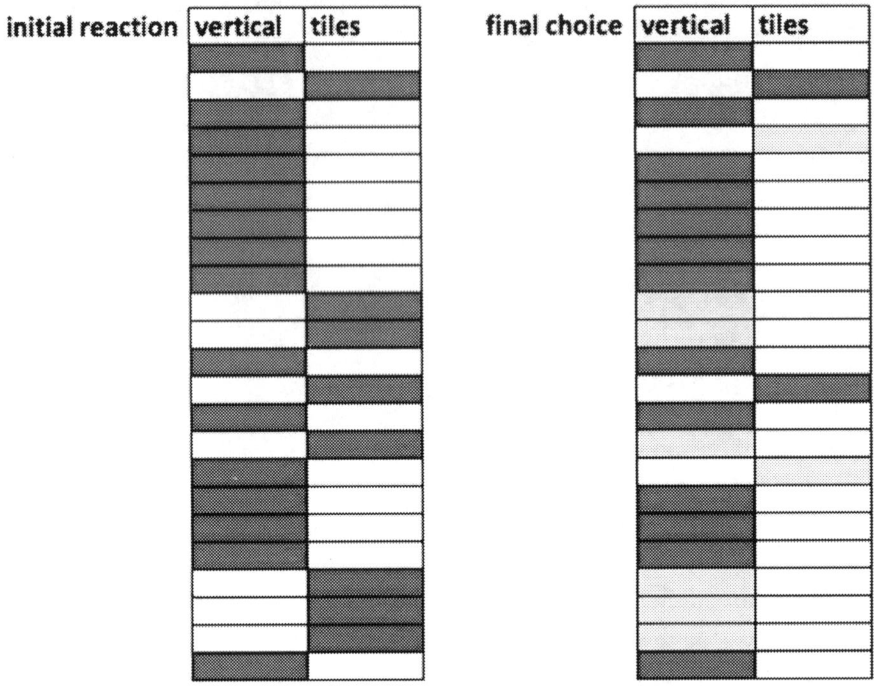

The table on the left displays the initial user preferences based on only the visual appearance of the menu-design. Green markings indicate the choice of each of the 23 participants. The table on the right shows the user preferences after they were able to test both clickable prototypes. The green markings indicate that this specific user made the same choice as before, while the yellow markings indicate that this specific user changed their opinion. The verbal feedback, opinions and information provided throughout this process was gathered as well and used to adapt future testing sessions accordingly and helped in understanding the preferences of this diverse user-group. The results showed that the users had a fairly strong preference towards the vertical menu-design, especially after performing tasks with the clickable prototype. Therefore, the project team decided to focus further implementation and design efforts into this type of menu-design.

Icon-Testing

Following the decision regarding the design of the menu, efforts were channeled to create an initial working and functional version of the portal. The design-team however refocused their efforts to improve the readability, usability and accessibility of the portals interface by reducing cognitive load and providing supportive elements. In a first and very important step, suitable icons as an important non-textual cue for the various menus and buttons had to be selected. While there were already icons used in the previous testing sessions, they were only choices made by the design-team and not by the special needs user group of the future portal. Therefore, a preliminary set of icons for each menu-item or button was established through the cooperation of the design team with specialists in usability, dyslexia and psychology. Ad-

Inclusion of Users with Special Needs in the Human-Centered Design of a Web-Portal

ditionally, an online testing session to gather feedback and preferences from users with dyslexia was set up. Figure 5 displays parts of this testing-tool in different languages.

The software was created in cooperation with dyslexia experts in order to make it as accessible and easy to use as possible. Additionally, it was translated into the native languages of the participants: Czech, Hungarian and Hebrew. In contrast to the previous testing sessions, this testing was not conducted in a face-to-face scenario but rather through a website. This allowed the project team to access a much larger pool of potential participants and also to gather all the information from the participating countries, Czech Republic, Hungary and Israel, in one centralized database. The testing was split into three steps but only took a couple of minutes to be completed. In the first screen the participants had to choose icons for the items in the vertical menu. Each item offered 4 to 6 options and the users were able to choose or change them by simply clicking on their preferred icon. This way they were able to "build" their preferred menu and also saw how the final menu-design would look. On the second screen users were provided with icon-options for the meta-menus "Settings" and "Login", which will be displayed in the top right corner of the screen. In the third and final step the participants were presented with their final menu with their chosen icons. Now they had the option to adjust the vertical as well as the meta-menu to a size they felt comfortable with. In total 128 dyslexic users from Hungary, Israel and the Czech Republic participated in this testing session. The chosen icons can be seen in Figure 6.

Figure 5. Icon-testing

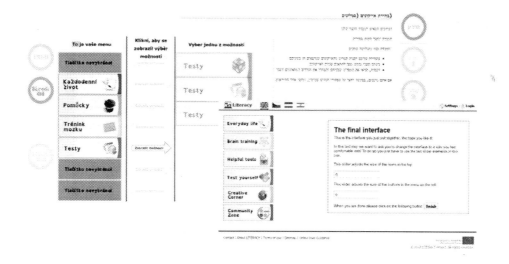

Figure 6. The LITERACY-portal

283

More information on how the icon-testing as well as the choice of menu-design influenced the overall design strategy of the web-portal can be found in the paper "Designing a web-portal supporting the social inclusion of a specific user group. A case study of the LITERACY-portal" (Hagelkruys, 2014).

Usability Testing

After defining the basic style of the menu as well as the icons to help in identifying the purpose of the specific areas of the portal, the next design-step was to test and improve the portal's navigation and usability. For this step an elaborated usability testing was set up. This testing consisted of three independent parts that every participant had to complete: a task based testing of an interactive portal prototype, filling out a specialized usability questionnaire, and participating in a group session with other testers. The combination of these three parts would allow the design team to derive a complex set of variables which in turn furthers the understanding of the specific design-needs of this diverse group of users.

The first part of this testing session was a task-based testing session, utilizing a "thinking aloud"-process, with individual users. For this purpose, an interactive prototype in English, Czech and Hungarian was created to allow for offline testing with the dyslexic users. Again, it was necessary to include experts from the fields of dyslexia, special education and psychology to set up suitable testing environments and to supervise the face-to-face testing sessions. The structure of the sessions was split into multiple parts and gave the participants the opportunity to assess the portal thoroughly. Each session started with some time for the participants to freely browse through the portal. This provided the content and design-teams with valuable information about which content initially appeals to the users. Thereafter the participants had to fulfill a list of tasks that had them navigate through different parts of the portal. Their progress, struggles and comments were noted by the supervisors and translated to be assessed by the design-team. In the last part of the testing-session the participants and the supervisor had a concluding talk about their experiences and feelings about working with the portal.

In the second part of the usability testing the participants had to fill out a usability questionnaire. Although there already exist a number of usability questionnaires, the process of choosing the right one, considering the purpose of the testing and the preconditions of the participants, proved to be difficult. A number of questionnaires, like for example "AttrakDiff" (User Interface Design GmbH, 2014), "System Usability Scale" (Brooke, 2004), "Computer System Usability Questionnaire" (Lewis, 1995), "ISONORM 9241-110" (Prümper), and "ISOMETRICS" (Gediga & Hamborg, 1999), were considered, but ultimately the project team decided that none of them were applicable with dyslexic users. Therefore, two suitable questionnaires based on the "ISONORM 9241-110"- and "System Usability Scale"-questionnaires were produced through collaboration of the design team with experts from the fields of usability, dyslexia, special education and psychology. These two questionnaires were translated into all portal languages and a specialized interface, again through consultation of experts from different fields, for online use was created. Creating these specialized questionnaires and a suitable web-interface to host them allowed the design-team to keep the cognitive strains on the participants low enough to let them fill out the questionnaires right after the task-based testing sessions. This also had the additional benefit for the dyslexic test-users of still having access to the supervisors, in case they needed any support.

The third and last part of this comprehensive usability testing was a group session which took place sometime after the first two parts. For this session, the participants of the first two parts were brought together to discuss their thoughts, results, struggles and ideas. The process was guided, supervised and journalized by experts in dyslexia, who tried to create a welcoming and open environment for the participants. Each of the three participating countries, Czech Republic, Hungary and Israel, conducted a separate group session with their respective testers.

Through the comprehensive feedback and information gathered in the usability testing the design team was able to identify problems and gained valuable insights for potential solutions. Furthermore, the results also showed that the majority of participants found the portal to be easy to use and that it does not require a lot or previous knowledge to operate and navigate, which was a main goal when designing the portal-interface. More detailed results and information about creating the questionnaires and specialized software tools for the usability testing can be found in the paper "Human-Centered Design in Action: Designing and Performing Testing Sessions with Users with Special needs" (Hagelkruys, 2015).

Dyslexia Contest

In an effort to include the targeted dyslexic user group not only into the design of the interface and navigation elements, a contest was created, which allowed the participants to actively get involved with the portal and help provide content that is helpful for people with dyslexia. The contest used the first running version of the portal and took advantage of one of the strengths of people with dyslexia – their creativity. Three similar but independent contests, which were open for single participants and groups, like for example school classes, were started in Austria, Hungary and the Czech Republic. The task for all participants was simple: "How do you use the LITERACY-Portal?". The participants created a variety of creative, fun and interesting contest-submissions that not only further opened the projects teams' eyes to the unique views and experiences of dyslexics, but also showcased examples of integration of dyslexics into a community through collectively participating in the Dyslexia contest. Detailed information about the contests in general as well as outcomes of the Austrian Dyslexia contest can be found in the paper "Can an Online Contest help to Build Awareness and Activate Users with Special Needs? The Case of the LITERACY-Contest" (Böhm, 2015).

Solutions and Recommendations

So far, carrying out the preparatory research, applying methods of direct user-inclusion proposed by the Human Centered Design process and creating national contests for the targeted user group, has lead to four main results.

First of all, a deeper level of understanding of people with dyslexia and their specific needs was reached. It became apparent how differently this user-group thinks, how this difference intertwines with their school-, work- and personal life and how they use the internet. For example, inquiries into internet usage helped to reveal that people with dyslexia mind long texts, prefer sans-serif fonts, and require consistency throughout a website. Implementing assistance for screen-reading is necessary and supportive tools and guides to using them are also welcome. Moreover, due to the variability of thinking styles and of manifestations of dyslexia, a high degree of personalization for a portal such as LITERACY seems to be critical. These and other findings not only support the design work and enforce a different style of thinking, but also showcase the potential that is in people with dyslexia. The design-team felt motivated to help users with dyslexia to develop their potential and to help them in maintaining a positive outlook on life. Therefore, the project team considers direct inclusion an essential part in meeting these goals.

Secondly, specific ideas were collected that were implemented in subsequent phases of the design process of the LITERACY Portal. Together with possible future users, the vertical expanding menu was chosen as the most suitable menu style and the users also reorganized the content, which will be provided on the portal, into 8 main categories. Furthermore, the dyslexic users provided some tips in naming the (sub)categories, such as turning "Assistive technology" into "Helpful tools".

Thirdly, an understanding of how the procedures of the HCD process can be applied in the case of users with special needs was formed. Interviews evolved and a successful guide was created. The design-team discovered that 60 cards in a card-sorting procedure was an appropriate number and it was not necessary to develop a lighter version with fewer cards. With the willingness and cooperativeness of the dyslexic interviewees on one hand and the appreciative and person-centered approach on the other, these procedures went smoothly and all combined into one session took up to 2 hours per person (plus more time for preparation and then processing and analysis). However, some flexibility should be built-in each plan, whereas people with dyslexia vary in their thinking and approach the questions and tasks they are given, creatively. For example, the interview guide focused on strategy of asking and suggests some topics, rather than providing a rigid structure of questions. Furthermore, it quickly became apparent, that it was crucial to include experts from various fields of expertise, like dyslexia, psychology or special education. These experts were needed to consult on creating suitable testing environments, including software artifacts, establish contact with test-users and help conducting testing sessions as supervisors. Additionally, these experts proved invaluable in assessing and analyzing results and putting them into the right perspective to find suitable solutions that help this individualistic and inhomogeneous user-group.

The final outcome of this phase of HCD in the LITERACY project is that the project-team has started to build a relationship between the future users and the LITERACY Portal. Including end-users and letting them experience first-hand that the design-team listens to their feedback and undertakes serious effort to consider their ideas and to implement as many of them as possible, is likely to have two major effects: It will increase the probability of the adoption of the final product and its world-wide dissemination to people with dyslexia. In this context, there is evidence that users from Europe, Israel, the U.S. and Mexico visited the portal in the final phase of the project. Moreover, the project's method of user inclusion will have made a positive difference to the self-image of those special needs users who cooperated with the design team because finally there was somebody who met them at eye-level and it was they themselves who were considered the experts on their condition and needs.

FUTURE RESEARCH DIRECTIONS

One of the outcomes of the LITERACY Project aims to be a "person-centered" portal, or, in other words, an online portal designed with a focus on empathic understanding and acceptance of its end-user. Further research should specify a person-centered portal in more detail, inquire how the person-centered approach overlaps with human-centered design, how does the final product of such a design process function and whether it promotes authenticity, inclusion and the affective needs of its user.

Also, preparation of the LITERACY Portal's piloting in four different languages and two alphabets inspires us to delve deeper into the language-specific strengths and weaknesses of ICT usage in the case of people with dyslexia. Extension of the portal to include both Spanish and German calls for more comprehensive research in this envisioned direction, too.

CONCLUSION

This chapter illustrated various design decisions, techniques and steps of including dyslexic youth and adults in the early design stages of the LITERACY Portal, an interactive web-application that is intended to support the social inclusion of users who are struggling readers. Basically, two forms of end-user inclusion were needed, an indirect one in which the design team studied the special cognitive and affective habits of dyslexic users from literature, web-resources and by talking to experts from pedagogy and psychology; and a direct one in which users were asked about key aspects of the Portal. The latter employed procedures such as semi-structured interviews, hands-on testing, card-sorting and questionnaires. The results and sample data gathered through these various means not only helped in achieving a better understanding of how an optimal interface for this specific user group should look, but also how testing sessions have to be adapted to generate the best results. The findings of each individual design-step influenced subsequent ones and therefore helped create more suitable test scenarios as well as estimate the limits of cognitive capabilities more closely or incorporate the creative tendencies of dyslexic users, which heavily influenced design decisions, into testing sessions. These gradual improvements were only possible thanks to the help of experts in various fields of expertise within the LITERACY-Consortium. Future design-steps will focus on direct inclusion in the form of testing-sessions regarding usability and satisfaction of users.

So far, the project-team has:

- Deepened its understanding of a person with dyslexia;
- Identified the most recurring difficulties people with dyslexia encounter online and collected ideas for phases of the interface-design;
- Learned about dyslexia-specific aspects of human centered design procedures; and
- Built relationships with future users of the LITERACY-portal.

In this way, the portal has a higher chance of being accepted by its users, in promoting inclusion of people with dyslexia and other reading difficulties and providing insights into human centered design and person-centered communication with people with special cognitive and affective needs.

ACKNOWLEDGMENT

This work was supported by the European Commission (Grant agreement no: 288596). The authors thank their consortium partners, in particular Vera Vojtova, Maud Kotasová, Éva Gyarmathy, Tsipi Egozi, Ofra Razel, Břetislav Beránek, Jakub Hrabec, Jakub Marecek, Ján Struhár and Kamila Balharová for their collaboration without which this paper could not have been written. Special thanks are due to the University of Vienna's Centre for Education for ongoing support in the context of the dissemination and extension of the LITERACY Portal with special focus on higher and K5-K12 education.

REFERENCES

Balharová, K., Motschnig, R., Struhár, J., & Hagelkruys, D. (2013). A Case Study of Applying Card-sorting as an Initial Step in the Design of the LITERACY – Portal for People with Dyslexia. In *Proceedings of the Conference Universal Learning Design*, Brno, Masaryk University (pp. 143–157).

Barret, F. J., & Fry, R. E. (2005). *Appreciative inquiry: a positive approach to building cooperative capacity*. Ohio: Chagrin Falls.

Bell, L. (2009). Web Accessibility: Designing for Dyslexia. Retrieved October 15, 2013 from http://lindseybell.com/documents/bell_dyslexia.pdf

Böhm, C., Hagelkruys, D., & Motschnig, R. (2015). Can an Online Contest help to Build Awareness and Activate Users with Special Needs? The Case of the LITERACY-Contest. In *Proceedings of World Conference on Educational Media and Technology 2015* (pp. 105-113). Association for the Advancement of Computing in Education (AACE).

British Dyslexia Association. (2007). Dyslexia Research Information. Retrieved October 15, 2013, from http://www.bdadyslexia.org.uk/about-dyslexia/further-information/dyslexia-research-information-.html

Brooke, J. (2004). SUS - A quick and dirty usability scale. *Usabilitynet.org*. Retrieved December 5. 2014, from http://www.usabilitynet.org/trump/documents/suschapt.doc

Gediga, G., & Hamborg, K.-C. (1999). IsoMetrics: An usability inventory supporting summative and formative evaluation of software systems. In H.-J- Bullinger & J. Ziegler (Eds.), *Human-Computer Interaction: Ergonomics and User Interfaces, Proceedings of HCI International '99*. New Jersey: Lawrence Erlbaum Associates.

Hagelkruys, D., & Motschnig, R. (2014). Designing a web-portal supporting the social inclusion of a specific user group. A case study of the LITERACY-portal. In *Proceedings of World Conference on Educational Multimedia, Hypermedia and Telecommunications 2014* (pp. 267-277). Chesapeake, VA: Association for the Advancement of Computing in Education (AACE).

Hagelkruys, D., Motschnig, R., Böhm, C., Vojtova, V., Kotasová, M., & Jurkova, K. (2015). Human-Centered Design in Action: Designing and Performing Testing Sessions with Users with Special needs. In *Proceedings of World Conference on Educational Media and Technology 2015* (pp. 446-455). Association for the Advancement of Computing in Education (AACE).

ISO 9241. (2010). Ergonomics of human-system interaction – Part 210: Human-centered design for interactive systems.

Lányi, C. S. (2009). Multimedia Software Interface Design for Special-Needs Users. In M. Khosrow-Pour (Ed.), *Encyclopedia of Information Science and Technology* (2nd ed., pp. 2761–2766). doi:10.4018/978-1-60566-026-4.ch440

Lee, Y. (2008). Designing with users, how? In *Investigate user's involvement tactics for effective inclusive design processes. Design Thinking: New Challenges for Designers, Managers and Organizations*. France: Cergy-Pointoise.

Lewis, J. (1995). IBM computer usability satisfaction questionnaires: Psychometric evaluation and instructions for use. *International Journal of Human-Computer Interaction, 7*(1), 57–78. doi:10.1080/10447319509526110

Liimatainen, J., Häkkinen, M., Nousiainen, T., Kankaanranta, M., & Neittaanmäki, P. (2012). A mobile application concept to encourage independent mobility for blind and visually impaired students. In *ICCHP'12 Proceedings of the 13th international conference on Computers Helping People with Special Needs* (Vol. 2, pp. 552-559). Berlin/Heidelberg: Springer Verlag. 10.1007/978-3-642-31534-3_81

McCarthy, J., & Swierenga, S. (2010). What we know about dyslexia and Web accessibility: A research review. *Universal Access in the Information Society, 9*(2), 147–152. doi:10.100710209-009-0160-5

Moser, C., Fuchsberger, V., Neureiter, L., Sellner, W., & Tscheligi, M. (2012, May 5-10). Revisiting personas: the making-of for special user groups. In CHI '12 Extended Abstracts on Human Factors in Computing Systems, Austin, Texas, USA.

Motschnig, R., & Nykl, L. (2011). *Komunikace zaměřená na člověka: rozumět sobě i druhým*. Prague: Grada.

Motschnig, R., & Nykl, L. (2014). *Person-centred Communication Theory, Skills and Practice*. Maidenhead, Berkshire: McGraw Hill.

Nielsen, J. (1993). *Usability Engineering*. Boston: Academic Press.

Norman, D. A. (2002). *The design of everyday things*. New York: Basic Books.

Overton, T. (2012). *Assessing Learners with Special Needs. An applied approach*. Boston: Pearson Education.

Prümper, J. (n. d.). Fragebogen ISONORM 9241/110-S. Beurteilung von Software auf Grundlage der Internationalen Ergonomie-Norm DIN EN ISO 9241-110. Retrieved December 5. 2014, from http://www.seikumu.de/de/dok/

Rogers, C. R., & Farson, R. E. (1987). Active Listening. In R. G. Newman, M. A. Danziger, & M. Cohen (Eds.), Communication in Business Today. Washington D.C: Heath and Company.

Rogers, C. R., & Roethlisberger, F. J. (1991). Barriers and Gateways to Communication. *Harvard Business Review*.

Rogers, Y., Sharp, H., & Preece, J. (2011). *Interaction Design: beyond human-computer interaction*. New York: Wiley.

Schikhof, Y., & Mulder, I. (2008). Under Watch and Ward at Night: Design and Evaluation of a Remote Monitoring System for Dementia Care. In *USAB '08 Proceedings of the 4th Symposium of the Workgroup Human-Computer Interaction and Usability Engineering* (pp. 475–486). Austrian Computer Society on HCI and Usability for Education and Work. Berlin/Heidelberg: Springer Verlag.

Thimbleby, H. W. (2008). Understanding User Centred Design (UCD) for People with Special Needs. In K. Miesenberger, J. Klaus, W. L. Zagler, & A. I. Karshmer (Eds.), *ICCHP* (pp. 1–17). Berlin, Heidelberg: Springer Verlag. doi:10.1007/978-3-540-70540-6_1

User Interface Design GmbH (2014). AttrakDiff. Retrieved December 5. 2014, from http://attrakdiff.de/

ADDITIONAL READING

Edmondson, W. H. (2001). *A Taxonomical Approach to Special Needs Design in HCI* (pp. 909–913). New Orleans, USA: Universal Access in Human-Computer Interaction.

Goldsmith, S. (2007). *Universal Design*. Great Britain: Taylor & Francis.

Spencer, D. (2009). *Card Sorting: Designing Usable Categories*. Brooklyn, New York, USA: Rosenfeld Media.

KEY TERMS AND DEFINITIONS

Accessibility: Accessibility describes the extent to which persons with special needs or people who use assistive technologies can use a product, like for example software.

Card Sorting: Card sorting is an interactive activity in which the participants choose cards from a set number of options with a specific goal in mind, like for example elements of a menu.

Dyslexia: Dyslexia can be characterized as a learning deficiency, which expresses itself in form of reading and writing difficulties.

Human-Centered-Design: Human-Centered-Design (HCD) is an iterative design approach that puts the focus on the users. A central part of HCD is the constant inclusion of end-users into the different steps of the design process.

IT for Inclusion: IT for inclusion means the use of information technologies to support the social inclusion of specific user groups, such as users with special needs.

Personas: Personas are fictional characters that represent a certain user group. They comprise certain characteristics that are representative for this user group.

Screen Design: Screen design includes all visual elements of an interface, including positioning of objects, color-schemes, fonts, styles, etc.

Social Inclusion: Social inclusion depicts a form of inclusion that helps people to take part in social activities, like for example social media or different forms of communication.

Task Analysis: Task analysis depicts the process of assessing and describing potential tasks that users need, have or want to perform with the product.

Usability: Usability describes the extent to which a product, like for example software, can be used to achieve specific goals in an effective, efficient, engaging, error tolerant and easy to learn way.

User Analysis: User analysis is the process of assessing users of a product regarding a variety of different aspects, e.g. age, knowledge of the product, skill-level, etc.

This research was previously published in the International Journal of People-Oriented Programming (IJPOP), 6(1); edited by Steve Goschnick; pages 1-18, copyright year 2017 by IGI Publishing (an imprint of IGI Global).

Chapter 15
Providing Quality Education for Persons With Disabilities Through the Implementation of Individual Educational Programs Managed by the Intelligent Agents in the Sliding Mode

Vardan Mkrttchian
HHH University, Australia

Ekaterina Aleshina
Penza State University, Russia

ABSTRACT

Professional education of persons with disabilities is an important sphere of education enabling psychically and physiologically impaired persons to get economic independence contributing to their integration in society. The quality of professional education for persons with disabilities is realized only in conditions considering specifics of communicative and cognitive activity of the students with different disability categories. The absence of these conditions in universities makes it impossible for this category of students to complete the programs of higher education. As a rule, the contents of the study programs and the study schedule do not take this category of students into consideration.

INTRODUCTION

In unequal conditions such students have weak motivation for study, insufficient level of professional skills, they develop a consumer position. Apart from this, the reasons hindering the process of learning include architectural unavailability, insufficient psychological, medical and pedagogical support of study process; uneasiness of the teaching staff for instructing persons with disabilities.

DOI: 10.4018/978-1-7998-1213-5.ch015

Therefore, in conditions of unequal starting opportunities the students of this category cannot compare their success with the rest of the class and lose the strife for life goal. There arises the contradiction between the necessity of the providing education to persons with disabilities and inadequacy of the study process organization in university.

Individual study programs are based on humanistic principles, personality- oriented, differentiating, subject approach which makes them an effective mechanism of professional education for persons with disabilities.

MAIN FOCUS IN CHAPTER

Solutions and Recommendations

We suppose that in the process of implementer individual study programs in university education will provide the following effects:

- Individual opportunities of students with disabilities will be considered;
- Study process will become personality-oriented;
- Students with disabilities will be more successful;
- The quality of education will not be evaluated in categories of formal academic success but also include achievements in development of creative potential, formation of the wide range of competences and socialization of students;
- There will be a professional dialog between the specialists realizing support of persons with disabilities and instructors working on increasing their professional competences.

In accordance with the above let us turn to the definition of the quality of education given in normative documents. The quality of education highlights the two aspects of education:

1. Correspondence of goals and results of education to the modern social demands connected with transition to the open democratic society with market economy demanding making independent decisions on the basis of social experience, living in the situation of social and labor mobility, increasing tolerance level;
2. Correspondence of conditions of educational activity to the demands of students' health preservation and maintaining psychological comfort for all participants of the study process.

Apart from that, we consider education as a common process of education and development, the quality of education – as a quality of personality, its moral and civilian development. The quality of education is viewed as a social category which defines the state and outcomes of educational process in society, its correspondence to demands and expectations of various social groups in developing civil, common and professional competences of the students.

Individual study track is defined as a projected differentiated study program making the student a subject in the situation of choosing the program, participating in its development and realization, with the instructors' support of his/ her self-realization. Individual study track is determined by educational needs, abilities and opportunities of the student with disabilities, and also existing standards of education content. Individual study track is a structured program of the student's actions at a certain stage of study.

Individual study programs in the university educational space realize educational needs and opportunities of the students with disabilities due to the functions they perform:

- Fixing students' load, defining the order of following the study schedule and helping with the choice of the study track;
- Defining the goals, values and results of the students' educational activity;
- Allowing for realization of the students' needs in self-realization on the basis of choice, etc.

Analyzing the above, the quality of professional education for persons with disabilities can be defined as a condition of organizing educational activity corresponding to the demands of the students' health preservation and maintaining the psychological comfort of all participants of the educational process; organization of the study process based on introduction of individual educational programs, definition of individual study track in accordance with individual possibilities of persons with disabilities.

It is important to find the forms of study activity which could make the student feel successful and at the same time, could create conditions for his/ her mastering the key competences.

Availability of higher professional education for persons with disabilities is maintained due to the three components: support, barrier-free environment and adaptive study process. The combination of these components enables the students with disabilities to successfully cover the educational standards and adapt themselves in society.

The indices of the high quality of professional education are:

- Availability for various categories of students;
- High demand in labor market;
- Correspondence of the education content to its goals and cognitive abilities of students with disabilities;
- Development of general cultural and professional competences of students;
- Formation of the skills necessary for acquiring knowledge in the course of life and information literacy.

Accordingly, the study process for persons with disabilities should be based on individual study programs for students with disabilities. Their use will provide for the high quality of education. Therefore, the development and construction of the individual study programs should follow the plan below:

- Defining the content of general educational programs;
- Developing and approving basis and working syllabi, and also the contents of the course programs, internships, final exams;
- Planning the contents of educational modules and academic load of the students and instructors;
- Appointing academic consultants for supporting the student with disabilities while planning and realizing the individual study track;
- Defining the methodological support of individually-oriented study process;
- Defining is the demands for material, technical and information support of the classes, etc.

Implementation of individual study programs in the process of learning for persons with disabilities should be backed up by the individual and differentiating approach. Differential of learning means considering individual and typological specificity of personality in the form of grouping the students and variability of the learning process in the groups. A differentiation of education highlights the introduction of certain changes in the course of study process for some groups of students. The term "differentiating approach" is defined as the approach to the process of learning based on differentiation in various kinds and forms.

Of special importance in the process of realization of individual educational programs is the choice of forms and methods of the study process organization. In classifying the methods of learning we followed our ideas (Mkrttchian et all, 2014; Mkrttchian, 2015) who singled out three groups of methods:

- Organizing the study activity;
- Stimulating the study activity;
- Controlling the efficiency of the study activity.

Most efficient are the methods of organizing the study activity of persons with disabilities based on the dialog communication of the students with disabilities, healthy students and the instructor with the view of mutual control, creation of situation of mutual participation, etc. Individuality of educational process is realized through various forms of working with the student: individual tasks, consultations, passing the test, organization of pair and group work, rehabilitation program, complex medical psychological and pedagogical support, etc. Implementation of individual education in quality education with both instructors and students involved should include the following stages:

- Revealing psychological and physiological specifics of the students with disabilities;
- Analyzing the results of the previous education of persons with disabilities;
- Developing methodological recommendations for education of persons with disabilities with selection of optimal instruction methods, the style of study interaction, the forms of knowledge control, etc.
- Constructing individual study programs on the basis of corrected syllabi in accordance with the needs and opportunities of the students;
- Advising the teaching staff realizing study programs on individual psycho-physical specificity of each student's development, its possibilities and limitations;
- Compiling a special schedule, individual load of the students; advising parents about their participation in the process;
- Implementing compulsory and voluntary assessment of the achievements of the persons with disabilities;
- Intermediate testing of students; searching for adequate means of control over covering the study program standards;
- Instructors' awareness of their activity being oriented to achievement of students' success, their development and socialization.
- Thus, implementation of the individual study track in the university educational process will result in the following changes:
- Increasing share of students successfully covering educational programs;

- Increasing number of psychologically protected students covering the programs according to their possibilities (extending the term of the programs, individual study schedule, etc.);
- Increasing share of successful students participating in compulsory and voluntary assessment of education quality.

CONCLUSION

Implementing individual programs in education process will result in satisfaction of education needs of students with disabilities which will allow for their passing to the new level of development, teach them to be responsible and independent in the future, to pursue their life goal.

REFERENCES

Mkrttchian, V. (2015, January-June). Use Online Multi-Cloud Platform Lab with Intellectual Agents: Avatars for Study of Knowledge Visualization & Probability Theory in Bioinformatics. *International Journal of Knowledge Discovery in Bioinformatics*, 5(1), 11–23. doi:10.4018/IJKDB.2015010102

Mkrttchian, V., Kataev, M., Shih, T., Misra, K., & Fedotova, A. (2014, July-September). Avatars HHH Technology Education Cloud Platform on Sliding Mode Based Plug- Ontology as a Gateway to Improvement of Feedback Control Online Society. *International Journal of Information Communication Technologies and Human Development*, 6(3), 13–31. doi:10.4018/ijicthd.2014070102

KEY TERMS AND DEFINITIONS

Control in E-Learning: Is the fundamental idea of control in learning is to reach the highest level of effectiveness in undertaking a task, which happens when individual's ability level is congruent with the level of challenge.

Didactic Method: Is a teaching method that follows a consistent scientific approach or educational style to engage the student's mind.

Learning Goals and Objectives: Is joint pedagogical aspects.

Online and Blended Learning of Adults: Is learners are adults, and training is carried out continuously throughout life. The purpose of adult education is closely associated with certain socio-psychological, occupational, household, personal problems, or factors or conditions with sufficiently clear ideas about further application of acquired knowledge, skills and qualities.

Studying and Training in Joint Activities: Is organizational aspects for training.

Virtual Assistant: Is special soft program creating in HHH University for training.

This research was previously published in Sliding Mode in Intellectual Control and Communication edited by Vardan Mkrttchian and Ekaterina Aleshina; pages 70-76, copyright year 2017 by Information Science Reference (an imprint of IGI Global).

Chapter 16
Digital Control Models of Continuous Education of Persons with Disabilities Act (IDEA) and Agents in Sliding Mode

Vardan Mkrttchian
HHH University, Australia

Ekaterina Aleshina
Penza State University, Russia

ABSTRACT

Currently higher professional education is defined as a sphere of nationwide strategic interests of the state whose priorities contain systemic approaches and solutions, values of world and national culture, humanist morals, civic consciousness, worldviews and methodological solutions targeted at training new generations of specialists capable of creative activity and professional responsibility. In this chapter of goals of education, processes of humanization and democratization in society have led to the extension of educational institutions' rights and the tendency to regionalization of education. Therefore, the role of educational institutions in the educational space has changed.

INTRODUCTION

We consider the problem of building up a whole educational space in the context of implementing the system of continuous professional education in an integrated educational institution. The pedagogical approaches to the realization of integration processes in the system of continuous education are based on the philosophic ideas considering the man as the highest value in society. So, the aim of societal development is a person's continues moral and spiritual, personal and professional perfection (Mkrttchian et al., 2016).

DOI: 10.4018/978-1-7998-1213-5.ch016

The defining condition of working out digital models for the system of continues professional development of persons with health limitations is based on our concept of continues professional education which is considered as an instrument of economic policy directed at increasing competitive capacity, full-time employment of the population and maintaining employees' professional mobility as connected with implementing new technologies. It is based on the following principles:

1. Basic property (basic education) realized through getting a ceratin educational start, that is basic training is regarded as a "matriculation certificate";
2. Multiple-level system presented by a number of levels and stages of education;
3. Diversification which supposes extension of the activity types of the education system as well as acquiring new forms and functions previously absent in the system;
4. Complementarity of basic and postgraduate education referring to the vector of professional skills and progression of a person in educational space – the idea is backed up by the fact that in the system of continues education a person has to continue his/ her education for life;
5. Flexibility of educational syllabi providing for a person's orientation in Educational space, professional re-orientation, for the possibility of changing activity sphere at a certain stage of life and at a certain level of education, or getting parallel education in two or more spheres;
6. Succession of educational programs necessary for a trainee, a student, a specialist to freely move in educational space;
7. Integration of educational structures viewed as integration of subsystems of education, turning of professional educational institutions into multi-specialized, multi-level, multi-stage educational institutions;
8. Flexibility of organization forms revealed through a person's free movement in educational space which ensures not only the diversity of education forms, but also their flexibility and variability.

Creating the system of quality of professional education is a very important direction of realization of models. We consider the problem of quality from three perspectives: the quality of specialists' technological training; the quality of their economic and market training; the quality of basic qualifications formed in them. From this viewpoint we state the necessity of quality education being aimed at marketing values completely different from the traditional training typical of former planned economy. With that, a graduate will possess basic qualifications including the training components off-professional or over-professional character (information technologies skills, foreign language skills, advertising marketing skills, etc.). In present-day conditions, such training is vital for a specialist in accordance with the "formula" of successful employment at the labor market: higher education (any), knowledge of a foreign language, computer skills.

MAIN FOCUS IN CHAPTER

Solutions and Recommendations

Our research has found out the following major directions of further improvement and modernization of professional education (Mkrttchian & Belyanina, 2016):

1. Realization of advanced professional education: the level of specialists' general and professional education, development of their professional qualities and personality as a whole should be ahead of development of industry and its technologies.
2. Innovative higher educational institutions integrating primary, secondary and higher professional education in one institution and legal fixation of their status. There are two possible variants of creating such integrated educational institutions:
   a. Based on a new type of college;
   b. Based on a higher education institution by means of integrating primary and secondary professional education.

The graduate of such an integrated educational institution has knowledge and skills of an integrated specialist according to the state standard is a practice-oriented specialist qualified as a worker and possessing fundamental knowledge and skills of a modern employee able to use information technologies and the knowledge of at least one foreign language on the professional basis in his/ her practical activity.

3. Personal orientation, differentiation and individualization of education backed by educational standards based on diversity and variability of educational institutions successfully implementing the above concept of continues professional education.
4. Creating information space in every educational institution and wide use of state-of-the-art pedagogical technologies in education process together with working out and accepting the corresponding standards for their realization.
5. Creating educational, study-research-industrial and sociocultural complexes, resource centers, training and consultation centers, development of distance learning, their regulation basis.
6. Introduction of subject-oriented instruction in senior grades and integration of high school into educational institutions of primary, secondary and higher professional education.

Modern system of continues professional education guarantees building up the efficient market of education services in accordance with the economy's demands for qualified staff as based on the constant monitoring of labour market. Continued education provides every person an institutional opportunity to form an individual education trajectory and get the professional training necessary for his/ her further professional, career and personal development. We are sure that researching into the ways of the system's evolution can contribute to the growth of education's adaptability to external demands including those of labor market.

Maintenance of the growing demands for constant professional development or re-training, in our view, necessitates creation of the infrastructure of the access to continues professional education during the whole of professional activity.

Defined below are the basic elements of this infrastructure:

- Programs of professional training, re-training and development based on module principles;
- Social and professional organizations whose activity is directed at formation of labor market-stated qualification demands for the specialists' level of training, search and choice of information technologies and also the evaluation (accreditation) of the syllabi quality;

- Common system of credits based on the modern information infrastructure of control, storage and accumulation of date on education and training obtained by a person in various educational organizations;
- Nationwide system of evaluating quality of education independent of organizations, aimed at providing unity of educational space through providing citizens with an opportunity of objective control of the knowledge and skills they got.

Our research has shown that formation of the efficient market of education services, ensuring competitiveness of national education and improving its quality requires reconsideration of the list of organizations entitled to providing educational services of continuous professional education. This list should include major industrial, commercial or other organizations possessing resources for realization of various educational programs in the framework of intercompany tuition. This necessitates improving the quality of state educational institutions activity which seems possible only through transition from managing educational institutions to managing educational programs. Therefore, such administrative functions as control, financing and assessment of activity quality change their nature and are realized in reference to educational programs. This requires creating crucially new mechanisms of evaluation and accreditation of educational programs which, in its turn, will require building up organization and legal conditions for development of social and professional organizations whose members will include representatives of professional associations, education community and employer associations. We have found out that the main task of such organizations is outlining the requirements for the level of necessary professional qualification, content and technologies and training, and also for the employees' competences. The above social and professional organizations are already able to ensure efficient control of the quality of educational process and adequacy of the trained staff to the dynamic perspective demands of the labor market.

The involvement of the employers into participation in the monitoring of the labor market and formation of the list of training specialties seems to be an innovative solution and greatly improves the quality of continues professional education. Creation of the common system of credits will ensure general recognition of the education outcomes, transition to managing education programs. Spreading of the module principle of building programs will guarantee an institutional opportunity for studying in various educational institutions within the framework of the same educational trajectory of a person. With that, the options of educational programs have extended, staff training have acquired a target character and have become more efficient. We propose creating an independent nationwide system for assessing quality of education which should become an inseparable part of continuos education infrastructure allowing for the unity of educational space and increase in objectivity of assessment procedures for an education level through their separation from the processes of training and preparation. This system may be supplemented by non-commercial organizations holding exams and certification of the citizens' education potential. These structures should organize exams after secondary and high school while getting to the second level of higher education.

Modern research enabled us to make a conclusion that in the process of continues professional education it is vital to reconstruct the system of primary and secondary professional education institutions. Formally various types of primary and secondary professional education institutions commonly realize a similar set of educational programs. Thus, the structure of professional education is being destroyed. Meanwhile, the loss of close ties with enterprises and organizations and aging of material and technical resources in the institutions does not let them guarantee the quality of graduates' preparation necessary for modern economy. Moreover, this system is burdened by social commitments. Institutions of this level concentrate a greater part of troubled youth, so the solution of social tasks often dominates in the process of highly-qualified staff training.

Most employers highlight the great deficiency in working staff accompanied by business expenditures caused by low-quality education.

With a view of providing modern quality staff preparation in the system of professional education we propose the following:

1. Creating conditions for productive interaction of enterprises and educational institutions to organize and manage study process based on the state-of-the-art technological base.
2. Distinguishing between the mechanisms of students' social support, providing general education and organizing professional training by working out and implementing mechanisms of separate financing of comprehensive syllabi and professional syllabi in institutions of professional education.
3. Creating organization and legal conditions for integrating educational programs of primary and secondary professional education into the system of continuous professional education together with spreading the module structure of programs for professions and specialties.

The law "On Education" describes the system of education as total of interacting successive educational programs and state education standards, as network of educational institutions realizing these programs and administrative bodies. This concept highlights not the organization and structural basis, as before in the centralized system of education, but, first of all, its content basis. Such understanding dictates the purposefulness of content and structural approach to constructing the system of continues education, supposing the priority of constructing the content of continues education over its organization forms. The concept of continues education may be referred to three objects (subjects):

- **Personality:** In this case it means that a person studies constantly either in educational institutions or in a self-instruction mode. This allows for three vectors of a person's movement in educational space. First, a person, staying at the same formal educational level, e.g. as a mechanic, a doctor or an engineer can improve his/ her qualification and professional skills. It may be conventionally called "forward movement vector". Secondly, ascending the steps and levels of professional education realizes the "vector of upward movement". With that, a person may gradually mount the levels of education or skip some of them. For example, a future student can continuously get primary, secondary and higher education or go to get higher education immediately after school. Thirdly, continues education supposes the opportunity not only of proceeding with, but also the change of the education major, presenting a possibility for an education maneuver at various levels of the lifetime according to the personality's demands, opportunities, social and economic conditions in the society. This is the "vector of horizontal movement".
- **Educational Processes (Educational Programs):** Continuity in the process of education is characterized by succession of the educational activity content in the process of transition from one kind of training to another, from one life stage to another;
- **Educational Institutions:** In this case continuity characterizes the network of educational institutions and their inter-connection creating the space of educational services able to satisfy all the variety of educational demands in the society as a whole and for every person in a certain area.

Presented below are the principles of continues education development which were separated on the basis of the dialectics category "content – form".

The content aspect, in its turn, is subdivided into two components: the "content" subsystem composition and its structural ties.

We find it important to highlight the principles of building content of continuos education corresponding to various vectors of a person's movement in the educational space:

- The principle of multi-level professional educational programs which supposes the presence of numerous levels and situations in professional education (the "upward movement vector");
- The principle of compensability of basic and postgraduate professional education (the "forward movement vector");
- The principle of study programs flexibility (the "horizontal movement vector").

Another direction of realization is considering the continuity of professional education as a system of educational processes (study programs) targeted at providing further development of the specialists according to their personal needs and social and economic demands of society.

We accept the following principles:

- The Principle of succession of educational programs which supposes their compatibility and correspondence to each other backed up by standartization of educational programs;
- The Principle of integration of professional education programs integration. Many lyceums and colleges realize study programs of primary and secondary professional education, often on 20-25 various specialties.

Thus, the integration of professional education subsystems and their organization structures seems inevitable contributing to the transformation of professional educational institutions into multi-level, multi-step and multi-multi-disciplinary institutions.

Otherwise, the possibility of the contrary process cannot be excluded. One and the same program can be realized in educational institutions of various types. This principle of organization forms flexibility ensures maximum variability of training forms.

The research has shown that the current trends in professional education include multi-disciplinarily and the structure with multiple levels. The education system comprises the following elements:

- "Multi-disciplinary" comprehensive schools are "common" schools, schools with in-depth study of certain subjects, lyceums, gymnasiums, etc. Apart from that, general education is realized according to majors in the institutions of primary and secondary professional education. A great degree of "specialization" is added to the content of secondary education by national, regional and local components;
- At least three steps in the institutions of primary professional education: training on the level of the first and second qualification labor grades; the level of primary professional education, qualification labor grades 3-4;
- The so-called "advanced level of primary professional education", qualification labor grades 4-5;
- At least two levels in institutions of secondary professional education: traditional and advanced, e.g. "technician" and "junior engineer" in technical colleges;

- In the institutions of higher professional education the system of higher education with 5 years of tuition and single qualification which was in action in previous years has been supplemented with a 4-year bachelor program and a 6-year master program;
- A 2-year educational program referring to the level of incomplete higher education has been introduced.

Compatibility of educational programs from the general education to postgraduate education is necessary for a student or a specialist to freely and confidently move in educational space through levels and steps (vertically) and stages and forms (horizontally).

Succession and compatibility mean that "coming out" from one stage of education must naturally "dock" with the "entrance" into the next stage. This necessitates transparent standardization of levels and steps of education is based on common goals of the whole system of continues education.

Multi-disciplinarily and multiple levels of educational programs are formed in institutions of general education, professional lyceums, colleges and universities. The paradox is connected with the fact that the links of education system, due to their traditional disconnection form multiple levels and multi-disciplinarily only for themselves, separately in general education, in professional education, in secondary and higher education. The institutions of postgraduate education, if any, work on their. As a result, with all the positive moments in growth of variety of educational systems and programs we face the situation of education space breakaway. Today, frequent are the cases when a student cannot be transferred from one school to another because different subjects are studied in different schools at different time even with the common state basic syllabus.

Many universities have started introducing entrance exams in the subjects not listen in the school syllabus. Additional entrance exams held by prestigious universities disorient general education schools and lead to the deformation of requirement for general education. Moreover, the results of the first university exams testify to the unsatisfactory selection of students.

The lists of specialties of training in primary, secondary and higher education do not agree with each other even in the names of professions.

So, lack of coordination in general educational programs on the all-state scale creates "educational dead ends", leads to other problems, particularly, conditions for corruption in education.

Nevertheless, succession of educational programs has begun to be formed partially, "from below" by the educational institutions themselves. Some schools, gymnasiums, professional lyceums, colleges make direct agreements with universities, create successive syllabi and programs and organize joint tuition of most capable students. There are numerous examples to this but the problem must be solved as a whole.

The above factors enabled us to make the following conclusions:

- In cultural and education environment of the state there have been formed the principles of continuous education system development;
- Partially built are multi-disciplinarily and multiple levels of educational programs, various forms of tuition are developing;
- Created is a network of educational institutions ensuring the succession of educational services.

Constructing a structural and functional model of the system of continues professional education for persons with health limitations means, firstly, creating conditions for its realization. The research on development of continues professional education and the structure of systemic theory of professional education development has revealed the main ideas of professional education evolution:

- Humanization of professional education (orientation to personality);
- Democratization of professional education (orientation to society and state);
- Advancing professional education (orientation to manufacture) is continuous professional education (orientation to system).

The data obtained from the research has allowed determining the main conditions for realization of the model of continues educations for persons with health limitations: humanization, democratization, advancement, continuity. These are the conditions necessary for the development of system of continuous professional education as a whole.

The problems of professional education humanization can be considered through humanization of education and fundamentally base, thus, necessitating the highlights on the general education component, the choice of either module or integration principle of content building, the transition to training the multi-discipline specialists, specification of basic training, strengthening the research potential and methodological preparation, socially-oriented and personalized and activity-oriented character of education and the teaching technologies used.

Consequently, the first condition for the system of the general model (set of models) of continues professional education is humanization which can be characterized as:

- Personal orientation of professional education for the persons with health limitations, the process and the result of the personality development, the means of its social and economic sustainability and social security in society;
- Modularity of professional education content;
- Strengthening the role of the independent education activity of the students with health limitations; providing freedom of choice of professional educational trajectories for students with health limitations;
- Formation of theoretical knowledge of the students with health limitations, with their practical professional demands and value orientations;
- Students' mastering the general competences for all kinds of professional activity (the skill of self-organization of study and professional activity, search for information, mastering new technologies, computer skills, foreign language knowledge, using databases, the knowledge of ecology, economics and business, financial knowledge, etc.).

The second condition for continues professional education is democratization considered as creating opportunities for each student with health limitations to realize own abilities in accordance with the demands of society and manufacture. Democratization of professional education supposes the necessity and possibility, and also means and conditions for realization of equal opportunities in getting professional education, its openness and variety of professional education institutions, cooperation of students and instructors, student self-administration, regionalization of professional education, international integration and cooperation, non-governmental forms of getting professional education with increasing authority at all levels.

Democratization supposes providing availability of professional education for all categories of youth and adults according to the principle of equal opportunities. Availability of education means a citizen's opportunity to get the quality education he/ she needs. Availability also means equality of education opportunities maintained through the following:

- Development of open distance education, extenuate, etc.
- Coordination of educational programs (the opportunities for mastering the new content, i.e. adequacy of educational standards);
- Social availability of professional education which includes both socially determined demands and traditions of education, and society's attitude to providing educational opportunities for persons with health limitations;
- Social partnership by means of attracting social professional associations to creating educational standards, organization of professional educational programs, to the assessment of professional education quality.

The advancing character of professional education can be considered as a condition for the future sustainable development of the country, its economy and social sphere and means reconsidering the content of professional education and technologies from the viewpoint of personality self-development, increase of population's education level, labor market monitoring, staff training in perspective directions, taking into account geographical location and perspective of the region's and the country's development as a whole.

Consequently, the third condition for continues professional education is the advancing continues professional education which means the following: the level of development of the system of general and professional education should be advanced and go ahead and form the level of personality development considering the advanced social order, implying forecasting, formation and advanced satisfaction of society's future needs for staff training. Advanced continues professional education is directed to the personality's self-development – self-development of intellect, will, emotions and sense motor sphere of students with health limitations.

The fourth condition is the continuity of professional education process which is understood as a possibility of the personality's multi-dimensional movement in educational space which means transition from the construction "education for lifetime" to the construction of "education through lifetime". Special interest presents vertical continuity (growth up the steps and levels of education with the change of education status). Continuity of professional education is ensured with the continuity of education content, education process, education organization, and also with flexibility of educational programs. The last condition can be realized with the module construction of proffessional education programs for their content to comply with other programs, levels and steps; creating conditions for parallel training in various educational institutions, in different programs of different levels.

For the student to freely move in educational space of continues education system, it is important to ensure agreement and compatibility of educational programs, their multi-level and successive character. Continuity in educational process becomes a characteristic of the personality's inclusion into education process at all the stages of its development. It is also linked to the succession in educational activity in transition from one its kind to another, from one life stage to another.

The fifth condition is diversification of professional education which supposes creating conditions for diversity of educational trajectories backed up by an unlimited number of educational programs considering individual characteristics and personal abilities within the framework of the new typology of professional educational institutions.

The sixth condition is the information of professional education which means development of modern information technologies and high-speed communication lines which expands the opportunities of using these technologies in professional education and research. This makes it necessary to develop territorial networks of data communication meant for maintaining educational organizations' access to Russian and international information networks, perfection of net infrastructure and information content, creating conditions for students' access to world information resources. This should result in the common information educational network in the region allowing for the use of cutting edge software for exchanging various data – from texts to video conferences, applying interactive multimedia technologies in education process. This will also make it possible to form inter-regional data of labor market, analyze perspective demands for professions and specialties.

The seventh condition is the integration of science and education:

- Working out mechanisms for formation and stimulation of solvent demand for high technologies and results of scientific research, selection and realization of most efficient achievements of science and technology on the basis of the federal contract system;
- Concentration of resources on priority directions of science and technology development; structural reconstruction of scientific research front, their priority support by the state in the spheres connected with the necessary and long-term vital interests of a person, society and state;
- Creating infrastructure providing for conducting and use of results of such research and their transformation into socially beneficial scientific and technical solutions, commercially efficient, ecologically safe and competitive technologies, commodities and services;
- Introduction of the system of effective stimuli on federal and regional levels for increasing the prestige of research, personnel retention, attraction of the young specialists to scientific, technical and innovative spheres; formation of necessary organization, economic, legal, information and other kinds of research activity of various centers and institutions with the view of approaching sustainable development of society.

The integration of science and education allows for development of scientific background of education system, to strengthen the potential of university research, to solve the tasks of staff training for innovative activity.

Working out the model of continues professional education necessitates analyzing problems in the sphere of continues education. The analysis of official statistics and the data of the questionnaires for enterprise management in the real economy sector made it possible to single out the trouble issues in education sphere negatively affecting further development of economy and business:

- Reduction of labor resource's growth resulting from the negative demographic situation in the period till 2015 (twice approximately);
- Difficulties in supplying real manufacture with qualified workers and specialists due to their deficiency in the labor market;
- Noncompliance of professional training of workers and specialists with the labor market demands;
- Absence of common strategy in staff training and realization of continuos education;
- Absence of the common system of certification for students and specialists.

Professionally competent specialist is characterized by a number of qualities:

- Education (knowledge, skills, intellectual interests, strives for and ability to constantly perfect knowledge, worldviews); social training (moral, aesthetic, physical, labor);
- Socialization (readiness for active professional and social activity, self-realization); culture (exteriorization of cultural values of humanity, culture of labor and communication);
- Articulated individual features (creativity, analytical skills, formed memory and thinking, etc.).

Consequently, at each stage of professional development one should consider not only formation of certain skills and knowledge, but also building up systemic qualities of the professional's personality.

Creating the common model consisting of separate interconnected models for the system of continues education is connected with solution of various tasks, among which are the following ones:

- Training highly qualified workers and specialists for most-demanded specialties on labor market in accordance with the region's interests;
- Providing for faster and more flexible adjustment of professional education system to labor market demands and changes;
- Compatibility of professional training levels within the framework of common educational programs;
- Multiple levels and openness of educational space;
- Completeness of each level of professional education (getting specialty, acquiring qualification); transition from one level of tuition to another according to the results of knowledge control on competitive basis;
- Diversity of forms and methods of training, creation and exploitation of new pedagogical technologies based on modern information and telecommunication resources;
- Providing for variability of educational process;
- Orientation to the development of fundamental and applied research as inseparable part of university specialist' training;
- Establishing close relationship with enterprise and labor market;
- Succession in the study of disciplines in professional education programs of different levels;
- Intensification of the process of the students' professional self-identification.

Construction of the model of the system of continues professional education makes it necessary to consider the previous experience in the system of education for persons with health limitations.

Educational practice reveals that most models of continuous professional education are regionally-oriented and realize career-orientation, training and profession-adaptation functions. The main idea of constructing such models is linked to the organization of education process, supposing the interaction of all the steps of professional education with each other and sectorial enterprises ensuring stimulation of students' professional self-determination, letting them build up an individual trajectory at any stage of professional and even pre-university training. In this case, professional orientation wills guarantee striving for efficiency of training and successful adaptation of young specialists in enterprise.

Methodological grounds of constructing models for continues professional education also present certain interest.

Most authors determine methodological approach as synergetic, resource, personality-oriented, context and competence approaches.

From the viewpoint of synergetic approach the modules of the continues professional education system are characterized by:

- Openness (determined by the links between educational institutions, enterprises and their environment);
- Dynamics (the model continuously adapts to the changing conditions);
- Ability to resist the outer destabilizing pressure.

Working out the model complies with the logics of resource approach which means creating necessary conditions for its realization. In reference to the student's personality as a subject of educational process in conditions of continues professional education there exist outer and individual resources. Considering the students' individual resources is based on their revealing, efficient use and providing conditions for their development. Outer resources include legal basis, material, technical and personnel-related background of the model.

The legal base for continues professional education model comprises:

- Legal documents of the ministry of education, regulating realization of the concept of continues professional education;
- Regional program of professional education development;
- Agreement on state corporate partnership in the sphere of professional education, professional training, re-training, professional development in the system of professional education;
- Agreement on cooperation of educational institutions with enterprises;
- Agreements of the university and schools on creation of profile classes;
- Agreements of the university with educational institutions in the sphere of professional training.

The functioning of the continues professional education model supposes involving into study process the teaching staff of general education institutions, university faculty, highly-qualified specialists from the allied spheres of industry and economy, heads of state and municipal bodies, guest professors from other regions and foreign faculty.

Material and technical support of the model in the study process supposes using laboratories of educational institutions, instructional classes, industrial platforms, etc. Thus, the model may be defined as an integral system developing through active use both of internal resources, and external opportunities of the environment. The essence of the model organization according to resource approach is concentrated around creating the conditions for its subjects' interaction which will ensure the development for each one.

- In creation of the general model we have used the personally-oriented approach according to which priority is given to the value and emotional sphere of personality, its activity and personal position. Main ideas of the personally-oriented approach as applied to construction the general model are as follows (Mkrttchian & Belyanina, 2016) The study process is filled with new personal ideas, values, relationships and supports the individuality and uniqueness of each student;
- Tuition is directed to formation of the vitally important knowledge, necessary for continues development;

- The learning process reveals the subject experience of each student;
- Tuition technologies consider the students' education abilities and the specificity of their major.

Another approach, the context one, is aimed at the students' preparation in accordance with their future profession. It supposes the student's personal inclusion into the processes of cognition and mastering the future profession and directly determines his/ her successful activity in the future.

The realization of the competence approach is linked to the urge to define the vital changes in professional training as determined by the transformation in society and economy. New quality of education is closely connected with the grounded forecasting, projecting, modeling of necessary competences of the student (Mkrttchian & Belyanina, 2016).

1. The basic principles of the model under consideration are as follows (Mkrttchian & Belyanina, 2016):Rationality supposing orientation in education organization and content to the local conditions and labor markets, dependency on concrete economic and social conditions of region development; the graduate's expanded professional profile as a feature in high demand in the market;
2. Integration supposing inclusion of all the system's elements into the process of professional training with the view of rational use of resources;
3. Succession consisting in the corresponding of the graduates' qualification characteristics to the demands of the customer enterprises;
4. Intensification of education consisting in raising efficiency of tuition by means of new technologies, forms and methods in educational process;
5. Differentiation expressed in realization of the students' right for choosing an individual educational and career trajectory;
6. Variability of educational programs providing the student with the free choice of individual education trajectory.

It is common knowledge that the staff professional training is based on the use of various technologies (personality-oriented, cooperation technologies, project and activity training); educational methods (problem method; searching method; the method of solving definite situational tasks; the method of doing creative tasks with research elements; project method); forms of study (individual; group; frontal method; self-education).

The research on integration in projecting educational systems showed that integration due to its dialectical and logical unity allows for reconstructing the unity of processes and systems necessary for solving education tasks. Integration approach is of great importance while building the model of specialists' training. It is determined by the development of the modern national economy as part of the world economy (Mkrttchian & Belyanina, 2016). Changing conditions of professional activity served the reason for a number of contradictions reflected on the sphere of education, particularly, for the discrepancy between changing demands for specialists in developing economy and reflecting new requirements in educational standards; between the market's need for specialists with practical professional background and the absence of this experience in graduates. These contradictions can be solved if the specialists' training is based on integration of professional education and professional practice. With that, the integration can be described as different stages of a single process: preparation for activity and activity itself.

The common ground for an individual's professional development is formed by means of social integration of the structure "school-university-postgraduate school" at the points "school-university" (lower step of professional training) and "university – postgraduate school" (higher step of qualification) – practical and research activities.

Social integration of school and university on the lower step of professional training provides for the continuity of going from one stage of personality development to another. Quantity accumulation of general knowledge, development of personality qualities and an individual's gnostic abilities leads to their quality transformation in professionally-oriented space. Strategic partnership contributes to realization of own functions for all the participants of study process which lets the partners to solve their problems. Thus, school can created a database for the students' self-determination in their further development based on the information of professional market, the role and place of professionals in national economy development.

Psychologically, professional orientation contributes to an individual's readiness for further learning by means of raising motivation for mastering professional skills.

The changing character of education, increase in the amount of self-study, activation of training and organization of stage communications allow for gradual introduction of the new tendencies in secondary school.

At the point of the university's transition to the practical activity sphere (here also refers the stage of post-graduate study) the integrated space is characterized by a brand new stage in personality development. It is determined by the discrepancy in the leading activity of the individual: between accumulation of professional knowledge and demand for their realization. This discrepancy is solved by means of transformation from the study to professional practice which proceeds with the process of the specialist's professional development.

The dialectics of development supposes the presence of some variants of entering the practical activity sphere: development follows a number of ways, not one. The dialectic ontogeny process continues at the postgraduate stage while combining research, teaching and practical activities.

The specialists from the sphere of professional activity return to this stage as development is not a straight line and not a move around the circle but a helix with a number of whorls. The cognition process sometimes repeats the past cycles but always on the new basis. The step of research activity in the system "school – university – postgraduate school" is determined logically and dialectically and presents the integration of study, research and practical activates.

Social integration of the university and organizations from the practical spheres lets the university flexibly structure the content of education with orientation to new scientific outcomes and demands of professional practice and labor markes. Internships bring corporate culture of strategic partners in the study process. In the process of tuition the students have the possibility of dealing with the strategic partners' corporate culture, of studying the rules of behavior in professional sphere and determining the potential workplace before graduation.

Connection with the corporate structure allows for development through educating staff, their getting additional qualifications in flexible conditions and forms of tuition.

Therefore, the model of special and structural integration of professional education and professional economic activity reflects the methodology, theoretical and methodological prerequisites for preparation of specialists with economics major. The key element of the model is the integration tools: internship bases, joint enterprises, workshops, students' professional activity. The mechanism of social integration of education and professional activity spheres is strategic partnership creating the field for developing the specilist's personality development in the common space of living. The social integration mechanism ensures the correspondence of the educational structure "school – university – postgraduate school" with the external environment (professional internship) and, being an open system, is able to develop and renew oneself under the influence of changing conditions.

Taking into consideration the accumulated experience in professional education system lets us turn to constructing own model of continuos education system for the persons with health limitations that will have its specificity determined by the specifics of this category of learners.

The model of continues professional education for the persons with health limitations, in our view, should be worked out in accordance with approaches to and demands for continues education system highlighted in the normative documents regulating the functioning of continues education for persons with health limitations; should consider conditions of its realization and contain components defining the contents of continues education for persons with health limitations.

Constructing the model of the system of continues education for persons with health limitations requires determining its structural components: the system of requirements for education; approaches and principles of creating the system of continues education; conditions for model realization; content of continuous professional education; complex support; creation of the environment free from barriers; the system of extracurricular activity; links of professional education institutions with labor market. Below are the characteristics of all the structural components of the model of continues professional education system for persons with health limitations (Mkrttchian & Belyanina, 2016). The first structural component of the model is the system of requirements. Normative documents prioritize the values of world and Russian culture, humanistic morals, civility, worldviews and methodological solutions, oriented to formation of new generations of specialists capable of creative, professional, responsible activity; provision of equal educational opportunities for persons with health limitations (Mkrttchian & Belyanina, 2016) .

The above enables us to determine requirements for the general model of the system of continues education for persons with health limitations: providing equal opportunities and conditions for persons with health limitations to get professional education aimed at training competitive specialists capable of responsible activity, oriented to general cultural and moral values, humanistic morals and civility.

- The second structural component of the general model of the system of continues a professional education for persons with health limitations is determining approaches to its organization. Generally, the main approaches are defined as an approach to the system of continues education for persons with health limitations (Mkrttchian & Belyanina, 2016) The aim of social development is a person's continues moral, personal and professional development;
- Continues education should provide each person with the institutional opportunity of forming an educational trajectory and of getting the professional training which is required for his/ her further professional, career and personal growth;
- Creating infrastructure of access to continues professional education throughout the period of professional activity.

The main approaches to constructing the general model of the continues professional education system may be summed up as follows: creating availability of professional education for persons with health limitations through formation of individual educational trajectory contributing to continues moral, personal and professional development in accordance with their abilities and possibilities.

- The third structural component of the model of the system of continues professional education for persons with health limitations is defining the principles of professional education organization. In

a general way, they may be presented as (Mkrttchian & Belyanina, 2016): Basic property, multiple levels, diversification, complementarity, flexibility, successive integration, availability;
- The possibility of changing the major at different life stages taking into account personality's demands and needs as well as social and economic conditions in society;
- Succession of educational activity content in transition from one kind to another, from one life stage to another;
- The space of educational services capable of satisfying all the number of educational needs arising in society as a whole, in a separate region as well as individually.

The above enables us to formulate the basic principles of constructing the model of continuous professional education for persons with health limitations: satisfying educational needs, in accordance with their possibilities, as based on multiple levels, diversification, complementarity, flexibility and succession of integration, flexibility and availability of the system of continues professional education.

The fourth structural component of the general system of continues professional education for persons with health limitations are conditions for realizations of continues professional education model (Mkrttchian & Belyanina, 2016).

Hereinafter mentioned are the main conditions for realization of the general model of continuous professional education:

- Personal orientation, differentiation and individualization of education backed up by state educational standards on the basis of diversity and variability of educational institutions;
- Creation of information environment in each educational institution and wide use in educational process of advanced pedagogical technologies; development and acceptance of corresponding norms of their realization;
- Integration of study programs of primary, secondary and higher professional education; spread of the module structure of programs of preparation in professionals and specialties;
- Creation of new mechanisms of assessment and accreditation of educational programs involving social and professional organizations, employers 'associations.

Conditions for realization of the model of continuous professional education system for persons with health limitations: personal orientation, differentiation and individualization of education as based on the use of advanced educational technologies, working out of the module structure of integrated educational programs, information of educational space and involving community into the process of the graduates' quality assessment.

The fifth structural component of the general model of the system of continuos professional education for persons with health limitations is the content of education (Mkrttchian & Belyanina, 2016).

The content of continues professional education includes:

- Continues professional training of the staff which is based on the use of various teaching technologies, teching methods (problem method, search method, method of solving definite practical tasks, method of doing creative works with research elements, project method), forms of tuition (individual, group, etc.);
- Development of open distance education, externate, etc.

- Agreement of educational programs (the possibility of covering new content – adequacy of educational standards);
- Personal orientation of professional education of persons with health limitations as means of its social sustainability and economic protection;
- Formation of theoretical knowledge of persons with health limitations in accordance with their practical professional needs and value orientations;
- Free choice of professional individual educational trajectories for students with health limitations;
- Modularity of professional education content;
- Students' mastering the competences common for all kinds of professional activity (skills of self-organization of study and professional activity, search for information, mastering new technologies of activity, computer skills, foreign language knowledge, data using skills, the knowledge of ecology, economics and business, etc.);
- Social availability of professional education which includes both socially determined needs and traditions of getting education, and the attitude of society and state to providing educational opportunities for persons with health limitations;
- Changing character of study, increase in the volume of independent work, activation of study activity and organization of step communications.

The content of the model of continues professional education system may be summarized as a process of formation of students' key competences on the ground of choosing individual educational trajectories, forms of study according to their possibilities, needs, values and personal orientation with a view of their social and economic sustainability and social security in society.

The sixth structural component of the model of continues professional education system for persons with health limitations is the complex of social and medical-psychological-pedagogical support including (Mkrttchian & Belyanina, 2016):

- Creation of integrated educational space as a complex of conditions for developing the personality's potential on the basis of implementing modern educational technologies including health-protecting, information technologies, pre-profile preparation and profile tuition;
- Maintenance of physical, psychic and social health, timely diagnostics and correction, systematic medical and psychological, pedagogical and social support for the students with health limitations;
- Individual program of rehabilitation;
- Career-oriented work for choosing the future specialty for persons with health limitations;
- Psychological and medical support for students with health limitations (psychologists, medical workers, social teacher).

Characteristics of complex social and medical psychological and pedagogical support for the persons with health limitations can be determined as a system of professional activity of different specialists on creating conditions for the subject's accepting optimal solutions for personality development through medical and psychological support, pedagogical support and professional adaptation.

The seventh structural component of the system of continues professional education for persons with health limitations is barrier-free environment (Mkrttchian & Belyanina, 2016):

- Required planning of study rooms, rampant and elevators;

- Equipping with informational technologies and adapted facilities (vision and hearing pathologies), free Internet access;
- Architecturally-available environment and special equipment (for students with loco motor system problems); equipped medical and rehabilitation rooms; equipped places for recreation;
- Study process is compliance with sanitation standards.

Characteristics of barrier-free environment for persons with health limitations are concentrated on creating conditions for equal opportunities and availability of professional education as backed up by modernization of educational institution infrastructure.

The eighth structural component of the model of the system of continues professional education for persons with health limitations is extracurricular pedagogical activity (Mkrttchian & Belyanina, 2016) . Theoretical background allows for stating that the main content of the university pedagogical activity comprises inclusion of a student with disability into educational and social life at university; application of personal growth programs with the use of active training methods; inclusion of students into student interest and hobby clubs, sport activity.

The main content of extracurricular activity of persons with disabilities is concentrated on inclusion of students with heath limitations into socially important cultural, creative and sport activity aimed at building their social and cultural competences for integration and adaptation in society.

The ninth structural component of the model of the system of continues professional education is connection with labor market expressed through (Mkrttchian & Belyanina, 2016):

- Mechanism of social integration of spheres of education and professional activity realized in strategic partnership creating the ground for developing the specialist's personality in the common space of its life activity;
- Integration of university and practical sphere organizations allowing for the university structuring the content of training in accordance with new research and professional practice as well as labor market demands.

The content of interacting with labor market is concentrated on forecasting, projecting, modeling of key competences for students with health limitations on the ground of changes taking place in society and demands for quality of education and professional training of persons with disabilities. Figure 1 shows the scheme of the general model of continues professional education for persons with health limitations consisting of worked out models (Mkrttchian & Belyanina, 2016).

Where block 1-1 shows the structural component of the general model generalizing "Demands of society, employers and students for professional education for persons with disabilities ", block 1-1 shows characteristics of structural component in general model, which generalizes "Ensuring equal opportunities in getting professional education for persons with disabilities aimed at training competitive specialists capable of professional responsibility, oriented to cultural and moral values, humanistic morals and civility", block 1-1 shows criteria of the general model "Share of students with disabilities having access to the system of continuos professional education".

Block 2-1 shows the structural component of the general model summarizing "Approaches to getting continues professional education for persons wih disabilities". Block 2-1 illustrates the characteristics of the structural component in general model which generalizes "Creating availability of professional education for persons with disabilities through formation of an individual educational trajectory providing for

Figure 1. The diagram a of the general model of continuing professional education of persons with disabilities Act (IDEA), consisting of designed models

Stages	Goals	Tasks
Preparatory stage	Block 1-1. Creating the normative basis for ODL use. Creating technical basis. Block 2-1. Creating course packet (of the net educational resource). Training the staff	- Formulating the goals of ODL usage, working out the model of DL in accordance with normative acts. - Defining the terms of educational process launch. - Creating the technical base for DL - Selecting/ developing the net educational resource. - Defining the principles of forming the study groups. - Defining the terms and succession of the courses. - Training net instructors, mentors, organizers, etc.
Stage 1 Realized before the academic year	Block 3-1. Questionnaire survey, revealing the students' educational needs. Block 4-1. Conducting the normative basis for ODL. Block 5-1. Compiling individual study plan. Compiling and correcting the students' study schedule. Block 6-1. Compiling the thematic outline.	- Study and analysis of the resource and course content - Studying the students' individuals needs. - Compiling individual study schedule considering the major and the study plan. - Meeting the study group -Compiling thematic schedule including: • preliminary defining the goals for each topic; • defining the academic hours for each topic; • defining the place of project and research activity; • a more detailed analysis of the program content; • defining the lesson types on the given topic including the venue for laboratory works, practical lessons, etc. • defining the venue for online lessons and their types; • defining the venue for discussions and conferences (both online и offline)
Stage 2 Realized before the start of each lesson and every topic	Block 7-1. Teacher's preparation for a certain lesson	• defining the goals of studying each topic in accordance with the major - defining the content of additional theoretical material on the given topic and preparing the list of sources of supplementary reading for students - Analysis of the system of tasks offered for solution in resource; defining the degree of its completeness, complexity of the offered tasks, the system of differentiating the tasks; its correspondence to the formulated goals. - Defining the necessity in additional set of tasks
	Block 8-1. Drafting instruction for the lesson Block 9-1. Working with home assignmentsP	- Planning the system of control and self-control of the students' mastering the content of the topic and achievement of the goals set - Selection of additional tasks to be solved in class and at home - Checking home assignments, assessment and commenting on home assignment

continues moral, personal and professional development of persons with health limitations, taking into account their possibilities and abilities", block 2-1 illustrates the criteria of the general model "Share of students with disabilities learning individually, in a distance mode".

Digital Control Models of Continuous Education

Block 3-1 shows the structural component of the general model summarizing "Principles of continues professional education for persons with disabilities", block 3-1 illustrates the characteristics of the structural component in general model which generalizes "Satisfying educational needs of persons with disabilities in accordance with their possibilities on the ground of multiple levels, diversification, completion, flexibility, succession, integration and flexibility and availability of continues professional education system", block 3-1 shows the criteria of the general model "Share of students with disabilities getting additional education. The level of satisfied educational is needs".

Block 4-1 illustrates the structural component of the general model summarizing "Conditions for realization of continues professional education for persons with disabilities", block 4-1 shows the characteristics of the structural component of the general which is generalized "Personal orientation, individualization of education for persons with disabilities based on using advanced technologies, working out the module structure of integrated educational programs, information of educational space and involving community into assessing the quality of graduates' preparation", block 4-1 shows such criteria of the general model "Developed methodological support for individually-oriented study processes of persons with disabilities".

Block 5-1 illustrates the structural component of the general model generalizing "Content of education of the system of continues professional education", bloc 5-1 shows the characteristics of the structural component of the general model which is summarized in "The process of building up the students' key competences on the basis of choosing the study content, individual educational trajectories and forms of tuition in accordance with their possibilities, needs, values, personal orientation with a view of providing their social and economic sustainability and social security in society", block 5-1 shows the criteria of the general model "Share of the students with disabilities included in various forms of education. High index of quality of education for persons with disabilities is during intermediate and final assessment".

Block 6-1 shows the structural component of the general model summarizing "Complex social, medical, psychological and pedagogical support of persons with disabilities", block 6-1 shows the characteristics of the structural component of the general model summarizing "The system of professional activity of various specialists creating conditions for the subject's taking optimal decisions for the development of the personality with disabilities through providing medical, rehabilitations, psychological support, pedagogical support", block 6-1 shows the criteria and indices of the general model "Share of the students with disabilities involved in complex social, medical, psychological and pedagogical support".

Block 7-1 shows the structural component of the general model summarizing "Barrier-free environment", block 7-1 shows the characteristics of the structural component of the general model summarizing "Creating conditions for equal opportunities and providing availability of professional education for persons with disabilities on the basis of modernized structure of the educational institution", block 7-1 shows the criteria and indices of the general model "Level of the students with disabilities' satisfaction with availability of educational environment and infrastructure".

Block 8-1 illustrates the structural component of the general model summarizing "Extracurricular activities", block 8-1 shows the characteristics of the structural component of general model summarizing "Inclusion of students with disabilities in social, cultural, sport activities aimed at building their sociocultural competences for integration and adaptation in society", block 8-1 shows such criteria and indices of the general model "Share of the students with disabilities involved in social, cultural, sport activities".

Block 9-1 shows the structural component of the general model summarizing "Links to labor market", block 9-1 shows the characteristics of the structural component of general model summarizing "Forecasting, projecting, modeling key competences of students with disabilities according to changes in society and requirements for the quality of education and professional training of persons with disabilities", block 9-1 shows such criteria and indices of the general model "The number of social partners and employers involved in assessing the quality of education of persons with disabilities". Figure 2 shows the structural and functional model of the system of continues education in sliding mode for persons with disabilities for solving tasks 1 through 7 with the use of the corresponding approaches and principles covered in Mkrttchian et al. (2016)

- **Task 1-1:** "Training of highly-qualified workers and specialists in most demanded specialties in labor market in accordance with the region's interests " is solved by means of approach and principle "Personal sense: realized tuition should be filled with personal senses, values and relationship of the person with disabilities".
- **Task 2-1:** "Considering labor market demands: the system's flexible adaptation of the system of professional education to labor market demands" is solved by means of approach "Individuality in education: education should support individual and uniqueness of each student with disabilities".
- **Task 3-1:** "Multiple levels and openness of educational space" is solved by means of approach and principle "Considering individual opportunities of students with disabilities and specifics of the major".
- **Task 4-1:** "Integration of resource opportunities of educational and sociocultural space" is solved by means of approach and principle "Succession as compliance of training in all educational levels and the correspondence of the graduates' qualification characteristics to the requirements of the enterprises".
- **Task 5-1:** "Establishing close links with industries and labor market" is solved by means of principle "Intensification of education consistent in increasing efficiency of learning through the use of new technologies, forms and methods in educational process".
- **Task 6-1:** "Diversity of forms and methods of training, creation and application of new pedagogical technologies based on modern informational and telecommunication resources" is solved by means of approach and principle "Differentiation expressed in the students' realization of the right for choosing the individual educational and career trajectory; the study should reveal each learner's subject experience".
- **Task 7-1:** "Succession in studying disciplines in professional educational programs of different levels" is solved by means of principle "Variability of educational programs; expansion of professional major as a demanded feature of the labor market".

CONCLUSION

Sliding mode can serve the ground for developing the model of continuous education for persons with disabilities. The sliding mode technique allows for taking decisions in invariant conditions, analysing the situation, evaluating the risks and, as a result, taking decisions in control and organization in the course of tuition. The system of continuous education is getting adapted to the requirements of the normative documents and the current trends, functions according to the logic of the sliding mode.

Digital Control Models of Continuous Education

Figure 2. Structural and functional scheme of the general model of continuous education of persons with disabilities controlled intelligent agents in the sliding mode

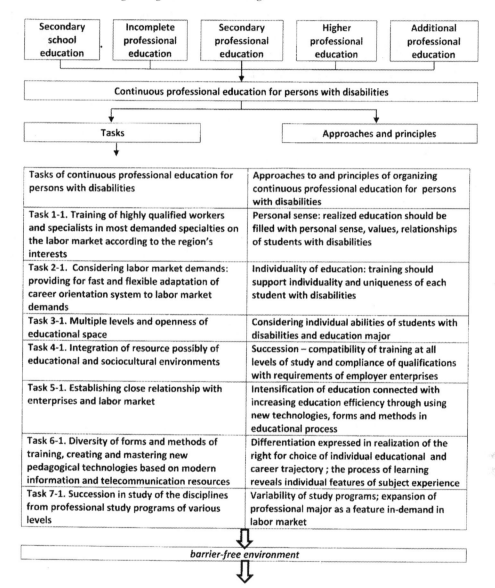

REFERENCES

Mkrttchian, V., & Belyanina, L. (2016). The Pedagogical and Engineering Features of E- and Blended Learning of Aduits Using Triple H-Avatar in Russian Fedreration. In V. Mkrttchian, A. Bershadsky, A. Bozhday, M. Kataev, & S. Kataev (Eds.), *Handbook of research on estimation and control techniques in e-learning systems* (pp. 61–77). Hershey, PA: IGI Global. doi:10.4018/978-1-4666-9489-7.ch006

Mkrttchian, V., Bershadsky, A., Bozhday, A., Noskova, T., & Miminova, S. (2016). Development of a Global Policy of All-Pervading E-Learning, Based on Transparency, Strategy, and Model of Cyber Triple H-Avatar. In Developing Successful Strategies for Global Policies and Cyber Transparency in E-Learning (pp. 207-221). Hershey, PA: IGI Global.

KEY TERMS AND DEFINITIONS

Education Technology: Are technical, biological and engineering systems for Education whose components are combined, controlled and generated using the aligned single processing core. All the components at all levels of interaction are combined in the network infrastructure. All components include built-in calculators, providing data processing in real-time.

Indicator of Sliding Mode: The software for control virtual research space, maintain it sliding mode.

Moderator Avatar: Personalized graphic file or rendering that represents a computer user used to represent moderator in an online environment.

Researcher Avatar: Personalized graphic file or rendering that represents a computer user used to represent researcher in an online environment.

Triple H-AVATAR Technology: The technology of modeling and simulation based on known technology of Avatar used in the HHH University since 2010.

Virtual Research Environment: The space where with the help of virtual reality creates a special environment for research.

This research was previously published in Sliding Mode in Intellectual Control and Communication edited by Vardan Mkrttchian and Ekaterina Aleshina; pages 31-62, copyright year 2017 by Information Science Reference (an imprint of IGI Global).

Section 3
Disabilities: Learning and Developmental

Chapter 17
Specific Learning Disabilities:
Reading, Spelling, and Writing Strategies

George Uduigwome
Los Angeles Unified School District, USA

ABSTRACT

This chapter discusses best practices in providing supports for students diagnosed with reading (dyslexia), writing (dysgraphia), and spelling (dysorthographia) deficits. It examines some impacts of these and associated conditions on learning. The recommended strategies for leveraging learning for the identified population are all evidence-based. Per the author, early intervention is key to providing students with learning disabilities a meaningful learning experience. An early intervention involves the use of multiple measures to diagnose a student's present level of performance primarily with a view to finding strengths (Strengths can be used to mitigate deficits) and learning gaps, utilizing evidence-based systematic instruction delivered with treatment fidelity, and an ongoing progress monitoring.

INTRODUCTION

A nation's ability to compete in an increasingly global economy depends on the quality of its labor force. Following Hanushek and Woßmann (2010) the quality of education, determined on an outcome basis of cognitive skills, has a considerable effect on economic development, although the macroeconomic effect of education relies on other complementary growth-enhancing policies and institutions. Education has the potential to reduce crime rate, increase productivity (Lochner, 2010), increase voter participation and civic awareness (Dee, 2010), equalize or disequalize inequality, promote human rights, increase life-expectancy; lower poverty; reduce public health, welfare, and prison costs, increase income, sales, and property tax receipts, yield positive environmental benefits, promote quality of life, and yield benefits to the larger society by the dissemination of technology from knowledge created by research and development in all academic fields (Blanden & Machin, 2010).

In the U.S. the Common Core State Standards (CCSS), a product of international benchmarking and a consequence of the desire to improve educational and economic competitiveness, were created to guide instruction and learning in math and English language arts from kindergarten through 12th grade.

DOI: 10.4018/978-1-7998-1213-5.ch017

Specific Learning Disabilities

The CCSS emphasize critical thinking and problem-solving skills, college- and career-readiness, and preparation for life in a technological society. The creation of these common standards has resulted in a paradigm shift whereby literacy development now, more than ever before, is predicated on a focused and coherent instructional approach by service providers working collaboratively. To that extent, the CCSS have become the fulcrum upon which the lever of instruction and learning must now pivot, and this comes with the expectation that they will have a longer shelf life than all their predecessors.

Although the CCSS stipulate grade-specific standards, they neither define intervention methods and materials nor proffer the supports necessary to leverage learning for struggling students. The additional challenge for service providers, therefore, is to close learning gaps by properly diagnosing needs or weaknesses and effectively matching them with evidence-based interventions.

Reading and mathematics skills are essential to success in many societies. However, not every child will start their academic career with the requisite literacy foundation. That notwithstanding, all students have a right to instruction that will help them rise to their full potential and service providers have a fiduciary duty to these and other students. The role of service providers is critical enough to warrant the multi-pronged approaches adopted by education systems to build and sustain capacity. This chapter focuses on best practices that can usher students with learning disabilities (LD) into a productive future.

The chapter examines:

- LD Definition
- Identification and Prevalence of LD
- Common Types of LD and Supports
- Some Associated Disorders and Supports

The concluding section reiterates the importance of early identification and intervention within the context of collaboration.

LEARNING DISABILITIES

The learning disabilities (LD) construct refers to a number of genetic, neurological, or injury-caused processing disorders that can hinder the acquisition of basic or higher level skills such as reading, writing, math, organization, time management, and abstract reasoning (British Columbia Ministry of Education, 2011; Cortiella & Horowitz, 2014). These deficits may impede learning in individuals who otherwise have average or above average abilities. LD are different from learning problems because they are not caused primarily by social maladjustment, lack of motivation, inadequate or insufficient instruction, intellectual disability, environmental, cultural or economic factors.

Individuals with LD may appear to be bright and intelligent when in reality there is a gap between their potential and actual achievement. LD often result in academic underachievement with varying impact on functions and the extent of severity on an individual. However, there is conclusive evidence in the body of literature that, with the right supports, affected students can become academically and socially successful (British Columbia Ministry of Education, 2011; Cortiella & Horowitz, 2014; Jacobs & Fu, 2014; Nies & Belfiore, 2006; Richie, 2005).

LD is sometimes associated with negative psychological and psychosocial ramifications. For example, La Greca and Stone (1990) reported that, compared to classmates with low and average reading achievement, students with LD had lower peer acceptance, lower feelings of self-worth, fewer positive nominations, and more negative self-perceptions regarding social acceptance. These students are more likely to receive behavior referrals, suspension from school, and are adjudicated delinquent at younger ages. They are also overrepresented in juvenile incarceration facilities for school-related infractions in a phenomenon known as school-to-prison pipeline (Chamberlain, Cheung-Chung, & Jenner, 1993; Holman & Ziedenberg, 2014; Mallett, 2014; U.S. Department of Education, 2014).

With respect to programming and placement, Smith (1980) reported the following: children with LD in regular classrooms exhibited negative self-regard; placement of children with LD in resource rooms with similarly handicapped children on a half day basis was associated with increased self-regard; and placement of children with LD into self-contained LD classrooms was associated with increased self-regard. When children with LD in self-contained LD classrooms were mainstreamed on a half day basis, their self-regard escalated dramatically; and when LD labeled children in self- contained LD classrooms were mainstreamed on a full day basis, their self-regard decreased.

The Individuals with Disabilities Education Improvement Act (IDEIA), a federal law, uses the term Specific Learning Disability (SLD) to qualify the LD condition, and it is one of 13 categories of disabilities under the IDEIA. IDEIA defines SLD as:

A disorder in one or more of the basic psychological processes involved in understanding or in using language, spoken or written, which disorder may manifest itself in the imperfect ability to listen, think, speak, read, write, spell, or do mathematical calculations. Such term includes such conditions as perceptual disabilities, brain injury, minimal brain dysfunction, dyslexia, and developmental aphasia. Such term does not include a learning problem that is primarily the result of visual, hearing, or motor disabilities, of mental retardation, of emotional disturbance, or of environmental, cultural, or economic disadvantage. (20 U.S.C. § 1401 [30])

An SLD diagnosis, according to the Diagnostic and Statistical Manual of Mental Disorders (DSM-5), is a condition involving persistent difficulties in reading, writing, arithmetic, or mathematical reasoning skills during the formal years of schooling. The listed symptoms include inaccurate or slow and effortful reading, poor written expression that lacks clarity, difficulties remembering number facts, or inaccurate mathematical reasoning with current academic skills being well below the average range of scores in culturally and linguistically appropriate tests of reading, writing, or mathematics. (American Psychiatric Association, 2013)

Identification and Prevalence

The LD category was once the fastest growing category of special education eligibilities with an increase of more than 300% between 1976 and 2000. However, as reported by Cortiella and Horowitz (2014), it has declined by almost 2% annually since 2002. They attributed the decline to an expansion of and attention to early childhood education, the use of early screenings and diagnostic evaluations to support school readiness, and the different approaches taken in the current identification of students with LD.

Recent changes to law and practice have resulted in significant changes to the SLD identification process. Following Tannock (2014), DSM-5 now employs one overarching category of SLD with specifiers to more precisely characterize the range of problems. The following four qualification criteria must also be met in lieu of the IQ-achievement discrepancy requirement: Criterion A: key characteristics of

SLD (at least one of six symptoms of learning difficulties that have persisted for at least 6 months despite the provision of extra help or targeted instruction). Criterion B: measurement of those characteristics to determine how they impair academic, occupational, or everyday activities. Criterion C: age at onset of problems, and Criterion D: specifies which disorders or adverse conditions must be ruled out before a diagnosis of SLD can be confirmed.

Changes to SLD identification brought about by the reauthorized IDEIA were discussed by Ihori and Olvera (2015) and Schultz, Simpson, and Lynch (2012) who noted that, in addition to a discrepancy model which contrasts intellectual and achievement test results, IDEIA now allows the use of a process which assesses a student's response to scientific, researched-based interventions (e.g., response-to-intervention [RtI]) and a third method which involves the use of multiple data sources in the review of a student's unique pattern of cognitive strengths and weaknesses (PSW) that result in academic deficits.

Additionally, when a student who appears to be otherwise capable manifests any of the following, it could be indicative of the existence of LD: frustration at own performance relative to peer's, processing difficulties, little or no engagement in learning situations, reluctance to take risks in learning situations, inability to cope with multi-step instructions, inappropriate behavior in an attempt to avoid an assigned task, sustaining and shifting attention which might be due to problems with self-regulation, physical discomfort or motivational factors, struggling with certain aspects of school, below average academic achievement, significant difference between achievement and ability, as well as an inability to perform certain tasks (British Columbia Ministry of Education, 2011; Cortiella & Horowitz, 2014; Jacobs & Fu, 2014).

COMMON TYPES OF LEARNING DISABILITIES

There are several types of LD and affected individuals usually manifest traits that are indicative of a disability in more than one area. The most common types of LD are reading disorder (Dyslexia), spelling disorder (Dysorthographia), writing disorder (Dysgraphia), and arithmetic disorder (Dyscalculia). Since the foci of this chapter are reading, spelling, and writing, dyscalculia will only be addressed in passing.

Reading Disorders (Dyslexia)

Recent findings seem to suggest that certain genes may predispose an individual to develop dyslexia. Etymologically, dyslexia means poor reading. Sometimes referred to as a language-based LD, it impairs a person's ability to read and its severity can differ in individuals. Individuals with dyslexia typically read at levels significantly lower than expected despite having normal intelligence. Dyslexia is sometimes confused with the lesser known Specific Reading Comprehension Deficits (S-RCD): A child with dyslexia has the tendency to confuse letters and struggles with sounding out words while one with S-RCD can decode but lacks the accompanying comprehension.

Dyslexia is usually characterized by difficulties with identifying, hearing, and manipulating individual sounds or phonemes in spoken words (phonemic awareness); difficulties with the meta-cognitive skill required to attend to, discriminate, remember, and manipulate sounds at the sentence, word, syllable, and phoneme or sound level (phonological awareness); difficulties with decoding words; reading fluently; understanding vocabulary; and text comprehension (Bosse, Tainturier, & Valdois, 2007; British Columbia Ministry of Education, 2011; Cortiella & Horowitz, 2014).

Evaluation for dyslexia is usually conducted by trained school staff or other competent personnel and it spans intellectual ability, academic skills, psycholinguistic processing, information processing, and overall performance. Due consideration is also given to the individual's family background

Strategies to Support Individuals with Dyslexia

Proficient reading requires a wide range of skills such as decoding, fluency, vocabulary, ability to extract and retain material in working memory (Ashby, Dix, Bontrager, Dey, & Archer, 2013; Harn, Stoolmiller, & Chard, 2008; Mihai, Friesen, Butera, Horn, Lieber & Palmer, 2015). Vaughn and Bos (2015) explained that "reading involves using the attentional, perceptual, memory, and retrieval processes necessary to automatically identify or decode words…thus a goal of reading and reading instruction is to decode effortlessly so that attention is on comprehension" (p. 243).

To improve reading skills in students, emphasis should be on strategies with the greatest potential for promoting the acquisition of skills in the areas of encoding, decoding, reading fluency, vocabulary, and text comprehension (Barnes, 1989; Burns, Hodgson, Parker, & Fremont, 2011; Chang & Millett, 2013; Duke & Pearson, 2009; Flett & Conderman, 2002). Additionally, teachers must be deliberate about creating and promoting opportunities for students to read independently.

Decoding

Decoding is the process of productively engaging one's knowledge of letters, sounds, and word patterns to decipher unfamiliar words. Effective decoding requires, among other things, a working knowledge of letter-sound relationships, word patterns, and the meanings of roots and affixes. Vaughn and Bos (2015) identified the following as effective strategies for decoding unknown words: phonic analysis (blending letter-sound correspondences), onset-rime (using knowledge of common spelling patterns), structural analysis (engaging knowledge of word structures such as affixes and roots), syllabication (using knowledge of common syllable types to decode multisyllabic words), automatic word recognition (recognizing high frequency words), syntax and context (using knowledge of word order and semantics), and the use of other resources such as asking someone or using a dictionary.

Strategies

1. **Phonological Awareness Activities**: Phonemic games or activities can be used to help students recognize how to segment words. One such activity is the *Head, Shoulders, Knees, and Toes* game where students are given a word with 1-4 phonemes (sounds), and while standing, touch their head, shoulders, knees, and toes as they say the sounds in words. Allor, Gansle, and Denny (2006) also discuss the *Stop and Go Phonemic Awareness Game,* a blending and segmenting intervention. When it was implemented an average of 26 minutes daily per student, all students made gains in phoneme segmentation fluency, with most reaching and exceeding the benchmark. To promote phonemic awareness, Flett and Conderman (2002) attested to the efficacy of activities such as teaching nursery rhymes, playing *I Spy* using initial sounds of words, creating a sound box, having students sort picture cards based on initial sounds, playing phoneme deletion games, and having students clap and count syllables.

Specific Learning Disabilities

Vaughn and Bos (2015) suggested the following phonological awareness activities: Listening for words that begin with the same sound (e.g., having all students whose name begins with /b/ line up); clapping the number of words in a sentence, syllables in words, and phonemes in words; blending: students say the sounds in a word and then say them fast while the teacher pushes blocks or letters together to demonstrate blending; segmenting: students say the word and then clap and say each syllable or sound (e.g., running is /run/ /ing/ is /r/ /u/ /n/ /i/ /ng/); deleting: students listen to words and say them without the first sound (e.g., bat becomes at); adding: students listen to words and add syllables (e.g., run becomes running, come becomes coming); substituting: students listen and change sounds (e.g., change /r/ in run to /b/ and make bun); transposing: students reverse the sounds (e.g., nat becomes tan).

2. **Cues**: Vaughn and Bos (2015) describe how a teacher can employ cues to help students use phonic analysis to decode words: Cue the students to say each sound, and then have them say it fast. Demonstrate and have students point to each letter sound as they say it, and then have them sweep their fingers under the word when they say it fast. Place letters apart when saying the sounds, and then push the letters together when saying it fast.
3. **Explicit Instruction**: Explicit instruction can be used to teach rhyming words, syllabication, and the identification of beginning, medial and final sounds in words. Spelling patterns are best taught by linking spelling and meaning. The acquired knowledge can then be employed as a tool for reading or writing new words. Lessons can be pre- or retaught one-on-one or in a small group setting as needed. Vaughn and Bos (2015) stressed the importance of teaching the meanings of affixes and inflectional endings along with how to decode them.

Several instructional programs have also been shown to be effective in beginning reading acquisition. For example, McIntyre, Protz, and McQuarrie (2008) reported positive gains in phonemic awareness and letter/sound correspondence for students deemed at-risk whose teachers used the LiPS program (Lindamood & Lindamood, 1998). The LiPS method of systematic instruction is based on a sensory-cognitive processing philosophy. It incorporates the constructs of reading deficit prevention and targets phonemic awareness development through five levels of progression using deliberate teaching methods.

Fluency

Fluency is the ability to read effortlessly with appropriate speed, accuracy,
expression, and understanding. Rasinski (2014) described reading fluency as comprising two distinct components at two ends of the reading spectrum – automaticity in word recognition and expression in oral reading that reflects the meaning of the text. In a sense, he noted, "reading fluency is the essential link between word recognition at one end of the spectrum and reading comprehension at the other" (p. 4). Struggling readers usually demonstrate a weakness in understanding text partly because working memory and attention are fully devoted to decoding at the expense of comprehension. The ability to read helps students access other content areas and it is often a predictor of future academic success.

It is important to correctly match readers with text in order for students to have productive reading experiences. Smith (2000) discussed the Lexile Framework which enables teachers to develop personalized instruction based on Lexile measures of reading ability and Lexiled reading lists. The Framework is a scale for determining a reader's skill level (Lexile reader measure) and a text's complexity (Lexile text measure). Lexile reader measures can range from below 200L (emergent readers) to above 1600L (advanced readers). BR is assigned to readers who score below 0L.

Strategies

1. **High-Frequency Word Cards**: This approach provides students with opportunities to interact with grade appropriate high-frequency words on a daily basis. Words can be written on index cards or presented in a matrix of three to five rows with each row containing lists of the same words presented in a different order. Students can practice with the teacher or with peers.
2. **Function Words**: Teachers should incorporate the teaching of function words (*e.g., might, which, enough*) into their schedule and teach them to automaticity. The functional category includes determiners, prepositions, auxiliaries, modals, complementers, conjunctions, and other types of particles. Students learn more about the syntactic/semantic identities of function words when they are embedded in printed sentences as opposed to studying the words in unstructured lists of words (i.e., in isolation) prior to listening to sentences comprised of them (Ehri & Wilce, 1980).
3. **Different Reading Approaches**: Increasing the level of instructional scaffolding makes challenging text accessible to struggling readers. Scaffolding is an instructional technique which involves the incremental structuring of instruction and interactions to enable a learner build on prior knowledge. Other evidence-based reading strategies include shared reading (Gill & Islam, 2011; Paige, 2011), echo reading (McIntyre, Rightmyer, Powell, Powers, & Petrosko, 2006), and timed repeated reading of short passages. Ideally, selected passages should be slightly above a student's present independent reading level (Ari, 2015; Chang & Millett, 2013; Strickland, Boon, & Spencer, 2013).
4. **Pre-Teach Target Words**: Prior to reading a passage, teachers can identify and teach target words from the selection while providing context practice opportunities to give students a clearer understanding of the meaning of the word. Preteaching equips students with the knowledge or skill required for meaningful engagement during the actual lesson although Livers and Bay-Williams (2014) cautioned against allowing the preteaching of an item or items to morph into preteaching content as this can lower the cognitive demand of the lesson, take time away from exploring and discussing the task at hand, as well as deprive students of the opportunity to first explore concept concretely and meaningfully.
5. **Reader's Theater (RT)**: RT has been identified (Doherty & Coggeshall, 2005; Rinehart, 2001) as an authentic and motivating literacy tool that can result in oral reading fluency growth in students regardless of reading abilities. Among other things, it provides ample opportunities for struggling readers to interact with text. According to Rinehart, RT involves choosing or preparing scripted text (preferably one with straightforward plot and interesting dialogue), practicing to read selected text aloud, and then interpreting the text for an audience. The instructional intent of this approach is the improvement of accurate oral reading and the modelling of effective phrasing and reading expression.
6. **Recorded Books**: Milani, Lorusso, and Molteni (2010) reported that the use of books recorded on digital media by pre-adolescents and adolescents with dyslexia resulted in a significant improvement in reading accuracy, reduced unease and emotional-behavioral disorders, as well as an improvement in school performance and a greater motivation and involvement in school activities. This approach, however, is not to be used in isolation. Greaney (2012) argued that while recorded stories may provide access to the meaning in the text, the listener has little or no involvement in any word solving strategies at the same time. Since the listener is not required to decode unfamiliar words during the listening process, there is also no incentive to develop any specific decoding strategies.

The key to a more effective use of recorded stories for students with severe reading difficulties, noted Greaney, is to "…provide opportunities for the student to also develop metacognitive word identification strategies" (p. 45).

Greaney (2012) recommended the use of audio-assisted readings as part of a three-stage integrated reading/language program:

a. Pre-listening/reading word list check (e.g., 10-12 words from the story that are most likely to cause problems for the student. The goal is the development of metacognitive decoding and spelling strategies).
b. Listening to the story (Regular story listening session. Students read along with a recording).
c. Post-listening/reading independent word analysis activities (Students write down the words from one of the pretaught words in a notebook).

Comprehension

Reading comprehension is a metacognitive process that involves the decoding and processing of text with the end goal of text understanding. It is "…the process of simultaneously extracting and constructing meaning through interaction and involvement with written language. It consists of three elements: the reader, the text, and the activity or purpose for reading" (RAND Reading Study Group, 2002, p.11). According to Duke and Pearson (2009), "…text processing occurs not only during 'reading' as we have traditionally defined it but also during short breaks taken during reading even after the 'reading' itself has commenced, even after the 'reading' has ceased" (p. 107). Vocabulary, prosody (i.e., patterns of stress and intonation), fluency, and background knowledge about the subject matter are reported to contribute to reading comprehension or the construction of meaning in written language (Kim, Wagner, & Lopez, 2012; Price, Meisinger, Louwerse & D'Mello, 2016; Veenendaal, Groen, & Verhoeven, 2014). Finally, good readers are able to automatically and effectively engage comprehension strategies to extract meaning text.

Strategies

1. **Think-Alouds**: Teachers can utilize think-alouds as a method of inquiry and as an instructional strategy. Ghaith and Obeid (2004) defined think-alouds as "the conscious disclosure of thought processes while reading…It is considered an effective technique in helping readers acquire a variety of metacognitive comprehension strategies such as evaluating understanding, predicting and verifying, and self- questioning before, during, and after reading" (p. 49). Think-alouds can result in an increased knowledge of reading strategies and the ability to use the strategies successfully to change overall reading behavior (Nash-Ditzel, 2010). Further, Ortlieb and Norris (2012) and Ness and Kenny (2016) revealed that using think-alouds as an instructional tool during reading activity significantly increases a student's comprehension. Using think-alouds requires teachers to first model the strategy. During reading, teachers can stop intermittently at points where they think students might be confused and vocalize what they are thinking "What is the importance of …," "I think the main character will…," and "What have I learned so far?"

2. **Read a Paragraph (RAP):** RAP was identified by Hagaman, Luschen, and Reid (2010) as an effective reading comprehension strategy for young students who exhibit reading comprehension problems. It is a three-step strategy: Read a paragraph; Ask yourself, "What was the main idea and two details?" and Put information into your own words, that requires student engagement in reading materials through questioning and paraphrasing to increase their comprehension of the material. Hagaman, Casey, Reid (2012) reported that the use of the RAP paraphrasing strategy increased reading comprehension as measured by the percentage of text recall and short-answer questions.
3. **Preview Selection**: This approach gives readers a sense of what a text is about and how it is organized before reading it closely and it is also a good time for purpose setting. According to Graves, Cooke, and Laberge (1983) and Erten and Karakas (2007), previewing a reading selection improves comprehension, recall, and reading attitudes of poor readers. When teachers preview text with students, they can draw attention to the text structure (i.e., organization of information), the sequence of events (based on illustrations), and so forth. Students may also be encouraged to talk about the illustrations, make predictions (and re-predict during the actual reading).
4. **Graphic Organizers**: There is a plethora of graphic organizers (GO) available for a variety of purposes. GO, such as Know–Wonder–Learn charts (K-W-L), can be used to keep track of reading as well as help students connect new and prior knowledge. GO can also be used for sequencing activities, identifying story elements, comparing and contrasting, and so forth and they are flexible enough for use in all content areas. According to Singleton and Filce (2015), GO that are predicated on the task at hand and the thinking and learning needs of the student using them help foster critical thinking. Similarly, Dexter and Hughes (2011) reported that across several conditions, settings, and features, the use of GO resulted in increases in vocabulary knowledge, comprehension, and inferential knowledge for students with LD. A study by Palmer, Boon, and Spencer (2014) compared the effects of the dictionary and the concept mapping models on the learning of vocabulary words. During the dictionary instruction phases, each student looked up a vocabulary word in the dictionary, defined the word, and then wrote the word in a sentence on his or her notebook paper. In the concept mapping phase, students completed a concept map (i.e., Frayer model) to display the definition of a word, wrote the word in a sentence, described what the word reminded them of based on their prior knowledge, and then drew a picture related to the vocabulary word. The concept-mapping model was found to be a more effective approach in students' learning of content area related vocabulary words.
5. **Visual Supports:** Teachers can use realia (i.e., objects and materials from everyday life), concept definition mapping, and examples and non-examples to reinforce learning. Rubinstein-Avila (2013) reported that content became more comprehensible when wait-time, think-pair-share, context setting, use of visuals/objects (e.g., realia), or modeling on overhead projector were used in conjunction with small groups and structured talk as instructional strategies.
6. **Inference Training**: Yuill and Oakhill (1998) reported gains in reading comprehension as a result of six 45-minute sessions of inference training delivered to small groups. The lexical inferencing tasks required children to select words from passages and explain how the words contributed to the overall meaning of sentences or stories. The children also generated questions about text and made predictions by trying to use context clues to decipher the meaning of hidden sentences.
7. **Think-Pair-Share (TPS):** TPS promotes student-to-student and student-to-teacher interactions in the classroom: Students are given a minute to think about a particular topic then they pair up with another student to discuss their ideas prior to sharing those ideas with the larger group. TPS was

Specific Learning Disabilities

found to be an effective strategy for improving students' speaking abilities (Usman, 2015), descriptive text writing skills (Sumarsih & Sanjaya, 2013), overall academic achievement (Ibe, 2009), and student engagement (Conderman, Brenahan, & Hedin (2011), with significant increases in critical thinking skills (Kaddoura, 2013).

8. **Activate Students' Background Knowledge**: According to Fisher, Frey, and Lapp (2011), teachers need to assess students' background knowledge for gaps or misconceptions and then provide instruction to build on that base. It is imperative for teachers to help students make connections to personal experiences, knowledge, and previous reading. It is also important to encourage students to make within-text connections and text-to-text connections. Examples of guiding questions in this regard are "What do the two characters have in common?" "How is the setting of this story different from that of the last story we read?" and "How is this story the same as the previous one?" Finally, it is important that students have structured time for independent reading.

9. **Explicit Instruction:** Explicit instruction has been found to significantly improve students' awareness of comprehension strategies and overall comprehension of text (Eilers & Pinkley, 2006; Martinez, 2011), reading comprehension of expository text following explicit vocabulary instruction (Kaldenberg, Watt, & Therrien, 2015), and vocabulary learning for struggling readers (Taylor, Mraz, Nichols, Rickelman & Wood, 2009).

Explicit systematic instruction, which can be one-to-one, small group or whole group, must be data-driven and targeted at areas where students struggle. For example, since it is often difficult for students with poor decoding skills to distinguish the orthographic boundaries in many unfamiliar words encountered during regular reading, Greaney (2012) recommended explicit instruction in assisting students to locate and highlight orthographic boundaries as a precursor to decoding. The most common groups of spelling patterns include consonant blends (e.g., *st, cl, str*), consonant digraphs (e.g., *sh, wr, ch*), vowel digraphs (e.g., *ee, ea, ai, ou*) and vowel phonograms (e.g., *ell, ight, um*).

10. **Skill-Related Activities**: Teachers can teach and provide activities that help students acquire desired skills. For example, an activity to promote a sequencing skill might have students work individually or with a partner to rearrange a cut-up version of the highlights of a selection. Similarly, an activity for summarizing might require students to read and summarize materials in chunks after which they will then put the summaries together to create a whole.

11. **Engagement through Multi-Modal Instruction**: Student engagement is one of the most well-established predictors of achievement (Harbor, Evanovich, Sweigart, & Hughes, 2015). Instruction needs to be age-appropriate. To promote student engagement while facilitating learning, teachers can intermittently change activities, alternate lesson pace, avoid unnecessarily restricting students' movement, employ various modes to present a concept, vary instructional grouping, and adopt a combination of brain-based teaching models like cooperative learning, memory model, and direct instruction. In terms of presentation, Schnotz, Mengelkamp, Baadte, and Hauck (2014) found a stronger modality effect (i.e., learner performance based on the presentation mode) for picture-related paragraphs (It increased with the level of picture novelty) over content-related ones.

12. **Retrospective Miscue Analysis (RMA)**: RMA is a meaning-constructing transactive process used to improve reading accuracy and comprehension. According to Woodley (1985), RMA is predicated on the following set of assumptions:
    a. Miscues are a natural part of reading,

    b.   All readers make miscues, and
    c.   Reading is a single process, whether it is done orally or silently.

The questioning technique in RMA, noted Woodley, encourages consideration of reading as a meaning-getting process as opposed to a process of seeking accuracy or perfection.

RMA combines the power of personal interaction with constructing knowledge in a social context (Theurer, 2002), and is most effective when used one-on-one or in small group settings. Although there are many variants of RMA, typical steps are: meeting one-on-one with a student (based on a predetermined frequency and duration), asking reading-related questions, and allowing the student to select and read a text which is recorded and later miscue-analyzed. The student retells the passage read prior to listening to a recording. While following along in the text, the student will stop if he or she hears something that does not match the text. The teacher then discusses the discrepancies or miscues noticed, self-corrections, and how the student can problem-solve whenever miscues that do not make sense are encountered.

RMA helps readers reappraise themselves as they develop greater confidence, become more conversant with the process of extracting meaning from text, and are better able to articulate the way in which they construct meaning while reading (Goodman & Paulson, 2000; Weaver, 1994; Wilson, 2005).

13. **Collaborative Strategic Reading (CSR)**: CSR is a hybrid of cooperative learning and reading comprehension strategy instruction that helps students improve their reading comprehension while maximizing engagement. It combines the elements of prior knowledge, vocabulary development, questioning techniques, and practice opportunities. The stages involved in CSR are: Discussion (Introduction of the strategy); Modeling (Teacher models each reading strategy and each group dynamics); Guided Practice (Students practice the strategies and roles); and Independent Practice (Students independently practice each strategy). Once students enter the independent phase and are able to operate in collaborative groups, the role of the teacher becomes one of a facilitator.

Although Hitchcock, Dimino, Kurki, Wilkins, and Gersten (2011) concluded that CSR did not appear to have any significant impact on student reading comprehension, a positive impact was reported by Annamma, Eppolito, Klingner, Boele, Boardman, and Stillman-Spisak (2011) and McCown and Thomason (2014) among others.

14. **Close Reading**: Close reading is a central focus of CCSS. It seeks to draw readers' attention to text features and language. Following Fisher and Frey (2014), close reading can be an effective intervention, with significant increases in student attendance, self-perception, and achievement.

According to the Partnership for Assessment of Readiness for College and Careers (PARCC, 2011), close, analytic reading stresses engaging with a text of sufficient complexity directly and examining meaning thoroughly and methodically, encouraging students to read and reread deliberately. Directing student attention on the text itself empowers students to understand the central ideas and key supporting details. It also enables them to reflect on the meanings of individual words and sentences; the order in which sentences unfold; and the development of ideas over the course of the text, which ultimately leads students to arrive at an understanding of the text as a whole.

Specific Learning Disabilities

15. **Clear and Concise Directions**: Flynn (2007) noted that engaging students productively requires giving effective directions, the components of which are: Telling students; Showing students; Rehearsing students; Helping students; and Letting students. Teachers should avoid giving multi-step directions as these can be confusing. To ensure students understand directions given, they could be encouraged to repeat or restate them to a peer or the teacher. A recorder can also be used to record directions, stories, and specific lessons so that students can replay them to clarify understanding of directions or concepts.
16. **Extended Time**: It is beneficial for students to have extended time allowance for assigned tasks. Lewandowski, Cohen, & Lovett (2013) found that when students with LD were given extended time, especially double time, they outperformed nondisabled peers on a reading comprehension test.

Spelling Disorder (Dysorthographia)

Accurate spelling requires cognitive and linguistic knowledge of the phonological, morphological, syntactical, and semantic principles of language (Beirne-Smith & Riley, 2009). Individuals with dysorthographia have difficulties with encoding (i.e., spelling) and understanding grammatical rules. The disorder affects phoneme conversion, segmentation of sentence elements, application of spelling rules, and grammar in varied proportions, and it usually stems from weak awareness or memory of language structures and letters in words. (British Columbia Ministry of Education, 2011).

Glenn and Hurley (1993) synthesized the results of research from the fields of psycholinguistics and education into the nature of the process of acquisition of spelling skills and concluded that the spelling difficulties experienced by some children may result from a combination of early adoption of an unusual reading strategy and/or children starting the reading process while in a state of phonological unreadiness.

Students with dysorthographia might demonstrate arbitrary misspellings such as additions, omissions, and/or substitutions of letters in words, reversals of vowels and/or syllables, slow, hesitant, or poor written expressions, errors in conjugation and grammar, phonetic spellings of non-phonetic words, and misunderstanding the correspondence between sounds and letters.

Strategies to Support Individuals with Dysorthographia

Nies and Belfiore (2006) compared the effects of two spelling strategies, Cover, Copy, Compare (CCC) and Copy Only (CO), used to enhance spelling performance in 3rd grade students with LD. In the CCC method, students were required to say the word, point to it, repeat it, cover it, print it, compare the word to the correct model, and correct errors if necessary. The CO method, on the other hand, required students to say the word, point to it, repeat it, and print it. Overall, CCC was found to be more effective in words learned and words retained. To improve spelling performance in the classroom, Nies and Belfiore recommended incorporating a simple, self-management component to spelling instruction. Jaspers, Williams, Skinner, Cihak, McCallum, and Ciancio (2012) also attested to the effectiveness of CCC and further reported an improvement in spelling and word reading when CCC was supplemented with sentence definition (i.e., providing students with a sentence containing a target word and a brief definition of the word).

Dysorthographia impedes students' overall literacy development because it adversely impacts the acquisition of both reading and writing skills. However, with the right supports in place, students can be taught to become better spellers, readers, and writers. Howard, DaDeppo and De La Paz (2008) described a study involving elementary-aged students with LD using a mnemonic approach to spelling sight words. The approach, called PESTS (i.e., 'words that bug you' because they are difficult to spell), included acrostics, pictorial representations, and stories. Instruction was applied to target words in daily instruction and compared to a traditional approach to spelling sight words. Spelling skills of each student improved significantly as determined by a standardized spelling test, a developmental spelling test, and a researcher-developed instrument.

Additional Strategies

The following additional strategies, while not exhaustive by any means, can be used to help students with dysorthographia:

1. **Extra Learning Sessions**: Teachers should be available to provide extra learning sessions while closely monitoring students' progress.
2. **Explicit Instruction**: The importance of direct instruction was discussed in some detail in the previous section. As students transition to upper grades, they need to learn about word structure or morphology. Word structure includes the study of compound words, root words, and affixes. According to Claravall (2016) and Goodwin and Ahn (2010), the knowledge and awareness of morphological structure provides a new light to help students with reading disabilities build skills in their word reading and spelling. Claravall further identified morphemic analysis, vocabulary and spelling, contextual reading, and written expression as four literacy components that teachers can focus on.

    Spelling rules: Teachers also need to design and implement activities which reinforce the acquisition of useful spelling rules, such as those for adding endings to words with a silent *e* (shake, shaking) or to closed syllables that end in a single consonant (hit, hitting). Use phonograms ending in *-gh* only at the end of base words or before the letter *T,* and so forth. Kemper, Verhoeven, and Bosman (2012) revealed that although explicit and implicit instruction of orthographical spelling rules are equally effective, explicit instruction is more useful when teaching spelling rules when generalization is the goal.

    Darch, Eaves, Crowe, Simmons, and Conniff (2006) compared rule- and activities-based instructional methods of teaching spelling to elementary students with LD. While the rule-based strategy group focused on teaching students rules based on the "Spelling Mastery Level D" program (a direct instruction curriculum designed to explicitly teach spelling skills to students in grades 1 through 6), the activities-based group provided students with an array of spelling activities, such as introducing the words in the context of the story, defining the meaning of the words, sentence writing, and dictionary skill training. Daily instructional sessions lasted for 30 minutes and were conducted over a period of 4 consecutive weeks with 4 different word types (i.e., regular, morphological, spelling rule, irregular) introduced as instruction progressed. Overall, the rule-based approach was more effective in increasing student spelling performance, particularly for the regular, morphological, and spelling-rule words.

3. **Word Sorting**: Word sorting is the process of grouping sounds, words, and pictures into three layers of English orthography, i.e., alphabet, pattern, and meaning. Teachers proceed by demonstrating how to sort pictures or word cards by sounds or patterns. As students sort word cards or picture

Specific Learning Disabilities

cards on their own, teachers help them make discoveries and generalizations about the conventions of English orthography or spelling. Finally, students compare and contrast word features, such as consonants and digraphs, so they can discover similarities and differences within the categories (Vaughn & Bos, 2009). Word sorting, as a teaching strategy, helps students develop more accurate and automatized word recognition and spelling abilities (Barnes, 1989; Greenwood & Bilbow, 2002).

4. **Multisensory Technique**: Fulk and Stormont-Spurgin (1995) reviewed 38 studies on spelling interventions designed for students with LD who were poor spellers, and concluded that instructional procedures (i.e., imitation modeling, analogy training), computer-assisted instruction, study strategies, and multisensory/modality training were all effective systematic techniques. Other studies (e.g., Donnell, 2007; Wadlington, 2000) have also provided conclusive evidence in support of instructional approaches that effectively engage the learning modalities (i.e., sensory channels or pathways through which they give, receive, and store information) of seeing, touching/tracing and hearing/repeating sounds or words.

Hands-on activities such as those involving writing or building printed words with letter tiles should be encouraged especially for younger learners. Teachers can also provide, for example, trays of salt or modeling clay for students to build words, print target words on strips of paper, and cut letters out and have students rearrange them to re-create words. Students can also be given opportunities to spell with magnetic letters.

5. **Daily Interaction with Print**: It is imperative to provide students with daily opportunities to interact with grade-appropriate high-frequency words. Words can be presented on index cards or in a list. Neumann, Summerfield, and Neumann (2015) revealed that although visual features of environmental print influence attention to words, children may preferentially attend to print according to their reading abilities. Print-salient environmental print, they concluded, may be more beneficial for enhancing pre-readers' visual attention to words, whereas print salience may be less important for beginning readers. Kuby and Aldridge (2004) also noted that indirect instruction with environmental print improved Kindergarten children's ability to read logos and aided them in making the transition from reading logos to reading logos in manuscript form. Students will also benefit from systematically decoding words on a daily basis.

6. **Accommodations and Modifications**: These should match a student's learning styles and interests. An accommodation is a tool for helping a student with special needs work around his or her disability. Students with LD often need academic accommodations to productively engage the curriculum. For a qualified student, for example, accommodations might be oral presentations instead of written responses, the use of a dictionary, word books, or computer spell-checkers or other assistive technology, such as those with predictive text. Modifications, on the other hand, reduce the cognitive demands or content of a task. An example of a modification is assigning fewer spelling words than those assigned to nondisabled peers.

Writing Disorder (Dysgraphia)

Dysgraphia is a neurological disorder typified by an inability to write despite thorough instruction. This disability varies in severity and can be characterized by an awkward pencil grip; unusual body, wrist, or paper position; poor spatial planning on paper; aversion to writing tasks; distorted or incorrect writing, such as incorrect letter orientation; an inability to retain motor patterns of letter forms; random mixture of uppercase and lowercase letters; poor letter formation; inappropriately sized letters; inconsistent spacing between letters or words; odd spelling; production of incorrect words; and a large gap between written ideas and understanding demonstrated through speech. Dysgraphia is typically identified by licensed psychologists (Chalk, J. C., Hagan-Burke & Burke, 2005; Cortiella & Horowitz, 2014; Crouch & Jakubecy, 2007; Datchuk & Kubina, 2013; *Dysgraphia Information*, n.d.).

Writing is important because, among other things, written responses demonstrate an understanding of text or instruction. Dysgraphia usually results in low classroom work productivity, incomplete homework assignments, and difficulty in focusing attention. Children with dysgraphia are usually the ones who spend a long time on writing tasks during the school day and end up having to take unfinished classwork home with them in addition to their daily homework.

Individual variations of dysgraphia include *dyslexic dysgraphia* where spontaneously written text is illegible accompanied by poor oral spelling and relatively normal finger-tapping speed (i.e., measure of fine-motor speed) with normal drawing and copying of written text; *motor dysgraphia* where spontaneously written and copied text may be illegible, oral spelling is normal, drawing is problematic, and finger-tapping speed is abnormal; and *spatial dysgraphia* where writing, whether spontaneously produced or copied, is illegible, oral spelling and finger-tapping speed are normal, but drawing is very problematic (International Dyslexia Association [IDA], 2000).

Following the National Institute of Neurological Disorders and Stroke (2011), the treatment for dysgraphia may include therapy for motor disorders to help control writing movements. Other treatments may be directed at impaired memory or other neurological problems. To avoid problems associated with handwriting, some physicians recommend that individuals with dysgraphia use computers.

Strategies to Support Individuals with Dysgraphia

According to some studies, many problems associated with dysgraphia can be prevented by early training. IDA (2000), for example, recommends teaching young children in kindergarten and grade one how to form letters correctly since kinesthetic memory is powerful and incorrect habits are very difficult to eradicate. Muscle training and over-learning good techniques (i.e. ongoing practice after achieving initial proficiency) are also beneficial.

As noted by Chalk, Hagan-Burke, and Burke (2005), many students with LD exhibit deficiencies in the writing process. In order to achieve an adequate level of writing competence, these students must apply strategies that enable them to effectively plan, organize, write, and revise a written product. Explicit strategy instruction involving a structured style of learning has been found to increase students' writing competence. Crouch and Jakubecy (2007) recommended a combination of drill and fine motor activities as these have the potential to significantly address problems associated with dysgraphia, especially in the area of handwriting.

Some writing programs have been found to be effective in helping individuals with writing challenges. For example, Walker, Shippen, Houchins, and Cihak (2007) found the direct-instruction writing program, *Expressive Writing*, to be effective in improving the writing skills of high school students with LD.

In a study involving 4th grade students with LD in two different writing situations (i.e., writing for test preparation and writing for digital stories), Jacobs and Fu (2014) concluded that classroom teachers can transform the teaching of writing by drawing on students' home literacies. They further observed

Specific Learning Disabilities

that while a test-driven teaching approach tends to limit students' ability as learners, instruction that values students' technological expertise energizes learning and helps students reach their potential while ensuring their school success.

Additional Strategies

1. **Accommodations**: Prater, Redman, Anderson, and Gibb (2014) observed that students with LD often need academic accommodations to be successful. It is the responsibility of the teacher, therefore, to ensure the accessibility of accommodations. Students should be able to avail themselves of options from a gamut of accommodations. A student might find it easier to dictate sentences into a tape recorder before writing them down. Another student might need wide-ruled or graph paper for visual guidance in aligning and spacing letters and numbers while yet another student might need pencil grips, pencils of different thicknesses, or any other specially designed writing aids to perform a task. Further, teachers can reduce the amount of writing a student needs to do by, for example, providing pre-printed worksheets where students fill in the blanks in passages from which some words have been omitted.

Additionally, students will benefit from teacher modelling of the use of graphic organizers to brainstorm ideas and create an outline (Singleton & Filce, 2015), availability of sentence frames (Donnelly & Roe, 2010) and a list of commonly used words. Finally, some students may need extended time to perform certain tasks. At the initial stage, however, neatness and spelling should not be a major grading consideration. The requirement can be refined with time.

2. **Peer Support**: Teacher and peer support are academic and social in nature and have unique implications for supporting motivation, engagement, and belonging in middle school (Kiefer, Alley & Ellerbrock, 2015). For example, McCurdy and Cole (2014) showed how support from typically developing peers can be effective in reducing off-task behaviors. The involvement of a peer note taker or teacher-provided notes or outlines can also be beneficial as these reduce writing demands.
3. **Self-Regulated Strategy Development (SRSD)**: SRSD is an instructional approach designed to help students learn, use, and adopt strategies employed by skilled writers. It adds the element of self-regulation to strategy instruction for writing by encouraging students to monitor, evaluate, and revise their writing, which in turn reinforces self-regulation skills and independent learning (Teaching Excellence in Adult Literacy, 2011). Elements of SRSD instruction are: discuss it, model it, make it your own, support it, and independent performance. Several studies (e.g., Asaro-Saddler, 2014; Hacker, Dole, Ferguson, Adamson, Roundy, & Scarpulla, 2015; Mason, Harris & Graham, 2011; McKeown, FitzPatrick, & Sandmel, 2014; Reid, Hagaman & Graham, 2014) have identified SRSD as an effective writing intervention.
4. **Practice**: Students need daily opportunities to work on letter and character formation. For example, they can practice formation of individual letters written in isolation. The importance of daily writing practice has been discussed by Kissel and Miller (2015), and Roth and Guinee (2011) among others.
5. **Modeling**: Following Troia (2002) and Regan and Berkeley (2012), explicit modeling and scaffolding of students' writing attempts are needed to support effective reading and writing instruction. Gerde, Bingham, and Wasik (2012) also stressed the importance of supporting children's literacy

development through the provision of multiple opportunities to observe teachers model writing, teacher support and scaffolding for children's writing attempts, and engaging children in meaningful writing in their play. Teacher can, for example, model writing to a prompt; provide students with rubrics, examples, and non-examples; and consult with them during the writing process. It is also advisable to expose students to different writing genres. Datchuk and Kubina (2013) revealed that students with writing difficulties and LD benefited from intervention, particularly in handwriting and sentence construction, and were able to transfer the acquired skills to more complex tasks like sentence writing and extended composition.

Some Associated Disorders

Auditory and visual processing disorders and executive functioning deficits are examples of disorders which, while not labeled as specific subtypes of LD, usually comorbid with it. Auditory, visual, and executive functioning disorders are discussed below along with some supports that could be put in place to support skill acquisition of affected individuals (Chermak & Musierk, 1992; Christmann, Lachmann & Steinbrink, 2015; Eilers & Pinkley, 2006).

Auditory Processing Deficits

There appears to be no consensus regarding a common definition of Auditory Processing and Auditory Processing Disorders (APD). However, the disorders are usually discussed in the context of a weakness in the ability to understand and use auditory information even though affected individuals appear to have adequate hearing abilities. An individual with APD might have trouble noticing, comparing, and distinguishing the distinct and separate sounds in words (auditory discrimination); picking out important sounds from a noisy background (auditory figure-ground discrimination); engaging short- and long-term memories to recall orally presented information (auditory memory); understanding and recalling the order of sounds and words; or following a sequence of activities (auditory sequencing).

Georgiou, Papadopoulos, Zarouna, and Parrila (2012) found that children with dyslexia did not demonstrate APD even though about half of them showed visual processing deficits. However, Christmann, Lachmann, and Steinbrink (2015) identified APD in most but not all participants with dyslexia and concluded that their results suggest the existence of a general auditory processing impairment in developmental dyslexia. Other studies reported that processing simultaneous auditory stimuli may be impaired in children with dyslexia regardless of phonological processing difficulties (Lallier, Donnadieu, & Valdois, 2013), and that language impairment and reading disorders commonly co-occur with auditory processing disorder (Sharma, Purdy, & Kelly, 2009).

Diagnosing auditory processing disorders, according to the National Coalition of Auditory Processing Disorders (2016), requires a comprehensive assessment to look at all of the following factors: 1) cognitive/behavioral testing by a psychologist, 2) language testing by a speech-language pathologist, 3) auditory processing testing by an audiologist, and 4) sensory systems assessment by an occupational therapist.

Strategies

Following McArthur, Ellis, Atkinson, and Coltheart (2008), auditory processing deficits can be treated successfully in children with specific reading disabilities (SRD) and specific language impairment (SLI) even though it is unlikely to help them with the acquisition of new reading, spelling, or spoken language skills. To improve auditory processing skills, Chermak and Musiek (1992) suggested a management approach that emphasizes the development of both specific and general problem-solving strategies in conjunction with self-regulation of strategy use. They observed that such an approach takes advantage of the functional plasticity of the maturing central nervous system in improving auditory processing skills.

Additional Strategies

1. **Cues**: Teachers can employ visual and gestural cues to engage diverse learners. Conderman and Hedin (2011) identified the use of cue cards as one of many effective instructional strategies for helping students with LD to succeed in school. They pointed out that cue cards help students:

    a. Learn academic and behavioral steps, principles, procedures, processes, and rules;
    b. Organize their approach to a task;
    c. Monitor their performance; and
    d. Become more independent learners.

Cognitive cue cards are valuable and result in improvements in the metacognitive capabilities of learners with LD (Richie, 2005), as well as providing an instructional structure for a wide variety of children and for multiple activities (McCoy, Mathur & Czoka, 2010).

2. **Ecological Considerations:** Ideally, learning spaces should be conducive to risk taking and learning. Due consideration also needs to be given to seating arrangements, zones of proximity, accessibility to locations and supplies, and the absence of clutter and distractions. Some students prefer to stand while working and others may be more productive if seating on, for example, a Pilate's ball in place of a regular chair.

"Preferential seating" refers to the seating accommodation allowed by teachers. Some students might do their best work if seating close to the teacher or away from a noise source in the classroom.

With respect to seating arrangements, Bicard, Ervin, Bicard, and Baylot-Casey (2012) found that disruptive behavior during group seating occurred at twice the rate when students were allowed to choose their seats with the likelihood of disruptive behavior increasing three-fold when students chose their seats during individual seating. When Wannarka and Ruhl (2008) examined three common seating arrangements (i.e., rows, groups, semi-circles), and found that students displayed higher levels of appropriate behavior during individual tasks when seated in rows. On the strength of their findings, they advised teachers to allow the nature of the task to dictate seating arrangements.

3. **Self-Regulation**: The teaching of self-regulation skills promotes on-task behavior. Self- regulation is positively associated with academic achievement (Duru, Duru, & Balkis, 2014). Self –regulation skills can be taught within or outside the classroom. Becker, McClelland, Loprinzi and Trost (2014) associated higher active play with better self-regulation, which in turn was associated with higher scores on early reading and math assessments. Hyndman (2015) explained that the use of school playground interventions has emerged as a critical strategy within schools to facilitate and develop children's active play via an informal curriculum.

4. **Pre-Teaching**: Pre-teaching activities have been associated with increased academic outcomes. Beck, Burns, and Lau (2009) investigated the effect of pre-teaching reading skills on-task behavior and observed that on-task time during reading instruction increased after a pre-teaching intervention. Burns, Hodgson, Parker, and Fremont (2011), also attested to the effectiveness of text previewing and the pre-teaching of keywords.
5. **Technology**: Technology such as computer-based training can be used to support students with APD. The National Coalition of Auditory Processing Disorders (2016) recommends the following: *Tomatis* (www.tomatis.com); the *Listening Program* (www.advancedbrain.com or www.thelisteningprogram.com); *Samonas* (www.samonas.com); *Therapeutic Listening* (www.vitallinks.com); *Earobics* (www.earobics.com); *Fast ForWord* (www.fastforword.com); and the *Lindamood-Bell Programs* (www.lindamoodbell.com).
6. **Task Analysis**: Task analysis is used to identify and teach discrete steps involved in a target skill. It is usually used where a skill consists of a series of connected discrete steps, as opposed to a skill involving multiple variables and/or outcomes. Szidon and Franzone (2009) noted that task analysis requires identifying a target skill (e.g., a goal from an IEP or IFSP); collecting a student's baseline data to determine if he or she has the prerequisite skills required to perform the task and ascertaining the availability of materials needed (i.e., depending on the student's unique needs as well as the available resources); breaking the skill into smaller steps for the student to follow; ensuring the component steps are accurately and completely represented; deciding the best approach to use in teaching the skill; and implementing and progress monitoring.
7. **Information Flow:** Information should be presented in manageable chunks so that student is not overwhelmed. Teachers should also speak slowly and clearly when presenting information or directions and have students repeat/rephrase the information. Students should be encouraged to clarify information as needed.
8. **Island of Competence**: Provide opportunities for students to thrive in their island of competence or areas of strength.

Visual Processing Deficits (VPD)

Visual processing deficits or perceptual disorders refer to the brain's inability to efficiently process information which is presented visually. VPD are not caused by a visual impairment and affected individuals usually have difficulty noticing, comparing, and contrasting features (visual discrimination); distinguishing a visual image from its background (visual figure-ground discrimination); specifying the location of an object in space in relation to a reference object (spatial relationships); identifying the sequential order of stimuli (visual sequencing); coordinating body movement based on visual feedback (visual motor processing); storing and retrieving information of what was seen (visual memory); and correctly perceiving a partly hidden object or word (visual closure). Individuals with VPD sometimes move the whole head (instead of just the eyes) while reading, experience double vision, squint, misjudge distance, fall or bump into objects due to poor spatial awareness, have eye tracking problems and demonstrate a lack of coordinated muscle movements (British Columbia Ministry of Education, 2011; Cortiella & Horowitz, 2014; Georgiou, Papadopoulos, Zarouna, & Parrila,, 2012; Neumann, Summerfield, & Neumann, 2015; Peyrin, Demonet, N'Guyen-Morel, Le Bas & Valdois, 2011).

Visual attention (VA) span was defined by Bosse, Tainturier, and Valdois (2007) as the amount of distinct visual elements that can be processed in a multi-element array. According to the VA span deficit hypothesis, letter string (i.e., strings of letters appearing in certain words, e.g., -unch, crunch, punch, brunch) deficits are a consequence of impaired visual processing. Peyrin, Demonet, N'Guyen-Morel, Le Bas, and Valdois (2011) reported that a VA span disorder is potentially responsible for the observed poor reading outcomes in children with dyslexia.

Although both orthographic processing and rapid automatized naming deficits are associated with dyslexia, their relationship with VPD is not so clear (Georgiou et al., 2012). According to Bogon, Finke, Schulte-Körne, Müller, Schneider, and Stenneken, (2014), slowed perceptual processing speed is a primary VA deficit in developmental dyslexia (DD), and reduced visual processing speed seems to modulate the difficulties in written language processing imposed by the disorder.

Supports

1. **Wait Time:** Wait time is the duration of pauses between teachers' and students' exchanges. According to Tobin (1987), wait time fosters higher cognitive level learning by giving teachers and students more time to think. However, Ingram and Elliott (2016) cautioned against maintaining extended wait times. They asserted that asking teachers to mechanically observe pauses of at least three seconds is not a productive strategy because it will focus their attention on the length of the pause rather than the desired student interactional behaviors. They further contended that unnecessarily extending wait time could result in an increase in unsolicited responses and, in some cases, the extension might be perceived as a signal of trouble, in which case participants are likely to self-select in an attempt to initiate a repair.

Additionally, in an attempt to improve the quality of classroom dialogue, teachers can prime students by informing them ahead of time that they will be answering the next question or performing the next task or, as advised by Ingram and Elliott, have students discuss questions in pairs before deciding on an answer.

2. **Explicit Structured Language Teaching**: Multisensory instructional approaches can be used to teach decoding, spelling, and math. It engages the visual (see), auditory (hear), and kinesthetic-tactile (touch) learning modalities in memory enhancement and learning. It is also good practice to incorporate these elements into lesson plans.
3. **Graphic Organizers**: Teachers can model and encourage the use of graphic organizers. Graphic organizers help students organize their thoughts, sequence events, compose paragraphs, compare and contrast, and identify story elements. They are also flexible enough for use in other content areas.
4. **Simplify Oral Directions**: Teachers should avoid giving convoluted directions. Rather, simplify oral directions and have students restate them to you or to a peer. Students should be encouraged to ask clarifying questions when in doubt. A graphic representation of steps involved in a task may also be provided.
5. **Cueing System**: Reinforce auditory cues with visual cues such as images and gestures.
6. **Models**: Provide models so students can see what a finished product looks like. Realia and authentic materials can also be used to reinforce learning.
7. **Students' Responses**: Provide students with a range of alternatives to traditional modes of responding to assigned tasks.

8. **Grouping**: Use instructional grouping approaches that are supportive of students' skill acquisition as well as those that allow for peer redirection when needed. Hollo & Hirn (2015) revealed that across elementary, middle, and high schools, whole-group instruction was the most frequently used format regardless of grade level, but individual opportunities to respond and active engagement were significantly higher during small-group lessons.
9. **Manage Tasks**: Break assignments into manageable steps and assign time frames for completing each step. Accommodations, variations, and modifications should also be given due consideration when assigning a task.
10. **Universal Design for Learning (UDL):** UDL is predicated on the architectural model of universal design. It guarantees access for diverse learners by addressing and redressing obstacles to learning. The three guiding principles of UDL are providing multiple means of representation (the "what" of learning), providing multiple means of action and expression (the "how" of learning), and the provision of multiple means of engagement (the "why" of learning). (Fact Sheet: Universal Design for Learning, [n.d]; Stockall, Dennis, & Miller, 2012).
11. **Track Reading**: Students can be shown how to use a ruler or some other straight-edged object to track reading. When this is used, however, it is advisable to place the ruler over – not under – the line being read.
12. **Highlighting**: Students will benefit from knowing how to identify and highlight pertinent portions of text. Important information may also be color-coded for easy retrieval. Yue, Storm, Kornell, & Bjork. (2015) examined highlighting in relation to distributed study and students' attitudes about highlighting as a study strategy. They concluded that highlighting can be beneficial for learning especially as the practice did not impair knowledge of non-highlighted information. They, consequently, argued that students should be trained in how to optimize the potential benefits of their highlighting behavior.
13. **Gradual Release of Responsibility:** Frey, and Fisher (2009) identified the four components of the gradual release of responsibility as focus lessons, guided instruction, collaborative tasks, and independent learning. It is imperative for teachers to structure instruction such that it creates the desired level of engagement as well as focus on the gradual transfer of the responsibility of learning from the teacher to the learner: "I do," "We do," "You do."
14. **Check for Understanding**: Checking for understanding is an important step in the teacher-student interaction. Teachers should employ different techniques (e.g., Timed-Pair-Share, Onion Ring, Project Study Group, journaling/quick writes) to check for understanding on an ongoing basis.
15. **Paraphrasing and Self-Verbalization**: Metacognitive awareness of reading strategies can be enhanced by the teaching of paraphrasing and self-verbalization techniques. As noted by Feitlera and Hellekson (1993), paraphrasing techniques taught as an integral part of a holistic supplemental reading program will produce positive growth in reading achievement. For multi-step tasks, some students will find it beneficial to verbalize each step. Having a checklist will also guide them through a task.
16. **Mnemonics**: Mnemonics introduced and taught as a memory enhancement strategy. Letter strategies, keyword-, and pegword methods of mnemonics are effective strategies in improving memory in content areas such as elementary life science, secondary social studies and anatomy, elementary social studies, elementary reading vocabulary, and secondary SAT vocabulary (Scruggs, Mastropieri, Berkeley, & Marshak, 2010).

Specific Learning Disabilities

17. **Reading Guide**: Teachers can create reading guides for different subjects and reading levels. This will improve comprehension and help students navigate text especially one that is above their independent reading level. Ortlieb, E. (2013) reported that the use of anticipatory reading guides resulted in significant gains across multiple subject areas for third grade struggling readers.
18. **Teach Organizational Strategies**: Teach organizational strategies and help students to know how to select the best strategy for a given task.
19. **Transitioning**: Teach students how to transition seamlessly from one activity or level to the next.

Executive Functioning Deficits

Executive functions (EF) are higher-level cognitive skills controlled by the frontal lobes of the brain. These functions can be organizational (e.g., acquiring, recalling, and retrieving information; sequencing; planning; abstract thinking; cognitive flexibility) or regulatory (e.g., task initiation, moral reasoning, self-regulation, monitoring, decision-making). Although some common characteristics are discussed in this chapter, care should be taken not to pathologize individual differences in development (British Columbia Ministry of Education, 2011; Cortiella, & Horowitz, 2014; Desoete, & De Weerdt, 2013).

Characteristics of EF deficits include weaknesses in the following areas: dealing with frustration, negotiating group dynamics, evaluating ideas, task initiation and completion, sequencing events or steps, staying on task, information processing and retrieval, engaging working memory in the temporary retention of new information, planning, organizing, self-monitoring, transitioning, time and space management, inappropriate behavior, abstract reasoning, verbal fluency, multi-tasking, and impulsive behaviors such as blurting out the answer to a problem without being called upon (British Columbia Ministry of Education, 2011; Cortiella, & Horowitz, 2014).

Although the literature is unclear about the mental processes involved in EF, they are important nonetheless for cognitive, affective, and conative development. Tests used to assess executive behavior include the Word Fluency Task, Stroop Test, Wisconsin Card Sorting Test, Trail Making Test, Category Test, Progressive Figures and Color Form Tests, Porteus Mazes, and the Behavior Rating Inventory of Executive Function (BRIEF).

Strategies

The following strategies can be employed to leverage learning for students with EF deficits:

1. **Single Step Directions**: Students find it easier to follow clear step-by-step directions especially when such directions are reinforced with multi-sensory cues. Written directions can be used in combination with spoken instructions and visual models or gestures. Implementing multi-sensory experiences has been found (Thompson, 2011) to increase the sustained focus of students with special needs.
2. **Organizers**: Teachers can introduce and encourage the use of checklists, visual schedules, organizers, computers, or visual timers. Waters, Lerman, and Hovanetz (2009) recommended the use of visual schedules in combination with extinction for helping students transition from one activity to the next.

3. **Break Up Tasks:** Some students will benefit from instruction on when and how to break large tasks into smaller manageable chunks. Some students might need extended time to produce their best work.
4. **Feedback**: It helps to give timely and productive feedback that is neither generic nor vague. According to Brookhart (2011), feedback for struggling students should be specific, concise, process-focused, and self-referenced to describe progress or capability, while checking for understanding. Feedback for successful students, on the other hand, should be descriptive while envisioning next steps for advancement or enrichment. Lalor (2012) also argued that giving students clear, high-quality feedback that is tied to learning targets, moves student learning forward. Conversely, when students are deprived of feedback or given feedback that is barely connected to learning targets, they get frustrated, lose sight of goals, and take many detours before they arrive at the desired learning.
5. **Workspace**: It is usually advantageous to have organized work areas that are clutter-free. It is also good practice to use labels to identify key areas and items in the classroom. Preferential seating may also be allowed as needed.
6. **Study Guides:** The diversity in general education classrooms requires teachers to continue to explore ways to support students' learning. According to Conderman and Bresnahan (2010), study guides support students in learning their material, focus their attention on important topics, and help them review for quizzes or tests. Teachers can provide study guides or, alternatively, encourage students to create their own.
7. **Highlighters**: Students can be taught to use highlighters to emphasize pertinent information as well as key or signal words in a passage.

CONCLUSION

According to the Least Restrictive Environment (LRE) component of IDEIA, children with disabilities should be educated with their non-disabled peers and their removal from the regular educational environment should occur only if the nature or severity of the disability is such that education in regular classes cannot be achieved satisfactorily even with the use of supplementary aids and services [20 United States Code (U.S.C.) Sec. 1412(a)(5)(A); 34 Code of Federal Regulations (C.F.R.) Sec.300.114]. The import of this requirement is that learners with special needs are spread across the placement gamut: from a general education setting with typical peers, to a more restrictive setting such as a special day class. Regardless of a student's setting, however, reason dictates that related services and intervention sessions, should not coincide with time slots when new material is being taught to other students.

Although the number of students with LD eligibility is declining, Cortiella and Horowitz (2014) estimated that about 42% of all students receiving special education services have an LD eligibility. Interestingly enough, some students with LD eligibility also find themselves in the English learner (EL) subgroup. Granted that there are several evidence-based practices that can be used to reroute the underachievement trajectory of struggling students, not all approaches will work for every learner. For example, the inability of some students with LD to, among other things, connect an existing knowledge base to new learning sometimes renders exploration or discovery methods of learning ineffective. Consequently, care has to be taken in the selection of interventions.

Research shows (e.g. Sexton, 2004) that teachers' prior educational experiences wield a strong influence on their approach to pedagogy. The task for many teachers, therefore, is how best to reconcile old practices and beliefs with the current realities of the profession. This recalibration will be easy for some and difficult, if not impossible, for others. In light of this, pre-service teachers must approach the profession with an open mind: willing to learn and make necessary adjustments by yielding to reason and evidence and it is the responsibility of teacher educators and veteran teachers to help these fledglings succeed in aligning practice with present demands.

Haager and Vaughn (2013) emphasized the need for special education teachers to develop

...a thorough understanding of the K-5 CCSS in order to facilitate access for students with disabilities within general education classroom, to assist classroom teachers in making appropriate adaptations and accommodations, and to design interventions that best prepare students to achieve competency across a wide range of literacy skills (p. 10).

Early intervention is key to providing students with LD a meaningful learning experience. An early intervention involves the use of multiple measures to diagnose a student's present level of performance primarily with a view to finding strengths (Strengths can be used to mitigate deficits) and learning gaps, utilizing evidence-based systematic instruction delivered with treatment fidelity, and an ongoing progress monitoring.

Finally, accommodations allowed for routine classwork should also be available to students during testing. To support present and future instructional planning, it is good practice to maintain a record of successful accommodations and modifications in a student's Individualized Education Program (IEP), Individual Family Service Plan (IFSP), or Cumulative Record. To reiterate, intervention needs to be individualized instead of generic and concern over students' academic and social progress should be generic instead of individualized. This just means that intervention must be customized to address identified needs while being tackled collaboratively by service providers as a collective enterprise.

REFERENCES

Allor, J. H., Gansle, K. A., & Denny, R. K. (2006). The stop and go phonemic awareness game: Providing modeling, practice, and feedback. *Preventing School Failure, 50*(4), 23–30. doi:10.3200/PSFL.50.4.23-30

American Psychiatric Association. (2013). *Diagnostic and statistical manual of mental disorders: DSM-5*. Washington, DC: American Psychiatric Association.

Anderson-Levitt, K. M. (2008). Globalization and curriculum. In F. M. Connelly, M. F. He, & J. I. Phillion (Eds.), *The SAGE handbook of curriculum and instruction* (pp. 349–368). Malden, MA: Sage. doi:10.4135/9781412976572.n17

Annamma, S., Eppolito, A., Klingner, J., Boele, A., Boardman, A., & Stillman-Spisak, S. J. (2011). Collaborative strategic reading: Fostering success for all. *Voices from the Middle, 19*(2), 27–32. Retrieved from http://www.ncte.org/journals

Ari, O. (2015). Fluency gains in struggling college readers from wide reading and repeated readings. *Reading Psychology, 36*(3), 270–297. doi:10.1080/02702711.2013.864361

Asaro-Saddler, K. (2014). Self-regulated strategy development: Effects on writers with autism spectrum disorders. *Education and Training in Autism and Developmental Disabilities, 49*(1), 78-91. Retrieved from http://daddcec.org/Publications/ETADDJournal.aspx

Ashby, J., Dix, H., Bontrager, M., Dey, R., & Archer, A. (2013). Phonemic awareness contributes to text reading fluency: Evidence from eye movements. *School Psychology Review, 42*(2), 157–170. Retrieved from http://www.nasponline.org/publications/

Barnes, W. G. W. (1989). Word sorting: The cultivation of rules for spelling in English. *Reading Psychology, 10*(3), 293–307. doi:10.1080/0270271890100306

Beck, M., Burns, M. K., & Lau, M. (2009). The effect of preteaching reading skills on the on-task behavior of children identified with behavioral disorders. *Behavioral Disorders, 34*(2), 91–99. Retrieved from http://www.ccbd.net/behavioraldisorders

Becker, D. R., McClelland, M. M., Loprinzi, P., & Trost, S. G. (2014). Physical activity, self-regulation, and early academic achievement in preschool children. *Early Education and Development, 25*(1), 56–70. doi:10.1080/10409289.2013.780505

Beirne-Smith, M., & Riley, T. F. (2009). Spelling assessment of students with disabilities: Formal and informal procedures. *Assessment for Effective Intervention, 34*(3), 170–177. doi:10.1177/1534508408318844

Bicard, D. F., Ervin, A., Bicard, S. C., & Baylot-Casey, L. (2012). Differential effects of seating arrangements on disruptive behavior of fifth-grade students during independent seatwork. *Journal of Applied Behavior Analysis, 45*(2), 407–411. doi:10.1901/jaba.2012.45-407

Blanden, J., & Machin, S. (2010). Education and inequality. In D. Brewer & P. J. McEwan (Eds.), *Economics of education*. Oxford, UK: Elsevier. doi:10.1016/B978-0-08-044894-7.01218-5

Bogon, J., Finke, K., Schulte-Körne, G., Müller, H. J., Schneider, W. X., & Stenneken, P. (2014). Parameter-based assessment of disturbed and intact components of visual attention in children with developmental dyslexia. *Developmental Science, 17*(5), 697–713. doi:10.1111/desc.12150

Bosse, M., Tainturier, M., & Valdois, S. (2007). Developmental dyslexia: The visual attention span deficit hypothesis. *Cognition, 104*(2), 198–230. doi:10.1016/j.cognition.2006.05.009

Boyles, N. (2013). Closing in on close reading. *Educational Leadership, 70*(4), 36–41. Retrieved from http://www.ascd.org

British Columbia Ministry of Education. (2011). *Supporting students with learning disabilities: A guide for teachers*. Author. Retrieved from http://www.bced.gov.bc.ca/specialed/docs/learning_disabilities_guide.pdf

Brookhart, S. M. (2011). Tailoring feedback: Effective feedback should be adjusted depending on the needs of the learner. *Education Digest: Essential Readings Condensed for Quick Review, 76*(9), 33-36. Retrieved from http://www.eddigest.com/

Burns, M. K., Hodgson, J., Parker, D. C., & Fremont, K. (2011). Comparison of the effectiveness and efficiency of text previewing and preteaching keywords as small-group reading comprehension strategies with middle-school students. *Literacy Research and Instruction*, *50*(3), 241–252. doi:10.1080/19388071.2010.519097

Chalk, J. C., Hagan-Burke, S., & Burke, M. D. (2005). The effects of self-regulated strategy development on the writing process for high school students with learning disabilities. *Learning Disability Quarterly*, *28*(1), 75–87. doi:10.2307/4126974

Chamberlain, L., Cheung-Chung, M., & Jenner, L. (1993). Preliminary findings on communication and challenging behavior in learning disabilities. *Behavior Journal of Developmental Disabilities*, *31*(77), 118–125. doi:10.1179/bjdd.1993.014

Chang, A., & Millett, S. (2013). Improving reading rates and comprehension through timed repeated reading. *Reading in a Foreign Language*, *25*(2), 126–148. Retrieved from http://www.afb.org/store

Cheng, Y. C. (2004). Fostering local knowledge and human development in globalization of education. *International Journal of Educational Management*, *18*(1), 7–24. doi:10.1108/09513540410512109

Chermak, G. D., & Musiek, F. E. (1992). Managing central auditory processing disorders in children and youth. *American Journal of Audiology*, *1*(3), 61–65. doi:10.1044/1059-0889.0103.61

Christmann, C., Lachmann, T., & Steinbrink, C. (2015). Evidence for a general auditory processing deficit in developmental dyslexia from a discrimination paradigm using speech versus nonspeech sounds matched in complexity. *Journal of Speech, Language, and Hearing Research: JSLHR*, *58*(1), 107–121. doi:10.1044/2014_JSLHR-L-14-0174

Claravall, E. B. (2016). Integrating morphological knowledge in literacy instruction: Framework and principles to guide special education teachers. *Teaching Exceptional Children*, *48*(4), 195–203. doi:10.1177/0040059915623526

Conderman, G., & Bresnahan, V. (2010). Study guides to the rescue. *Intervention in School and Clinic*, *45*(3), 169–176. doi:10.1177/1053451209349532

Conderman, G., Bresnahan, V., & Hedin, L. (2011). Promoting active involvement in today's classrooms. *Kappa Delta Pi Record*, *47*(4), 174–180. doi:10.1080/00228958.2011.10516587

Conderman, G., & Hedin, L. (2011). Cue cards: A self-regulatory strategy for students with learning disabilities. *Intervention in School and Clinic*, *46*(3), 165–173. doi:10.1177/1053451210378745

Cortiella, C., & Horowitz, S. H. (2014). *The state of learning disabilities: Facts, trends, and emerging issues*. New York: National Center for Learning Disabilities. Retrieved from https://www.ncld.org/wp-content/uploads/2014/11/2014-State-of-LD.pdf

Crouch, A. L., & Jakubecy, J. J. (2007). Dysgraphia: How it affects a student's performance and what can be done about it. *Teaching Exceptional Children Plus*, *3*(3), Article 5. Retrieved from http://escholarship.bc.edu/education/tecplus/vol3/iss3/art5

Darch, C., Eaves, R. C., Crowe, D. A., Simmons, K., & Conniff, A. (2006). Teaching spelling to students with learning disabilities: A comparison of rule-based strategies versus traditional instruction. *Journal of Direct Instruction, 6*(1), 1–16. Retrieved from http://www.adihome.org

Datchuk, S. M., & Kubina, R. M. (2013). A review of teaching sentence-level writing skills to students with writing difficulties and learning disabilities. *Remedial and Special Education, 34*(3), 180–192. doi:10.1177/0741932512448254

Dee, T. S. (2010). Education and civic engagement. In D. Brewer & P. J. McEwan (Eds.), *Economics of education*. Oxford, UK: Elsevier. doi:10.1016/B978-0-08-044894-7.01228-8

Dexter, D. D., & Hughes, C. A. (2011). Graphic organizers and students with learning disabilities: A meta-analysis. *Learning Disability Quarterly, 34*(1), 51–72. doi:10.1177/073194871103400104

Doherty, J., & Coggeshall, K. (2005). Reader's Theater and Storyboarding: Strategies That Include and Improve. *Voices from the Middle, 12*(4), 37–43.

Donnell, W. J. (2007). The effects of multisensory vowel instruction during word study for third-grade students. *Reading Research Quarterly, 42*(4), 468–471. doi:10.1598/RRQ.42.4.2

Donnelly, W. B., & Roe, C. J. (2010). Using sentence frames to develop academic vocabulary for English learners. *The Reading Teacher, 64*(2), 131–136. doi:10.1598/RT.64.2.5

Duke, N. K., & Pearson, P. D. (2009). Effective practices for developing reading comprehension. *The Journal of Education, 189*(1/2), 107–122. Retrieved from https://lincs.ed.gov/professional-development/resource-collections/profile-348

Duru, E., Duru, S., & Balkis, M. (2014). Analysis of relationships among burnout, academic achievement, and self-regulation. *Educational Sciences: Theory and Practice, 14*(4), 1274–1284. doi:10.12738/estp.2014.4.2050

Dysgraphia Information. (n.d.). Retrieved from http://www.ninds.nih.gov/disorders/dysgraphia/dysgraphia.htm

Dysgraphia. (n.d.). Retrieved from http://www.dyslexiasd.org/factsheets/dysgraphia.pdf

Ehri, C., & Wilce, L. S. (1980). Do beginners learn to read function words better in sentences or in lists? *Reading Research Quarterly, 15*(4), 451–476. doi:10.2307/747274

Eilers, L. H., & Pinkley, C. (2006). Metacognitive strategies help students to comprehend all text. *Reading Improvement, 43*(1), 13–29. Retrieved from http://www.projectinnovation.biz/ri.html

Erten, I. H., & Karakas, M. (2007). Understanding the divergent influences of reading activities on the comprehension of short stories. *The Reading Matrix, 7*(3), 113–133. Retrieved from http://www.readingmatrix.com/journal.html

Executive Function Fact Sheet. (2008). Retrieved from http://www.ldonline.org/article/24880/

Executive Functions Development and Learning Disabilities. (2016). Retrieved from http://ldaamerica.org/executive-functions-development-and-learning-disabilities/

Fact Sheet: Universal Design for Learning. (n.d.). Retrieved from https://teal.ed.gov/tealguide/udl

Feitler, F. C., & Hellekson, L. E. (1993). Active verbalization plus metacognitive awareness yields positive achievement gains in at-risk first graders. *Reading Research and Instruction*, *33*(1), 1–11. doi:10.1080/19388079309558139

Fisher, D., & Frey, N. (2014). Close reading as an intervention for struggling middle school readers. *Journal of Adolescent & Adult Literacy*, *57*(5), 367–376. doi:10.1002/jaal.266

Fisher, D., Frey, N., & Lapp, D. (2012). Building and activating students' background knowledge: It's what they already know that counts. *Middle School Journal*, *43*(3), 22–31. doi:10.1080/00940771.2012.11461808

Flett, A., & Conderman, G. (2002). 20 ways to promote phonemic awareness. *Intervention in School and Clinic*, *37*(4), 242–245. doi:10.1177/105345120203700409

Flynn, R. M. (2007). Giving directions: A teaching art. *Teaching Artist Journal*, *5*(1), 37–46. doi:10.1080/15411790709336714

Frey, N., & Fisher, D. (2009). The release of learning. *Principal Leadership*, *9*(6), 18–22.

Fulk, B. M., & Stormont-Spurgin, M. (1995). Spelling interventions for students with disabilities: A review. *The Journal of Special Education*, *28*(4), 488–513. doi:10.1177/002246699502800407

Gargiulo, R. M. (2015). *Special education in contemporary society: An introduction to exceptionality* (5th ed.). Thousand Oaks, CA: SAGE.

Georgiou, G. K., Papadopoulos, T. C., Zarouna, E., & Parrila, R. (2012). Are auditory and visual processing deficits related to developmental dyslexia? *Dyslexia (Chichester, England)*, *18*(2), 110–129. doi:10.1002/dys.1439

Gerde, H. K., Bingham, G. E., & Wasik, B. A. (2012). Writing in early childhood classrooms: Guidance for best practices. *Early Childhood Education Journal*, *40*(6), 351–359. doi:10.100710643-012-0531-z

Ghaith, G., & Obeid, H. (2004). Effect of think alouds on literal and higher-order reading comprehension. *Educational Research Quarterly*, *27*(3), 49–57.

Gill, S. R., & Islam, C. (2011). Shared reading goes high-tech. *The Reading Teacher*, *65*(3), 224–227. doi:10.1002/TRTR.01028

Glenn, P., & Hurley, S. R. (1993). Preventing spelling disabilities. *Child Language Teaching and Therapy*, *9*(1), 1–12. doi:10.1177/026565909300900101

Goodman, Y. M., & Paulson, E. J. (2000). *Teachers and students developing language about reading through retrospective miscue analysis*. Urbana, IL: National Council of Teachers of English Research Foundation.

Goodwin, A. P., & Ahn, S. (2010). A meta-analysis of morphological interventions: Effects on literacy achievement of children with literacy difficulties. *Annals of Dyslexia*, *60*(2), 183–208. doi:10.100711881-010-0041-x

Graves, M. F., Cooke, C., & Laberge, M. (1983). Effects of previewing difficult short stories on low ability junior high school students' comprehension, recall, and attitudes. *Reading Research Quarterly, 18*(3), 262–276. doi:10.2307/747388

Greaney, K. (2012). Developing word knowledge within tape assisted and/or other audio recorded reading programmes. *Kairaranga, 1*(1), 44-49. Retrieved from http://www.massey.ac.nz/massey/learning/departments/school-curriculum-pedagogy/kairaranga/kairaranga_home.cfm

Greenwood, S., & Bilbow, M. (2002). Word identification in the intermediate and middle grades: Some tenets and practicalities. *Childhood Education, 79*(1), 26–31. doi:10.1080/00094056.2002.10522760

Haager, D., & Vaughn, S. (2013). The common core state standards and reading: Interpretations and implications for elementary students with learning disabilities. *Learning Disabilities Research & Practice, 28*(1), 5–16. doi:10.1111/ldrp.12000

Hacker, D. J., Dole, J., Ferguson, M., Adamson, S., Roundy, L., & Scarpulla, L. (2015). The short-term and maintenance effects of self-regulated strategy development in writing for middle school students. *Reading & Writing Quarterly, 31*(4), 351–372. doi:10.1080/10573569.2013.869775

Hagaman, J., Casey, K., & Reid, R. (2012). The effects of the paraphrasing strategy on the reading comprehension of young students. *Remedial and Special Education, 33*(2), 110–123. doi:10.1177/0741932510364548

Hagaman, J., Luschen, K., & Reid, R. (2010). The "RAP" on reading comprehension. *Teaching Exceptional Children, 43*(1), 22–29. doi:10.1177/004005991004300103

Hanusek, E. A., & Woßmann, L. (2010). Education and economic growth. In D. Brewer & P. J. McEwan (Eds.), *Economics of education* (pp. 60–67). Oxford, UK: Elsevier.

Harbour, K. E., Evanovich, L., Sweigart, C. A., & Hughes, L. E. (2015). A brief review of effective teaching practices that maximize student engagement. *Preventing School Failure, 59*(1), 5–13. doi:10.1080/1045988X.2014.919136

Harn, B. A., Stoolmiller, M., & Chard, D. J. (2008). Measuring the dimensions of alphabetic principle on the reading development of first graders: The role of automaticity and unitization. *Journal of Learning Disabilities, 41*(2), 143–157. doi:10.1177/0022219407313585

Hitchcock, J., Dimino, J., Kurki, A., Wilkins, C., & Gersten, R. (2010). *The impact of collaborative strategic reading on the reading comprehension of grade 5 students in linguistically diverse schools. (NCEE 2011-4001)*. Washington, DC: U.S. Department of Education.

Hollo, A., & Hirn, R. G. (2015). Teacher and student behaviors in the contexts of grade-level and instructional grouping. *Preventing School Failure, 59*(1), 30–39. doi:10.1080/1045988X.2014.919140

Holman, B., & Ziedenberg, J. (2014). *The dangers of detention: The impact of incarcerating youth in detention and other secure facilities*. Washington, DC: Justice Policy Institute.

Howard, S., DaDeppo, L. M. W., & De La Paz, S. (2008). Getting the bugs out with PESTS: A mnemonic approach to spelling sight words for students with learning disabilities. *Teaching Exceptional Children Plus, 4*(5), Article 3. Retrieved from http://escholarship.bc.edu/education/tecplus/vol4/iss5/art3

Hunter, M. (1993). *Enhancing teaching*. Englewood Cliffs, NJ: Prentice Hall.

Hyndman, B. (2015). Where to next for school playground interventions to encourage active play? An exploration of structured and unstructured school playground strategies. Journal of Occupational Therapy. *Schools & Early Intervention, 8*(1), 56–67. doi:10.1080/19411243.2015.1014956

Ibe, H. (2009). Metacognitive strategies on classroom participation and student achievement in senior secondary school science classrooms. *Science Education International, 20*(1-2), 25-31. Retrieved from http://icaseonline.net

Ihori, D., & Olvera, P. (2015). Discrepancies, responses, and patterns: Selecting a method of assessment for specific learning disabilities. *Contemporary School Psychology, 19*(1), 1–11. doi:10.100740688-014-0042-6

Individuals with Disabilities Education Improvement Act (IDEIA). 2004. P.L. 108- 446, 20 U.S. Code § 1401 et seq.

Ingram, J., & Elliott, V. (2016). A critical analysis of the role of wait time in classroom interactions and the effects on student and teacher interactional behaviors. *Cambridge Journal of Education, 46*(1), 37–53. doi:10.1080/0305764X.2015.1009365

Jacobs, P., & Fu, D. (2014). Students with learning disabilities in an inclusive writing classroom. *Journal of Language and Literacy Education, 10*(1), 100–113. Retrieved from http://olle.coe.uga.edu/wp-content/uploads/2014/04/Students-with-Learning-Disabilities-Jacobs.pdf

Jaspers, K. E., Williams, R. L., Skinner, C., Cihak, D., McCallum, R., & Ciancio, D. (2012). How and to what extent do two cover, copy, and compare spelling interventions contribute to spelling, word recognition, and vocabulary development? *Journal of Behavioral Education, 21*(1), 80–98. doi:10.100710864-011-9137-6

Kaddoura, M. (2013). Think pair share: A teaching learning strategy to enhance students' critical thinking. *Educational Research Quarterly, 36*(4), 3–24. Retrieved from https://www.questia.com/library/journal/1P3-3007248671/think-pair-share-a-teaching-learning-strategy-to

Kaldenberg, E. R., Watt, S. J., & Therrien, W. J. (2015). Reading instruction in science for students with learning disabilities. *Learning Disability Quarterly, 38*(3), 160–173. doi:10.1177/0731948714550204

Kaufmann, L. (2008). Dyscalculia: Neuroscience and education. *Educational Research, 50*(2), 163–175. doi:10.1080/00131880802082658

Kemper, M. J., Verhoeven, L., & Bosman, A. M. T. (2012). Implicit and explicit instruction of spelling rules. *Learning and Individual Differences, 22*(6), 639–649. doi:10.1016/j.lindif.2012.06.008

Kennedy, M. M. (1999). The role of preservice teacher education. In L. Darling-Hammond & G. Sykes (Eds.), *Teaching as the learning profession: Handbook of teaching and policy* (pp. 54–86). San Francisco: Jossey Bass.

Kiefer, S. M., Alley, K. M., & Ellerbrock, C. R. (2015). Teacher and peer support for young adolescents' motivation, engagement, and school belonging. *RMLE Online: Research in Middle Level Education, 38*(8). Retrieved from http://files.eric.ed.gov/fulltext/EJ1074877.pdf

Kim, Y., Wagner, R., & Lopez, D. (2012). Developmental relations between reading fluency and reading comprehension: A longitudinal study from grade 1 to grade 2. *Journal of Experimental Child Psychology, 113*(1), 93–111. doi:10.1016/j.jecp.2012.03.002

Kissel, B. T., & Miller, E. T. (2015). Reclaiming power in the writers' workshop: Defending curricula, countering narratives and changing identities in prekindergarten classrooms. *The Reading Teacher, 69*(1), 77–86. doi:10.1002/trtr.1379

Kuby, P., & Aldridge, J. (2004). The impact of environmental print instruction on early reading ability. *Journal of Instructional Psychology, 31*(2), 106–114. Retrieved from http://www.projectinnovation.biz/jip.html

La Greca, A. M., & Stone, W. L. (1990). LD status and achievement: Confounding variables in the study of children's social status, self-esteem, and behavioral functioning. *Journal of Learning Disabilities, 23*(8), 483–490. doi:10.1177/002221949002300806

Lallier, M., Donnadieu, S., & Valdois, S. (2013). Developmental dyslexia: Exploring how much phonological and visual attention span disorders are linked to simultaneous auditory processing deficits. *Annals of Dyslexia, 63*(2), 97–116. doi:10.100711881-012-0074-4

Lalor, A. (2012). Keeping the destination in mind. *Educational Leadership, 70*(1), 75–78.

Landerl, K., Fussenegger, B., Moll, K., & Willburger, E. (2009). Dyslexia and dyscalculia: Two learning disorders with different cognitive profiles. *Journal of Experimental Child Psychology, 103*(3), 309–324. doi:10.1016/j.jecp.2009.03.006

Lewandowski, L., Cohen, J., & Lovett, B. J. (2013). Effects of extended time allotments on reading comprehension performance of college students with and without learning disabilities. *Journal of Psychoeducational Assessment, 31*(3), 326–336. doi:10.1177/0734282912462693

Livers, S. D., & Bay-Williams, J. M. (2014). Vocabulary support: Constructing (not obstructing) meaning. *Mathematics Teaching in the Middle School, 20*(3), 153-159.

Lochner, L. (2010). Education and crime. In D. Brewer & P. J. McEwan (Eds.), *Economics of education* (pp. 93–98). Oxford, UK: Elsevier.

Mallett, C. A. (2014). The "learning disabilities to juvenile detention" pipeline: A case study. *Children & Schools, 36*(3), 147–154. doi:10.1093/cs/cdu010

Martínez, A. (2011). Explicit and differentiated phonics instruction as a tool to improve literacy skills for children learning English as a foreign language. *GIST Education and Learning Research Journal, 5*, 25-49. Retrieved from http://files.eric.ed.gov/fulltext/EJ1062615.pdf

Mason, L. H., Harris, K., & Graham, S. (2011). Self-regulated strategy development for students with writing difficulties. *Theory into Practice, 50*(1), 20–27. doi:10.1080/00405841.2011.534922

McArthur, G. M., Ellis, D., Atkinson, C. M., & Coltheart, M. (2008). Auditory processing deficits in children with reading and language impairments: Can they (and should they) be treated? *Cognition, 107*(3), 946–977. doi:10.1016/j.cognition.2007.12.005

McCown, M. A., & Thomason, G. B. (2014). Informational text comprehension: Its challenges and how collaborative strategic reading can help. *Reading Improvement, 51*(2), 237–253. Retrieved from http://www.ingentaconnect.com/contentone/prin/rimp/2014/00000051/00000002/art00003?crawler=true

McCoy, K. M., Mathur, S. R., & Czoka, A. (2010). Guidelines for creating a transition routine: Changing from one room to another. *Beyond Behavior, 19*(3), 22–29. Retrieved from http://www.ccbd.net/beyondbehavior/index.cfm?categoryID=D646D293-C09F-1D6F-F9C4E203B21F5EB8

McCurdy, E., & Cole, C. L. (2014). Use of a peer support intervention for promoting academic engagement of students with autism in general education settings. *Journal of Autism and Developmental Disorders, 44*(4), 883–893. doi:10.100710803-013-1941-5

McIntyre, E., Rightmyer, E., Powell, R., Powers, S., & Petrosko, J. (2006). How much should young children read? A study of the relationship between development and instruction. *Literacy Teaching and Learning, 11*(1), 51-72. Retrieved from http://www.readingrecovery.org/rrcna/journals/ltl/index.asp

McIntyre, L., Protz, S., & McQuarrie, L. (2008). Exploring the potential of LiPS instruction for beginning readers. *Developmental Disabilities Bulletin, 36*(1-2), 18–48. Retrieved from http://files.eric.ed.gov/fulltext/EJ828948.pdf

McKeown, D., FitzPatrick, E., & Sandmel, K. (2014). SRSD in practice: Creating a professional development experience for teachers to meet the writing needs of students with EBD. *Behavioral Disorders, 40*(1), 15–25. doi:10.17988/0198-7429-40.1.15

Michaelson, M. T. (2007). An overview of dyscalculia: Methods for ascertaining and accommodating dyscalculic children in the classroom. *Australian Mathematics Teacher, 63*(3), 17–22. Retrieved from http://www.aamt.edu.au

Mihai, A., Friesen, A., Butera, G., Horn, E., Lieber, J., & Palmer, S. (2015). Teaching phonological awareness to all children through storybook reading. *Young Exceptional Children, 18*(4), 3–18. doi:10.1177/1096250614535221

Milani, A., Lorusso, M. L., & Molteni, M. (2010). The effects of audiobooks on the psychosocial adjustment of pre-adolescents and adolescents with dyslexia. *Dyslexia (Chichester, England), 16*(1), 87–97. doi:10.1002/dys.397

Nash-Ditzel, S. (2010). Metacognitive reading strategies can improve self-regulation. *Journal of College Reading and Learning, 40*(2), 45–63. doi:10.1080/10790195.2010.10850330

National Coalition of Auditory Processing Disorders. (2016). *What is APD?* Retrieved from National Coalition of Auditory Processing Disorders website: http://www.ncapd.org/What_is_APD_.html

National Research Council. (1998). *10 recommendations for practice and research. Preventing Reading Difficulties in Young Children.* Washington, DC: The National Academies Press.

Ness, M., & Kenny, M. (2016). Improving the quality of think-alouds. *The Reading Teacher, 69*(4), 453–460. doi:10.1002/trtr.1397

Neumann, M., Summerfield, K., & Neumann, D. (2015). Visual attention to print-salient and picture-salient environmental print in young children. *Reading and Writing: An Interdisciplinary Journal, 28*(4), 423–437. doi:10.100711145-014-9531-2

Nies, K. A., & Belfiore, P. J. (2006). Enhancing spelling performance in students with learning disabilities. *Journal of Behavioral Education, 15*(3), 162–169. doi:10.100710864-006-9017-7

Ortlieb, E. (2013). Using anticipatory reading guides to improve elementary students' comprehension. *International Journal of Instruction, 6*(2), 145–162.

Ortlieb, E., & Norris, M. (2012). Using the think-aloud strategy to bolster reading comprehension of science concepts. *Current Issues in Education, 15*(1), 1-9. Retrieved from http://cie.asu.edu

Paige, D. D. (2011). "That sounded good!": Using whole-class choral reading to improve fluency. *The Reading Teacher, 64*(6), 435–438. doi:10.1598/RT.64.6.5

Palmer, J., Boon, R. T., & Spencer, V. G. (2014). Effects of concept mapping instruction on the vocabulary acquisition skills of seventh-graders with mild disabilities: A replication study. *Reading & Writing Quarterly, 30*(2), 165–182. doi:10.1080/10573569.2013.818890

Partnership for Assessment of Readiness for College and Careers. (2011). *PARCC model content frameworks: English language arts/literacy grades 3–11*. Retrieved from http://www.parcconline.org/sites/parcc/files/PARCCMCFELALiteracyAugust2012_FINAL.pdf

Peyrin, C., Demonet, J. F., N'Guyen-Morel, M. A., Le Bas, J. F., & Valdois, S. (2011). Superior parietal lobule dysfunction in a homogeneous group of dyslexic children with a visual attention span disorder. *Brain and Language, 118*(3), 128–138. doi:10.1016/j.bandl.2010.06.005

Prater, M., Redman, A., Anderson, D., & Gibb, G. (2014). Teaching adolescent students with learning disabilities to self-advocate for accommodations. *Intervention in School and Clinic, 49*(5), 298–305. doi:10.1177/1053451213513958

Price, K. W., Meisinger, E. B., Louwerse, M., & D'Mello, S. (2016). The contributions of oral and silent reading fluency to reading comprehension. *Reading Psychology, 37*(2), 167–201. doi:10.1080/02702711.2015.1025118

RAND Reading Study Group. (2002). *Reading for understanding: Toward a research and development program in reading comprehension*. Santa Monica, CA: Office of Education, Research and Improvement.

Rasinski, T. (2014). Fluency matters. *International Electronic Journal of Elementary Education, 7*(1), 3–12.

Regan, K., & Berkeley, S. (2012). Effective reading and writing instruction: A focus on modeling. *Intervention in School and Clinic, 47*(5), 276–282. doi:10.1177/1053451211430117

Reid, R., Hagaman, J., & Graham, S. (2014). Using self-regulated strategy development for written expression with students with attention deficit hyperactivity disorder. *Learning Disabilities (Weston, Mass.), 12*(1), 21–42. Retrieved from http://www.cec.sped.org/AM/Template.cfm?Section=Publications1

Richie, G. (2005). Two interventions that enhance the metacognition of students with disabilities: Cognitive cue cards and correspondence training. *Kairaranga, 6*(2), 25-32. Retrieved from http://www.massey.ac.nz/massey/learning/departments/school-curriculum-pedagogy/kairaranga/kairaranga_home.cfm

Rinehart, S. D. (2001). Establishing guidelines for using reader's theater with less-skilled readers. *Reading Horizons, 42*(2), 65–75.

Roth, K., & Guinee, K. (2011). Ten minutes a day: The impact of interactive writing instruction on first graders' independent writing. *Journal of Early Childhood Literacy, 11*(3), 331–361. doi:10.1177/1468798411409300

Rubinstein-Avila, E. (2013). Scaffolding content and language demands for "reclassified" students. *Voices from the Middle, 20*(4), 28–33. Retrieved from http://www.ncte.org/journals

Schnotz, W., Mengelkamp, C., Baadte, C., & Hauck, G. (2014). Focus of attention and choice of text modality in multimedia learning. *European Journal of Psychology of Education, 29*(3), 483–501. doi:10.100710212-013-0209-y

Schultz, Simpson, & Lynch. (2012). Specific learning disability identification: What constitutes a pattern of strengths and weaknesses? *Learning Disabilities: A Multidisciplinary Journal, 18*(2), 87-97.

Scruggs, T. E., Mastropieri, M. A., Berkeley, S. L., & Marshak, L. (2010). Mnemonic strategies: Evidence-based practice and practice-based evidence. *Intervention in School and Clinic, 46*(2), 79–86. doi:10.1177/1053451210374985

Sexton, S. S. (2004). Informing how post-graduate teacher candidates see teaching and themselves in the role as the teacher. *International Education Journal, 5*(2), 205–214.

Sharma, M., Purdy, S., & Kelly, A. (2009). Comorbidity of auditory processing, language, and reading disorders. *Journal of Speech, Language, and Hearing Research: JSLHR, 52*(3), 706–722. doi:10.1044/1092-4388(2008/07-0226)

Singleton, S. M., & Filce, H. (2015). Graphic organizers for secondary students with learning disabilities. *Teaching Exceptional Children, 48*(2), 110–117. doi:10.1177/0040059915605799

Smith, R. R. (2000). How the Lexile Framework Operates. *Popular Measurement, 3*(1), 18–19.

Snow, C. E., Burns, M. S., & Griffin, P. (Eds.). (1998). *Preventing reading difficulties in young children.* Washington, DC: National Academy Press.

Stahl, K. (2012). Complex text or frustration-level text: Using shared reading to bridge the difference. *The Reading Teacher, 66*(1), 47–51. doi:10.1002/TRTR.01102

Stockall, N. S., Dennis, L., & Miller, M. (2012). Right from the start: Universal design for preschool. *Teaching Exceptional Children, 45*(1), 10–17. doi:10.1177/004005991204500103

Strickland, W., Boon, R., & Spencer, V. G. (2013). The effects of repeated reading on the fluency and comprehension skills of elementary-age students with learning disabilities (LD), 2001-2011: A review of research and practice. *Learning Disabilities (Weston, Mass.), 11*(1), 1–33. Retrieved from http://www.ldam.org

Sumarsih, M., & Sanjaya, D. (2013). TPS as an effective technique to enhance the students' achievement on writing descriptive text. *English Language Teaching, 6*(12), 106–113. doi:10.5539/elt.v6n12p106

Szidon, K., & Franzone, E. (2009). *Task analysis*. Madison, WI: National Professional Development Center on Autism Spectrum Disorders, Waisman Center, University of Wisconsin.

Taylor, D., Mraz, M., Nichols, W., Rickelman, R., & Wood, K. D. (2009). Using explicit instruction to promote vocabulary learning for struggling readers. *Reading & Writing Quarterly, 25*(2-3), 205–220. doi:10.1080/10573560802683663

Teaching Excellence in Adult Literacy. (2010). *Self-regulated strategy development. TEAL Center Fact Sheet No. 2*. Retrieved from https://teal.ed.gov/sites/default/files/Fact-Sheets/2_TEAL_UDL.pdf

Teaching Excellence in Adult Literacy. (2011). *Self-regulated strategy development. TEAL Center Fact Sheet No. 10*. Retrieved from https://teal.ed.gov/sites/default/files/Fact- Sheets/10_TEAL_Self_Reg_Strat_Dev_0.pdf

Theurer, J. L. (2002). The power of retrospective miscue analysis: One preservice teacher's journey as she reconsiders the reading process. *The Reading Matrix, 2*(1). Retrieved from http://www.readingmatrix.com/articles/theurer/

Thompson, C. J. (2011). Multi-Sensory Intervention Observational Research. *International Journal of Special Education, 26*(1), 202–214.

Tobin, K. (1987). The role of wait time in higher cognitive level learning. *Review of Educational Research, 57*(1), 69–95. doi:10.3102/00346543057001069

Troia, G. A. (2002). Teaching writing strategies to children with disabilities: Setting generalization as the goal. *Exceptionality, 10*(4), 249–269. doi:10.1207/S15327035EX1004_3

Understanding Visual Processing Issues. (n.d.). Retrieved from http://www.ncld.org/types-learning-disabilities/adhd-related-issues/visual-processing-disorders

U.S. Department of Education. (2014). *Appendix 1: U.S. Department of Education: Director of Federal School Climate and Discipline Resources*. Washington, DC: Author.

Usman, A. (2015). Using the think-pair-share strategy to improve students' speaking ability at Stain Ternate. *Journal of Education and Practice, 6*(10), 37–45. Retrieved from http://iiste.org/Journals/index.php/JEP

Vaughn, S. R., & Bos, C. S. (2015). *Strategies for teaching students with learning and behavior problems* (9th ed.). Austin, TX: Pearson.

Veenendaal, N. J., Groen, M. A., & Verhoeven, L. (2014). The role of speech prosody and text reading prosody in children's reading comprehension. *The British Journal of Educational Psychology, 84*(4), 521–536. doi:10.1111/bjep.12036

Visual Processing Disorder. (n.d.). Retrieved from http://www.ncpd.org/sites/default/files/Visual%20Processing%20Disorder%200213.pdf

Wadlington, E. (2000). Effective language arts instruction for students with dyslexia. *Preventing School Failure*, *44*(2), 61–65. doi:10.1080/10459880009599785

Walker, B. D., Shippen, M., Houchins, D., & Cihak, D. (2007). Improving the writing skills of high school students with learning disabilities using the expressive writing program. *International Journal of Special Education*, *22*(2), 66–76. Retrieved from http://www.internationaljournalofspecialeducation.com

Wannarka, R., & Ruhl, K. (2008). Seating arrangements that promote positive academic and behavioral outcomes: A review of empirical research. *Support for Learning*, *23*(2), 89–93. doi:10.1111/j.1467-9604.2008.00375.x

Waters, M. B., Lerman, D. C., & Hovanetz, A. N. (2009). Separate and combined effects of visual schedules and extinction plus differential reinforcement on problem behavior occasioned by transitions. *Journal of Applied Behavior Analysis*, *42*(2), 309–313. doi:10.1901/jaba.2009.42-309

Weaver, C. (1994). Reconceptualizing reading and dyslexia. *Journal of Childhood Communication Disorders*, *16*(1), 23–35. doi:10.1177/152574019401600103

What is APD? (2016). Retrieved from http://www.ncapd.org/What_is_APD_.html

Wilson, J. L. (2005). Interrupting the failure cycle: Revaluing two seventh-grade struggling readers. *Voices from the Middle*, *12*(4), 25–30. Retrieved from http://www.ncte.org/journals

Wollak, B. A., & Koppenhaver, D. A. (2011). Developing technology-supported, evidence-based writing instruction for adolescents with significant writing disabilities. *Assistive Technology Outcomes and Benefits*, *7*(1), 1-23. Retrieved from http://www.atia.org/i4a/pages/index.cfm?pageid=3305

Woodley, J. W. (1985, March). *Retrospective miscue analysis as a tool in teacher preparation in reading*. Paper presented at the 4th Annual Meeting of the National Council of Teachers of English Spring Conference, Houston, TX.

Yue, C. L., Storm, B. C., Kornell, N., & Bjork, E. L. (2015). Highlighting and its relation to distributed study and students' metacognitive beliefs. *Educational Psychology Review*, *27*(1), 69–78. doi:10.100710648-014-9277-z

Yuill, N. M., & Oakhill, J. V. (1988). Effects of inference awareness training on poor reading comprehension. *Applied Cognitive Psychology*, *2*(1), 33–45. doi:10.1002/acp.2350020105

This research was previously published in Preparing Pre-Service Teachers for the Inclusive Classroom edited by Jennifer Courduff, Patricia Dickenson, and Penelope Keough; pages 170-205, copyright year 2017 by Information Science Reference (an imprint of IGI Global).

Chapter 18
Coping Strategies of Primary School Students With Specific Learning Disabilities

Karin Bagnato
University of Messina, Italy

ABSTRACT

This article focuses on proving whether there are differences among children with or without learning disabilities when choosing coping strategies that may be functional to solve problematic situations. The participants were 32 children with learning disabilities and 32 children without learning disabilities aged between 8 and 11. Results show that children with learning disabilities have less often coping behaviour rather than their peers with typical development. This demonstrates the need to opt for educational actions as soon as possible fostering suitable strategies in order to face problematic situations.

1. BACKGROUND THEORY

The phrase Specific Learning Disabilities (SLD) refers to a heterogeneous group of evolutionary disorders, which affect some basic psychological processes, such as listening, thinking, reading, language, writing, handwriting and computing (American Psychiatric Association, 2014). In particular, the term specific refers to the fact that only certain abilities are compromised which prevent total self-sufficiency in learning (Cornoldi, 2007; Stella, 2004).

The evolutionary deficit is found in individuals whose intelligence is within the norm and who are educated; it does not concern skills lost because of traumatic events, but it concerns the lack of development of skills never acquired. Furthermore, such disorders are intrinsic to the individual and can show throughout his/her lifetime, as well as represent a potential element of vulnerability.

These disorders "…cannot be explained as intellectual disabilities, altered visual or auditory acuity, other mental or neurological disorders, psychosocial difficulties, [...] general delay in the development, movement disorders…" (American Psychiatric Association, 2014, p. 77, 80). Because of such peculiarities, SLD cannot be considered an illness, the result of various types of traumas, the reaction to unfavourable

DOI: 10.4018/978-1-7998-1213-5.ch018

environment conditions, the result of incorrect didactics, the consequence of poor commitment from the individual or the result of psychological, behavioural, educational or relational problems.

"The specific learning disability is a disorder of the neurodevelopment of biological origin [...] which includes the interaction of genetic, epigenetic and environmental factors, which affect the ability of the brain to perceive and process verbal and non-verbal information in an efficient and precise manner..." (American Psychiatric Association, 2014, p. 79). In other words, the individual receives the information coming from the surrounding environment, but shows difficulties integrating, processing and filing it. This, in turns, causes an issue in the way this information is reproduced in the form of writing, reading or computing: that is, reading, writing and computing skills are compromised (American Psychiatric Association, 2014).

Apart from the specific cognitive difficulties that characterise the various learning disabilities, individuals with SLD can show a variety of problems associated to their disorder and the impact that such disorder has on their surrounds; among these:

- Psychological distress (Ryan, 2006; Gersten et al., 2006);
- High levels of anxiety and frustration towards academic tasks (Sawyer et al., 1996; Dyson, 1996; Maag and Reid, 2006; Mahmoud and Saber, 2004; Pattison, 2005);
- Learned helplessness, bad self-esteem, lack of motivation at school and poor self-efficacy (Bender, 2008; Elliott, 2000; Hallahan et al., 2009; Lackaye and Margalit, 2006; Gans et al., 2003; Ghisi et al., 2016);
- Low self-esteem deriving from various school-related failures and frequent rejections from their peers (Bear et al., 2006; Swanson et al. 2006; Tarver-Behring and Spagna, 2004);
- Internalising problems (anxiety, depression, withdrawal from society etc.) and externalising problems (aggression, anger, behavioural problems, etc.) (Halonen et al., 2006);
- Socio-emotional and behavioural difficulties (Bryan et al., 2004; Mugnaini et al., 2009);
- Inadequate social skills and relationship problems (Tarabia and Abu-Rabia, 2016; Panicker and Chelliah, 2016; Leichtentritt and Shechtman, 2010).

These situations cause a condition of deep suffering, which along with the poor knowledge of the problem and the lacking perception of control over events, can trigger inadequate coping strategies when facing situations that are perceived as problematic and/or stressful.

There exist many studies on this topic, which have focused their attention on adolescents and university students with SLD. These studies have highlighted that such individuals see themselves as less competent, both academically and socially, due to their cognitive, behavioural and social disorders. This means that they show greater difficulty in adapting socially and seem incapable to show adaptive coping mechanisms in comparison to their peers without SLD (Shulman et al., 1994; Cheshire and Cambell, 1997; Shessel and Reiff, 1999; Firth et al., 2008; Givon and Court, 2010).

Based on these assumptions it is possible to speculate that also children with SLD can show a deficiency in the skills needed to approach a problem, evaluate it and identify multiple and different strategies to solve it (Singer, 2005; Pavri and Monda-Amaya, 2010). This is because of lacking social skills, which could affect both interpersonal and intra-personal relationships. In particular, the tendency these individuals have to be pessimistic towards future successes could lead them to withdraw from difficult situations (i.e. Forness and Kavale, 1996; Pavri and Monda-Amaya, 2010).

The work presented below belongs to this search term and aims to offer further contribution to the analysis of coping mechanisms used by children with Specific Learning Disabilities.

2. RESEARCH METHODS

2.1. Aims of the Research

My research aims to examine the coping styles shown by children with Specific Learning Disabilities. In particular, it aims to:

- Identify the main responsive behaviours in children with SLD;
- Check the existence of differences between children with and without SLD when choosing coping mechanisms to deal with difficult situations.

The existing literature suggests that when it comes to solving problematic situations, children with SLD show adaptive coping strategies less frequently than children with typical development.

2.2. Participants, Tools and Procedure

Participants: the research involved 32 individuals with SLD and 32 individuals without SLD, aged between 8 and 11 (A = 9.30; SD = 1,164), who attended various Rehabilitation Centres in the city of Messina.

Tools: the "Scala di Valutazione del Coping 8-11" (SVC8-11) (Rating Scale of Coping) (Bagnato, Marino, in press) was applied to the whole group. The SVC8-11 applies to individuals aged 8 to 11 and aims to identify the main coping styles adopted in problematic situations where the interaction partners are peers or adults.

The SVC8-11 consists of 32 likely problematic situations and is divided into 4 categories, based on the interaction partner: classmates, friends, teachers and family. Each category is made of eight possible problematic situations where the interaction partner does something wrong to the main character (the person who fills the SVC8-11), either intentionally or unintentionally. There are therefore four intentional situations and four non-intentional situations for each category.

Each problematic scenario also foresees five response options, which make reference to the traditional coping mechanisms: active, distraction, escape, request for help and aggression. Next to each of these response options a 10-point thermometer is found, which is used to track how frequently each coping mechanism is used.

Each individual, once given a problematic scenario, is asked to state the degree of probability of using each coping mechanism.

Procedure: the SVC8-11 was used individually and presented using a PowerPoint slideshow. I chose to use a computer and colour images in order to catch the children's attention and motivate them to complete the test.

Given that, all individuals involved in the research were minors, all parents were asked to sign an informative consent form before the Ladder was used with their children.

3. ANALYSIS OF THE RESULTS

A first objective of the research was to identify the main coping strategies used by children with SLD to solve problematic situations.

As it can be seen in Table 1, the results indicate that, in order to cope with difficulties, individuals with SLD state that they mainly implement *active* coping and *distraction* modalities independently of the interaction partner (peers and adults). While they report to use less often *escape, help-seeking* and *aggressive* behaviour.

A further objective of the research was to verify if there were differences between subjects with SLD and subjects with typical development in the choice of coping styles functional to the resolution of problematic situations.

From the analysis of multivariate variance (MANOVA) (Table 2), a significant main effect at the multivariate level attributable to the group emerges [Lambda = .76; F (5.58) = 3.60; p = .007]: in the distraction [F (1.62) = 10.27; p = .002] the group with typical development reports higher scores (A = 234.75; SD = 46.67) than the group with SLD (A = 179.37; SD = 85.90). Also in *active* coping strategies [F (1.62) = 13.33; p = .001] it was found that subjects with typical development obtain higher scores (A = 249.25; SD = 34.13) than those with SLD (A = 195.13; SD = 76.61). In the other coping behaviours, no significant group effects are shown.

From a more detailed analysis, which has examined possible differences between the various interaction partners within each coping strategy, it emerged that there are significant differences between the groups only in the adoption of some coping styles (Table 3).

For what concerns the issue of distraction coping with peers and adults, the multivariate variance analysis (MANOVA) highlights a significant main effect at the multivariate level attributable to the

Table 1. Average (A) and Standard Deviation (SD) of the answers of children with SLD concerning the probability of issuing coping strategies

			Aggressive Coping	Escape Coping	Distraction Coping	Active Coping	Help-Seeking Coping
SLD	PEERS	A	40.78	64.62	91.56	95.16	40.09
		SD	39.25	42.65	38.64	34.97	36.96
	AdultS	A	24.84	44.91	92.81	99.97	35.16
		SD	37.86	41.53	43.36	44.77	38.00

Table 2. Average (A) and standard deviation (SD) of the answers of children with SLD and typical development concerning the probability of issuing coping strategies

		Aggressive Coping	Escape Coping	Distraction Coping	Active Coping	Help-Seeking Coping
SLD	A	65.69	142.09	179.37	195.13	75.31
	SD	82.17	56.77	85.90	76.61	73.53
TYPICAL DEVELOPMENT	A	65.62	109.53	234.75	249.25	102.56
	SD	73.15	79.82	46.67	34.13	81.63

Table 3. Average (A) and Standard Deviation (SD) of the answers of children with SLD and typical development concerning the probability of issuing each coping strategy with peers and adults

			Aggressive Coping	Escape Coping	Distraction Coping	Active Coping	Help-Seeking Coping
PEERS	SLD	A	40.78	84.25	91.56	95.16	40.09
		SD	39.25	27.14	38.64	34.96	36.95
	TYPICAL DEVELOPMENT	A	36.53	64.62	110.09	118.56	56.13
		SD	42.77	42.65	23.34	19.28	40.04
AdultS	SLD	A	29,31	44.91	92.81	99.97	35.16
		SD	41.54	41.53	43,36	44,77	38.00
	TYPICAL DEVELOPMENT	A	24.84	63.06	124.66	130.69	46.44
		SD	37,86	32.24	25.96	21,09	45.00

group [Lambda = .80; F (2.61) = 7.51; p = .001]: in the use of distraction with peers [F (1.62) = 5.39; p = .024] the typical development group reports higher scores (A = 110.09; SD = 23.34) than those with SLD (A = 91.56; SD = 38.64). The same occurs when choosing the mode of distraction with adults [F (1.62) = 12.70; p = .001]: the typical development group reports higher scores (A = 124.66; SD = 25.96) than the group with SLD (A = 92.81; SD = 43.36).

A similar picture also occurs in relation to the use of *active* coping conducts with peers and adults. In fact, the analysis of multivariate variance (MANOVA) results in a significant main effect at the multivariate level referable to the group [Lambda = .82; F (2.61) = 6.51; p = .003]: in *active* coping with peers [F (1.62) = 11; p = .002] subjects with typical development return higher scores (A = 118.56; SD = 19.28) than those with SLD (A = 95.16; SD = 34.97). A similar situation occurs in *active* coping with adults [F (1.62) = 12.33; p = .001]: the typical development group recorded higher scores (A = 130.69; SD = 21.09) than those with SLD (A = 99.97; SD = 44.77).

In relation to escape behaviour, instead, the analysis of multivariate variance (MANOVA) does not reveal any significant main effect at the multivariable level attributable to the group [Lambda = .92; F (2.61) = 2.52; p = .089]. However, at the univariate level a significant difference emerges between the groups in the manifestation of the escape behaviour with peers [F (1.62) = 4.82; p = .032]. In fact, the group with SLD records higher scores (A = 84.25; SD = 27.14) than the group with typical development (A = 64.62; SD = 42.65).

In the other coping behaviours, there are no significant group effects. It is, however, possible to observe further important data: the group of SLD states to implement to a greater extent, compared to the group with typical development, both aggressive behaviours with peers and adults and escape strategies in interactions with peers, while the subjects with typical development claim to make more use of the *help-seeking* strategy than their peers with SLD.

4. DISCUSSION

Data analysis has shown that children with SLD declare to choose mainly, both with their peers and with adults, adaptive coping styles mainly related to active and distraction behaviours. This data would seem to indicate that the subjects with SLD are competent in solving problematic situations and that therefore the condition of learning disability does not compromise their ability to choose suitable behaviours to face the problem.

However, the significant differences found between children with and without SLD are certainly indicative of the different frequency with which adaptive coping strategies are put in place: in fact, the issue of active and distraction coping is less frequent in subjects with SLD, and this would let us suppose that this condition and/or the problems associated with it could somehow favour restrictions in the choice of strategies functional to solving the problem.

Less significant results, but which deserve to be commented, are those related to aggressive, escape and help-seeking behaviour.

With regard to aggressive behaviour, the fact that children with SLD adopt them more frequently than those with typical development could be due to the inability to implement behaviours that meet common interests. That is, referring to schemes developed in past experiences there would be a greater probability of responding to problematic situations in an aggressive manner. The question then that aggressive strategies are mainly used with peers could lead to the hypothesis that it is easier to address hostile actions to peers rather than to adults, but also that previous experiences have consolidated the idea that hostility can somehow discourage others from engaging in disturbing actions.

With regard to the escape coping, it was found that subjects with SLD in interactions with peers use this more frequently. This choice could be because children with SLD pay special attention to social relationships with friends and classmates because they are afraid of cracking their interpersonal relationships and perhaps being rejected by their peers.

Finally, a different picture is presented for the help-seeking coping that records a greater frequency in subjects with typical development. The reason why people with SLD use it less frequently could be that asking others for help, especially peers, can be interpreted in a negative way. As if the request for support, advice and help to solve problematic situations could be something to be ashamed of.

These results confirm, therefore, the hypothesis according to which children who have Specific Learning Disorders issue, with less frequency, adaptive coping modalities compared to their peers with typical development.

The condition of SLD, in fact, already at an early age and in the long term, could lead to a profound suffering that can compromise the ability to control events and, consequently, favour the adoption of inadequate coping modalities. In fact, as Ryan (2006) states, the presence of SLD increases the possibility of psychological distress because the subjects face school, relational and educational experiences that often place them in a disadvantaged and stressful situation compared to their peers. In addition, if this condition evolves over time and is managed in an inadequate way, it can lead to forms of psychosocial maladjustment, which, according to Halonen and collaborators (2006), can give rise to internalizing and externalizing problems.

5. CONCLUSION: THE POTENTIAL OF INFORMATION AND COMMUNICATION TECHNOLOGIES (ICT)

The condition of SLD significantly affects the well-being of the individual because the difficulties faced by the subjects are very complex and include cognitive, behavioural and emotional aspects.

Mostly children with SLD suffer for all the difficulties related to the disorder and are convinced that events happen regardless of their will and that, therefore, it is useless to try to find solutions to solve the problem because they are not so much able to do it.

It is therefore necessary to implement, as soon as possible, educational actions that promote the construction of an adequate repertoire of social skills functional both to ensure effective perception of control of events and to promote the implementation of appropriate strategies to solve the problems that can occur with peers and adults.

It is, however, necessary to point out that, being in full developmental age, children manifest coping behaviours that cannot be considered permanent, but transitory. Consequently, in this phase of development, the methods of coping cannot be considered predictors of future behavioural outcomes. However, this does not mean that children's coping strategies can be disregarded as they are subject to constant variations. Indeed, for those working in the educational field it is of fundamental importance to know and examine the child's coping styles early, as only in this way they will help to improve the strategies of coping, to increase self-esteem, to enhance the problem-solving process, etc. Naturally, bearing in mind that these are transitory strategies that are gradually changing according to their experiences.

Educational interventions, in particular, should take into account that all responses are conditioned by the expectations and evaluations that the individual implements on information deriving from the external environment. Therefore, we should act on all the factors that contribute to the implementation of a specific behaviour: cognitive sphere (dysfunctional thoughts, self-esteem, problem solving, etc.), behavioural dimension (communication, social, study abilities, etc.) and reference context (surrounding environment, socio-environmental factors, family dynamics, etc.). This proves to be of fundamental importance because the goal is not only to achieve an adequate repertoire of social skills, but also to facilitate self-knowledge in the participants.

In an increasingly digital and technological society, which calls for the knowledge and use of the various information and communication technologies (ICT) in different life contexts, it could be particularly profitable and interesting to foresee the implementation of educational actions that aim to improve the strategies for dealing with problematic/stressful situations with ICT.

ICTs have gradually and inevitably changed both the way of managing information and knowledge and the cognitive styles and mental structures of the individuals involved in their use, determining new ways of learning and building knowledge. Today, cognitive processes are improved and developed with crossmediality, multitasking, participation and sharing among users and are directed towards the construction of shared educational paradigms. From this point of view, therefore, ICT can offer a varied range of tools that can contribute to the creation of effective learning environments.

Among the many different ICTs, we find the Virtual Reality (VR) that, in the specific case of coping strategies, could represent a suitable tool to build an adequate repertoire of social skills.

The VR is a simulated reality, a three-dimensional environment that can be explored and with which it is possible to interact using different and multiple computer devices (viewers, gloves, earphones, etc.) that transport the subject in a context as realistic as to seem true. Precisely for this reason, the VR is defined as "immersive", insofar as it isolates the individual from the external environment, projecting it into a parallel reality that completely absorbs it (Fedeli, 2013).

In the VR, there is nothing that cannot be done, everything becomes possible and there are no limits of any kind.

The subject enters the virtual environment bringing with it their personal history, their own desires and their own cognitive and emotional peculiarities. Moreover, they do not passively "undergo" the stimuli and information they encounter, but they implement intentional choices. All these characteristics give life to that sense of presence that characterises the VR (Riva et al., 2003; Ijsselteijn, 2004).

It must be stressed that VR is not only synonymous with entertainment, but also has an educational value. In fact, there have been and there are still now different applications: in the psychotherapeutic field, it has been mainly used in the management of emotions and in the treatment of phobias, eating disorders, anxiety, stress, aggressive behaviour, etc. (i.e. Wiederhold and Wiederhold, 2005; Moore et al., 2002; Riva et al., 2004; Pull et al., 2005; Rizzo et al., 2005;); in the clinical field, it has been used for neuro-psychological evaluation and for physical and neurological rehabilitation (i.e. Morganti, 2004; Lam et al., 2006; Holden, 2005).

In addition to these purely clinical applications, VR has also been used in educational settings and, more specifically, in the area of learning and training. In these processes, the VR presents significant advantages related to the construct of experiential learning, according to which knowledge begins with action (Bruner, 1996) and, from this point of view, VR can be a very significant tool.

Since VR has proved particularly effective in the management of anxiety, stress and emotions (especially negative ones) and all these aspects are closely related to the issue of adequate coping strategies, it is plausible to assume that the VR can be helpful in the fulfilment of intervention trainings that aim at the manifestation of appropriate strategies to face problematic situations. Specifically, the use of the VR could be profitable with children not only because it is appealing to their eyes, but also because it would overcome a set of limits inherent in the "traditional" intervention trainings and open new scenarios and "places" in which children can experience first-hand emotions, feelings, anxieties, fears and find new cognitive, emotional and behavioural solutions.

An interesting proposal could be to "build" virtual problematic situations in which children can immerse in having an active role in living the experience. Such situations could occur in the family and at school, since they represent the main educational agencies with which children interact most of their time, and refer to fairly common and frequent circumstances. From this point of view, the three-dimensional and realistic visualization of the "own" context, leads the subject to have the feeling of being really in that environment because they do not have to make the effort to imagine the situation and to identify with it.

Furthermore, different levels of complexity of problematic situations could be foreseen that lead to different outcomes, the subject could interact with both peers and adults, we could "build" intentional and unintentional problematic situations [the interaction partner (adult or peer) wrongs the protagonist of the story (the subject who participates in the VR) in an intentional and unintentional way]. Someone who "guides" the VR and that, consequently, can increase or decrease the risk of unpredictable effects would manage all these aspects.

The possibility of virtual experiences, in which specific skills related to the management of emotions and anxiety are acquired, is fundamental because it determines the increase in the sense of self-efficacy, favours the issue of adequate coping strategies and prepares the subject to face also real situations. In fact, once acquired, these skills can be generalized in other life contexts. In other words, the implementation of virtual problematic situations creates the conditions for the participants to perceive themselves as competent, effective and able to control the event.

From what has been said so far, it emerges that VR, as well as other information and communication technologies, should not be interpreted as "special" technologies, but as new and unprecedented "places" of learning. In fact, these can facilitate learning itself, encourage active participation in social life and promote the acquisition of an adequate repertoire of social skills necessary for the physical, psychological and emotional well-being of the subject. In particular, in the educational field, the intrinsic potentials of

ICT are considerable and the way to explore them is long and fascinating, even if it is not without limits and risks. Only through research and practice is it possible to familiarise with ICT and exploit it to the full in order to promote and improve the quality of life of both children and adults.

REFERENCES

American Psychiatric Association. (2014). *Manuale diagnostico e statistico dei disturbi mentali (DSM-5)*. Milano: Raffaello Cortina.

Bagnato, K., & Marino, F. (in press). *Scala di Valutazione del Coping 8-11 (SVC8-11)*. Trento: Erickson.

Bear, G. G., Kortering, L. J., & Braziel, P. (2006). School completers and noncompleters with learning disabilities: Similarities in academic achievement and perceptions of self and teachers. *Remedial and Special Education*, 27(5), 293–300. doi:10.1177/07419325060270050401

Bender, W. N. (2008). *Learning disabilities: characteristics, identification, and teaching strategies*. Boston: Allyn and Bacon.

Bruner, J. (1996). *La cultura dell'educazione*. Milano: Feltrinelli.

Bryan, T., Burstein, K., & Ergul, C. (2004). The social-emotional side of learning disabilities: A science-based presentation of the state of the art. *Learning Disability Quarterly*, 27(1), 45–51. doi:10.2307/1593631

Cheshire, G., & Cambell, M. (1997). Adolescent coping: Differences in the styles and strategies used by learning disabled compared to non-learning disabled adolescents. *Australian Journal of Guidance & Counselling*, 5(1), 65–73. doi:10.1017/S1037291100001254

Cornoldi, C. (a cura di) (2007). Difficoltà e disturbi dell'apprendimento. Bologna: Il Mulino.

Dyson, L. L. (1996). The experiences of families of children with learning disabilities: Parental stress, family functioning, and sibling self-concept. *Journal of Learning Disabilities*, 29(3), 280–286. doi:10.1177/002221949602900306 PMID:8732889

Elliott, J. G. (2000). The psychological assessment of children with learning difficulties. *British Journal of Special Education*, 27(2), 59–66. doi:10.1111/1467-8527.00161

Fedeli, L. (2013). *Embodiment e mondi virtuali. Implicazioni didattiche*. Milano: FrancoAngeli.

Firth, N., Frydenberg, E., & Greaves, D. (2008). Perceived control and adaptive coping: Programs for adolescent students who have learning disabilities. *Learning Disability Quarterly*, 31(3), 151–165.

Forness, S. R., & Kavale, K. A. (1996). Treating social skill deficits in children with learning disabilities: A meta-analysis of the research. *Learning Disability Quarterly*, 19(1), 2–13. doi:10.2307/1511048

Gans, A. M., Kenny, M. C., & Ghany, D. L. (2003). Comparing the self-concept of students with and without learning disabilities. *Journal of Learning Disabilities*, 36(3), 287–295. doi:10.1177/002221940303600307 PMID:15515648

Gersten, R., Baker, S. K., Smith-Johnson, J., Dimind, J., & Peterson, A. (2006). Eyes on the prize: Teaching complex historical content to middle school students with learning disabilities. *Counsel for Exceptional Children, 72*(3), 264–280. doi:10.1177/001440290607200301

Ghisi, M., Bottesi, G., Re, A. M., Cerea, S., & Mammarella, I. C. (2016). Socioemotional features and resilience in Italian university students with and without dyslexia. *Frontiers in Psychology, 7*. doi:10.3389/fpsyg.2016.00478 PMID:27065220

Givon, S., & Court, D. (2010). Coping strategies of high school students with learning disabilities: A longitudinal qualitative study and grounded theory. *International Journal of Qualitative Studies in Education: QSE, 23*(3), 283–303. doi:10.1080/09518390903352343

Hallahan, D. P., Kuuffman, J. M., & Pullen, P. C. (2009). *Exceptional learners: introduction to learning disabilities*. Boston: Allyn and Bacon.

Halonen, A., Aunola, K., Ahonen, T., & Nurmi, J. E. (2006). The role of learning to read in the development of problem behaviour: A cross-lagged longitudinal study. *The British Journal of Educational Psychology, 73*(3), 517–534. doi:10.1348/000709905X51590 PMID:16953960

Holden, M. K. (2005). Virtual environments for motor rehabilitation [review]. *Cyberpsychology & Behavior, 8*(3), 187–211. doi:10.1089/cpb.2005.8.187 PMID:15971970

IJsselsteijn, W. A. (2004). *Presence in depth. The Nederlands*. Technische Universiteit Eindhoven Press.

Lackaye, T. D., & Margalit, M. (2006). Comparison of achievement, effort, and selfperceptions among students with learning disabilities and their peers from different achievement groups. *Journal of Learning Disabilities, 39*(5), 432–446. doi:10.1177/00222194060390050501 PMID:17004675

Lam, Y. S., Man, D. W., Tam, S. F., & Weiss, P. L. (2006). Virtual reality training for stroke rehabilitation. *NeuroRehabilitation, 21*(3), 245–253. PMID:17167194

Leichtentritt, J., & Shechtman, Z. (2010). Children with and without learning disabilities: A comparison of processes and outcomes following group counseling. *Journal of Learning Disabilities, 43*(2), 169–179. doi:10.1177/0022219409345008 PMID:19890074

Maag, J. W., & Reid, R. (2006). Depression among students with learning disabilities: Assessing the risk. *Journal of Learning Disabilities, 39*(1), 3–10. doi:10.1177/00222194060390010201 PMID:16512079

Mahmoud, A., & Saber, S. (2004). Some psychological and behavioral characteristics among children with learning disabilities. *Journal of Arab Children, 5*(19), 8–21.

Moore, K., Wiederhold, B. K., Wiederhold, M. D., & Riva, G. (2002). Panic and agoraphobia in a virtual world. *Cyberpsychology & Behavior, 5*(3), 197–202. doi:10.1089/109493102760147178 PMID:12123240

Morganti, F. (2004). Virtual interaction in cognitive neuropsychology. *Studies in Health Technology and Informatics, 99*, 55–70. PMID:15295146

Mugnaini, D., Lassi, S., La Malfa, G., & Albertini, G. (2009). Internalizing correlates of dyslexia. *World Journal of Pediatrics, 5*(4), 255–264. doi:10.100712519-009-0049-7 PMID:19911139

Panicker, A. S., & Chelliah, A. (2016). Resilience and stress in children and adolescents with specific learning disability. *Journal of the Canadian Academy of Child and Adolescent Psychiatry, 25*(1), 17–23. PMID:27047553

Pattison, S. (2005). Making a difference for young people with learning disabilities: A model for inclusive counseling practice. *Counselling & Psychotherapy Research, 5*(2), 120–130. doi:10.1080/17441690500258735

Pavri, S., & Monda-Amaya, L. (2010). Loneliness and students with learning disabilities in inclusive classrooms: Self-perceptions, coping strategies, and preferred interventions. *Journal Learning Disabilities Research & Practice, 15*(1), 22–33. doi:10.1207/SLDRP1501_3

Pull, C. B. (2005). Current status of virtual reality exposure therapy in anxiety disorders: Editorial review. *Current Opinion in Psychiatry, 18*(1), 7–14. PMID:16639177

Riva, G., Bacchetta, M., Cesa, G., Conti, S., & Molinari, E. (2004). The use of VR in the treatment of eating disorders. *Studies in Health Technology and Informatics, 99*, 121–163. PMID:15295149

Riva, G., Davide, F., & IJsselsteijn, W. A. (Eds.). (2003). *Being there: concepts, effects and measurements of user presence in synthetic environments*. Amsterdam: Ios Press.

Rizzo, A. A., Pair, J., McNerney, P. J., Eastlund, E., Manson, B., Gratch, J., ... Swartout, B. (2005). Development of a VR therapy application for Iraq war military personnel with Ptsd. *Studies in Health Technology and Informatics, 111*, 407–413. PMID:15718769

Ryan, M. (2006). Problemi sociali ed emotivi legati alla dislessia. *Dislessia, 3*(1), 29–35.

Sawyer, V., Nelson, J. S., Jayanthi, M., Bursuck, W. D., & Epstein, M. H. (1996). Views of students with learning disabilities of their homework in general education classes: Student interview. *Learning Disability Quarterly, 19*(2), 70–85. doi:10.2307/1511249

Shessel, I., & Reiff, H. B. (1999). Experience of adults with learning disabilities: Positive and negative impacts and outcomes. *Learning Disability Quarterly, 22*(4), 305–315. doi:10.2307/1511264

Shulman, S., Carlton-Ford, S., Levian, R., & Hed, S. (1994). Coping styles of learning disabled adolescents and their parents. *Journal of Youth and Adolescence, 24*(3), 281–294. doi:10.1007/BF01537597

Singer, E. (2005). The strategies adopted by Dutch children with dyslexia to maintain their self-esteem when teased at school. *Journal of Learning Disabilities, 38*(5), 411–423. doi:10.1177/00222194050380050401 PMID:16329442

Stella, G. (2004). *Dislessia*. Bologna: Il Mulino.

Swanson, H. L., Harris, K. R., & Graham, S. (2006). *Handbook of learning disabilities*. New York: The Guilford Press.

Tarabia, E., & Abu-Rabia, S. (2016). Social competency, sense of loneliness and self-image among reading disabled (RD) arab adolescents. *Creative Education, 7*(9), 1292–1313. doi:10.4236/ce.2016.79135

Tarver-Behring, S., & Spagna, M. E. (2004). Counseling with exceptional children. *Focus on Exceptional Children*, *36*(8), 1–12.

Wiederhold, B. K., & Wiederhold, M. D. (2005). *Virtual reality therapy for anxiety disorders: advances in evaluation and treatment*. Washington: American Psychological Association. doi:10.1037/10858-000

This research was previously published in the International Journal of Digital Literacy and Digital Competence (IJDLDC), 8(4); edited by Antonio Cartelli; pages 39-52, copyright year 2017 by IGI Publishing (an imprint of IGI Global).

Chapter 19
School Bullying and Students with Intellectual Disabilities

Michelle F. Wright
Masaryk University, Czech Republic

ABSTRACT

School bullying research began in the 1970s through seminal research conducted on these experiences among Norwegian boys. From this initial research, multiple studies have been conducted over the past forty years, revealing the nature, extent, causes, and consequences of school bullying. More recent investigations have also focused on cyberbullying, bullying using information and communication technologies (e.g., cell phones). Little attention has been given to school bullying involvement among students with disabilities, particularly those with intellectual disabilities. These studies suggest that these students experience internalizing (e.g., depression, anxiety, loneliness) and externalizing (e.g., aggression, antisocial behaviors) difficulties associated with their involvement in school bullying. The aim of this chapter is to review multidisciplinary research concerning school bullying among students with intellectual disabilities and to make recommendations for public policy and prevention programs as well as future research.

INTRODUCTION

Students with disabilities benefit from inclusion in the same schools as their nondisabled peers. Research findings also suggest that nondisabled peers benefit from this inclusion as well (Buckley, Bird, Sacks, & Archer, 2002; Lindsay & McPherson, 2012; Richardson, 1996; Sailor, Wolf, Choi, & Roger, 2009; Tomasik, 2007). Therefore, disabled and nondisabled students benefit from having an inclusive school environment where there is potential for social interactions among a variety of students with different backgrounds. There is also evidence that such inclusion does not reduce test scores, grades, or instructional time, further suggesting the necessity of inclusion for students with disabilities (Sirlopu et al., 2008; Stahmer, Carter, Baker, & Miwa, 2003; Salend & Duhaney, 1999; York, Vandercook, MacDonald, Heise-Neff, & Caughey, 1992).

DOI: 10.4018/978-1-7998-1213-5.ch019

The total number of students with disabilities in inclusion education varies based on students' location within the United States. In particular, students from the Eastern United States are more frequently assigned to segregated classrooms (Kurth, 2014). In addition, some states (e.g., Iowa, Minnesota, West Virginia) favor inclusion, while other states (e.g., Florida, New Jersey, South Carolina) prefer the restrictive setting for students with disabilities. Overall, 50% of disabled students from the ages of 6 to 11 are in regular classrooms around 80% of the day, while 30% of disabled students from the ages of 12 and higher are in such classrooms (Maryland Coalition for Inclusive Education, 2011). Regardless of the differences in these rates, it is clear that a variety of students with disabilities spend some time learning in the regular classroom.

Although there are benefits to the inclusion of students with disabilities in the school environment, additional attention is needed to promote a more welcoming environment as these students are often victims of school bullying (Mishna, 2003). Welcoming school environments are not always something students with disabilities experience as bullying is frequently a direct result of their disability, especially if the students' disability is more visible in inclusion environments (Verdugo, Bernejo, & Fuertes, 1995; Waldman, Swerdloff, & Perlman, 1999; Whitney, Smith & Thompson, 1994). In addition, students with disabilities are also rejected by their peers, a risk factor associated with victimization and bullying perpetration (Fox, 1989; Kistner & Gatlin, 1989; Martlew & Hodson, 1991; Morrison, Furlong, & Smith, 1994). Being rejected by one peers can lead to isolation and other consequences, such as depression, loneliness, and anxiety. Furthermore, peer rejection can affect academic engagement and achievement, which are vital to the long-term functioning of these students.

Some students with disabilities are also vulnerable to school bullying involvement because they have inadequate protection in the inclusion environment and due to their tendency to react aggressively (Lagerheim, 1986; Nabuzoka & Smith, 1993; Sprafkin & Gadow, 1987). Many times this inadequate protection stems from these students being socially rejected by their peers, which diminishes their odds of having good quality friendships, a protective factor associated with reduced bullying incidences. Reacting aggressively to benign situations or in situations when it is not warranted increases children's and adolescents' risk of being rejected by their peers. This increased risk also makes them vulnerable to victimization and aggression. Students with intellectual disabilities are also at risk for victimization because they have fewer resources to cope with this experience (Cunningham, Clark, Heaven, Durrant, & Cunningham, 1989; Lagerheim, 1986; Nabuzoka & Smith, 1993; Zeitlin & Williamson, 1990).

The purpose of this chapter is to examine school bullying perpetration and victimization among students with intellectual disabilities in elementary, middle, and high schools. The chapter utilizes multidisciplinary qualitative, quantitative, and mixed-design research methodologies drawn from psychology, special education, sociology, social work, and criminology to review research on students with intellectual disabilities' involvement in school bullying, incorporating both cross-sectional and longitudinal research designs. This chapter has six main purposes, including describing:

1. **The Nature of School Bullying:** Discussion of the definition, forms and types, prevalence rates, and associated psychosocial adjustment difficulties;
2. The prevalence and consequences of school bullying among students with disabilities;
3. The predictors of school bullying among students with intellectual disabilities;
4. **Solutions and Recommendations:** Description of public policy and school bullying prevention programs concerning students with intellectual disabilities;

5. **Future Research Directions:** The focus is on longitudinal research designs as well as recommending more research dedicated to understanding risk factors and protective factors associated with school bullying involvement among students with intellectual disabilities;
6. **Conclusion:** Final remarks concerning the state of the literature on school bullying among students with intellectual disabilities.

THE NATURE OF SCHOOL BULLYING

School bullying is a common experience for many students in the United States and throughout the world. It is defined as the intentional use of physical force or power against another person or group (Espelage & Swearer, 2003; Hemphill, Tollit, Kotevski, & Florent, 2015; Hong et al., 2014). It includes behaviors which cause physical and/or psychological harm and that are perceived as unwanted by the target of these behaviors. Over the last forty years, research on school bullying has been evolving, providing an important foundation for understanding the nature, extent, causes, consequences, intervention strategies, and the prevention of these behaviors (Hymel & Swearer, 2015). The recent attention given to school bullying by the public is the result of many high profile cases and news reports regarding school shootings and victims committing suicide. Although some of the research awareness and concern over school bullying is the result of the 1999 Columbine school shooting, the study of school bullying began in Norway during the 1970s. This systematic study of school bullying began with Olweus's 1973 book, *Aggression in the Schools: Bullies and Whipping Boys*. In his book, Olweus described boys' experiences with school bullying in Scandinavian countries. Most of the earliest research spurred by Olweus's book occurred across Europe as a result of the 1978 translation of his book into English. The book generated further interest and 10 years later the first European conference was held on school bullying. At this time, Olweus developed an intervention campaign designed to prevent school bullying among Norwegian students. Other European countries, like England, Wales, and Scotland, launched similarly designed intervention programs. A couple of years later, research and awareness began in Canada, the United States, Australia, and New Zealand. Most current research has focused attention on school bullying in Asia, Africa, and South America.

The typically used definition of school bullying comes from Olweus's work (1993). Like the definition provided in the previous paragraph, Olweus's definition emphasizes three essential elements of school bullying, including:

1. The behavior is aggressive and negative (i.e., it is unwanted and causes emotional distress to the victim),
2. The behavior is carried out repeatedly (i.e., it occurs often and over time), and
3. The behavior occurs in a relationship where there is an imbalance of power between the individuals involved.

School bullying behaviors are further delineated into two modes, direct and indirect. Direct forms of school bullying include physical aggression in which the victim is openly attacked, while indirect forms include social exclusion or social rejection. Indirect forms of bullying are often employed by girls while direct forms are more often used by boys (Banks, 1997; Brighi, Guarini, Melotti, Galli, & Genta, 2012; Carbone-Lopez, Esbensen, & Brick, 2010; Carney & Merrell, 2001; Crick & Grotpeter, 1995; Ericson,

2001). Socialization processes throughout childhood and adolescence are thought to account for gender differences in the usage of direct and indirect forms of bullying. As a result of these gender differences in bullying involvement, researchers argue that it is important to distinguish between indirect and direct forms of school bullying.

Other researchers, like Underwood and colleagues (2001), suggest that referring to some school bullying behaviors as indirect implies that the behavior does not involve direct or overt interaction with the victim, which might diminish beliefs about the severity of this type of bullying. By diminishing the belief that indirect forms of bullying are severe, schools, parents, and students might not take these behaviors seriously and consider them harmful to victims' well-being. Instead of using the terminology of indirect bullying, some researchers utilize social aggression to categorize the indirect forms of school bullying that Olweus described. As a result of the different forms of school bullying, researchers have categorized these behaviors into four types, including physical (e.g., pushing, hitting), verbal (e.g., name-calling), relational (e.g., exclusion, spreading rumors), and damage to property (Olthof & Goossens, 2008; Wang, Iannotti, Luk, & Nansel, 2010). Bullying can also include bullying in other contexts, such as those behaviors which occur electronically. Electronic forms of bullying are referred to as cyberbullying, and typically these behaviors are perpetrated or experienced through social networking websites, email, chatrooms, or chat programs (Lapidot & Dolev-Cohen, 2015; Waasdorp & Bradshaw, 2015). Sexual bullying is another type of bullying which can occur in the school setting. It occurs when a person is bullied based on his or her sex or sexual activity, and it can include physical, verbal, or emotional forms (Duncan, 1999).

Another important element of the school bullying definition is that the behaviors occur among school-aged students, 5 to 18 years of age, and it doesn't include aggression or bullying perpetrated by siblings. The definition also does not include bullying that might occur within romantic relationships. Furthermore, the definition excludes any bullying and abuse which might be perpetrated by adults or behaviors directed to adults. Children and adolescents can hold a variety of different roles in the bullying situation. They can be victims, bullies, bully-victims (both victim and perpetrator), bystanders (i.e., witnesses to the bullying situation), and uninvolved (Noorden, Haselager, Cillessen, & Bukowski, 2015; Psalti, 2012). Students experience a variety of academic and psychosocial adjustment consequences associated with the specific role they have in school bullying. In particular, bully-victims usually have the worst psychological, social, behavioral, and academic outcomes when compared to victims, bullies, bystanders, and uninvolved children and adolescents, with victims having worse outcomes than the other roles.

Prevalence rates of school bullying vary, depending on the definitions employed, samples used, the measurement of school bullying, and the age of the participants. Variations found in the general population range from 13% to 75% based on a variety of factors that impact students' reporting of school bullying, such as the definitions used, the measurement of school bullying, and their reluctance to admit to perpetrating and/or experiencing school bullying (Swearer, Siebecker, Johnsen-Frerichs, & Wang, 2010). Usually, researchers report prevalence rates between 30% and 32%, with 10.6% of students categorized as victims, 13.0% as bullies, and 6.3% as bully-victims (Dinkes, Kemp, Baum, & Snyder, 2009; Nansel et al., 2001). Research has also revealed that boys were more likely to report victimizing others when compared to girls while girls were more likely to report being victimized (Charach, Pepler, & Ziegler, 1995; Craig & Pepler, 1995). However, when researchers specified different forms of bullying, girls were more often involved in relational forms, while boys were more often engaged in physical forms (Banks, 1997; Brighi et al., 2012; Carbone-Lopez et al., 2010; Carney & Merrell, 2001; Crick & Grotpeter, 1995; Ericson, 2001). Furthermore, relational forms of school bullying increase in adolescence, while physical forms tend to decrease from childhood into adolescence (Boyes, Bowes, Cluver, Ward, & Badcock, 2014; Bradshaw, Waasdrop, & Johnson, 2015; Ryoo, Wang, & Swearer, 2015). Findings from these studies underscore the importance of consideration both gender and age when examining school bullying involvement.

Researchers, parents, and educators are particularly concerned with school bullying because of its linkages to academic (e.g., poor academic achievement, lower academic engagement), behavioral (e.g., delinquency), and psychosocial (e.g., depression, anxiety, loneliness) adjustment difficulties. School bullying victimization is a strong predictor of interpersonal problems and internationalizing emotional problems, such as anxiety, depression, and loneliness (Graham, Bellmore, & Mize, 2006; Hawker & Boulton, 2000; Kelly et al., 2015; Nishina, Juvonen, & Witkow, 2005; Perren, Dooley, Shaw, & Cross, 2010; Thomas et al., 2015). Such psychosocial problems contribute to victimized students' poor academic performance, often as a result of frequent absences from school and impaired concentration (Card & Hodges, 2008; Espelage, Low, & Jimerson, 2014; Hong et al., 2014; Nishina et al., 2005). Victims might not attend school because they fear further victimization. In addition, their concentration is impaired because they might repeatedly ruminate over their experience and be concerned about the chances of experiencing other attacks. Victimized students are also at risk for psychiatric problems and suicidal ideation (Dickerson Mayesa et al., 2014; Kumpulainen, Rasanen, & Puura, 2001; Rigby & Slee, 1991; Skapinakis et al., 2011). It is unclear whether victimization is a cause of psychiatric problems and suicidal ideation or whether psychiatric problems and suicidal ideation reduce children's and adolescents' coping abilities, leading them to be vulnerable to victimization. Many victimized children believe that they deserve to be bullied, which further contributes to the helplessness they feel, creating a vicious cycle of peer victimization. This cycle might make it difficult for them to believe that they can ever escape victimization.

Students who bully others also experience depression and suicidal ideation, and they are also at risk for antisocial behavioral tendencies, such as abusing drugs, drinking alcohol, and property theft (Hertz, Donato, & Wright, 2013; Kaltiala-Heino, Rimpela, Marttunen, Rimpela, & Rantanen, 1999; Cummings, Pepler, Mishna, & Craig, 2006). They also engage in academic misconduct, such as cheating and skipping school, and have lower academic achievement (Atik & Guneri, 2013; Berthold & Hoover, 2000; Carlson & Cornell, 2008; Rigby & Cox, 1996). Later in life, bullies are likely to be diagnosed with a psychiatric problem and to engage in substance abuse and criminal misconduct (Baldry & Farrington, 2000; Kumpulainen et al., 2001; Luukkonen, Riala, Hakko, & Rasanen, 2010; Nansel et al., 2001; Radliff, Wheaton, Robinson, & Morris, 2012; Rigby & Cox, 1996). Although there are overlaps in negative adjustment consequences between bullies and victims, there are differences in the type of consequences experienced. For instance, bullies typically experience more externalizing problems, while victims usually experience more internalizing problems.

Bully-victims experience the highest levels of these externalizing (e.g., antisocial behavior, rage, anger) and internalizing (e.g., depression, anxiety, loneliness) behaviors when compared to students who are either bullies or victims only (Kelly et al., 2015; Marini et al., 2009; Ozdemir & Stattin, 2011; Sansone & Sansone, 2008). Given that bully-victims experience elevated levels of internalizing and externalizing problems when compared to bullies and victims, it is imperative that researchers consider the multiple roles that students can have in school bullying. Nowadays, the education of students with disabilities occurs in schools with their peers without disabilities. Because peer victimization is a concern in the school environment, researchers began to focus their attention on investigating the school bullying experiences of disabled students.

PREVALENCE AND CONSQUENCES OF SCHOOL BULLYING AMONG STUDENTS WITH INTELLECTUAL DISABILITIES

Although many studies have been conducted on school bullying involvement among the general population of students, less attention has been given to examining students with disabilities' involvement in these behaviors, especially those with intellectual disabilities. The lack of attention to these students might be the result of the mistaken belief that such students cannot adequately express their opinions about their experiences with peers. As a result, some researchers might not include students with disabilities in their samples. Furthermore, ethical considerations might require special provisions for including students with disabilities in research, and many researchers might not have the resources necessary to ensure that they have the tools to aid in data collection that would allow these students' participation.

Most of the research on school bullying among students with disabilities utilizes school-aged samples of children and adolescents with disabilities between the ages of 5 and 18. Such research is important as there are consistent findings concerning students with disabilities being at an increased risk for school bullying when compared to their peers without disabilities (Rose, Espelage, & Monda-Amaya, 2009; Rose, Monda-Amaya, & Espelage, 2011; Sheard, Clegg, Standen, & Cromby, 2001). In particular, some research indicates that these students are more vulnerable to school bullying in comparison to nondisabled peers, while other research suggests that there are no differences in their risk for experiencing school bullying. The researchers that conclude that students with disabilities are more prone to school bullying propose that these students are at an increased risk for peer victimization because they have fewer resources to cope with this experience. Having better coping strategies makes it easier for students with disabilities to handle the challenges that they encounter and to "bounce back" from such challenges.

When compared to the general population of students, students with disabilities are 5 times more likely to report victimization by school bullying (Rose et al., 2009; Rose et al., 2011). In addition, research indicates that students with disabilities were more likely to experience peer victimization when placed in remedial classes and regular education classes when compared to students without disabilities. To explain these results, Rose and colleagues (2009; 2011) proposed that these students' physical or mental disability makes them particularly salient in the classroom, increasing the likelihood that they will be noticed and that others will be aware that they are different in some way. Being different from the average, might heightened the chance that students with disabilities will be victimized.

In one of the few longitudinal studies to examine school bullying among students with disabilities, students between the ages of 3 and 6 were followed for three years (Son, Parish, & Peterson, 2012). Employing parent reports, Son and colleagues found that 19% of 3 and 4 year olds experienced one or more types of peer victimization, and that 25% of 5 year olds experienced one or more types of peer victimization. The experience of peer victimization increased to 30% at the age of 6. The developmental trajectory of peer victimization reveals increases in these experiences from elementary to middle school, with declines beginning in early high school. Similar to their peers without disabilities' experiences with school bullying, peer victimization peaks in middle school. The patterns concerning the increase in peer victimization experiences from ages 3 to 6 is not unique among students with disabilities, but the odds of exposure are a bit higher than among students without disabilities. In particular, 34.1% of students with disabilities in one sample reported peer victimization compared with 24.5% in elementary school and 26.6% in high school (Blake et al., 2012). Other research revealed that rates of victimization among children with disabilities peaked in 3rd grade and declined afterward, somewhat in contrast to findings from the previous research (Bear, Mantz, Glutting, Yang, & Boyer, 2015). So far, only one study has examined the prevalence rates of cyberbullying involvement among students with intellectual disabilities.

In their study, Didden et al. (2009) found that between 4% and 9% of students with intellectual disabilities were involved in cyberbullying as either the perpetrator or the victim.

Students with disabilities are also at an elevated risk of school bullying perpetration (Carter & Spencer, 2006; Doren, Bullis, & Benz, 1996; Estell et al., 2009; Rose et al., 2009; Whitney et al., 1994). Students with disabilities also report more incidences of physical bullying, sexual abuse, and emotional abuse (Cappadocia, Weiss, & Pepler, 2012; Mishna, 2003; Reiter, Bryen, & Shachar, 2007). For example, Whitney and colleagues (1994) found that one-third of students with disabilities in their sample engaged in school bullying perpetration when compared to one-sixth of students without disabilities. In another study comparing prevalence rates between students with disabilities and students without, Dickson and colleagues (2005) found that 28% of students with disabilities in their sample reported being victims of school bullying when compared to 9.8% of students without. Given that students with disabilities are more likely to be exposed to school bullying, they might experience extreme distress from such exposure. This distress might reduce their ability to deal with peer victimization, making them utilize ineffective coping strategies. One such way they might cope with peer victimization is by aggressing against others, maybe even those responsible for their victimization.

Thus far, much of the research reviewed on school bullying perpetration among students with disabilities did not specify whether school bullying was a function of revenge, meaning that the bully was retaliating against someone who had previously bullied him or her first. This provoked type of school bullying is more common among students with disabilities, and they are more often classified as bully-victims (Carter & Spencer, 2006; Reiter & Lapidot-Lefler, 2007; Roberts & Smith, 1999; Whitney et al., 1994; Van Cleave & Davis, 2006). Considering that students with disabilities are at risk for being bully-victims, it is important for research to focus more attention on these students' experiences with school bullying as bully-victims experience the worse psychological, social, behavior, and academic consequences. Thus, students with disabilities who are bully-victims might be at an elevated risk for these consequences.

The statistics discussed in the previous paragraphs involve studies in which researchers combined samples of students with physical disabilities as well as intellectual and social disabilities without delineating different types of disability (Dawkins, 1996; Llewellyn, 2000). Such a consideration is important as risk factors associated with disability, like aggressiveness, anger, hostility, low impulsive control, hyperactivity, poor social information processing, poor social skills, low self-esteem, and social rejection, are what contribute to school bullying involvement, and these factors vary depending on the specific type of disability (Kavale & Forness, 1995; Kavale & Forness, 1996; Lewandowski & Barlow, 2000; McNamara, Willoughby, Chalmers, & YLC-CURA, 2005; Nabuzoka, 2003; Rose & Espelage, 2012). Therefore, it is important to take into consideration the type of disability that students might have when examining their experience of school bullying.

Students with intellectual disabilities typically have more problems with anger, aggression, information processing, and self-control than students with other types of disabilities (Jahoda, Pert, & Trower, 2006a; Jahoda, Pert, & Trower, 2006b; Novaco & Taylor, 2004). Among students with mild developmental and intellectual disabilities, Reiter and Lapidot-Lefler (2007) found that half of the 12 through 18 year old students in their sample were involved in school bullying as perpetrators. About 83% of students in their sample were victims of physical, social, and verbal forms of school bullying. Similar patterns were found in later studies, citing prevalence rates between 50% and 80% among students with mild developmental and intellectual disabilities (Emerson, 2010; Glumbic & Zunic-Pavlovic, 2010). Variations in prevalence rates might be the result of measurement and definitional differences among the studies. Despite such variations, it is clear that researchers need to delineate the type of disability when examining school bullying. Such a consideration is also important for research comparing students with disabilities to students without disabilities.

The research is mixed as to whether students with intellectual disabilities are more at risk for peer victimization in special education placement settings or inclusive placement settings. In particular, research indicates that rates of peer victimization are much higher in more restrictive special education placements (Norwich & Kelly, 2004; Rose et al., 2009), while other studies reveal that inclusive placements relate to greater school bullying involvement (Sterzing, Shattuck, Narendorf, Wagner, & Cooper, 2012; Whitney, Nabuzoka, & Smith, 1992; Zablotsky, Bradshaw, Anderson, & Law, 2013). Furthermore, research on cyberbullying suggested that placement in special education settings increased the risk of cyberbullying involvement among students with intellectual disabilities (Didden et al., 2009). Additional research attention should be given to understanding their experience of cyberbullying as children and adolescents, even students with intellectual disabilities, are spending more time utilizing information and communication technologies, a known risk factor associated with cyberbullying involvement (Flander, Stimac, Bagaric, & Vinscak, 2014; Kopecky, 2014; Lindfors, Kaltiala-Heino, & Rimpela, 2012; Mishna, Khoury-Kassabri, Gadalla, & Daciuk, 2012; Sourander et al., 2010).

Students with disabilities are at risk for a variety of adjustment difficulties resulting from their involvement in school bullying. In this literature, students with disabilities experience depression, anger, hostility, and lower self-esteem as a result of their bullying involvement, no matter their role as victims or perpetrators (Bauminger, Solomon, & Rogers, 2010; Larkin, Jahoda, MacMahon, & Pert, 2012; Rose, Forber-Pratt, Espelage, & Aragon, 2013). Similar patterns were found for victims and perpetrators of cyberbullying (Didden et al., 2009). They also experience increased levels of loneliness, delinquency, greater difficulties in their social interactions with their peers, and higher levels of social exclusion and peer rejection (Andreou, Didaskalou, & Vlachou, 2013; Jahoda et al., 2012; Nadeau & Tessier, 2006; Pearl & Bay, 1999). In addition, Davis and Nixon (2010) found that students with disabilities were more likely to experience severe trauma as a result of peer victimization when compared to students without disabilities. The associations between adjustment difficulties and school bullying are much stronger when students with disabilities are identified as bully-victims. In particular, Farmer and colleagues (2012) found that students with disabilities who were classified as bully-victims were at an increased risk for experiencing emotional (e.g., depression) and behavioral (e.g., antisocial behavior) problems when compared to students who were identified as either victims or bullies. Taken together, this research indicates that more consideration should be given to predictors of students with disabilities' involvement in school bullying as understanding such predictors can help to identify students who are at an increased risk for experiencing these behaviors. Identification of these students is important as specific intervention strategies can be implemented to mitigate their involvement in school bullying. In addition, identifying such students could help with including them in school bullying prevention programs.

PREDICTORS OF SCHOOL BULLYING AMONG STUDENTS WITH INTELLECTUAL DISABILITIES

Little attention has been given to the risk factors related to students with intellectual disabilities' involvement in school bullying. In the literature, behavioral problems (e.g., uncontrolled anger) are risk factors associated with school bullying perpetration among students with disabilities (Reiter & Lapidot-Lefler,

2007). In particular, temper tantrums, unruly and quarrelsome behavior, and a tendency to lie and steal increase these students' school bullying involvement as bullies and as bully-victims. Other findings revealed that emotional and interpersonal problems (e.g., poor social skills) increase these students' vulnerability to peer victimization. Their higher levels of depression, anxiety, and loneliness, and frequent conflicts within their friendships are significant predictors of peer victimization as well (Matheson, Olsen, & Weisner, 2007; Zeedyk, Rodriguez, Tipton, Baker, & Blacher, 2014). Students with intellectual disabilities also have lower adaptive behaviors and poorer social skills (i.e., social problems, social withdrawal), which increase their risk for peer victimization (Neece & Baker, 2008). Because they have lower adaptive behavioral skills, they might not be able to effectively deal with changes in their routine, which could reduce their ability to cope with changes. Their reduced capacity to cope might increase their susceptibility to peer victimization. Furthermore, having poorer social skills might also make students with intellectual disabilities particularly salient to the peer group as well. Some members of this group might notice the lack of social skills among students with intellectual disabilities, making them perceive these students as targets, especially easy targets, for school bullying. Another study found that poor social skills increased students with intellectual disabilities' susceptibility to peer victimization from middle childhood through early adolescence (Christensen, Fraynt, Neece, & Baker, 2012). Given that bullying increases in early adolescence, it might be likely that having poor social skills makes these students particularly vulnerable to peer victimization. Findings from Christensen et al. (2012) demonstrate the need for social skills training programs for these students as a lack of such skills perpetuates the cycle of peer victimization. Therefore, it is important for schools, parents, researchers, and the government to join together to help mitigate students with disabilities' involvement in school bullying.

SOLUTIONS AND RECOMMENDATIONS

To better understand and prevent school bullying among students with intellectual disabilities, federal programs should be developed to help fund research and bullying prevention incentives (Flynt & Morton, 2007). Access to funding can make conducting research on bullying among students with intellectual disabilities more feasible for researchers who might not have the funds necessary to revise data collection tools to fit this population. Furthermore, increased funding can also help researchers design more large-scale projects devoted to understanding more about school bullying among students with intellectual disabilities.

Research plays a major role in the development of bullying prevention programs and additional funds should be allocated to better serve students with intellectual disabilities in anti-bullying efforts. Individualized Education Programs could also be a source of bullying prevention. Expanding technical assistance within these programs can help to protect students with intellectual disabilities from school bullying involvement as well as provide effective ways for addressing specific bullying behaviors related to students' disabilities. Furthermore, school-wide bullying prevention programs should be modified to accommodate students with intellectual disabilities in an effort to guarantee that these students benefit from such programs. Most bullying prevention and intervention strategies have not be empirically evaluated for application to students with intellectual disabilities. However, the available programs do have some evidence that they decrease anger as well as school bullying victimization and perpetration among students with intellectual disabilities (Rose, West, & Clifford, 2000; Whitney et al., 1994).

School Bullying and Students with Intellectual Disabilities

Many programs are designed and implemented for use with students without disabilities. Therefore, the application and effectiveness of such programs for students with intellectual disabilities is untestable, making the implementation of these programs particularly problematic, especially if the cost of implementation is high.

Social policy should also mandate the development of a system used to notify parents of incidences involving school bullying. The aims of such a system would be to notify parents of their children's involvement in bullying, as either victims or perpetrators, as well as when other children are involved in these incidences. This notification system might be especially important for students with intellectual disabilities who might have communication issues which could prevent their reporting of school bullying incidences to their parents. For instance, an incident might have occurred at school, but parents could only have an awareness of the event, not really knowing what happened. It might be difficult for a student with intellectual disabilities to explain the event to their parents, which might make parents panic. Receiving information from the notification system might reduce parents' worries and their complaints to schools.

FUTURE RESEARCH DIRECTIONS

Based on the literature reviewed in this chapter, there are some clear gaps concerning students with intellectual disabilities' involvement in school bullying that should be addressed in future research. First, much of the literature involves cross-sectional designs, making it difficult to draw conclusions concerning the long-term extent, causes, and consequences of school bullying among students with intellectual disabilities. Such research can help to determine the risk factors associated with school bullying involvement and the long-term outcomes of students with intellectual disabilities' involvement as bullies and victims. Furthermore, this longitudinal research will shed light on whether students with intellectual disabilities experience more severe consequences associated with their involvement in school bullying when compared to their peers without intellectual disabilities. Longitudinal designs will also be helpful for testing prevention and intervention programs that are specifically designed to be sensitive to students with intellectual disabilities.

Second, much of the research does not compare school bullying involvement among students with different intellectual disabilities, which is important as some individuals might be more susceptible to these behaviors when compared to other individuals with intellectual disabilities. That is, students with physical disabilities might experience school bullying at different rates when compared to students with intellectual disabilities. This knowledge might also be important for the development of more sensitive prevention and intervention programs. In addition, some disabilities might differentially relate to different risks for school bullying involvement from childhood to adolescence. For example, students with physical disabilities might experience different levels of psychological, social, behavioral, and academic difficulties after experiencing school bullying in comparison to students with intellectual disabilities.

Another topic worth investigating is the role of protective factors. It is currently unknown whether there are protective factors associated with school bullying among students with intellectual disabilities. Understanding these protective factors might benefit the development of prevention programs and intervention strategies as they can be promoted to reduce these students' involvement in school bullying.

CONCLUSION

In summary, the literature reveals that students with intellectual disabilities are involved in school bullying as victims, perpetrators, and bully-victims. Furthermore, the research also suggests that they experience victimization by school bullying more often than their peers without intellectual disabilities. They also have similar risk factors and adjustment difficulties related to their experience of school bullying as their nondisabled peers. More research needs to be conducted to provide a better understanding of students with disabilities' involvement in school bullying and the associated risk factors and psychosocial adjustment difficulties. Such research is important as it serves as a foundation for the much needed policies and prevention and intervention programs aimed at reducing school bullying involvement among students with intellectual disabilities.

ACKNOWLEDGMENT

This work was supported by the project "Employment of Best Young Scientists for International Co-operation Empowerment" (CZ.1.07/2.3.00/30.0037), co-financed from European Social Fund and the state budget of the Czech Republic.

REFERENCES

Andreou, E., Didaskalou, E., & Vlachou, A. (2013). Bully/victim problems among Greek pupils with special educational needs: Associations with loneliness and self-efficacy for peer interactions. *Journal of Research in Special Educational Needs*.

Atik, G., & Guneri, O. Y. (2013). Bullying and victimization: Predictive role of individual, parental, and academic factors. *School Psychology International*, *34*(6), 658–673. doi:10.1177/0143034313479699

Baldry, A. C., & Farrington, D. (2000). Bullies and delinquents: Personal characteristics and parental styles. *Journal of Community & Applied Social Psychology*, *10*(1), 17–31. doi:10.1002/(SICI)1099-1298(200001/02)10:1<17::AID-CASP526>3.0.CO;2-M

Banks, R. (1997). *Bullying in Schools*. Washington, DC: U.S. Government Printing Office.

Bauminger, N., Solomon, M., & Rogers, S. J. (2010). Externalizing and internalizing behaviors in ASD. *Autism Research*, *3*(3), 101–112. doi:10.1002/aur.131 PMID:20575109

Bear, G. G., Mantz, L. S., Glutting, J. J., Yang, C., & Boyer, D. E. (2015). Differences in bullying victimization between students with and without disabilities. *School Psychology Review*, *44*(1), 98–116. doi:10.17105/SPR44-1.98-116

Berthold, K., & Hoover, J. (2000). Correlates of bullying and victimization among intermediate students in Midwestern USA. *School Psychology International*, *21*(1), 65–79. doi:10.1177/0143034300211005

Blake, J. J., Lund, E. M., Zhou, Q., Kwok, O., & Benz, M. (2012). National prevalence rates of bully victimization among students with disabilities in the United States. *School Psychology Quarterly, 27*(4), 2100–2222. doi:10.1037pq0000008 PMID:23294235

Boyes, M. E., Bowes, L., Cluver, L. C., Ward, C. L., & Badcock, N. A. (2014). Bullying victimization, internalizing symptoms, and conduct problems in South African children and adolescents: A longitudinal investigation. *Journal of Abnormal Child Psychology, 42*(8), 1313–1324. doi:10.100710802-014-9888-3 PMID:24882504

Bradshaw, C. P., Waasdorp, T. E., & Johnson, S. L. (2015). Overlapping verbal, relational, physical, and electronic forms of bullying in adolescence: Influence of school context. *Journal of Clinical Child and Adolescent Psychology, 44*(3), 494–508. doi:10.1080/15374416.2014.893516 PMID:24738548

Brighi, A., Guarini, A., Melotti, G., Galli, S., & Genta, M. L. (2012). Predictors of victimization across direct bullying, indirect bullying and cyberbullying. *Emotional & Behavioural Difficulties, 17*(3-4), 375–388. doi:10.1080/13632752.2012.704684

Buckley, S., Bird, G., Sacks, B., & Archer, T. (2002). A comparison of mainstream and special school education for teenagers with Down syndrome: Effects of social and academic development. *Down's Syndrome: Research and Practice, 2*(2), 46–54.

Cappadocia, M. C., Weiss, J. A., & Pepler, D. (2012). Bullying experiences among children and youth with autism spectrum disorders. *Journal of Autism and Developmental Disorders, 42*(2), 266–277. doi:10.100710803-011-1241-x PMID:21499672

Carbone-Lopez, K., Esbensen, F. A., & Brick, B. T. (2010). Correlates and consequences of peer victimization: Gender differences in direct and indirect forms of bullying. *Youth Violence and Juvenile Justice, 8*(4), 332–350. doi:10.1177/1541204010362954

Card, N. A., & Hodges, E. V. E. (2008). Peer victimization among schoolchildren: Correlations, causes, consequences, and considerations in assessment and intervention. *School Psychology Quarterly, 23*(4), 451–461. doi:10.1037/a0012769

Carlson, I. W., & Cornell, D. W. (2008). Differences between persistent and desistent middle school bullies. *School Psychology International, 29*(4), 442–451. doi:10.1177/0143034308096433

Carney, A., & Merrell, K. (2001). Bullying in schools: Perspectives on understanding and preventing an international problem. *School Psychology International, 21*(3), 364–382. doi:10.1177/0143034301223011

Carter, B. B., & Spencer, V. G. (2006). The Fear Factor: Bullying and Students with Disabilities. George Mason University. *International Journal of Special Education, 21*(1). Retrieved from http://www.forockids.org/PDF Docs/Bullying.pdf

Charach, A., Pepler, D., & Ziegler, S. (1995). Bullying at school. *Education Canada, 37*, 12–18.

Christensen, L., Fraynt, B., Neece, C. L., & Baker, B. L. (2012). Bullying adolescents with intellectual disability. *Journal of Mental Health Research in Intellectual Disability, 5*(1), 49–65. doi:10.1080/19315864.2011.637660

Craig, W. M., & Pepler, D. J. (1995). Peer processes in bullying and victimization: An observational study. *Exceptionality Education Canada, 5*, 81–95.

Crick, N. R., & Grotpeter, J. K. (1995). Relational aggression, gender, and social-psychological adjustment. *Child Development, 66*(3), 710–722. doi:10.2307/1131945 PMID:7789197

Cummings, J., Pepler, D. J., Mishna, F., & Craig, W. M. (2006). Bullying and victimization among children with exceptionalities. *Exceptionality Education Canada, 16*, 193–222.

Cunningham, C. E., Clark, M. L., Heaven, R. K., Durrant, J., & Cunningham, L. H. (1989). The effects of coping-modelling problem solving and contingency management procedures on the positive and negative interactions of learning disabled and attention deficit disordered children with an autistic peer. *Child & Family Behavior Therapy, 11*(3-4), 89–106. doi:10.1300/J019v11n03_06

Davis, S., & Nixon, C. (2010). *The youth voice research project: Victimization and strategies*. Retrieved from: http://njbullying.org/documents/YVPMarch2010.pdf

Dawkins, J. L. (1996). Bullying, physical disability and the pediatric patient. *Developmental Medicine and Child Neurology, 38*(7), 603–612. doi:10.1111/j.1469-8749.1996.tb12125.x PMID:8674911

Dickerson Mayes, S., Baweja, R., Calhoun, S. L., Syed, E., Mahr, F., & Siddiqui, F. (2014). Suicide ideation and attempts and bullying in children and adolescents: Psychiatric and general population samples. *Crisis, 35*(5), 301–309. doi:10.1027/0227-5910/a000264 PMID:25115491

Dickson, K., Emerson, E., & Hatton, C. (2005). Self-reported anti-social behaviour: Prevalence and risk factors amongst adolescents with and without intellectual disability. *Journal of Intellectual Disability Research, 49*(11), 820–826. doi:10.1111/j.1365-2788.2005.00727.x PMID:16207279

Didden, R., Scholte, R. H. J., Korzilius, H., De Moor, J. M. H., Vermeulen, A., O'Reilly, M., ... Lancioni, G. E. (2009). Cyberbullying among students with intellectual and developmental disability in special education settings. *Developmental Neurorehabilitation, 12*(3), 146–151. doi:10.1080/17518420902971356 PMID:19466622

Dinkes, R., Kemp, J., Baum, K., & Snyder, T. (2009). *Indicators of school crime and safety: 2009 (NCES 2010–012/NCJ 228478)*. Washington, DC: National Center for Education Statistics, Institute of Education Sciences, U.S. Department of Education, and Bureau of Justice Statistics, Office of Justice Programs, U.S. Department of Justice.

Doren, B., Bullis, M., & Benz, M. R. (1996). Predictors of victimization: Experiences of adolescents with disabilities in transition. *Exceptional Children, 63*, 7–18.

Duncan, N. (1999). *Sexual bullying: Gender conflict and pupil culture in secondary schools*. New York, NY: Routledge.

Emerson, E. (2010). Self-reported exposure to disablism is associated with poorer self-reported health and well-being among adults with intellectual disabilities in England: A cross-sectional survey. *Public Health, 124*(12), 682–689. doi:10.1016/j.puhe.2010.08.020 PMID:21035153

Ericson, N. (2001). *Addressing the problem of juvenile bullying.* Washington, DC: U.S. Government Printing Office. doi:10.1037/e317892004-001

Espelage, D. L., Low, S. K., & Jimerson, S. R. (2014). Understanding school climate, aggression, peer victimization, and bully perpetration: Contemporary science, practice, and policy. *School Psychology Quarterly, 29*(3), 233–237. doi:10.1037pq0000090 PMID:25198615

Espelage, D. L., & Swearer, S. M. (2003). Research on school bullying and victimization: What have we learned and where do we go from here? *School Psychology Review, 32*, 365–383.

Estell, D. B., Farmer, T. W., Irvin, M. J., Crowther, A., Akos, P., & Boudah, D. J. (2009). Students with exceptionalities and the peer group context of bullying and victimization in late elementary school. *Journal of Child and Family Studies, 18*(2), 136–150. doi:10.100710826-008-9214-1

Farmer, T. W., Irvin, M. J., Motoca, L. M., Leung, M., Hutchins, B. C., Brooks, D. S., & Hall, C. M. (2015). Externalizing and internalizing behavior problems, peer affiliations, and bullying involvement across the transition to middle school. *Journal of Emotional and Behavioral Disorders, 23*(1), 3–16. doi:10.1177/1063426613491286

Farmer, T. W., Petrin, R., Brooks, D. S., Hamm, J. V., Lambert, K., & Gravelle, M. (2012). Bullying involvement and the school adjustment of rural students with and without disabilities. *Journal of Emotional and Behavioral Disorders, 20*(1), 19–37. doi:10.1177/1063426610392039

Flander, G. B., Stimac, D., Bagaric, E. S., & Vinscak, M. (2014). Patterns of and copying with cyberbullying in Croatia. *The International Journal of Person Centered Medicine.*

Flynt, S. W., & Morton, R. C. (2007). Bullying prevention and students with disabilities. *National Forum of Special Education Journal, 19*(1), 1-6.

Fox, C. L. (1989). Peer acceptance of learning disabled children in the regular classroom. *Exceptional Children, 56*(1), 50–59.

Glumbic, N., & Zunic-Pavlovic, V. (2010). Bullying behavior in children with intellectual disability. *Procedia: Social and Behavioral Sciences, 2*(2), 2784–2788. doi:10.1016/j.sbspro.2010.03.415

Graham, S., Bellmore, A. D., & Mize, J. (2006). Peer victimization, aggression, and their co-occurrence in middle school: Pathways to adjustment problems. *Journal of Abnormal Child Psychology, 34*(3), 363–378. doi:10.100710802-006-9030-2 PMID:16648999

Hawker, D. S., & Boulton, M. J. (2000). Twenty years' research on peer victimization and psychosocial maladjustment: A meta-analytic review of crosssectional studies. *Journal of Child Psychology and Psychiatry, and Allied Disciplines, 41*(4), 441–455. doi:10.1111/1469-7610.00629 PMID:10836674

Hemphill, S. A., Tollit, M., Kotevski, A., & Florent, A. (2015). Bullying in schools: Rates, correlates and impact on mental health. In J. Lindert & I. Itzhak (Eds.), *Violence and mental health: Its manifold faces* (pp. 185–205). Springer. doi:10.1007/978-94-017-8999-8_9

Hertz, M. F., Donato, I., & Wright, J. (2013). Bullying and suicide: A public health approach. *The Journal of Adolescent Health, 53*(1), S1–S3. doi:10.1016/j.jadohealth.2013.05.002 PMID:23790194

Hong, J. S., Davis, J. P., Sterzing, P. R., Yoon, J., Choi, S., & Smith, D. C. (2014). A conceptual framework for understanding the association between school bullying victimization and substance misuse. *The American Journal of Orthopsychiatry, 84*(6), 696–710. doi:10.1037/ort0000036 PMID:25545436

Hong, J. S., Peguero, A. A., Choi, S., Lanesskog, D., Espelage, D. L., & Lee, N. Y. (2014). Social ecology of bullying and peer victimization of Latino and Asian youth in the United States: A review of the literature. *Journal of School Violence, 13*(3), 315–338. doi:10.1080/15388220.2013.856013

Hymel, S., & Swearer, S. M. (2015). Four decades of research on school bullying. *The American Psychologist, 70*(4), 293–299. doi:10.1037/a0038928 PMID:25961310

Jahoda, A., Pert, C., & Trower, P. (2006a). Socioemotional understanding and frequent aggression in people with mild to moderate intellectual disabilities: Recognition of facial affect and role-taking abilities. *American Journal of Mental Retardation, 111*(2), 77–89. doi:10.1352/0895-8017(2006)111[77:SUAFAI]2.0.CO;2 PMID:16466287

Jahoda, A., Pert, C., & Trower, P. (2006b). Frequent aggression and attribution of hostile intent in people with mild to moderate intellectual disabilities: An empirical investigation. *American Journal of Mental Retardation, 111*(2), 90–99. doi:10.1352/0895-8017(2006)111[90:FAAAOH]2.0.CO;2 PMID:16466288

Kaltiala-Heino, R., Rimpela, M., Marttunen, M., Rimpela, A., & Rantanen, P. (1999). Bullying, depression, and suicidal ideation in Finnish adolescents: School survey. *British Medical Journal, 319*(7206), 438–451. doi:10.1136/bmj.319.7206.348 PMID:10435954

Kavale, K. A., & Forness, S. R. (1995). Social skill deficits and training: A meta-analysis of the research in learning disabilities. *Advances in Learning and Behavioral Disabilities, 9*, 119–160.

Kavale, K. A., & Forness, S. R. (1996). Social skill deficits and learning disabilities: A meta-analysis. *Journal of Learning Disabilities, 29*(3), 226–237. doi:10.1177/002221949602900301 PMID:8732884

Kelly, E. V., Newton, N. C., Stapinski, L. A., Slade, T., Barrett, E. L., Conrod, P. J., & Teesson, M. (2015). Suicidality, internalizing problems and externalizing problems among adolescent bullies, victims and bully-victims. *Preventive Medicine: An International Journal Devoted to Practice and Theory, 73*, 100–105. doi:10.1016/j.ypmed.2015.01.020 PMID:25657168

Kistner, J. A., & Gatlin, D. F. (1989). Sociometric differences between learning-disabled and nonhandicapped students: Effects of sex and race. *Journal of Educational Psychology, 81*(1), 118–120. doi:10.1037/0022-0663.81.1.118

Kopecky, K. (2014). Cyberbullying and other risks of internet communication focused on university students. *Procedia: Social and Behavioral Sciences, 112*, 260–269. doi:10.1016/j.sbspro.2014.01.1163

Kumpulainen, K., Rasanen, E., & Puura, K. (2001). Psychiatric disorders and the use of mental health services among children involved in bullying. *Aggressive Behavior, 27*(2), 102–110. doi:10.1002/ab.3

Kurth, J. A. (2014). Educational placement of students with autism: The impact of state of residence. *Focus on Autism and Other Developmental Disabilities*.

Lagerheim, B. (1986). Preparing disabled children for coping with adolescent stress. *International Journal of Adolescent Medicine and Health*, *2*(4), 309–316.

Lapidot-Lefler, N., & Dolev-Cohen, M. (2015). Comparing cyberbullying and school bullying among school students: Prevalence, gender, and grade level differences. *Social Psychology of Education*, *18*(1), 1–16. doi:10.100711218-014-9280-8

Larkin, P., Jahoda, A., MacMahon, K., & Pert, C. (2012). Interpersonal sources of conflict in young people with and without mild to moderate intellectual disabilities at transition from adolescent to adulthood. *Journal of Applied Research in Intellectual Disabilities*, *25*(1), 29–38. doi:10.1111/j.1468-3148.2011.00652.x PMID:22473946

Lewandowski, L. J., & Barlow, J. R. (2000). Social cognition and verbal learning disabilities. *Journal of Psychotherapy in Independent Practice*, *4*(4), 35–47. doi:10.1300/J288v01n04_04

Lindfors, P. J., Kaltiala-Heino, R., & Rimpela, A. H. (2012). Cyberbullying among Finnish adolescents – a population-based study. *BMC Public Health*, *1*. PMID:23176715

Lindsay, S., & McPherson, A. C. (2012). Strategies for improving disability awareness and social inclusion of children and young people with cerebral palsy. *Child: Care, Health and Development*, *38*(6), 809–816. doi:10.1111/j.1365-2214.2011.01308.x PMID:21880056

Llewellyn, A. (2000). Perceptions of mainstreaming: A systems approach. *Developmental Medicine and Child Neurology*, *42*(2), 106–115. doi:10.1017/S0012162200000219 PMID:10698328

Luukkonen, A. H., Riala, K., Hakko, H., & Rasanen, P. (2010). Bullying behavior and substance abuse among underage psychiatric inpatient adolescents. *European Psychiatry*, *25*(7), 382–389. doi:10.1016/j.eurpsy.2009.12.002 PMID:20435448

Marini, Z. A., Dane, A. V., Bosacki, S. L., & Cura, Y.-. (2006). Direct and indirect bully-victims: Differential psychosocial risk factors associated with adolescents involvement in bullying and victimization. *Aggressive Behavior*, *32*(6), 551–569. doi:10.1002/ab.20155

Martlew, M., & Hodson, J. (1991). Children with mild learning difficulties in an integrated and in a special school: Comparisons of behavior, teasing and teachers' attitudes. *The British Journal of Educational Psychology*, *61*(3), 355–372. doi:10.1111/j.2044-8279.1991.tb00992.x PMID:1786214

Maryland Coalition for Inclusive Education. (2011). *Quality indicators for inclusive building based practices*. Retrieved from: http://www.mcie.org/usermedia/application/8/quality-indicators---building-based-practices-(2011).pdf

Matheson, C., Olsen, R. J., & Weisner, T. (2007). A good friend is hard to find: Friendship among adolescents with disabilities. *American Journal of Mental Retardation*, *112*(5), 319–329. doi:10.1352/0895-8017(2007)112[0319:AGFIHT]2.0.CO;2 PMID:17676957

McNamara, J. K., Willoughby, T., & Chalmers, H. (2005). Psychosocial status of adolescents with learning disabilities with and without comorbid attention deficit hyperactivity disorder. *Learning Disabilities Research & Practice*, *20*(4), 234–244. doi:10.1111/j.1540-5826.2005.00139.x

Mishna, F. (2003). Learning disabilities and bullying: Double jeopardy. *Journal of Learning Disabilities*, *36*(4), 336–347. doi:10.1177/00222194030360040501 PMID:15490906

Mishna, F., Khoury-Kassabri, M., Gadalla, T., & Daciuk, J. (2012). Risk factors for involvement in cyber bullying: Victims, bullies, and bully-victims. *Children and Youth Services Review*, *32*(1), 63–70. doi:10.1016/j.childyouth.2011.08.032

Morrison, G. M., Furlong, M. J., & Smith, G. (1994). Factors associated with the experience of school violence among general education, leadership class, opportunity class, and special day class pupils. *Journal of Education and Treatment of Children*, *17*, 356–369.

Nabuzoka, D. (2003). Teacher ratings and peer nominations of bullying and other behavior of children with and without learning difficulties. *Educational Psychology*, *23*(3), 307–321. doi:10.1080/0144341032000060147

Nabuzoka, D., & Smith, P. K. (1993). Sociometric status and social behaviour of children with and without learning difficulties. *Journal of Child Psychology and Psychiatry, and Allied Disciplines*, *34*(8), 1435–1448. doi:10.1111/j.1469-7610.1993.tb02101.x PMID:8294529

Nadeau, L., & Tessier, R. (2006). Social adjustment of children with cerebral palsy in mainstream classes: Peer perception. *Developmental Medicine and Child Neurology*, *48*(05), 331–336. doi:10.1017/S0012162206000739 PMID:16608539

Nansel, T. R., Overpeck, M., Pilla, R. S., Ruan, W. J., Simons-Morton, B., & Scheidt, P. (2001). Bullying behaviors among US youth: Prevalence and association with psychosocial adjustment. *Journal of the American Medical Association*, *285*(16), 2094–2100. doi:10.1001/jama.285.16.2094 PMID:11311098

Neece, C., & Baker, B. L. (2008). Predicting maternal parenting stress in middle childhood: The roles of child intellectual status, behavior problems and social skills. *Journal of Intellectual Disability Research*, *52*(12), 1114–1128. doi:10.1111/j.1365-2788.2008.01071.x PMID:18513339

Nishina, A., Juvonen, J., & Witkow, M. (2005). Sticks and stones may break my bones, but names will make me sick: The consequences of peer harassment. *Journal of Clinical Child and Adolescent Psychology*, *34*, 37–48. doi:10.120715374424jccp3401_4 PMID:15677279

Noorden, T. H. J., Haselager, G. J. T., Cillessen, A. H. N., & Bukowski, W. M. (2015). Empathy and involvement in bullying in children and adolescents: A systematic review. *Journal of Youth and Adolescence*, *44*(3), 637–657. doi:10.100710964-014-0135-6 PMID:24894581

Norwich, B., & Kelly, N. (2004). Pupils' views on inclusion: Moderate learning difficulties and bullying in mainstream and special schools. *British Educational Research Journal*, *30*(1), 43–65. doi:10.1080/01411920310001629965

Novaco, R. W., & Taylor, J. L. (2004). Assessment of anger and aggression among male offenders with developmental disabilities. *Psychological Assessment*, *16*(1), 42–50. doi:10.1037/1040-3590.16.1.42 PMID:15023091

O'Brennan, L. M., Bradshaw, C. P., & Sawyer, A. L. (2009). Examining development differences in the social-emotional problems among frequent bullies, victims, and bully/victims. *Psychology in the Schools*, *46*(2), 100–115. doi:10.1002/pits.20357

Olthof, T., & Goossens, F. A. (2008). Bullying and the need to belong: Early adolescents' bullying-related behavior and the acceptance they desire and receive from particular classmates. *Social Development*, *17*(1), 24–46.

Olweus, D. (1978). *Aggression in the schools: Bullies and whipping boys*. Washington, DC: Hemisphere Press.

Olweus, D. (1993). *Bullying at school: What we know and what we can do*. Blackwell Publshing.

Ozdemir, M., & Stattin, H. (2011). Bullies, victims, and bully-victims: A longitudinal examination of the effects of bullying-victimization experiences on youth well-being. *Journal of Aggression, Conflict and Peace Research*, *3*(2), 97–102. doi:10.1108/17596591111132918

Pearl, R., & Bay, M. (1999). Psychosocial correlates of learning disabilities. In V. L. Schwean & D. H. Saklofske (Eds.), *Handbook of psychosocial characteristics of exceptional children* (pp. 443–470). New York, NY: Kluwer Academic / Plenum Publishers. doi:10.1007/978-1-4757-5375-2_17

Perren, S., Dooley, J., Shaw, T., & Cross, T. (2010). Bullying in school and cyberspace: Associations with depressive symptoms in Swiss and Australian adolescents. *Child and Adolescent Psychiatry and Mental Health*, *23*(4), 28. doi:10.1186/1753-2000-4-28 PMID:21092266

Psalti, A. (2012). Bullies, victims, and bully-victims in Greek schools: Research data and implications of practice. *Hellenic Journal of Psychology*, *9*(2), 132–157.

Radliff, K. M., Wheaton, J. E., Robinson, K., & Morris, J. (2012). Illuminating the relationship between bullying and substance use among middle and high school youths. *Addictive Behaviors*, *37*(4), 569–572. doi:10.1016/j.addbeh.2012.01.001 PMID:22277772

Reiter, S., Bryen, D., & Shachar, I. (2007). Adolescents with intellectual disabilities as victims of abuse. *Journal of Intellectual Disabilities*, *11*(4), 371–387. doi:10.1177/1744629507084602 PMID:18029413

Reiter, S., & Lapidot-Leflet, N. (2007). Bullying among special education students with intellectual disabilities: Differences in social adjustment and social skills. *Journal of Intellectual & Developmental Disability*, *45*(3), 174–181. doi:10.1352/1934-9556(2007)45[174:BASESW]2.0.CO;2 PMID:17472426

Richardson, S. O. (1996). Coping with dyslexia in the regular classroom: Inclusion or exclusion. *Annals of Dyslexia*, *46*(1), 37–48. doi:10.1007/BF02648170 PMID:24234266

Rigby, K., & Cox, I. K. (1996). The contributions of bullying and low self-esteem to acts of delinquency among Australian teenagers. *Personality and Individual Differences*, *21*(4), 609–612. doi:10.1016/0191-8869(96)00105-5

Rigby, K., & Slee, P. T. (1991). Bullying among Australian school children: Reported behaviour and attitudes to victims. *The Journal of Social Psychology*, *131*(5), 615–622. doi:10.1080/00224545.1991.9924646 PMID:1798296

Roberts, C. M., & Smith, P. R. (1999). Attitudes and behavior of children towards peers with disabilities. *International Journal of Disability Development and Education, 46*(1), 35–50. doi:10.1080/103491299100713

Rose, C. A., & Espelage, D. L. (2012). Risk and protective factors associated with the bullying involvement of students with emotional and behavioral disorders. *Behavioral Disorders, 37*(3), 133–148.

Rose, C. A., Espelage, D. L., & Monda-Amaya, L. E. (2009). Bullying and victimization rates among students in general and special education: A comparative analysis. *Educational Psychology, 29*(7), 761–776. doi:10.1080/01443410903254864

Rose, C. A., Forber-Pratt, A. J., Espelage, D. L., & Aragon, S. R. (2013). The influence of psychosocial factors on bullying involvement of students with disabilities. *Theory into Practice, 52*(4), 272–279. doi:10.1080/00405841.2013.829730

Rose, C. A., Monda-Amaya, L. E., & Espelage, D. L. (2011). Bullying perpetration and victimization in special education: A review of the literature. *Remedial and Special Education, 32*(2), 114–130. doi:10.1177/0741932510361247

Rose, J., West, C., & Clifford, D. (2000). Group intervention for anger in people with intellectual disabilities. *Research in Developmental Disabilities, 21*(3), 171–181. doi:10.1016/S0891-4222(00)00032-9 PMID:10939316

Ryoo, J. H., Wang, C., & Swearer, S. M. (2015). Examination of the change in latent statuses in bullying behaviors across time. *School Psychology Quarterly, 30*(1), 105–122. doi:10.1037pq0000082 PMID:25111466

Sailor, W., Wolf, N., Choi, H., & Roger, B. (2009). Sustaining positive behavior support in a context of comprehensive school reform. In W. Sailor, G. Dunlop, G. Sugai, & R. Horner (Eds.), *Handbook of positive behavior support* (pp. 633–669). New York: Springer Publishing. doi:10.1007/978-0-387-09632-2_26

Salend, S. J., & Duhaney, L. M. G. (1999). The impact of inclusion on students with and without disabilities and their educators. *Remedial and Special Education, 20*(2), 114–126. doi:10.1177/074193259902000209

Sansone, R. A., & Sansone, L. A. (2008). Bully victims: Psychological and somatic aftermaths. *Psychiatry, 5*(6), 62–64. PMID:19727287

Sheard, C., Clegg, J., Standen, P., & Cromby, J. (2001). Bullying and people with severe intellectual disability. *Journal of Intellectual Disability Research, 45*(5), 407–415. doi:10.1046/j.1365-2788.2001.00349.x PMID:11679046

Sirlopu, D., Gonzalez, R., Bohner, G., Siebler, F., Ordonnez, G., Millar, A., ... De Tezanos-Pinto, P. (2008). Promoting positive attitudes toward people with Down syndrome: The benefit of school inclusion programs. *Journal of Applied Social Psychology, 38*(11), 2710–2736. doi:10.1111/j.1559-1816.2008.00411.x

Skapinakis, P., Bellos, S., Gkatsa, T., Magklara, K., Lewish, G., Araya, R., ... Mavreas, V. (2011). The association between bullying and early stages of suicidal ideation in late adolescents in Greece. *BMC Psychiatry, 11*(1), 1–9. doi:10.1186/1471-244X-11-22 PMID:21303551

Son, E., Parish, S. L., & Peterson, N. A. (2012). National prevalence of peer victimization among young children with disabilities in the United States. *Children and Youth Services Review, 34*(8), 1540–1545. doi:10.1016/j.childyouth.2012.04.014

Sourander, A., Klomek, A. B., Ikonen, M., Lindroos, J., Luntamo, T., Koskelainen, M., ... Helenius, H. (2010). Psychosocial risk factors associated with cyberbullying among adolescents: A population-based study. *Archives of General Psychiatry, 67*(7), 720–728. doi:10.1001/archgenpsychiatry.2010.79 PMID:20603453

Sprafkin, J., & Gadow, K. (1987). An observational study of emotionally disturbed and learning-disabled children in school settings. *Journal of Abnormal Child Psychology, 15*(3), 393–408. doi:10.1007/BF00916457 PMID:3668086

Sterzing, P. R., Shattuck, P. T., Narendrof, S. C., Wagner, M., & Cooper, B. P. (2012). Bullying involvement and autism spectrum disorders: Prevalence and correlates of bullying involvement among adolescents with an autism spectrum disorder. *Archives of Pediatrics & Adolescent Medicine, 166*(11), 1058–1064. doi:10.1001/archpediatrics.2012.790 PMID:22945284

Swearer, S. M., Siebecker, A. B., Johnsen-Frerichs, L., & Wang, C. (2010). Assessment of bullying/victimization: The problem of comparability across studies and across methodologies. In S. R. Jimerson, S. M. Swearer, & D. L. Espelage (Eds.), *Handbook of bullying in schools: An international perspective* (pp. 305–327). New York, NY: Routledge.

Tomasik, M. (2007). Effective inclusion activities for high school students with multiple disabilities. *Journal of Visual Impairment & Blindness, 101*(10), 657–659.

Underwood, M. K., Galen, B. R., & Paquette, J. A. (2001). Top ten challenges for understanding gender and aggression in children: Why can't we all just get along? *Social Development, 10*, 248–266.

Van Cleave, J., & Davis, M. M. (2006). Bullying and peer victimization among children with special health care needs. *Pediatrics, 118*(4), 1212–1219. doi:10.1542/peds.2005-3034 PMID:17015509

Verdugo, M. A., Bermejo, B. G., & Fuertes, J. (1995). The maltreatment of intellectually handicapped children and adolescents. *Child Abuse & Neglect, 19*(2), 205–215. doi:10.1016/0145-2134(94)00117-D PMID:7780782

Waasdorp, T. E., & Bradshaw, C. P. (2015). The overlap between cyberbullying and traditional bullying. *The Journal of Adolescent Health, 56*(5), 483–488. doi:10.1016/j.jadohealth.2014.12.002 PMID:25631040

Waldman, H. B., Swerdloff, M., & Perlman, S. P. (1999). A "dirty secret": The abuse of children with disabilities. *ASDC Journal of Dentistry for Children, 66*(3), 197–202. PMID:10476359

Wang, J., Iannotti, R. J., Luk, J. W., & Nansel, T. R. (2010). Co-occurrence of victimization from five subtypes of bullying: Physical, verbal, social exclusion, spreading rumors, and cyber. *Journal of Pediatric Psychology, 35*(10), 1103–1112. doi:10.1093/jpepsy/jsq048 PMID:20488883

Whitney, I., Nabuzoka, D., & Smith, P. K. (1992). Bullying in schools: Mainstream and special needs. *Support for Learning, 7*(1), 3–7. doi:10.1111/j.1467-9604.1992.tb00445.x

Whitney, I., Smith, P. K., & Thompson, D. (1994). Bullying and children with special educational needs. In P. K. Smith & S. Sharp (Eds.), *School bullying: Insights and perspectives* (pp. 213–240). London: Routledge.

York, J., Vandercook, T., MacDonald, C., Heise-Neff, C., & Caughey, E. (1992). Feedback about integrating middle school students with severe disabilities in general education classes. *Exceptional Children*, *58*(3), 244–257. PMID:1839896

Zablotsky, B., Bradshaw, C. P., Anderson, C., & Law, P. A. (2013). The association between bullying and the psychological functioning of children with autism spectrum disorders. *Journal of Developmental and Behavioral Pediatrics*, *34*(1), 1–8. doi:10.1097/DBP.0b013e31827a7c3a PMID:23275052

Zeedyk, S. M., Rodrigeuz, G., Tipton, L. A., Baker, B. L., & Blacher, J. (2014). Bullying of youth with autism spectrum disorder, intellectual disability, or typical development: Victim and parent perspectives. *Research in Autism Spectrum Disorders*, *8*(9), 1173–1183. doi:10.1016/j.rasd.2014.06.001 PMID:25285154

Zeitlin, S., & Williamson, G. (1990). Coping characteristics of disabled and nondisabled young children. *The American Journal of Orthopsychiatry*, *60*(3), 404–411. doi:10.1037/h0079183 PMID:2143354

ADDITIONAL READING

Basquill, M., Nezu, C. M., Nezu, A. M., & Klein, T. L. (2004). Aggression-related hostility bias and social problem-solving deficits in adult males with mental retardation. *American Journal of Mental Retardation*, *109*(3), 255–263. doi:10.1352/0895-8017(2004)109<255:AHBASP>2.0.CO;2 PMID:15072517

Ebeling, H., & Nurkkala, H. (2002). Children and adolescents with developmental disorders and violence. *International Journal of Circumpolar Health*, *61*(0), 51–60. doi:10.3402/ijch.v61i0.17502 PMID:12585820

Fenning, R. M., Baker, J. K., Baker, B. L., & Crnic, K. A. (2007). Parenting children with borderline intellectual functioning: A unique risk population. *American Journal of Mental Retardation*, *112*(2), 107–121. doi:10.1352/0895-8017(2007)112[107:PCWBIF]2.0.CO;2 PMID:17295551

Horner-Johnson, W., & Drum, C. E. (2006). Prevalence of maltreatment of people with intellectual disabilities: A review of recently published research. *Mental Retardation and Developmental Disabilities Research Reviews*, *12*(1), 57–69. doi:10.1002/mrdd.20097 PMID:16435331

Loveland, K. A., & Kelley, M. L. (1988). Development of adaptive behavior in adolescents and young adults with autism and Down syndrome. *American Journal of Mental Retardation*, *93*, 84–92. PMID:2970861

Luckasson, R., Borthwick-Duffy, S., Buntinx, W. H. E., Coulter, D. L., Craig, E. M., Reeve, A., ... Tasse, M. J. (2002). *Mental retardation: Definition, classification, and systems of supports*. Washington, DC: American Association on Mental Retardation.

Mitchell, L. M., & Buchele-Ash, A. (2000). Abuse and neglect of individuals with disabilities: Building protective supports through public policy. *Journal of Disability Policy Studies*, *10*(2), 225–243. doi:10.1177/104420730001000206

Murphy, N. (2011). Maltreatment of children with disabilities: The breaking point. *Journal of Child Neurology, 26*(8), 1054–1056. doi:10.1177/0883073811413278 PMID:21775619

Nettelbeck, T., & Wilson, C. (2002). Personal vulnerability to victimization of people with mental retardation. *Trauma, Violence & Abuse, 3*(4), 289–306. doi:10.1177/1524838002237331

Olweus, D. (1991). Bully/victim problems among school children: Some basic facts and effects of a school-based intervention program. In D. Pepler & K. Rubin (Eds.), *The development and treatment of childhood aggression* (pp. 411–448). Hillsdale, NJ: Erlbaum.

This research was previously published in the Handbook of Research on Diagnosing, Treating, and Managing Intellectual Disabilities edited by Rejani Thudalikunnil Gopalan; pages 33-53, copyright year 2016 by Information Science Reference (an imprint of IGI Global).

Chapter 20
Marginality and Mattering:
The Experiences of Students With Learning Disabilities on the College Campus

Wanda Hadley
Western Michigan University, USA

Jennifer Hsu
Grand Valley State University, USA

Mark Antony Addison
Western Michigan University, USA

Donna Talbot
Western Michigan University, USA

ABSTRACT

Students with learning disabilities are the fastest growing at-risk population transitioning to higher education institutions. This chapter explores the academic adjustment issues students with learning disabilities experience in their transition to the college environment. Their experiences are explored and reported through the context of student development theory of marginalization. The chapter discusses students' access and adjustment to the campus culture and how this experience influences their identity development.

INTRODUCTION

There is an increase in students with learning disabilities' enrollment in colleges and universities in the United States (Agarwal, Calvo, & Kumar, 2014; Grant, 2011; Herbert et al., 2014; Hollins & Foley, 2013). A student with a learning disability is defined as having one or more of the following conditions: "a specific learning disability, a visual handicap, hard of hearing, deafness, a speech disability, an orthopedic handicap, or a health impairment" (U.S. Department of Education, 2013). Learning disabilities are

DOI: 10.4018/978-1-7998-1213-5.ch020

intrinsic to the student and may continue throughout their life span. Even though students with learning disabilities continually enroll in colleges and universities, they generally have trouble successfully assimilating in the college environment, persevering and graduating. Students with learning disabilities might meet general university admissions requirements and many colleges and universities do provide a number of services to support their persistence. However, this population will still possibly experience a variety of academic and social challenges while in the college culture. In addition to diagnosed learning disabilities, students' transition might be challenging because they move from the structured high school environment to the more autonomous environment of college.

Once the student enrolls in the university and their disability is documented, the higher education institution is required by law to reasonably accommodate the student and provide academic accommodations. Examples of academic accommodations in the college environment include, but are not limited to, extended time for exams, tape recording lectures, note takers, or sign language interpreters. However, higher education institutions are not required to provide accommodations that are unduly burdensome, nor are they required to "fundamentally alter" academic programs (Geier & Hadley, 2015). Students with learning disabilities transition to college from a high school background that provides a tremendous amount of oversight and support due to their learning disability (Eckes & Ochoa, 2005). Whereas learning to manage the disability is the first concern, a primary skill for students with learning disabilities to acquire during their developmental years is to learn how to advocate for their own education. Many of these students enter college with no experience self-advocating. By contrast to their high school experience, in their transition to college, they are expected to self-advocate and practice self-determined behavior. Students with learning disabilities associate the skill of self-advocacy to better understanding their disabilities, more confidence and better able to set goals for themselves. But previous to their college experience they may have little or no experience practicing such behavior. Without the expectation of advocating for services in high school, students with learning disabilities enter college lacking such skills.

SELF-ADVOCACY AND SELF-DETERMINATION SKILLS

Students who practice both self-advocacy and self-determination are stronger at requesting services and supports on campus (Finn, Getzel, & McManus, 2008). Ankeny and Lehman (2011) defined self-advocacy and self-determination as constructs that relate to the student's understanding of their learning disability, their ability to value themselves despite their learning disability and their willingness to set forth and act on plans for their future. Self-advocacy and self-determination might be complex skillsets to develop because along with the student's learning disability, students may have other diagnosis such as attention-deficit-disorders, depression, emotional problems and/or anxiety disorders (Anctil, Ishikawa & Scott, 2008). Ankeny and Lehman further noted the significance of students with learning disabilities growing their self-knowledge about how their disability may impact their learning. They stressed that students need continuing opportunities to develop self-knowledge, including an understanding of their specific learning disability and how it influences their persistence in their college experience. Concentrating on self-advocacy and self-determination skills as students with learning disabilities transition from high school to college is necessary. Encouraging students with learning disabilities to practice self-advocacy and self-determination to contend with university obstacles can increase student retention and persistence in the college setting (Hadley, 2009). An important feature of self-advocacy and self-determination is self-awareness or "knowing yourself." Because students with learning disabilities are required to request accommodations, they must be knowledgeable about specific needs and strengths in relation to their disabilities. In particular students should be able to explain to campus administrators, staff and faculty what their disability is and how it impacts their academic performance. Finn, Getzel and McManus (2008) reported that a shared characteristic of students who successfully access and complete programs of study in college is that of practicing self-advocacy and self-determination skills. They further pointed out that there is a connection between self-determination, career development and post-college employment.

In secondary school systems, students with learning disabilities are provided special accommodations and services that are not generally available when they transition to college. Consequently, students may perceive the university culture as unwelcoming as well as challenging. It is, therefore, important to understand university culture and how it shapes students' experiences. Most definitions of university culture are largely influenced by Schein's work (1969, 1988) on organizational culture, which defines culture as shared values, assumptions and beliefs. Within an organization or university, messages about what is valued, believed and assumed are conveyed through its people (faculty and staff), structures (buildings, statues, and grounds), policies (mission, student code of conduct, handbooks, and syllabi) and symbols (signs, artwork, language, and attitudes). Unlike other organizational cultures such as businesses, universities are more loosely coupled--they have many functions and serve a diverse set of constituents. Sporn (1996) helps us understand why university culture is so complex and may be slow to respond to various populations' needs by summarizing the following characteristics:

Their goals are more ambiguous; their focus is on people not on profit; their techniques are unclear and non-routine; they are vulnerable to environmental changes and experts dominate the decision-making process. (p. 43)

Wilson, Getzel and Brown (2000) found specific attributes of institutional culture that determines whether or not a campus is perceived by students to be disability-friendly; these attributes have both academic and non-academic (or social) components. For instance, academic components relate to the structure and flexibility of programs/classes (e.g., philosophy of the program, availability of course waivers and substitutions, faculty awareness and support, faculty development/training, testing accommodations, time to degree requirements, tutoring and writing support), while co-curricular and non-academic factors focus on all the parts of campus life that impact students' sense of belonging, feelings of being understood and accepted, development of self-determination skills, and subsequently comfort in asking for accommodations for a disability. It is important to note that the attributes of institutional culture defined in these studies are based on current practice and realities which often are embedded in legal requirements, and not necessarily guided by models of social justice.

STUDENTS WITH LEARNING DISABILITIES: A SOCIAL JUSTICE PERSPECTIVE

To understand how students with learning disabilities experience higher education institutions (HEIs), it is necessary to understand the context and history through which the concept of disability is framed and understood. The larger disabilities rights movement has changed the landscape for how disabilities are perceived and interpreted by society, which has in turn impacted how HEIs manage services for students with disabilities. Disabilities have largely been interpreted through two dominant models, the individual (medical) model and social model (Oliver, 1983). The modern understandings of the differences between these models were primarily brought to light by disability rights organizations. In 1975, the Union of Physically Impaired Against Segregation, a disability rights organization in the United Kingdom, released the following statement:

In our view, it is society which disables physically impaired people. Disability is something imposed on top of our impairments by the way we are unnecessarily isolated and excluded from full participation in society. Disabled people are therefore an oppressed group in society (UPIAS, 1976, pp. 3-4).

Following the release of the UPIAS statement and building on the concepts contained therein, Oliver (1983) coined the term "social model of disability" to explicate the ways in which society creates barriers that make institutions and social experiences inaccessible. The social model of disability shifts the focus from disability as an individual concept and suggests that social institutions, such as universities create restricting environments. This is in contrast to the individual or medical model that focuses the intervention on an individual's functional limitations and the need for medical care or rehabilitation. The social model has undergirded much of the UK disability rights movement's efforts to remove disabling barriers (Oliver, 2013).

Some critics have argued that the dichotomous views of the social and medical model have limited the advancement of the disability rights movement. According to Shakespeare and Watson (2002), "social model theory in the UK rests on a distinction between impairment, an attribute of the individual body or mind, and disability, a relationship between a person with impairment and society." Shakespeare and Watson (2002) argue that the social model ignores the ways in which people, their bodies, their multiple identities and experiences are constantly interacting with the environment around them which necessitates new models that consider these multiple dimensions of being. Oliver (2013) argues that the social model continues to be an effective tool with which to improve students' lives in the absence of other models and that the model does not exist in exclusion to impairment and difference. Rather, the social model provides advocates with a model that unites people with disabilities toward the elimination of barriers rather than imposing the divisive burden of being individual victims of impairment (Oliver, 2013). The social model of disability has been understood through multiple approaches, often varying by geography and informed by its sociocultural contexts. While the UK social model largely relies on situating impairment and disability as dichotomous, the Nordic social model situates impairment and disability as interacting with one another while still framing people with disabilities as flawed and less able, and the North American social model, aligning closely with the US Civil Rights Movement of the 1960s, maintains that the social environment fails to adapt to citizens with disabilities and subsequently segregates and discriminates against them (Owens, 2015). Students with learning disabilities might experience this very dynamic on the university campus.

Many higher education institutions continue to operate from a medical model of disability, largely guided by the need to adhere to legal compliance requirements. Loewen and Pollard (2010) highlight that even with reasonable accommodations, students may not be fully included in the classroom and often feel stigmatized having to request accommodations. By having to make special requests, the burden is on the individual student rather than HEIs. As such, they contend that there continues to be a need to reframe disability access in higher education from an individual (medical) model of providing accommodations to a social justice model that emphasizes access as a necessary human right and the lack thereof as discrimination (Loewen & Pollard, 2010). This shift allows higher education institutions to move away from a social welfare model of addressing students' needs on an individual, at-request level to one in which systems and structures are systematically changed to provide broader access to students of many different abilities (Marks, 2008). One example of implementing social justice approaches to higher education include the concept of universal design, in which classroom instruction is pre-emptively designed to be accessible and useful to students with a variety of disabilities, including those with learning disabilities. Researchers have found that universal design instruction can improve classroom experiences for both students and instructors (McGuire & Scott, 2006). Moving toward universal design instruction is a clear implementation of a social justice model, where the higher education institution changes their structure to meet the needs of all students, with consideration given to students of diverse abilities. Beyond this, however, the implications of a social justice model of disability in higher education institutions are varied. Guzman and Balcazar (2010) found that while the vast majority of disability service providers in higher education understand and speak from a social justice framework, the services they provide reflect the medical model of disability and are focused on addressing individual limitations.

Higher education institutions can support students with disabilities in many other ways by shifting the focus of their services and support. The social justice model of disability can support students' social integration on campus. While significant research has demonstrated the importance of social belonging on student persistence and success, few disability service offices prioritize social supports as part of their outreach with students. Litner, Mann-Feder, and Guerard, (2005) noted that a key to successful adjustment on campus for students with learning disabilities is participating in non-academic, co-curricular activities. The researchers further pointed out that these engagements in-turn contributed to the development of a positive self-identity and supported their academic achievements. In a review of existing research on underrepresented students in higher education, Leake and Stodden (2014) suggest that the relative lack of research on social integration issues for students with disabilities stem from the focus on academic and physical accommodations and less on social acceptance. They urge a future focus on including disability as a diversity issue in higher education, ensuring accessible co-curricular experiences, and supporting student activism to effect changes in policy and practice. The focus must be placed on providing all students and the whole student an opportunity to feel included and welcome in higher education institutions. The social justice model of disability also serves to address students' multiple identities. Students with multiple oppressed, social identities often experience compounded effects of discrimination. Crenshaw (1989) coined the term intersectionality, as a way of understanding and analyzing how multiple oppressed identities such as sex and race operate together to oppress Black women in a way that is greater than the sum of its individual identities. Liasidou (2013) explains, "intersectional understandings of disability can make more salient the wider sociopolitical and cultural contextual factors that collude towards creating subordinated subject-positions as gauged against conventional ability, ethnic or social class norms (p. 302)." As such, educational policies to address disabilities must take into consideration the broader contexts and experiences of the student more holistically.

STUDENT WITH LEARNING DISABILITIES: MULTIPLE IDENTITIES

It is important to review Schlossberg's theory of marginality and mattering when examining students' transition to the college culture (Patton, et al., 2016). According to Schlossberg (1989) marginality has to do with the student's sense of not "fitting in" in their new environment. Schlossberg theorized that the feeling may be temporary for students from the dominant population, but can be a permanent feeling and/or condition for minority groups of students such as students with learning disabilities. According to Schlossberg, when students feel insignificant they began to worry about whether they matter to others. Furthermore, mattering is the belief, whether right or wrong, that individuals matter/connect to someone else. Marginalization and/or disenfranchisement describes the practice of consciously and/or unconsciously excluding students with learning disabilities from the mainstream of the campus culture - placing them on the margins/fringes of the main culture (Gil-Kashiwabara, et al., 2007). When students with learning disabilities are marginalized, they might be more susceptible to negative outcomes in their transition to college. Gill (1997) questioned if it is wise for students with disabilities to call attention to their differences in a culture that may use nonconformity as a basis for discrimination. Schlossberg (1989) specifically identifies students in transition as prone to feelings of marginality and pronounces that those feelings of marginality and mattering may influence campus involvement. Marginality and mattering conceptual frame also includes the notion that the more support students have in the campus culture, the less they will feel marginalized.

Agarwal, Calvo, and Kumar (2014) point to the diversity and multiple identities of students with disabilities as being similar to that of their peers without disabilities. Students with disabilities differ in type of disability, age, gender and ethnic background. It is imperative, then, for institutions of higher learning to "foster an inclusive and equitable environment for all students" (p. 34). Institutions create environments that are conducive to learning and success for students with learning disabilities by having inclusive language in its mission statement, while demonstrating the importance of its values through the creation and maintenance of robust and inclusive student support services. This requires higher education institutions to offer greater efforts than the minimum requirements of Section 504 of the Rehabilitation Act and the Americans with Disabilities Act (ADA) that just seek equal access for all students. Kurth and Mellard (2006) reported that an institution which performs minimally in order to meet the basic requirements of equal access laws limits the success potential of the college and its students" (p. 83). On the other hand, an institution which invests in an accommodation process, considerate of the "entire context of student life...incorporates system wide universal design concepts" to achieve profound results (Kurth & Mellard, 2006, p.83). In order to implement accommodation processes for students with learning disabilities, who also possess other identities, it is important to learn about the group and understand the social and academic challenges they face before the administration acts.

Some literature has contributed useful knowledge and understanding of the types of learning disabilities that students identify with, as well as the challenges that hinder them academically. Hollins and Foley (2013) noted that college students with Attention Deficit Hyperactivity Disorder (ADHD) and learning disabilities identified issues such as "inadequate study skills, poor note-taking abilities, and difficulty with test-taking" (p. 608) as negatively influencing their academic performance. According to the Learning Disability Association of America (LDA, 2016), the student's ability to read, write, speak, spell, and compute math may with varying degrees be compromised by the characteristic and severity of a particular learning disability. Such findings have led to improved classroom technology, academic liaisons within disabilities services offices, faculty training to promote awareness of needs for students with learning disabilities, and extended time for students with learning disabilities during test-taking. Conversely, there is very little known about the social implications for students with learning disabilities on college campuses, especially those students with additional historically marginalized or underserved identities such as first-generation status, students from minority racial and ethnic backgrounds, students who identify as lesbian, gay, bisexual, and transgender (LGBT), and student athletes with learning disabilities to name a few.

Reynolds, Cooper and Hadley (2014) noted that in addition to finding it difficult to complete their academic programs, students with learning disabilities reported feelings of marginalization and a lack of acceptance by the campus culture. Archer and Hadley (2014) added that as an at-risk population, student athletes with learning disabilities not only academically struggle, they often identify as having low self-confidence which leads to emotional and psychological distress and possible academic failure. Concurrently, Reynolds, Cooper and Hadley (2014) found that African American college students with learning disabilities who also identify as Lesbian, Gay, Bisexual or Transgender (LGBT) as a sub-culture of students with learning disabilities have received very little attention in the literature. The duality of minority status or identities could lead to double experiences of marginality and oppression for students with learning disabilities that identify as LGBT. Such negative consequences could adversely affect the academic adjustment and performance of students with learning disabilities who identify as LGBT. Leake, Burgstaher, and Izzo (2011) informed that students with learning disabilities from culturally and linguistically diverse backgrounds in particular are less likely to enroll in and complete college. Leake, Burgstaher, and Izzo found that culturally and linguistically diverse students with learning disabilities are more likely to come from poor upbringings and experience its damaging effects. They further offered that students may be subjected to discrimination and experience low expectations due to their learning disability and being of culturally and linguistically diverse backgrounds.

It is imperative to mention the lack of research that assess the impact of multiple identities on the success of students with learning disabilities in higher education, especially when those identities relate to social characteristics such as race, sexual orientation, socioeconomic status, and student-athlete status. Henry, Fuerth, & Figliozzi (2010) noted the mistake made by previous academic inquiries that tend to analyze the impact of these social characteristics on educational success in isolation of one another. There should be more attention paid to the combined social impact of these identities, especially when students with learning disabilities incur challenges as members of more than one historically marginalized group. Lombardi, Murray, and Gerdes (2012) conducted research that looked at the impact of social factors associated with being first-generation college student and a student with a learning disability. Their research reported that students with learning disabilities are at risk of successfully transitioning to and completing college due to factors such as limited peer support (i.e. emotional support from peers and ability to make friends), family support (i.e. help and support from family members during college), and use of accommodations (i.e. requesting accommodations regardless of academic or social performance). Evidence has shown that strong family support, as a social support factor, is related to positive experiences for college students especially those students from historically underserved populations (Freeman, Stoch, Chan, & Hutchinson, 2004).

Lombardi, Murray, and Gerdes (2012) further discovered that there are, in fact, additional social and economic challenges that accompany their status as 'first generation' resulting in lower graduation rates in comparison with their peers who do not have learning disabilities and continuing generation (a student who has at least one parent with a bachelor's degree). First generation status as a risk factor for completing a four-year college degree presents a disturbing reality that deserves institutional awareness. Lombardi, Murray, and Gerdes (2012) propose that universities must take into consideration the characteristic of first generation status when designing support services for students with learning disabilities as this factor can determine overall success for students with learning disabilities. When it comes to student athletes with learning disabilities, researchers (Clark & Parette,(2002; Stokowski & Hardin, 2014) shared the extremely harmful stigma of "the dumb jock" that is attached to the identity of student-athletes and the threat it creates for students with learning disabilities. Stokowski and Hardin (2014) found that the

Marginality and Mattering

stereotypes attached to being a student-athlete and a student with a learning disability (especially those participating in a high profile sport such as football, behaved favorably to those stereotypes) hindered that population from performing to their highest abilities. This is a growing group and support services must ensure that student-athletes with learning disabilities are not overlooked.

Strayhorn (2006) found that the race and ethnic identity of a student, coupled with other underserved identities significantly predicts success at the college level. These students who face "familial, cultural, and social transitions that may make the transition to, and completion of, postsecondary school challenging" (Lombardi et al., 2012, p. 811). Other research (Henry, Fuerth, & Figliozzi, 2010) has noted the mistake made by previous academic inquiries that tend to analyze the impact of these social characteristics on educational success in isolation of one another. The authors point out that students with multiple minority identities need services that cater to their unique challenges, as well as advocates who understand the nature of such challenges. Henry, Fuerth, and Figliozzi (2010) reviewed the experiences of a gay male student with learning disabilities in order to add to the topic in higher education. The experiences of gay students with learning disabilities have historically included "oppressions of heterosexism and ableism (p. 360)." The more alarming information gathered during the research is the student's indication that "limited services within the university environment, such as counseling, have restricted [his] growth as a multiple minority" (p. 381). Brown and Broido (2015) identified three important aspects of university-wide dynamics that create "a welcoming and supportive campus: upper-level leadership, community orientation and cross-campus collaboration, and supportive policies" (p. 196). Brown and Broido proposed the creation of a campus committee consisting of faculty, staff, and students dedicated to improving institutional commitment to students with learning disabilities. A dedicated committee could consist of individuals (employees and students) with learning disabilities that would contribute personal experiences to the dialogue, as well as propose institutional changes that promote effective support services.

FUTURE RESEARCH DIRECTIONS

Generally speaking, higher education institutions are driven by a traditional measure of success, i.e., student completion of degrees and/or graduation. Consequently, attempts to create campuses that are viewed as welcoming to students with learning disabilities often place more emphasis on academic issues than social factors. This emphasis overlooks the importance that students with learning disabilities place on non-academic factors in helping them to be successful in college. Denhart (2008) noted that as early as the middle 1990s students with learning disabilities have voiced feelings of being misunderstood on the college campus. Despite the importance to students with learning disabilities to have faculty, staff and peers understand and validate their needs and challenges, little has changed on college campuses. The impact of "non-academic" issues on whether or not students with learning disabilities remain in college cannot be underestimated. Fear of being misunderstood or judged negatively, especially by faculty, has deterred students with learning disabilities from disclosing and asking for accommodation (Gans, Kenney, & Ghany, 2003), which ultimately may have a negative impact on their ability to be successful. This challenge is foundational in disability theory which emphasizes the belief that "social intolerance of human variation creates disability" (Denhart, 2008, p. 493). Similarly, when students with learning disabilities are interacting with peers, if they do not disclose some of their disabilities and coping strategies, their behaviors may seem odd or inappropriate, leading to misunderstanding and/ or further isolation. Once again, the fear of disclosing may create unwanted consequences. While these social factors may not directly relate to academic success, they can determine whether or not a student stays in college. Compounded with issues brought about by multiple marginalized identities, students with learning disabilities might be even more challenged in college learning environments.

CONCLUSION

This chapter has emphasized the importance for higher education institutions to set the tone for creating welcoming and supportive environments in their educational endeavors for students with learning disabilities, who may also belong to other historically underserved groups. These educational efforts must be extended to the campus community at large, as the issues presented thus far, have presented a variety of social concerns. We are reminded by Denhart's (2008) description of disability theory, as cited earlier in this chapter, that it "demonstrates how social intolerance of human variation creates disability (p. 493)." Students with learning disabilities are the least likely to ask for accommodations due to the debilitating effects of social stigma that they perceive to be the way society views them (Denhart, 2008). Such stigma is validated through ablest language that impact all aspects of life and lack of institutional support. To that effect, our efforts to change campus culture in order to reflect acceptance and accommodation of students with learning disabilities and their needs must include education for all members of campus. Senior level administrators must encourage and provide opportunities for collaboration among disabilities services offices and other departments such as multicultural affairs, Greek life, athletic department, and student leadership organization programs. To that extent, the achievements of such campus-wide endeavors must be celebrated alongside, and in the same manner in which we celebrate milestones in athletics, academics, and in student leadership programs. The fact remains that students with non-visible disabilities, such as learning disabilities, contribute in to our achievements in all of those areas.

Active intervention strategies such as "validation" may be needed to encourage at-risk populations such as students with learning disabilities to feel accepted and to engage in the campus culture. Patton et al (2016) informed that validation early in the college experience of students who feel marginalized by the campus culture can be important to their success. In addition, Maramba and Palmer (2014) stressed the importance of such support for students who may doubt their ability to succeed. Trainor et al. (2008) highlighted the impact of cultural beliefs and values on the student's transition to higher education. Differences in beliefs and values between diverse students with disabilities and educators may create additional obstacles to successful transition to college for students. Cultural diversity has to do with the student's racial/ethnic identities, religion, traditions and socioeconomic backgrounds. Trainor et al. (2008) further noted that diversity can also include majority students who have faced economic marginalization and lack of opportunity because of poverty or other conditions. Students with learning disabilities from low socioeconomic backgrounds, those who are African American, Latino, Native American Indian as well as those who speak English as a second language and face documentation and immigration issues are particularly at-risk in their transition to college (Shalhout, Simmons, & Hadley, 2015; Trainer, et al. 2008). Trainor et al. (2008) added that high school graduation rates, postsecondary outcomes and employment outcomes for students with disabilities differ according to disability type, socioeconomic class, gender and race/ethnicity. Hadley (2009) emphasized that it is the responsibility of the university culture to ensure that students with learning disabilities are accepted in the college community and have every opportunity to pursue their goals and be successful as their peers without learning disabilities.

REFERENCES

Agarwal, N., Calvo, B. A., & Kumar, V. (2014). Paving the road to success: A students with disabilities organization in a university setting. *College Student Journal*, *48*(1), 34–44.

Anctil, T. M., Ishikawa, M. E., & Scott, A. T. (2008). Academic identity development through self-determination: Successful college students with learning disabilities. *Career Development for Exceptional Individuals*, *31*(3), 164–174. doi:10.1177/0885728808315331

Ankeny, E. M., & Lehmann, J. P. (2011). Journey toward self-determination: Voices of students with disabilities who participated in a secondary transition program on a community college campus. *Remedial and Special Education*, *32*(4), 279–289. doi:10.1177/0741932510362215

Archer, D. E. & Hadley, W. M. (2014). College athletes and learning disabilities: An underexplored, at-risk population. *American College Personnel Association (ACPA): Standing Committee on Disability (SCD) Newsletter*.

Brown, K., & Broido, E. M. (2014). Engaging students with disabilities. In S. J. Quaye & S. R. Harper (Eds.), *Student engagement in higher education* (2nd ed.; pp. 187–207). New York: Routlege.

Clark, M., & Parette, P. (2002). Student athletes with learning disabilities: A model for effective supports. *College Student Journal*, *36*(1), 47–61.

Cornett-Devito, M. M., & Worley, D. W. (2005). A Front Row Seat: A Phenomenological Investigation of Learning Disabilities. *Communication Education*, *54*(4), 312–333. doi:10.1080/03634520500442178

Crenshaw, K. (1989). Demarginalizing the intersection of race and sex: A black feminist critique of antidiscrimination doctrine, feminist theory, and antiracist politics. *University of Chicago Legal Forum*, *14*, 538–554.

Denhart, H. (2008). Deconstructing barriers: Perceptions of students with labeled with learning disabilities in higher education. *Journal of Learning Disabilities*, *41*(6), 483–497. doi:10.1177/0022219408321151 PMID:18931016

Eckes, S. E., & Ochoa, T. A. (2005). Students with disabilities: Transitioning from high school higher education. *American Secondary Education*, *33*(3), 6–20.

Evans, N. J., Forney, D. S., Guido, F. M., Patton, L. D., & Renn, K. A. (2010). *Student development in college: Theory, research and practice* (2nd ed.). San Francisco: Jossey-Bass.

Evans, N. J., Forney, D. S., & Guido-DiBrito, F. (1998). *Student development in college: Theory, research and practice*. San Francisco: Jossey-Bass.

Finn, D., Getzel, E. E., & McManus, S. (2008). Adapting the self-determined learning model for instruction of college students with disabilities. *Career Development for Exceptional Individuals*, *31*(2), 85–93. doi:10.1177/0885728808318327

Freeman, J. G., Stoch, S. A., Chan, J. S., & Hutchinson, N. L. (2004). Academic resilience: A retrospective study of adults with learning difficulties. *The Alberta Journal of Educational Research*, *50*(1), 5–21.

Gans, A. M., Kenney, M. C., & Ghany, D. L. (2003). Comparing the self-concept of students with and without LD. *Journal of Learning Disabilities, 36*, 287-295.

Geier, B., & Hadley, W. M. (2015). Students with disabilities transitioning to higher education: Legal differences. *American College Personnel Association (ACPA): Standing Committee on Disability (SCD) Newsletter.*

Gil-Kashiwabara, E., Hogansen, J. M., Geenen, S., Powers, K., & Powers, L. E. (2007). Improving transition outcomes for marginalized youth. *Career Development for Exceptional Individuals, 30*(2), 80–91. doi:10.1177/08857288070300020501

Gill, C. J. (1997). Four types of integration in disability identity development. *Journal of Vocational Rehabilitation, 9*, 39–46. doi:10.1016/S1052-2263(97)00020-2

Grant, K. T. (2011). *Challenges and success strategies for college students with learning disabilities: with implications and recommendations for practice* (Doctoral dissertation). Retrieved from ProQuest. (UMI No: 3500008)

Guzman, A., & Balcazar, F. (2010). Disability services' standards and the worldviews guiding their implementation. *Journal of Postsecondary Education and Disability, 23*(1), 50–63.

Hadley, W. M. (2009). The transition and adjustment of first-year students with specific learning disabilities: A longitudinal study. *The Journal of College Orientation and Transition, 17*(1), 31–44.

Hadley, W. M. (2015). *Students with intellectual disabilities on campus.* National Association for Student Personnel Administrators blog: http://www.naspa.org/about/blog/students-with-intellectual-disabilities-on-campus

Henry, W. J., Fuerth, K., & Figliozzi, J. (2010). Gay with a disability: A college student's multiple cultural journey. *College Student Journal, 44*(2), 377–388.

Herbert, J. T., Hong, B. S., Byun, S., Welsh, W., Kurz, C. A., & Atkinson, H. A. (2014). Persistence and graduation of college students seeking disability support services. *Journal of Rehabilitation, 80*(1), 22–32.

Hollins, N., & Foley, A. R. (2013). The experiences of students with learning disabilities in a higher education virtual campus. *Educational Technology Research and Development, 61*(4), 607–624. doi:10.100711423-013-9302-9

Kurth, N., & Mellard, D. (2006). Student perceptions of the accommodation process in postsecondary education. *Journal of Postsecondary Education and Disability, 19*(1), 71–84.

Leake, D. W., Burgstahler, S., & Izzo, M. V. (2011). Promoting transition success for culturally and linguistically diverse students with disabilities: The value of mentoring. *Creative Education, 2*(2), 121–129. doi:10.4236/ce.2011.22017

Leake, D. W., & Stodden, R. A. (2014). Higher education and disability: Past and future of underrepresented populations. *Journal of Postsecondary Education and Disability, 27*(4), 399–408.

Liasidou, A. (2013). Intersectional understandings of disability and implications for a social justice reform agenda in education policy and practice. *Disability & Society, 28*(3), 299–312. doi:10.1080/09687599.2012.710012

Litner, B., Mann-Feder, V., & Guerard, G. (2005). Narratives of success: Learning disabled students in university. *Exceptionality Education Canada, 15*(1), 9–23.

Loewen, G., & Pollard, W. (2010). The Social Justice Perspective. *Journal of Postsecondary Education and Disability, 23*(1), 5–18.

Lombardi, A. R., Murray, C., & Gerdes, H. (2012). Academic performance of first-generation college students with disabilities. *Journal of College Student Development, 53*(6), 811–826. doi:10.1353/csd.2012.0082

Maramba, D. C., & Palmer, R. T. (2014). The impact of cultural validation on the college experiences of Southeast Asian American students. *Journal of College Student Development, 55*(6), 515–530. doi:10.1353/csd.2014.0054

Marks, J. (2008). *Post-secondary education disability services in the United States*. Disability Information Services. Retrieved from http://www.dinf.ne.jp/doc/english/resource/dss_um.html

McGuire, J. M., & Scott, S. S. (2006). Universal design for instruction: Extending the universal design paradigm to college instruction. *Journal of Postsecondary Education and Disability, 19*(2), 124–134.

Oliver, M. (1983). *Social Work with Disabled People*. Basingstoke, UK: Macmillan. doi:10.1007/978-1-349-86058-6

Oliver, M. (2013). The social model of disability: Thirty years on. *Disability & Society, 28*(7), 1024–1026. doi:10.1080/09687599.2013.818773

Owens, J. (2015). Exploring the critiques of the social model of disability: The transformative possibility of Arendts notion of power. *Sociology of Health & Illness, 37*(3), 385–403. doi:10.1111/1467-9566.12199 PMID:25524639

Patton, L. D., Renn, K. A., Guido, F. M., & Quaye, S. J. (2016). *Student development in college: Theory, research and practice* (3rd ed.). San Francisco: Jossey-Bass.

Rendon, L. I. (1994). Validating culturally diverse students: Toward a new model of learning and student development. *Innovative Higher Education, 19*(1), 33–51. doi:10.1007/BF01191156

Reynolds, J., Cooper, S. & Hadley, W. M. (Summer, 2014). African American college students with learning disabilities that identify as LGBT. *American College Personnel Association (ACPA): Standing Committee on Disability (SCD) Newsletter*.

Schein, E. H. (1969). *Process consultation: Its role in organization development*. Reading, MA: Addison-Wesley.

Schein, E. H. (1988). *Process consultation* (2nd ed.). Reading, MA: Addison-Wesley.

Schlossberg, N. K. (1989). Marginality and mattering: Key issues in building community. In D. C. Roberts (Ed.), *Designing campus activities to foster a sense of community* (pp. 5–15). San Francisco: Jossey-Bass. doi:10.1002s.37119894803

Shakespeare, S., & Watson, N. (2002). The social model of disability: An outdated ideology? *Research in Social Science and Disability*, 2, 9–28. doi:10.1016/S1479-3547(01)80018-X

Shalhout, F., Simmons, R., & Hadley, W. M. (Summer, 2015). Undocumented students with learning disabilities transitioning to higher education. *American College Personnel Association (ACPA): Standing Committee on Disability (SCD) Newsletter*.

Sporn, B. (1996). Managing university culture: An analysis of the relationship between institutional culture and management approaches. *Higher Education*, 32(1), 41–61. doi:10.1007/BF00139217

Stokowski, S., & Hardin, R. (2014). Stereotype threat in academic experiences of student-athletes with learning disabilities. *Research Quarterly for Exercise and Sport*, 85(S1), A102–A103.

Strayhorn, T. L. (2006). Factors influencing the academic achievement of first-generation college students. *NASPA Journal Online*, 43(4), 82–111.

The Learning Disabilities Association of America. (2016). *Support and resources for parents*. Retrieved from https://ldaamerica.org/parents/

Trainor, A. A., Lindstrom, L., Simon-Burroughs, M., Martin, J. E., & McCray Sorrells, A. (2008). From marginalized to maximized opportunities for diverse youths with disabilities. *Career Development for Exceptional Individuals*, 31(1), 56–64. doi:10.1177/0885728807313777

UPIAS. (1976). *Fundamental Principles of Disability*. London: Union of the Physically Impaired Against Segregation.

U.S. Department of Education, National Center for Education Statistics. (2013). *Digest of Education Statistics, 2012 (NCES 2014-015)*. Retrieved from: https://nces.ed.gov/fastfacts/display.asp?id=60

ADDITIONAL READING

Hadley, W. M., & Archer, D. E. (in press). College students with learning disabilities: An at-risk population absent from the conversation of diversity. In K. Eunyoung & K. C. Aquino (Eds.), *Disability as Diversity in Higher Education: Policies and Practices to Enhance Student Success*. New York: Taylor and Francis.

Perez, R. J., Woojeong, S., King, P. M., & Baxter Magolda, M. B. (2015). Refining King and Baxter Magoldas model of intercultural maturity. *Journal of College Student Development*, 56(8), 759–777. doi:10.1353/csd.2015.0085

Stewart, S., Doo Hun, L., & Kim, J. (2015). Factors influencing college persistence for first-time students. *Journal of Developmental Education*, 38(3), 12–20.

Strayhorn, T. L. (2012). *College students sense of belonging: A key to educational success for all students*. New York, NY: Routledge.

Torres, V., Howard-hamilton, M. F., & Cooper, D. L. (2003). *Identity development of diverse populations: Implications for teaching and administration in higher education*. San Francisco: Jossey-Bass.

Vaccar, A., Daly-Cano, M., & Newman, B. M. (2015). A sense of belonging among college students with disabilities: An emergent theoretical model. *Journal of College Student Development*, *56*(7), 670–686. doi:10.1353/csd.2015.0072

Wernersbach, B. M., Crowley, S. L., Bates, S. C., & Rosenthal, C. (2014). Study skills course impact on academic self-efficacy. *Journal of Developmental Education*, *37*(3), 14–23.

KEY TERMS AND DEFINITIONS

Accommodations/Services: Assistance for classes such as "notetakers" or "extra time" to complete assignments or tests.

Learning Disability: The difference between the student's aptitude and achievement.

"Medical Model" of Learning Disability: Student is tested and diagnosed with a learning disability.

Self-Advocacy: The student identifying as having a learning disability and discussing their learning disability with administrators and faculty.

Self-Determination: The student engaging in their educational process.

"Social Justice Model" of Learning Disability: Student is viewed as other marginalized/underrepresented groups in society.

University Culture: The common beliefs and values held within the institution

---

This research was previously published in Student Culture and Identity in Higher Education edited by Ambreen Shahriar and Ghazal Kazim Syed; pages 180-193, copyright year 2017 by Information Science Reference (an imprint of IGI Global).

Chapter 21
Understanding Nonverbal Learning Disabilities in Postsecondary Students with Spina Bifida

Carol Russell
Emporia State University, USA

ABSTRACT

Transitioning to life after high school can be challenging for most young adults, even more so for individuals with a nonverbal learning disability (NLD). However, careful planning can lead to success. Friends, family members, employers, college instructors, therapists, and other service providers need information and methods to support individuals with NLD, particularly those with spina bifida (SB). A review of NLD characteristics, effects on student learning, non-awareness and misconceptions of NLD, and effective supports for individuals with NLD (e.g., accommodations, agendas and checklists, assistive technology) will be illustrated via the example of one young college student with NLD and SB. MAP (Making Action Plans) and PATH (Planning Alternative Tomorrows with Hope)—research-based strategies and tools for transition planning and progress monitoring of teens and young adults with NLD and SB—as well as methods to self-advocate to obtain assistance from others academically, physically, socially, and emotionally will be demonstrated.

INTRODUCTION

Caitlyn, age 18, returns home from her full day of classes as a college freshman. She does not yet have a driver's license, so her father transports her in their wheelchair-accessible van. She glares at her mother with her dark eyes, reporting that she got lost on campus today. Close to tears, she relays that they also had a substitute professor in orchestra, and they had not set up a wheelchair lift to the stage for the pre-concert practice. The substitute professor told her to go to a practice room or sit and watch the rest of the orchestra practice. On top of that, her dad was a few minutes late to pick her up, and she had a paper to write that night on a topic that was confusing for her—intelligent design. Caitlyn continues to ruminate over these things and gets even more upset. Her mom knows that unless she intervenes, Caitlyn will continue to perseverate on these events in her mind until she gags and throws up. She encourages Caitlyn to take deep, slow breaths and breathes along with her while talking about what's for dinner, what came in the mail, and plans for the weekend. Caitlyn calms down a bit, but throughout the evening, she continues to bring up each of these events that were changes from her normal routine. While trying to focus on her paper, Caitlyn expresses that she feels confused and overwhelmed by the events of the day. Her mom, careful not to let her get too upset, listens but is ready to intervene with more controlled breathing, if needed. She repeatedly cues Caitlyn to stay focused on her paper until she finally completes it, after which they resume their evening routine, which is what Caitlyn needs most. As Caitlyn gets ready for bed, she reviews her day again with frustration and some tears. Her mother listens, reassures, and reminds her that things should be better tomorrow. Caitlyn soon falls asleep, exhausted.

Change comes easier for some people than others. The events that were out of routine for Caitlyn might frustrate any student during the day. Any college freshman may share these experiences and be upset (although not all would be excluded from a class experience due to lack of wheelchair accessibility). However, the interpretation and response to people's actions and events of the day differ for students with NLD (nonverbal learning disabilities). New, novel, and out-of-routine events can be overwhelming, even exhausting. Caitlyn, who thrives on routine, could not "let it go." Her response was much more intense and long lasting than would be the case for a student without NLD.

One of Caitlyn's doctors summarized this challenge by stating that Caitlyn uses her full energy—physically, neurologically, and emotionally—just to make it through her day. Changes (even seemingly small ones) take longer to process neurologically, cause anxiety and fear, and are generally avoided if possible. Routine is essential. Although Caitlyn copes better with change than she did in elementary and high school, substantial mental and physical energy is still needed just to manage the variations of her day. Adding to that are the physical challenges that come with having spina bifida (SB) and other medical conditions. Caitlyn is often fatigued by evening, even on a typical day. When the routine changes, she may be able to "hold it in" for the day, which also requires much energy, but the emotional explosion occurs once she is home (Tyler & Russell, 2005).

Caitlyn is not alone with her daily challenges; these experiences and reactions are common for individuals with NLD. This chapter provides information about NLD in general as well as characteristics of NLD specific to individuals with SB. Also included are explanations about how NLD impacts learning and all areas of development in addition to various tools, supports, and resources to optimize these students' learning experiences. Postsecondary educators, college administrators, professionals in other disciplines, family members, and students with NLD themselves would benefit from knowledge about this learning disability and the use of strategies, tools, and resources referenced. Students with special needs can best advocate for themselves if they have full knowledge of their disability, how it impacts their learning and daily needs, and how best to convey this information to others. Self-disclosure is also essential to obtain appropriate supports. Postsecondary faculty, staff, administrators, student support providers, and family members must recognize the neurologically based nonverbal learning needs in students with NLD and appropriately support them to foster their success in the postsecondary learning environment and in life. This chapter will provide the following:

1. A review of characteristics, non-awareness, and misconceptions of NLD; effects on student learning; and effective ways to support individuals with NLD (e.g., accommodations, agendas and checklists, assistive technology).
2. Background of one young college student with NLD and SB to illustrate the importance of assessment, diagnosis, and awareness among family members, educators, and therapists.
3. Specific research-based strategies and tools for young adults and teens with NLD and SB to assist them with transition planning, self-planning, and monitoring progress towards life's goals and dreams.
4. Effective ways to share these tools and strategies with supportive individuals such as friends, extended family members, employers, college instructors, personal care assistants (PCAs), therapists, and other service providers.
5. Ways to customize information, tools, and strategies for teens and young adults in order for them to better understand themselves and help others to support them academically, physically, socially, and emotionally.

BACKGROUND

What is NLD?

In the early 1970s, nonverbal learning disabilities were first noticed when researchers observed large discrepancies between the verbal and performance IQ scores of some children with learning disabilities (Myklebust, 1975). NLD syndrome was described in detail in the late 1980s (Rourke, 1987), and various articles and two major books were dedicated to descriptions of the disorder (Rourke, 1989; 1995). Roman (1998) wrote, "There is no formal provision under United States federal special education law recognizing the existence of nonverbal learning disability as a handicapping condition" (p. 1). However, according to the Learning Disabilities Association of America (2014), "In Federal law, under the Individuals with Disabilities Education Act (IDEA), the term is 'specific learning disability,' one of 13 categories of disability under that law. 'Learning Disabilities' is an 'umbrella' term describing a number of other, more specific learning disabilities, such as dyslexia and dysgraphia" (para. 7). Although we currently have many more diagnostic distinctions related to NLD in the medical and neuropsychological fields, and students in the United States could be served under the IDEA "umbrella" definition of learning disabilities, sadly, families in the United States report that the schools and special education laws tend to lag behind, may not recognize, or even resist accepting the clear and validated professional diagnosis and data (Russell & Russell, 2012).

Thompson (1997) also noted that unfortunately, over 30 years later (at the time of her writing), many professionals and educators had not heard of NLD. "Current evidence and theories suggest destruction, disorder or dysfunction of the white matter (long myelinated fibers in the brain) in the right hemisphere could be the cause for nonverbal learning disorders" (p. 11). Researchers have observed NLD in individuals with neurological insults such as moderate to severe head injuries, repeated radiation treatments, congenital absence of the corpus callosum (often found with individuals with SB), insertion of a shunt to treat hydrocephalus (95% of individuals with SB have shunted hydrocephalus), and removal of brain tissue from the right hemisphere (Davis & Broitman, 2011; Thompson, 1997).

Characteristics of NLD

According to Thompson (1997), there are three categories of dysfunction apparent in individuals with NLD:

1. **Motoric:** Lack of coordination in both fine- and gross-motor skills; potential for severe balance problems.
2. **Visual-spatial-organizational:** Difficulty with visual recall, spatial perception, and spatial relations.
3. **Social:** Lack of ability to comprehend nonverbal communication; difficulty adjusting to transitions and novel situations; significant challenges with social judgment and interactions (also Little, 1993).

Thompson (1997) offers a comprehensive checklist for each of the above areas in *The Source for Nonverbal Learning Disorders* (pp. 40–42). Davis and Broitman (2011) also offer a comprehensive list in *Nonverbal Learning Disabilities in Children: Bridging the Gap Between Science and Practice.* Table 1 displays a list of the typical characteristics and performance of a student with NLD, offered by Russell and Russell (2012).

Table 1. Typical characteristics and performance of a student with NLD

Typical NLD Characteristics and Performance of Student
Motoric: poor psychomotor coordination, severe balance problems, and difficulties with fine motor skills: • Hesitates to explore environment (symptomatic of NLD; affected by wheelchair accessibility/proximity) • Talks through motor tasks • Difficulty in writing (e.g., printing, cursive)
Visual-Spatial Organization: difficulty changing from one activity to another or moving from one place to another: • Verbally labels everything • Uses counting • Prefers routine • Neglects spatial reference **Difficulty with:** • Spatial relations and perceptions (e.g., difficulty with directions; for some, black and white patterns can cause disorientation and nausea. See below)  • Recognition (e.g. facial expressions, buildings, directions, maps) and organization • Memory visualization • Copying from a board or from text • Remembering sequences • Higher level reasoning
Social: Misinterpretations of body language and or tone of voice, inability to perceive subtle cues in their environment: • Inability to discern nonverbal cues • Ineffective at recognizing facial expressions, tone of voice, verbal and nonverbal gestures • Inability to understand deceit and manipulation; tendency to naively trust others

In regard to the contrasting patterns pictured in Table 1, Russell (in Russell & Russell, 2012)—who has been diagnosed with NLD—stated in a presentation given with the author,

Sometimes when I go places or meet new people, I think PLEASE, PLEASE, PLEASE don't wear a pattern of black and white. It makes me nauseous. If they do, I try really hard to just look at their faces, their hair, or over their heads. I've tried desensitizing myself by looking at black and white patterns more often, it doesn't work!

To illustrate the noted social aspects, Russell (in Russell & Russell, 2012) also said,

Sometimes I have to think about what was really meant by something someone says. I often give people blank stares, because I'm trying to figure out what they mean. People who know me and understand my NLD, take time to explain or break down what they are saying. . . . I might find the way some things are said, as offensive, because my brain may incorrectly interpret the way something is said, even though it's not meant that way. I have to think about what people are saying. Subtleties and sarcasm stink!

Non-Awareness and Misconceptions of NLD

NLD can be invisible to the casual observer, and it takes an experienced neuropsychologist to diagnose NLD. With reference to the young lady described in the chapter introduction, throughout Caitlyn's elementary and secondary education, teachers would often say, "But she speaks so well, how can she have a learning disability?" A "false illusion of giftedness" may result from a well-developed vocabulary coupled with the appearance of competence in students with NLD, making it difficult for educators to appreciate the debilitating nature of NLD (Tanguay, 2002, p. 26).

Rissman (2006) found a "compelling need to raise educator awareness about the range of cognitive, learning and social problems associated with shunted hydrocephalus and spina bifida" (p. iii). Rissman's case studies of five students in Australia included interviews from all support sources—parents, teachers, and teacher aides. Findings revealed a misunderstanding or non-awareness of NLD. According to Rissman, teachers were frustrated with the students' poor organization, decision making, task completion, problem solving, and social competence. Students were perceived as "lazy," and family members were often blamed for "molly-coddling" or overprotecting the young person.

In the presentation by Russell and Russell (2012), one speaker stated, "Because NLD is not easily noticed, it's important to help people understand, so they can make sense of the effects it has on me. When my family and friends understand my NLD moments, they make appropriate accommodations."

Another misconception is that the child or young adult with NLD would be more successful if she or he would just put in more effort. A strict, firm approach or "tough love" is also mistakenly thought of as the best method for students with NLD. Brett Mills, a young man with NLD, addressed this well in the afterword section of Davis and Broitman's (2011) book, *Nonverbal Learning Disabilities in Children: Bridging the Gap Between Science and Practice*:

The most insulting and hurtful thing that you can say to someone with a learning disorder is that they are lazy or should work harder. You have no idea how hard they are working, and those words will inspire nothing. Tough love is misplaced in this kind of a situation. I can only imagine the kind of frustration that I have put many a teacher through, and yet I think that the ones who served me best are the ones who displayed patience and understanding. They created a safe environment where I could express confusion and frustration. If I encountered a situation where I felt judged, I usually became too scared to speak up and just let myself get further and further behind while just nodding "yes" to everything that the teacher said. (p. 99)

Effects of NLD on Student Learning

Neuropsychological testing of students with NLD has identified difficulty with the following:

- Impulsivity.
- Attention to tasks.
- Memory.
- Sequencing.
- Organization.
- Visual-perceptual skills.

Similarly, higher order conceptual reasoning can be difficult for individuals with NLD and SB. These difficulties may influence

- Efficiency of processing.
- Mental flexibility.
- Conceptualization.
- Problem-solving abilities (Rowley-Kelly & Reigel, 1993; Sandler, 1997).

Some research indicates that NLD is a common coexisting disorder in people who have attention-deficit/hyperactivity disorder (ADHD; Semrud-Clikeman & Bledsoe, 2011). Other research states that individuals with Asperger syndrome (AS) fit the criteria for NLD and that a diagnosis of AS is often preferred (Fitzgerald & Corvin, 2001). Margaret Semrud-Clikeman states in her foreword of Davis and Broitman's (2011) book, "There are many thorny issues that are unresolved regarding the diagnosis of NVLD [nonverbal learning disability]" (p. vii). Semrud-Clikeman goes on to say, ". . . one important unresolved issue is knowledge of the differences between NVLD, high functioning autism, and Asperger's syndrome" (p. vii). Research at Michigan State University identified some clear distinctions between NLD and Asperger syndrome, with the majority in areas of behavior and math (Davis & Broitman, 2011). NLD can also occur with other disorders and on a spectrum. Those affected may experience a range of symptoms manifested to varying degrees. As stated earlier, the focus of this chapter is on NLD in individuals with SB.

Students with SB have often had learning needs that resulted in a diagnosis of attention deficit disorder (ADD) or ADHD. This can be confusing to some, as there are some distinct differences between NLD and ADHD. Numerous children with SB are diagnosed with ADHD in error, when in actuality they have NLD. A comprehensive comparison of ADD/ADHD and NLD is offered by Thompson (1997, p. 54) in an effort to differentiate between the two (see Table 2).

Table 2. Comprehensive comparison of ADD/ADHD and NLD

Characteristics of ADD/ADHD	Characteristics of NLD
• Difficulty following through	• Slow or arduous performance of tasks
• Easily distracted	• Faulty spatial perceptions
• Difficulty playing quietly	• Talks through activities
• Seeks out novelty, surprise, newness	• Avoids novelty
• Does not seem to listen	• Misreads nonverbal communications
• Manipulates situations	• Cannot comprehend personal manipulation or deception

Thompson (1997, p. 45) also included a comparison chart of various syndromes involving social incompetencies, including autism, Asperger's syndrome, Williams syndrome, pervasive developmental disorder, hyperlexia, and nonverbal learning disabilities. The chart clearly differentiates these syndromes and disabilities, comparing areas of speech, IQ, motor, and behavior domains.

Appropriate diagnosis of NLD should be accompanied by recommendations to support the students in all domains and aspects of their lives. Identification and support services for students with NLD are urgent due to the risk of depression, withdrawal, panic attacks, anxiety, and even suicide (Thompson, 1997). The reader is referred to Thompson's (1997) book, *The Source for Nonverbal Learning Disorders*, for detailed illustrations of compensations, accommodations, modifications, and strategies.

NLD Specific to Students with SB

Most individuals with SB who have lesions (openings on the spine) in the lumbar or above areas also have a brain structure abnormality called Arnold Chiari II malformation (brain stem elongation). Most also have hydrocephalus (excessive cerebral spinal fluid in the ventricles), which requires a shunt—usually placed in the right side of the brain—to drain hydrocephalic fluid into the stomach. Many individuals with SB are also born with a little corpus callosum, the wide band of neural fibers interconnecting the two cerebral hemispheres of the brain (Rowley-Kelly & Reigel, 1993; Sandler, 1997).

According to Thompson (1997) and Russell and Russell (2012), effects of NLD in students with SB permeate all areas of their lives, including the following:

- **Self-Care:** Challenges scheduling, remembering, and sequencing self-care tasks, managing health care needs, and taking preventive measures.
- **Cognitive:** Challenges understanding concepts and homework expectations, remembering information and sequences, and completing tasks that require visual-spatial skills.
- **Physical:** Difficulty with handwriting, copying, motor planning, and following sequences.
- **Social:** Problems making and keeping friends and understanding inferences, subtleties, jokes, and movie plots.
- **General Life Skills:** Difficulty with organization of time and schedules, money, and social relationships. For example, in the presentation given by Russell and Russell (2012), Russell stated, "Learning new skills, for example, self-catheterization, or taking new meds can be not only physically, but mentally difficult to change routine."

Background of One Young College Student with NLD and SB

The opening scenario of this chapter describes a typical day for Caitlyn, a young adult with NLD. In first grade, Caitlyn was evaluated and diagnosed with ADHD. Medication was discussed as a treatment, but Caitlyn's family wanted to try non-medication strategies first. After third grade, the family moved from South Dakota, USA, to Kansas, USA, and Caitlyn had another neuropsychological evaluation conducted at a rehabilitation institute, the outcome of which was a diagnosis of NLD. The more Caitlyn's family read and learned about NLD, the more it connected with aspects of Caitlyn's life, learning, behaviors, and responses to events. The family described an "ah-ha" moment when they could finally connect the dots and understand reasons behind her behavior. Caitlyn's family had assistance presenting this information to her school's Individualized Education Plan (IEP) team. An IEP is a legal document in the United States that defines a child's special education program. The IEP, which includes specific services and accommodations that the IEP team will provide based on the child's disability and needs, was not well received. Although her IEP was clear about physical accommodations due to SB, Caitlyn and her family struggled to have accommodations related to NLD included on her IEP. The NLD diagnosis was not validated on her IEP until high school. The family stated that throughout elementary and middle school, the school district and many of Caitlyn's teachers, therapists, and other professionals did not understand her difficulties and misinterpreted many of her behaviors, responses, and needs. For example, when Caitlyn was in fourth grade, the school nurse was convinced that she should know how to get back to her classroom from the nurses' office. Caitlyn would get confused and sometimes go in the opposite direction and then get lost, even in the middle or end of the school year.

Russell (in Russell & Russell, 2012) stated,

Response to change can take much longer and be more intense for a child or adult with NLD. Children and adults with NLD cannot neurologically "let it go." New, novel, and out-of-routine events can be overwhelming, even exhausting. Learning new skills, for example, self-care, or taking new meds can be not only physically, but mentally difficult to change routine. Routine is KEY!!! If not, your WHOLE life will go haywire!

Attention to transitions and organization is important for individuals with NLD and their families, and advanced planning is needed for success. According to Russell and Russell (2012), transitions can be difficult, with major ones potentially causing more stress and anxiety. Therefore, planning well in advance can help make the transitions as seamless as possible. Transitions and novel situations can be anticipated through the use of "social stories," which help individuals prepare for these situations by seeing photos, settings, and examples of what is to come in advance, making the unfamiliar more approachable. Russell stated, "Social stories offer some predictability by helping individuals take things slowly and break tasks down into individual steps. Planning ahead definitely makes transitions easier." For example, when describing an international trip, Russell recalls that "planning and making a trip to Sydney, Australia, took months to plan and strategize, with all the parts and pieces it took to get here!" (Russell & Russell, 2012).

Children and adults with NLD often have organizational problems such as difficulty remembering to hand in completed homework, knowing what is relevant information and what is not, and prioritizing tasks. The concept of time and money can also be overwhelming. These individuals need assistance to break things down into manageable parts, and they manage the changes in routine only if they are prepared and the steps are repeatedly rehearsed. The need for organization permeates all areas of the child's or adult's life; therefore, supports are needed in all environments. This includes everything from medication to self-care schedules, from homework to social schedules, from scheduling personal care assistance to finding one's way around campus or throughout a school building, and from paying bills to ordering medical supplies. Russell (in Russell & Russell, 2012) shares, "Without assistance with organization in my college life, I could not survive the day. Looking at the whole picture can be overwhelming, and I might shut down. If someone breaks it down into understandable parts, it's then doable. I cannot do this on my own!" To foster success, it is important to respect children and adults with NLD, meet them where they are, and note their understanding at the time. It is essential that they be a part of making that plan, because input leads to ownership (Russell & Russell, 2012).

Perseveration is a common characteristic of individuals with NLD, as noted in research since the mid-1960s (Johnson & Myklebust, 1967; Myklebust, 1975; Roman, 1998). There are pros and cons to perseveration. As illustrated in the introductory example, perseveration can be difficult when a child or adult with NLD is not able to "turn the page" or "put it in a bubble" and move on. As stated earlier, individuals with NLD cannot neurologically "let it go." It takes validation, redirection, and patience. On the positive side, perseveration can be beneficial if it feeds into determination for working on an assignment or reaching toward a goal (Russell & Russell, 2012).

Validation and redirection can be powerful. Validating one's feelings tends to validate the individual as a person, as Russell (in Russell & Russell, 2012) explains:

It's important to be validated, whatever your feelings are. Because it makes me know that people are at least trying to understand my challenges and feelings, and are there to help me get through them. When my feelings are not validated, with comments like, "Everything is fine ... You're OK ... Don't worry about it ... It's not that bad," it escalates my feeling and response into something that you do not want to see or experience. I don't get violent or anything, I just end up getting [sic] more upset, screaming or crying. An EXTREME NLD MOMENT! Validating my feelings helps me try to move forward ... although slowly. Without the validating, I get stuck, and perseverate on the same thing or feeling. When feelings are validated, it opens the door to redirection.

Before the "extreme NLD moment" (as described above), it is important to intervene and attempt to redirect. This redirection needs to occur when the child or adult first shows signs of frustration. Once the extreme NLD moment occurs, it is too late. One great method of redirection is blowing bubbles. This works particularly well for children; however, it can be wonderfully effective for all ages. Russell states, "For me, bubbles work to redirect me. Seeing something move, like bubbles, or blowing in my face works!" (Russell & Russell, 2012).

The opportunity for breaks is another critical need for individuals with NLD. Russell (in Russell & Russell, 2012) stated,

Brain breaks are important. Right now my computer games, playing my violin, and even my Sign Language is a brain break. Also playing with my puppy or hanging out with my horse is a great stress reliever. When I was in school, working on homework right after I came in the door, and after a short break helped me get it done. I could not do it late in the evening. My brain shut off from any additional information at that point. It was what I call, 'NLD Overload!"

Again, NLD permeates all areas of an individual's life, not just academic, but social, emotional, physical, and adaptive behavior as well.

SOLUTIONS AND RECOMMENDATIONS

Suggestions to Best Support Students with NLD and SB

It is important to note two things:

1. The neurological condition of NLD does not go away; one does not grow out of it.
2. A college/postsecondary student with NLD and SB has worked very hard physically, cognitively, emotionally, and socially through elementary, middle, and high school years. It is a great accomplishment for this student to be able to walk or wheel through the classroom door. This student will need support and accommodations.

Learning by observing is difficult and sometimes impossible for individuals with NLD. Fittingly, Thompson's (1997) book, *The Source for Nonverbal Learning Disorders*, was formerly titled, *I Shouldn't Have to Tell You*. Professionals, family members, and friends *do* need to tell these individuals everything. "We must try to explain and break down the subtleties, inferences, and nonverbal communication in life. We must also break down assignments, the plot of a movie, or the social response (or non-response) of a friend" (Russell, 2004). Assignment specifics, a detailed class syllabus, lecture notes copied for the student ahead of class, and taping lectures can be helpful.

Another valuable resource, *Spinabilities: A Young Person's Guide to Spina Bifida*, edited by Lutkenhoff and Oppenheimer (1997), has helpful tools to assist young people with NLD and SB. The information is easy to read and understand, and materials are broken down. Included are tools such as self-care charts for monitoring skin care and hygiene, tips for organizing school/campus life, writing tips, and a checklist for work readiness.

Sue Thompson has been a leader in interpreting needs of individuals with NLD. In *IEP for NLD: A Compilation of IEP Suggestions for Kids with NLD*, Thompson (2012a) lists suggested accommodations to include on a child's IEP. The following are some examples of her recommendations:

- Due to a deficit in recognizing nonverbal cues, facial expressions, or tone of voice, the child with NLD may have difficulty interpreting the words spoken. Words directed to this child need to be concrete and straight forward.
- A child with NLD has good rote memory; however, the teaching approach needs to be decelerated, repetitive, and redundant.
- Role modeling with verbal descriptions is necessary to demonstrate expectations.
- Due to difficulty with handwriting and speed, quantity of homework will need to be accommodated and "be used as a reinforcement for already-learned material" (p. 1).
- Organizational skills are challenging; therefore, duplicate textbooks should be kept at home.
- A clear daily checklist system is needed for homework due/completed, for clarity of what has been accomplished and what is expected.

- Because "the development of good self-esteem is always at risk, especially for the child with learning disabilities, teachers need to increase verbal and physical rewards for jobs completed and jobs well done, remembering that it takes many positives to undo one negative" (p. 1).

In addition to the above recommendations, more IEP recommendations are offered by Caitlyn's family, who advocated for appropriate accommodations for her in her high school years. The following is a general list of recommendations from Caitlyn's high school IEP:

- Provide extra time for in-class tests and assignments.
- Provide extra assistance with understanding material (break it down, assist with highlighting, note general area and page numbers to assist with referencing, locate textbooks on tape).
- Provide enough time to respond, to compensate for processing speed, both verbally and in writing. (It is not uncommon for students to want to contribute in class, raise their hands to give an answer, but forget what they were going to say when called on.)
- Provide assistance with note taking to compensate for a decrease in mental processing speed and decreased memory.
- Modify assignments that have copying as the main component.
- Keep requirements for written output to a minimum. Try not to let motor deficits block learning and academic success.
- Preview material and use supplemental aids such as outlines, study guides, and highlighting to allow student to benefit from instruction.
- Provide assistance with organization of materials on a daily basis.
- Use verbal strengths (such as self-talk) to help with organization, problem solving, and learning.
- Provide a structured, predictable environment.
- Ensure that student has pathways throughout the classroom.
- Specifically discuss and prepare the student for transition and changes. It is often helpful to write out changes in the schedule, which the student can refer to when there is a question.
- Verbally teach the student things that other students learn intuitively.
- Be aware that student may be absent due to medical appointments or needs and may therefore need help catching up with material.
- Provide accommodations for testing:
  - Minimize visual confusion on tests and answer sheets.
  - Use verbal testing as needed.
  - Modify or eliminate timed tests.
  - Eliminate or break down word problems and abstract questions to a concrete level with extraneous information eliminated.
- Provide encouragement to participate in structured extracurricular peer groups.
- Provide verbal interpretation of visual cues to help student understand social situations. Movies can offer useful practice for this.
- Review with student classroom emergency procedures for physical needs and mental understanding.

This last recommendation is essential. With the increase in recent years of campus violence, bomb threats, and natural disasters, students with physical or cognitive challenges are at even greater risk of harm. These children and adults need individualized emergency plans that they, the instructor, administration, and the students' families clearly understand.

Accommodations that are needed academically for the student with NLD are also needed in all other aspects of life. If the student needs a note taker/scribe or topics and essay questions broken down in a class setting, he or she will also need this kind of assistance in a club or student organization and in social settings.

Stress management is a key to a positive academic outcome and success in life. Most people have daily challenges dealing with stress and have not successfully learned the art of relaxation within the confines of a busy schedule. As noted earlier, students with NLD are at even greater risk for stress, depression, and suicide, and may be naive to social manipulations. Thompson (2012b) stated,

It's not hard to imagine how a child who doesn't see the "whole picture," who is constantly confused by his surroundings and his interactions with others, and who is unable to anticipate what will happen next, could experience a disproportionate amount of stress in his everyday experiences, such as attending school or shopping at a mall. Add to this the perfectionistic and obsessive/compulsive tendencies of many students with NLD, and the immense pressure this child faces should be obvious. (para. 4)

These challenges are exacerbated in students with SB, due to their physical limitations. Counseling is therefore essential.

It is best if the student with NLD has a clear transition plan developed in high school. This requires careful collaboration and specific planning with the student, family, and high school and postsecondary school personnel. The change of environments, individuals in those environments, and routines can cause stress and anxiety. Therefore, planning well in advance can help make the transitions as seamless as possible. The disability services personnel from the postsecondary school are a fundamental part of this process. With current technology, their participation could occur virtually or by phone. Students with NLD and SB have to stay on top of, and may need support in, many areas including organization, class accommodations, hiring and organizing schedules of personal assistants, assistive technology, health care, transportation, and daily living skills. The disability services personnel from the postsecondary school must gather the evaluation results, consider adaptations from students' high school IEPs, and translate this information into accommodations and modifications that are appropriate for this student in the new setting, with new instructors, and possibly in a new living environment and community. This is vital. If this sounds overwhelming for the professional, consider what it might feel like to the young adult with NLD and SB.

When modifying the above accommodations list into a postsecondary format, some accommodations will be appropriate for a tutor or an assistant to the student to implement, while others are to be implemented by the instructor. Disclosure is paramount. Below are some additional considerations regarding accommodations and modifications:

- A letter from the disability services office, clearly stating the accommodations and modifications needed, is often helpful.
- Different situations lend themselves to different accommodations and supports.

- The student may need an attendant for some classes, but not for others. It is better to give more support at the beginning to determine the level of assistance, and then taper off the support, than to offer no beginning support, with the risk of failing early on.
- The student will need assistance with organizing material, prioritizing assignments, editing papers, and remembering to hand in work on time (he or she may have it completed but forget to turn it in).
- An electronic organizer helps enable independence, but assistance may be needed to set up and individualize the technology.

Tables 3, 4, and 5 are examples of accommodation lists utilized by Caitlyn and shared in various college classes and settings. The first is a general list of accommodations, compiled from her last IEP and other records that was shared with the disability service office and used to generate her letter from this office; the next list describes accommodations to support Caitlyn while she assisted in the campus preschool; and the third example was provided to her violin professor. Caitlyn received assistance putting these lists together, and she delivered these, along with her letter from the disability services office, to each instructor on or before the first day of classes. Instructors are asked to sign a form stating they received a copy of the letter.

The general academic accommodations for NLD provided in Table 3 resulted and accumulated from family members and professionals who worked with Caitlyn throughout her education.

While working at the preschool on campus, Caitlyn needed several accommodations specific to this environment (see Table 4). Many centered around safety of the children as well as physical access and space. However, to assist her with issues directly related to her NLD, she also needed accommodations including prompts and assistance dealing with details, sequencing, directions, and breaking information down into steps. For example, to remember information, Caitlyn needed to repeat it to indicate her understanding. Better yet, having someone put the information in writing or prompt her to write it down aided in understanding. Written combined with auditory input offered Caitlyn maximum opportunity for understanding.

Caitlyn enjoyed playing violin. However, to be a part of the orchestra and have successful violin lessons, several accommodations were needed due to her NLD. Table 5 displays a list of accommodations that she provided to her college orchestra director and violin instructor.

Table 3. General academic accommodations for NLD

1. Modify assignments that have copying as a main component
2. Keep requirements for written output to a minimum (don't let motor deficits block learning and academic success)
3. To compensate for processing speed, provide sufficient time to respond to both verbal and written questions
4. Provide a system of monitoring organizational skills on a daily basis
5. Specifically discuss and prepare student for transition and changes
6. Accompany oral instructions with diagrams, maps, drawings, symbolic figures, and designs
7. Verbally teach things that other students learn intuitively or through observation
8. Don't make the mistake of thinking student can be left to his or her own resources when faced with new and/or complex situations
9. Provide verbal interpretation of visual cues to help student understand social situations
10. Preview material and use supplemental aids (e.g., outlines, study guides) to allow student to benefit from instruction
11. Specifically teach study skill techniques.

Table 4. Accommodations for Caitlyn while working at the campus preschool

Things I can help with:
1. Table-top projects such as art, manipulatives, etc., as I cannot transfer to the floor
2. Reading to children
3. Assisting with group times
4. Assisting with setting up snacks
5. Assisting with coats, jackets, etc.
6. Assisting children with computers if at my level
7. Facilitate dramatic play, science, cooking, etc. if at my level
8. General caring interaction, as I enjoy children

Things that would be challenging for me:
1. The playground, as it is not really accessible, but I can help on flat surfaces
2. Areas not accessible in room
3. Helping in bathroom
4. Handling difficult behavior
5. Field trips, depending on where you are going, I will need accessible transportation. If walking, I may need assistance with directions
6. I cannot be left alone with children, as I cannot independently, safely, and physically take care of them

Suggestions to help me assist you, please:
1. Explain things in detail and break them down. It helps if I can repeat it to you so you know that I understand
2. Write it down for me, or prompt me to write it, so I can remember or understand better
3. Be patient with my medical needs. I may need to be absent (due to appointments from time to time) or leave due to them. I will let you know if I need medical attention
4. I have a latex allergy, so I must be careful with erasers, balloons, rubber bands, etc., and I need to avoid activities that have these materials
5. Water requirement and overheating, especially when outside, due to medication. I cannot be outside above 85-90 degrees
6. Know that I need pathways throughout the classroom
7. Review with me classroom emergency procedures. I need them in writing too
8. Know that I am really excited to be here, and will do the best to assist you and your class. Thank you!

Table 5. Accommodations for Caitlyn's violin lessons

Suggestions to help you assist me, please:
1. Explain things in detail and break them down. It helps if I can repeat it to you so you know that I understand;
2. Write down assignment for me, or prompt me to write it and check for accuracy, so I can remember or better understand;
3. Sometimes I need music numbered and modified;
4. It helps if I hear the music first, and if I can tape record the music, it will help me practice with it;
5. Although I'm working on it, I have trouble reading music, and this helps;
6. Sometimes it takes me a bit longer to catch on to the pace of some songs;
7. Be patient with my medical needs. I may need to be absent (due to appointments from time to time) or leave due to them. I will let you know if I need medical attention;
8. Know that I need pathways and safe, accessible access to stage areas;
9. Know that I am really excited to be taking lessons, and will do my best.
Thank you!

Table 6. provides an example of a detailed schedule that assists Caitlyn in her daily routine indicating the amount of supports needed throughout the day. Routines are essential to the success of the activity, assignment, or day. This example is a detailed schedule of a typical day for Caitlyn during her first semester of college.

Agenda and Checklists

An organized agenda with checklists is essential. Most students with NLD will need assistance with this as well as with time management. Caitlyn has used a notebook agenda but will be transitioning to

Figure 1. With accommodations, participation in academic and community activities can be successful for students with NLD

an electronic organizer soon. Small agendas can be frustrating because the notebook needs to be large enough to allow for ample writing space. Caitlyn's classes are listed on each day, as are the times to leave for class. Additionally, she keeps the schedule shown in Table 6 in the notebook pocket for easy access. Under each class she indicates when something is due and what needs to be done for the next class session. On violin lesson day, space is left in the agenda for the professor, himself, to list the items to practice, for clarity. This allows Caitlyn to be independent and not need an assistant for this class. On Friday, the items that need to be completed over the weekend are listed, in addition to long-term projects or papers. Caitlyn usually works with her assistant to create this list and prioritize tasks, which can be a great challenge for students with NLD. Emergency numbers are in the back of the agenda. Social activities and appointments are also noted. Caitlyn primarily writes in the agenda herself, unless she asks someone to write for her. She does need assistance with the overall class schedule and checking for accuracy. Fine-motor tasks can be difficult for students with SB and fatiguing for those with NLD and visual-spatial challenges.

Caitlyn also uses a checklist for personal care and tasks of daily living. This daily checklist offers an organized way for Caitlyn to complete daily living skills, some of which she can accomplish independently, some requiring interdependence and assistance. She also has her medications in an organized, plastic bubble-type dispenser, with the date and AM or PM listed. This, too, aids with independence and organization.

Understanding Nonverbal Learning Disabilities in Postsecondary Students with Spina Bifida

Table 6. Example of Caitlyn's typical day with college classes

Time	Event(s)
7:00 am	• Get Ready for Class • Needs assistance with: Dressing, transferring, hair care, bathroom, hygiene, meds • Cannot eat breakfast due to gag reflex, needs mid-morning snack • Transportation • Feed Beta (on own) and Hedgehog (with assistance) • Feed Midnight (Caitlyn's horse) with assistance
8:30 am	• Leave for Campus Preschool • Needs assistance with: Transport and getting into campus preschool
9:00-11:30 am	• Working at Campus Preschool • (Mom in class at 10:00 [location], call Dad if needing help)
11:30 am	• To Mom's Office (location) • Needs assistance with: Getting to Mom's office; self-care and lunch with Dad in office or Union • Work on journaling with laptop • Any additional homework • Sign Language practice.
1:30 pm	• Violin lesson • Music Building #___ • Needs assistance with: transportation to lesson
2:00 pm	• Back Home • Needs assistance with: Transportation home • Practice violin • Practice Sign Language • Journaling and materials
3:30 pm	• Self-care • Needs assistance with: ROM (range of motion)
4:45 pm	Assistance with feeding Midnight (Caitlyn's horse)
5:00 pm	Assistance with self-care
5:30 pm	• Supper • Needs assistance with: Meal preparation; transportation.
6:15 pm	• Self-care • Needs assistance with: ROM (range of motion)
6:30 pm	• Leave for evening class • Needs assistance with: Transportation to class
7:00-9:00 pm	• Sign Language Class • Needs assistance with (Mom assists): Note taking • Alternative time to take Sign quiz each week.
9:15 pm	• Transportation back home • Needs assistance with: Transportation home
10:00 pm	• Bedtime routine • Needs assistance with: Dressing, bathroom, tooth brushing, hygiene, ROM • Check skin for pressure sores • Transfers
colspan	• Needs assistance at times in the night to reposition, as both hips are dislocated and she has contractures in both legs. • Both Mom and Dad's schedules are listed, with locations and cell phone numbers in case of emergencies.

Assistive Technology

Assistive technology allows students with NLD and SB to enter and participate in the classroom, have access to the class notes, get to class and complete assignments on time, and manage general organizational requirements of life. Examples of assistive technology that Caitlyn uses on a daily basis include the following:

- A tape recorder to tape lectures.
- Lecture notes from the professor, sent electronically ahead of class sessions.
- Technology for note taker for some classes (needs to be someone familiar with the student, trained, and familiar with NLD). Typed notes versus written ensures clarity of information and allows use of technology for auditory version of notes.
- Textbooks on tape.
- Organized agenda on electronic calendar.
- Organized medication dispenser (discussed above).
- Reacher attached to chair to pick up small items (e.g., pen, paper, etc.).
- Reacher holder attached to chair, also holds pens and pencils for easy access.
- Folders and notebooks color-coded for each class.
- Cell phone for emergencies and notifying about transportation needs.
- Laptop computer for assignments and communicating with professors, peers, and family members.
- A power wheelchair to conserve physical strength.
- A manual wheelchair for non-accessible locations, visiting friends/families' homes that are not accessible, for physical education classes and recreational activities, and for a backup to the power wheelchair.
- A van with a lift for transportation.
- Accessible features at home for independence and access.
    - roll under sink.
    - roll under stovetop.
    - roll under countertop for work area.
    - side opening oven.
    - side by side (with indoor water/ice dispenser) refrigerator for access.
    - pocket doors for easy access and space saving.
    - accessible trays in various areas for eating, paperwork, etc.
    - roll under computer table.
    - desk with height and width to roll under.
    - portable cart (with roller) to organize textbooks and papers to load backpack each day.
    - side railing on bed for safety (with paralysis, she cannot feel if she is falling out of bed).
    - accessible bathroom.
    - ramps to access home.
    - decking around three sides of house, with multiple doors on each side for emergency exits.

Helpful Resources for Individuals with NLD, their Families, Educators, and Service Providers

The "Additional Reading" section at the end of this chapter lists several useful sources that readers can access for additional information about NLD. The best resource, though, is the students with NLD themselves, and it is essential to listen to them. The family can be a very helpful source of support throughout the individual's life. However, according to the United States Department of Education (2014), the Family Education Rights and Privacy Act (FERPA) prevents parents' and other caregivers' involvement in postsecondary settings without the student's permission.

Two invaluable tools for transition and future planning are Making Action Plans (MAP) and Planning Alternative Tomorrows with Hope (PATH), developed in the 1990s in Toronto, Canada (O'Brien, Pearpoint, & Kahn, 2010). According to Pearpoint, O'Brien, and Forest (n.d.) of North Star Facilitators, "It was originally developed as a person-centered planning process designed to level the playing field for people with disabilities to co-plan their ways forward with their network of community/support" (http://www.northstarfacilitators.com/services/customized-group-facilitation/strategic-planning/the-path-process/). Below is a brief description of each tool; more details and information can be found through the North Star Facilitators website provided above.

MAP

MAP is a tool developed by Forest and Pearpoint in the 1990s to assist teams in planning for children with special needs and their families, as well as with IEP or IFSP (Individualized Family Service Plan) development (O'Brien et al., 2010). It is a collaborative process that brings the key people in a child or young adult's life together to create an action plan. MAP is not an IEP or IFSP, but it can lead directly to the formulation of these plans. Two people facilitate it, one being the "host" and another the recorder. A personal and informal, relaxed atmosphere is essential to this process. The MAP is created through eight questions:

1. What is a map? Discuss the characteristics of a map (e.g., shows direction, how to find stuff, where to go).
2. What is your story?
3. What is your dream?
4. What is your nightmare?
5. Who is this child?
6. What are her or his strengths, talents, and unique gifts?
7. What are her or his needs and what do we need to do to meet these needs?
8. What is the plan of action to avoid the nightmare and to make the dream come true? (O'Brien et al., 2010, p. 16)

PATH

PATH is another tool to assist teams in planning for children with special needs and their families and to assist with IEP development (O'Brien et al., 2010). There are seven steps in the PATH process:

1. *Touching the Dream:* The dream(s) can be formulated from the MAP process. These should be presented at the developmental level of the individual. Some additional questions that can assist a person with identifying his or her Dream might include the following: What would you like to do in life? What values do you want to guide you? What gives directions to your life? What motivates you?
2. *Sensing the Goal: Imagine/tell us what happened, Positive and Possible:* The second step is to look backwards from a future date (a year or two), describing the positive outcome and desirable future as if it had already occurred. How does it feel? Articulating this creates the Goals on which to focus. It is important to remember that this needs to be from a POSITIVE and POSSIBLE future.
3. *Grounding in the NOW:* Step three brings participants back to the current reality. What is it like now? This is just a snapshot of life as it is now. The objective is to get from NOW to the GOAL.
4. *Enroll - Who do we need?*: This step is a core of the PATH planning process. No one can do this work alone. Who are the key people who need to be involved to make change possible and to achieve your goal? Who are those who are not currently involved but may be committed to the process? It is important to strive not only for independence where possible but also for interdependence.
5. *Recognizing Ways to Build Strength*: The fifth step is about what the group needs, as well as noting individual needs in order to reach the goals. This step is important, as this discussion is often ignored and can make the difference in reaching goals.
6. *Let's Do It:* Step six looks at the strategies needed to move the work forward and charts action for the next few months. Facilitators will again focus the group through backward thinking; however, now the "future" is much closer.
7. *Planning the next month's work:* Step seven is a repeat of the sixth step except that the time is closer, such as one to three months from today. Vital to this seventh step is considering more specifics of the strategies to include who will do what, how, when, and where. This step is also used to identify specifics for the more immediate future and can be used to measure people's true commitment.
8. *Committing to the first step:* Step eight is really the first step. This includes actions that can be taken almost immediately, by tomorrow or next week. If the process is going to begin, it's essential that it begin NOW. It may be talking with, emailing, or calling someone. Whatever this step is, the person who is willing to make this first critical step happen must be identified (O'Brien et al., 2010).

Additional information about these tools can be found on the following websites:

- http://www.inclusion.com/path.html
- http://www.inclusion.com/maps.html

Caitlyn's family has found the PATH tool to be particularly helpful during her postsecondary years. Caitlyn's PATH, completed while in college, is shared in Table 7 with her permission.

The results of the individual's MAP and PATH can be shared with all who are supportive in the individual's life: friends, extended family members, employers, college instructors, PCAs, doctors, therapists, and other service providers. These tools may enhance the ability of teens and young adults to use the checklists, schedules, and strategies noted earlier in this chapter to better understand themselves, to be more independent, and to help convey how others can support them academically, physically, socially, and emotionally.

Table 7. Caitlyn's PATH: Planning Alternative Tomorrows with Hope

Step Number and Description	Caitlyn's Response

Step 1: Touching the Dream! Some of the questions that can assist a person to identify their Dream may be: What ideals do you most want to realize? What values do you want to guide you? What gives directions to your life? What motivates you?	• Own a car?
	• Learn to drive?
	• Study and pass Sign language Interpreter state exam
	• Sign Language interpreter with young children
	• A phone for organization and emergencies. This is something that I already have but there is a continued need
	• Move away from my parents (not in the immediate future)
	• Assistance to keep pets healthy - a continued need
	• Sea World or Harry Potter theme park
	• Go to St. Louis
	• Travel more
	• Vegas – DONE! Want to go again
	• Write a book about my life (in progress)
	• Write children's books:
	  o Midnight – in progress
	  o Wheels and accessibility awareness
	• Keep collecting rocks
	• Keep presenting nationally on topics such as NLD, accessibility, AT, advocacy

Step 2: Sensing the Goal/Imagine/Tell us what happened/Positive and Possible The second step is to choose a time in the future that is just beyond the comfortable reach of predictability, such as a year or two from now, or maybe six months from now. This articulation of what has happened creates the GOALS for the focus person. Remember events from a POSITIVE and POSSIBLE future.	• Keep friendships, make new friends
	• Experience new things, even though it's hard sometimes
	• Sign Language interpreter – prepare for licensure test
	• Move away from my parents (not in the immediate future)
	• Keep pets healthy
	• Work with children in educational setting
	• Sea World or Harry Potter theme park
	• Go to St. Louis
	• Travel more
	• Las Vegas – DONE! Want to go again
	• Write a book– DONE! Working on:
	  o Writing a book about my life (in progress)
	  o Write children's books:
	    ■ Midnight, the horse
	    ■ Wheels and accessibility awareness
	• Keep collecting rocks
	• Keep presenting on topics such as NLD, accessibility, AT, advocacy
	• Need Vocational Rehabilitation help to meet goals. Keep updating with them, and utilize their assistance
	• Get counseling when needed
	• Stay healthy
	• Own a car
	• Learn to drive, or have reliable transportation

Step 3: Grounding in the NOW Step three focuses the group in the current reality. A snap shot of the current picture of the person's PRESENT is the purpose of this step. The remaining five steps will formulate the development of the action plan. The objective is to get from NOW to the GOAL.	• Graduated from Emporia State University and took 3 Sign classes from the Deaf Culture Center in Olathe, Kansas • Talks regularly with friends online • Occasionally go out • Love going down to pond, reflecting, and feeding fish and turtles • Looking for someone to really focus on Sign Language. Reviewing for exam preparation • Live part time in own apartment, when PCAs are available • Enjoy being with horse and puppy at home • Enjoy working with children • Enjoy meeting actors from Wicked, the Musical (from the Broadway hit) • Reflecting about Australia trip and connections (went last year) • Enjoy writing about experiences • Co-authored Rocks book for children • Working on marketing Rock book • Dreaming of going to Sea World or Harry Potter theme park • Need financial support and help managing finances • See counselor as needed • Trying to stay on top of and prevent health problems

continued on following page

Table 7. Continued

Step Number and Description	Caitlyn's Response

Step 4: Enroll/Who do we need?
Step four is based on the assumption deeply embedded in the PATH planning process, that is, no one can do this work alone. Therefore, identifying who needs to be included is an important step of the PATH. This means the person is committed to making a difference in the person's life.
	• Sign Language interpreter – preparing for licensure test:
	  o ME
	  o Someone specializing in Sign to assist with studying
	  o Mom and Dad
	  o Internet - $ support for online connection
	  o Time to practice
	  o People to practice with
	  o Vocational Rehabilitation (VR) support
	• Work with children in educational setting:
	  o ME
	  o VR support
	  o Transportation
	  o School for the Deaf (to observe interpreters)
	  o Preschool (to observe interpreters)
	  o Other job shadowing?
	• Smartphone for organization, making appointments, reminders for meds, emergencies, etc.
	  o Assistive Technology for Kansans
	  o Vocational Rehabilitation assistance
	• Keep apartment – need support for utilities
	  o Mom and Dad
	  o Other sources?
	• Market our children's book
	• Own a car
	• Explore possibility of learning to drive:
	  o VR
	  o Mom and Dad
	  o Rehab Center
	• Keep friendships, make new friends:
	  o Everyone
	  o Transportation
	  o Places to go
	  o Technology (computer and cell phone)
	• Experience new things, even though it's hard sometimes:
	  o Ideas from family and friends
	  o My positive attitude
	• Keep pets healthy:
	  o Dad and Mom
	  o ME
	  o Sisters
	• Sea World, Harry Potter theme park, Go to St. Louis, Travel more:
	  o $$$$$$$$$$$$$$
	  o Transportation
	  o Time
	• Write a book about therapy horse and dog
	  o Me and Mom
	• Keep collecting rocks
	• Take classes at art center
	  o Mom and Dad - Need to help check options and enrolling
	  o Director at community art center
	• Keep presenting on topics such as NLD, accessibility, AT, advocacy
	  o Mom and Dad – arrange and transportation
	  o Other support people
	  o Explore and locate other places to present
	• Counseling as needed
	  o College counselor
	  o Others?
	  o Art therapy with student therapist
	  o Mom to help with scheduling
	• Stay healthy
	  o Family
	  o Family Physician
	  o Specialists
	  o Gillette adult clinic

Step 5: Recognizing Ways to Build Strength The fifth step is about what the group will need or to have or to do that will keep them strong and allow them to do the hard work that it will take move forward as a team. What do we need to do as a group, team, and/or family, in order to be strong enough to reach the goal and keep this team moving forward?	• Still in progress

continued on following page

Table 7. Continued

Step Number and Description	Caitlyn's Response
Step 6: Let's Do It/Charting Action for the Next Few Months Step six looks at the strategies that can be used to move the work forward. The facilitators will again focus the group through backward thinking. This time the "future" is much closer (e.g., 6 months)	• Within 6 months, Caitlyn will have: ○ Met with VR about next step ○ Sent diploma and transcript to VR Counselor ○ Name on list at Housing and Urban Development (housing assistance) ○ Sign up for LIEKP (assistance program for power and heating) ○ Check insurance after age of 26? ○ Has a new smart phone – VR Counselor will check on this and talk with ATK ○ Connected with more friends, go out once or twice per month ○ Connected with what classes to take at Art Center ○ Has found person to assist with Sign Language ○ Has timeline for studying and taking Sign Language interpreter licensure test ○ Explored possibility of learning to drive ○ Kept pets healthy ○ Checked out preschool as possibility of working with Sign and children ○ Made appointment with Gillette adult clinic
Step 7: Planning Next Month's Work Step seven is a repeat of step six, but time is closer yet, (e.g., 1 or 3 months from today). This must be specific, include steps: Who will do what? When will they do it? Where?	**Prioritized list:** • Sent diploma and transcript to Counselor at VR ○ Caitlyn and Mom print out and mail by Dec. 1 • Name on list at US Housing and Urban Development ○ Dad and Caitlyn go and apply by Dec. 15 • Sign up for LIEKP ○ Dad and Caitlyn go and apply by Dec. 15 • Check insurance after 26? ○ Dad and Mom check with Mom's insurance by Dec. 15 • Gotten a new smart phone ○ Vocational Rehabilitation will check on this and talk with Assistive Technology for Kansans • Has found person to assist with Sign Language ○ Caitlyn and Mom contacted Sign Language interpreters or others by Dec. 15 ○ Caitlyn and Mom contacted person by Dec. 30 ○ Caitlyn and person have timeline for studying starting in Jan. ○ Caitlyn and person have calculate timeline/goal for taking Sign Language interpreter licensure test • Checked out preschool as possibility of working with Sign and children ○ Caitlyn and Mom contacted school district by Dec. 15 • Made appointment with Gillette adult clinic by end of year • Connected with more friends, go out once or twice per/month • Connected with what classes to take at Art Center • Explored possibility of learning to drive • Kept pets healthy
Step 8: Committing to the First Step The final step, step eight, is the first step. This is an action that can be taken right now. This action should be taken almost immediately, by tomorrow or next week. It does not need to be gigantic – but if the process is going to begin, it's essential that it begin NOW.	• See Caitlyn's prioritized list above

FUTURE RESEARCH DIRECTIONS

After high school, young adults with NLD need more tools, strategies, supports, options, and opportunities to choose from in order to achieve their goals. More research is needed to explore the success of various strategies to support individuals with NLD who are transitioning from high school into postsecondary education and adult life. Specific suggestions for future research in this area include the following:

1. Longitudinal studies of individuals with NLD, measuring their progress towards goals and dreams (e.g., measuring process and progress of PATH).
2. Case studies of individuals with NLD who have completed college and are successfully employed to determine key areas that contributed to their success.

Figure 2. Proud college graduation day. What a journey—and the journey continues!

3. Further research to identify empirically-based strategies to assist teens and young adults with NLD and SB, including methods to self-advocate and assist others in supporting them academically, physically, socially, and emotionally.
4. Studies aimed at developing more effective ways to disseminate resources and information to individuals with NLD who are transitioning from high school into postsecondary education and adult life and to clarify misconceptions of NLD.
5. Research to measure the use and success of social stories to prepare individuals with NLD for new and novel situations.

CONCLUSION

This chapter presented specific characteristics and misconceptions of NLD, effects on student learning, and effective ways to support an individual with NLD (e.g., accommodations, agendas and checklists, assistive technology). A description of one young college student with NLD and SB was offered to illustrate the importance of neuropsychological assessment, diagnosis, and promoting awareness among family members, educators, therapists, and other service providers. Specific transition- and self-planning strategies and tools were provided for teens and young adults with NLD and SB to assist them in reaching their goals and dreams. Also presented were effective ways to share this information with those who are supportive in their lives in order to strengthen them academically, physically, socially, and emotionally.

The author of this chapter is a parent of a young adult with NLD and SB as well as a professor of early childhood, elementary, and special education. As a parent, she knows firsthand how valuable this information is; it has changed her daughter's and family's life. This information has shed new light and hope for her daughter and her family, who more fully understand her learning needs. With an understanding of NLD, the family has changed their whole outlook as well as their strategies and responses to her needs. This young lady has recently graduated from college. As an educator, this author is compelled to share this information with professionals working with young adults with NLD and SB to help educators and families *make sense of what does not make sense* to individuals with NLD. Educators and families need to validate and respond to the neurologically based, nonverbal learning needs of postsecondary students with NLD and appropriately support them to foster their success in learning and in life.

REFERENCES

Davis, J. M., & Broitman, J. (2011). *Nonverbal Learning Disabilities in Children: Bridging the Gap between Science and Practice*. New York, NY: Springer Publishing. doi:10.1007/978-1-4419-8213-1

Fitzgerald, M., & Corvin, A. (2001). Diagnosis and differential diagnosis of Asperger syndrome. *Advances in Psychiatric Treatment*, 7(4), 310–318. doi:10.1192/apt.7.4.310

Johnson, D. J., & Myklebust, H. R. (1967). Nonverbal disorders of learning. In D. J. Johnson & K. R. Myklebust (Eds.), *Learning disabilities: Educational principles and practices*. New York, NY: Grune & Straton.

Learning Disabilities Association of America. (2014). *Types of learning disabilities*. Retrieved from http://ldaamerica.org/types-of-learning-disabilities/

Little, S. (1993). Nonverbal learning and socioemotional functioning: A review of recent literature. *Journal of Learning Disabilities*, 26(10), 653–665. doi:10.1177/002221949302601003 PMID:8151205

Lutkenhoff, M., & Oppenheimer, S. G. (Eds.). (1997). *Spinabilities: A young person's guide to Spina Bifida*. Bethesda, MD: Woodbine House.

Martin, M. (2007). *Helping children with nonverbal learning disabilities to flourish: A guide for parents and professionals*. London: Kingsley Publishing Company.

Murphy, M. B., & Shapiro, G. R. (2008). NLD from the inside out: Talking to parents, teachers, and teens about growing up with nonverbal learning disabilities (2nd ed.). Booklocker.com Incorporated.

Myklebust, H. R. (1975). Nonverbal learning disabilities: Assessment and intervention. *Progress in Learning Disabilities, 3*, 85–121.

O'Brien, J., Pearpoint, J., & Kahn, L. (2010). *The PATH and MAPS handbook: Person-centered ways to build community*. Toronto, Canada: Inclusion Press International.

Pearpoint, J., O'Brien, J., & Forest, M. (n.d.). *Making action plans (MAPS) and planning alternative tomorrows with hope (PATH)*. Retrieved from http://www.northstarfacilitators.com/services/customized-group-facilitation/strategic-planning/the-path-process/

Rissman, B. (2006). *They didn't ask the question . . . An inquiry into the learning experiences of students with spina bifida and hydrocephalus* (Doctoral dissertation). Retrieved from http://eprints.qut.edu.au/16528/

Roman, M. A. (1998). The syndrome of nonverbal learning disabilities: Clinical description and applied aspects. *Current Issues in Education, 1*, 1–16. Retrieved from http://cie.asu.edu/ojs/index.php/cieatasu

Rourke, B. P. (1987). Syndrome of nonverbal learning disabilities: The final common pathway of white-matter disease/dysfunction? *Clinical Neuropsychologist, 1*(3), 209–234. doi:10.1080/13854048708520056

Rourke, B. P. (1989). *Nonverbal learning disabilities: The syndrome and the model*. New York, NY: Guilford Press.

Rourke, B. P. (1995). *Syndrome of nonverbal learning disabilities: Neurodevelopmental manifestations*. New York, NY: Guilford Press.

Rowley-Kelly, F. L., & Reigel, D. H. (1993). *Teaching the student with spina bifida*. Baltimore, MD: Brookes.

Russell, C. L. (2004). Understanding nonverbal learning disorders in children with spina bifida. *Teaching Exceptional Children, 36*(4), 8–13. Retrieved from http://w.teachingld.net/pdf/teaching_how-tos/nonverb_dis.pdf

Russell, C. L., & Russell, T. L. (2012, October). *Understanding Nonverbal Learning Disorder*. Paper presented at Australian Masterclass: Symposium conducted at the International Spina Bifida Conference, Sydney, Australia.

Sandler, A. (1997). *Living with spina bifida: A guide for families and professionals*. Chapel Hill, NC: University of North Carolina Press.

Semrud-Clikeman, M., & Bledsoe, J. (2011). Updates on attention deficit/hyperactivity disorder and learning disorders. *Current Psychiatry Reports, 13*(5), 364–373. doi:10.100711920-011-0211-5 PMID:21701839

Tanguay, P. (2000). *Nonverbal learning disabilities at home: A parent's guide*. London: Kingsley Publishing Company.

Tanguay, P. (2001). *Nonverbal learning disabilities at school: Educating students with NLD, Asperger syndrome and related conditions*. London: Kingsley Publishing Company.

Tanguay, P. (2002). *Nonverbal learning disabilities at school*. London: Kingsley Publishing Company.

Thompson, S. (1997). *The source for nonverbal learning disorders*. East Moline, IL: LinguiSystems.

Thompson, S. (2012a). *IEP for NLD: A compilation of IEP suggestions for kids with NLD*. Retrieved from http://www.nldontheweb.org/nldentrylevelreading/nldcharacteristics.html

Thompson, S. (2012b). *Stress, anxiety, panic and phobias: Secondary to NLD*. Retrieved from http://www.nldontheweb.org/nldadvancedreading/stressanxietypanic.html

Tyler, J., & Russell, T. (2005, September). *Overview of neuropsychological effects of spina bifida*. Paper presented at Emporia High School, Emporia, KA.

U.S. Department of Education. (2014). *Family Educational Rights and Privacy Act (FERPA)*. Retrieved from http://www2.ed.gov/policy/gen/guid/fpco/ferpa/index.html

ADDITIONAL READING

Martin, M. (2007). *Helping children with nonverbal learning disabilities to flourish: A guide for parents and professionals*. London, England: Kingsley Publishing Company.

Murphy, M. B., & Shapiro, G. R. (2008). NLD from the inside out: Talking to parents, teachers, and teens about growing up with nonverbal learning disabilities (2nd ed.). United States: Booklocker.com Incorporated.

O'Brien, J., Pearpoint, J., & Kahn, L. (2010). *The PATH and MAPS handbook: Person-centered ways to build community*. Toronto, Canada: Inclusion Press International.

Porter, P., & Obst, B. (2009). *A guide for school personnel working with students with spina bifida. (2009)*. Baltimore: Maryland State Department of Education Division of Special Education/Early Intervention Services.

Tanguay, P. (2000). *Nonverbal learning disabilities at home: A parent's guide*. London, England: Kingsley Publishing Company.

Tanguay, P. (2001). *Nonverbal learning disabilities at school: Educating students with NLD, Asperger syndrome and related conditions*. London, England: Kingsley Publishing Company.

KEY TERMS AND DEFINITIONS

Arnold Chiari II Malformation: Brainstem elongation, usually caused by structural defects in the brain and spinal cord.

Attention-Deficit/Hyperactivity Disorder (ADHD): A problem involving inability to focus, overactivity, inability to control behavior, or a combination of these.

Disability Services Office: An office located on most college campuses (with this or a similar title) that coordinates accommodations for students with documented disabilities.

Making Action Plans (MAP): A tool developed by Forest and Pearpoint in the 1990s to assist teams in planning for children with special needs and their families.

Planning Alternative Tomorrows with Hope (PATH): A tool developed by Pearpoint, O-Brien, and Forest in the 1990s to assist teams in planning for children with special needs and their families.

Social Stories: A concept devised by Carol Grey in 1991 to improve the social skills of people with autism spectrum disorders (ASD). Social stories help prepare children for situations through describing scenarios and modeling appropriate interactions. See http://thegraycenter.org/social-stories/what-are-social-stories

Hydrocephalus: A condition involving too much cerebral spinal fluid in the ventricles of the brain. Congenital hydrocephalus is caused by a buildup of excess cerebrospinal fluid in the brain at birth.

Spina Bifida (SB): A condition caused by a type of birth defect called a neural tube defect. It occurs when the bones of the spine (vertebrae) do not form properly around part of the spinal cord. Spina bifida can be mild or severe.

Transition: In education, the move from one grade level or school to the next. Noting and planning for transitions is important, particularly for postsecondary school. This requires careful collaboration and specific planning with the child, the family, the sending program, and the receiving program.

This research was previously published in Medical and Educational Perspectives on Nonverbal Learning Disability in Children and Young Adults edited by Barbara Rissman; pages 164-190, copyright year 2016 by Information Science Reference (an imprint of IGI Global).

Chapter 22
Use of Assistive Technology to Empower Persons with Intellectual Disabilities

Sanjeev Kumar Gupta
All India Institute of Speech and Hearing, India

ABSTRACT

This chapter focuses on the use of assistive technology in persons with Intellectual Disabilities (IDs). Persons with IDs have significant limitations, both in intellectual functioning and in adaptive behaviors. The use of assistive technology is essential to help persons with IDs and make them independent in all spheres of life. Assistive technology devices and services can be used to teach, train, rehabilitate, and empower persons in a variety of daily activities viz. new learning, home living, employment, health and safety, communication, social activities, protection and leisure. Empirical studies suggest that assistive technology is effective in improving the quality of life of persons with IDs and make them less dependent on others. This chapter investigates the available research evidence on the use of assistive technology in IDs, discusses utilizations, impediments/barriers, implications and suggests recommendations for future research.

INTRODUCTION

In today's world, technology has become an integral part of human life impacting every sphere of daily living. For example, people are purchasing everything from cookies to clothes, movie tickets to flight tickets online; using elevator and escalators, using smart phones to send instant group messages, photos, videos, and files; to name a few. Technology has also become an integral part of the advancement of medical diagnostic assessment and treatment. Telemedicine has reached remote areas of villages. But, there is a common concern that persons with disabilities in general, are among the most excluded ones in the process of development of the country. Technology has changed and continues to change the way people manage things in both, their personal as well as professional lives. So, the natural extension of that

DOI: 10.4018/978-1-7998-1213-5.ch022

is to see the impact and the integration of technology in the empowerment of persons with disabilities in the same way as it has been in other areas of life (Alnahdi, 2014).

The focus on technology being used by people with intellectual disabilities (IDs) is a fairly recent phenomenon (Wehmeyer & Smith, 2004). The American Association on Intellectual and Developmental Disabilities (2009), defined Intellectual disability as a "disability characterized by significant limitations, both in intellectual functioning (reasoning, learning, problem solving) and in adaptive behavior, which covers a range of everyday social and practical skills. This disability originates before the age of 18". Technology has the potential to contribute to a better quality of life for persons with IDs, which is more than just a matter of convenience (Wehmeyer, Palmer, Smith, Davies, & Stock, 2008). Use of technology is indispensable in persons with IDs, particularly in the area of early disability detection, prevention, identification, assessment and rehabilitation.

According to the Census of India 2011, there are 26.81 million persons with disabilities in India who constitute 2.21% of the total population. Out of the total persons with disabilities, 1.5 million (5.61%) are mentally retarded or intellectually disabled in India. The distribution of the population suffering from mental retardation is shown in Table 1 (Census of India, 2013). However, estimates vary across sources. A new World Bank Report (O'Keefe, 2009) on disabled persons in India, has observed that there is growing evidence that people with disabilities comprise between 5 and 8 per cent of the Indian population (around 55-90 million individuals). The prevalence of IDs is calculated to be 1 to 3% in developed countries (Petterson, Bourke, Leonard, Jacoby, & Bower, 2007). Millions of people worldwide are affected by IDs which burdens not only the people who suffer from it, but also the family and society as a group (Katz & Lazcano-Ponce, 2008). The development of assistive technology devices and equipments has made significant contributions towards improving lives of people with IDs and reducing the burden on their families and society (Table 1).

The term "assistive technology" (AT) refers to a variety of tools, devices, equipments or instruments that help persons with IDs to educate, empower, improve, rehabilitate, train and adjust within their daily context and achieve a superior quality of life. AT includes many resources, which are expected to create positive and vital behavioral as well as social profits for the users by reducing the negative impact of their problems and related difficulties (Bauer, Elsaesser, & Arthanat, 2011; Reichle, 2011). AT can be a device or a service. An *assistive technology device* is any item, piece of equipment, or product system that is used to increase, maintain, or improve functional capabilities of persons with IDs, whereas an *assistive technology service* refers to any service that helps an individual with IDs to select, acquire, or use an assistive technology device (P.L. 103-218: The Tech Act amendments in 1994). AT devices and services can be used in a variety of daily activities viz. education, new learning, home living, employment, health and safety, communication, social activities, protection, sports, recreation and leisure, and

Table 1. Population suffering from mental retardation

Gender	Total	Rural	Urban
Persons	15,05,624	10,25,560	4,80,064
Males	8,70,708	5,91,408	2,79,300
Females	6,34,916	4,34,152	2,00,764

Census of India, 2013.

in medical services. Persons with IDs should receive AT that is best suited to their characteristics, tasks, and environments (Bauer et al., 2011; Borg, Larson, & Östegren, 2011).

The mere use of AT may not be sufficient to guarantee a positive outcome. Such an outcome is more likely to occur if one adds, to the provision of technology, an explicit and carefully designed intervention aimed at ensuring that the persons learn how to use it effectively (Lancioni, Sigafoos, O'reilly, & Singh, 2013). When one thinks of issues pertaining to technology and IDs, it is within the context of a class of high-and-low tech devices that fall under the category of *assistive technology* (Wehmeyer, Smith, Palmer, Davies, & Stock, 2004). This chapter aims to serve as a general review on the use of assistive technology to empower persons with intellectual disabilities. Especially, this chapter aims to:

1. Identify key assistive technology services for persons with intellectual disabilities,
2. Identify key assistive technology devices for persons with intellectual disabilities,
3. Compiling recent studies on assistive technology and intellectual disabilities,
4. Discuss impediments, and
5. Recommend directions for future research.

ASSISTIVE TECHNOLOGY SERVICES FOR PERSONS WITH INTELLECTUAL DISABILITIES

The Tech Act defines the term assistive technology service as any service that directly assists an individual with a disability in the selection, acquisition, or use of assistive technology devices. The term includes:

1. Evaluating the needs of an individual in the individual's customary environment.
2. Purchasing, leasing, or otherwise providing for the acquisition of AT devices by individuals with disabilities.
3. Selecting, designing, fitting, customizing, adapting, applying, maintaining, repairing, or replacing assistive technology devices.
4. Coordinating and using other therapies, interventions, or services with assistive technology devices, such as those associated with existing education and rehabilitation plans and programs.
5. Training or technical assistance for an individual with disabilities or, where appropriate, the family.
6. Training or technical assistance for professionals, employers, or other individuals who provide employment services or are involved in the major life functions of individuals with IDs.

ASSISTIVE TECHNOLOGY DEVICES FOR PERSONS WITH INTELLECTUAL DISABILITIES

AT devices enables an individual to perform functions that can be achieved by no other means. These devices help to access for participation in programs or activities which otherwise would be closed to the individuals with IDs. There are many AT devices that can be useful for persons with IDs. Few devices/technology have been discussed here:

1. **Computer-Aided Instruction:** Okolo, Bahr, and Reith (1993) have defined Computer-Aided Instruction (CAI) as "the use of a computer or other associated technology with the intention of improving students' skills, knowledge, or academic performance". CAI devices aimed at providing verbal or pictorial cues to support persons through the performance of multistep activities (Sigafoos et al., 2009). Traditional CAI programs are mostly presented in a linear format, involving text or still pictures, and give little control of the process to students. Whereas, contemporary CAI programs are different from traditional ones, in the way they involve sound, video or animation, and also allow a range of interaction. With the help of CAI, young children with disabilities can learn word recognition and transfer acquired skills to functional materials (Lee & Vail, 2005).

2. **Microswitches and Microswitch Clusters:** Microswitch devices can be activated with minimal responses and are used in combination with an electronic control system and basic software (Lancioni, O'Reilly, & Basili, 2001). Microswitches have been used among people with severe/profound intellectual or multiple disabilities to help reduce isolation and increase their interaction with the surrounding world such as obtaining environmental stimulation independently or requesting for it efficiently (Lancioni et al., 2001). Microswitches aimed at allowing the persons to access environmental stimulation with minimal responses. Microswitch clusters devices are useful to strengthen adaptive responses and inhibit problematic behaviour (Lancioni et al., 2008).

3. **Portable Electronic Devices:** Portable electronic devices (PEDs) are a type of electronic device having the capacity to record, store, and transmit text, video or audio data. PEDs include iPad, iPhone, iPod, cellular/smartphones, digital watches, portable digital assistant, laptops, media players with audio playback, and handheld video players. Use of PEDs by persons with IDs is gaining increasing research attention. These devices and apps clearly have a role within the spectrum of augmentative and alternative communication devices currently available. They may have some distinct advantages in cost, ease of use and acceptability, but more research into their use is needed (Mechling, 2011). Thus, the proper use of PEDs can be helpful for persons with IDs or multiple disabilities.

4. **Mobile Technology:** Recent developments in mobile technology (m-technology), including the introduction of the iPad and other smartphone and tablet devices, have provided important new tools for communication (McNaughton & Light, 2013). The m-technology revolution has had dramatic effects on the lives of many individuals with complex communication needs, including those with developmental disabilities (Flores et al., 2012). The use of technology-based interventions for persons with IDs is evident by the support of various studies (Goldsmith & LeBlanc, 2004; Mechling, 2011). Hernández, Zorrilla, and Zapirain (2012) presented a technological solution to promote independent living for persons with IDs and used Android Smartphones to support them for daily tasks and found that it meets the needs of persons with IDs perfectly. Mobile-learning can bring the learning experience to a whole new level if used wisely and appropriately. Indeed, with the proliferation of m-technologies, such as cellphones/smartphones, personal digital assistants and tablets, or mobile applications, many on-the-go services are now offered (Metcalf & Marco, 2006).

5. **Speech Generating Devices:** Speech-generating devices (SGDs), also known as voice output communication aids, are programmable digital devices that provide voice output in the form of digitized or synthesized speech when activated (Trottier, Kamp, & Mirenda, 2011). SGD are aimed at allowing the persons to translate their simple motor responses into the production/utterance or

verbal message (Rispoli, Franco, van der Meer, Lang, & Camargo, 2010; Sigafoos et al., 2009) and vary greatly in terms of features, cost, and appearance (Sigafoos, Didden, & O'Reilly, 2003).

6. **Spatial Orientation System:** These devices are aimed at helping the persons navigate when they are indoors by the use of auditory or visual direction cues or through corrective feedback (Lancioni et al., 2007).

Assistive Technology devices can further be divided into two- low tech and high tech devices (Franklin, 1991). Examples of low and high tech devices that might be useful for persons with IDs have been listed in Table 2.

RECENT INVESTIGATIONS ON ASSISTIVE TECHNOLOGY AND INTELLECTUAL DISABILITIES

The main objectives of recent studies on assistive technology and IDs is to compile the evidenced-based studies and use the finding to empower and enable persons with IDs. In one study, Lancioni, Oliva, and Bracalente (1995) assessed the effectiveness of an orientation system, consisting of a programmable control device linked to acoustic and light sources, for facilitating independent indoor navigation and activity in two persons with profound intellectual disability and blindness respectively. The control device was programmed to activate the acoustic or light sources that led the persons to their desired destination automatically (i.e., after a preset time was arrived at from previous trials of the persons reaching the destinations successfully). One person was exposed to two baseline phases without the system being alternated between two orientation phases; the other person received only one baseline and one orientation phase. Results showed that during the orientation phases, both persons benefited from the use of the system and could reach the destinations successfully and carry out the activities.

Derer, Polsgrove, and Rieth (1996) investigated the use of AT in classrooms through surveying teachers who worked with students with IDs. The results of the study indicated that 10% to 23% of the students with IDs were using AT, and 34% students were using some form of AT. The researcher identified six barriers to technology use for students with IDs, including locating and procuring equipments; lack of time for training students and teachers to use the equipment as well as time to obtain and prepare equipment for use; high cost of devices and the lack of funds to access devices or services, and

Table 2. Examples of low and high tech devices

Low Tech	High Tech
Note-taking voice recorders or Audionote	Optical character recognition
Pencil grips	Talking Calculator
Non-Carbon paper/Copy machine	Electronic spell and grammar checker
Simple switches	Word prediction
Head pointers	Voice recognition
Picture boards	Speech synthesizers
Taped instructions	Augmentative communication devices (e.g. Liberator)
Workbooks	Alternative keyboards (e.g. Portable, Touch window, PowerPad, intellikeys)

teacher's knowledge about and training in the area of AT. Lesar (1998) conducted a study that aimed at providing state-of-the-art descriptive information regarding preparation needs, concerns, and perceived barriers to the use of assistive technology for young children with disabilities. Surveys were completed by 62 early childhood special education professionals in 2 south eastern states. The findings indicated that respondents had frequent and significant concerns about their knowledge and utilization of AT.

Mechling, Gast, and Barthold (2003) studied the effectiveness of a multimedia program (interactive computer program, video captions, and still photographs) to teach 3 students with moderate IDs to make purchases using a debit card and an automated payment machine (APM). A multiple probe design across participants was used to evaluate the effectiveness of the multimedia program. All instructional sessions occurred through simulations using video captions and still photographs replicating operation of the APM. Generalization of skills was assessed through purchasing at community stores. Results showed that the multimedia program alone was effective in teaching generalized operation of APMs with a debit card.

Holburn, Nguyen, and Vietze (2004) conducted a study on five adults with profound physical and intellectual disabilities, in which they were taught to respond to photographs of preferences embedded in Microsoft PowerPoint presentations by operating microswitches that functioned as mouse clicks. Rate of responding was generally correlated with changes in types of presentation, although variability in rate was often high, and session durations were quite short. Two participants showed substantial increases in responding when fitted with switches that were easier to manipulate. This exploratory study demonstrates that people with extremely limited physical and cognitive abilities can be taught to operate switches that produce changes in visual arrays on a computer screen.

Today's electronic technologies, including computers, cell phones, Internet, and electronic organizers, hold great promise for individuals with IDs, yet little research has been conducted to explore patterns of use among this population. Drawing upon a survey of 83 adults with IDs, Carey, Friedman, and Bryen (2005) examined factors affecting use of three key electronic technologies: computer, Internet, and electronic organizers. Forty-one percent of participants used a computer; 25%, the Internet; and 11%, electronic organizers. Primary barriers reported by participants included lack of access, training and support, and expense of technologies. Interest in using such technologies was high, and participants offered suggestions for improved accessibility.

Hoppestad (2007) conducted an online comprehensive search of literature pertaining to computer access for persons with severe and multiple disabilities to provide a review of the contemporary literature regarding computer access for persons with severe and multiple disabilities using AT. The study depicts the evolution from a 'medical model' to a 'social model' in rendering AT services for these individuals. Prescribing the proper device to enable computer access to persons with severe disabilities is a complex undertaking, and services have been inadequate. Technological advances that enable access to computers for persons with disabilities have not reached those persons that need it most, particularly those with severe disabilities, for a number of reasons. The literature is replete with explanations for the underutilization of AT for computer access including prejudicial views towards persons with disabilities, inadequate assessments, lack of a person-centered approach, and methods for practice that are not evidence based.

Rai (2008) investigated the effectiveness of a treatment package that included video technology (e.g., video modelling and video prompting) to teach three self-help skills (e.g., cleaning sunglasses, putting on a wrist watch, and zipping a jacket) to three elementary school students with mental disabilities in a small group setting. Using a constant time delay procedure, observers measured the percentage of steps of the task analysis performed correctly before and after a video model prompt. A multiple probe design across behaviors, replicated across participants, demonstrated experimental control. The results indicate that an instructional package that includes video technology can be an effective method for teaching self-help skills to students with mental disabilities.

Selecting an appropriate mode of communication is an important clinical decision when beginning an AAC intervention. In the present study, Cannella-Malone, DeBar, and Sigafoos (2009) investigated whether two boys with significant IDs would show a preference for using one of the three AAC devices. Initially, the boys were taught to use three AAC devices (i.e., Cyrano CommunicatorTM, Mini-MessageMateTM, and a Picture Communication Board) using a multiple-probe-across-devices design. One participant was successful with only one device, while the other was successful in acquiring basic use of all three devices (i.e., making a request using the device and demonstrating correspondence between the picture icon and the item requested). The child who acquired basic use of all three devices participated in the second phase. A choice assessment was conducted using a free operant paradigm to determine which of the three devices he preferred. In the final phase, the most preferred device was targeted for more specific instruction (i.e., retrieving the device from a distance, turning the device on, approaching a communication partner, getting the communication partner's attention, and using the device to make a request), using a changing criterion design. Results for this participant indicated that he had a clear preference for one device and was able to learn how to use it in a more functional manner.

Many people with IDs also have physical difficulties which prevent them from using standard computer control devices. Custom made alternative devices for those with special needs can be expensive and the low unit turnover makes the prospect unattractive to potential manufacturers. One solution is to explore the potential of devices used in contemporary gaming technology, such as the Nintendo Wii. This study evaluated the feasibility of using the Nunchuk by comparing its performance as a switch with the participant's usual switch. Twenty-three volunteers aged between 17 and 21 years with intellectual and physical disabilities completed a single switch performance test using the new device and their familiar device. For most functions of the switch, there was no significant difference between the participants' performance using the Nunchuck and their familiar device. Additional analysis found that some participants' performance did improve whilst using the Nunchuck, but this was not significantly related to physical or cognitive ability. Those whose performance was better with the Nunchuk were more likely to hold it in the conventional way than were those who had better performance with their familiar device. This merits it being offered as a possible alternative to currently available switches for those with physical difficulties affecting their grip (Standen, Camm, Battersby, Brown, & Harrison, 2011)

Davidson (2012) studied the application of collaborative action research to the use of iPods by a small group of adults with IDs. The study was aimed at developing abilities to become autonomous using videos with mobile computing devices. Davidson produced instructional videos, which uploaded onto iPods. The iPods were lent to the young adults with IDs for a period of ten weeks, to try to develop abilities needed for autonomous living such as cooking, using a stove, using a washing machine and keeping oneself safe. The results of focus groups conducted at the end of the collaborative action research during which participants voiced their opinion about the project and revealed their true interests with regards to mobile technologies.

Computer and computer-aided instruction can be used as a high tech device to teach mathematics for persons with IDs, as demonstrated by Singh and Agarwal (2013). In their study wherein, they investigated whether computer games help in teaching mathematics to children with IDs and whether computer games help both boys and girls equally. The quasi-experimental two-group pre & post test design was used for the study. The results obtained through ANCOVA were in favour of Computer games for both boys and girls. However, boys seemed to benefit more from computer games.

UTILIZATION OF ASSISTIVE TECHNOLOGY FOR PERSONS WITH INTELLECTUAL DISABILITIES

AT can be used as device and service in many ways, such as in communication, learning and education, employment, home living, health and medical services, mobility and sports and recreation.

- **Communication:** Augmentative and alternative communication (AAC) includes methods of communication for those with difficulty on the production or comprehension of spoken and written language. AAC systems are extremely varied and dependent on the capabilities of the individual. They may be as basic as pictures on a board that are used to request eatables, beverages or other needs; or they can be advanced speech generating devices, which are based on speech synthesis, that are capable of storing hundreds of phrases and words. Thus, AAC ranges from low technology message boards to computerized voice output communication aids and synthesized speech for those who cannot use vocal communication.
- **Learning and Education:** Education is the most effective vehicle of socio-economic empowerment. Computer-aided instruction can help in many areas, including word recognition, mathematics, spelling and even social skills for individuals with IDs. Portable electronic devices have been found to promote social interaction with peers/friends.

Assistive technology for cognition is the use of technology to augment and assist cognitive processes such as attention, memory, self-regulation, navigation, emotional recognition and management, planning, and sequencing activity. Systematic reviews of the studies have found that the development and use of assistive technology for cognition is growing rapidly. It was also found that a lot of scope still exists in the development of new assistive technology for cognition, specifically, in the areas of memory and planning, such as NeuroPage which prompts users about meetings.

- **Employment:** Video-aided instruction/training can be used for job training and job skill development and to teach higher order functioning and complex skills for appropriate job behavior and social interaction. Prompting systems like voice recorders and computer-based prompting devices have been used to help individuals stay on task, and manage their time in scheduling job activities respectively.
- **Home Living:** AT is helping persons with IDs to successfully complete day to day tasks of self-care. For instance, automated and computerized dining devices allow an individual to eat more independently. Audio prompting devices may be used to assist a person with memory difficulties in completing a task or to follow a certain sequence of steps from start to finish. Video-based instructional materials can help people learn functional life skills such as cooking food, grocery shopping, writing a cheque, paying the bills or using the ATM machine (Jeyachandran, Gadkari, & Mishra, 2009).
- **Health and Medical Services:** Recent advances in medical technology are revolutionizing services to persons with IDs and have focused on cost reduction. Medical technology may broadly include medical devices, information technology and healthcare services. Advances in mapping techniques have allowed good progress toward the specific goals of the Human Genome Project and are also providing strong corollary benefits throughout biomedical research (Olsen, 1993).

Developments of affordable, cost-effective and user friendly assistive and augmentative devices need to be undertaken such as the Hawking Communicator.

- **Mobility:** Wheelchairs are devices that include a seating system and are designed to be a substitute for the normal mobility of individuals with disabilities or those in their old age. These devices allow individuals to perform activities of daily living that require mobility, such as feeding, toileting, dressing, grooming and bathing. The device comes in a number of variations where they can be handled manually or by motors wherein, the user uses electrical controls to manage motors and seating control actuators through a joystick, sip-and-puff control, or other input devices. Often there are handles behind the seat for someone else to manually handle the device or input devices for caregivers.
- **Sports and Recreation:** Toys can be fitted with switches and other technologies to facilitate play among children with IDs. Computer or video games help children learn cognitive and visual-motor coordination skills. Specially designed software can help people with IDs access the World Wide Web. Exercise and physical fitness can be supported by audio and video-based technology. Bailey (1994) suggested that toys using switches and other technologies encourage young children to play, motivate and support cause-effect learning. Switches are simple, intuitive and can be mastered with low physical and mental effort.

An increasing number of people with disabilities are participating in sports, leading to the development of new assistive technology. Use of assistive technology can be found in sports ranging from local community recreation to the elite Paralympics Games.

IMPEDIMENTS

Copley and Ziviani (2004) reviewed the literature on AT in order to identify current barriers to its effective integration within schools for children with multiple disabilities. These barriers were lack of appropriate staff training and support, negative staff attitudes, inadequate assessment and planning processes, insufficient funding, difficulties procuring and managing equipment and time constraints. Wehmeyer (1999) found that the main impediments or barriers about the devices are lack of information on the availability of AT devices, cost and complexity of the devices, training assessment and limited training in their use.

FUTURE RESEARCH DIRECTIONS

At present, the use of technology is associated with intervention and in learning/education as aids for persons with IDs which will become wider in scope and more encompassing in its dimensions. Future research studies can assess the efficacy and impact of various types of available assistive technologies for enhancing the adaptive behaviour, abilities and overall quality of life of persons with IDs. Some research areas that have been identified are as follows:

1. Effect of the level of cognitive development in the understanding of working with the portable electronic devices among children.

2. The most appropriate age, and the best way to introduce portable electronic devices into the learning and educational process.
3. Developing cost-effective and easy to use portable electronic devices for better communication, leisure activity, social and occupational life of persons with IDs or multiple disabilities.
4. Developing new and better computer-aided instruction materials.
5. Developing new technology approaches and solutions.

Research on adaptive technology that focuses on enhancing personal mobility, verbal/non-verbal communication, design changes in articles of every day usage, etc., with a view to develop cost effective, user-friendly and durable aids & appliances is the need of the hour. Appropriate hardware and software suitable for persons with IDs to ensure access to information technologies have to be developed.

CONCLUSION

In Conclusion, AT can be useful for persons with IDs if it is provided as per their learning and working ability, need, characteristics, and environments. The use of AT in persons with IDs would help them to lead an independent life to some extent and also reduce the caregiver's burden. However, further research studies can examine the impact, efficacy and effectiveness of various types of available AT devices and services for enhancing the abilities and overall quality of life of persons with IDs and their family as a whole.

REFERENCES

Alnahdi, G. (2014). Assistive Technology in Special Education and the Universal Design for Learning. *The Turkish Online Journal of Educational Technology*, *13*(2), 18–23.

American Association on Intellectual and Developmental Disabilities. (2009). *Frequently Asked Question on intellectual disability*. Retrieved from http://www.aamr.org/content_104.cfm

Bailey, D. M. (1994). Technology for adults with multiple impairments: A trilogy of case reports. *The American Journal of Occupational Therapy*, *48*(4), 341–345. doi:10.5014/ajot.48.4.341 PMID:8059867

Bauer, S. M., Elsaesser, L. J., & Arthanat, S. (2011). Assistive technology device classification based upon the World Health Organization's, International Classification of Functioning, Disability and Health (ICF). *Disability and Rehabilitation: Assistive Technology*, *6*(3), 243–259. doi:10.3109/17483107.2010.529631 PMID:21446850

Borg, J., Larsson, S., & Östergren, P. O. (2011). The right to assistive technology: For whom, for what, and by whom? *Disability & Society*, *26*(2), 151–167. doi:10.1080/09687599.2011.543862

Cannella-Malone, H. I., DeBar, R. M., & Sigafoos, J. (2009). An examination of preference for augmentative and alternative communication devices with two boys with significant intellectual disabilities. *Augmentative and Alternative Communication*, *25*(4), 262–273. doi:10.3109/07434610903384511 PMID:19883289

Carey, A. C., Friedman, M. G., & Bryen, D. N., S. J. (2005). Use of Electronic Technologies by People with Intellectual Disabilities. [PubMed]. *Mental Retardation, 43*(5), 322–333.

Census of India. (2013). *Disabled population by type of Disability, age, and sex.* Office of the Registrar General & Census Commissioner.

Copley, J., & Ziviani, J. (2004). Barriers to the use of assistive technology for children with multiple disabilities. [PubMed]. *Occupational Therapy International, 11*(4), 229–243. doi:10.1002/oti.213

Davidson, A. L. (2012). Use of Mobile Technologies by Young Adults Living with an Intellectual Disability: A Collaborative Action Research Study. *Journal on Developmental Disabilities, 18*(3), 21–32.

Derer, K., Polsgrove, L., & Rieth, H. (1996). A survey of assistive technology applications in schools and recommendations for practice. *Journal of Special Education Technology, 13*, 62–80.

Flores, M., Musgrove, K., Renner, S., Hinton, V., Strozier, S., Franklin, S., & Hil, D. (2012). A comparison of communication using the Apple iPad and a picture-based system. *Augmentative and Alternative Communication, 28*(2), 74–84. doi:10.3109/07434618.2011.644579 PMID:22263895

Franklin, K. S. (1991). Supposed employment and assistive technology-a powerful partnership. In L. Griffin & W. G. Revell (Eds.), *Rehabilitation counselor desktop guide supported employment*. Richmond, VA: Virginia Commonwealth University, Rehabilitation Research and Training Center on Supported Employment.

Goldsmith, T. R., & LeBlanc, L. A. (2004). Use of technology in interventions for children with autism. *Journal of Early and Intensive Behavior Intervention, 1*(2), 166–178. doi:10.1037/h0100287

Hernández, F. J., Zorrilla, A. M., & Zapirain, B. G. (2012). Management Platform to Support Intellectually Disabled People Daily Tasks Using Android Smartphones. In *Ambient Intelligence-Software and Applications* (pp. 119–128). Springer Berlin Heidelberg. doi:10.1007/978-3-642-28783-1_15

Holburn, S., Nguyen, D., & Vietze, P. M. (2004). Computer-assisted learning for adults with profound multiple disabilities. *Behavioral Interventions, 19*(1), 25–37. doi:10.1002/bin.147

Hoppestad, B. S. (2007). Inadequacies in computer access using assistive technology devices in profoundly disabled individuals: An overview of the current literature. *Disability and Rehabilitation: Assistive Technology, 2*(4), 189–199. doi:10.1080/17483100701249540 PMID:19263537

Jeyachandran, P., Gadkari, J. P., & Mishra, S. K. (2009). *Mental Retardation, Status of Disability in India-2007*. New Delhi: Rehabilitation Council of India. Retrieved from http://www.rehabcouncil.nic.in/writereaddata/mr.pdf

Katz, G., & Lazcano-Ponce, E. (2008). Intellectual disability: Definition, etiological factors, classification, diagnosis, treatment and prognosis. *Salud Pública de México, 50*, s132–s141. doi:10.1590/S0036-36342008000800005 PMID:18470340

Lancioni, G. E., O'Reilly, M. F., & Basili, G. (2001). Use of microswitches and speech output systems with people with severe/profound intellectual or multiple disabilities: A literature review. *Research in Developmental Disabilities, 22*(1), 21–40. doi:10.1016/S0891-4222(00)00064-0 PMID:11263629

Lancioni, G. E., O'Reilly, M. F., Singh, N. N., Sigafoos, J., Oliva, D., Antonucci, M., ... Basili, G. (2008). Microswitch-based programs for persons with multiple disabilities: An overview of some recent developments. *Perceptual and Motor Skills*, *106*(2), 355–370. doi:10.2466/pms.106.2.355-370 PMID:18556894

Lancioni, G. E., O'Reilly, M. F., Singh, N. N., Sigafoos, J., Oliva, D., Bracalente, S., & Montironi, G. (2007). Orientation systems to support indoor travel by persons with multiple disabilities: Technical aspects and applicability issues. *Technology and Disability*, *19*(1), 1–6.

Lancioni, G. E., Oliva, D., & Bracalente, S. (1995). An acoustic orientation system to promote independent indoor travel in blind persons with severe mental retardation. *Perceptual and Motor Skills*, *80*(3), 747–754. doi:10.2466/pms.1995.80.3.747 PMID:7567392

Lancioni, G. E., Sigafoos, J., O'reilly, M. F., & Singh, N. N. (2013). *Assistive technology: Interventions for individuals with severe/profound and multiple disabilities*. New York: Springer. doi:10.1007/978-1-4614-4229-5

Lee, Y., & Vail, C. O. (2005). Computer-based reading instruction for young children with disabilities. *Journal of Special Education Technology*, *20*(1), 5–18.

Lesar, S. (1998). Use of Assistive Technology with Young Children with Disabilities Current Status and Training Needs. *Journal of Early Intervention*, *21*(2), 146–159. doi:10.1177/105381519802100207

McNaughton, D., & Light, J. (2013). The iPad and mobile technology revolution: Benefits and challenges for individuals who require augmentative and alternative communication. *Augmentative and Alternative Communication*, *29*(2), 107–116. doi:10.3109/07434618.2013.784930 PMID:23705813

Mechling, L. C. (2011). Review of twenty-first century portable electronic devices for persons with moderate intellectual disabilities and autism spectrum disorders. *Education and Training in Autism and Developmental Disabilities*, 479-498.

Mechling, L. C., Gast, D. L., & Barthold, S. (2003). Multimedia computer-based instruction to teach students with moderate intellectual disabilities to use a debit card to make purchases. *Exceptionality*, *11*(4), 239–254. doi:10.1207/S15327035EX1104_4

Metcalf, D. S., & De Marco, J. M. (2006). mLearning: Mobile learning and performance in the palm of your hand. Amherst, MA: HRD Press.

O'Keefe, P. (2009). *People with disabilities in India: from commitments to outcomes. Human Development Unit, South Asia Region*. The World Bank.

Okolo, C. M., Bahr, C. M., & Rieth, H. J. (1993). A retrospective view of computer-based instruction. Journal of Special Education Technology, 12(1), 1-27.

Olson, M. V. (1993). The human genome project. *Proceedings of the National Academy of Sciences of the United States of America*, *90*(10), 4338–4344. doi:10.1073/pnas.90.10.4338 PMID:8506271

Petterson, B., Bourke, J., Leonard, H., Jacoby, P., & Bower, C. (2007). Co-occurrence of birth defects and intellectual disability. *Paediatric and Perinatal Epidemiology*, *21*(1), 65–75. doi:10.1111/j.1365-3016.2007.00774.x PMID:17239182

P.L. 103-218. (1994). *Technology-related Assistance for Individuals with Disabilities Act Amendments of 1994*. Author.

Rai, K. (2008). Technology to teach self-help skills to elementary students with mental disabilities. *Journal of the Indian Academy of Applied Psychology, 34*(2), 201–214.

Reichle, J. (2011). Evaluating assistive technology in the education of persons with severe disabilities. *Journal of Behavioral Education, 20*(1), 77–85. doi:10.100710864-011-9121-1

Rispoli, M. J., Franco, J. H., van der Meer, L., Lang, R., & Camargo, S. P. (2010). The use of speech generating devices in communication interventions for individuals with developmental disabilities: A review of the literature. *Developmental Neurorehabilitation, 13*(4), 276–293. doi:10.3109/17518421003636794 PMID:20629594

Sigafoos, J., Didden, R., & O'Reilly, M. (2003). Effects of speech output on maintenance of requesting and frequency of vocalizations in three children with developmental disabilities. *Augmentative and Alternative Communication, 19*(1), 37–47. doi:10.1080/0743461032000056487

Sigafoos, J., Green, V. A., Payne, D., Son, S. H., O'Reilly, M., & Lancioni, G. E. (2009). A comparison of picture exchange and speech-generating devices: Acquisition, preference, and effects on social interaction. *Augmentative and Alternative Communication, 25*(2), 99–109. doi:10.1080/07434610902739959 PMID:19444681

Singh, Y. P., & Agarwal, A. (2013). Teaching Mathematics to Children with Mental Retardation using Computer Games. *Educationia Confab, 2*(1), 44–58.

Standen, P. J., Camm, C., Battersby, S., Brown, D. J., & Harrison, M. (2011). An evaluation of the Wii Nunchuk as an alternative assistive device for people with intellectual and physical disabilities using switch controlled software. *Computers & Education, 56*(1), 2–10. doi:10.1016/j.compedu.2010.06.003

Trottier, N., Kamp, L., & Mirenda, P. (2011). Effects of peer-mediated instruction to teach use of speech-generating devices to students with autism in social game routines. *Augmentative and Alternative Communication, 27*(1), 26–39. doi:10.3109/07434618.2010.546810 PMID:21284561

Wehmeyer, M. L. (1999). Assistive technology and students with mental retardation: Utilization and barriers. *Journal of Special Education Technology, 14*, 50–60.

Wehmeyer, M. L., Palmer, S. B., Smith, S. J., Davies, D. K., & Stock, S. (2008). The efficacy of technology use by people with intellectual disability: A single-subject design meta-analysis. *Journal of Special Education Technology, 23*, 21–30.

Wehmeyer, M. L., & Smith, S. J. (2004). Introduction to the special issue on technology use by students with intellectual disabilities. *Journal of Special Education Technology, 19*(4), 5–6.

Wehmeyer, M. L., Smith, S. J., Palmer, S. B., Davies, D. K., & Stock, S. E. (2004). Technology use and people with mental retardation. In L. M. Glidden (Ed.), *International review of research in mental retardation*. Elsevier Academic Press. doi:10.1016/S0074-7750(04)29009-7

KEY TERMS AND DEFINITIONS

Assistive Technology Device: An object or a machine designed for a special purpose to increase, maintain or improve activities of daily living of individuals with disabilities.

Assistive Technology Services: It helps individuals with disabilities to use a set of articles or devices to help them in the area of daily living, education, etc.

Disability: A sensory, physical or mental condition and may be present from birth, or occur during person's lifetime.

Empowerment: To equip persons with qualities or abilities and essential skills so they can take initiative and make decisions to solve problems and improve performance in personal and professional life.

Independent Living: The ability or skill to live and cope up independently in the social system.

Quality of Life: The general well-being or the standard of health, comfort, and happiness experienced by an individual or group.

Technology: The application of the knowledge and usage of tools or device and techniques to control one's environment.

This research was previously published in the Handbook of Research on Diagnosing, Treating, and Managing Intellectual Disabilities edited by Rejani Thudalikunnil Gopalan; pages 331-345, copyright year 2016 by Information Science Reference (an imprint of IGI Global).

APPENDIX: LIST OF ASSISTIVE TECHNOLOGY VENDORS

The following list provides the name of vendors with websites/URLs that carry assistive technology products. Listing the vendors name does not recommend an endorsement by the author or publisher.

- **AbleNet, Inc.**
  - Website: https://www.ablenetinc.com/
  - AbleNet, Inc. provides a wide range of products such as switches, speech generating devices, accessible toys, and apps and software. AbleNet also conduct webinars and onsite training programs for professionals and parents.
- **Adaptivation, Inc.**
  - Website: http://www.adaptivation.com/
  - Adaptivation, Inc. is the producer of electronic communication aids, environmental controls, switches and other assistive technology for individuals with special needs.
- **Barrier Break**
  - Website: http://barrierbreak.com/
  - Barrier Break provides a variety of assistive technology products for visual, hearing, learning and mobility, and for elderly. These products are helpful to users for daily living skills or other routine task.
- **Boundless**
  - Website: http://www.boundlessat.com/
  - Boundless Assistive Technology offers with over 3,000 products, complete PC and Mac systems, and bundled tablets, access solutions meet the needs of virtually any ability.
- **EnableMart**
  - Website: https://www.enablemart.com/
  - EnableMart is provider of products for people with special needs and providing solutions in learning curriculum, adaptive equipment, and therapy products. EnableMart is also conduct free webinar covering a variety of products and brands related to special education, speech therapy and assistive technology.
- **Prentke Romich Company**
  - Website: http://www.prentrom.com/
  - Prentke Romich Company (PRC) is a member of a consortium of companies that are pioneers in the field of assistive technology and augmentative communication. The mission of PRC is to help people with disabilities achieve their potential in educational, vocational, and personal pursuits. Products include augmentative communication devices, computer access technology and switches. PRC provides practical and clinically sound product training and AAC implementation classes based on years of client support.
- **Vitasta India**
  - Website: http://vitastaindia.com/
  - Vitasta India (originally known as Vitasta Healthcare International) is involved in marketing and selling of Tobii eye tracking Technology Devices for analytical and assistive use. It also provides alternative and augmentative communication devices, products for Child Therapy of Timocco to increase children's motivation for physical, cognitive and social activities and medical devices for healthcare professional's safety.

Chapter 23
The Use of iPad® Devices and "Apps" for ASD Students in Special Education and Speech Therapy

Johnny R. O'Connor Jr.
Lamar University, USA

Keonta N. Jackson
Texas A&M University – Commerce, USA

ABSTRACT

This chapter presents an examination of the various uses of iPads and applications ("apps") for students with Autism Spectrum Disorder (ASD) in special education and speech therapy settings. Although many individuals view these technologies as less academic and as more entertainment or "busy tasks," if appropriately vetted, and with proper training, they can serve a significant purpose in the lives of individuals with ASD. Using this technology in educational and therapeutic environments can further extend the often static approach to education and therapy treatments to a more fluid and flexible approach meeting the varied and individualized needs of students with ASD.

INTRODUCTION

As the number of autism cases continues to rise, many agencies have begun to take interest in the condition, raising millions of dollars for research related to identifying causes and treatments (Glicksman, 2012). Specifically, autism spectrum disorder (ASD) is an inclusive term that describes a set of neurological conditions that affect an individual's ability to process information. ASD conditions manifest themselves differently and distinctively in each individual and can often influence an individual's behavior patterns, as well as the ability to engage in social communication and interactions (American Psychiatric Association, 2013; National Institute of Mental Health, 2016). These manifestations often lead to individuals with ASD being misunderstood. However, during this time of rapid advancement in

DOI: 10.4018/978-1-7998-1213-5.ch023

technology, it has become more imperative that educators and speech therapists take the opportunity to understand the evolution of technology and its potential effectiveness in the treatment of students with ASD in both educational and therapeutic settings. It is critically important that ASD be considered a lifelong disorder. Despite this, many individuals with ASD have been known to live independent and productive lives (Benson, 2016).

BACKGROUND

Although many may view technology as less academic or therapeutic and as more of a source for entertainment or as "busy work," researchers have found that the use of emerging technologies, as well as related app software, show promise for the developmental progress of students with ASD (Ploog, Scarf, Nelson, & Brooks, 2012). Emerging technologies include iPads and other tablet devices that are considered more portable and convenient than computers. Tablet apps include software that accompany iPads and allow access to gaming and the completion of communicative and instructional tasks. If properly vetted and implemented, this technology can be used as an alternative to the more traditional approach to intervention, providing a flexible way of meeting the varied needs of students with ASD. The importance of this will become more evident as the use of technology with this population continues to steadily increase (Odom et al., 2015). This chapter will explore the various uses of technology and apps for students with ASD in special education and speech therapy settings. Although both settings are unique, many of the practices as they relate to the implementation of innovative technologies share basic concepts.

TECHNOLOGY AND ASD STUDENTS

Historical Perspective of Technology and the Needs of Students with ASD

The availability of innovative technologies has grown exponentially. This has provided a new and exciting set of communication tools with varied levels of power, portability, and network ability. These technologies have transformed the way that individuals with ASD communicate and perform daily tasks, allowing them access to more mainstream tools, as well as increased functionality (McNaughton & Light, 2013). As an added benefit, the ability to use more current iPad/tablet devices has increased social acceptance, minimizing the stigma often attached to using more traditional assistive technology (Kagohara et al., 2013). Various types of technology continue to be identified in the ASD research literature, putting in perspective the relevance of its use in educational and therapeutic settings (Odom et al., 2015). Given this, it is important to discuss the evolution of technology as it relates to students with ASD. This evolution can be best presented in three phases: Phase I: No-Tech/Low-Tech, Phase II: High-Tech Traditional, and Phase III: High-Tech – Innovative.

Phase I: No-Tech/Low-Tech Devices

Developed out of a need for individuals to communicate expressively, low-tech assistive technology paved the way for individuals with disabilities to communicate with those around them in the most basic form. Specifically, in the '80s and '90s, this technology demonstrated an increased potential for use among individuals with ASD (Shane et al., 2012). Conventionally, the term assistive technology refers to augmentative and alternative communication (AAC) and speech-generating devices used primarily by nonverbal individuals (Knight, McKissick, & Sanders, 2013). Early on, AAC used by individuals with ASD were developed with none to low levels of technology. This included manual signs or graphics that served as points of communication by way of pointing to or exchanging symbols (Shane et al., 2012). These devices provided basic access to a student's ability to answer yes or no questions and assisted others in understanding their basic wants and needs and in academic decision making.

However, low-tech devices provided limited opportunities to assist with higher-level thinking and age-appropriate communication skills. Furthermore, the labor-intensive and rigid nature of this type of communication rendered social, therapeutic, and academic interactions difficult. Ultimately, the use of low-tech forms of assistive technology addressed the fundamental purpose of communication, but failed to provide individuals with ASD a more advanced opportunity to engage in more academically and socially meaningful interactions. This, in turn, resulted in a more high-tech approach to communication.

Phase II: High-Tech Traditional Devices

More traditional high-tech options found their way into educational and therapeutic settings due to the limitations associated with low-tech choices. These high-tech options included traditional desktops and laptop devices that allowed individuals to communicate using both pictures and written language to address communication needs. This technology definitely offered more options for communication and creativity compared with basic no-tech or low-tech options, offering more flexibility and creative opportunities for individuals with ASD to use materials across multiple or varied settings. The advancement of desktops and laptops facilitated the ease of communication in both educational and therapy settings.

However, similar to the phase-out of low-tech devices, this segment of high-tech devices presented challenges. These challenges included a lack of portability, which made it difficult to change locations, limited software options, and high hardware and software costs. Given this, it did not come as a surprise when teachers and speech language pathologists (SLPs) began to take interest in the sleeker and more portable devices when considering the intervention needs of students with ASD (Clark, Austin, & Craike, 2015).

Phase III: High-Tech Innovative Devices

As technology continued to advance, more innovative devices became available. These high-tech devices offered a more adaptable approach to alternative communication. This innovative technology included the iPad and tablet tools, which have become popular with individuals both with and without disabilities (Murdock, Ganz, & Crittendon, 2013). These tools offered portability and convenience of use, something that was missing in previous AAC devices (Clark et al., 2015). Consequently, practitioners began to favor this newer and more affordable technology (Simmons, 2014). In addition to this, Stockall and Dennis (2013) found other advantages to this type of technology that included the opportunity to customize and generalize skills across multiple settings and touch-screen capability, which allows for multisensory engagement and immediate feedback. Given this, these devices began to emerge in the ASD literature as tools to consider (Clark et al., 2015; Hennessy, Ruthven, & Brindley, 2005; McNaughton & Light, 2013 Kagohara et al., 2013).

Technology has been known to be an effective means of providing interventions for students with ASD (King, Thomeczek, Voreis, & Scott, 2014). This may explain the phenomena of the growing use of iPads/tablets and related apps in educational and therapeutic settings (Grynszpan, Weiss, Perez-Diaz, & Gal, 2014). Given this, it is important to explore this type of innovative technology in depth to further explain its significance in ASD interventions.

ASD Student Response to Innovative Technology

When considering tools and related apps for students with ASD, it is important to address how ASD students respond to this technology. In 21st-century classrooms, students have become accustomed to using innovative technology to meet daily academic and social needs (Boyd, Barnett, & More, 2015). These devices are considered routine fixtures in the school, home, and therapeutic environments. In the absence of technology, students often find tasks dull and stagnant (Cafiero, 2008). When given a choice, adolescents with ASD prefer to access and use technology related to their leisure activities (Odom et al., 2015). Furthermore, adolescents with ASD prefer a visual presentation of information as a means of instruction and learning (Shane & Albert, 2008). In this context, research has found that apps and other mobile technologies have the potential to improve the social and life skills of students with ASD (Mintz, Branch, March, & Lerman, 2012).

ASD and Technology: Parental and Professional Response to Innovative Technology

So, how do parents respond to this technology? Do they agree with the implementation of emerging technologies with ASD students? What about the professionals who work with these students? Do they find value in this technology? According to a research study conducted by Clark et al. (2015), both parents and professionals positively perceived innovative technology. Moreover, parent attitudes toward the use of technology was found to be positively related to their child's use of iPad applications. In fact, as it relates to speech therapy, it was suggested that parents support the use of technology. In some instances, parents have been documented to hand tablet devices to SLPs, with the expectation that he or she will know how to assist a child in communication, cognition, social skills, and motor development by using this device. This has prompted the eagerness of SLPs to quickly embrace the learning of these new technologies (DeCurtis & Ferrer, 2011).

iPads and Apps: Tools for Managing the Instruction and Treatment Delivery of ASD

As previously mentioned, applications, or apps, as they are commonly known, are downloaded software that present as rectangular icons on an iPad or other tablet device. What makes apps so appealing for use with ASD students are their low cost, convenience, and the many options they present as they relate to interventions. Many companies have created communication-related apps that address behavior, social skills, and other aspects of language development. In fact, a recent search of these apps suggests that there are hundreds available (Boyd, Barnett, & More, 2015). Given this, one must be able to discern the most appropriate applications by completing a careful review before implementing them for academic and/or speech therapy use. Each consideration must be guided by evidence-based practices, under the expectation that simply providing a device does not ensure effective communication or outcomes (McNaughton & Light, 2013).

In the context of practical implementation, both special education teachers and speech pathologists, in their respective settings, have found significant uses for these apps. Special education teachers are highly qualified instructors that specialize in academic content delivery to students with disabilities, whereas, SLPs are highly credentialed therapists who evaluate and develop and implement treatment plans for individuals with a variety of disabilities, as appropriate. Mark Coppin (2012) established a pedagogy wheel that systemically identifies apps based on six core areas of difficulty for students with ASD. These areas include difficulty with traditional learning, behavior, sensory sensitivity, routines, communication, and social skills. Although this wheel offers a sampling of actual applications, it more importantly serves as a basis for decision making or analysis when it comes to app selection. Using this wheel as a guide increases the likelihood that the type of app selected will sufficiently meet the students' needs.

Considerations for iPad/Tablet and App Use

Although research suggests that technology can be a valuable tool in supporting educators and practitioners in the treatment of students with ASD, one must proceed with caution and careful consideration (More & Travers, 2013). This can be done by developing a set of guidelines for the review and selection of technology and software apps. In fact, several authors have provided guidelines for selecting tools for students with ASD. Boyd, Barnett, and More (2015) suggest the following when selecting technology hardware (iPad/tablet) to support the needs of students with ASD:

- The ability to customize;
- User motor skills;
- Time required to orient the user;
- Affordability of technology.

However, although guidelines for selecting hardware are important, they should also be considered when selecting related software applications supporting these devices. In fact, More and Travers (2013) propose the following considerations when evaluating educational apps for practice:

- Accessibility;
- Alignment to developmentally appropriate practice (DAP);
- Appropriateness of the content;
- Significance to the educational needs.

Lee and Kim (2015) conducted a study to develop a tool to evaluate educational apps for the enhancement of education. This study recognized the value of considering both hardware and app software in decision making. Consequently, findings from this study concluded that evaluative factors should include criteria for teaching and learning, screen design, technology, and economy and ethics. Although many of the factors in this model can be found in the literature, screen design and ethics appear to have unique findings. With regard to screen design, this suggests that the physical makeup of the device may influence the efficacy of tool use in educational and therapeutic settings. Furthermore, ethical considerations include checking for morally biased or other questionable material that may be embedded within the app.

So why is all of this important? Why can't I just select an app that "looks good?" The answer is simple: children with ASD, as well as other disorders, require specific pedagogy that holds true to the foundational characteristics of ASD. Additionally, it is important to note that although many considerations are given to the use of this technology, without the appropriate supporting research, practitioners may experience problems with implementation (More & Travers, 2013).

ASD Related Apps for Use in the Classroom and Speech Therapy

The foundation of the evaluative criteria for apps is heavily grounded in the individual needs of each student. The unique nature of each application lends itself to addressing varied academic and therapeutic levels, as well as curricula and behavioral needs. Given this, it is difficult to provide a definitive list of apps that address the needs of "all" ASD students (Simmons, 2014). Despite this, the following information highlights several apps that are available for use in both academic and therapeutic settings and meet several elements of the aforementioned criteria.

iPrompts® by Hanhold Adaptive, LLC.

Students with ASD often struggle in unfamiliar surroundings and with changing routines (Benson, 2016). This research-based app is suited to meet the educational and social needs of ASD students. It offers the opportunity to build a platform to support the need for visual awareness and firm routines (Hagedorn, 2004). Students with ASD often have difficulty processing various contexts (Lopez & Leekam, 2003). This app offers the ability to build context based on organization, sequencing, routines, and generalization of skills and actions. Furthermore, the expandable image library allows users to add their own images and captions from day-to-day interactions at home, school, and other social environments. According to Simmons (2014), visuals are important elements in helping individuals with ASD understand the demands of the environment and in expressing needs and wants. iPrompts® supports the learning domains of behavior and social skills and meets the following selection criteria: accessibility to curriculum, alignment to DAP, appropriateness of content, and significance to the educational needs of the student.

Behavior Tracker Pro by Marz Consulting, Inc.

The behavior of students with ASD is often unpredictable (Janzen, 1996). Teachers, parents, and speech pathologists often encounter distinct student behaviors, depending on the setting and task demands. In fact, over the past two decades, research has focused on identifying approaches to managing learning and behaviors in ASD students (Howlin, Maglati, & Charman, 2009). Behavior Tracker Pro is a practitioner's support tool used to collect, track, and analyze behavior information. This app allows the end user to capture and record behavior data with ease and is fully customizable. Additionally, Behavior Tracker Pro organizes data so that behavioral characteristics can be documented and viewed at a glance, along with the setting and time. This increases the ability to provide real-time support and redirection that will improve the likelihood of appropriate behavior outcomes. Its features promote consistent usage across multiple settings, with the ability to share information with all appropriate stakeholders. Behavior Tracker Pro supports the learning domains of behavior and social skills and meets the following selection criteria: accessibility to curriculum, relationship to DAP, appropriateness of the content, and significance to the educational needs of the student.

Articulation Scenes by Smarty Ears

Students with ASD often suffer from communication deficits (Boucher, 1976; Koegel, Camarata, Koegel, Ben-Tall, & Smith, 1998). Articulation Scenes is an application with a cinematic theme that provides users with fun and interesting ways to practice the production of phonemes. Both interesting and engaging, this app employs the use of visual and auditory effects. Its interactive platform invites users to hear the accurate sound productions, followed by opportunities to practice and record independently produced phonemes. Additionally, this app allows modeling and practice opportunities that can be used to support the individual needs of the student beyond traditional speech therapy sessions. Given its intuitive nature, students can use Articulation Scenes to engage in drill and practice activities independently. Activities found in this application support sentence production, generalization, and carryover into real-world situations. This app supports the learning domain of communication and meets the following selection criteria: accessibility to curriculum, relationship to DAP, appropriateness of content, and significance to the educational needs of the students.

Special Words by Special iApps

A defining characteristic of ASD is its impact on one's language abilities. Individuals with ASD often require unique learning and communication methods (Hagedorn, 2004). Special Words is designed to support learners who have difficulty acquiring and learning vocabulary using traditional methods. It promotes early vocabulary development by prompting users to recognize written words and use those words in day-to-day activities. Information in this app is presented in the format of a game with increasing levels of difficulty and can be viewed in different languages. Users can add personalized pictures and words to the app to meet distinctive needs. Moreover, the app design successfully meets the unique motor skills of users through the use of built-in features that allow access via assistive switches or Bluetooth-connected switches. This app supports the learning domain of communication and difficulty with traditional learning approaches and meets the following selection criteria: accessibility to curriculum, relationship to DAP, appropriateness of the content, and significance to the educational needs of the student.

Relax Melodies Premium HD by iLBSOFT

Students with ASD often suffer from various sensory-related difficulties (Robertson & Simmons, 2013). Relax Melodies supports individuals with ASD who suffer from sensory sensitivity deficits that disrupt the ability to sleep. This app consists of music, sounds, and brainwave beats that support relaxation and improved sleeping habits. Users have the ability to select songs and sounds to create personal mixes that can be played for predetermined times or continuously depending on the need. These mixes can be created, saved, and sorted in multiple ways and played as background music while other apps are being accessed. This app supports the learning domain of sensory sensitivity and meets the following selection criteria: accessibility to curriculum, relationship to DAP, appropriateness of content, and significance to the educational needs of the student.

Emotions from I Can Do Apps by I Can Do Apps

Difficulty with socialization is a well-documented characteristic of students with ASD; therefore, academic goals and objectives should be accompanied by setting social goals (Sweeney, 2013). Specifically, this can affect a student's ability to interpret facial expressions and emotions, in turn impeding their ability interact socially with others (Lierheimer & Stichter, 2011). Emotions from I Can Do provides students with an innovative and fun option to practice the interpretation and delivery of appropriate emotions, while integrating pictures of real faces. This app provides auditory reinforcement, options to supplement pictures with written text, data collection, and varied levels of difficulty. Additionally, it is aligned with the Common Core Standards (CCS); supports the learning domain of social skills; and meets the selection criteria of accessibility, developmentally appropriate content, and significance to the educational needs of the student.

Before utilizing apps, practitioners must ensure that assistive technology and/or other supplements have been properly considered per each student's individualized needs (Sweeney, 2013). The previous examples showcase only a few of the hundreds of apps that may be helpful to students with ASD (Simmons, 2014). Apps have a unique place in the instruction of students with ASD, in that, when used in concert with an iPad/tablet, they can support classroom participation and assist in the teaching of target skills (King et al., 2014).

Innovative Technologies and ASD: Educational /Therapeutic Settings

Educators and therapists significantly influence the integration of technology (Clark, Austin, & Craike, 2015). Based on this, it is important to take a methodical approach to each aspect of the process, including the context in which the technology will be used. This type of attention will further enhance the overall quality of education or therapy provided to students with ASD.

Special Education Settings: An Educator's Perspective

Technology and applications in educational settings have provided high-leveraged tools to enhance learning (McTighe & March, 2015). These tools have become staples in the classroom. Special education teachers of students with ASD typically provide instruction within a self-contained setting, often using technology to differentiate and manage instruction. In order for the teacher to employ effective use of differentiated instruction using technological supports, he or she must consider the following questions:

- What is the role of the teacher?
- What is the role of the student?
- How does the technology align with student goals and objectives for learning?
- How will the efficacy of implementation be monitored?

What is the role of the teacher? The primary role of the special education teacher is differentiated instruction. In the context of using technology for students with ASD, a teacher must determine what area of the learning process to address, employing tools that best meet the needs of the student. The identified need should be supported with previous academic performance data that identify the specific area of the lesson cycle that would benefit the student. The teacher must determine if it is most appropriate to alter content delivery, instructional activities presented throughout lesson cycles, or the means in which students demonstrate understanding and mastery of the concept. For example, should the pace of content delivery be altered or enhanced with additional visual and auditory supports?

An equally important issue is whether the instructional activities provided as part of the lesson cycle should be embedded with scaffolds via technology. These scaffolds may include changes to readability level, use of text to voice, and preteaching of difficult or concept-specific vocabulary. The flexibility of innovative technologies assists the teacher in easily modifying content and lessons to support the individualized learning needs of students with ASD.

What is the role of the student? In the educational setting, the student must be an active participant in the use of tools and applications. Students must be trained in and use technology devices as intended. This requires a certain level of responsibility. However, given the nature of ASD, expectations may need to be modified. This will look differently for each child.

How does the technology align with ASD student goals and objectives for learning? Technology selected for use must be aligned with student goals and objectives for learning. The use of technology must be customized to suit the needs of the student. This can only occur after an in-depth review of a student's academic performance and trends across settings. The technology tools and applications must be relevant to teaching or remediating the particular skills stated in the student's academic or behavioral goals and learning objectives. Technology tools cannot be used as one-size-fits-all tools and must have the ability to be flexible in both the planning and learning process.

How will the efficacy of implementation be monitored? The efficacy of implementation of technology tools and applications in the classroom can be monitored in the traditional ways. Traditionally, efficacy is measured by student performance in activities designed to determine the understanding of the concept taught. Additionally, teacher observations and anecdotal notes throughout the lesson cycle can provide relevant information in terms of effective use of technology. Finally, technology tools and applications have built-in features that provide pertinent information in terms of time spent on specific skills, the student's baseline performance, projected performance gains, and actual performance. This monitoring should also evaluate student use of any applicable technology.

Therapeutic Settings: The Speech Language Pathologist's Perspective

Similar to that of the classroom teacher, SLPs have found use for apps within therapeutic settings when providing interventions to students with ASD (DeCurtis & Ferrer, 2011). In support of this, a study completed at MIT related to speech therapy games with children on the autism spectrum found that students were more engaged during computerized speech therapy versus traditional speech therapy (Hoque, Kaliiouby, Goodwin, & Picard, 2009). This is valuable information in that many SLPs are continuously looking for ways to improve therapy with ASD students. Based on this, careful consideration should be given to the use of technology and other applications when treating students with ASD.

So what does this look like in therapy? Providing speech therapy to students with ASD should never look the same. Any implemented technology interventions should have clear relevance to the treatment session. When considering whether or not technology or related applications are a "good fit," the following questions must be answered:

- What is the role of the SLP?
- What is the role of the student?

- How does the technology align with the stated goals and objectives?
- How will the efficacy of implementation outcomes be monitored?

What is the role of the SLP? As with most things, having the right person for the job is the key. The role of the SLP has been well documented in the literature. This role consists of the evaluation and treatment of speech, language, and swallowing disorders (American Speech Language and Hearing Association, 2016). Specifically, SLPs are tasked with providing intervention in terms of an individual treatment plan to address any communicative deficiencies. As this relates to a student with ASD, an SLP may target any pragmatic or other language deficiencies that may be documented during an evaluation (Plumb & Plexico, 2013). Although similar to the role of a teacher, an SLP has been trained to assess and treat a variety of communicative disorders at a more granular level. In terms of integrating technology, he or she must possess proper training in order to ensure the appropriate use and selection of technology tools. The good news is that most of the iPad/tablets and applications are intuitive and require little training. However, an SLP still must draw upon his or her foundational training, primarily in articulation and language disorders/delays, to ensure proper alignment and implementation.

What is the role of the student? The consideration of the role of a student with ASD in speech therapy is underrepresented in the literature. In fact, some may even argue that the consideration of the student's role is irrelevant. The general response to this question is that students need only "attend therapy sessions." However, this is not completely true. Student ownership in treatment is important, especially when integrating innovative technologies, but it would be prudent to consider that expectations should be individualized and will range from simple attendance to initiating some of the tasks involved.

Specifically, embedded skills may manifest within a given role in therapy, adding more value to treatment. For example, in traditional treatment, the student role has been historically established as the learner, with the SLP being the lead facilitator of the session. Given that students with ASD often struggle with the social aspects of speech and routines, something as simple as turning on technology and initiating an application may align with treatment outcomes. This turns the actual technology itself into a teaching tool by elevating the student's responsibility.

How does the technology align with the stated goals and objectives? Technology should always align with treatment goals and objectives. This holds true whether selecting hardware or software devices. If the selected technology serves no purpose, this could be damaging to the overall intent of the session and brings into question ethical concerns with the clinician. Some students with ASD require structure and continuity. Technology selection should not be random and should be executed with a purpose in mind to ensure that any use will increase the likelihood of positive outcomes. The iPad and apps offer the type of flexibility required to address within a session an array of communicative needs.

How will the efficacy of implementation be monitored? Like the discussion of the student role, the monitoring efficacy of the tools used with ASD students is underrepresented in the research. However, if the overall intent of treatment is to enhance student outcomes, SLPs are compelled to periodically monitor the use of hardware and related applications for quality, fidelity, and efficacy in treatment. Although research may suggest that technology is valuable, it does not state that it will work for all students with ASD. As it relates to tracking student progress—both individually and in groups—with therapeutic interventions, many apps have built-in functions that assist SLPs in monitoring this.

The following are considerations when monitoring implementation of technology in education and therapy settings:

- iPad/Tablet:
  - Was the student able to manipulate the device?
  - Was the device responsive to the needs of the student?
- Apps:
  - Did the app actually target the desired objective?
  - Did the student show progress?
  - Was there ease of implementation without excessive downtime for transitions, etc.?
  - What was the student's level of frustration when using the app?

It is important to note that although many of the technology platforms are intuitive and self-facilitating, many ASD students have needs that require the personal assistance of a teacher or SLP.

Improving Educational/Therapeutic Outcomes for Students with ASD

Improving the educational and therapeutic outcomes of students with ASD takes a multifaceted approach, which can be significantly supported by the use of innovative technology. Technology often serves as a mitigating medium that can improve student language, as well as academic and behavior performance across multiple academic and social settings. The tools in question are embedded with opportunities to provide immediate feedback, positive reinforcement, and collection of data and to model appropriate language, academic, and behavior skills.

Immediate feedback is paramount, especially in situations where teaching is indirect in nature and facilitated with the use of technology. When feedback is specific and timely, it supports the retention of information. In support of this, research cites that when provided with timely and explicit feedback, learners demonstrate an increase in performance (Opitz, Ferdinand, & Mecklinger, 2011). The iPad and app directly provide this opportunity. Additionally, feedback, if appropriately applied, can serve as a form of positive reinforcement that improves the user's motivation to complete learning tasks. When teachers or practitioners use positive reinforcement as a means to provide feedback, the learners are more likely to demonstrate desired skills (Conroy, Sutherland, Snyder, Hendawi, & Vo, 2009). This type of motivation is even more critical when engaging students with ASD. It is noteworthy that many tools and applications provide positive reinforcements through embedded features that present at varied times throughout the learning activities. These features encourage individuals to continue working diligently toward achieving a desired outcome.

When programmed and applied correctly, iPad/tablet devices and apps collect unique and invaluable data related to student performance that may be difficult to obtain during face-to-face interactions. Technology devices have the ability to easily track time spent on activities, the number of attempts per item, and performance trends over time (Linder-VanBerschot & Summers, 2015). Practitioners and educators can analyze data to design tailored educational and therapeutic opportunities for students with ASD.

Finally, technology tools and applications can be used to provide individuals with ASD models of appropriate academic and social behaviors. In particular, technology may provide an opportunity to present students with video models of various skills. These are skills that can be presented for replication by focusing on language concepts, social interactions, life skills, and behavior management (Shane et al., 2012). The primary benefit of using innovative technology and applications is its flexibility. This can ultimately assist individuals with ASD in the processing, retention, and generalization of information across settings. Overall, the impact of iPad/tablets devices and applications in educational and therapeutic settings is powerful and ever changing.

However, before the true impact can be established, one must recognize that students with ASD are a heterogeneous group, often requiring various intervention approaches and a comprehensive support system. As previously stated, with this comes careful consideration and decision making. Iovannone, Dunlap, Huber, & Kincaid (2003, p. 153) suggest addressing six essential components when considering programs for students with ASD:

- Individual supports and services for families;
- Systemic instruction;
- Structural environments;
- Functional approach to behaviors;
- Family involvement.

Both special education teachers and speech pathologists must consider these elements before evaluating and establishing a plan to integrate technology with these students. More importantly, innovative technology tools possess the flexibility to support a structured and functional program at all levels.

A Holistic Approach to Integrating Innovative Technologies

The importance of building a continuum of support, as it relates to the integration of technology with ASD students, is extremely important (Hennessy et al., 2005). From an organizational perspective, whether in a PK–12 or therapeutic setting, it is critical to make sure that intervention programs are built to encourage and not impede student growth. A holistic approach to addressing the integration of innovative technologies in education and therapy settings takes a broad perspective that extends beyond the individual level—that is, how individual efforts are affected by the actions of others. In this context, a discussion will ensue presenting a holistic approach in terms of the elements necessary to ensure the sustainability and effectiveness of technology practices for programs involving ASD students. With this in mind, the following issues should be considered when taking a holistic approach:

- Continuum of support;
- Training.

Continuum of Support

For the purpose of this discussion, a continuum of support will be defined as a collaborative stakeholder support system intended to ensure continuous evidence-based educational and therapeutic programming for students with ASD. In this context, a continuum should include support from the student, parent/guardian, special education teacher, general education teacher, and any other relevant support staff or leadership, as appropriate (Tucker & Schwartz, 2013). The collaboration of stakeholders can improve the appropriateness of student goals, functional use of skills, evidence-based strategies, and negative behaviors (Donaldson & Stahmer, 2014). Additionally, a more holistic approach can foster positive relationships. This is significant because parents of students with ASD have reported displeasure when being excluded from a collaborative process (Tucker & Schwartz, 2013). This supports the foundational need to keep all stakeholders informed and is critically important when considering the overall impact and implementation of technology with students diagnosed with ASD.

Shared ownership is important when introducing technology as an intervention (Hennessy et al., 2005). The connection between parents, speech therapists, and other educational professionals should be encouraged, given the level of technology present in schools and therapy today. ASD students will ultimately benefit from this continuum of stakeholders, given that this type of interest will be crucial to the development and carryover of skills for students with ASD. The importance of this shared ownership is further embedded within the fact that many students with ASD have difficulty with change. If all stakeholders are aligned, the efficacy of any technology or application use in schools or speech therapy will improve significantly. It is important to recognize that each participant along the continuum offers important information.

Training

Training is paramount when addressing ASD. It has been suggested that as the number of individuals with ASD entering educational settings continues to rise, the need for training will become more critical (Alexander, Ayres, & Smith, 2015). In fact, it has been cited that many SLPs graduating from programs of study require more intensive training in ASD-related treatments. This is significant because parents expect SLPs to be well trained and ready to implement an array of treatments (Cascella & Colella, 2004; Plumb and Plexico, 2013). However, regardless of the lens, training with students, staff, and teachers is critical to sustaining the high-quality implementation of innovative technologies with students on the ASD spectrum. This should include baseline student training and readiness, parent training focused on carryover and support, and teacher/clinician training related to best practices in the implementation of innovative technologies for students with ASD.

FUTURE RESEARCH DIRECTIONS

The use of innovative technologies in the intervention of ASD will require more research and review. Although it has been well established that many of the uses of this technology support the needs of students with ASD, there is still much to be explored as it relates to the impact of app use on learning and the sustainability of skills versus the more traditional approach (King, et al, 2014). Additionally, research as it relates to the proper implementation of apps must also be addressed if innovative technologies continue to be routine in the classroom and therapy settings. This type of research will assist in providing practitioners with valuable insight as it relates to the fidelity of implementation. Despite this, it is clear that this approach to pedagogy provides value to both the education and speech therapy professions.

CONCLUSION

Innovative technologies and applications have provided an opportunity to enhance special education and speech therapy services for students with ASD. Moving forward, organizations, as well individual professionals, will have to make decisions regarding specific interventions or treatment protocols. When considering the use of technology and related applications in these settings, considerations must be made, keeping the individual needs of the student at the forefront. Innovative technologies such as the iPad and apps appear to be here to stay and offer the unique opportunity to extend the reach of academics and speech therapy. However, in order for this to take place, a true commitment to planning, training, and collaboration must be present. If this commitment remains intact, the possibilities will be unlimited. The goal of technology interventions in ASD should be sustainability. Sustainability increases the likelihood that individuals with ASD will have the necessary supports in place to facilitate daily living.

REFERENCES

Alexander, J. L., Ayres, K. M., & Smith, K. A. (2015). Training teachers in evidence-based practice for individuals with autism spectrum disorder: A review of the literature. *Teacher Education and Special Education*, *38*(1), 13–27. doi:10.1177/0888406414544551

American Psychiatric Association. (2013). *Diagnostic and statistical manual of mental disorders* (5th ed.). Arlington, VA: American Psychiatric Publishing.

American Speech Language and Hearing Association. (2016). *Scope of Practice in Speech Language Pathology*. Retrieved February 15, 2016 from http://www.asha.org/policy/SP2016-00343/#Definitions

Benson, S. (2016, February). *What is autism spectrum disorder?* Retrieved February 15, 2016 from https://www.psychiatry.org/patients-families/autism/what-is-autism-spectrum-disorder

Boucher, J. (1976). Articulation in early childhood autism. *Journal of Autism and Childhood Schizophrenia*, *6*(6), 297–302. doi:10.1007/BF01537907 PMID:1036736

Boyd, T. K., Barnett, J. E. H., & More, C. M. (2015). Evaluating iPad technology for enhancing communication skills of children with autism spectrum disorders. *Intervention in School and Clinic*, *51*(1), 19–27. doi:10.1177/1053451215577476

Cafiero, J. M. (2008). Technology supports for individuals with autism spectrum disorders. *TAM Technology in Action*, *3*(3), 1–12.

Cascella, P. W., & Colella, C. S. (2004). Knowledge of autism spectrum disorders among connecticut school speech-language pathologists. *Focus on Autism and Other Developmental Disabilities*, *19*(4), 245–252. doi:10.1177/10883576040190040601

Clark, M. L. E., Austin, D., & Craike, M. J. (2015). Professional and parental attitudes toward iPad application use in autism spectrum disorder. *Focus on Autism and Other Developmental Disabilities*, *30*(3), 174–181. doi:10.1177/1088357614537353

Conroy, M., Sutherland, K. S., Snyder, A., Al-Hendawi, M., & Vo, A. (2009). Creating a positive classroom atmosphere: Teachers' use of effective praise and feedback. *Beyond Behavior*, *18*(2), 18–26.

Coppin, M. (2012). *Apps for Students with Autism Spectrum Disorder* [Data file]. Retrieved from https://www.autismspeaks.org/sites/default/files/pedagogy_wheel.pdf

DeCurtis, L. L., & Ferrer, D. (2011). Toddlers and technology: Teaching the techniques. *The ASHA Leader*, (16). Retrieved February 16, 2016from http://leader.pubs.asha.org/article.aspx?articleid=2280052&resultClick=1

Donaldson, A. L., & Stahmer, A. C. (2014). Team collaboration: The use of behavior principals for serving students with ASD. *Language, Speech, and Hearing Services in Schools*, *45*(4), 261–276. doi:10.1044/2014_LSHSS-14-0038 PMID:25091620

Glicksman, E. (2012). Catching autism earlier. *Monitor on Psychology*, *43*(9), 56.

Grynszpan, O., Weiss, P. L., Perez-Diaz, F., & Gal, E. (2014). Innovative technology-based interventions for autism spectrum disorders: A meta-analysis. *Autism*, *18*(4), 346–361. doi:10.1177/1362361313476767 PMID:24092843

Hagedorn, V. S. (2004). Special learners: Using picture books in music to encourage participation of students with autistic spectrum disorder. *General Music Today*, *17*(2), 46–51. doi:10.1177/10483713040170020108

Hennessy, S., Ruthven, K., & Brindley, S. (2005). Teacher perspective on integrating ICT into teaching: Commitment, constraints, caution, and change. *Journal of Curriculum Studies*, *37*(2), 155–192. doi:10.1080/0022027032000276961

Hoque, M., Lane, J. K., Kaliouby, R., Goodwin, M., & Picard, R. W. (2009). Exploring speech therapy games with children on the autism spectrum. *Proceedings from 10th Annual Conference of the International Speech Communication Association, INTERSPEECH 2009*.

Howlin, P., Maglati, I., & Charman, T. (2009). Systemic review of early intensive behavioral interventions for children with autism. *American Journal of Intellectual and Developmental Disabilities*, *114*(1), 23–41. doi:10.1352/2009.114:23-41 PMID:19143460

Iovannone, R., Dunlap, G., Huber, H., & Kincaid, D. (2003). Effective educational practices for students with autism spectrum disorders. *Focus on Autism and Other Developmental Disabilities*, *18*(2), 150–165. doi:10.1177/10883576030180030301

Janzen, J. E. (1996). *Understanding the nature of autism: A practical guide*. San Antonio, TX: Therapy Skill Builders.

Kagohara, D. M., Meer, L., Ramdoss, S., O'Reilly, M. F., Lancioni, G. E., Davis, T. N., ... Sigafoos, J. (2013). Using iPods and iPads in teaching programs for individuals with developmental disabilities: A systematic review. *Research in Developmental Disabilities*, *34*(1), 147–157. doi:10.1016/j.ridd.2012.07.027 PMID:22940168

King, A. M., Thomeczek, M., Voreis, G., & Scott, V. (2014). iPad use in children and young adults with autism spectrum disorder: An observational study. *Child Language Teaching and Therapy*, *30*(2), 159–173. doi:10.1177/0265659013510922

Kinght, V., McKissick, B. R., & Saunders, A. (2013). A review of technology-based interventions to teach academic skills to students with autism spectrum disorder. *Journal of Autism and Developmental Disorders*, *43*(11), 2628–2648. doi:10.100710803-013-1814-y PMID:23543292

Koegel, R. L., Camarata, S., Koegel, L. K., Ben-Tall, A., & Smith, A. E. (1998). Increasing speech intelligibility in children with autism. *Journal of Autism and Developmental Disorders, 28*(3), 241–251. doi:10.1023/A:1026073522897 PMID:9656136

Lee, J.-S., & Kim, S. W. (2015). Validation of a tool evaluating educational apps for smart education. *Journal of Educational Computing, 52*(3), 435–450. doi:10.1177/0735633115571923

Lierheimer, K., & Stichter, J. (2011). Teaching facial expressions of emotion. *Beyond Behavior, 21*(1), 20–27.

Linder-VanBerschot, J. A., & Summers, L. L. (2015). Designing instruction in the face of technology transience. *The Quarterly Review of Distance Education, 16*(2), 107–117.

Lopez, B., & Leekam, S. (2003). Do children with autism fail to process information in context? *Journal of Child Psychology and Psychiatry, and Allied Disciplines, 44*(2), 285–300. doi:10.1111/1469-7610.00121 PMID:12587864

McNaughton, D., & Light, J. (2013). The iPad and mobile technology revolution: Benefits and challenges for individuals who require augmentative and alternative communication. *Augmentative and Alternative Communication, 29*(2), 107–116. doi:10.3109/07434618.2013.784930 PMID:23705813

McTighe, J., & March, T. (2015, May). Choosing apps by design. *Educational Leadership*, 36–41.

Mintz, J., Branch, C., March, C., & Lerman, S. (2012). Key factors mediating the use of a mobile technology tool designed to develop social and life skills in children with autistic spectrum disorders. *Computers & Education, 58*(1), 53–62. doi:10.1016/j.compedu.2011.07.013

More, C. M., & Travers, J. C. (2013). What's app with that? Selecting educational apps for young children with disabilities. *Young Exceptional Children, 16*(2), 15–32. doi:10.1177/1096250612464763

Murdock, L. C., Ganz, J., & Crittendon, J. (2013). Use of iPad play story to increase play dialogue of preschoolers with autism spectrum disorders. *Journal of Autism and Developmental Disorders, 43*(9), 2174–2189. doi:10.100710803-013-1770-6 PMID:23371509

National Institute of Mental Health. (2016). *What is autism spectrum disorder?* Retrieved from http://www.nimh.nih.gov/health/topics/autism-spectrum-disorders-asd/index.shtml

Odom, S. M., Thompson, J. L., Hedges, S., Boyd, B. A., Dykstra, J. R., Duda, M. A., ... Bord, A. (2015). Technology-aided interventions and instruction for adolescents with autism spectrum disorder. *Journal of Autism and Developmental Disorders, 45*(12), 3805–3819. doi:10.100710803-014-2320-6 PMID:25468409

Opitz, B., Ferdinand, N. K., & Mecklinger, A. (2011). Timing matters: The impact of immediate and delayed feedback on artificial language learning. *Frontiers in Human Neuroscience, 5*, 8. doi:10.3389/fnhum.2011.00008 PMID:21344008

Ploog, B. O., Scharf, A., Nelson, D., & Brooks, P. J. (2012). Use of computer-assisted technologies (cat) to enhance social, communicative, and language development in children with autism spectrum disorders. *Journal of Autism and Developmental Disorders, 43*(2), 301–322. doi:10.100710803-012-1571-3 PMID:22706582

Plumb, A. M., & Plexico, L. W. (2013). Autism spectrum disorders: Experience, training, and confidence levels of school-based speech-language pathologists. *Language, Speech, and Hearing Services in Schools, 44*(1), 89–104. doi:10.1044/0161-1461(2012/11-0105) PMID:23087159

Robertson, A. E., & Simmons, D. R. (2013). The relationship between sensory sensitivity and autistic traits in the general population. *Journal of Autism and Developmental Disorders, 43*(4), 775–784. doi:10.100710803-012-1608-7 PMID:22832890

Shane, H. C., & Albert, P. D. (2008). Electronic screen media for persons with autism spectrum disorders: Results of a survey. *Journal of Autism and Developmental Disorders, 38*(8), 1499–1508. doi:10.100710803-007-0527-5 PMID:18293074

Shane, H. C., Laubscher, E. H., Schlosser, R. W., Flynn, S., Sorce, J. F., & Abramson, J. (2012). Applying technology to visually support language and communication in individuals with autism spectrum disorders. *Journal of Autism and Developmental Disorders, 42*(6), 1228–1235. doi:10.100710803-011-1304-z PMID:21691867

Simmons, K. D. (2014). Apps for communication and video modeling for middle school students with autism spectrum disorders. *Journal of Instructional Psychology, 41*(1–4), 79–82.

Stockall, N., & Dennis, L. (2013). Using pivotal response training and technology to engage preschools with autism in conversations. *Intervention in School and Clinic, 49*(4), 195–202. doi:10.1177/1053451213509486

Sweeney, S. (2013). Apps for high schoolers with autism: Bolster curriculum access, organizational skills and social learning among older students. *The ASHA Leader, 18*, 34.

Tucker, V., & Schwartz, I. (2013). Parents' perspectives of collaborations with school professionals: Barriers and facilitators to successful partnerships in planning for students with ASD. *School Mental Health, 5*(1), 3–14. doi:10.100712310-012-9102-0

KEY TERMS AND DEFINITIONS

Apps: Gaming, educational or other productivity software available for iPad and tablet technologies.

Augmentative and Alternative Communication (AAC): Communication generated by low-tech or high tech devices.

High Tech Innovative: Technology that assists in facilitating the communicative and educational needs of students with ASD. This technology includes iPads, Tablets, and app software.

High Tech Traditional: Technology that assists in facilitating the communicative and educational needs of students with ASD. This technology includes desktops/laptops.

Holistic Approach: Represents a broad perspective of collaborative planning.

Innovative Technology: Technologies that include iPad, tablets, apps, or any other streamlined technology devices.

iPad/Tablet: Computer technology used to facilitate educational and therapeutic interventions.

No Tech/Low Tech: Basic technology that assists in facilitating the communicative and educational needs of students with ASD. Includes sign language and basic graphics.

Special Education Setting: Setting where many students with ASD receive specialized academic services.

Speech Therapy Setting: Setting where many students with ASD receive speech and language therapy.

This research was previously published in Supporting the Education of Children with Autism Spectrum Disorders edited by Yefim Kats; pages 267-283, copyright year 2017 by Information Science Reference (an imprint of IGI Global).

Chapter 24
Handmade Content and School Activities for Autistic Children with Expressive Language Disabilities

Shigeru Ikuta
Otsuma Women's University, Japan

Ryoichi Ishitobi
University of Tsukuba, Japan

Fumio Nemoto
University of Tsukuba, Japan

Chiho Urushihata
University of Tsukuba, Japan

Kyoko Yamaguchi
Abiko Special Needs Education School for the Mentally Challenged, Japan

Haruka Nakui
Abiko Special Needs Education School for the Mentally Challenged, Japan

ABSTRACT

Original teaching materials with dot codes, which can be linked to multimedia such as audio, movies, Web pages, html files, and PowerPoint files were created for use with autistic children with intellectual and expressive language disabilities. A maximum of four audio recordings can be linked to one dot code icon. One of the authors (S. I.) also created "Post-it" icons, on which dot codes were printed, and shared these with teachers of children with Autism Spectrum Disorders (ASD). As part of this project, many activities using dot code materials were successfully conducted at special needs and general schools. Basic information on the creation of these materials and their use in schools are presented in this paper.

DOI: 10.4018/978-1-7998-1213-5.ch024

Handmade Content and School Activities for Autistic Children with Expressive Language Disabilities

INTRODUCTION

Some children with Autism Spectrum Disorders (ASD) do not have the ability to express themselves clearly and therefore, find it difficult to express their needs to others. Consequently, they often become frustrated and treat their classmates and teachers harshly. With the assistance of information communication technology (ICT) tools, such children are able to communicate their needs. Original teaching materials with dot codes and e-books with Media Overlays were created by the authors, who then conducted activities in schools for students with intellectual and expressive language disabilities. By repeatedly touching a card using a sound pen to hear the sounds, long-term use of these activities has allowed some students at these special needs schools to understand the functions of the dot-coded illustrated cards. Teachers have also assisted these students in acquiring understanding using simultaneous body language and mouthing of the words. Over time, the students were able to learn to select a suitable card from many cards to express their needs to others. The children were at first surprised at the function of the sound pen, but soon understood how this method could allow them to communicate with others. A few students were able to correctly say several key words and phrases necessary for daily life, such as "Good morning!" "Let's eat lunch," and "Goodbye." The dot code activities developed for use by autistic children showed that these original teaching materials and tools, with the associated school activities, were very useful in enriching the students' understanding of words and phrases and improving their speaking ability (Ikuta et al., 2013; Ikuta et al., 2015).

Autistic students are often unable to understand what is going on in their classes at school or preschool and thus, become frustrated and sometimes panic. Handmade sheets with dot codes developed by the authors were put on the wall in the classrooms, and by touching the sheets with a sound pen; these students could listen to each day's schedule and confirm it with other classmates at the school's morning meeting. Various sheets were also developed for use during classes to assist the autistic students in keeping calm and understanding the appropriate behavior required in class and school.

One of the authors, Shigeru Ikuta (S. I.), from the Otsuma Women's University, Japan, has been involved in organizing a worldwide collaborative research group to develop original handmade teaching materials using advanced ICT tools, and has conducted school activities both at special needs and general schools in partnership with the Japanese companies Gridmark Inc. (Gridmark, 2009), FUSE Network Inc. (FUSE Network, Inc., 2010), and Apollo Japan (Apollo Japan, 2005). The funding provided by the Japanese Ministry of Education, Culture, Sport, Science and Technology and by the Otsuma Women's University has been crucial for the continuation and extension of this important research project.

In this chapter, we discuss the methods for the development of original ICT-based teaching materials, provide guidance on the creation of focused materials, and provide an overview of useful and helpful school activities for autistic students.

Background

More than ten years ago, we started helping students with various disabilities use a sound pen to trace two-dimensional dot codes printed on paper to reproduce sound. Scan Talk code developed by Olympus Co., Japan (Olympus, 1999) was first used, in which the voices/sounds were encoded and printed directly on paper as two-dimensional dot codes. To reproduce the voices and/or sounds, the students had to trace the fairly long dot codes with great care using a Scan Talk Reader and Sound Reader.

Use of this first system demonstrated that it was a very powerful tool for students with disabilities, as the specially designed software could be used to create original handmade teaching material focused on individual needs and desires, was easy to use, and was free of charge for schools. However, some mentally and severely hand- and finger-challenged students at special needs schools were unable to trace the long, straight Scan Talk codes correctly and were therefore unable to join in with class activities. Therefore, we sought alternative systems so that students could easily touch the dot codes with a sound (speaking) pen to reproduce the voices/sounds clearly, which would allow a greater number of disabled students to learn to use the dot code content. S. I. started collaborating with two companies, Apollo Japan Co. and Gridmark Inc., both of which had separately developed new dot codes. Apollo Japan had developed the new dot codes named ScreenCodes (ApolloJapan, 2005), but the software needed to create original content for the sound pen was costly (approximately USD 3,000), meaning that few schools could afford it. Therefore, S. I. decided to create content based on the schools' requirements, which would then be given to the schools without charge.

Gridmark Inc. had originally developed the GridOnput dot codes (Gridmark, 2009), in which a maximum of four audio recordings could be linked to each dot code symbol icon by recoding the software. With the assistance of S. I., Gridmark Inc provided schools with non-commercial assembly software free of charge, meaning they could create their own original content. Gridmark Inc. then developed easy-to-handle non-commercial software to allow a maximum of four voice/sound audio files to be linked to each dot code. Okidata Co. Japan, in collaboration with Gridmark Inc., had also developed software (*GridLayouter* (Okiata, 2009)) that overlaid the GridOnput dot codes on texts and illustrations, so they could be printed on ordinary paper. Okidata has further developed their software (*GridContentStudio* (Okiata, 2009)) so that it can also link the dot codes with multimedia such as movies, html files, Web pages, and PowerPoint files. Since Okidata stopped distributing their software, *GridLayouter and GridContentStudio*, to the public, Gridmark Inc. is now preparing new software (noted *Gridmark Authoring Tool* hereafter) to overlay the GridOnput dot codes on texts and illustrations.

S. I. has recently created original sheets (called "magical sheets") with a "Post-it"-like removable sticker icon overlaid with the dot codes, which have been given to schools with the accompanying easy-to-use software. Now schoolteachers are able to create their own original GridOnput booklets for disabled students without needing to buy costly software or printers. The teachers can remove the "Post-it" sticker icons from the magical sheets and affix them to any real items they wish to link with voice or sound. By simply touching the symbol icons affixed to the real item with a sound pen such as G-Talk, students are able to hear the voices/sounds very clearly. Further, using a scanner pen, such as the G-Pen, connected to a tablet or PC can activate multimedia such as movies.

S. I. has established two collaborative research groups: a regional research group for schoolteachers working mainly in general schools near Otsuma Women's University and a worldwide group for schoolteachers from Japan, the USA, the United Arab Emirates (UAE), and Oman. Schoolteachers in Japan have been creating various handmade teaching materials using recently developed ICT like dot code, EPUB3 (International Digital Publishing Forum, 2011), Augmented Reality (hp next, 2015), and Paper Application (developed by Ricoh Co., Japan) (Ricoh, 2015) to assist student learning at both general and special needs schools, and many fruitful school activities have already been developed. The worldwide research group has been creating original content mainly using dot code technology and has conducted plenty of activities in participating schools.

Funds for these projects were provided by the Ministry of Education, Culture, Sports, Science and Technology, Japan, and by Otsuma Women's University, which has allowed for the purchase of the necessary tools and software for the collaborative research work. Gridmark Inc. also supports the research projects by providing the non-commercial software free of charge and discounting tools such as the sound and scanner pens.

MAIN FOCUS OF THE CHAPTER

1. General Problems for Children with ASD

The wide variety symptoms of autism led to the classification of ASD. Autism Spectrum Disorders affect three areas of a child's life: social interaction, communication (both verbal and nonverbal), and behavior and interests. Each ASD child has a unique pattern of autism; sometimes, a child's development is delayed from birth, some children seem to develop normally before they suddenly lose their social or language skills, and others appear to have normal development until they have enough language to communicate their unusual thoughts and preoccupations. All autistic people, however, have some core verbal and nonverbal communication symptoms, such as a delay in learning to talk or a complete lack of verbal ability. As many as 40% of autistic people never speak, and others who have a milder form of autism often have difficulties continuing a conversation after it has begun, and may repeat a phrase they have heard previously over and over. Most autistic students have some trouble relating to others (WebMD, 2015).

2. Problems for Autistic Children with Intellectual and Expressive Language Disabilities

In some children, the loss of language is a major impairment. An autistic child may never speak or they may repeat a certain phrase and over. As a result, they are often frustrated at school as they are unable to express their needs to teachers or classmates.

How can students actively participate in class activities, demonstrate knowledge and understanding, make choices, express their opinions, reveal their interests, or socialize and develop friendships if they cannot speak? The inability to communicate often leads to intolerable frustrations that in many students with autism or severe cognitive disabilities lead to temper tantrums, screaming, biting, and self-abusive behavior. Unfortunately, many people in our society, including education professionals, tend to equate an inability to speak with an inability to think. They often have very low expectations for these children and, as a result, do not offer them any challenging educational opportunities. One of the most powerful applications of ICT has been the development and ongoing refinement of devices that can speak. The technical term for this technology is "alternative and augmentative communication," which is shortened to "augmentative communication" for convenience, and is designed to assist individuals who cannot speak in their interactions with others. One of the interventions based on applied behavior analysis includes teaching languages using a sequenced curriculum that guides nonverbal children from simple verbal behaviors to more functional communication skills through techniques such as errorless teaching and prompting (NIH, 2015).

We have been creating original teaching materials using dot codes, EPUB3 e-books, and Augmented Reality, and have conducted useful and effective school activities at both general and special needs schools. In this paper, we discuss the creation of the materials with dot codes and the school activities we conducted for students with intellectual and expressive language disabilities.

3. ICT to Support Students with Various Difficulties

ICT often stimulates schoolteachers to develop new teaching materials and new tools for disabled students. There are several tools that can help severely disabled students, where, for example, a student who needs to remain in bed and can only move their eyes or cheeks, can select characters and words simply by moving their eyes very slightly. Students with hand or finger disabilities may not be able to scroll through the pages of a book, but they can now read e-books easily using, for example, iPad/iBooks, with their auto-page-scroll functionality (Ikuta & Kasai, 2014). Some students with reading disabilities can read ordinary books and textbooks affixed with dot-code symbol icons quite effectively using a sound pen.

In this chapter, we discuss the creation of materials and the school activities we conducted for students with intellectual and expressive language disabilities using dot codes that can handle multimedia like movies, Web pages, html files, and PowerPoint files, in addition to multiple voices or sounds.

4. The Importance of Individual Handmade Teaching Materials and Tools for Each Student with Various Difficulties

Every year, teachers at special needs schools consider whether the teaching materials and tools that had been effective for previous students are appropriate for new students, because the needs, desires, personality, and character of each autistic student tend to be unique to that student. Therefore, teaching materials and/or tools that had been effective for one student are sometimes not suitable for use with other students, so content and access tools need to be prepared individually for each student.

5. Scope of the Present Chapter

S. I. has been collaborating with a Japanese venture business company, Gridmark Inc., which developed GridOnput dot codes. Both domestic and foreign collaborative teacher research groups have focused on the development of original teaching materials and have been conducting activities at both general and special needs schools. Three of the other authors (F. N., R. I., and C. U.) are teachers at the School for the Mentally Challenged at Otsuka, University of Tsukuba, while Kyoko Yamaguchi and Haruka Nakui are teachers at the Abiko Special Needs Education School for the Mentally Challenged. These teachers conduct their school activities for students with different levels of autism by creating original content using the dot code technology. S. I., with assistance from the participating companies, provides the software and hardware to the collaborating teachers free of charge. In this chapter, we describe the recent software and hardware developments, describe the creation of the original teaching materials using the dot code technology, and give useful hints about using these activities at special needs schools.

SOLUTIONS AND RECOMMENDATIONS

1. Dot Code Technology

"Invisible" dot codes "GridOnput" (Gridmark, 2009), developed by Gridmark Inc., is novel two-dimensional code technology consisting of extremely small dots. Small dot codes printed in a 2.0-square-millimeter Grid are so tiny that such dot codes can invisibly overlay any graphically printed letters, photos, and illustrations and never affect the designed images, meaning that letters, photos, and illustrations can be changed into information-trigger icons. A maximum of four voices/sounds can be linked to each icon as well as other media, such as movies, Web pages, html files, and PowerPoint files. Gridmark Inc. is the only company that provides this valuable software free of charge to teachers so that they can create original content.

Simply touching the dot codes printed on ordinary paper with a sound pen (G-Talk or G-Speak) and a scanner pen (G1-scanner and G-Pen) enables disabled students to directly access the digital information.

S. I. has created an original sheet (called a "magical sheet") that can be overlaid with GridOnput dot codes, as shown in Figure 1 with G-Talk and G-Pen. Each sheet has 117 "Post-it" sticker icons that can be taken off and pasted on any real items. Each sticker icon is linked with up to four voices/sounds and multimedia such as movies, Web pages, html files, and PowerPoint files. The sheet also has paper controller icons on the lower part that can change a mode, and record and delete the voice/sound linked to each icon. Teachers are able to obtain these magical sheets from S. I. free of charge.

There are two methods for the creation of the GridOnput content for a sound pen.

1. The first method is very simple. Voices can be easily recorded with the microphone installed in the sound pen and then linked to a "Post-it" sticker icon as follows:
    a. Touch the "Start REC" icon on the paper controller on the magical sheet.

Figure 1. Original "Magical Sheet" with dot code symbol icons, a sound pen (G-Talk), and a scanner pen (G-Pen)

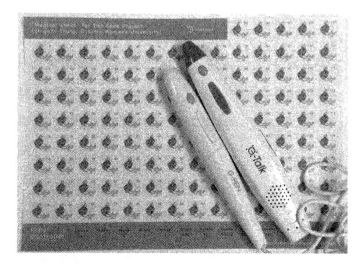

Handmade Content and School Activities for Autistic Children with Expressive Language Disabilities

    b. Once a red LED lamp on the sound pen appears, the voice can be recorded using the microphone on the sound pen.

    c. After recording, touch a "Post-it" sticker icon (No. 1) and the first voice is then linked to the sticker icon.

    d. Steps (a) through (c) can be repeated as many times as needed. The second voice recording should be linked to the next "Post-it" sticker icon, as shown in "No. 2."

2. The second method has less noisy voices/sounds. In the following example, content with 30 voices/sounds is recorded.

    a. First the software and sample files needed to create the original content are distributed to collaborating schoolteachers free of charge by S. I., in cooperation with Gridmark Inc. The demo_1 folder in the sample files (Figure 2) includes sample audio files, a linkage table file (filelist.csv), and the software (*NANA.exe*) needed to create content, where only a single audio file is linked to each "Post-it" symbol icon. The linkage table file in the demo_2 folder, on the other hand, is a sample file, where double audio files are linked to each "Post-it" symbol icon. The manual.doc and manual.pdf files in Figure 2 are instruction manuals for the GridOnput dot code trial. The "Movies" folder includes all the files, including an executable file, a linkage table file, and the files needed to reproduce multimedia such as movies, Web pages, html files, and PowerPoint files on a tablet or PC screen connected to a scanner pen, such as the G-Pen, by touching the "Post-it" symbol icons.

    b. First, open a "demo_1" folder and find the *twenty*-mp3 audio files, filelist.csv, and the *NANA.exe* files, as shown in Figure 3.

    c. To create content with the thirty mp3 audio files, create ten more MP3 voices/sounds similar to the 21.mp3, 22.mp3, and 30.mp3, as shown in Figure 4. Audio files can be recorded, edited, and saved in mp3 format using software such as Audacity (Audacity, 2015).

    d. The linkage table, filelist.csv, can be edited using Microsoft Excel software, as shown in Figure 5. In the table, there is only data in three columns (A, B, and C). In each of the cells in the A column, input 1, which indicates only a single audio file, is linked to each of the 20 "Post-it" sticker icons. Numbers in the B column correspond to the "Post-it" sticker number, and each mp3 file-name in the C column corresponds to the linked real audio file, respectively. Data can be increased to 30 lines in the filelist.csv file, as shown in Figure 6.

    e. Executing a *NANA.exe* file by double-clicking produces a content folder, *Private*, for the sound pen, as shown in Figure 7.

    f. Finally, the created content is copied onto a Micro SD card or into the internal memory of the sound pen, G-Talk. If copying the content to the internal memory, copy only the *GMVRC* folder in the *Private* content folder. Two content files can be copied to the Micro SD card and the internal memory at the same time, but the content on the Micro SD card has priority over that in the internal memory. To reproduce the content installed in the internal memory, take out the Micro SD card from the sound pen first. (Sound pens as G-Talk and G-Speak are available from S. I., but can also be bought directly from Gridmark Inc.)

Using the magical sheets, very simple software (filelist.csv and *NANA.exe*), and the sound pen, any teacher can create original content with audios for their class. Furthermore, using the software *Grid Content Studio* (Figure 8), executable files can be created that reproduce the multimedia files linked to

Figure 2. Distributed SD card file content

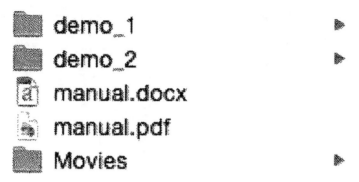

Figure 3. Demo_1 folder file content

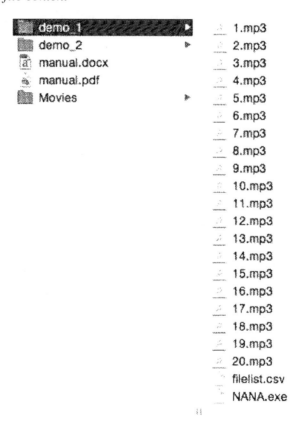

each dot code on the screen of a tablet or PC connected to a G-Pen scanner. Once an executable file is created (which could be included in the *Movies* folder as shown in Figure 2), any new movies can be added by replacing the existing files.

Gridmark Inc. is preparing to sell commercial software to link audio files (*SoundLinker*) and multimedia files (*FileLinker*) such as movies, Web pages, html files, and PowerPoint files to the corresponding dot code stickers for the sound and scanner pens, respectively. On the other hand, the more expensive software (*Gridmark Authoring Tool*) can also be used soon to overlay GridOnput dot codes at any part

Figure 4. Ten voices/sounds added to demo_1 folder

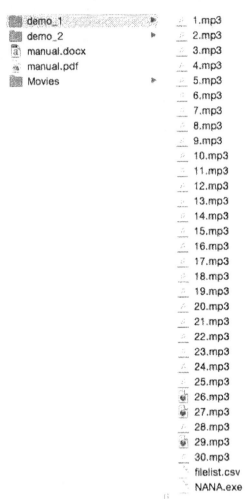

of an illustration, and the text and figures in the illustration can be used as triggers to reproduce audios and multimedia. Figure 9 shows a Snapshot of the *Gridmark Authoring Tool*. The Japanese version of the *Gridmark Authoring Tool* can easily be changed into English one.

2. Handmade Teaching Materials and School Activities

There are 1,114 special needs education schools in Japan (Statistics Japan, 2015); however, there exist only a few schools for children with ASD. Some children with Autistic behaviors attend special or ordinary classes at general schools, others overlapped with a mental disorder attend special needs education schools (532 schools) for the mentally challenged.

Figure 5. filelist.csv file in the demo_1 folder

	A	B	C
1	1	1	1.mp3
2	1	2	2.mp3
3	1	3	3.mp3
4	1	4	4.mp3
5	1	5	5.mp3
6	1	6	6.mp3
7	1	7	7.mp3
8	1	8	8.mp3
9	1	9	9.mp3
10	1	10	10.mp3
11	1	11	11.mp3
12	1	12	12.mp3
13	1	13	13.mp3
14	1	14	14.mp3
15	1	15	15.mp3
16	1	16	16.mp3
17	1	17	17.mp3
18	1	18	18.mp3
19	1	19	19.mp3
20	1	20	20.mp3

SCHOOL ACTIVITY AT ABIKO SPECIAL NEEDS EDUCATION SCHOOL FOR THE MENTALLY CHALLENGED

For more than two years, the teachers at the Abiko Special Needs Education School for the Mentally Challenged have been conducting a long-term school activity with a sound pen for a 15-year-old autistic male student. He has basic exercise abilities, such as walking and running, and he is capable of following the teachers' rough exercises, such as putting his hands up and down, swinging his hands left and right, and jumping, but cannot follow the teachers' smaller, less physical exercises. He can dress by himself, but does not understand the front and back of clothes nor recognize when clothes are inside out. He can eat food with chopsticks and use the bathroom by himself.

He has an expressive language disability; that is, he pronounces no words, but only utters sounds like "ba," "ya," and "ka." He can, however, understand the meaning of the words spoken to him in his daily life and understand real items, and can indicate their respective positions in photos and on cards. He usually expresses his desires with gestures such as "I do not like" and "I want to go to a bathroom," and takes the teachers to his favorite items and places. He can compare and check two similar illustration cards and assemble simple jigsaw puzzles.

He likes public vehicles very much, and often looks at his favorite train in a picture book by tapping his favorite trains. He often demands that teachers memorize a train's name by pointing to the train with

Figure 6. Revised filelist.csv file in the demo_1 folder

	A	B	C
1	1	1	1.mp3
2	1	2	2.mp3
3	1	3	3.mp3
4	1	4	4.mp3
5	1	5	5.mp3
6	1	6	6.mp3
7	1	7	7.mp3
8	1	8	8.mp3
9	1	9	9.mp3
10	1	10	10.mp3
11	1	11	11.mp3
12	1	12	12.mp3
13	1	13	13.mp3
14	1	14	14.mp3
15	1	15	15.mp3
16	1	16	16.mp3
17	1	17	17.mp3
18	1	18	18.mp3
19	1	19	19.mp3
20	1	20	20.mp3
21	1	21	21.mp3
22	1	22	22.mp3
23	1	23	23.mp3
24	1	24	24.mp3
25	1	25	25.mp3
26	1	26	26.mp3
27	1	27	27.mp3
28	1	28	28.mp3
29	1	29	29.mp3
30	1	30	30.mp3

Figure 7. Created content folder (private) in the demo_1 folder

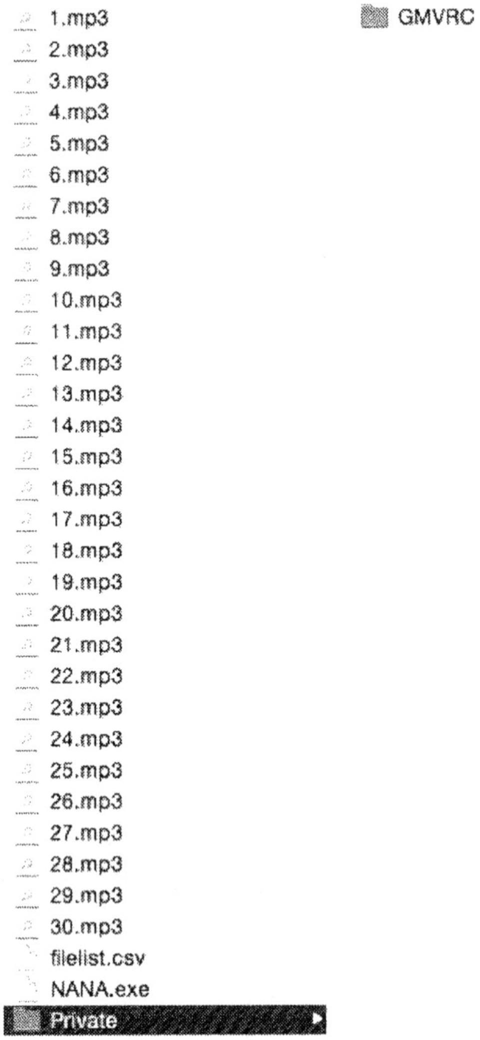

1.mp3
2.mp3
3.mp3
4.mp3
5.mp3
6.mp3
7.mp3
8.mp3
9.mp3
10.mp3
11.mp3
12.mp3
13.mp3
14.mp3
15.mp3
16.mp3
17.mp3
18.mp3
19.mp3
20.mp3
21.mp3
22.mp3
23.mp3
24.mp3
25.mp3
26.mp3
27.mp3
28.mp3
29.mp3
30.mp3
filelist.csv
NANA.exe
Private ▶

GMVRC

his finger. During school breaks, he passes the time by hitting a little bit hard picture cards each other. He cries loudly when he encounters difficulty and during new experiences. In a group activity, he often leaves the group, covers his ears with his hands, and closes his eyes.

The Abiko Special Needs Education School for the Mentally Challenged, Abiko, Chiba Prefecture, Japan, has 140 students (from 1st to 9th grades), all with various levels of disability. After arriving at school, they change their clothes, hand teachers their teacher-parent correspondence notebooks, and study their own individual study assignments by themselves. Later, every class has a morning meeting, the steps for which are 1) opening the morning meeting (exchanging very friendly morning greetings with each other), 2) calling the roll, 3) verification of both the daily schedule and the day's school lunch menu, 4) checking personal appearance (dress check), 5) a short teacher's speech, and 6) cheerfully closing the morning meeting. Every day, the two students on day duty chair the meeting in rotation.

Figure 8. Snapshot of Grid Content Studio for multimedia linking

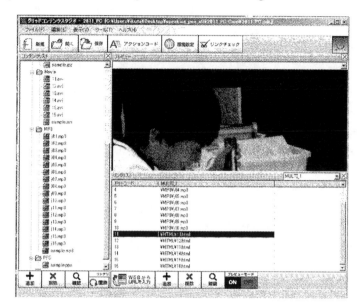

Figure 9. Snapshot of Gridmark Authoring Tool

Students with expressive language disabilities are usually unable to say what they want to others when they join the morning meetings. Therefore, the teachers (three teachers in each class) felt it was important that these students understood how the other students communicate with each other. The teachers created a booklet that included all the steps of these morning meetings, where each step in a booklet was overlaid with dot codes of the teachers' voices, so by touching the symbol icons beside the photos and texts with a sound pen, each step was reproduced with the corresponding voices.

First Step: May to June 2013

Understanding How to Use a Sound Pen

In the beginning, the teachers were not convinced that the student was interested in the sound pen and would be able to operate it. The teachers first made several cards overlaid with dot codes linked to his favorite songs. Surprisingly, he at once understood that by touching these cards with the sound pen with the help of the teachers, he could reproduce and listen to the songs. He touched the cards by himself and listened to the song, and then put the sound pen to his ear (Figure 10). Soon, he also put the sound pen to his mouth as if he were speaking on his own. The teachers realized that he was able to handle a sound pen by himself and would be able to preside as chair over a morning meeting.

Second Step: July 2013 to March 2014

Improvement in Teaching Materials and Student Transformation

The teachers created original content illustrating all the steps in both the morning and farewell meetings using text and photos with dot codes icons. It was designed as a booklet with rings that could easily turn the pages of the booklet, where the blank book to create an original picture book was used. This content had the following steps for the morning meeting: greeting each other, calling the roll, the day's schedule,

Figure 10. The student put the sound pen to his ear.

the day's lunch menu, a teacher's speech, and the closing. For two of the steps, calling the roll and the teacher's speech, all the class students' photos and the teachers' photos were put on the sheets. The sheets had easy-to-understand words and phrases, with Japanese Hirakana characters placed alongside their corresponding illustrations. For example, on the first sheet, the voice said "Let's start today's morning meeting" and was linked to the respective Japanese Hirakana characters. The size of the booklet was 19 cm by 21 cm (Figure 11).

The student was then able to conduct the morning meeting by tapping the dot code symbols with a sound pen with the help of the teacher. The autistic student soon realized that the sound pen could reproduce voices, so he could tap the steps in the right order for the morning meeting, and when calling the roll, he could tap the dot code symbols placed by the side of each classmate's photo one by one, in the right order. Sometimes, the sound pen failed to reproduce the voices, but he learned that he could touch the symbol icon again. Previously, he had to use a stick on the daily schedules pinned on the board in order to confirm the daily activities, but now he touched the symbol icons overlaid with dot codes one by one using the sound pen, which he could easily turn on and off.

Third Step: April 2014 to March 2015

When calling the roll at the morning meeting, after touching the dot code icons placed by the side of photos and reproducing the name of the classmate, he began looking at the faces and pointing. In the middle of the first school term (around May/June 2014), after finishing his preparation for school in the morning, he often took out the booklet for the morning meeting and proceeded with each step by touching the dot code symbols with the sound pen, and practiced the morning meeting by himself. He could now understand how to preside over the morning meeting using the handmade booklet and the sound pen.

Once they have mastered how to do something, autistic students tend to do the task in their own way. For the morning meeting, he took the booklet and proceeded to tap the symbol icons in his own way and when calling the roll, he began to tap the dot code symbol icons without looking at the faces. The

Figure 11. Booklet for morning meeting

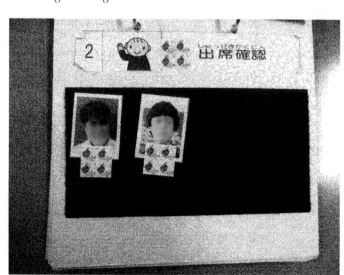

teachers advised him not to behave in such a selfish way, but he ignored the teachers' advice, lost his temper, and shouted. In a meeting about this problem, the teachers recreated some of the pages of the booklet; for example, the classmates' photos used at the calling of the roll, the illustrations used to check personal appearance, and the photos of the teacher speaking at the day's speech could be removed from the booklet. Before touching them with a sound pen, he had to place the removed photos and illustrations in their correct positions, which made him look at the classmates' faces again when calling the roll. Even now, he sometimes displays the following behavior: When a response from a classmate is slightly delayed, he proceeds calling the roll his own way; for the teacher's speech, he does not understand who is giving that day's speech; and when checking personal appearance, he takes his handkerchief from his pocket and checks the state of his fingernails (Figure 12).

During the time when these activities were undertaken, Gridmark Inc. released a new sound pen (G-Speak), but the student would not change from the older sound pen (G-Talk) to the new one. (He still uses the older type of sound pen.)

At the Abiko Special Needs Education School for the Mentally Challenged, volunteers come to pick up the students who go to an after-school care center and school buses take the other students directly to their homes. Every day, at the farewell meeting, the two students on day duty ask every student how they are getting home. Some students say that they are going to the after-school center and others say they are catching the school bus. The student with autistic behavior one day suddenly replied "ba (like *bus*)," expressing that he wanted to choice the school *bus*. After that day, he expressed himself by saying "ba" to the teachers and classmates, when he wanted to select the school *bus*; he had started to utter the corresponding sounds when he wanted to express his real desire.

Figure 12. Sheet to check personal appearance

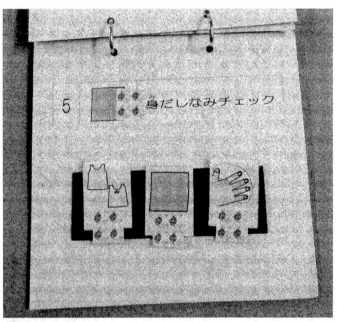

Outcomes from the Present Activities and Possible Future Problems

The autistic student could easily understand how to handle the sound pen and the relationships between the photos and illustrations in the booklet and the corresponding voices that linked the photos and illustrations. He was able to preside at the morning and farewell meetings with his teachers' help, and he and some of the other students began putting the sound pen to their ears to listen to the voices very carefully, and they also put the sound pen to their mouths so it looked as if they were speaking. He also came to understand the connections between the names of his classmates and the actual people, and the connections between the names of objects, such as handkerchief, shirt, and so on, and the actual objects. He now listens to the sound pen very carefully, and has begun to understand that words and phrases have real meanings. His understanding of words and phrases has been significantly extended through repeated listening using the sound pen. He has also developed the knowledge that he is able to express his meaning at the daily farewell meetings through the utterance "ba." First, with the teachers' help, he learned to tap the dot code symbol icons placed beside the illustrations to hear the sound, but soon he was able to determine the correct symbol dot code icons to proceed with the morning meeting one item at a time. When calling the roll, he only once touched the icons at the side of the classmates' photos. To present the daily schedule, typical school routines and transitions, he was able to tap the dot code symbol icons placed on the daily schedule sheets from the top down. He could also understand the order of the morning meeting.

He is now able to undertake many activities without the teachers' help, but help is still needed when it comes to his relationships with others. The teachers are still wondering how to create additional booklets that are more suitable for him to use at the morning meeting, as he is able to understand the situations and patiently waits for his classmates' replies when calling the roll. The teachers now know that he understands the beginning and the end of each action. When calling the roll, for example, each student first has their own photo, and the autistic student needs to take this photo from the classmate and place it in the proper position, after which he touches the symbol icons overlaid with the dot codes to call the roll.

Because of the success of this first school activity for the autistic student at Abiko Special Needs Education School, the teachers wanted him to extend and improve his communication and relationship skills. The handmade content for the morning meeting improved his communication skills and he acquired a few utterances that had real meaning. However, he refuses to use the sound pen for other events and situations. To overcome this difficulty, the teachers created content in collaboration with his family and asked him to take them home, but he never used them at home. The teachers are still trying to develop new content, as he understands that he is able to express his desires to others by touching the symbol icons.

SCHOOL FOR THE MENTALLY CHALLENGED AT OTSUKA, UNIVERSITY OF TSUKUBA

The teachers at the School for the Mentally Challenged at Otsuka, University of Tsukuba, want the autistic students to gain experience from others, so the teachers encourage them to communicate and share their experiences with their classmates and families. It is very difficult for these students to understand beyond the task they are engaged in at the present moment, and if asked about what comes next, they often exhibit fear and are unable to remain calm. Therefore, they show weakness when asked to do activities outside their school, and often show significant reluctance to become involved, especially if it is an activity requiring them to stay overnight. On the way to an off-campus activity, autistic students are often fearful and may start crying, panicking, deliberately hurting themselves, or damaging other items.

The First Activity at the School for the Mentally Challenged at Otsuka, University of Tsukuba: Extramural Activities with Handmade Content and a Sound Pen

At the School for the Mentally Challenged at Otsuka (that has preschool and elementary, junior high, and senior high school), there are several off-campus activities, such as junior and senior high school three-day ski camps, school excursions in the second and third grades at junior and senior high school, and twice-yearly senior high school campus athletics activities at the University of Tsukuba.

The senior high school teachers were informed that many of the autistic students did not like going on the ski camps and that they had cried during the three days at camp. The goal of the first activity was to provide these students with an individual booklet with the various illustrations linked to corresponding voices that gave an introduction and overview of the ski camp, so that the students would be encouraged to look forward to it.

Ryoichi Ishitobi, one of the authors, created the ski camp booklet with dot codes for the autistic students so that they would stay calm and have as pleasant a time as possible. In the booklet, various daily activities were drawn with the corresponding illustrations overlaid with dot codes showing the time (using a clock face) so that the student could become familiar with the daily schedule of activities at the ski camp. The dot codes were linked to both the teachers' and students' voices and, in addition to the voice explanations for each activity, several short slogans (with dot codes) like "It's 7 am. Good morning. Go for it for the whole day today!" were added to each process to stimulate students' excitement. Each linked student explained their aim for the ski camp, the ski camp schedules, attendee photos, the belongings that they should bring, and the ski camp song. (Figure 13) Every sheet included the dot code symbols beside the corresponding photos and sentences. The teachers hoped that all students could enjoy every page of the individual booklet and feel excited in learning about the camp in advance using their own booklet and a sound pen, so that all students were able to look forward to and be eager to attend the ski camp.

First, the teacher gave the handmade booklet to an autistic student and asked him to touch the symbols with dot codes and listen to the reproduced voices. This autistic student did not pronounce any of the words and could only utter sounds such as "u-," and usually expressed his needs through gestures. However, he was able to understand the messages given to him by his parents and teachers. From his previous activities with a sound pen, he understood that he was able to let his classmates, teachers, and parents know his needs through use of the sound pen.

He enjoyed listening to the various explanations in the ski camp booklet using the sound pen and repeatedly touched the dot codes. His classmates soon gathered around him with interest and looked at his handling of the sound pen as they listened to the recordings. He took the lead in learning the ski camp schedule, as the teachers had expected. (Figure 14) During the ski camp, when he felt fear in the bus or hotel, the teachers recommended that he use the book to calm himself down by listening to the aims and explanations. The teachers suggested that the finished portions of the schedules should be crossed out in the booklet, so that he would know when the ski camp was coming to an end. The dot-coded booklet really helped him understand and prepare for the next step. During the three-day ski camp, the booklet assisted him in remaining calm, as he could see what was coming next and was able to prepare for it. After the camp ended, he continued to use the booklet to recall the pleasant time he had had.

For an off-campus athletics activity held at the University of Tsukuba, a similar handmade dot-coded booklet was developed for the same student (Figure 15). The teachers suggested that he use the booklet in advance and on the day of the activity. He was able to understand the daily schedule of the athletics activity from the dot-coded booklet by touching the symbol icons with the sound pen, and was therefore able to approach the activity with a calm mind.

The Second Activity at the School for the Mentally Challenged at Otsuka, University of Tsukuba

A second activity was developed for three first-year students in the high school. Student A has Down's syndrome, and on formal occasions is often unable to speak due to nerves resulting from his poor speech articulation and poor memory. With repetition, however, he was able to master the activity well. Student B also has Down's syndrome in addition to hearing sensitivity and can become physically violent when tired or frustrated. Whilst he is able to read and pronounce simple words and phrases, when he tries to

Figure 13. Sheets for ski camp with dot codes: (a) own objectives, (b) daily schedule, (c) own things, and (d) songs for ski camp

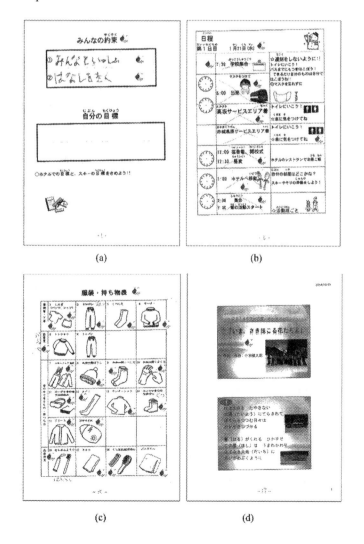

Figure 14. Photos at school activity: (a) listening to audio by putting the sound pen to the ear, (b) classmates surrounding student, (c) taking the lead in the learning, and (d) enjoying the progress of the learning

Figure 15. Timetable sheets for off-campus athletics activities

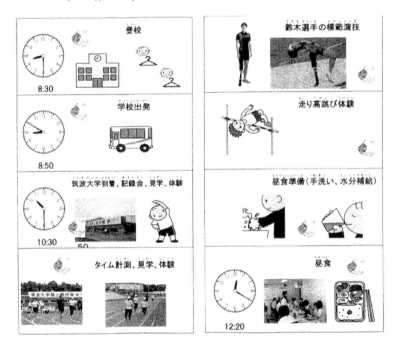

let people know what he wants, his speech is often ambiguous and he is not well understood. Student C displays autistic behavior and is unable to pronounce words clearly, instead using grunts or single sounds and gestures to communicate to others what he wants. When his wishes are not met or his actions prevent or restrict him in some way, he panics and may hurt himself or damage surrounding items.

Throughout the ten-month activity in the class, the three students became worried about their classmates who did not come to school, could not enjoy sports in the breaks, and were unable to join in school events, such as athletics or bowling meets. The three students were also able to understand each other's

Handmade Content and School Activities for Autistic Children with Expressive Language Disabilities

likes and dislikes and favorite things, and enjoyed talking together. However, most of these conversations were supported and prompted by the teachers, but in the absence of the teachers, these students found communication difficult and frustrating.

The teachers wanted to ensure that the students were aware of the upcoming school activities and wished them to become more involved in their own growth over the course of the year to have motivation for the following year and to gain confidence. The teachers praised each student and took photos when they made an effort and talked with each other without the teachers' assistance.

The teachers used the following procedures to develop individually focused handmade content (Figure 16) for these three students: 1) Each student wrote down what they felt they had achieved in the past year on a worksheet. 2) The teachers then distributed a questionnaire to the parents about their child's goals, the activities the student had found successful, the student's favorite things, the student's strong points, and the kind of help the parents received from the student at home. The teachers also asked the parents for photos of the students' activities. 3) The teachers also listed the points each student had learned and then tried to do at school and also took group photos of the students, taken at some of the group works where the behaviors and appearances of the students could not see each other. 4) The teachers put the symbol icons, overlaid with dot codes, beside the photos with the corresponding texts from steps 2) and 3) and created content sheets such as "Let's look for the good points of our classmates." The teachers also created sheets that allowed each student to record and present their own good points to their classmates. 5) Finally, the teachers created new sheets so that each student could present their own impressions of the good points that had been pointed out by their classmates.

Each student gave a presentation with the corresponding sheets and the sound pen. Before the class, Student A did the exercises and then recorded the good points of his classmates clearly and loudly and repeatedly used the sound pen. At the real presentation, he was able to give his presentation using his own voice because he was confident that he could use a sound pen if he became too nervous to speak. Student B also prepared in advance. After recording himself, he listened to his voice again and again, and examined his recordings again when the teachers asked him if he thought that the content was adequate. He listened to the recorded voices and put the sound pen on his mouth and repeated the recordings with his own voice. Student C did not say any of the words, but he told the teachers that he wanted to use his friends' voices in addition to the teachers' to create his content. He took a communication board with his classmates' photos and names, and asked the teachers to record his favorite friends (Figure 17).

Throughout this second school activity, the students were able to understand their own good points from their own introspection and the comments of their classmates, which gave them all confidence and a sense of achievement. Recording their own voices with the sound pen meant that each student tried to speak more clearly and began to understand their own behavior. Presenting thoughts and feelings in front of a live audience was not easy for these students, as they often find it difficult to speak because of stress. However, because they had had the opportunity to record and link their own voice to the dot-coded symbol icons, they were much more relaxed as they knew that they could use these recordings in the event that they became too nervous. For Student C, who always had great difficulty presenting his thoughts and feelings in the class, the sound pen recording functionality was very convenient, as his friends or teachers were able to record his thoughts and feelings for him and, using these recordings, he could present his own thoughts and desires. Doing this presentation using the sound pen and the dot-coded symbol icons allowed the students to overcome their language disabilities and enable them to be involved in the class with the help of their classmates, teachers, and parents.

Figure 16. Sheets for looking for good points with dot codes: (a) looking for wonderful points, (b) presenting their own growth, and (c) presenting their own feelings

The Third Activity at the School for the Mentally Challenged at Otsuka, University of Tsukuba: Work Experience Activities using Handmade Content and Sound Pen

At the School for the Mentally Challenged at Otsuka, University of Tsukuba, the teachers created content for the mentally challenged and autistic students to learn about the workplace. Every first- and second-year high school student has workplace experiences to prepare them for the world of work after graduation. The students work for between one and two weeks at general companies and special workplaces for the handicapped, where they do the same jobs as the regular staff. Depending on the parents' and students' wishes, the teachers decide on workplaces for the students and the final workplace is sometimes decided after a one-day trial experience.

Figure 17. Photos of school activities: (a) checking sheet with symbol icons, (b) putting sound pen to mouth, and (c) selecting the classmate to record the voices

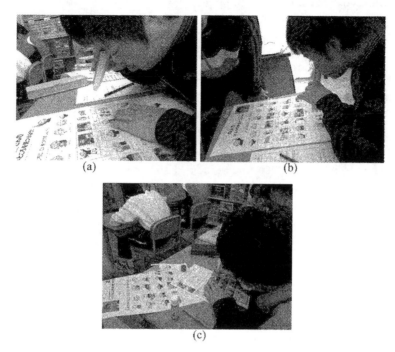

It is always very difficult for mentally challenged and autistic students to cope with these workplace experiences because it is in an unknown place, with unfamiliar people, and new activities. After deciding on the workplace, the students are interviewed by the staff and practice using handmade content focused on their workplace experience aims. In spite of these efforts, the students suffer many workplace experience frustrations every year. During the real workplace experience, teachers can only monitor each student's workplace twice, spending only around one hour each time. Some students are unable to get to the workplace by themselves, which puts a heavy burden on the parents as they have to transport them every day.

Therefore, in this third activity, the teachers hoped that the autistic student would be able to go to the workplace by himself and tackle the workplace experience, so they developed a special learning unit for him and his classmates. In the handmade content for the unit, the following content was included: information on the workplace, working procedures, and the student's aims for the work experience. After the work experience, a review of the "work experience" was conducted, in which the students presented the skills they felt they had gained through the work experience placement.

The teachers had the following three targets for the unit: 1) the students were able to go to their workplace easily because of this pre-work experience learning, 2) through learning about the workplace and the work experience duties and requirements, each student could develop their own objectives and present these to their classmates at the send-off party, and 3) after the work experience, each student was able to present their work experience impressions and future targets. All students from 1st to 12th grades and their parents attended both the send-off and reporting events.

The teachers, therefore, created three activity workbooks to ensure smooth and effective lessons. The first activity was "Let's find out about the workplace and the work experience duties" (Figures 18 and 19).

Photos of the workplace and the tools that the students would use were taken by the teachers on a visit and were then printed. On each side of the photo, a dot code symbol was added so the student could listen to the linked voice using a sound pen. The students could take their own content and the sound pen home so that they could use it anywhere and anytime. The second activity was called "Go for it," in which the work experience duties and each student's targets were printed with the dot code symbols. The teachers told the student what content they needed, which they then presented at the send-off party. The third activity was named "Looking back," in which the photos taken during the work experience were included and the degree of achievement for each student's objective was developed into a table with the dot code symbols.

The teachers gave the activity sheets for "Let's find out about the workplace and the work experience duties" to the autistic student, along with a sound pen. He was able to easily touch the dot-coded symbol icons while he turned the pages of the booklet. He listened to the recordings and then repeated them to his classmates using the sound pen. He reproduced phrases such as "I will work here and have a workplace experience soon," and pointed out the pictures with his finger. At home, he showed the booklet to his parents and introduced the workplace and work experience duties using the sound pen, which made his parents praise him. At both the send-off party and the reporting event, with the help of his classmates, he tried to present his thoughts and feelings. At the send-off party, he performed the presentation with his friend turning the pages of the booklet. However, except for the use of the sound pen, he did not need any other help at the reporting event (Figure 20).

Throughout the activity, the teachers confirmed that a sound pen with suitable content was a useful tool for the autistic students as they were able to communicate their feelings and wishes. The reproduced voices allowed them to communicate their thoughts and feelings to classmates, teachers, and parents by putting the sound pen to their ears or mouth.

In September 2014, the students in 10th grade successfully performed a two-week workplace experience at two welfare facilities. In June 2015, the autistic student and 11th-grade students also completed a workplace experience at a working facility for the handicapped; before he went to the facility, the teacher had explained to the staff that the autistic student usually used the booklet and a sound pen.

Figure 18. Sheets to understand the workplace

Handmade Content and School Activities for Autistic Children with Expressive Language Disabilities

Figure 19. Sheets for work experience placement in 11th grade: (a) workplace duties, (b) objectives before the work experience, (c) objectives after the work experience, and (d) own future objectives

Figure 20. Photos of school activity in 11th grade: (a) helping classmates, (b) striking a victory pose, and (c) presentation

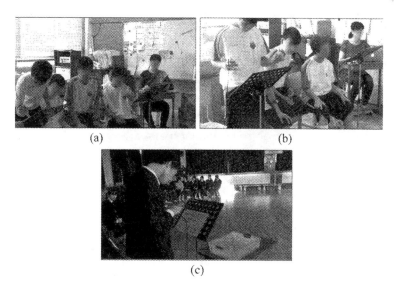

FUTURE RESEARCH DIRECTIONS

Future Research Directions for Software and Hardware

Up to now, Gridmark Inc. had not put the dot code software on the market and only provided companies with packaged content and sound pens. Gridmark Inc., however, is now preparing software onto the market that can easily create content using *SoundLinker* and *FileLinker*. This *SoundLinker* and *FileLinker* software is not cheap (approximately USD 350 each), and may be therefore mostly out of the reach of the average teacher. The non-commercial (*NANA.exe*) software that Gridmark Inc. kindly provided us with is different from the commercial software. *NANA.exe* is free and is very easy to use for teachers who are not good with ICT. The authors have asked Gridmark Inc. to consider reducing the price of the commercial software and the sound pens (G-Talk and G-Speak), which cost about USD 50 each, so that they are more accessible to teachers.

Further, as we have used the sound pens widely for many activities, we were able to notice that some changes were needed. We asked Gridmark Inc. to change the positions of the buttons on the G-Speak pen, as the students, especially those with disabilities, often make errors by accident. Easier to use, cheaper software and hardware are required, especially for teachers.

Future Research Directions for Original Handmade Contents

We have been collaborating with schoolteachers for nearly ten years in the creation of *original* handmade content and conducting school activities for students with disabilities. These long-term collaborations have been supported by the Japanese venture business companies, Gridmark Inc., Apollo Japan Co., and FUSE Network Inc. The funds provided by the Ministry of Education, Culture, Sports, Science and Technologies and the Otsuma Women's University have been crucial in enabling us to start, develop, and continue our present collaborations. The present collaborations are not restricted to students with autistic behavior, but are also for use with students with various disabilities, such as the mentally challenged, students with Down's syndrome, and the physically handicapped. Activities for visually impaired students have recently been started at the Osaka Prefectural Special Needs Education School for the Visually Impaired. University students have been collaborating to create handmade content and to conduct school activities for young students in collaboration with teachers at both special needs and general schools.

Content that is useful and effective for one student is not always useful for other students, as each student has a different set of needs and desires, degree of disability, and learning history. Therefore, teachers need to create independent content suitable for each student. Therefore, we feel that developers need to develop the software and hardware so that collaborative content and activities can be developed, which may provide developers with guidance as to how to adapt and improve their products.

With the support of S. I., teachers in the USA, the UAE, and Oman are now developing content and conducting school activities using materials with dot code symbols, the results of which may extend the collaboration internationally.

Future Research Directions for School Activity for Students with Autistic Behavior

We have conducted many long-term school activities for autistic students in addition to the cases presented in this chapter. Each autistic student has responded to these activities with confidence and joy, proving that such long-term school activities could also improve the students' composition and speaking.

Autistic students often have other disabilities. Therefore, the various effects noticed during the running of the school activities should be carefully analyzed and classified for each kind of disability, so as to be able to focus the activities more precisely. Teachers at special needs schools need to collaborate more with the software and hardware producers so that these producers can carefully analyze the experimental data gathered during school activities in order to develop attractive and easy-to-use software and hardware. More university professors should lend support to the development of teachers' content at both special needs and general schools.

CONCLUSION

Teaching materials created with dot-code technology and long-term school activities for autistic students are quite useful and effective in the promotion of communication skills. It is crucial that teachers develop *original* content for each student in their class, as each student has different thoughts, feelings, and learning histories. Students with expressive language disabilities, in particular, are unable to express what they want to say, which often results in violent and frustrated outbursts. In such cases, tools such as sound pens that can reproduce the recorded voices of teachers, classmates, and parents are often very effective. Some students were able to understand that tools such as the sound pen were able to assist them in making their desires known to others, and they often put the sound pen to their ear or mouth. Through long-term school activities, some of the students were able to master phrases such as "Good morning," "May I start?" and "Goodbye."

Collaboration with software and hardware houses is an important issue for the development of focused school activities. Support given by Grants-in-Aid for Scientific Research and the Institute of Human Culture Studies, Otsuma Women's University, are also important to ensure continuation of the development of useful and effective content and to conduct appealing school activities. University student help is a strong motivation for the development of individual content, and collaboration with teachers from various special needs and general schools may provide useful insights for the learning classification of each disability, which would assist in the development of more focused software and hardware and assist in the sharing of activities for autistic students. International collaboration with foreign teachers and researchers could also lead to new developments in materials for disabled students around the world.

ACKNOWLEDGMENT

Shigeru Ikuta thanks "Grant-in-Aids for Scientific Research" (C) (#22530992) and "Otsuma Grant-in-Aid for Individual Exploratory Research (Grant Numbers: s2605 and s2713)." The authors thank all the students and teachers at the School for the Mentally Challenged at Otsuka, University of Tsukuba and Abiko Special Needs Education School for the Mentally Challenged, Chiba Prefecture. The authors would like to thank Enago (www.enago.jp) for the English language review.

REFERENCES

Apollo Japan. (2005). *ScreenCode*. Retrieved September 5, 2015, from http://www.apollo-japan.ne.jp/sccd_en.html

Audacity. (2015). *Audacity is free, open source, cross-platform software for recording and editing sounds*. Retrieved September 5, 2015, form http://audacityteam.org

FUSE Network, Inc. (2010). *FUSEe*. Retrieved September 5, 2015, from http://fusee.jp/news/index.php?pageID=21

Gridmark Inc. (2009). *GridOnput*. Retrieved September 5, 2015, from http://www.gridmark.co.jp/english/gridonput

HP Next. (2015). *Post tagged Augmented Reality*. Retrieved September 5, 2015, from http://www8.hp.com/hpnext/tags/augmented-reality#.Vc_R6LS06-Q,2015

Ikuta, S., Endo, E., Nemoto, F., Kaiami, S., & Ezoe, T. (2013). School Activities Using Handmade Teaching Materials With Dot-codes. In D. G. Barres, Z. C., Carrion, & R. L.-C. Delgado (Eds.), Technologies for Inclusive Education: Beyond Traditional Integration Approaches (pp. 220-243). Hershey, PA: IGI Global. doi:10.4018/978-1-4666-2530-3.ch011

Ikuta, S., & Kasai, M. (2014). Reading activity using e-books with Media Overlays [in Japanese]. *Int. J. Hum. Cult. Stud*, *24*(24), 160–167. doi:10.9748/hcs.2014.160

Ikuta, S., Morton, D., Kasai, M., Nemoto, F., Ohtaka, M., & Horiuchi, M. (2015). School Activities with New Dot code Handling Multimedia. In L. Lennex, & K. Nettleton (Eds.), Cases on Instructional Technology in Gifted and Talented Education (pp. 314-340). Hershey, PA: IGI Global. doi:10.4018/978-1-4666-6489-0.ch015

International Digital Publishing Forum (IDPF). (2011). *EPUB 3.0*. Retrieved September 5, 2015, from http://idpf.org/epub/30

National Institute of Mental Health (NIH). (2015). *What is Autism Spectrum Disorders?* Retrieved September 5, 2015, from http://www.nimh.nih.gov/health/topics/autism-spectrum-disorders-asd/index.shtml

Okidata Co. (2009). *GridLayouter & GridContentStudio*. Retrieved September 5, 2015, from http://www.okidata.co.jp or http://www.gridmark.co.jp/english/casestudy.html

Olympus Co. (1999). *ScanTalk, Scan Talk Reader, & Sound Print Kobo*. Retrieved September 5, 2015, from http://www.olympus.co.jp/jp/news/1999b/nr990823r300j.jsp

Ricoh Co. Ltd. (2015). *Paper Application*. Retrieved September 5, 2015, from http://www.ricoh.co.jp/rental/paper_app/

Statistics Japan. (2015). *Report on School Basic Survey*. Retrieved September 5, 2015, from http://www.e-stat.go.jp/SG1/estat/List.do?bid=000001061937&cycode=0

WebMD. (2015). *Autism Spectrum Disorders Health Center*. Retrieved September 5, 2015, from http://www.webmd.com/brain/autism/autism-spectrum-disorders#1

ADDITIONAL READING

Amaral, D. G., Dawson, G., & Geshwind, D. H. (2011). *Autism Spectrum Disorders*. Oxford, UK: Oxford University Press. doi:10.1093/med/9780195371826.001.0001

Autismnetworking.org (2013). Retrieved September 5, 2015, from http://ww1.autismnetwork.org

Beard, L. A., Carpenter, L. A. B., & Johnston, L. B. (2011). *Assistive technology: Access for all students* (2nd ed.). Upper Saddle River, NJ: Pearson Education.

Beukelman, D. R., & Mirenda, P. (2012). *Augmentative and alternative communication: supporting children and adults with complex communication needs* (4th ed.). Baltimore, MD: Paul H. Brookes Pub. Co.

Brewer, N., & Young, R. L. (2015). *Crime and Autism Spectrum Disorder: Myths and Mechanism*. London, UK: Jessica Kingsley Publishers.

Castro, E. (2011). *epub straight to the point*. Retrieved September 5, 2015, from http://www.elizabethcastro.com/epub

Dell, A. G., Newton, D. A., & Petroff, J. G. (2012). *Assistive technology in the classroom: Enhancing the school experiences of students with disabilities* (2nd ed.). Upper Saddle River, NJ: Pearson Education.

Goldstein, S., & Naglieri, J. A. (2013). *Interventions for Autism Spectrum Disorders: Translating Science into Practice*. New York, NY: Springer. doi:10.1007/978-1-4614-5301-7

Hardy, C., Ogden, J., Newman, J., & Cooper, S. (2002). *Autism and ICT: A Guide for Teachers and Parents*. London, UK: David Fulton Publishers Ltd.

Hulit, L. M., & Howard, M. R. (2002). *Born to talk: An introduction to speech and language development* (3rd ed.). Boston, MA: Allyn & Bacon.

Ikuta, S. (2008). School activities with audios for the students with disabilities. In K. Koreeda (Ed.), *Examples of school activities useful for the special needs education* (pp. 72–73). Tokyo, Japan: Gakken. [in Japanese]

Ishitobi, R., Ezoe, T., & Ikuta, S. (2010). "Tracing" is "speaking": Communicating and learning using supportive sound books [in Japanese]. *Computers & Education, 29*, 64–67.

Kaneko, S., Ohshima, M., Takei, K., Yamamoto, L., Ezoe, T., Ueyama, S., & Ikuta, S. (2011). School activities with voices and sounds: Handmade teaching materials and sound pens [in Japanese]. *Computers & Education, 30*, 48–51.

Lindfors, J. W. (1987). *Children's language and learning* (2nd ed.). Boston, MA: Allyn & Bacon.

Mesibov, G., & Howley, M. (2015). *Accessing the Curriculum for Learners with Autism Spectrum Disorders Using TEACCH programme to help inclusion* (2nd ed.). London, UK: Routledge.

Morrison, S. (2015). *Autism: The Ultimate Guide To Parenting An Autistic Child How To Understand And Help Your Son Or Daughter Cope With Disorder*. Amazon Service International, Inc.

Ohshima, M., Shimada, F., Yamamoto, L., Nemoto, F., Ezoe, T., Suzuki, J., & Ikuta, S. (2007). Use of "Sound Pronunciation System" in elementary schools [in Japanese]. *Computers & Education, 23*, 76–79.

Okawara, H., Uchikawa, T., Shiraishi, T., Kaneko, S., Sugibayashi, H., Hara, Y., ... Ikuta, S. (2008). Use of "Sound Pronunciation System" for students with physically handicapped [in Japanese]. *Computers & Education, 24*, 40–43.

Sicile-Kira, C. (2014). Autism Spectrum Disorder: Complete Guide to Understanding Autism. New York, NY: A Perigee Book.

Speaking of Speech.com Inc. (2013). Retrieved September 5, 2015, from http://www.speakingofspeech.com

Sussman, F., & Lewis, R. B. (2012). *More Than Words: A Parents Guide to Building Interaction and Language Skills for Children with Autism Spectrum Disorder or Social Communication Difficulties* (2nd ed.). Toronto, Ontario: The Hanen Centre.

Theng, L. B. (2011). *Assistive and augmentative communication for the disabled: Intelligent technologies for communication, learning and teaching*. New York, NY: Information Science Reference. doi:10.4018/978-1-60960-541-4

Wendt, O., Quist, R. W., & Lloyd, L. L. (2011). *Assistive technology: principles and applications for communication disorders and special education*. Bingley, United Kingdom: Emerald Group Pub. Ltd.

Wetherby, A. M., & Prizant, B. M. (2000). *Autism Spectrum Disorders: A Transactional Developmental Perspective*. Baltimore: Brooks.

KEY TERMS AND DEFINITIONS

Dot Code: Invisible dot codes developed by Gridmark Inc. are a novel two-dimensional code technology consisting of extremely small dots. Each symbol icon with dot codes can be linked to up to four audios. Multimedia such as movies can be also linked to the same symbol icon. A simple touch by sound and scanner pens on the symbol icons enables a link between the paper and digital content.

Handmade Content: Original handmade teaching content plays a key role in learning, as each student has different thoughts, feelings, needs, and desires. Independent teaching material should be prepared and used for individuals, especially in preschool and special needs classrooms.

Magical Sheet: This specially designed sheet has the order for each dot code imprinted on each symbol icon. The sheet has additional symbol icons with audio recording functionality and mode changing. The icons can then be taken off and pasted onto a target object and touched with the sound and scanner pens. The "magical sheet" enables the costly GridOnput system to be used at any school at a low cost.

Scanner Pen: The Scanner-pen like G-Pen can read the dot codes printed on paper and play back multimedia (such as movies) on the screen of a G-Pen connected to a tablet or personal computer.

School Activity: School activities at special needs school can be improved through the use of *original* and *individual* handmade teaching materials and aids suitable for each student with disabilities.

Sound Pen: The G-Talk and G-Speak pens reproduce original voices and sounds by simply touching the dot-coded symbol icons or the dot codes directly printed on paper. In the present GridOnput system, up to four audios can be linked to each symbol icon, and multimedia in addition to audio can be linked to the same symbol.

Work Experience: The students in the high school at the School for the Mentally Challenged at Otsuka, University of Tsukuba, have work experiences from one week to two weeks in duration at general companies and special workplaces for the handicapped, where they do the same jobs as the regular staff. The teachers select and decide on the workplace in consultation with the parents and students.

This research was previously published in Supporting the Education of Children with Autism Spectrum Disorders edited by Yefim Kats; pages 85-115, copyright year 2017 by Information Science Reference (an imprint of IGI Global).

Section 4
Disabilities: Physical

Chapter 25
Improving Access to Higher Education With UDL and Switch Access Technology:
A Case Study

Luis Perez
Eye on Access, USA

Ann Gulley
Auburn University at Montgomery, USA

Logan Prickett
Auburn University at Montgomery, USA

ABSTRACT

This chapter presents an in-depth case study of the creative use of a mobile technology system by a diverse learner who is also one of the authors of the chapter. This learner is blind, has significant fine and gross motor impairment, and speaks in a whisper that is not understood by today's speech recognition technology. The learner's inclusion as an author is, in itself, a testimony to the empowerment the mobile communication system has brought to his life, which in turn has allowed him to be an active participant in the design of a learning environment based on Universal Design for Learning (UDL) principles. More specifically, the chapter details the ongoing development of a system for making math content more accessible not only to the individual learner who is the focus of the case study, but to other learners who struggle with higher level math content in higher education.

BACKGROUND STUDENTS WITH DISABILITIES AND HIGHER EDUCATION

According to the National Center for Educational Statistics (NCES), the proportion of college undergraduates with disabilities increased dramatically in the space of just a decade, going from approximately 6 percent in 1999 to 11 percent of all college students in 2012 (U.S. Department of Education, 2013). This

DOI: 10.4018/978-1-7998-1213-5.ch025

trend is likely to continue due to two factors: the impact of the Individuals with Disabilities Education Act (IDEA) and returning veterans continuing their education (National Council on Disability, 2015).

About 60 percent of special education students (those receiving services under IDEA) attend some kind of postsecondary educational program after high school, a rate only slightly lower than that of their non-disabled peers (at 67 percent) (Newman et al, 2011). However, despite attending postsecondary education at rates just slightly lower than non-disabled students, students with disabilities continue to face barriers that make it less likely they will complete their undergraduate education when compared to their peers who do not have disabilities. Only 34 percent of students with disabilities are able to complete a four-year degree within eight years, compared to 51.2 percent of the general population (Newman et al, 2011). These lower rates of college graduation then translate into lower participation in the workforce. On average, only one-third of working-age people with disabilities (32 percent) are employed compared to over two-thirds of people without disabilities (72.7 percent) (U.S. Department of Labor, 2014).

The pattern of exclusion is just as pronounced when careers in STEM (Science, Technology, Engineering and Mathematics) are considered. This is important because STEM-related fields have received considerable attention and funding in recent years due to concerns about economic competitiveness. Only 10% of undergraduate STEM majors report having a disability, and participation in STEM fields for students with disabilities decreases significantly at the graduate level, where only 5% of all graduate students in STEM (and only 1% of those receiving doctorates) have a disability (Moon, Todd, Morton and Ivey, 2012). This all translates to low rates of employment for individuals with disabilities in STEM-related jobs, where they make up only 2% of the workforce (Moon, Todd, Morton and Ivey, 2012). Opening up careers in STEM to learners who have disabilities would not only benefit the learners themselves (by providing access to good jobs), but it would also increase the talent pool needed for continued innovation in these fields.

While all learners with disabilities face challenges in pursuing STEM fields, those who are blind are at an even greater disadvantage due to the visual nature of much of the work done in these fields. Graphically conveyed information, such as charts, graphs, diagrams, schematics, and 3-D simulations all present significant challenges if an alternative representation is not provided for those who are not able to see. A number of tools and techniques are available to make this kind of content accessible, ranging from raised line drawings to physical models, but faculty may not always be aware of their existence, know where to procure them, or have the skill needed to implement them effectively during instruction. For example, Nemeth Code is an excellent tool for math accessibility for those who are blind, but its use is often limited to students who have been enrolled in a school for the blind and who have received training in its use. Even then, math content may remain completely inaccessible to a student who is both blind and mobility impaired.

The problem is compounded by the fact that solutions are often implemented in an "ad hoc" basis when faculty encounter individual learners with visual disabilities in their classes. A more proactive approach based on providing multiple representations of key information, would benefit not only those learners who have sensory limitations, but also those who just need these multiple representations as an aid to understanding. This proactive approach to planning more inclusive instruction, known as Universal Design for Learning, is explained in more detail in the next section.

Universal Design for Learning

Universal Design for Learning (UDL) is a set of curriculum design principles the Center for Applied Special Technology developed with the goal of providing all individuals with equal opportunities to learn (CAST, 2011). UDL seeks the development of expert learners who are motivated and purposeful, knowledgeable and resourceful, and strategic and goal directed (Meyer, Rose and Gordon, 2014). To this end, UDL begins with the steps educators can take to reduce barriers to learning before moving on to the metacognitive skills learners themselves must develop to take ownership of their own learning. This outward to inward move mirrors the development of UDL itself, which was inspired by the Universal Design movement in architecture but is today more closely aligned with instructional design and the learning sciences. As with the Universal Design movement in architecture, with UDL barriers to learning are considered from the start, and the goal is to develop instructional goals, methods, materials and assessments that work for everyone, rather than one-size-fits-all solutions. Thus, an emphasis is placed on flexibility through the application of three key principles (CAST, 2011; Meyer, Rose and Gordon, 2014):

- **Multiple Means of Engagement:** Learning is made relevant and meaningful by appealing to learners' interests and passions. Furthermore, learners are encouraged to develop self-determination and autonomy as they make choices in what they want to learn, how they want to go about learning it (individually or in small groups, online or face to face), and the tools they use to interact with the learning environment. Collaboration and formative feedback are used to support learners as they not only master the content but also develop a number of coping skills that help them overcome frustration and persist when learning becomes challenging.
- **Multiple Means of Representation:** Information is presented in a variety of formats to account for the different ways in which learners perceive and process information. For example, a student who is blind or who has a visual impairment may need information to be available in an alternative format, such as audio or Braille. Likewise, a student who is deaf may need captions in order to access the information in a video shown in the classroom. Other students may need supports, such as a dictionary to look up unfamiliar words as they read or a graphic organizer to help them notice important relationships in the content.
- **Multiple Means of Action and Expression:** Learners are provided with options for demonstrating their understanding. For example, rather than requiring learners to only submit an essay on a topic discussed in class, they may instead be given the option of making a video as another way to show their understanding of key concepts and ideas.

The UDL principles are grounded in insights from the learning sciences which point to a more complex picture when it comes to the internal makeup of individual learners. These insights, which have been facilitated by the development of brain imaging technology, call into question the concept of an "average learner" and indicate that variability among learners is instead the norm (National Center on Universal Design for Learning, 2012). More specifically, learners vary along three dimensions that correspond to the three primary networks of the brain: they vary in how they are motivated to engage with learning and how they persist when challenges arise (the affective network); in how they can access information and turn it into meaningful knowledge (the recognition network); and in how they can organize themselves for purposeful action upon the environment (the strategic network).

To guide educators in addressing the variability of learners along these three dimensions, CAST developed the UDL guidelines. These guidelines, which can be downloaded from the CAST website at www.cast.org, make the three UDL principles more concrete for practitioners. They identify a number of tools and methods educators can implement to support the varied ways in which diverse learners are motivated to learn, process information, and demonstrate their understanding.

While UDL is first and foremost about creating a more flexible pedagogy to address learner variability, technology can play an important role in the implementation of UDL by providing educators with more flexibility in how they present information and how they allow learners to demonstrate their understanding. For example, technology can lessen educators' dependence on print as the primary or only way information is presented to learners. Print is a fixed format that can put certain learners (such as those with dyslexia or other processing difficulties) at a disadvantage, whereas digital content can incorporate a number of features that make it a more flexible format capable of accommodating a variety of learner needs.

Digital resources such as the latest generation of ebooks can include a number of universal design features, such as the ability to adjust the size of the text, have the content read aloud with text to speech, or adjust the colors to make it easier to read. Similarly, learners who have motor challenges that make writing difficult can use dictation (speech to text) or word prediction to record their answers during assessments. With these features and the many apps that can be installed on mobile devices, educators have at their disposal a toolkit for designing more flexible learning environments that will work for more learners in accordance to the UDL principles. The only limitation is their creativity in integrating technology in a meaningful and pedagogically sound way.

Much research on the scientific basis for UDL has taken place in the neurosciences, but a similar body of empirical research about the impact of UDL implementation on learning outcomes is only starting to emerge. This is in part due to the fact that UDL emphasizes the contextual nature of learning. Thus, empirical studies based on traditional experimental designs would have to be conducted under constraints that are antithetical to the premise of UDL: that the curriculum should be designed with flexibility and creativity to meet the variability learners bring to every classroom. This need for flexibility can often be at odds with the type of standardization required by experimental research.

Despite the challenges of researching UDL as a whole, researchers at CAST and elsewhere continue to explore ways to empirically demonstrate the impact of specific aspects of UDL on learning. For example, two recent studies followed an experimental design to compare the impact of using digital resources designed according to UDL (and supported within UDL designed lessons) and more traditional methods. In both studies, learners in the experimental group who used the UDL resources did better on standardized measures than those in the control group who did not (Coyne, Pisha, Dalton, Zeph and Smith, 2013; Rappolt-Schlitmann et al, 2013). In one of these studies (Rappolt-Schlitmann et al, 2013) researchers also examined the perceptions and experiences of both teachers and learners. Not only did both groups demonstrate a high level of interest and excitement for the UDL digital resources, but learners who used those resources showed a higher level of ownership in their work and felt more competent in their knowledge. This research supports the important role digital materials designed according to UDL principles can play in the creation of learning environments that work for more learners.

Further developing the empirical research base for UDL implementation is an important goal, but so is addressing the needs of individual learners who can more immediately benefit from learning environments based on UDL. For this reason, the authors believe a better model for conducting research on UDL implementation is through case studies comparing an individual's implementation of a new technology

Improving Access to Higher Education

or instructional method based on UDL with traditional methodology over the course of time. This type of case study can not only address the immediate needs of the individual learner, but also produce both quantitative and qualitative data leading to insights that speed the process of innovation for others who are not yet fully included in our education system.

CASE DESCRIPTION

Logan is an academically gifted college student who was homeschooled during much of his early childhood. Growing up on a farm, he was an active child who enjoyed a number of outdoor activities. At the age of thirteen, in the fall of Logan's eighth grade year, he suffered an anaphylactic reaction to the contrast dye in an MRI, causing him to go into full respiratory and cardiac arrest for forty-five minutes. After Logan's heartbeat returned, he was comatose and the medical prognosis was that Logan would live in a persistent vegetative state for the remainder of his life. When Logan finally regained consciousness twelve days later, he emerged from his coma with cortical blindness, significant fine and gross motor mobility impairments, and a voice that could not exceed a whisper due to damage to his vocal cords during lifesaving measures. Remarkably, despite having suffered a global ischemic event, Logan retained his intelligence, and with time he applied himself fully to his schoolwork and once again excelled academically.

Despite Logan's academic achievements and his ability to re-engage in many activities he loved, Logan was increasingly out of step with his peers due to his inability to access technology independently. Logan's limited access to technology included a Morse code device that had been adapted for his motor capabilities the year after his injury. During the years subsequent to Logan's injury, the use of personal computers, tablets, and smartphones has increased dramatically for American teens. According to a recent Pew Research Center study, nearly three-quarters of teens say they own or have access to a smartphone, and 92% report going online daily (including 24% who say they go online "almost constantly.") (Lenhart, 2015). Communication through email, text messaging, and social media apps play a significant role in the lives of Logan's peers, but these have been largely inaccessible to Logan. Thus, much of Logan's communication has been filtered through assistants who speak or write for him.

When Logan began college in the fall of 2014, his education paradigm changed dramatically from high school to college. While in high school, the expectation was that others would advocate for Logan. In college, the expectation was that Logan would advocate for himself. This is consistent with the experience of many students with disabilities making this transition to postsecondary education (Sparks, 2015). Although Logan would receive accommodations in college including note takers, lab assistants, additional access to on campus tutoring services, and extended time on tests, he would no longer have an Individualized Education Program (IEP) created by the school to help him succeed.

As one of the accommodations available to him, Logan would take all of his tests in the Center for Disability Services with a proctor employed by the university. While this accommodation met an immediate need of allowing Logan to complete assessments, it did not address all of his accessibility needs. During Logan's first semester, two specific areas of concern emerged. The first area was the continued lack of access to technology that distanced Logan from his peers and compromised his ability to engage with his instructors and the curriculum. The second area, of far greater concern due to academic requirements Logan had to meet as a student, was the lack of accessibility to higher level math.

PROCESS-DRIVEN MATH

Despite Logan's intelligence, higher level math threatened to place before him a wall he could not climb that would prevent him from persisting in his education. As the complexity of math increases, the accessibility to the subject decreases for students who are blind, have low vision, are mobility impaired, or are challenged with other disabilities. Math problems may have multiple levels, multiple parentheses, long square roots, logarithmic functions, trigonometric functions, several exponents, or any or all of the above in combination. Due to Logan's mobility impairment, Nemeth Code, the math equivalent of Braille, was unavailable to him as a tool for success in math.

Another accessibility technology, math problems spoken by a screen reader, was also inadequate. The screen reader did not accurately represent the complex problems, and there was no software available to allow the student who is both blind and mobility impaired to systematically work through complex math problems to a final solution. While screen reader technology has improved to more accurately describe mathematical expressions, that improvement alone will not solve the accessibility problem for students like Logan. The complexity of the syntax in a single problem still renders the subject inaccessible to many students with visual disabilities who either cannot or have not been trained to use Nemeth Code.

When Logan enrolled in Intermediate Algebra during his second semester, the math services coordinator with the university's Learning Center worked with the math department to provide a learning environment that would make college level math more accessible to Logan. Logan was given permission to attend class with the math services coordinator functioning as his supplemental instructor. This model allowed for instruction to take place in a quiet environment that would accommodate Logan's low whisper and allow him to interact with his supplemental instructor. However, it also meant that Logan was receiving math instruction separately from his peers.

Logan, the math services coordinator, and a student tutor worked together between fifteen and thirty hours each week to develop a fully audio method of math instruction and assessment that would allow Logan to fully drive all the intellectual processes involved in simplifying and solving algebraic expressions and equations. The methodology, which they called Process-Driven Math, was a tool that allowed Logan to learn and succeed in his Intermediate College Algebra class and the next semester his Pre-Calculus with Trigonometry class. When asked about how Process-Driven Math has impacted his life, Logan asserted, "I could not have gotten through Intermediate Algebra and Pre-Calc with Trig without it."

With the goal of automating Process-Driven Math, collaborations were established with several universities and the staff who were supporting Logan as he pursued his studies. The group, which came to be known as The Logan Project, is now reaching out to help others on campus who are visually impaired meet their core math requirement. The goal of making higher level math more accessible to students who are blind or low-vision expanded with the input of others who reviewed the method. The Logan Project subsequently developed a version of Process-Driven Math for sighted learners, with the hypothesis that it could be an effective tool for sighted learners, especially those with dyslexia, dyscalculia, auditory or visual processing disorders, or deafness. The future development of Process-Driven Math into software with a Universal Design for Learning focus would provide the opportunity for students who are blind, low vision, or otherwise disabled to learn higher level math alongside their peers in an inclusive, educational setting.

Logan's involvement in the research project has had a significant impact on his college experience. He states:

Improving Access to Higher Education

Everyone on campus knows me because of The Logan Project. Being on a research team and making presentations has really gotten my name out there. The thought of making math accessible to other people is just awesome. If I get to help another student I will be happy.

Logan is also looking forward to his role in the research project changing in the years to come. Logan was recently hired at the university's Learning Center to train tutors to work with other students who are blind using Process-Driven Math. After putting over 500 hours into the completion of his core math requirement, there is no one more qualified than Logan to do this job. Logan responded to his expanded responsibilities for The Logan Project saying, "I like the idea of having a part time job in college, but I never thought I would be working in math." When asked about his long-term goals with the project, Logan said, "I anticipate being one of the designers of the assistive technology, and I hope to be helping with it until it is done."

User-Centered Design

The ongoing development of Process-Driven Math was only one component of The Logan Project. The core values of The Logan Project were also the catalyst for the development of a mobile technology and communication system for Logan. One of those core values is User Centered Design (UCD), where the needs, wants, and desires of the person who will use the technology drive its development (Dorrington, Wilkinson, Tasker and Walters, 2016). To remain faithful to this approach that puts the individual with the disability at the heart of the research being conducted, Logan needed the best access possible to the team's technology and communication. An iPhone 6+ mounted on the wheelchair allowed the team to communicate through Skype and FaceTime (two video chat apps), and Logan was able to be right there in the middle of it, no matter where he was.

The decision to select Apple products as the foundation for Logan's mobile technology system was based on the advances made to the Switch Control feature that is available on Apple's mobile devices as a built-in option. Switch Control provides an alternative for the many multi-touch gestures that are the basis for most interactions with a touchscreen device. For example, to launch an app by "tapping" its icon on the Home screen, the switch user waits for a cursor to scan through the options on the screen until the desired app is selected. At that point, the switch user will press a switch to bring up a menu with actions he or she can perform, such as "tapping." Switch Control relies on a switch interface to make the connection between the switches and the mobile device. This interface translates each switch press into a command the mobile device can understand, allowing the user to perform a number of actions that would normally not be possible without this technology (including the many flick and swipe gestures used on touchscreen interfaces).

Most of the available switch interfaces available on the market rely on Bluetooth technology to establish a wireless connection between the interface and the mobile device, but a number of hardwired options are also now available. While the reliability of Bluetooth has improved with the latest updates to this technology, it is still not as dependable as a hardwired solution. Using a hardwired system, four switches were connected to Logan's mobile device, with each switch having both a short and a long press function. Thus, the system had eight separate actions with which Logan could control the functions of his mobile device. These actions were: home, select, next, previous, tap, volume down, volume up, and a scanner menu giving him access to his device's settings. In addition, provision was made to increase the volume of Logan's low whisper for in person conversations.

Working with an engineer, Logan's four switches were mounted in a custom console no larger than a watch. This design was chosen so that Logan's technology would look similar to the technology others were using with the advent of the smartwatch and other wearables. Logan's mobility was optimized with switches controlled by small buttons mounted close together. The console was attached to the armrest of Logan's wheelchair and he could grasp the underneath of the armrest with his four fingers and use small movements with his thumb to press the four buttons controlling his phone (Figure 1). A fifth button to control a custom microphone switching device was added to Logan's technology. This allowed him to redirect his microphone from his phone to two small speakers mounted on his wheelchair (Figure 2) so that the volume of his whisper was increased, providing for greater engagement for in person conversations.

Prior to Logan's matriculation, he was without access to technology, despite having had several technology assessments done by the state. In talking about his experience with technology, Logan stated, "Nothing worked. Nothing helped. I left everything technology based to helpers, like going on the internet or having homework done on the computer. I couldn't use the phone by myself so I had to ask helpers to call people or send text messages for me."

Apple's Switch Control with the speech option turned on provided a solution that allowed Logan to become more independent in his use of technology. Switch Control allowed Logan to sequentially move through the items on the screen as he pressed a switch, and to hear each item identified by the screen reader. Logan worked with an assistive technology consultant who gave him the training he needed to become an effective Switch Control user. Many tasks that could have required upward of 100 button clicks for Logan to execute were greatly simplified using the Workflow app. With this powerful tool, initial workflows were built that enabled Logan to place phone calls and send pre-written text messages to every person in his contacts, often requiring fewer than ten button presses to execute the action. A voice cancelling microphone connected to his phone and mounted on his wheelchair with a flexible gooseneck arm (Figure 3) allowed for Logan to speak directly to people on the phone without relying on a personal assistant to listen and speak on his behalf.

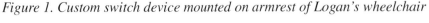
Figure 1. Custom switch device mounted on armrest of Logan's wheelchair

Figure 2. Small speakers mounted on Logan's wheelchair make it easier for others to hear his speech

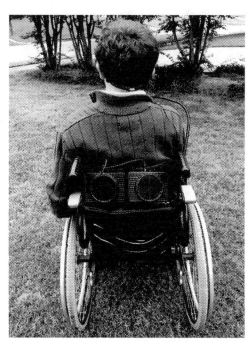

Figure 3. Microphone mounted on flexible gooseneck arm facilitates communication for Logan

The ability to communicate independently provided the inspiration for Logan's enthusiastic practice with this new technology. On his own, Logan discovered that predictive text gave him the help he needed to send his own unique text messages or emails, a huge advance from the pre-written messages he started with. In evaluating this new skill, Logan stated, "It's awesome. When I send a text message I don't have to keep repeating myself because people can't hear me." Logan also noted, "Before I could only talk to people if it was face to face." With his technology system in place, Logan says he is better able to maintain the relationships that are important to him. In addition, Logan is using his ability to text to manage his daily schedule. Logan no longer asks his mom to contact his personal assistant on his behalf to find out when she is coming. Logan uses text messaging to manage his own communication with his personal assistant and make the plan for the day.

Since Logan was dependent on others for his transportation needs, he was not always available for in-person meetings. His mobile system was employed to give him full access to The Logan Project meetings. From anywhere, Logan was able to engage in conversations that were held with math accessibility experts from around the country using his mobile technology. Logan conducted interactive demonstrations from remote locations using his mobile technology, an element that was critical to the establishment of collaborative partners for The Logan Project.

Logan's mobile technology has allowed him to give lengthy presentations without the need for intervention from an assistant during his speech. Audio prompts for Logan's speeches are placed on his phone as the titles to "dummy apps" created for the sole purpose of giving Logan audio cues during his talks. While using Switch Control with speech turned on, Logan advances through these files and hears the titles through his bone conduction headset, allowing him to stay on track while speaking publicly. Recently, Logan spoke for fifteen minutes during a presentation at the National Science Foundation using this application of his technology. Previously, Logan would have had an assistant sitting next to him whenever he spoke publicly for any significant length of time in order to give him cues for the content he was speaking. The person giving Logan these reminders was a distraction to the audience, and the setup gave the impression that Logan was less capable than his peers who could independently use print or Braille cards for their presentations. Logan's perspective on this use of his technology is:

It makes it a lot simpler when I can just click and have a voice speak in my ear. Having this mobile technology setup that lets me speak without having to ask someone else what I am supposed to say next looks much more impressive to an audience.

As Logan's confidence and experience with Switch Control advanced, additional skills were added. Logan began checking his own email and commented:

It really helps. Now I don't have to ask my mom to check it, so it helps other people too. I heard the other day on my email that there was going to be a quiz in biology that I had not known about, so it is giving me more independence in my schoolwork. I like the fact that I know what is happening and I can do something about it.

The Workflow app was used extensively, giving Logan the ability to execute complex tasks such as retrieving and listening to articles placed in his Pocket app, creating audio files and storing them in Dropbox, retrieving documents from Dropbox, sending audio files as text messages and emails, and placing email attachments into the Voice Dream reader app.

While Logan's mobile communication system has given him more options for communication and allowed him to become more independent, a number of challenges remain to be addressed to make the system an even more powerful solution for him. One of these challenges relates to the tension between security and accessibility. The technology that protects people's information may also create barriers that deny assistive technology users access into protected cyber environments. A switch control user with limited mobility to efficiently enter usernames and passwords may find that the amount of time it takes to enter that information will render the environment inaccessible, especially since the password field disables predictive text input.

The "remember me" function can be a simple fix for many apps, but larger corporate, government, and academic institutions often opt to use an external authenticator for the sign in process in order to provide more comprehensive protection over the many portals housing private information within their systems. An external authenticator often does not allow a "remember me" function, and that is the case with Logan's access into the university's academic portal. Switch Control should theoretically allow Logan to input a password that has been copied onto his device's clipboard. However, for a Switch Control user who is blind, the Switch Control screen reader does not always read options like "paste" that appear on a popover menu. This may just be an oversight in the design of the screen reader that will be addressed in future updates. Without knowing when "paste" is available to him, Logan is not able to successfully enter a password that has been copied to the clipboard. In this way, his inability to log in excludes him from the portal where much of the work of his courses takes place.

One possible solution to the tension between security and accessibility would be if the authentication systems used on some portals would support the latest security technologies available on mobile devices. For example, iOS devices such as the iPad and the iPhone now include a TouchID sensor that allows the user to unlock his or her device by simply placing a finger on top of the sensor (which is located underneath the device's Home button). Many of the portals used in higher education now provide an app for mobile access in addition to the standard web interface for those accessing the system on a computer. If the portal is designed to support TouchID (as a number of shopping apps already do) it would not only enhance access for those users who rely on assistive technology, it would be a convenience for all students accessing the portal on a mobile device.

Access to secure environments is not the only obstacle facing the Switch Control user who is blind. Competing voices, inconveniently placed user controls, and the lack of efficiency for a switch user who is typing are all areas that need improvement. Apps that have their own built-in speech, which includes many of the apps for accessing print materials, can be confusing and difficult to use. These apps can be confusing because the blind Switch Control user could have the device's built-in voice and the app's voice speaking simultaneously. Another issue is that the layout of the interface, especially the location of playback controls, can make the app difficult to use for a switch user. Often, these playback controls are located at the bottom of the screen, requiring many switch presses before they can be reached with the Switch Control cursor. Switch Control does include a Point Mode that allows the user to go directly to any point on the screen, but this feature requires that the user have some vision to use it.

Another usability challenge for a blind Switch Control user is the effort required to enter text when speech recognition is not an option, as is the case due to Logan's low whisper. With iOS 8, Apple made it possible for third party keyboards to be installed on iOS devices. A number of these third-party keyboards provide layouts that are designed specifically for switch users, including ones that place the keys in an ABC arrangement or by their frequency of use. Even with these alternative layouts, the process of entering text still requires a great deal of effort on the part of the switch user, as it takes many switch presses to enter even a short phrase.

A solution could be to bring back mobile technologies that actually predate the smartphone. As documented on the Continuous Path website (www.continuouspath.org), the T9 text entry method used on many feature phones (those using a physical keyboard instead of a touchscreen for text entry) was originally created to allow individuals with mobility impairments to type using only eight keys. At the height of the feature phone's popularity, this technology was installed in over 5 billion devices (Continous Path, n.d.), but once smartphones took over, the T9 text entry was phased out of the cell phone industry and has since been dormant. Recently, the developers of T9, who would go on to adapt this technology for smartphones and release it as the Swype third party keyboard, have created a foundation that seeks to return these commercial technologies back to the accessibility community (Continous Path, n.d.). This would be a positive development, as text entry remains a significant challenge for both switch and screen reader users.

The issues related to the usability of apps for Switch Control users could be addressed through a combination of better awareness on the part of developers and improvements to Switch Control itself. In the case of developers, they could make the apps easier to use for switch users by placing important controls (such as those for playback) toward the top of the screen. This simple change would dramatically reduce the number of switch presses required to interact with the app. With regard to Switch Control, there is now a feature called Recipes (introduced in iOS 9) for repetitive actions, but this feature requires the user to enter a special mode where scanning is disabled and each press of the switch performs the same action (flip a page, tap a point on the screen). While Recipes may be an option for Logan, switching between modes would require some practice, and it carries a greater cognitive load, especially for someone who is not able to see the screen. Finally, developing an alternative for text entry that requires less effort from switch and screen reader users would go a long way toward allowing those users to more efficiently use their devices to write papers, complete online forms, participate in social media and many other tasks that ensure their equal participation in the academic and social life of their universities.

CONCLUSION

Despite a number of challenges that still need to be addressed, there is no doubt that the accessibility features built into Logan's mobile communication system have already had a positive impact on his life. These features, Switch Control in particular, have not only improved his ability to communicate and provided him with more independence, they have also allowed him to enjoy better access to academic content. More importantly, in keeping with the core value of User Centered Design, his mobile communication system has allowed him to be an active participant in the ongoing development of Process-Driven Math. In the process, he has gained a number of important skills while presenting about Process-Driven Math to a number of different audiences and has even allowed him to contribute as an author to this book chapter.

Logan's empowerment shows what is possible when there is synergy between accessible content and the assistive technologies used by students with disabilities. Without his mobile device communication system, Logan would not have been able to play a central role in the development of Process-Driven Math as a Universal Design for Learning solution that will not only expand accessibility to higher level math for other college students like himself, but also for non-disabled peers who struggle with this subject.

REFERENCES

CAST. (2011). Universal Design for Learning Guidelines version 2.0. Wakefield, MA: CAST.

Continuous Path. (n.d.). *Our History*. Retrieved April 20, 2016, from http://continuouspath.org/3.html

Coyne, P., Pisha, B., Dalton, B., Zpeh, L. A., & Smith, N. C. (2012). Literacy by design: A universal design for learning approach for students with significant intellectual disabilities. *Remedial and Special Education, 33*(3), 162–172. doi:10.1177/0741932510381651

Dorrington, P., Wilkinson, C., Tasker, L., & Walters, A. (2016). User-centered design method for the design of assistive switch devices to improve user experience, accessibility, and independence. *Journal of Usability Studies, 11*(2), 66–82.

Lenhart, A. (2015). *Teen social media and technology overview 2015*. Washington, DC: Pew Research Center. Retrieved from http://www.pewinternet.org

Meyer, A., Rose, D. H., & Gordon, D. (2014). *Universal design for learning: Theory and practice*. Wakefield, MA: CAST.

Moon, N., Todd, R., Morton, D., & Ivey, E. (2012). *Accommodating students with disabilities in science, technology, engineering, and mathematics (STEM): Findings from research and practice for middle grades through university education*. Atlanta, GA: Center for Assistive Technology and Environmental Access.

National Center on Universal Design for Learning. (2012). *Learner Variability and UDL* [Online seminar presentation]. UDL Series, No. 1. Retrieved from http://udlseries.udlcenter.org

National Council on Disability. (2015). *Briefing paper: Reauthorization of the Higher Education Act (HEA): The implications for increasing the employment of people with disabilities*. Retrieved from http://www.ncd.gov

Newman, L., Wagner, M., Knokey, A. M., Marder, C., Nagle, K., Shaver, D., ... Schwarting, M. (2011). The Post-High School Outcomes of Young Adults With Disabilities up to 8 Years After High School. A Report from the National Longitudinal Transition Study-2 (NLTS2) (NCSER 2011-3005). Menlo Park, CA: SRI International.

Rappolt-Schlitmann, G., Daley, S., Lim, S., Lapinski, S., Robison, K., & Johnson, M. (2013). Universal design for learning and elementary school science: Exploring the efficacy, use, and perceptions of a web-based science notebook. *Journal of Educational Psychology, 105*(4), 1210–1225. doi:10.1037/a0033217

Sparks, S. (2015, May 29). After K-12, students must be self-advocates. *EdWeek, 34*(33), 8.

U.S. Department of Education. (2015). Digest of Education Statistics 2013 (2015-011). Author.

U.S. Department of Labor. (2014). *Economic Picture of the Disability Community Project: Key Points Document*. Retrieved from http://www.dol.gov/odep/pdf/20141022-KeyPoints.pdf

KEY TERMS AND DEFINITIONS

Braille: A form of written language for blind and visually impaired people, in which characters are represented by patterns of raised dots that are felt with the fingertips.

Nemeth Code: A form of Braille used to encode mathematical or scientific notation so that it can be understood by people who are blind or who have visual impairments.

Screen Reader: Software that describes what is shown on a display to someone who is blind by using synthesized speech to read the content aloud.

Switch Access: An alternative method of access for those who are not able to use a traditional mouse or a keyboard. In its most basic form a switch allows a person with only minimal voluntary control of their muscles to tap a button in order to perform an action, usually make a selection from a menu of options shown on a computer or mobile device's display.

Switch Interface: A device that translates switch presses into commands a mobile device or computer can understand. Each switch press is assigned the equivalent of a keyboard shortcut the operating system can recognize and convert into actions such as moving a cursor or making a selection from a menu.

Universal Design: A design philosophy that seeks to make the environment more accessible and easier to use for all people. From its origins in architecture, universal design has been taken up in fields as diverse as industrial and instructional design.

Universal Design for Learning (UDL): The Center for Applied Special Technology (CAST) defines UDL as a framework to improve and optimize teaching and learning so that it works for all people. With UDL, this is accomplished through proactive planning to ensure all aspects of a given lesson address the variability all learners bring into the classroom.

User-Centered Design (UCD): The idea that people with disabilities should be at the center of the design process for assistive technology, by providing input and feedback at every step of development.

This research was previously published in Empowering Learners With Mobile Open-Access Learning Initiatives edited by Michael Mills and Donna Wake; pages 13-30, copyright year 2017 by Information Science Reference (an imprint of IGI Global).

Index

A

ability level 295, 947, 961, 971
ableism 41, 43, 397, 514, 525, 534, 738, 740
accessibility needs 10, 52, 55, 58, 60-64, 68, 74, 499
Accommodation or Modification 238
Accommodations/Services 403
action research 437, 891, 893, 895-896, 904, 911, 925, 929
ADA 3-5, 11, 19-20, 22-23, 25, 28-30, 35-36, 220, 223, 225, 238-239, 395, 510, 513-518, 521, 523-526, 595
adaptive behavior 413, 432, 556, 578, 950, 971
adolescents 357, 369, 371-373, 375, 449
African Americans 652, 685, 689, 691, 695, 713-714, 716-718, 723, 747, 807, 1025-1026
Alberta Education 1000, 1011, 1020-1021
Americans with Disabilities Act 4-5, 19-20, 35, 37, 223, 395, 510, 513, 551, 579, 595
anxiety 108, 190, 363, 368-369, 372, 376, 391, 405, 410-411, 415, 564, 633, 673, 695, 891, 893, 896-898, 902, 904, 956, 1014
apps 19-20, 30, 446-447, 449-456, 458-459, 462, 498-499, 501, 503-505, 523, 667, 672, 675, 978
Arnold Chiari II Malformation 410, 429
Asperger syndrome 409, 581, 595-596
assistive technology (AT) 513, 526, 549
Assistive Technology Device 432, 444
Assistive Technology Services 433, 444
ATAG 58, 69, 78
auditory processing 336-337
autism spectrum disorder 446, 585, 595, 941
Aversive Racism 688, 699, 711

B

backward design 761, 766, 780
banzhuren 865-867, 870-886, 890
barrier-free 293, 312-313, 315, 509-510, 512, 517-522, 534

Barrier-Free (BF) concepts 510, 517, 534
behavior management 126, 171, 456, 771
Behavioral Consultation 167, 177
bilingualism 632, 636
blind users 63-65, 535-536, 541-543, 547
blindness 27, 73, 142, 435, 499, 540, 549, 553-554, 691-692, 899, 944, 967-968
Bloom's Taxonomy 180, 183, 185-186, 195
Braille 25, 53, 208, 500, 504, 507, 513-514, 521, 523, 549, 945, 967-968
bullying 108-109, 368-378, 621, 782, 790, 1008-1009

C

campus climate 693, 699, 712, 714-715, 719-725, 1022-1025, 1028-1029, 1035-1037
Card Sorting 280, 290, 341
Chinese education 203, 866-867, 870, 872-873, 884, 890
chronic disabilities 557, 560-561, 567-568, 570, 573, 575
Classroom Communities 102
coaching 147-148, 150, 155, 230, 520, 770, 906-907, 912, 917-921, 923, 927
cognitive functioning 950, 971, 1010
College Entrance Examination 198, 204-205
colorblindness 690-691, 696, 894, 899
Common Core State Standards 152, 179, 182, 185-186, 188, 190-191, 195, 243, 320, 591, 846
community partnerships 13, 757, 762, 816
Constructivism 183-184, 195
Control in E-Learning 295
coordinated instruction 143, 153-156
coping strategies 356-359, 361-363, 373-374, 397, 1008
co-teacher-educators 767, 773-774, 780
Co-Teaching Model 971
critical literacy 629, 782, 791-792
critical reflection 613, 615, 617-618, 636, 1016
critical theory 738-741, 750, 753, 756
Crockett 122, 124, 126, 142, 784

Index

Cross-Cultural Dissonance 821
cultural border crossing 613
cultural diversity 398, 631, 635-636, 644, 651-652, 657, 659, 787, 807, 823, 840
Cultural Mismatch 808, 821
culturally affirming education 899
culturally competent 649, 655-656, 791, 821, 918
culturally diverse 630, 632, 635-636, 638, 640, 644, 655-658, 686, 768, 806, 814, 821
culturally relevant pedagogy 629, 651
culturally responsive pedagogy 614-616, 623-624, 629, 786-787, 894, 915
culturally responsive teaching 613, 620-621, 649, 651, 653, 659, 666, 668-671, 673, 782, 806, 809, 817, 899
culture of learning 822-837, 840
Curbcuts or Curbramps 534

D

data analysis 144, 171, 360, 617, 630, 827, 846, 848-849, 851, 853-856, 896, 898, 1006
data collection 144, 226, 239, 250, 276, 373, 376, 453, 617, 637, 668, 826-827, 871, 895, 898, 973, 975, 977, 986-988
data system 8, 846-849, 853, 856, 862-863
data use 843, 845-849, 856-858
data-based 126, 130, 165, 170, 177, 244, 757, 771, 973
data-based decision making 130, 170, 177, 244, 771
Data-driven decision-making 862
data-informed decision-making 844, 847, 856, 862
Deficit vs. Difference 238
depression 62, 106, 108-109, 368-369, 372, 375-376, 391, 410, 415, 695, 948, 965
Didactic Method 295
disability disclosure 226-227, 230, 239
disability discrimination 21-22, 220, 510, 514-515, 525, 534
Disability Prevalence 239
disability services office 230, 416, 429
disclosure 35, 226-227, 230, 239, 415, 738, 742, 744, 750, 753
discrimination 4-6, 21-22, 25, 35-36, 53, 83, 92, 199-200, 219-220, 223, 238, 246, 336, 338, 393-396, 509-510, 512, 514-515, 525, 534, 566-567, 572, 582, 595, 615, 624, 658, 684, 686, 688-689, 691, 693, 695, 711, 721-723, 739, 784, 786, 788, 811-812, 890, 1023, 1025
disproportionate representation 718, 812, 821, 910
diverse learners 35, 37-38, 52, 55, 60, 74, 153, 498, 614, 622, 660, 762, 810, 818, 891-899, 902-903
diversity and equity 613-614, 644, 757, 762-763

dot code 464-466, 468-469, 471, 477, 479-480, 486, 488, 492-493
dysgraphia 274, 320, 323, 333-334, 406
dyslexia 62, 64-65, 70, 72, 272-287, 290, 320, 322-324, 334, 336, 339, 406, 498, 500, 591, 957
dysorthographia 320, 323, 331-332

E

Education Technology 6, 318
educational attainment 197-198, 200, 210-211, 816
Educational Creativity 890
educational rights 3, 199, 208, 550-551, 574, 784
effective leadership 126, 141
elderly 52, 54-55, 60, 62, 276, 676
elementary school 373, 436, 630-631, 633, 771, 818, 868, 883, 885
emotional segregation 684-685, 699
empathy 109, 228, 630, 632-636, 640-644, 667, 684-685, 744, 793, 822, 825, 948
English language learners 40, 151, 596, 620, 892, 902, 908, 926
English Learner 342, 780, 843, 845, 856
essentialist 822, 824-825, 827, 829, 834, 836-837, 840
evidence-based practices 123, 144-145, 153, 165, 241, 244-245, 251, 262, 342, 449, 774, 927
exceptionality 808, 940-941, 944, 946, 948, 950, 952-953, 955, 958, 963-965, 967, 971
executive functions 39, 184, 189, 341, 965
expressive language disability 473
Eye-Gaze Technology 523, 534

F

field experiences 660, 757, 759, 761, 763, 898, 1030
field-based teacher education 757-760, 762, 765, 767-768, 773, 776-777, 781
field-experiences 763, 768
finance 1, 7, 12, 18, 95, 208
footer 850, 852, 862
foreign students 52, 55, 60, 725, 831
Forensic psychology 697
Free and Appropriate Education (FAPE) 596
Fullan 124, 132, 134-136, 141, 921
Fullan's Framework for Leadership 135, 141

G

giftedness 408, 996-1000, 1005-1013, 1020-1021
grade level 127, 180, 186, 241, 244, 247-248, 262, 430, 564, 587-588, 623, 649-650, 653-654, 947, 949, 971, 987

H

handmade content 464, 479-480, 483-485, 488, 492
handmade teaching material 466
Hargreaves 132-133, 921
HCI 57, 78
Health Impaired 550-551, 553, 563
help system 848, 862
High Incidence Disability 971
High Tech Innovative 462
High Tech Traditional 462
higher education 1-15, 18, 28-29, 34-37, 44-47, 53, 80-86, 88-92, 94-96, 126, 190-191, 197-201, 203-211, 215, 219, 221, 223, 225, 227-233, 238, 291, 297, 299, 302, 390-398, 495, 505, 509-511, 513, 517, 534, 593, 599, 649, 653-658, 660-662, 683, 686, 690-693, 695, 697, 699, 713, 719-720, 723, 726, 741, 748, 751, 753, 822, 890, 892-894, 1022, 1024-1025, 1027-1029, 1033, 1036-1037
higher education institutions 3-7, 10, 12-14, 53, 199-200, 204-206, 208-209, 211, 221, 390-395, 397-398, 649, 653-658, 660-662, 741, 1022, 1024-1025, 1027, 1037
holistic approach 9, 23, 46, 457, 462
Human-Centered-Design 290
hydrocephalus 406, 408, 410, 430

I

Identification of Giftedness 1021
IEP Goal 186, 195
inclusion 34-35, 42, 46-47, 52, 54, 60, 74, 107-108, 147, 201, 215, 218, 221-222, 231, 233, 238, 240, 254, 256, 272-277, 280, 284-287, 290, 304, 308, 313, 315, 368-369, 495, 509, 511-513, 515, 517-518, 520, 524-526, 534, 552, 558-559, 565, 574, 599-600, 602-603, 607-608, 653, 655-656, 697, 787, 867-868, 884, 891-892, 894, 907, 910-911, 919, 922-923, 925-927, 929, 951, 972, 991, 995, 1016, 1032
inclusive classroom 102-103, 190-191, 240, 865-867, 871, 875-879, 881-882, 884-886, 890-891, 896, 898, 902-904, 972-973, 979, 1016
inclusive education 45, 106, 198, 200-201, 208, 369, 509, 514, 579, 584, 600-601, 606, 865-873, 875, 885-886, 890, 910-912, 919, 1016
inclusive environment 103, 107, 109, 111, 211, 940, 1027, 1036, 1040
inclusive practices 123, 526, 599, 608, 785, 906-907, 914, 916, 918-920, 922-923, 927, 929
independent living 2, 444, 510, 519, 554, 814, 967

Indicator of Sliding Mode 318
Individual Education Plan (IEP) 179, 191, 958
Individualized Education Plan (IEP) 411, 565, 581, 596
Individuals with Disabilities Education Act (IDEA) 4, 22, 126-127, 142, 144, 195, 241, 406, 496, 551-552, 589, 596, 812, 821, 971
Individuals with Disabilities Education Improvement Act (IDEIA) 177, 322
Innovative Practice 866, 890
innovative technology 448-449, 456-457, 462
institutes of higher education 510
institutional racism 680, 683-684, 691, 693, 695-697, 699, 711, 899, 1024
Institutions of Higher Education (IHE) 510, 534
International Baccalaureate 772, 781, 1003
international students 37, 712-715, 719-720, 723, 725, 822-823, 832
internationalisation 822, 824-825, 834, 836, 840
intersectionality 42, 394, 1040
IT for inclusion 290

L

language and literacy 629, 771
Language Disorder 821
law 1, 3-7, 18-19, 21-22, 25, 44, 127, 142, 180, 198, 200-202, 207-208, 220, 224, 300, 322, 375, 391, 406, 512-514, 551-554, 557-560, 566, 579, 582-585, 595-596, 666, 675, 689, 697-698, 717-718, 721, 740, 821, 825, 899
leadership 11, 13, 121-126, 130, 134-135, 141, 182-183, 397-398, 457, 618, 621, 651, 680-683, 686-688, 690, 697, 699, 711, 724, 746-748, 762, 765-766, 768, 771, 790, 866, 868, 872-874, 918, 998, 1026, 1036
learning disability 36, 38, 40, 126-127, 142, 144, 165, 227, 229, 242, 248, 320-323, 356-358, 361, 390-398, 403-410, 514, 552-554, 567, 574, 582, 585, 870, 878, 883, 957
learning goals 295, 649, 668, 672-673, 766
learning management system 20, 25, 862
learning objectives 454, 748
lesson study 151, 153, 906, 912, 915-916
linguistic diversity 600, 630-631, 637, 640, 758
linguistically diverse 396, 614, 630-631, 638, 640, 644, 653, 659, 758-759, 770-771, 808-809, 811-818, 821, 902, 906-907
Local Educational Agency 596
loneliness 368-369, 372, 375-376, 676
Low-Incident Disability 971

M

magical sheet 469, 493
Making Action Plans (MAP) 421, 430
mathematics 144-146, 148, 150-153, 156, 182, 240-257, 261-262, 321-322, 437, 496, 588, 590, 596, 652, 772, 783, 785, 844-845, 914-915, 919, 949, 961
media representations 712-714, 716-718, 721, 723-725
medical model 198, 200-202, 211, 251, 393-394, 403, 436
mental retardation 142, 322, 432, 552-554, 890
Microaggression 691-693, 699, 711, 899, 1040
micro-aggressions 740, 746, 750, 752-753, 756
mobile technologies 437, 449, 505, 666-668, 671-673, 675-677
Model Minority 693-694
Moderator Avatar 318
MOOCs 6-7, 20, 52, 54-55, 57, 59-60, 62-63, 65, 67, 72-74, 535-537, 544
motor impairment 62, 495
multicultural education 43, 632, 643, 657, 660, 782, 786-788, 806-808, 818, 821
Multi-Disciplinary Team (MDT) 178
Multi-Tiered System of Support 105, 240-241, 244
Mutually Beneficial Partnership 772, 781

N

narrative 11, 146, 149, 616-618, 629, 676, 738-739, 741-742, 744, 747-748, 750-753, 756, 918
Narrative Pedagogy 617, 629, 747
National Universities Commission 84
Nemeth Code 496, 500, 507
Nigeria 80-86, 88-96, 901
No Child Left Behind (NCLB) Act 123, 165, 552, 579, 596, 940, 974
No Tech/Low Tech 462
non-essentialist 822-827, 834, 840

O

Online and Blended Learning of Adults 295
organizational culture 392, 680, 683, 687, 689, 698, 711
overrepresentation 103, 717, 821
Over-the-Counter Data 856, 862

P

peaple/person with disabilities 2, 10, 14, 22, 41-42, 52, 60, 86, 197-205, 207-208, 210-211, 216-224, 226, 228, 231, 233, 393, 421, 432, 439, 496, 508, 510, 520, 548, 567, 595

pedagogy 35, 38, 43, 152-155, 277, 279, 287, 342, 450-451, 458, 498, 600, 602, 605, 608, 614-618, 623-625, 629, 631, 651, 653, 657, 671, 698, 711, 714, 738-739, 744, 746-748, 784, 786-788, 793-794, 817-818, 869, 892-894, 896-897, 899, 901, 907, 912, 914-916, 918-921, 925, 928, 1037
peer rejection 369, 375
Personas 273, 276, 290
Planning Alternative Tomorrows with Hope (PATH) 421, 430
postsecondary 3-9, 12-15, 18, 34-38, 42-47, 210, 219, 229, 241, 397-398, 404-405, 415, 421-422, 425, 427, 430, 496, 499
pre-service teachers 163, 171, 182, 188, 343, 630-632, 641, 644, 657-659, 661, 760, 789-790, 793, 795, 891-894, 897, 902, 904, 925-926, 940-941, 966, 968-969, 999
Prevalence 103, 127-128, 216-217, 239, 274, 322, 371, 373-374, 432, 511, 562, 940-941, 944, 946, 948, 950, 952-953, 955, 958, 963, 967, 971
problem based learning 631, 634-636, 643-644, 666, 668, 670-671, 673, 676
problem-solving 62, 124, 128-129, 163, 165, 167-171, 321, 337, 362, 653, 656, 667, 759, 914, 919
professional development (PD) 143, 145, 847, 862, 907
Professional Development Schools (PDS) 907
professional education 200, 291-293, 296-315
professional learning 148-151, 155-156, 622-623, 761, 772, 906-909, 912, 915, 917-918, 921, 926, 984
Professional Learning Communities (PLCs) 761, 907

Q

quality of life 54, 320, 364, 431-432, 439-440, 444, 514, 974
quota system 81, 84-85, 89, 93-94, 692

R

Racial Identity 1040
racism 43, 601, 656-657, 675, 680-693, 695-699, 711, 713, 716, 721-725, 738-744, 746, 748-753, 756, 782, 788, 894, 899, 901, 923, 1024
racist ideology 739-740, 745
reading disorder 323
reference guide 848, 862
reference sheet 848, 850, 862
Rehabilitation 2, 4, 7, 20, 22, 36, 217, 223, 294, 358, 363, 393, 395, 411, 432, 509-510, 512-513, 520, 550-552, 554, 559, 566-567, 572, 579, 582, 589, 595

Rehabilitation Act 4, 20, 22, 36, 223, 395, 509-510, 512-513, 550-552, 554, 566-567, 572, 579, 582, 589, 595
Religious Tenets 1025, 1040
Repressive Tolerance 741, 753, 756
Researcher Avatar 318
Response to Intervention 105, 121-123, 126-129, 133, 142-144, 164-165, 181, 244, 983
Response-to-Intervention (RTI) 105, 121-123, 126-129, 133, 142-144, 163-165, 178, 181, 244, 323, 914, 983

S

scanner pen 466, 469, 493
Scholarly Personal Narrative 747, 756
school activity 473, 479, 482-483, 487, 489, 493
screen design 275, 277, 279-281, 290, 450
screen reader 5, 9, 500, 502, 504-507, 549
SEL 102
self-advocacy 43, 391-392, 403, 591
self-determination 249, 306, 309, 391-392, 403
self-esteem 109, 362, 374-375, 579, 657, 695, 699, 807, 956, 967, 996
self-study 309, 765-767, 773, 776, 829-831
sense of belonging 54, 106, 392, 721, 1009, 1024, 1028, 1033-1034, 1040
social and emotional learning 102-112
social inclusion 275, 284, 287, 290, 599, 607-608
social justice 10, 12, 14, 18, 41-43, 46-47, 201, 392-394, 403, 515, 519, 619, 632, 655, 666-667, 670, 672, 697, 724, 726, 784-788, 790-793, 893-894, 898, 901, 925, 996-997, 1022, 1026, 1040
social justice model 393-394, 403
social skills 107, 109-111, 357, 362-363, 374, 376, 430, 449-451, 453, 564, 941, 949, 951, 966-967, 974
Social stories 411, 430
sound pen 465-466, 468-470, 473, 475-486, 489, 493
special education 13, 22, 103-105, 107, 121-130, 132-133, 136, 142-148, 150-151, 153-154, 156-157, 163-167, 169-170, 179-185, 190-191, 195-196, 198, 201-202, 208-210, 240-245, 251-256, 262, 284, 286, 322, 342-343, 369, 375, 406, 411, 427, 436, 446-447, 450, 453, 457-458, 463, 496, 522, 550-560, 562-565, 568, 572, 574-575, 578-579, 582-584, 586, 590-593, 596, 607, 654, 763, 766-767, 770, 806-808, 811-815, 821, 847, 853, 862, 866-868, 886, 890, 892-893, 910, 922-923, 926-928, 940-941, 944, 946-948, 950-953, 955, 958, 960, 963-965, 967, 972-973, 995-997, 1010-1011, 1021

Special Education Administrator 142
special education collaboration 927
Special Education Setting 163, 463
specially-designed instruction 245
specific learning disabilities 36, 242, 320, 356, 358, 406, 552, 585
speech therapy 446-447, 449, 451-452, 454-455, 458-459, 463, 560
Speech Therapy Setting 463
Spelling Disorder 323, 331
spina bifida (SB) 404-405, 430
stereotype 688, 694-695, 711, 998
struggling learners 123, 144-145, 149, 151-156, 923
Stuart Hall 712
student development 390, 751, 865, 872, 884-885, 890
student identity 41
student mobility 822-827, 832, 834-837, 840
Student Study Team (SST) 164, 166, 169, 178
student with a disability 25, 47, 142, 534, 554, 560, 570, 575, 583-584, 596, 971
study groups 40, 150, 906, 912, 914, 916, 927, 929
Switch Access 495, 507
Switch Interface 501, 507

T

task analysis 273, 276, 290, 436
teacher candidate 657, 762, 781
teacher education 146, 171, 630-632, 634, 636, 638, 642-644, 651, 656-657, 660-661, 690, 696, 698, 757-760, 762, 765-768, 771, 773-777, 781, 785-786, 790, 795, 847-849, 854, 892, 925, 927, 968, 1025, 1030
teacher knowledge 146, 148-150, 156, 908, 914
teacher learning 147-148, 150-151, 153, 155-156, 657, 761, 908, 917, 923, 925
teacher practice 910
teacher preparation programs 44, 217, 658, 775, 847, 928
team teaching 738, 748-749, 751-753, 756
Techies 549
technology devices 5, 62, 431-433, 435, 454, 456, 462, 513
Technology Services 15, 433, 444
transition planning 404
transitioning 230, 261, 341, 390, 396, 404, 417, 425, 673, 770
Triple H-AVATAR Technology 318

Index

U

UAAG 58, 79
unconscious racism 680, 683, 689, 699
underrepresentation 211, 694, 815, 821, 899
Universal Design (UD) 35, 517, 521, 534
Universal Design for Learning (UDL) 38, 179-181, 186, 495, 497, 508, 522
university culture 392, 398, 403
urban education 656, 782-783, 789
User analysis 290
User-Centered Design (UCD) 508

V

victimization 106, 109, 369, 372-376, 378, 654
Virtual Assistant 295
Virtual Research Environment 318
Visual Impaired 537-539, 549

W

WAI 23, 58, 79
WCAG 19-20, 23-27, 29-30, 58, 60-61, 72, 79
Web Accessibility 20-21, 23, 58, 73, 79, 275-276
White supremacy 690, 716, 721, 739-744, 750, 753, 756, 892
Whitten 122-123, 128-129
work experience 484-487, 493
workforce development 215-226, 229-233
Writing Disorder 323, 333

Purchase Print, E-Book, or Print + E-Book

IGI Global's reference books are available in three unique pricing formats:
Print Only, E-Book Only, or Print + E-Book.
Shipping fees may apply.

www.igi-global.com

Recommended Reference Books

ISBN: 978-1-5225-9348-5
© 2019; 454 pp.
List Price: $255

ISBN: 978-1-5225-7763-8
© 2019; 253 pp.
List Price: $175

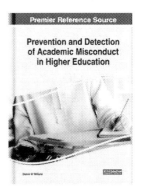

ISBN: 978-1-5225-7531-3
© 2019; 324 pp.
List Price: $185

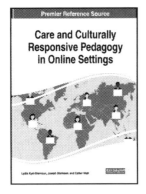

ISBN: 978-1-5225-7802-4
© 2019; 423 pp.
List Price: $195

ISBN: 978-1-5225-6246-7
© 2019; 610 pp.
List Price: $275

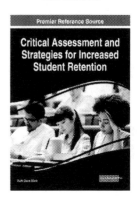

ISBN: 978-1-5225-2998-9
© 2018; 352 pp.
List Price: $195

Do you want to stay current on the latest research trends, product announcements, news and special offers?
Join IGI Global's mailing list today and start enjoying exclusive perks sent only to IGI Global members.
Add your name to the list at **www.igi-global.com/newsletters**.

Publisher of Peer-Reviewed, Timely, and Innovative Academic Research

IGI Global
DISSEMINATOR OF KNOWLEDGE

www.igi-global.com   Sign up at www.igi-global.com/newsletters   facebook.com/igiglobal   twitter.com/igiglobal   linkedin.com/igiglobal

Ensure Quality Research is Introduced to the Academic Community

Become an IGI Global Reviewer for Authored Book Projects

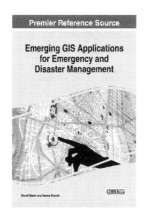 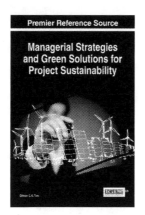  

The overall success of an authored book project is dependent on quality and timely reviews.

In this competitive age of scholarly publishing, constructive and timely feedback significantly expedites the turnaround time of manuscripts from submission to acceptance, allowing the publication and discovery of forward-thinking research at a much more expeditious rate. Several IGI Global authored book projects are currently seeking highly-qualified experts in the field to fill vacancies on their respective editorial review boards:

Applications and Inquiries may be sent to:
development@igi-global.com

Applicants must have a doctorate (or an equivalent degree) as well as publishing and reviewing experience. Reviewers are asked to complete the open-ended evaluation questions with as much detail as possible in a timely, collegial, and constructive manner. All reviewers' tenures run for one-year terms on the editorial review boards and are expected to complete at least three reviews per term. Upon successful completion of this term, reviewers can be considered for an additional term.

If you have a colleague that may be interested in this opportunity,
we encourage you to share this information with them.

IGI Global Proudly Partners With eContent Pro International

Receive a 25% Discount on all Editorial Services

Editorial Services

IGI Global expects all final manuscripts submitted for publication to be in their final form. This means they must be reviewed, revised, and professionally copy edited prior to their final submission. Not only does this support with accelerating the publication process, but it also ensures that the highest quality scholarly work can be disseminated.

English Language Copy Editing

Let eContent Pro International's expert copy editors perform edits on your manuscript to resolve spelling, punctuaion, grammar, syntax, flow, formatting issues and more.

Scientific and Scholarly Editing

Allow colleagues in your research area to examine the content of your manuscript and provide you with valuable feedback and suggestions before submission.

Figure, Table, Chart & Equation Conversions

Do you have poor quality figures? Do you need visual elements in your manuscript created or converted? A design expert can help!

Translation

Need your documjent translated into English? eContent Pro International's expert translators are fluent in English and more than 40 different languages.

Hear What Your Colleagues are Saying About Editorial Services Supported by IGI Global

"The service was very fast, very thorough, and very helpful in ensuring our chapter meets the criteria and requirements of the book's editors. I was quite impressed and happy with your service."

– Prof. Tom Brinthaupt,
Middle Tennessee State University, USA

"I found the work actually spectacular. The editing, formatting, and other checks were very thorough. The turnaround time was great as well. I will definitely use eContent Pro in the future."

– Nickanor Amwata, Lecturer,
University of Kurdistan Hawler, Iraq

"I was impressed that it was done timely, and wherever the content was not clear for the reader, the paper was improved with better readability for the audience."

– Prof. James Chilembwe,
Mzuzu University, Malawi

Email: customerservice@econtentpro.com

www.igi-global.com/editorial-service-partners

www.igi-global.com

Celebrating Over 30 Years of Scholarly Knowledge Creation & Dissemination

InfoSci®-Books

A Database of Over 5,300+ Reference Books Containing Over 100,000+ Chapters Focusing on Emerging Research

GAIN ACCESS TO **THOUSANDS** OF REFERENCE BOOKS AT **A FRACTION** OF THEIR INDIVIDUAL LIST **PRICE**.

InfoSci®-Books Database

The **InfoSci®-Books** database is a collection of over 5,300+ IGI Global single and multi-volume reference books, handbooks of research, and encyclopedias, encompassing groundbreaking research from prominent experts worldwide that span over 350+ topics in 11 core subject areas including business, computer science, education, science and engineering, social sciences and more.

Open Access Fee Waiver (Offset Model) Initiative

For any library that invests in IGI Global's InfoSci-Journals and/or InfoSci-Books databases, IGI Global will match the library's investment with a fund of equal value to go toward **subsidizing the OA article processing charges (APCs) for their students, faculty, and staff** at that institution when their work is submitted and accepted under OA into an IGI Global journal.*

INFOSCI® PLATFORM FEATURES

- No DRM
- No Set-Up or Maintenance Fees
- A Guarantee of No More Than a 5% Annual Increase
- Full-Text HTML and PDF Viewing Options
- Downloadable MARC Records
- Unlimited Simultaneous Access
- COUNTER 5 Compliant Reports
- Formatted Citations With Ability to Export to RefWorks and EasyBib
- No Embargo of Content (Research is Available Months in Advance of the Print Release)

*The fund will be offered on an annual basis and expire at the end of the subscription period. The fund would renew as the subscription is renewed for each year thereafter. The open access fees will be waived after the student, faculty, or staff's paper has been vetted and accepted into an IGI Global journal and the fund can only be used toward publishing OA in an IGI Global journal. Libraries in developing countries will have the match on their investment doubled.

To Learn More or To Purchase This Database:
www.igi-global.com/infosci-books

eresources@igi-global.com • Toll Free: 1-866-342-6657 ext. 100 • Phone: 717-533-8845 x100

www.igi-global.com

Publisher of Peer-Reviewed, Timely, and Innovative Academic Research Since 1988

IGI Global's Transformative Open Access (OA) Model:
How to Turn Your University Library's Database Acquisitions Into a Source of OA Funding

In response to the OA movement and well in advance of Plan S, IGI Global, early last year, unveiled their OA Fee Waiver (Offset Model) Initiative.

Under this initiative, librarians who invest in IGI Global's InfoSci-Books (5,300+ reference books) and/or InfoSci-Journals (185+ scholarly journals) databases will be able to subsidize their patron's OA article processing charges (APC) when their work is submitted and accepted (after the peer review process) into an IGI Global journal.*

How Does it Work?

1. When a library subscribes or perpetually purchases IGI Global's InfoSci-Databases including InfoSci-Books (5,300+ e-books), InfoSci-Journals (185+ e-journals), and/or their discipline/subject-focused subsets, IGI Global will match the library's investment with a fund of equal value to go toward subsidizing the OA article processing charges (APCs) for their patrons.

   Researchers: Be sure to recommend the InfoSci-Books and InfoSci-Journals to take advantage of this initiative.

2. When a student, faculty, or staff member submits a paper and it is accepted (following the peer review) into one of IGI Global's 185+ scholarly journals, the author will have the option to have their paper published under a traditional publishing model or as OA.

3. When the author chooses to have their paper published under OA, IGI Global will notify them of the OA Fee Waiver (Offset Model) Initiative. If the author decides they would like to take advantage of this initiative, IGI Global will deduct the US$ 1,500 APC from the created fund.

4. This fund will be offered on an annual basis and will renew as the subscription is renewed for each year thereafter. IGI Global will manage the fund and award the APC waivers unless the librarian has a preference as to how the funds should be managed.

Hear From the Experts on This Initiative:

"I'm very happy to have been able to make one of my recent research contributions, 'Visualizing the Social Media Conversations of a National Information Technology Professional Association' featured in the *International Journal of Human Capital and Information Technology Professionals*, freely available along with having access to the valuable resources found within IGI Global's InfoSci-Journals database."

— **Prof. Stuart Palmer**, Deakin University, Australia

For More Information, Visit: www.igi-global.com/publish/contributor-resources/open-access or contact IGI Global's Database Team at eresources@igi-global.com.

Are You Ready to Publish Your Research?

IGI Global offers book authorship and editorship opportunities across 11 subject areas, including business, computer science, education, science and engineering, social sciences, and more!

Benefits of Publishing with IGI Global:

- Free one-on-one editorial and promotional support.
- Expedited publishing timelines that can take your book from start to finish in less than one (1) year.
- Choose from a variety of formats including: Edited and Authored References, Handbooks of Research, Encyclopedias, and Research Insights.
- Utilize IGI Global's eEditorial Discovery® submission system in support of conducting the submission and blind review process.
- IGI Global maintains a strict adherence to ethical practices due in part to our full membership with the Committee on Publication Ethics (COPE).
- Indexing potential in prestigious indices such as Scopus®, Web of Science™, PsycINFO®, and ERIC – Education Resources Information Center.
- Ability to connect your ORCID iD to your IGI Global publications.
- Earn royalties on your publication as well as receive complimentary copies and exclusive discounts.

Get Started Today by Contacting the Acquisitions Department at:
acquisition@igi-global.com

Printed in the United States
By Bookmasters

Section B (partial)
...ENFORCEMENT
County Police

	205
	207
	207
	207
	209
	212
	214
	214
	214
	216
	221
	221
	222
	225
	228
	230
	233
	236
	238
	239
	240
	240
	243
	245
	247
	250
	252
	254
	255
	255
	256
	257
	258
	262
	263
	265
	267
	268
	271
	271
	272
	274
	276
	283
	284
	285
	287
	288
	290
	292

Section C
CORONERS & MEDICAL EXAMINERS
County & Precinct

ALABAMA	295
ALASKA	296
ARIZONA	296
ARKANSAS	296
CALIFORNIA	297
COLORADO	298
CONNECTICUT	299
DELAWARE	299
DIST OF COLUMBIA	299
FLORIDA	299
GEORGIA	299
HAWAII	302
IDAHO	302
ILLINOIS	303
INDIANA	304
IOWA	306
KANSAS	307
KENTUCKY	308
LOUISIANA	310
MAINE	311
MARYLAND	311
MASSACHUSETTS	311
MICHIGAN	311
MINNESOTA	312
MISSISSIPPI	313
MISSOURI	314
MONTANA	316
NEBRASKA	317
NEVADA	318
NEW HAMPSHIRE	319
NEW JERSEY	319
NEW MEXICO	319
NEW YORK	319
NORTH CAROLINA	320
NORTH DAKOTA	320
OHIO	321
OKLAHOMA	322
OREGON	322
PENNSYLVANIA	323
RHODE ISLAND	324
SOUTH CAROLINA	324
SOUTH DAKOTA	325
TENNESSEE	326
TEXAS	327
UTAH	338
VERMONT	338
VIRGINIA	338
WASHINGTON	338
WEST VIRGINIA	339
WISCONSIN	339
WYOMING	340

Section D
PROSECUTORS
County & District

ALABAMA	341
ALASKA	342
ARIZONA	342
ARKANSAS	343
CALIFORNIA	344
COLORADO	345
CONNECTICUT	346
DELAWARE	347
FLORIDA	347
GEORGIA	348
HAWAII	351
IDAHO	351
ILLINOIS	352
INDIANA	354
IOWA	357
KANSAS	359
KENTUCKY	361
LOUISIANA	364
MAINE	365
MARYLAND	365
MASSACHUSETTS	366
MICHIGAN	366
MINNESOTA	368
MISSISSIPPI	370
MISSOURI	372
MONTANA	375
NEBRASKA	376
NEVADA	377
NEW HAMPSHIRE	378
NEW JERSEY	378
NEW MEXICO	378
NEW YORK	379
NORTH CAROLINA	380
NORTH DAKOTA	382
OHIO	383
OKLAHOMA	384
OREGON	386
PENNSYLVANIA	387
RHODE ISLAND	389
SOUTH CAROLINA	389
SOUTH DAKOTA	390
TENNESSEE	391
TEXAS	393
UTAH	399
VERMONT	399
VIRGINIA	400
WASHINGTON	402
WEST VIRGINIA	402
WISCONSIN	404
WYOMING	405

Sect
CHILD S
ENFOR

CHILD SUPPORT ENF